BUSINESS ETHICS

BUSINESS ETHICS

DENIS COLLINS
EDGEWOOD COLLEGE

WILEY
John Wiley & Sons, Inc.

VICE PRESIDENT AND PUBLISHER George Hoffman

EXECUTIVE EDITOR Lise Johnson

ASSISTANT EDITOR Sarah Vernon

EDITORIAL ASSISTANT Melissa Solarz

MARKETING MANAGER   Kelly Simmons

MEDIA EDITOR Elena Santa Maria

CREATIVE DIRECTOR Harold Nolan

SENIOR DESIGNER Maureen Eide

PHOTO EDITOR Sheena Goldstein

PRODUCTION MANAGER Dorothy Sinclair

SENIOR PRODUCTION EDITOR Trish McFadden

PRODUCTION MANAGEMENT SERVICES Laserwords Private Ltd.

COVER/INTERIOR DESIGN Tamara Newman

COVER PHOTO Wataru Yanagida/Getty Images, Inc.

CHAPTER OPENER PHOTOS © ooyoo/iStockphoto

This book was set in Sabon 10/12 by Laserwords Private Ltd. and printed and bound by Quad/Graphics. The cover was printed by Quad/Graphics, Versallles.

This book is printed on acid free paper. ∞

ISBN-13 9780470639948

ISBN-10 0470639946

Printed in the United States of America

10 9 8 7 6

DEDICATION

To my children, Seth and Anna Collins. While writing this book, I had a small note next to my computer screen that said: "What do Seth and Anna need to know to create an ethical organization?" This book contains my best efforts for them, and all college students.

To Bob Simler, a former manager and student who died of cancer during the writing of this book. I am a terminal cancer survivor, 16 years and counting, and there is no better way to spend time on Earth than to help create ethical organizations and an ethical society.

PREFACE

Topic Importance and Relevance

"How many of you would like to work for an ethical organization?" I ask my students the first day of class. They all raise their hands. "How many of you work for an ethical organization?" Some raise their hands, and some do not.

"How many of you want to work for an ethical boss?" Once again, all hands shoot up in the air. "And how many of you work for an ethical boss?" Some hands remain in the air, and some disappointingly are lowered.

All organizations can be of high integrity. But doing so requires planning and effort due to competing pressures and human flaws. This textbook is aimed at helping students to create and reinforce high integrity organizations and to become managers of high integrity.

This is a major undertaking. Every year has its own unique set of high profile business scandals and tragedies. In early 2010, British Petroleum (BP) was ranked among the top 100 largest and most respected companies in the world by *Barron's* and first among the ten largest oil companies for managing social and environmental issues by Tomorrow's Value Rating.[1] Then on April 20, 2010, BP's Gulf of Mexico oil rig exploded, killing 11 people and causing the largest oil spill in U.S. history. A government investigation concluded that BP continually risked employee lives in designing and building the oil rig to save money.[2]

Every day some employees struggle with work issues that can have major ethical ramifications. For security reasons, a bank branch manager knows the first three numbers to the cash vault and the assistant manager knows the second three numbers. This way nobody knows all six numbers. Unexpectedly, the branch manager is unable to arrive on time to jointly open the vault. Customers will be waiting for service. Should the branch manger violate policy and tell the assistant manager the first three numbers to the vault? Should the assistant manager accept the numbers? For the sake of customer service, they did. The bank's security cameras filmed my student, the assistant manager, opening the vault on his own. Both he and the branch manager were fired, despite years of admirable service.

A Pragmatic and Proactive Approach

The first two habits of Stephen Covey's *The 7 Habits of Highly Effective People* are "Be Proactive" and "Begin with the End in Mind."[3] Beginning with the end in mind, it is possible to create businesses that are profitable and ethical. Managers must be proactive to achieve these highly desired end goals; they do not happen by accident. Yet many organizations struggle with ethics. According to the Ethics Resource Center, approximately half of survey respondents observed at least one type of major ethical misconduct in the workplace during the previous year, and nearly half of these violated the law.[4]

What can be done to fix the moral ills of organizations?

A doctor applying the scientific method to a sick patient defines the illness, determines the causes of the illness, envisions a healthy patient, and then prescribes medicines that will generate health. The same scientific method can be pursued for addressing the moral ills of organizations:

- First, managers must recognize and indentify the moral problem. Moral imperfections are not limited to a handful of renegade CEOs, financiers, or subordinates. We are all morally imperfect people and, by extension, every organization is morally imperfect.
- Second, managers must understand the causes of organizational moral imperfections. Many people who behave unethically believe they are doing the right thing based on how they view the world or frame the tradeoffs.
- Third, managers must have a vision, and understand the benefits, of a morally healthy organization.
- Fourth, managers must understand and implement strategies that will result in achieving the vision of a morally healthy organization.

That is what this book does. The textbook takes a pragmatic and proactive organizational systems approach based on the best practices in business ethics organized around an Optimal Ethics Systems Model:

- Recruit individuals who demonstrate and sustain ethical behavior over time.
- Orient new employees to the organization's Code of Ethics, Code of Conduct, and ethical decision-making framework.
- Respect employee and customer diversity.
- Report ethical misbehaviors.
- Foster ethical leadership.
- Design work goals and performance appraisals that reward ethical behaviors.
- Engage and empower employees to achieve superior performance.
- Manage the organization's interactions with the natural environment.
- Conduct meaningful community outreach.

By the end of the book, students will know how to design and manage ethical organizations and work units, how to make ethical decisions, and how to be a virtuous person. Students will be equipped with an array of best practices in business ethics that can be implemented immediately or soon after graduation.

General Overview

Chapter 1: Unethical Behavior in Organizations and Human Nature. Managers must recognize that moral imperfection is a fact of life and then develop systems and checks and balances to minimize the exercise of moral imperfections within their own organization. This chapter discusses research and insights on human nature, six stages of moral development, why good people occasionally behave unethically, and workplace implications.

Chapter 2: An Historical Perspective on Business Ethics. People engaged in business activities have been acting ethically and unethically since the beginning of human history. This chapter describes some prominent business ethics issues related to economic growth during pivotal historical moments prior to, and after, the formation of the United States. The chapter discusses Adam Smith's ethical defense of capitalism and culminates with the Optimal Ethics Systems Model as a conceptual framework for maximizing ethical behavior and reducing ethical risks in organizations.

Chapter 3: Hiring Ethical People. Hiring just one employee with an unethical value system—someone whose sense of morality and justice does not match that of a high-integrity work culture—can corrupt an organization. This chapter reviews the current research on a variety of ethics-related job-screening techniques, such as background checks and integrity tests, to determine which methods are more likely to differentiate between ethical and unethical job candidates. A six-step process for evaluating the ethics of job candidates is provided.

Chapter 4: Codes of Ethics and Codes of Conduct. Ethical dilemmas arise because people have different ethical beliefs, and many situations are ambiguous. An organization's Code of Ethics serves as its conscience and provides employees with a common ethical reference point. The chapter explains the differences between a Code of Ethics and a Code of Conduct, summarizes their prevalence and content, and describes how to use a Code of Ethics to assess and improve ethical performance.

Chapter 5: Ethical Decision Making. Employees need to know how to independently derive a moral answer to business issues. This chapter explores a variety of factors that influence whether a person decides to behave ethically or unethically. People quickly form an ethical intention based on moral intuitions and then sometimes make a revision by applying a rational ethical decision-making process. The chapter provides a systematic seven-question ethics decision-making framework grounded in moral philosophy and a critical thinking decision-making process to help derive moral conclusions.

Chapter 6: Ethics Training. Ethics training initiates dialogue at work around contentious issues and helps create a culture of trust. This chapter provides 10 ethics training workshops that can be conducted at work.

Chapter 7: Respecting Employee Diversity. The population of the United States continues to diversify, as do the employees and customer base of organizations. This chapter examines the most common types of workplace discrimination and the best operational practices for enhancing and managing diversity, including a 10-step process for implementing a diversity initiative. Instructions are offered for conducting a series of diversity training workshops that increase social group self-awareness, explore specific issues, and help employees manage different communication styles.

Chapter 8: Ethics Reporting Systems. Managers must be made aware of, and employees need to discuss, ethical issues as they arise. This chapter examines why some employees maintain silence when they observe ethical misconduct and what management behaviors and internal mechanisms can elicit such essential information. The chapter explores three alternative internal communication mechanisms for obtaining information about unethical behavior: an ethics and compliance officer, an ombudsperson, and an assist line. A failure in these internal communication systems can result in external whistle-blowing, which is damaging for both the organization and the whistle-blower.

Chapter 9: Managers as Ethical Leaders and Role Models. Three aspects of daily organizational life significantly impact an employee's ethical performance: the direct supervisor's behaviors, work goals, and performance appraisals. This chapter explores how managers are ethical role models and how to be an ethical leader. Managers can reinforce ethical behavior among employees through work goals and performance appraisals that encourage and reward ethical behaviors. Several surveys are provided to help managers evaluate themselves and others in terms of ethical leadership and behaviors.

Chapter 10: Engaging and Empowering Ethical Employees. Managers must develop workplaces where employees are fully engaged with their job tasks and empowered to make decisions. This chapter examines how to engage employees by meeting essential human needs, ensuring organizational justice, and providing meaningful work. The chapter also explores how to empower employees by giving them decision-making authority, providing relevant information about organizational operations, and sharing financial benefits generated by their efforts.

Chapter 11: Environmental Management. Environmental management is a competitive advantage that saves the organization money, enhances its reputation, and attracts and motivates employees. This chapter summarizes environmental problems and efforts by organizations, government, and businesses to address them. It also explores how superior environmental performance can be achieved by screening suppliers, adopting an Environmental Management System and the Natural Step framework, conducting environmental risk assessments, designing eco-friendly products, operating in green buildings, and monitoring environmental performance indicators.

Chapter 12: Community Outreach and Respect. The well-being of the host community profoundly impacts an organization, and vice versa. This chapter describes the business case for community involvement, how managers can engage multiple stakeholders on a wide variety of issues, and how to develop a diverse portfolio of giving opportunities. The chapter also examines how to align community outreach with the company's mission and assets, choose a strategic partner, administer the community involvement process, and assess and report social performance.

In addition, Chapter 12 contains a section on international corporate citizenship and discusses the United Nations Global Compact Principles and problems associated with applying cultural relativism internationally. The organizational processes described throughout this textbook are universal. They can and should be applied in organizations located in any nation. International issues are also addressed in many of the 17 in-depth case studies.

Features of the Book

Each chapter in the book contains three unique real life ethical dilemmas, specific examples of best practices in use, student questions that highlight chapter content, and ancillary materials for further understanding topics relevant to business ethics. Seventeen cases are also available for more in-depth analysis. Twelve in the back of the book and an additional five online at www.wiley/college/collins.

Ethical Dilemmas

What Would You Do?—The "What Would You Do?" vignettes are real-life ethical dilemmas experienced by my students. The "What Would You Do?" dilemma begins every chapter and is related to the chapter content. Some details have been modified to protect identities and to enrich understanding. After the facts of the case, students are provided with several decision options to choose from and asked why they would choose that particular option. Other potential courses of action can be elaborated during class discussions. A blog with recent newspaper articles related to ethical dilemmas in business, organizations, and government is available at http://deniscollins.tumblr.com/.

In the Real World: Enron—This textbook focuses on best practices in business ethics. Enron is one of the largest business scandals in U.S. history, and it serves as a balance to the best practice approach. Enron's story is timeless because ethical problems experienced at Enron have existed in some variation for centuries, such as how to respond to unethical workplace bullies or the temptation to manipulate financial results, and will exist for centuries to come. Some organizations do a good job addressing these issues; Enron did not.

It is important to note that Enron's collapse in December 2001 was not inevitable, nor did it happen overnight. At any point between 1985 and 2001, Enron's misdirected evolution could have been corrected by applying different aspects of the Optimal Ethics Systems Model. Key decisions are presented in chronological order from several perspectives, including those of Ken Lay, Jeff Skilling, accountants, and investment bankers. Students are challenged to decide what they would have done if employed by, or doing business with, Enron, and to learn from Enron's tragic mistakes. Students can get a better feel for the personalities at Enron by watching *Enron: The Smartest Guys in the Room*, a 2005 documentary film based on a book with a similar title by Bethany McLean and Peter Elkind.

Let's Build a Building—The construction industry is among the largest industries in the United States, and its activities cut across all sectors of the economy. At some point in their careers, students will likely experience building remodeling or expansion or new construction. This series of real-life vignettes chronologically educates students about a wide range of ethical issues during the course of a building project, including purchasing land, building design, choosing contractors, employee issues, environmental issues, and payment issues. A 2004 FMI/CMAA report, *Survey of Construction Industry Ethical Practices,* is available at http://cmaanet.org/user_images/ethics_survey.pdf.

Best Practice in Use

Every chapter highlights a company implementing the best practices discussed in the textbook. "Best Practice in Use" exhibits include Starbucks' *Global Responsibility Report 2009* efforts, REI's employee benefits, Ben & Jerry's social mission, the Gap's gratuities Code of Conduct, Coca Cola's Code of Conduct ethics training exercise, Wells Fargo's diversity initiatives, Whole Foods' employee engagement activities, Walmart's Supplier Sustainability Index, and Timberland's community service toolkit.

Ancillary Materials

Best Place to Work Video—Link to *Fortune* magazine videos for nine companies in its annual "Best Places to Work For" rankings and other best practices videos, including Google, Dreamworks, and REI. Three videos are interviews with CEOs, Ben & Jerry's Ben Cohen and Jerry Greenfield, Whole Foods' John Mackey, and Malden Mills' Aaron Feuerstein. The videos range from 5 to 10 minutes.

Business Ethics Issue Video—Links to *Frontline* documentaries about business ethics topics. *Frontline* is a public affairs series on the Public Broadcasting System. Topics include BP's oil spill, the 2008 financial crisis, Bernie Madoff's ponzi scheme, and international bribery. The documentaries range between one and two hours.

TEDTalks Videos—Links to the award-winning "TEDTalks" video site. TED is a nonprofit organization that hosts conferences featuring talks about innovative ideas. General topic areas include human nature, happiness, decision making, leadership, diversity, environment, and philanthropy. Talks range between 12 and 76 minutes.

Conversations with Charlie Rose—Links to the Public Broadcasting System's award-winning conversations conducted by Charlie Rose. These one-on-one interview and roundtable discussion topics include ethics, business scandals, the 2008–10 financial crisis, and business innovations that have social benefits. The conversations range between 15 and 60 minutes.

Student and Instructor Resources—Found on the password-protected website www.wiley.com/college/collins, Wiley supplies a comprehensive learning package to assist the instructor and the student.

Videos—Set of short video clips from CBS News helps students visualize critical issues discussed in the text and the cases and provides an excellent starting point for lectures and general classroom discussion.

Video Guide—Contains a brief description of the videos and 2 to 5 discussion questions with answers relating the video to content in the text.

Instructor's Manual—Offers helpful teaching ideas, advice on course development, sample assignments, and chapter-by-chapter text highlights, learning objectives, lecture outlines, class exercises, lecture notes, answers to end-of-chapter material, and tips on using cases.

Test Bank—The test bank contains approximately 80 questions per chapter, including multiple choice, true/false, and short essay questions with suggested responses.

Websites to Explore—Links to websites related to the chapter topic.

Management Weekly Updates—Keep you and your students updated and informed on the very latest in business news stories. Each week you will find links to 5 new articles, video clips, business news stories, and so much more with discussion questions to elaborate on the stories in the classroom. http://wileymanagementupdates.com.

Power Point Slides—Provides lecture/interactive slides for each chapter to enhance students' overall experience in the management classroom.

Web Quizzes—Students will have the ability to test themselves on text concepts and content with 15 to 25 questions per chapter, including true-false and multiple choice questions.

In-Depth Case Studies

This textbook contains 17 in-depth case studies on a wide range of topics, many of them from an international perspective. Twelve of these cases can be found in the back of the printed text, and an additional five are posted online at www.wiley.com/college/collins. The cases include socially irresponsible behaviors in the oil industry (British Petroleum), socially responsible behaviors in New Zealand's mining industry (Newmont), the largest Ponzi scheme in history (Bernie Madoff), the largest civil fine in the Securities and Exchange Commission's history (Goldman Sachs), Canada's version of Enron and WorldCom (Nortel), attempts to regulate cigarettes (United States) and fast food (San Jose, California), asbestos compensation in Australia (James Hardie Group), terrorist threats in Colombia (Chiquita), human trafficking in Africa (Plan Togo), employees with physical disabilities in Mexico (Movimiento Congruencia), remnants of Holocaust involvement in Germany (Degussa), providing loans to entrepreneurs in developing nations (Kiva), fair trade products in the United Kingdom (Cafédirect), trademark disputes (Apple and Cisco), China's economic development evolution, and the ethics of experimenting on monkeys.

Acknowledgments

I would like to thank my Edgewood College colleagues for taking on the challenge of teaching about business ethics across the Business School curriculum.

I am indebted to Lise Johnson of John Wiley & Sons for her continual enthusiastic support for this project. I want to thank Sarah Vernon and Rebecca Lazure for their editorial assistance. I also thank Dianne Jenkins, Ginny Gilbert, Ken Spuda, Sheena Smith, and my many undergraduate and graduate students at Edgewood College for their ideas, advice, and encouragement. Last, I offer a special thanks to workshop participants and clients for accepting the challenge to implement the best practices discussed in this book.

NOTES

[1] "The World's Most Respected Companies," *MSN Money Central,* February 15, 2010, available at http://articles.moneycentral.msn.com/Investing/Extra/the-worlds-most-respected-companies.aspx?page=3, accessed 4/11/11; Two Tomorrow's, *2010 Tomorrow's Value Rating of the World's Largest Oil and Gas Companies: Summary Report,* available at http://www.tomorrowsvaluerating.com/Page/OilandGas, accessed 4/11/11.

[2] Representative Henry A. Waxman and Representative Bart Stupak, "Letter to Tony Hayward, CEO of BP," June 14, 2010, available at http://energycommerce.house.gov/documents/20100614/Hayward.BP.2010.6.14.pdf, accessed 4/11/11.

[3] Stephen R. Covey, *The 7 Habits of Highly Effective People* (New York: Simon & Schuster, 1989).

[4] Ethics Resource Center, *2009 National Business Ethics Survey,* available at http://www.ethicsworld.org/ethicsandemployees/nbes.php#new09, accessed 4/11/11.

REVIEWERS

I'm pleased to express my appreciation to the following reviewers for their contributions to this book.

Anke U. Arnaud, Embry Riddle University
Carolyn Ashe, University of Houston–Downtown
Gay Birkholz, Purdue University (North Central)
Bonnie S. Bolinger, Ivy Tech State College
Michael B. Burns, Lone Star College–University Park
Nicole Buzzetto-More, University of Maryland–Eastern Shore
Laura Dendinger, Wayne State College
Leeanne Eagleson, Univeristy of La Verne
Linda Enghagen, University of Massachusetts, Amherst
Don Fisher, Dixie State College
Jessica Gosnell, St. Ambrose University
Melanie Hilburn, Lone Star College–North Harris
Janet Knight, Purdue University (Porter County)
Melodee Lambert, Salt Lake Community College
David Levy, State University of New York–Geneseo
Nancy Lindsey Fregoso, Pima Community College
Michael Littman, Buffalo State College
Pauline Magee-Egan, St. John's University–Queens
Jessica McManus Warnell, University of Notre Dame
Madhavi Mentreddy, Central Georgia Technical College
Stephen Mumford, Gwynedd-Mercy College
John Felder Osoinach, University of Delaware
Margot Palermo, Stony Brook University
John Thomas Perry, Pennsylvania State University–Harrisburg
Joseph Petrick, Wright State University
Dr. W. Trexler Proffitt Jr., Franklin & Marshall
Timothy Reymann, Franklin University
Richard Rosen, Pima Community College
Wendy Smith, Southwestern Illinois College
Feliz Tabak, Towson University
Neal Thompson, Columbus State University
Mohamed Zainuba, University of Arkansas

ABOUT THE AUTHOR

Denis Collins is a tenured professor of management in the School of Business at Edgewood College and has been teaching business ethics in undergraduate and graduate programs for more than 20 years. He received a Ph.D. in business administration from the University of Pittsburgh and is considered a leader among business ethics professors. He has published numerous books and articles. Dr. Collins currently serves on the editorial boards of several academic journals and has served on the board of governance for several professional organizations.

Dr. Collins is the recipient of the 2010 MBA Outstanding Faculty Award and the 2009 Estervig-Beaubien Outstanding Professor Award, School of Business, Edgewood College, for excellence in teaching and mentoring. Three times he was voted the outstanding MBA faculty member at the University of Wisconsin–Madison in Business Week's survey of alumni. Dr. Collins was a finalist for the Academy of Management's Distinguished Educator Award.

BRIEF TABLE OF CONTENTS

TABLE OF CONTENTS

CHAPTER 2

An Historical Perspective on Business Ethics 39

CHAPTER 6

Ethics Training   169

CHAPTER 7

Respecting Employee Diversity   201

CHAPTER 9

Managers as Ethical Leaders and Role Models   267

CHAPTER 10

Engaging and Empowering Ethical Employees   301

Part Four: Being a Good Citizen   333

CHAPTER 11

Environmental Management   335

CHAPTER 12

Community Outreach and Respect   373

CASES

Environmental Issues

Financial and Accounting Issues

Health and Safety Regulations

Political Issues

Employee Issues

Community Concerns

Marketing Issues

Online Cases

LIST OF EXHIBITS

PART I

Background

CHAPTER OUTLINE

1

UNETHICAL BEHAVIORS IN ORGANIZATIONS AND HUMAN NATURE

What would you do?

Product Design

Upon graduation, you obtain a job as a marketing manager for a retail clothing store in a college community. Among the store's high profit margin items are artistic t-shirts with witty slogans. The best-selling t-shirts have sexual innuendos, put-downs of conference sports competitors, and references to high-profile political or media events. The t-shirts attract a lot of customers to the store and lead to sales of other store products.

Unfortunately, the community has experienced a burglary spree over the past six months that has received a tremendous amount of local media coverage. The thief, a college dropout who escaped from a drug rehabilitation house, has become a local counterculture antihero. He breaks in and steals money and jewelry from unoccupied high-scale homes in the morning and afternoon, and businesses after they close at night, including some on the street where your store is located. He occasionally steals high-end automobiles and abandons them after running out of gas. The thief leaves signed apology notes at crime scenes and teases the understaffed police department

about its inability to find him. His antics remind people of the real-life thief Leonardo DeCaprio played in the hit movie *Catch Me If You Can*. Fan clubs at local high schools and colleges have been formed in his honor.

A local t-shirt supplier, who provides your best-selling t-shirts, visits the store and shows you pictures of his latest creation. The supplier contract provides you with the right of first refusal for her latest creations, and exclusive three-month rights on designs you purchase. Nearby stores sometimes purchase designs you reject.

The supplier's latest samples are all variations of an artistic t-shirt design that says "FAN CLUB" below the counterculture antihero's picture. You show the design to a few customers. They laugh and say "that's cool, where can I buy it?" It's obvious that the t-shirt will quickly become the newest best seller and positively impact your year-end sales target bonus.

College students represent a key target market. The market demand will be high, as will profits. But the t-shirt glorifies a thief, and he's robbed from a few stores in your shopping area. Other variations of the t-shirt theme will not sell as well. You are pretty sure that a nearby competitor will purchase the design if you don't.

What would you do? Would you
1) Purchase the design?
2) Not purchase the design?
   Why?

Chapter Objectives

After reading this chapter, you will be able to

- Explain the competitive advantages of creating and maintaining an ethical organization
- Appreciate that unethical behaviors occur in all organizational operations
- Identify common types of unethical behaviors

- Understand that unethical behaviors can be very costly to organizations
- Describe different theories of human nature and the stages of moral development
- Discuss why good people occasionally behave unethically

Businesses significantly improve the quality of life by providing goods and services that fulfill consumer needs. Service to others, one of the most admirable ethical standards, is at the heart of business operations. The financial well-being of organizations depends on employees serving the needs of customers, owners, and other employees.

Look around. A business built the house you live in, the alarm clock that wakes you up, the bed you sleep in, the clothes you wear, the periodicals you read, the computer you work on, the chair you sit in, the food you eat, the music you listen to, and the car you drive to school or work.

Providing goods and services is just one ethical aspect of organizational operations. Assume you have an idea for a new business. You will need people to help with product development, marketing, accounting, and management. You will be interacting with suppliers as well as customers. Doing business involves a network of human interactions. Some of these people may have high ethical standards; some may not.

Managers must manage their organization's ethical environment. Due to imperfections in human nature and inappropriate management control systems, many organizations are ethically challenged. Every day media outlets report the latest organizational misbehaviors. The judicial system overflows with lawsuits for alleged wrongdoings filed against organizations by employees, customers, and other organizations.

Federal, state, and local governments, along with regulatory agencies, create new rules and regulations to ensure that stakeholders are treated appropriately. A stakeholder is any person or organization that is affected by, or could affect, an organization's goal accomplishment. Regulators make sure that employees are fairly treated by employers, customers and suppliers are dealt with honestly, and the natural environment is not ruined. Some owners and managers choose to surpass the minimum requirements of existing rules and regulations, operating in a manner that continually benefits all stakeholders. Some choose to meet existing rules and regulations, while others continually exploit loopholes in existing rules and regulations.

This chapter discusses why appropriately managing ethics is essential for every organization. The prevalence and costs of unethical behaviors at work can be substantial. In addition, appropriately managing ethics provides ethical organizations with many competitive advantages. Despite these competitive advantages, however, unethical behaviors continue to occur because every person is morally imperfect. The chapter reviews different theories of human nature and the six stages of moral development and explores why good people occasionally behave unethically.

Daily Occurrence of Ethical Dilemmas

Ethics is similar to breathing and blinking, with a slight twist. We breathe and blink subconsciously, unaware that the average adult on a daily basis takes 18,000 breaths and blinks 15,000 times. Similarly, we are unaware that every decision made during a day has ethical ramifications. All decisions are initiated by motives and result in consequences: were our motives and intentions good or bad, and were the consequences and outcomes good or bad? Unlike breathing and blinking, which are automatic, human beings possess free will and can choose to behave ethically or unethically in a particular situation. Even if the decision maker believes he or she is being ethical, someone harmed by the action may think otherwise.

When an organization employs someone, that individual brings to work not only unique job skills, but also his or her ethics. Ethics is the set of principles a person uses to determine whether an action is good or bad. Interactions involving owners, customers, employees, lenders, suppliers, and government officials have an ethical dimension.

People experience a multitude of ethical dilemmas on a daily basis. Almost every decision and action a person makes impacts other people:

- Should you arrive at work early, on time, or late?
- Should you submit adequate work that meets a deadline or submit the highest-quality work possible and miss the deadline?
- Should you inform your boss about your colleague's questionable work habits?
- Should the organization incur additional costs for environmental protection technologies not required by law?
- Should you leave work at the designated time or cancel after-work plans and stay late to finish a project?

Each of these decisions and actions is subject to ethical analysis that considers competing obligations and outcomes. Even if an employee does not think the decision is an ethical issue, the person benefitted or harmed may think so. Arriving late to work may seem deserving after laboring hard the previous day. But other employees may be waiting for essential information that only the late arrival possesses.

Some decision choices are obviously right or wrong, while others are questionable. Ethical analysis takes into consideration all aspects of an action sequence. An action sequence consists of the motivation behind the act, the act itself, and the consequences of the act. Acts are morally neutral. There is nothing inherently right or wrong with a manager speaking to an employee. It is the motivation that led to the act, and the consequences of the act, that carry ethical weight. In this sense, actions and behaviors are surrounded, or sandwiched, by ethics.

For instance, is it ethical for a manager to inform a subordinate about upcoming layoffs? It depends. If the manager has permission to share the information and doing so improves the subordinate's performance, then it is ethical. However, if sharing the information violates a confidentiality agreement and the subordinate is likely to misuse the information, then it is unethical.

An ideal ethical situation is one in which a person has good motives and the act results in good consequences. When this alignment occurs, people often do not realize the act has an ethical dimension. On the other extreme, the most unethical situation is one in which a person has bad motives and the act results in bad consequences. Those committing these acts often realize what they are doing is wrong, but do so anyway, maybe to achieve some personal gain at the expense of others. Many action sequences fall within these two ethical extremes, and either motives or consequences fall short of the ideal.

Sometimes, good motives can generate bad consequences. Trying to help a colleague perform one task, for example, might distract the person from meeting an important deadline. Sometimes, bad motives can generate good consequences. An employee's selfish refusal to assist an annoying colleague may result in the colleague obtaining assistance from an even more qualified person. When evaluating these less-than-ethically-ideal situations, some people place greater ethical weight on having proper motives, while others place greater weight on achieving favorable consequences.

Unethical Behaviors at Work

Extent

Every organization is confronted with ethical and unethical behaviors. What is the extent of unethical behaviors at work? The Ethics Resource Center surveyed more than 3,010 employees in 2009 about work-related ethical issues.[1] Approximately half of the respondents observed at least one type of major ethical misconduct in the workplace during the past year, and nearly half of these violated the law.

Some employees are ambivalent about being ethical at work and fail to learn lessons from unethical predecessors. During 2008, Lehman Brothers declared bankruptcy in part for having hidden $50 billion in bad assets, using some of the same complicated financial statement gimmickry that destroyed Enron earlier in the decade.[2]

Among respondents to the 2003 Ethics Resource Center survey, 25 percent reported that their peers were not committed to ethics. Despite the high-profile scandals of the early 2000s, with prison terms exceeding 20 years issued to former WorldCom CEO Bernie Ebbers and Enron CEO Jeff Skilling, the lack of commitment to ethics increased in subsequent Ethics Resource Center surveys. The number of respondents claiming that their peers were not committed to ethics rose to 34 percent in 2005 and 39 percent in 2007.

In 2009, the types of ethical misconduct survey respondents observed most within the previous 12 months included the following:[3]

- Company resource abuse (23%)
- Abusive or intimidating behavior toward employees (22%)
- Lying to employees (19%)
- Email or Internet abuse (18%)

- Conflicts of interest (16%)
- Discrimination (14%)
- Lying to outside stakeholders (12%)
- Employee benefit violations (11%)
- Employee privacy breach (10%)
- Improper hiring practices (10%)
- Falsifying time or expenses (10%)

These ethical misconducts were observed in both large firms (27 percent) and small firms (16 percent), and in all sectors examined, including government agencies (29 percent reporting ethical misconducts), nonprofit organizations (26 percent), publicly traded for-profit firms (25 percent), and privately held for-profit firms (25 percent).

During a five and a half year period, 2000 to mid-2005, forty Fortune 100 companies either pled guilty to a crime; were found guilty of a crime; or agreed to settle a case out of court for acts such as fraud, discriminatory practices, undisclosed executive pay, antitrust violations, and patent infringements.[4] Some of the Fortune 100 companies committed multiple offenses and promoted products that contributed to multiple deaths.

These survey results help explain why businesses score so poorly on Gallup Poll public trust surveys. In 2009, only 16 percent of the respondents expressed confidence in "Big Business," compared to 82 percent in the military and 67 percent in small businesses.[5] In 2008, when asked to evaluate the honesty and ethical standards of different professions, 83 percent of the respondents rated nurses as either having high or very high ethical standards, followed by 66 percent for pharmacists. Business executives were rated much lower, at just 12 percent, followed by 10 percent for insurance salespeople, 9 percent for stockbrokers, and 7 percent for car salesmen.[6]

Even the most admirable organizations can engage in ethical misconduct. Fannie Mae, the government-sponsored home mortgage company, was rated the #1 "Best Corporate Citizen" by *Business Ethics* magazine over a five-year time horizon, 2000 through 2004, based on data gathered from seven different stakeholder perspectives.[7] Yet, in 2006, Fannie Mae's CEO, CFO, and former controller were found to have manipulated company earnings from 1998 through 2004 to maximize their bonuses. In addition, Fannie Mae's many bad loans in the subprime mortgage market contributed significantly to the onset of the 2008 worldwide financial crisis and recession. Millions of people lost their jobs. Consequently, Fannie Mae was put into conservatorship.[8] Similarly, Xerox, despite having won many awards for its excellent diversity programs, was fined $12 million in 2008 for racial discrimination.[9]

Managers as Victims

Managers and owners are also victims of unethical behaviors. Researchers estimate that 20 percent to 44 percent of all resumes contain lies about work histories, educational background, or other credentials.[10] One out of three employees calling in sick is really tending to personal needs, family needs, or stress or feels entitled to a day off.[11]

The percentage of employees engaged in theft is a staggering 60 percent.[12] In addition to the usual pilfering of pens and paper, the most common employee misuses of corporate assets for personal use are:[13]

- Email: 63%
- Web Browser: 45%
- Fax Machine: 45%
- Software: 33%
- Mail/Overnight Delivery: 23%
- Wireless Phone: 22%
- Digital Copier: 18%

Profession and Industry Issues

Every profession and industry experiences ethical problems. In the accounting profession, a client audit contains opportunities for a wide range of deviant employee behaviors.[14] Unethical activities among auditors include falsifying reimbursement or time reports, working slowly without concern for budget limits, excessively surfing the web, using company resources for personal purpose, and ignoring manager input. Deviant behaviors against auditing coworkers include spreading rumors, cursing or harshly criticizing them, blaming them when things go wrong, and claiming credit for their work. When interacting with clients, some audit employees might bad-mouth audit firm managers, convey confidential or private information, or break client protocol for acceptable behavior.

The misuse of billable hours is also a problem in the legal profession. To maximize profits, and obtain partner status, lawyers are rewarded for charging as many hours as possible to clients. This has led some lawyers to delay concluding a case, overbill clients for services rendered, or charge clients for hours worked on other issues.[15] One egregious case involved a lawyer charging a client 3,500 billable hours for one year's work, which averages out to almost 10 hours a day, 7 days a week, every week of the year.[16]

The construction industry represents a significant part of the economy, accounting for 4 percent to 5 percent of gross domestic product. When surveyed by a construction industry association, 84 percent of the respondents reported that they personally experienced, encountered, or observed unethical industry-related acts or transactions during the past year, with 34 percent claiming this happened many times.[17] The top five major issues were (1) bid shopping [divulging solicited bids as leverage with contractors to get lower prices], (2) change orders [changing a contract order in the last moment to get a better price], (3) overbilling, (4) unreliable contractors, and (5) questionable claims.

Public relations and sales are two professions in which employees experience significant pressure to fudge the truth. According to a survey of 1,700 public relations executives, 25 percent lied on the job and 39 percent exaggerated the truth.[18] A survey of sales and marketing representatives revealed that 79 percent heard a salesperson make an unrealistic promise on a sales call, and 78 percent caught a competitor lying about his or her company's products and services.

Government agencies are not immune. According to the 2007 Ethics Resource Center survey, 52 percent of federal government employees, 57 percent of state government employees, and 63 percent of local government employees saw at least one form of ethical misconduct within the previous 12 months.[19] An audit of federal government agencies found that more than 40 percent of $14 billion in credit-card purchases from 2005 to 2006 violated purchasing procedures. Federal employees used government credit cards for a range of unethical and illegal expenses, including Internet dating services, luxury hotels, extravagant clothing, and unauthorized technology purchases.[20] An Agricultural Department employee fraudulently wrote 180 checks totaling more than $640,000 to her live-in boyfriend over a period of six years.

Army personnel, who operate under a stringent code of ethics, cheated on online testing programs used for promotions, including subject areas for explosives and demolitions, detecting mines, chemical detection, and air defense artillery.[21] Free test copies were available on a website called ShamSchool, which had more than 2 million hits during a 6-month period and 200,000 downloads of test answers during an 11-month time period. Army exams were also purchased on eBay.

Even medical researchers, whose findings influence health care delivery, engage in unethical behaviors. A prominent anesthesiologist falsified 21 medical studies on pain killers that were published in medical journals over a 12-year period of time.[22] The Food and Drug Administration relied on the fraudulent research to determine product safety and effectiveness.

As highlighted in Exhibit 1.1, small businesses are just as prone to experience unethical behaviors as large corporations.

Exhibit 1.1 But What If I'm a Small Business?

Small businesses make up approximately 90 percent of all businesses worldwide and account for more than 50 percent of all employees.* Many of the problems associated with managing morally imperfect employees and unethical behaviors are more, not less, prominent for small businesses.

In a survey of small business professionals, more than 25 percent reported ethical conflicts with customers, employees, and competitors.** The major issues were gift giving/kickbacks, honesty in contracts and agreements, honesty in internal communications, and granting pay raises. By 1995, just four years after the Federal Sentencing Guidelines went into effect, 56 percent of the businesses prosecuted had fewer than 20 employees.***

By nature of their limited size, small businesses may be more prone to bullying from a large unethical customer or supplier. Costs associated with lawsuits create a bigger burden for small businesses.

It may be easier to monitor employee behaviors in a small business. However, small businesses are more likely to employ high school and college students on a part-time basis, a group of employees more prone to doing favors for friends and less committed to the organization.

---

* Heledd Mair Jenkins, "A Critique of Conventional CSR Theory: An SME Perspective," *Journal of General Management*, 29, 4 (2004), 55–75.
** Scott J. Vitell, Erin Baca Dickerson, and Troy A. Festervand, "Ethical Problems, Conflicts and Beliefs of Small Business Professionals," *Journal of Business Ethics*, 28, 4 (2000), 15–24.
*** O. C. Ferrell, Debbie Thorne LeClair, and Linda Ferrell, "The Federal Sentencing Guidelines for Organizations: A Framework for Ethical Compliance," *Journal of Business Ethics*, 17, 4 (1998), 353–363.

Operation Areas

Every employee level and operational area is confronted with ethical issues. Unethical discriminatory practices based on race or gender can occur in dealings with suppliers, employees, customers, the government, or the public. Unethical discrimination can occur at any level of the organization—board of directors, executives, middle managers, staff, or production employees—or in any department—accounting, finance, human resources, or marketing.

Some operation areas engage in contradictory unethical game playing. According to a survey of chief financial officers, 67 percent had been pressured to misrepresent corporate results.[23] Some accountants under a CFO's span of control are pressured to overreport revenue to maximize profits and impress investors, while other accountants are pressured to underreport revenue to minimize taxable income.

Middle-level managers must balance productivity demands from superiors with job and resource limitations. To avoid appearing incompetent or to respond to requests from superiors, 25 percent of middle managers admit to having written a fraudulent internal report.[24] The pressure to accomplish "more with less" is particularly stressful during economic downturns, when layoff survivors are asked to pick up the responsibilities of those dismissed.

Secretaries have their own set of ethical issues. According to a 2003 survey, 57 percent of the secretaries had either been asked, or observed someone else being asked, by their boss to lie. Forty-three percent of the secretaries were asked to sign someone else's name to a legal document, and 36 percent were asked to prepare a document that included false or misleading information.[25] Harassment is another major problem among secretaries, with 36 percent reporting that they were verbally harassed and 21 percent sexually harassed at work. In terms of their own misbehaviors, 17 percent shared confidential information about an employee's salary, and 15 percent shared confidential information about hirings, firings, and layoffs.

The most economically vulnerable employees are low-wage workers. A survey of more than 4,000 low-wage workers found that during the previous week, 68 percent had experienced at least one pay-related violation.[26] Illegal immigrant women experienced the most pay violations.

Costs Associated with Unethical Behaviors

Managers often underestimate the costs associated with unethical behaviors. The most direct cost is lost business. It takes only one unethical behavior for an organization to lose a key customer or find itself sued by an aggrieved party. The Quadrangle private equity fund lost a $5 billion client, New York City Mayor Michael Bloomberg, for its involvement in a state pension fund scandal.[27] The $5 billion accounted for half of the firm's current assets. Arthur Andersen's $9.3 billion revenue stream evaporated after the federal government indicted the accounting firm for its involvement in the Enron scandal.

Other costs associated with unethical behaviors include legal costs, theft, recruitment and turnover costs, monitoring costs, reputation costs, and abusive treatment costs.

Legal Costs

Lawsuits are one of the most easily quantifiable costs associated with unethical behaviors. In a 2007 survey, 40 percent of the 250 largest U.S. corporations had at least one new lawsuit filed against them worth $20 million within the past year, and 20 percent spent at least $5 million for outside counsel.[28] The median award for employment civil rights cases settled in U.S. district courts between 2006 and 2007 was $158,000.[29]

Tobacco companies long avoided lawsuits for wrongful death or injury from customers who smoked. That changed in 1992 when the U.S. Supreme Court ruled that the Surgeon General's health warning on cigarette packages did not negate lawsuits against tobacco companies. In 1997, tobacco companies and state attorney generals reached a $368.5 billion settlement originated from lawsuits filed to pay Medicare costs for treating sick smokers.[30] In 2002, a jury ruled that Phillip Morris was liable for $28 billion in punitive damages to a smoker dying of lung cancer.[31] Following an extensive appeal process on the excessiveness of the damage award, in 2009 a new jury reduced the penalty to $13.8 million. There is no end in sight for this saga. In 2010, President Barack Obama's administration sought $300 billion in damages for a half-century of deception that either killed or damaged the health of millions of people.[32]

Prior to the 2008 financial crisis, there was a general sense in the financial industry that large credit rating agencies such as Moody's and Standard & Poor's intentionally overvalued high-risk securities to win future business from firms financially benefitting from high ratings, such as the banks selling the securities.[33] A Standard & Poor's employee encapsulated this game playing in an email noting that a deal "could be structured by cows and we'd rate it."[34] The unethical behavior was tolerated until the economy collapsed and billions of dollars of triple-A rated bonds disintegrated, ruining pension funds. Then large customers, including the California Public Employees Retirement System and the state of Ohio, filed lawsuits against the now beleaguered rating agencies.

The Equal Employment Opportunity Commission (EEOC) maintains an annual database of charges filed and resolved under various antidiscrimination laws, such as age discrimination or sexual harassment.[35] Exhibit 1.2 summarizes the totals for fiscal year 2009 and offers a comparison to fiscal year 1997. The discriminations are listed according to the number of cases filed in 2009, with 33,579 racial discrimination filings leading the pack. In terms of costs, organizations paid $121.5 million in fines for gender discrimination.

Exhibit 1.2 EEOC Charges and Resolutions 1997 and 2009

Type of Discrimination	Fiscal Year 1997	Fiscal Year 2009		
	Number of Cases Filed	Number of Cases Filed	Number of Cases Resolved	Monetary Benefits Determined by EEOC (excludes other forms of litigation)
Race	29,199	33,579	31,129	$82.4 million
Gender	24,728	28,028	26,618	$121.5 million
Age	15,785	22,778	20,529	$72.1 million
Disability	18,108	16,470	21,451	$67.8 million
Sexual Harassment	15,889	12,696	11,948	$51.5 million
National Origin	6,712	11,134	9,644	$25.7 million
Pregnancy	3,977	6,196	5,594	$16.8 million
Religion	1,709	3,386	25,958	$7.6 million
Equal Pay and Compensation	1,134	942	991	$4.8 million

Employee Theft

Theft represents a cost directly incurred by the organization for hiring untrustworthy employees. Employees can steal money, products, or time. Theft-related costs that are individually minimal—doing personal emails, Internet searchers, and phone calls on company time—become substantial when aggregated across an entire workforce. For instance, the U.S. Department of Interior calculated that non-work-related Internet usage by its employees cost taxpayers $2 million and a loss of 104,221 work hours annually.[36]

The biggest source of retail industry theft is employees, not customers. A missing product is 5 times more likely the result of an employee than a professional thief, and 15 times more likely the result of an employee than a shoplifter.[37] The U.S. Chamber of Commerce attributes one-third of annual business failures to employee theft and other personnel crimes.[38] The Association of Certified Fraud Examiners estimated that $994 billion is lost from the economy as a result of frauds, equivalent to 7 percent of the gross domestic product.[39] According to an annual survey conducted for the National Retail Federation, retail stores lost more than $41 billion from theft and fraud in 2006, 1.5 percent of total sales.[40] Approximately $20 billion of the losses, or 50 percent, were attributed to employees. In the construction industry, for every $1 million spent on a project, $5,000 to $50,000 is "unaccounted for."[41]

Theft can occur at all levels of an organization. Dennis Kozlowski, one of the highest paid CEOs in the world, and other Tyco executives defrauded shareholders of more than $600 million. Tyco had established an employee benefit that provided key employees with low-interest loans to pay taxes when stock options were exercised. Kozlowski misused this employee benefit to purchase a $15 million yacht and spent $72,042 for jewelry, $155,067 for clothing, $96,943 for flowers, $60,427 for club memberships, and $52,334 for wine.[42] He also used the low-interest loans to purchase a $90,000 Porsche Carrera and a $5 million diamond ring for his long-term mistress.

Monitoring Costs

Organizations incur monitoring costs when they employ, or do business with, unethical individuals. Once an employee has lied, he or she needs to be more closely monitored until trust is restored. According to an electronic monitoring and surveillance survey conducted by the American Management Association, 76 percent of the responding organizations monitor and review email, 51 percent use video surveillance, and 36 percent monitor employee computer time.[43]

An unethical organization incurs additional monitoring costs from increased scrutiny and requests by clients, auditors, or government regulators. In the construction industry, 74 percent of the surveyed owners do not trust contractors, and 60 percent of contractors do not trust design professionals.[44] The lack of trust results in additional costs due to heightened supervision and new layers of rules and regulations aimed at preventing unethical behaviors.

Reputation Costs

An organization's reputation is one of its most important assets. Reputation management is a high priority for many corporations and accounts for 63 percent of their market value.[45] Employees, customers, and investors consider organizational reputation when making employment and purchasing decisions.[46] An organization's reputation can be severely damaged when lawsuits and accusations of unethical behavior appear in the media, or when customers register complaints with the Better Business Bureau. Researchers report strong correlations between the frequency of Occupational Health and Safety Administration and Environmental Protection Agency violations and declines in organizational reputation.[47]

Continuous negative publicity creates substantial barriers for consumer engagement. Goldman Sachs announced a $3.46 billion profit for the first quarter of 2010, a time when Wall Street investors anxiously sought good news. But instead of being rewarded, Goldman Sachs stock price declined by 2 percent because of negative publicity surrounding the sale of bonds brokers expected to decline in value.[48] Consumer damage is lessoned if the organization has a history of being socially responsible prior to the wrongdoing.[49]

Abusive Treatment Costs

Managers are mistaken if they think the costs noted earlier pertain only to the most egregious unethical behaviors, such as blatant employee discrimination, customer fraud, or health and safety violations. Researchers attribute a wide range of costs to less egregious unethical behaviors, such as a verbally abusive manager.

Researchers report that abusive supervision affects approximately 13 percent of U.S. workers.[50] Costs in terms of absenteeism, health care costs, and lost productivity have been estimated to be $23.8 billion annually. Employees managed by an abusive boss respond in a variety of ways that result in additional costs to organizational operations. Some employees "get even" with the abusive boss by stealing money or product from the organization. Others may work less diligently when the abusive supervisor is not closely monitoring their activities.[51] Disgruntled current and former employees express their negative views on Internet blogs and community forums and engage in other activities that sabotage customer relations.[52] Employees can also release the abuse they incur on others, such as colleagues, subordinates, or customers requesting help. The stress associated with working for an abusive boss can lead to reduced productivity, additional health care costs, absenteeism, and turnover.[53]

Customers who have been mistreated by a belligerent manager or employee also have a variety of ways to "get even." According to medical malpractice research studies, the most prevalent predictor of lawsuits is not the doctor's skills or training. Instead, it is the quality of the relationship between doctor and patient. Potential litigants tend not to sue doctors they like.[54]

Recruitment and Turnover Costs

Unethical organizations cannot be trusted. As will be discussed in the following section, unethical organizations incur greater costs recruiting employees, customers, suppliers, and investors, and they must provide some premium to offset their ethical deficiencies. The lack of loyalty between an unethical organization and its key constituents is mutual, resulting in higher turnover among employees, customers, suppliers, and investors.

Competitive Advantages of Ethical Organizations

Whereas unethical behavior has a negative impact on organizational operations, ethical behavior can have a very positive impact on an organization's bottom line. A growing amount of research on organizational performance has shifted the theoretical debate from choosing between ethical performance and financial performance to choosing ethical performance because of its contributions to financial performance.[55]

How much ethics enhances financial performance depends on a wide range of issues. For instance, bankruptcy of a major customer and other market factors can overwhelm the financial benefits associated with being ethical. The linkage between

---

Exhibit 1.3 Competitive Advantages of Being Ethical and Trustworthy

Ethical organizations, compared to unethical organizations, are more likely to

1. Attract and retain high-quality employees
2. Attract and retain high-quality customers
3. Attract and retain high-quality suppliers

4. Attract and retain high-quality investors

5. Earn good will with community members and government officials

Organizations that attract and retain high-quality employees, customers, suppliers, and investors, and earn good will with community members and government officials, are more likely to have

6. Greater trustworthy information for decision making

7. Higher product and service quality

8. Higher levels of employee productivity

9. Less employee theft

10. Less need for employee supervision

11. Increased flexibility from stakeholders in times of emergency

ethical performance and financial performance is multifaceted, as outlined in Exhibit 1.3.

If you were a *job applicant*, would you rather work for an ethical or an unethical organization?

Ethical organizations, compared to unethical organizations, are more likely to attract high-quality employees, have higher levels of employee satisfaction, and greater employee commitment to both the organization and product or service quality.[56] If the pay is similar, job candidates consistently choose the ethical organization rather than the unethical organization. Individuals choose job offers from unethical organizations only if pay and benefits are substantially higher.

High-quality applicants seek employment with organizations on annual "best places to work" lists published by the federal government,[57] *Fortune* magazine,[58] and the Great Place to Work® Institute.[59] These organizations are characterized by high levels of employee empowerment, fairness, job satisfaction, and employee benefits. High-quality applicants also seek employment at organizations that perform well in an area of social responsibility uniquely important to them, such as best places to work for working mothers[60] or gays and lesbians.[61]

Researchers report that 94 percent of surveyed Americans believe it is "critical" or "important" to work for an ethical company and 33 percent have left a company because they disagreed with its business ethics.[62] A survey of MBA students found that 94 percent of them would accept an average of 14 percent lower pay to work for an organization with a reputation for high ethical standards.[63]

If you were a *customer*, would you rather purchase products or services from an ethical or unethical organization?

A stellar ethical reputation is priceless marketing and leads to higher levels of customer satisfaction and loyalty. When product price and quality are similar, potential customers consistently choose the ethical organization over the unethical organization. A consumer survey found that 70 percent of Americans had not purchased a company's product because of its questionable ethics, and that 72 percent were willing to pay a modest premium for products and services supplied by an ethical company.[64] An unethical organization wins out over an ethical organization only if its prices are substantially lower.

Persuading Employees of the Importance of Being Ethical

Being ethical is the right thing to do, but telling that to someone who is not concerned about ethics, or is considering an unethical act, will likely fall on deaf ears. Instead, build a business case linking ethical behavior to profitability or other performance measures. That usually gets the person's attention.

Begin by developing a list of reasons why being ethical is good for your organization's bottom line. Compelling reasons typically include customer and employee retention, lower costs, higher product quality, and employee morale. Then share a list of costs attributed to unethical behaviors, such as monitoring, reputation, turnover, and legal costs.

If you were a *supplier*, would you rather sell your products and services to an ethical or unethical organization?

An ethical organization attracts high-quality suppliers and has higher levels of supplier satisfaction and loyalty. Potential suppliers consistently choose to sell to the ethical organization that pays a fair price rather than the unethical organization. Suppliers depend on their customers to pay their bills on time and prefer to partner with customers they trust.

If you were an *investor*, would you rather do business with an ethical or unethical organization?

High-quality investors are attracted to ethical organizations, which leads to higher levels of investor satisfaction and loyalty. If anticipated return-on-investments (ROIs) are similar, potential lenders and investors consistently choose the ethical organization rather than the unethical organization. Investors are drawn to organizations that adopt best practices in corporate governance.[65] According to researchers, Wall Street investors respond favorably when new accounting laws requiring financial transparency, such as the Sarbanes-Oxley Act of 2002, are legislated.

If you were a *community leader or government official*, would you rather interact with an ethical or unethical organization?

Ethical organizations honestly communicate with stakeholders and pay their fair share of taxes. In return, ethical organizations earn the respect of, and gain access to, community leaders and government officials. When problems arise between a company and powerful constituency groups, politicians are more likely to provide a sympathetic perspective to the company if it has a stellar community service reputation.

Finally, there are a host of secondary performance benefits that ethical organizations achieve because they attract high-quality employees and are trusted by customers, suppliers, investors, and government officials.

People tend to treat others as they want others to treat them. The reverse is also true. People who are treated fairly and truthfully tend to reply in a fair and truthful manner. Managers can make better informed decisions when they know that the information supplied by others is trustworthy. The honest flow of ideas and high levels of employee loyalty, commitment, and satisfaction result in better quality consumer products and services, higher levels of employee productivity, less employee theft, and less need for employee supervision. In addition, in times of emergency, stakeholders are more likely to be flexible in their interactions with ethical organizations.

Starbucks, which in 2009 had more than 10,000 retail stores and 150,000 employees, considers its core mission to be to "inspire and nurture the human spirit." The company exhibits and monitors its socially responsible behaviors in five key areas: ethical sourcing, environment, community service, customer wellness, and diversity. The results are published in an annual *Global Responsibility Report* (see "Best Practice in Use" exhibit).[66]

BEST PRACTICE IN USE

Starbucks 2009 *Global Responsibility Report*

Ethical Sourcing   We're committed to buying and serving the highest-quality, responsibly grown, ethically traded coffee to help create a better future for farmers.

- Eighty-one percent of total coffee purchased was third-party verified or certified through Coffee and Farmer Equity (C.A.F.E) Practices, Fairtrade, or another externally audited system that ensures safe, fair, and humane working conditions and ecologically friendly growing methods.
- Provided $14.5 million in loans to 72,000 farmers in six countries to finance preharvest activities, make operational improvements, and cover export costs.

Environment   We're finding ways to minimize our environmental footprint, tackle climate change, and inspire others to do the same.

- Engaged 29 coffee-growing communities in pilot programs to reduce carbon emissions.
- Customers brought their own tumblers into stores more than 26 million times, keeping 1.2 million pounds of paper out of landfills.
- Completed installation of energy efficient lighting in more than 1,000 stores in the United States.
- Purchased renewable energy certificates equivalent to 25% of energy use.
- Reduced water use by 4.1%.

Community   As good neighbors we get involved with local efforts to bring people together and create positive change whenever we can.

- Employees and customers contributed 186,011 hours of community service.
- Awarded $2 million in Starbucks Shared Planet Youth Action Grants that engaged 20,868 young people in community activities.

Given the many financial benefits associated with ethical behavior, and the many costs associated with unethical behavior, why don't all organizations excel in ethics? The core of the problem can be found in the nature of human beings.

Let's Build a Building

Land for Sale

You work for a technical college that wants to expand operations into another city. In October 2012, you are assigned responsibility for finding land to build a new one-story 18,000 square foot building with state-of-the-art classrooms that would be completed on time for the fall 2014 academic year.

You drive by a parcel of land for sale and call the broker. He notes that this would be a reasonable location for your school, but he has two or three other properties that would be even better locations. The broker takes you to more expensive vacant land at a newly developed business park, anchored by a large stable corporation and other businesses that would be excellent prospects for supplying students and hiring your graduates.

You purchase the land in November 2012 and send out a call for proposals to architects for the $3 million building. The architect drawings are completed in November 2013 with the intent to start construction in December. The technical college has also hired a marketing firm to begin recruiting students.

You take the architect's drawings to city hall to apply for the building permit. The city reviews your materials and then shows you the Planned Use Development documents for the business park. To your shock, the college building violates zoning restrictions. The business park documents note that tenants are limited to office buildings and their ancillary uses. "There's no way a technical college counts as

an ancillary use," the city official explains. "The broker and business park manager should have known. I guess they just weren't paying attention."

You go back to the broker, who is surprised by the ruling. The broker informs the business park owner, who says he will fight for you with city hall to rezone the land, but these things take time and meeting your scheduled fall 2014 opening may no longer be reasonable. After a heated discussion, the business park owner offers to put lobbying to rezone high on his busy agenda if you make environmentally friendly design adjustments that would cost an additional $15 a square foot, raising the price to $3.275 million. Meanwhile, you've already incurred costs for purchasing the land, the architectural drawings, and marketing campaign.

What would you do? Would you

1. Sue the broker to recover your costs, sell the land, and build elsewhere?
2. Sue the business park owner to recover your costs, sell the land, and build elsewhere?
3. Agree to make the $275,000 building modifications to ensure that the business park owner uses all his lobbying power to immediately rezone so the technical college can open on time for the fall 2014 term?
4. Stay with the original $3 million building plan, negotiate with the business park owner and city to rezone, and delay the opening to the fall 2015?

Why?

Human Nature

Managing ethics entails understanding human nature. Are employees, customers, and suppliers inherently selfish or altruistic, can they be trusted or do they have to be carefully monitored? Why are human beings morally imperfect? From a managerial perspective, what are the most important features of our moral imperfection? Answers to these questions influence how managers can efficiently and effectively address ethical problems at work.

Human nature refers to the moral, psychological, and social characteristics of human beings. Philosophers, theologians, anthropologists, sociologists, and psychologists have explored and debated for centuries the moral dimensions of human nature at birth. No consensus has been achieved. Their responses, derived through both reason and faith, can be categorized into four areas: infants are born with prior knowledge of right and wrong, good, with inherited sin, and/or morally neutral.

Born with Prior Knowledge of Right and Wrong

Among the ancient Greek philosophers, Socrates (469–399 BC) and Plato (427–347 BC) theorized that individuals are born with a soul—consisting of mind, emotions, and desires—that forms an individual's inner essence.[67] The mind, filled with ideas, preexisted in a spiritual realm and joined the body at birth. With age and experience, individuals rediscover what they already knew about the world at the time of birth.

Born Good

The second perspective on human nature tends to be grounded in religious faith.[68] Theologians in a variety of faith traditions maintain that all individuals are born in the image of God, or with a conscience, which is good. The Book of Genesis in the Old Testament describes God blowing the breath of life into man's nostrils. Islam teaches that the human soul is a part of God within us. The soul is pure and sinless at birth and seeks perfect goodness. Conscience, in this context, is the voice of God, or pure goodness, within us. Individuals possess free will and can act in accordance with the goodness embodied within their soul or conscience, or they can choose to do wrong. People remain connected to their original God essence through righteous living. According to the philosopher Jean-Jacques Rousseau (1712–78), children are born good and then learn immoral behaviors from morally corrupt adults and institutions.[69]

Individuals often express a "gut" feeling or moral intuition that something is right or wrong, although they are unable to articulate the reasoning that led to their moral conclusion. University of Virginia psychology professor Jonathan Haidt attributes the moral conclusion to an individual's innate moral sense that is part of our psychological makeup.[70] Psychology researcher Paul Bloom traces moral sense to birth. Within the first year of life, infants exhibit a preference for helpful behaviors, compassion, and other pleasant situations, and an aversion to mean behaviors.[71] Dacher Keltner claims that positive emotions, such as kindness, are at the core of human nature and part of our DNA.[72]

According to Haidt's conception of a "moral sense," infants are born with five senses—sight, hearing, touch, smell, and taste—that enable them to perceive and interpret outside stimuli. Haidt maintains that infants are also born with a "moral sense" consisting of four groups of emotions that help individuals differentiate right from wrong: (1) other-praising emotions: gratitude and moral awe; (2) other-condemning emotions: contempt, anger, and disgust; (3) other-suffering emotions: sympathy, compassion, and empathy; and (4) self-conscious emotions: guilt, shame, and embarrassment. These emotions are developed over time, inform our sense of right and wrong, and guide people along a moral path.

Born with Inherited Sin

Others believe that individuals are born morally imperfect, or with inherited sin. This does not mean individuals are born evil, just morally imperfect. Due to inherited sin, a morally damaged soul joins the body at birth and needs to be healed.

Roman Catholics and many Protestants trace inherited sin to Adam and Eve's disobedience to God's will. Adam and Eve birthed children prior to becoming one with God and every person born since then begins life distant from the original source of goodness. According to Saint Augustine (354–430), original sin is physically transmitted through sexual intercourse, which weakens a person's will to deny evil temptations.[73] By choosing to do good, individuals restore the original essence that existed prior to Adam and Eve's fall from grace and reconcile with God.

Hindus and Buddhists believe that a morally imperfect soul is reincarnated from one individual to another.[74] The soul of a morally imperfect person departs a body at death and then reenters the body of a newborn baby. The individual currently embodying the soul is challenged to purify the inherited moral imperfections of the individual who previously embodied the soul. The soul no longer returns to Earth after an individual achieves enlightenment, a state of oneness with God consciousness in which all desires are appropriately managed and kindness to all things has been mastered.

Born Morally Neutral

Last, some philosophers maintain that individuals are born morally neutral. Aristotle (384–322 BC) disagreed with his teacher Plato's view that infants possessed preexisting ideas and argued that at birth the mind is an "unscribed tablet."[75] Many centuries later, John Locke (1632–1704) referred to this as a "tabula rasa," or blank slate, on which people store moral rules and knowledge based on life experiences.[76] Infants are born with moral capacities but are not preprogrammed with a set of moral principles. Their sense of morality is shaped by culture. Moral principles are learned through parental influence, experiences, and reason.

Cognitive Development

Whether born morally perfect, imperfect, or neutral, children are born into a particular family, neighborhood, and culture that influence their moral judgment. According to researchers, infants are born with a still developing three-pound brain, consisting of 100 billion neurons, which controls our central nervous system and houses our thinking process. A child's brain receives and analyzes information and formulates decisions.

With the passage of time, these decisions tend to form a pattern. One particular pattern found among children, and adults, is a desire to experience pleasure and avoid pain. Newborn babies cry because they feel hunger, anger, or pain and desire to be fed and comforted, which brings them pleasure.[77] Infants are born with a sense of justice; they smile when good things occur and frown when bad things occur.[78]

Parents are a child's most direct role model and shape the child's environmental experiences. Some infants are born to kind parents who view the newborn as a gift to be cherished and fulfill a baby's physical and emotional needs. These infants demonstrate emotional security, grow up trusting their surroundings, and maintain positive emotions and relationships. Other infants are emotionally neglected by their parents, who treat the newborn as a nuisance. These infants become emotionally insecure, distrust their surroundings, and maintain negative emotions and relationships.

Jean Piaget (1896–1980) was among the first psychologists to outline stages of cognitive development based on patterns he observed in children, including his own.[79] During the first two years of life, the child has an egocentric understanding of the world—the belief that what he or she sees, hears, feels, and thinks is what everyone else sees, hears, feels, and thinks. Infants express a social smile by six weeks of age; laughter and curiosity by three months; anger by eight months; and fear of social events, strangers, and separation from caregiver by the age of one, when they are also able to speak their first coherent words.[80] These are key milestones because the child is learning to differentiate situations and people, and to express his or her feelings to others.

At 18 months, children exhibit self-awareness, and feelings of pride, shame, and embarrassment. Around age two, through play and other activities, the child becomes more socio-centric and realizes that other people see, hear, feel, and think differently. By two-and-a-half years of age, the child understands what it means to be good or bad, and by age three can empathize with another child's situation. As the child's conscience forms, the child becomes more capable of self-regulating emotions and behaviors. Mental scripts are developed that enable the child to generalize appropriate behaviors for different situations, such as "If someone helps me I should say thank you"; "When I grab other children's toys they get mad and I should give it back instead of hitting them."

Stages of Moral Development

Everyone has the potential to be kind or cruel to others. Why do some people make decisions that take into consideration only their own interests while others continually make decisions based on living for the sake of others? Harvard psychologist Lawrence Kohlberg (1927–87), influenced by the writings of Jean Piaget, sought to answer this question by analyzing how children and adults from many cultures formed moral judgments in response to a series of ethical dilemmas. The most famous of these ethical dilemmas is a situation involving Heinz, a fictional person who stole a highly priced rare drug from a pharmacist to save his dying wife (see Exhibit 1.4).[81]

Exhibit 1.4 The Heinz Dilemma

In Europe, a woman was near death from a special kind of cancer. There was one drug that doctors thought might save her. It was a form of radium that a druggist in the same town had recently discovered. The drug was expensive to make, but the druggist was charging 10 times what the drug cost him to make. He paid $2,000 for the radium and charged $20,000 for a small dose of the drug. The sick woman's husband, Heinz, went to everyone he knew to borrow the money, but he could only get together about $10,000, which is half of what it cost. He told the druggist that his wife was dying, and asked him to sell it cheaper or let him pay later. But the druggist said, "No, I discovered the drug and I'm going to make money from it." Heinz got desperate and broke into the man's store to steal the drug for his wife.

Should the husband have done that?

Based on extensive research, patterns emerged in terms of how people reasoned through the ethical dilemmas. According to Kohlberg, people sequentially progress through a continuum of six stages of moral development, beginning with egocentric punishment avoidance and culminating at the level of universal ethical principles. An individual might stop progress at any point along the stages of moral development. As shown in Exhibit 1.5, the six stages are subdivided according to three levels: Preconventional, Conventional, and Postconventional.

Exhibit 1.5 Stages of Moral Development for Heinz Dilemma

Level	It is "*Right*" for Heinz to Steal the Drug because...	It is "*Wrong*" for Heinz to Steal the Drug because...
Preconventional Level: Moral reasoning is based on what benefits the individual. Only my interests exist and matter. Moral determination is based on my own needs and wants.		
Stage 1: *Obedience-and-Punishment orientation*. Right is determined by obeying rules from a superior authority and avoiding punishment.	If Heinz lets his wife die, he might be punished. People will think he killed her.	Heinz will get caught and be punished in jail.
Stage 2: *Instrumental orientation*. Right is determined by a selfish desire to obtain rewards and benefits from others. You should be nice to other people so that they will be nice to you.	Heinz needs his wife's companionship. If Heinz is caught, he can pay the money back, serve a short jail term, and still have his wife.	Heinz's wife will probably die before he gets out of jail. It will not do him any good.
Conventional Level: Moral reasoning is based on applying a social role or group membership analysis. The interests of other people must be considered. Moral determination is based on performing good or right roles, pleasing others, and maintaining societal order.		
Stage 3: *Good Boy–Nice Girl orientation*. Right is determined by winning the approval, and avoiding the disapproval, of others. You should be concerned about the feelings of other people and keep loyalty and trust with partners.	Heinz's family will think he's a bad husband if he doesn't do everything he can to save his wife's life.	Everyone will think Heinz is a criminal. Heinz will feel bad bringing dishonor and shame to his family.
Stage 4: *Law-and-Order orientation*. Right is being a dutiful citizen who follows societal rules and maintains social order.	Heinz might be held legally responsible for not saving his wife.	Heinz is breaking the law.
Postconventional Level: Moral reasoning is based on applying abstract universal principles. There are societal and beyond societal perspectives that matter. Moral determination is based on abiding by abstract principles applied to society.		

Stage 5: *Social contract orientation.* Right is determined by preserving mutually agreed upon human rights and changing unjust laws for the sake of community welfare. Individual freedom should be limited only when such freedom interferes with other people's freedom.	The law was not fashioned for situations in which an individual would forfeit life by obeying the rules. The wife's right to life is more important than profits.	Others may also have great need for the drug. Heinz is being carried away by his emotions and needs to take a long-range point of view.
Stage 6: *Universal ethical principles orientation.* Right is determined by following abstract universal ethical principles (such as justice, the Golden Rule, equality, and respect for life). These principles represent a universal consciousness that all humanity should follow.	Heinz would not have lived up to the standards of his conscience, such as respect for life, if he allowed his wife to die.	Heinz did not live up to the standards of his conscience, such as being honest or doing to others as he would want done to him, when he stole from the pharmacist.

Each of the three levels is distinguishable by an individual's perceived relationship with society's rules and expectations. At the preconventional level, the individual is not perceived as being part of a broad community with rules and regulations. Instead, the right thing to do is that which generates personal pleasure and avoids pain. At the conventional level, societal roles and agreements matter a great deal to the individual. The right thing to do is to be a good role model and maintain societal order. At the postconventional level, the individual delves into the principles that govern societal roles and order. The right thing to do is to abide by abstract universal ethical principles, such as justice for everyone associated with the issue, that should be the basis of, but may conflict with, particular societal rules and regulations.

An individual's sequential passage through the six stages of moral development is influenced by three factors: age, respect for people at the next higher stage, and moral discomfort.

First, progression is somewhat dependent on age because the mind becomes more capable of understanding abstract thoughts over time. Kohlberg and other researchers report that most children under the age of nine, some adolescents, and some adults (particularly criminals) reason at the *preconventional* level. All pleasure-seeking pursuits are good until the pain associated with a scolding parent or authority figure outweighs the pleasure. Most adolescents and adults reason at the *conventional* level, which is why this level is called conventional or ordinary. They want others to perceive them as being good, and they understand the importance of laws for maintaining societal order and peace. Some adults, and a few adolescents, reason at the *postconventional* level. They are compelled to follow the dictates of their conscience, which are based on universal ethical principles.

Second, people predominantly apply one stage of moral reasoning, are comfortable applying lower stages, admire people one stage higher, and consider people two stages higher ethically naïve. A manager who reasons primarily at the "Good Boy–Nice Girl" stage will occasionally justify actions based on concern for punishment and rewards, admires managers who apply "law-and-order" concerns, and thinks managers who apply concern for universal human rights to decision making do not understand how businesses should operate.

Third, moral discomfort plays a key factor in explaining why some adults never progress beyond the preconventional level (Stages 1 and 2), and most adults stop moral reasoning progress at being a good group member (Stage 3) or law-abiding citizen (Stage 4).[82] If an individual is always content with the conclusions a particular level of moral reasoning generates, then there is little motivation to advance to the next higher sequential stage.

Cognitive dissonance occurs when an individual holds inconsistent or contradictory attitudes and beliefs, which creates an unpleasant state of mind. Individuals relieve this moral discomfort by reasoning at the next higher stage of moral development, which they admire.

For instance, a manager could be comfortable with the conclusions generated using Stage 3 "Good Boy–Nice Girl" moral reasoning. The manager observes how other managers behave and adopts their behaviors. If other managers work hard to maximize revenue, that is what the manager does. If one method other managers use to generate revenue involves selling faulty product without informing consumers of the potential dangers, which is a violation of the law, then the manager does so as well because that is what is expected of a "good" manager in this organization.

But one day the manager becomes upset when a customer is seriously harmed by the product, creating cognitive dissonance. The previous moral script the manager followed—do what the other mangers do—now creates psychological pain. An emotional crisis occurs because applying the usual pattern of decision making led to a blameworthy, rather than a praiseworthy, outcome. The manager might progress to the next higher stage of moral reasoning (Stage 4 "Law-and-Order"), which the manager admires, and start informing customers of the potential dangers because it would generate more psychological peace for the manager.

Lies and Cheating

Managers need honest information from other employees and stakeholders to achieve optimal organizational performance. Yet, truthfulness is particularly challenging for many people. "Do not lie" and "do unto others as you want done to you" are two moral imperatives, principles compelling people to action, found in all cultures and major world religions. Despite these often-repeated moral messages, children and adults conceal and falsify the truth on a daily basis and lie when it is to their advantage. For instance, people commonly lie about health issues, alcohol consumption, income level, weight, age, and sexual encounters to impress others, avoid punishment, or protect the feelings of others.

At what age do individuals begin to lie? Children lie and deceive others as soon as they can formulate and articulate alternative strategies, which is soon after they can speak. According to psychiatrist Charles Ford, "it is apparent that all children lie and that lying is to a large extent sanctioned, taught, and encouraged by those with whom the child comes in contact."[83] A child will deny having eaten forbidden food if the consequence of truth telling is punishment. If a forbidden activity is fun, children try to experience the forbidden activity beyond parental observation and then deny having done so if asked.

For 90 minutes, Anne Wilson and her colleagues videotaped interactions within 40 different families that had a two- and a four-year old child in a home setting, and then videotaped them again two years later, when the children were four and six years old.[84] Ninety-six percent of the children lied at least once during these two observations. Researchers report that as a child ages, lying to help a peer group member avoid punishment outweighs being honest with a parent, teacher, or anyone in authority.[85]

Lying and cheating continue through high school. The 2006 *Josephson Institute Report Card on the Ethics of American Youth* provides sobering statistics based on a survey of 36,000 high school students.[86] Their aspirations are appropriate—98 percent said that it was important to be a person of good character. Their moral contentment is solid—92 percent were satisfied with their personal ethics and character. Their parental guidance is in the right direction—90 percent said that their parents always want them to do the right thing, no matter the cost. But, within the past year, 82 percent admitted having lied to a parent about something significant and 62 percent lied to a teacher. In a different study of high-achieving high school students, 80 percent cheated at least once the past year.[87]

Cheating patterns continue in college, where cheating is rather widespread.[88] In a sample of nearly 2,400 respondents representing 260 business schools, approximately 52 percent had cheated on a test or written assignment and more than 70 percent personally observed another student cheating on an exam or written assignment. Ironically, more than 50 University of Wisconsin–Madison upper-level accounting students cheated on a take-home exam immediately after hearing an ethics presentation by Enron whistle-blower Sherron Watins.[89]

As demonstrated by Exhibit 1.6, moral challenges continue into adulthood. Research by Bella DePaulo and her colleagues found that adults lied on average once a day and told one lie for every five social interactions lasting more than 10 minutes.[90] The IRS estimates that more than 10 million Americans purposely underpay their income taxes, a $200 billion annual revenue loss to the federal government.[91] A whistle-blower for the Swiss bank UBS informed authorities that 52,000 American clients hid income in offshore accounts to avoid paying taxes.[92]

Exhibit 1.6 The Day Americans Told the Truth

In one of the most extensive studies documenting adult moral challenges, researchers surveyed thousands of people in person and through telephone interviews.* The findings follow:

• 91% lied regularly	• 25% cheated on income taxes
• 35% stole office supplies	• 22% lied to the boss
• 33% lied on a job application	• 22% stole from a store
• 31% cheated on his or her spouse	• 20% exaggerated an insurance claim

---

* James Patterson and Peter Kim, *The Day America Told the Truth* (New York: Prentice Hall Press, 1991).

Moral imperfection, however, is just a small aspect of human activity. If adults lie once a day, then they are honest and truthful hundreds or thousands of times every day. At any given moment, hundreds of millions of acts of kindness take place around the world. All children may lie in certain circumstances when it benefits them, but, according to developmental psychologist Michael Tomasello, helping behaviors are also innate because preverbal children exhibit them prior to being taught rules of polite behavior by their parents.[93]

Researchers report that by 18 months of age, toddlers exhibit altruistic behaviors, the deliberate pursuit of actions intended to benefit the interests or welfare of others. In one revealing study, a researcher purposely struggled performing ordinary tasks in front of 24 toddlers. Every time a book was "accidentally" knocked over or a towel dropped, the toddler responded in a helpful manner. By the age of two, some children exhibit feelings of guilt when breaking someone else's toy.[94] Other research revealed that preschoolers spontaneously help, without being asked, those struggling to reach for paint or trying to tie an apron.[95]

These helping behaviors continue throughout adulthood. People open doors for strangers, set aside time to help friends and family members, and make philanthropic donations, sometimes anonymously. Nearly half of all Americans perform a volunteer service, with 30 percent volunteering at least once a month.[96] In 2008, Americans donated $229 billion to nonprofit organizations, which is an average of 2.2 percent of personal disposal income.[97] Living for the sake of others is a time-honored tradition that everyone does sometimes, and some individuals do often.[98] As shown in Exhibit 1.7, many people will return a lost wallet to its owner, but not all of them.[99]

Exhibit 1.7 What Would Happen if You Lost Your Wallet?

Have you ever wondered what the odds were of a stranger returning your lost wallet with money in it? 74 percent. On 100 different occasions in various public places, a researcher strategically left an inexpensive wallet containing $2.10; a fake $50 gift certificate redeemable by calling a phone number; and an identification card with the wallet owner's name, address, and phone number. The ensuing events involving the lost wallet were filmed with a hidden camera and are available for viewing on the Internet. Within 30 days, 74 percent of the finders returned the lost wallet. A greater percentage of women than men returned the wallet, 86 percent to 61 percent. Three of the 26 people who did not return the wallet attempted to redeem the stolen $50 gift certificate.

Why Do Good People Behave Unethically?

Ethics would be easy to manage if it were simply a matter of detecting and dismissing evil people. But that is not the nature of life in organizations. Most employees are good people; otherwise, they would be in jail rather than being employed. Good people occasionally make ethical mistakes, which at times can be very costly for an organization.

There are four general reasons why good people occasionally behave unethically. First, a good person may not have intended to generate the resultant unethical outcome. Second, a good person may choose one set of values over a competing set of values. Third, a good person may justify the unethical behavior based on a reason considered more compelling, such as organizational survival. Fourth, a good person may choose not to prevent an unethical behavior for compelling reasons, such as fear of being fired or retaliation.

Unintended Unethical Behaviors

Unintended unethical behaviors could result from insufficient knowledge, situational ambiguity, or a misaligned management system.[100] Sometimes a person may have good motives, but insufficient knowledge or awareness. For instance, the manager of a retail clothing store may generously donate damaged products to Goodwill to assist people in need. Some of the used clothing is then purchased in bulk and sent to illegal street vendors in San Salvador. As a result, legitimate small retailers in San Salvador, who cannot compete on price with the illegal street vendors, go bankrupt. The manager donating damaged clothing did not intend to bankrupt the San Salvador retailer, but that is the action sequence consequence.

Sometimes the ethics of a situation are ambiguous or complex. Assume a colleague is obviously overwhelmed by work deadlines that, if not met, could result in being terminated. Should you proactively take on some of the colleague's work, ask others to provide assistance, or do nothing? Providing assistance may seem to be the ethical response. Indeed, the colleague may accuse you of being unethical for not providing the necessary assistance. However, many contextual issues must be considered before reaching a quick moral judgment. Providing assistance could be unethical if the work you set aside is even more important, or if your assistance makes the matter worse because you lack adequate skills or knowledge.

Lastly, the unintended unethical behavioral outcome could result from a misaligned management system rather than the fault of a particular employee. Managers in publicly held organizations have a fiduciary duty to maximize shareholder wealth. Managers may be able to achieve higher sales and profits by using extravagant packaging and junk mail marketing. The manager does not intend to reduce the quality of life for future generations by contributing to landfill scarcity and climate change, but that is the action sequence consequence.

Choosing Between Competing Values

Sometimes ethical dilemmas arise and the decision maker must choose between two competing values, both of which are morally appropriate. But in choosing one set of moral values over another, those not benefitted from the decision might claim the choice was unethical. Rushworth Kidder notes that "The *really* tough choices, then, don't center upon right versus wrong. They involve right versus right."[101]

Kidder identifies four types of ethical dilemmas based on competing values:

- *Truth versus Loyalty*: A manager possesses confidential information that will have a negative impact on another employee. The soon-to-be negatively impacted employee asks the manager about the confidential information. Should the manager tell the truth to the employee or maintain loyalty to the company by not sharing the confidential information? Similarly, a manager questions an employee about the recent poor performance of the employee's best friend and colleague. Should the employee tell the manager about the colleague's recent alcohol problem or maintain loyalty to the friend?

- *Individual versus Community*: A company has scarce resources. Should the scarce resource be given to the one person who could most benefit from it or be shared equally among everyone in the work group? Similarly, a subordinate has a privacy right to not share life-threatening health care information with other employees. But some employees would want to help if they knew about the life-threatening illness. Should the manager respect the subordinate's right to privacy or inform the other employees?

- *Short Term versus Long Term*: An employee's future promotion depends on earning an MBA degree. It will take several years to graduate from a part-time evening and weekend MBA program. The employee also has three young children who immediately benefit from parental interactions. Should the employee focus on immediate family needs or enroll in an MBA program that would financially benefit the family in the long term? Similarly, during a recession, should a company sit on cash reserves to ensure current stability or make a substantial investment in a project that may yield favorable financial benefits in a few years?

- *Justice versus Mercy*: A talented, accomplished, and well-respected employee has violated company policy. Fortunately, the damage was minimal. The employee admitted the mistake and promised never to violate the policy again. According to the company's policy violation standards, any employee violating the policy must be terminated. If not terminated, other employees will complain about preferential treatment. Should the manager uphold the policy and exercise justice by firing the talented, accomplished, and well-respected employee or forgive the employee's mistake?

All four types of ethical dilemmas represent hard choices in which an aggrieved party can claim that the decision maker has behaved unethically even though the decision maker thoughtfully made what he or she considered to be a highly ethical decision.

Intentional Unethical Behaviors

People provide a wide range of reasons for behaving unethically. The most basic justification for behaving unethically, as suggested by Kohlberg's theory of moral development, is to avoid punishment and receive praise. A salesperson may declare more sales than actually achieved in a month to obtain a bonus or avoid being fired. Or, the salesperson may offer an even nobler justification, such as helping the work unit or organization meet its goals. In either case, the salesperson performs a cost-benefit analysis and concludes that the benefits of behaving unethically outweigh the costs.

On a broad contextual level, some good people attribute their occasional unethical misbehaviors on an organizational culture that either encourages or tolerates them. A salesperson, who in other aspects of life may be an outstanding citizen and role model, might lie to customers about product quality to meet weekly, monthly, or annual revenue goals. The salesperson might justify the unethical behavior on the grounds that other salespeople in the organization, or in similar organizations, do it. Although the behavior is unethical, the salesperson reasons, it not only goes unpunished, but is rewarded with bonuses and promotions.

Some good people behave unethically as a result of feeling pressured to do so. A survey conducted by the Society for Human Resource Management and the Ethics Resource Center found that 24 percent of the respondents were pressured to compromise ethical standards either periodically, fairly often, or all the time. Of those feeling pressured, the top five organizational sources were:[102]

1. Following the boss's directives (experienced by 49%)

2. Meeting overly aggressive business or financial objectives (48%)

3. Helping the organization to survive (40%)

4. Meeting schedule pressures (35%)

5. Wanting to be a team player (27%)

Stanley Milgram, a professor of social psychology, conducted a series of troubling social experiments demonstrating how good people are capable of physically harming others if directed to do so by someone in authority willing to take responsibility for the act.[103] New Haven, Connecticut, residents were recruited as research subjects to participate in a learning experiment being designed by the Yale University Psychology Department. The research subjects were instructed by an experimenter wearing a scientific laboratory coat to administer a shock to a learner strapped in an electric chair by pressing a switch on a shock generator machine every time the learner gave an incorrect answer. The punishment level was increased by 15 volts after each subsequent wrong answer, up to 450 volts. The shock generator machine's control panel clearly labeled 195 volts as "Very Strong Shock," 255 volts as "Intense Shock," 315 volts as "Extreme Intensity Shock," and 375 volts as "Danger: Severe Shock."

Unknown to the research subject, the learner faked being hurt by the shocks. The learner began complaining about pain from the shocks at 120 volts, demanded that the experiment end after 150 volts, and let out agonizing screams at 270 volts. If a research subject hesitated to administer the next level of shock following a wrong answer, the experimenter directed the research subject to continue. The results: 65 percent of the research subjects proceeded, at 15 volt increments of increasing severity, to the maximum 450 volts of punishment despite the learner's agonizing pleas to stop. During the post-experiment debriefing, research subjects reported that they continued to obey the experimenter's commands even though their own conscience urged them to stop physically harming the learner.

Behaving unethically to be a team player highlights the importance of an employee's sense of belongingness.[104] If everyone else in the organization is falsifying expense reports or stealing product, then to do otherwise creates isolation by bringing attention to behaving differently. This justification is particularly compelling if the individual has low self-esteem, a weak sense of moral identity, lacks moral courage, or has low tolerance for conflict with others. For instance, although people agree that they should not take company property without permission, hotel staff may steal an occasional pastry when invited to do so by coworkers. Otherwise, it could create interpersonal conflict and lead to ostracism from the group.

Finally, a good person may behave unethically because the end goal is so essential that the ends justify the means. Executives may provide false financial statements to the public because they believe this is the only way their companies can survive a difficult financial situation. An employee might provide a boss with false performance information so as to protect his or her job status. Such short-term thinking damages years of trust building. For instance, despite overwhelming scientific evidence of climate change, years of research were called into question when a computer hacker released emails written by leading scientists that referenced manipulating or censoring some contrary evidence.[105] Both the researchers and the computer hacker behaved unethically for what they considered a noble cause.

Failure to Report Unethical Behaviors

Why would a good person remain silent about unethical activities at work? Based on in-depth interviews with employees, researchers found that 85 percent had not raised an important issue or concern to their bosses on at least one occasion. The top reasons for not informing a manager about unethical behaviors were[106]

- Fear of being labeled or viewed negatively by others, such as being considered a troublemaker, tattletale, or complainer
- Fear of damaging relationships with the person committing the unethical act
- Fear of retaliation or punishment from the person committing the unethical act
- Fear of negatively impacting the life of the person committing the unethical act
- Fear of being blamed for the problem
- Belief that management would not act on the issue if informed

The justifications provided earlier for unintended unethical behaviors and intentional ethical behaviors also justify remaining silent. These justifications for inaction are apparent in Good Samaritan research studies that examine whether a person's willingness to assist a stranger is based on personality characteristics, issue sensitivity, or a contextual factor, such as time.[107] In the original study, researchers informed students attending Princeton Theological Seminary that they would be participating in a preaching contest in another building. The researchers measured personality by gathering volunteer service information from the participants along with other common personality measures. Issue sensitivity was measured based on the content of the sermon participants would practice. Half the students were told to prepare a sermon on the Good Samaritan, thus sensitizing them to the issue, and the other half were assigned a nonrelated topic. The time factor was measured based on instructions regarding when the sermon had to be given. After practicing for the contest, half the students were told they had 20 minutes to arrive at the contest room. Researchers told the other half that they were already late.

Along the path to the other building, a research confederate moaning in pain requested help from each passer-by. Some seminarians behaved as Good Samaritans; others did not. Researchers examined what attributes best predicted which seminarians ignored the person's pleas for help. Seminarians in a hurry were the least likely to help, even if they had scored highly for serving others or had just practiced giving a sermon on the Good Samaritan. Time pressures, and other situational factors, can blind good people to the ethical ramifications of their decisions or influence them to behave unethically.

SUMMARY

Organizations are complex human endeavors. Individuals have a dual nature. Individuals are primarily honest but also lie when it is beneficial. Individuals care primarily for their own welfare but also for the welfare of others. Individuals are kind to others but can also be cruel at times. In a general sense, individuals seek to experience pleasure and avoid pain; have a sense of right and wrong; and are influenced by reasons and emotions, their conscience, and their peers. Nobody is morally perfect, although some people are more ethical than others.

Every day newspapers document the best and worst of humanity, and many of these situations are work related. Managers typically underestimate the prevalence of work-related ethical problems and the financial costs associated with unethical behaviors. Recognizing that all humans are morally flawed may seem slightly depressing. But recognizing human frailty enables managers to make informed plans that are more likely to succeed. As highlighted in this chapter, appropriately managing ethics can create many competitive advantages that lead to superior organizational and financial performance.

KEY WORDS

Stakeholder; ethics; action sequence; human nature; conscience; inherited sin; tabula rasa; Jean Piaget; Lawrence Kohlberg; stages of moral development; cognitive dissonance; moral imperatives; altruistic behaviors; Good Samaritan

CHAPTER QUESTIONS

1. What are the most common types of unethical behaviors in organizations?
2. In what ways do unethical behaviors increase organizational costs?
3. What are the competitive advantages of creating and sustaining an ethical organization?
4. Describe the six stages of moral developments.
5. Why do good people occasionally behave unethically?

In the Real World: Enron

Merger Opportunity—1985

In 1985, corporate raider Irwin "The Liquidator" Jacobs proposed a hostile takeover of the financially troubled InterNorth, an Omaha, Nebraska, firm that operated the largest national gas pipeline in North America. InterNorth's CEO contacted Ken Lay, the CEO of a regional company called Houston Natural Gas (HNG), about a potential merger to prevent the hostile takeover. InterNorth proposed purchasing HNG's $47 stock at $70 a share, for a total price tag of $2.4 billion, much of it borrowed money. Jacob's hostile takeover of InterNorth would be prevented because, even if he sold all the newly combined company's corporate assets, Jacobs could not profitably pay off its huge debt.

(Continued)

The merger proposal made strategic sense for the regional HNG. The federal government was in the process of deregulating the energy industry and the combined entity would be a dominant force in the natural gas market. In addition, Lay and other executives could sell their HNG stock options at the premium price being offered by InterNorth.

But there were some potential negative merger ramifications for Lay to consider. The InterNorth/ HNG entity would have to manage a daunting $4.3 billion debt. Also, it would be a merger of unequal partners. InterNorth, with $7.5 billion in revenue, was three times larger than HNG. Such a size disparity typically resulted in the smaller firm being taken over by the larger

one. Bureaucratic redundancies would be eliminated to achieve cost reductions. Only one CEO would be needed, not two, and corporate control would transfer from Houston to Omaha.

DECISION CHOICE. If you were the CEO of HNG, would you

1. Reject InterNorth's proposal to protect your job and keep HNG headquartered in Houston?
2. Merge with North America's largest natural gas pipeline company, although it means the risk of managing a large debt, relocating corporate headquarters to Nebraska, and losing jobs due to redundancies?

Why?

ANCILLARY MATERIALS

Websites to Explore

- Business Ethics surveys
  - Ethics Resource Center, available at http:// www.ethics.org/topic/national-surveys.
  - Josephson Institute, available at http:// josephsoninstitute.org/.
  - Gallup Poll business ethics surveys, available at http://www.gallup.com/search/default .aspx?q=business+ethics&s=&p=1.
- Government statistics
  - Bureau of Justice, available at http://bjs.ojp .usdoj.gov/.
  - U.S. Equal Employment Opportunity Commission, "Discrimination by Type," available at http://www.eeoc.gov/laws/ types/index.cfm.
- 100 Wallets Dropped in Front of Hidden Cameras to Test Honesty, available at www .wallettest.com.

Best Place to Work Video

- Best Place to Work—SAS, available at http:// money.cnn.com/video/fortune/2010/01/20/ f_bctwf_sas.fortune/.

Business Ethics Issue Video

- "The Spill," *Frontline,* about the BP Oil Spill, October 26, 2010, 54 minutes, available at http://www.pbs.org/wgbh/pages/frontline/ the-spill/?utm_campaign=viewpage&utm_ medium=grid&utm_source=grid.

TEDTalks Videos

- *Born with Blank Slate Mind and Innate Traits:* Steven Pinker talks about his book *The Blank Slate,* which argues that all humans are born with some innate traits; February, 2003, 22 minutes, available at http:// www.ted.com/talks/steven_pinker_chalks_ it_up_to_the_blank_slate.html.
- *Human Beings Compared to Animals:* Jane Goodall, the primatologist, says the only real difference between humans and chimps is our sophisticated language; March 2002, 28 minutes, available at http://www.ted .com/talks/lang/eng/jane_goodall_on_what_ separates_us_from_the_apes.html.

Conversations with Charlie Rose

- A conversation about how the brain controls social behavior; January 19, 2010,

53 minutes, available at http://www.charlie rose.com/view/interview/10820.

- A conversation with former Secretary of Education William Bennett about his book *Our Sacred Honor*, which offers pieces of moral wisdom from the country's founding fathers; October 1, 1997, 31 minutes, available at http://www.charlierose .com/view/interview/5333.

NOTES

1 Ethics Resource Center, *2009 National Business Ethics Survey,* available at http://www.ethicsworld .org/ethicsandemployees/nbes.php#new09, accessed 10/15/10; a list of Ethics Resource Center surveys with links is available at http://www.ethics.org/topic/ national-surveys.

2 Louise Story, "Crisis Panel to Probe Window-Dressing at Banks," *New York Times,* May 4, 2010.

3 "Ethics Resource Center Publishes 2009 National Ethics Survey," available at http://www.ethicsworld .org/ethicsandemployees/nbes.php#new09, accessed 10/15/10; *2009 National Business Ethics Survey* is available at http://www.ethics.org/nbes/downloadnbes .html, accessed 10/15/10.

4 Ronald W. Clement, "Just How Unethical is American Business?" *Business Horizons,* 49, 4 (2006), 313–327.

5 Lydia Saad, "Americans' Confidence in Military Up, Banks Down," *Gallup,* June 24, 2009, available at http://www.gallup.com/poll/121214/ Americans-Confidence-Military-Banks-Down .aspx, accessed 10/15/10.

6 Lydia Saad, "Honesty and Ethics Poll Finds Congress' Image Tarnished," *Gallup,* December 9, 2009, available at http://www.gallup.com/ poll/124625/Honesty-Ethics-Poll-Finds-Congress-Image-Tarnished.aspx, accessed 10/15/10.

7 "29 Firms Make 100 Best Corporate Citizens Last Five Years in a Row," Press Release, *Business Ethics Magazine,* May 2, 2004.

8 Zachary A. Goldfarb, David Cho, and Binyamin Appelbaum, "Treasury to Rescue Fannie and Freddie," *Washington Post,* September 7, 2008.

9 Kathryn A. Canas and Harris Sondak, *Opportunities and Challenges of Workplace Diversity* (Upper Saddle River, NJ: Pearson Prentice Hall, 2008).

10 Susan Bowles, "Background Checks: Beware and Be Prepared," *USA Today,* April 10, 2002.

11 Sue Shellenbarger, "From Pilfering Pens to Padding Expense Accounts—We're Lying More at Work," *Wall Street Journal,* March 24, 2005.

12 Luis R. Gomez-Mejia, David B. Balkin, and Robert L. Cardy, *Managing Human Resources,* 5th ed. (Upper Saddle River, NJ: Pearson Prentice Hall, 2007).

13 John Galvin, "Cheating, Lying, Stealing," *Ziff Davis Smart Business for the New Economy,* 13, 6 (2000), 86+.

14 Ronald Jelinek and Kate Jelinek, "Auditors Gone Wild: The 'Other' Problem in Public Accounting," *Business Horizons,* 51, 3 (2008), 223–233.

15 Michael A. Hitt, Leonard Bierman, and Jamie D. Collins, "The Strategic Evolution of Large U.S. Law Firms," *Business Horizons,* 50, 1 (2007), 17–28.

16 Aaron Bernstein and Michael Arndt, "UAL Lawyers: Eight Days A Week," *Business Week,* April 4, 2005.

17 FMI/CMAA, *Survey of Construction Industry Ethical Practices,* 2004, available at http://cmaanet.org/ user_images/ethics_survey.pdf, accessed 10/15/10.

18 Chad Kaydo and Andy Cohen, "Are Your PR People Lying for You?" *Sales & Marketing Management,* July 2000, 16+.

19 Ethics Resource Center, *2007 National Government Ethics Survey,* available at http://www.ethics .org/files/u5/The_National_Government_Ethics_ Survey.pdf, accessed 10/15/10.

20 Hope Yen, "GAO: Millions Wasted on Government Cards," Associated Press, April 10, 2008.

21 Bryan Bender and Kevin Baron, "Army Knew of Cheating on Tests for Eight Years," *Boston Globe,* December 16, 2007.

22 Keith J. Winstein and David Armstrong, "Top Pain Scientist Fabricated Data in Studies," *Wall Street Journal,* March 11, 2009.

[23] Advertising Supplement, *Business Week,* July 13, 1998.

[24] Joseph L. Badaracco and Allen Webb, "Business Ethics: The View from the Trenches," *California Management Review,* 37, 2 (1995): 8–28.

[25] Nan Demars, "Taking the Ethics Pulse," *Office Pro,* May 2003, 24–27.

[26] Steven Greenhouse, "Low-Wage Workers Are Often Cheated, Study Says," *New York Times,* September 2, 2009.

[27] Louise Story and Michael Barbaro, "Bloomberg Shifts $5 Billion out of Friend's Firm," *New York Times,* February 20, 2010.

[28] "Fulbright & Jaworski Litigation Survey Reports Drop in Number of New Lawsuits and Regulatory Actions Filed Against U.S. Companies," October 15, 2007, available at http://www.businesswire.com/portal/site/home/perma link/?ndmViewId=news_view&newsId=20071015 005270&newsLang=en, accessed 10/15/10.

[29] Tracey Kyckelhahn and Thomas H. Cohen, "Bureau of Justice Statistics Special Report: Civil Bench and Jury Trials in State Courts, 2005, Table 7, August 2008," available at http://bjs.ojp.usdoj.gov/content/pub/pdf/cbjtsc05.pdf, accessed 10/15/10.

[30] John Broder, "Cigarette Makers in a $368 Billion Accord to Curb Lawsuits and Curtail Marketing," *New York Times,* June 21, 1997.

[31] Anonymous, "Jury Awards $13.8 Million in Cigarette Suit," *Associated Press,* August 24, 2009.

[32] Anonymous, "Tobacco Fight Comes to Supreme Court," *Associated Press,* February 19, 2010.

[33] Arthur Levitt and Paula Dwyer, *Take on the Street: What Wall Street and Corporate America Don't Want You to Know* (New York: Pantheon Books, 2002).

[34] David Segal, "Ohio Sues Rating Firms for Losses in Funds," *New York Times,* November 22, 2009.

[35] "Discrimination Type," U.S. Equal Employment Opportunity Commission, available at http://www.eeoc.gov/laws/types/index.cfm, accessed 10/15/10.

[36] Jelinek and Jelinek, "Auditors Gone Wild."

[37] Kevin R. Murphy, *Honesty in the Workplace* (Pacific Grove, CA: Brooks/Cole, 1993).

[38] Jeffrey J. Walczyk, Jonathan P. Schwartz, Rayna Clifton, Barett Adams, Min Wei, and Peijia Zha, "Lying Person-to-Person About Life Events: A Cognitive Framework for Lie Detection," *Personnel Psychology,* 58, 2 (2005), 141–170.

[39] Association of Certified Fraud Examiners, *2008 Report to the Nation on Occupational Fraud & Abuse,* available at www.acfe.com/documents/2008-rttn.pdf, accessed 10/15/10.

[40] Kathy Grannis, "Retail Losses Hit $41.6 Billion Last Year, According to National Retail Security Survey," *National Retail Federation,* June 11, 2007.

[41] FMI/CMAA, *Survey of Construction Industry Ethical Practices.*

[42] Chad Bray, "Tyco Ex-Officer Tells of Fund Transfers," *Wall Street Journal,* December 3, 2002.

[43] Anonymous, "The State of Surveillance," *Business Week*, August 8, 2005.

[44] FMI/CMAA, *Survey of Construction Industry Ethical Practices.*

[45] Ronald Sims, "Toward a Better Understanding of Organizational Efforts to Rebuild Reputation Following an Ethical Scandal," *Journal of Business Ethics,* 90, 4 (2009), 453–472.

[46] Daniel B. Turban and Daniel W. Greening, "Corporate Social Performance and Organizational Attractiveness to Prospective Employees," *Academy of Management Journal,* 40, 3 (1997), 658–672.

[47] Robert J. Williams and J. Douglas Barrett, "Corporate Philanthropy, Criminal Activity, and Firm Reputation: Is There a Link?" *Journal of Business Ethics,* 26, 4 (2000), 341–350.

[48] Nelson D. Schwartz, "Goldman's Earnings Fail to Shift Focus From Case," *New York Times,* April 20, 2010.

[49] Joelle Vanhamme and Bas Grobben, "Too Good to Be True! The Effectiveness of CSR History in Countering Negative Publicity," *Journal of Business Ethics,* 85, 2 (2009), 273–283.

[50] Bennett J. Tepper, "Abusive Supervision in Work Organizations: Review, Synthesis, and Research Agenda," *Journal of Management,* 33, 3 (2007), 261–289.

[51] Bennett J. Tepper, Christine A. Henle, Lisa Schurer Lambert, Robert A. Giacalone, and Michelle K. Duffy, "Abusive Supervision and Subordinates' Organization Deviance," *Journal of Applied Psychology,* 93, 4 (2008), 721–732.

[52] Lloyd C. Harris and Emmanuel Ogbonna, "Service Sabotage: The Dark Side of Service Dynamics," *Business Horizons,* 52, 4 (2009), 325–335.

53 Bennett J. Tepper, "Consequences of Abusive Supervision," *Academy of Management Journal*, 43, 2 (2000), 178–190.

54 Malcolm Gladwell, *Blink* (New York: Back Bay Books, 2007).

55 Joshua D. Margolis and James P. Walsh, "Misery Loves Companies: Rethinking Social Initiatives by Business," *Administrative Science Quarterly*, 48, 2 (2003), 268–305; Marc Orlitzky, Frank L. Schmidt, and Sara L. Rynes, "Corporate Social and Financial Performance: A Meta-Analysis," *Organization Studies*, 24, 3 (2003), 403–441.

56 Randy Myers, "Ensuring Ethical Effectiveness," *Journal of Accountancy*, 195, 2 (2003), 28–33; Charles H. Schwepker, "Ethical Climate's Relationship to Job Satisfaction, Organizational Commitment, and Turnover Intention in the Salesforce," *Journal of Business Research*, 54, 1 (2001), 39–52.

57 "Welcome to the 2010 Best Places to Work Rankings," available at http://bestplacestowork.org, accessed 10/15/10.

58 "100 Best Companies to Work For," *Fortune*, available at http://money.cnn.com/magazines/fortune/bestcompanies/2009/, accessed 10/15/10.

59 Great Place to Work Institute website, available at http://www.greatplacetowork.com/, accessed 10/15/10.

60 "Best Companies," *Working Mother*, available at http://www.workingmother.com/BestCompanies/, accessed 10/15/10.

61 "Best Places to Work for LGBT Equality," available at http://www.hrc.org/issues/workplace/11832.htm, accessed 10/15/10.

62 Dov L. Seidman, "Corporate Culture: The Ultimate Driver of Business Performance," *Boards & Directors*, February 2007.

63 David Montgomery and Catherine A. Ramus, "Corporate Social Responsibility: Reputation Effects on MBA Job Choice," in Gregory T. Papanikos and Cleopatra Veloutsou (Eds.), *Global Issues of Business*, 2, Athens Institute for Education and Research (2003): 289–298.

64 Seidman, "Corporate Culture."

65 Robert Neal and Philip L. Cochran, "Corporate Social Responsibility, Corporate Governance, and Financial Performance: Lessons from Finance," *Business Horizons*, 51, 6 (2008), 535–540.

66 Starbucks, Global Responsibility Report 2009, available at http://assets.starbucks.com/assets/ssp-g-p-full-report.pdf , accessed 10/10/10; Starbucks,

"Being a Responsible Company," available at http://www.starbucks.com/responsibility, accessed 10/10/10.

67 David Bostock, *Plato's Phaedo* (Oxford: Clarendon Press, 1986).

68 Houston Smith, *The World's Religions* (New York: HarperOne, 1991).

69 Jean Jacques Rousseau, *Emile* (Amherst, NY: Prometheus Books, 1762/2003).

70 Jonathan Haidt, *The Happiness Hypothesis* (New York: Basic Books, 2006).

71 Paul Bloom, *How Pleasure Works* (New York: W. W. Norton & Company, 2010).

72 Dacher Keltner, *Born to Be Good* (New York: W. W. Norton & Company, 2009).

73 Augustine, *The City of God* (New York: Penguin, 426/2003).

74 Smith, *The World's Religions*.

75 Martha C. Nussbaum and Amelie Okesenberg Rorty (Eds.), *Essays on Aristotle's De Anima* (Oxford: Clarendon Press, 1992).

76 John Locke, *An Essay Concerning Human Understanding* (London: Oxford University Press, 1690/1979).

77 Lynn Twarog Singer and Philip Sanford Zeskind, *Biobehavioral Assessment of the Infant* (New York: The Guilford Press, 2001).

78 Bloom, *How Pleasure Works*.

79 Jean Piaget, *The Child's Conception of the World* (London: Routledge and Kegan Paul, 1928).

80 Kathleen Stassan Berger, *The Developing Person* (New York: Worth Publishers, 2005).

81 Lawrence Kohlberg, *The Philosophy of Moral Development* (San Francisco: Harper & Row, 1981), p. 12. Note: The original prices have been multiplied by a factor of ten to maintain the financial realism of the original dilemma. In 2009, one gram of radium cost approximately $25,000.

82 James Weber and Janet Gillespie, "Differences in Ethical Beliefs, Intentions, and Behaviors," *Business and Society*, 37, 4 (1998), 447–467.

83 Charles V. Ford, *Lies! Lies!! Lies!!!: The Psychology of Deceit* (Washington, DC: American Psychiatric Press, 1996), pp. 84–85.

84 Anne E. Wilson, Melissa D. Smith, and Hildy S. Ross, "The Nature and Effects of Young Children's Lies," *Social Development*, 12, 1 (2003), 21–45.

85 Genyue Fu and Lingfend Wang, "The Moral Understanding and Evaluation of Lying or Truth

Telling of Primary School Children under the Circumstances of Individual Benefit or Collective Benefit," *Psychological Science,* 28, 4 (2005), 859–862.

[86] Josephson Institute of Ethics, *2006 Josephson Institute Report Card on the Ethics of American Youth: Part One—Integrity,* available at http://josephsoninstitute.org/pdf/ReportCard_press-release_2006-1013.pdf, accessed 10/15/10.

[87] Carolyn Kleiner and Mary Lord, "The Cheating Game: Cross-National Exploration of Business Students' Attitudes, Perceptions, and Tendencies Toward Academic Dishonesty," *Journal of Education for Business,* 74, 4 (1999), 38–42.

[88] S. R. Premeaux, "Undergraduate Student Perceptions Regarding Cheating: Tier 1 Versus Tier 2 AACSB Accredited Business Schools," *Journal of Business Ethics,* 62, 4 (2005), 407–418.

[89] Karen Rivedal, "Faculty Member Cites 'Overwhelming Evidence of Collusive Behavior,'" *Wisconsin State Journal,* April 24, 2003.

[90] Bella M. DePaulo, Deborah A. Kashy, Susan E. Kirkendol, Melissa M. Wyer, and Jennifer A. Epstein, "Lying in Everyday Life," *Journal of Personality and Social Psychology,* 70, 5 (1996), 979–995.

[91] Anonymous, "Simplify Tax Code to Help Catch Cheats," *Wisconsin State Journal,* April 21, 2003.

[92] Lynnley Browning, "Ex-UBS Banker Seeks Billions for Blowing Whistle," *New York Times,* November 27, 2009.

[93] Michael Tomasello, *Why We Cooperate* (Cambridge, MA: MIT Press, 2009).

[94] Grazyna Kochanska, Robin A. Barry, Natasha B. Jimenez, Amanda L. Hollatz, and Jarilyn Woodard, "Guilt and Effortful Control: Two Mechanisms That Prevent Disruptive Developmental Trajectories," *Journal of Personality and Social Psychology,* 97, 2 (2009), 322–333.

[95] Nancy Eisenberg, Carlos Valiente, and Claire Champion, "Empathy-Related Responding," in Arthur G. Miller (Ed.), *The Social Psychology of Good and Evil* (New York: The Guilford Press, 2004), pp. 386–415.

[96] Independent Sector, *Giving and Volunteering in the United States: Findings from a National Survey* (Washington, DC: Independent Sector, 2001).

[97] "U.S. Charitable Giving Estimated to Be $307.65 Billion in 2008," Giving USA Foundation, June 10, 2008, available at http://www.philanthropy.iupui.edu/News/2009/docs/GivingReaches300billion_06102009.pdf, accessed 4/30/10.

[98] C. Daniel Batson, Nadia Ahmad, and E. L. Stocks, "Benefits and Liabilities of Empathy-Induced Altruism," in Miller (Ed.), *The Social Psychology of Good and Evil,* pp. 359–385.

[99] "100 Wallets Dropped in Front of Hidden Cameras to Test Honesty," available at www.wallettest.com, this website includes the videos, accessed 10/15/10.

[100] Lynn Sharp Paine, *Leadership, Ethics, and Organizational Integrity* (New York: Irwin, 1997).

[101] Rushworth M. Kidder, *How Good People Make Tough Choices* (New York: William Morrow and Company, 1995), p. 18.

[102] Anonymous, "How to Help Reinvigorate Your Organization's Ethics Program," *HR Focus*, June 2003, 7–8.

[103] Stanley Milgram, *Obedience to Authority* (New York: Harper & Row, 1974).

[104] Roy F. Baumeister and Mark R. Leary, "The Need to Belong: Desire for Interpersonal Attachments as a Fundamental Human Motivation," *Psychological Bulletin*, 117, 3 (1995), 497–530.

[105] Andrew C. Revkin, "Hacked E-Mail Is New Fodder for Climate Disputer," *New York Times,* November 21, 2009.

[106] Frances J. Milliken, Elizabeth W. Morrison, and Patricia F. Hewlin, "An Exploratory Study of Employee Silence: What Employees Do Not Say to Their Bosses and Why," *Journal of Management Studies,* 40, 6 (2003), 1453–1476.

[107] Malcolm Gladwell, *The Tipping Point* (New York: Back Bay Books, 2002).

CHAPTER OUTLINE

2

AN HISTORICAL PERSPECTIVE ON BUSINESS ETHICS

What would you do?

Unfinished Work in a Union Setting

Upon graduation, you obtain a mid-level management job at a manufacturing facility. The company works two shifts, 8 a.m. to 4 p.m. and 4 p.m. to midnight. All production employees are unionized. The union contract forbids you to perform any work that is the responsibility of a union employee, but you have been trained to perform all manufacturing tasks in case of an "extreme emergency," such as when someone's personal safety is at risk.

You are responsible for managing the evening shift. After three weeks, you have already used up the allotted monthly overtime budget. Your boss is beginning to question your ability to appropriately manage the workflow. "Under no circumstance, and I mean no circumstance," he emphasizes, "can anyone on your shift work overtime the rest of the month." You agree.

Halfway through the evening shift, Jessica, the most productive union employee, informs you that it will be impossible for her to achieve this evening's production goal. Several problems had arisen, plus her assigned goal was extremely ambitious. "I hate to tell you," she tells you, "but it'll take an additional five hours after my normal shift to finish the work."

If her work is not completed, the efficiency of the morning shift's work assignments, which is dependent on her work outcome, will be ruined. This will not only earn you a reprimand from your boss, but also make it nearly impossible for you to accomplish your goals for tomorrow evening.

Jessica's work is highly specialized and you are the only other person who knows how to efficiently perform her tasks. You can complete the work when the shift ends, but the union representative will file a grievance because, according to the union contract, this does not count as "an extreme emergency." Another option is to confidentially ask Jessica to stay when the evening shift ends to complete the work "off the books" with the promise of providing her an equivalent amount of paid time off on a less hectic day or pay her with your own money. She would probably accept the offer, but both of these options violate union rules and would lead to a grievance if the union representative found out.

What do you do? Would you

1) Leave the work undone to avoid violating your boss's absolutely no overtime command?

2) Ask Jessica to work paid overtime to complete the work and find some other way to reduce the labor budget?

3) Ask Jessica to confidentially work unpaid overtime and give her equivalent paid time off on a less hectic day?

4) Ask Jessica to confidentially work overtime and pay her with your own money?

5) Complete the work yourself after everyone leaves at midnight and hope nobody finds out?

Why?

Chapter Objectives

After reading this chapter, you will be able to:

- Describe salient business ethics issues in precapitalist America
- Understand the ethical foundation of capitalism as argued by Adam Smith in the 1700s
- Appreciate the delicate balance between economic growth and stakeholder rights,

particularly labor issues, throughout U.S. history

- Benchmark an organization to the Ethics Compliance Program best practices outlined by the Federal Sentencing Guidelines
- Conceptualize how to maximize ethical behaviors in organizations based on an Optimal Ethics Systems Model

Business ethics must be understood from a historical perspective to appreciate how the current economic system and regulatory system has evolved over time. Arnold Toynbee, the noted historian, said, "Civilization is a movement and not a condition, a voyage and not a harbor."[1] The movement of history has been toward the creation of a wealthy *and* just society, which requires balancing economic growth and respect for people. Our current mix of ethical issues in the business sector has grown out of the nation's unique historical evolution.

Throughout the history of the United States, progress in business ethics has been achieved by extending "rights" to an increasing number of stakeholders, and by the maturation of democracy and the justice system. Government laws and regulations are often a response to business owners and managers exercising their freedom in a way detrimental to the well-being of employees, customers, community, and the natural environment. The executive branch of government serves as an umpire, arbitrating competing stakeholder claims. Congress has the ability to change rules considered to be unfair or harmful to their constituents by passing new legislation or approving new regulations.

This chapter begins with a description of some prominent business ethics issues related to economic growth during pivotal historical moments prior to the formation of the United States, with a focus on Christopher Columbus, colonial settlements at Jamestown and Plymouth, and the buildup to the Revolutionary War. The philosophically inclined founders of the United States, wanting to create the most just political and economic systems in the world, chose capitalism for the new nation's economy because of its emphasis on liberty. The nation's historical struggle to develop an ethical business sector is examined through the Industrial Revolution, formation of labor unions, wage issues, and expansion of stakeholder rights and culminates in the 1991 Federal Sentencing Guidelines. The chapter concludes with an Optimal Ethics Systems Model as a conceptual framework for maximizing ethical behavior and reducing ethical risks in organizations.

Economic Growth and Business Ethics in Precapitalist America

Some people tend to blame capitalism for unethical business practices.[2] But Adam Smith conceptualized capitalism in the 1700s as a response to what many people back then considered to be unethical business practices under mercantilism, the economic system preceding capitalism. This section spotlights four pivotal historical periods leading up to the formation of the United States: Christopher Columbus's arrival, the Roanoke and Jamestown settlements, the Plymouth settlement, and the buildup to the Revolutionary War. These events were associated with economic growth and entangled in a web of ethical issues prior to, during, and after their occurrence. Their culmination led political leaders to choose capitalism as the economic system for the newly formed United States.

Christopher Columbus's Arrival

For several centuries, Constantinople, the capital of the Byzantine Empire, was called the gateway to the Orient because of its strategic location, situated where European merchants entered Asia. In 1453, the Ottoman Turks conquered Constantinople. The overland spice trade routes linking Europe to India fell under the auspices of Ottoman government officials who began charging European traders exorbitant taxes for business passing through the city.[3] Products were confiscated when Europeans resisted payment.

The Christian rulers of Europe declared it unethical to enrich an Islamic military power that already controlled land in southern Spain and wanted to conquer the rest of Europe. The Italian navigator Christopher Columbus proposed an alternative trade route based on sailing west to India rather than east by land or sea. Columbus secured financial funding for the never before undertaken risky adventure from King Ferdinand and Queen Isabella, who had developed Spain into a commercial leader and military power. The monarchs provided Columbus with three boats and 39 crew members and agreed to fund half the remaining costs, with the other half coming from Italian private investors.

King Ferdinand's instructions to Columbus were straightforward: "Get gold, humanely if possible, but at all hazards—get gold."[4] Columbus signed a lucrative contract that entitled him to the rank of admiral, governor of any new lands discovered, and 10 percent of the revenues generated by the new lands.[5]

Columbus bravely weathered storms and a potential mutiny before landing on Caribbean islands assumed to be off the coast of either India or China. After exploring the modern-day Bahamas, Cuba, Haiti, and the Dominican Republic, Columbus concluded that the indigenous people would be relatively easy to conquer, enslave, and Christianize. Columbus kidnapped 20 indigenous people and boarded them on his return ship to Spain. Only eight indigenous people survived the voyage. Some Spanish sailors were left behind to establish a trading outpost on Haiti. They raped indigenous women and enslaved their husbands and children. The indigenous people responded by attacking the Spanish fort and killing all of its inhabitants.

Columbus undertook three additional Caribbean voyages in search of spices, gold, farmland, and slaves, who became a valued export. Altogether, Columbus shipped 500 slaves back to Spain, of which 200 died on the trip. The surviving slaves were sold at auctions. Within two years of Columbus's initial contact, half of Haiti's 250,000 indigenous population died, mostly from new diseases caused by European viruses.

Roanoke and Jamestown Settlements

England, France, and the Netherlands competed with Spain to find riches in "America," a name derived from the Amerigo Vespucci, an Italian explorer and mapmaker. In the 1580s, Queen Elizabeth I of England granted Walter Raleigh and his business associates a charter to establish a colony in the area of modern-day Virginia and North Carolina to trade, search for minerals, and plunder Spanish merchant ships.[6]

Charters granted by the British government allowed several people to create an organization by pooling their financial resources, which enabled bigger and riskier business projects to be undertaken. Chartered organizations had to serve a specific public good, such as transportation or insurance, and were limited in terms of function, size, and longevity. Owners of chartered organizations were exempt from debtor's prison if the business venture failed.

Life on Roanoke Island was harsh. English colonists stole from indigenous tribes when food supplies ran low. Warfare ensued when indigenous tribes realized that the Europeans intended to settle on the land, rather than merely trade. By 1591, all English settlers on the island had died as a result of bad weather conditions or from an attack by indigenous people or Spanish sailors.

King James succeeded Queen Elizabeth and chartered the Virginia Company of London to search for gold and gems, and trade in furs and spices in the same geographic area.[7] One hundred and fifty Virginia Company employees landed in April 1607 and created the Jamestown settlement, named in honor of King James. The laborers consisted mostly of indentured servants who came from England's "excess population" of landless tenants, beggars, and criminals.[8] They were required to serve their masters for seven years in exchange for transportation, food, clothing, lodging, and eventual freedom.

Many Jamestown colonists died from starvation or in military battles with indigenous tribes that opposed encroachment on their lands and the kidnapping of their children to Christianize them. The colonists began exporting tobacco to England in 1614. Lacking a sufficient number of laborers, the colonists enslaved indigenous men and women to work the tobacco plantations. The market for tobacco continued to grow in England and, in 1619, plantation owners began importing slaves from Africa to meet labor needs.

Plymouth Settlement

The Pilgrim settlement at modern-day Plymouth, Massachusetts, was also a business venture. The Plymouth Company, an association of merchants in England, obtained a charter to establish a trading colony on the northeast coast of America and recruited the Pilgrims as its settlers.[9] The Pilgrims were willing to take on the risk for religious and economic reasons.

The Church of England had separated from Roman Catholicism in 1534 and operated under the domain of the English monarch. The Puritans were a group within the Church of England who believed the church still needed to purify itself of some Catholic dogma and practices. The Pilgrims were a radical group within the Puritan movement who sought total separation from the Church of England, which they considered corrupt. Political and church authorities responded by fining, imprisoning, or executing Pilgrims for not attending official Church of England services. The Pilgrims fled to the Netherlands but had difficulty financially sustaining their community. The Plymouth Company owners, some of whom were Puritans, offered the Pilgrims shares of company stock and transportation to "New England" where they could create their god-centered community in the American wilderness.[10] In return, the Pilgrims had to work off their travel and relocation debts by exporting goods back to England.

The Mayflower left England in September 1620 with 102 adults and children. Twenty-seven of the 70 adults on the ship were Pilgrims. The other passengers were explorers and indentured servants. The Mayflower eventually anchored in southeastern Massachusetts, near corn fields that had been harvested by indigenous tribes for thousands of years. Peaceful relations with indigenous tribes ended when, following a harsh winter, Pilgrims violated fur trading pacts and land agreements, stole food, and failed in an effort to broker hostilities between warring indigenous tribes.

Many more colonists risked their lives travelling across the turbulent Atlantic Ocean to settle in New England. The new arrivals, not wanting to live according to the Pilgrims' strict religious lifestyle, created their own colonies. By 1640, 20,000 people from England pursued new business opportunities and religious freedom on land previously inhabited by indigenous people.

Buildup to the Revolutionary War

By 1774, more than 2.3 million European colonists participated in highly regulated business activities along the eastern section of America. A sense of American nationalism grew among several generations of English settlers who had experienced life only in America and felt limited loyalty to England.

Business and tax policies exacerbated anti-England sentiments.[11] The British government placed restrictions on entrepreneurship, trade, travel, and political activities. The Currency Act of 1764 restricted the power of colonies to issue paper money. The Sugar Act of 1764 made colonialists accountable to judicial and tax administrators the British controlled in Nova Scotia. The British Parliament passed the Stamp and Quartering Act of 1765 and Townsend Acts of 1767 to fund continually increasing colonial administrative costs.

Wealthy colonial farmers and merchants protested that they wanted greater say in self-government. Britain's taxing polices were unethical, they claimed, because no elected colonialist served in the British Parliament. Taxation without representation violated the British Constitution. British troops occupied Boston to silence colonial dissent, which worsened the situation. In 1770, a dispute between a colonial apprentice and a British military officer over the payment of a bill escalated into the Boston Massacre.

The Boston Tea Party, the next major colonial incident, was the result of the East India Company's monopolistic business practices.[12] The East India Company, approximately one-third owned by members of the British Parliament, had become the world's most dominant multinational corporation, with its own army, judicial system, and foreign policy.[13] In 1773, a worldwide financial panic threatened to bankrupt the company. Parliament passed the Tea Act of 1773, which allowed the East India Company to sell tea on consignment directly to select, and usually politically well-connected, colonial merchants at prices below that of Dutch tea smugglers. The colonial tea merchants not part of the East India Company's distribution network now faced bankruptcy.

In mid-December 1773, three British ships packed with tea cargo anchored in Boston Harbor. A large mob of politically agitated colonialists demanded that the ships return the tea cargo to England, which is what happened at harbors in Philadelphia, New York, and Charleston. The Massachusetts governor, loyal to England, refused to let the ships depart. During the standoff, a group of radical colonialists snuck on the ships late at night and dumped the tea, which accounted for 8 percent of the tea consumed in colonial America, into Boston Harbor.[14]

Acts of civil disobedience intensified and, within two years, the colonists declared war against their English ancestors. On July 4, 1776, colonial leaders declared political independence from Britain, an act of treason punishable by death.

Freedom, Rights, and the Ethics of Capitalism

In composing the Declaration of Independence, Thomas Jefferson, James Madison, and Benjamin Franklin outlined an extensive list of legislative, judicial, and military abuses imposed on colonialists by King George III. Many of the colonial leaders were well educated in philosophy. They wanted a government based on the consent of the governed, a claim they grounded in fundamental human rights. The declaration's second sentence declared: "We hold these truths to be self-evident, that all men are created equal, that they are endowed by their Creator with certain unalienable rights, that among these are life, liberty, and the pursuit of happiness."

Approximately 25,000 colonists died for these rights during the victorious Revolutionary War. Emboldened by defeating Europe's largest military power, the nation's founders set out on a utopian experiment to create a government based on individual liberty. Such a government would have limited power, protect the rights of people, and be accountable to laws established by the people.

These rights, elaborated by James Madison in the Bill of Rights, took effect in 1791.[15] The rights included freedom of speech, freedom of the press, freedom of religion, freedom to petition the government, freedom to keep and bear arms, and freedom from unreasonable search and seizure. Property rights, a core value for conducting commerce, are contained in the Fifth Amendment to the U.S. Constitution: "[nor should any person] be deprived of life, liberty, or property, without due process of law." Freedom to be who you want to be and do the things you want to do had historically belonged to the ruling monarch, and political and business elites. These rights and freedoms would now be disbursed more broadly.

Adam Smith's Capitalism

Victory in the Revolutionary War meant abandoning England's government-controlled mercantilist system for commercial laws that encouraged and protected liberty in the business sector. Being pragmatic, the nation's founders needed evidence that economic liberty would grow the economy. Being philosophical, they also needed to justify that such a system was not only grounded in ethics, but would enhance ethics. James Madison, Benjamin Franklin, and Alexander Hamilton relied on the writings of Scottish philosopher Adam Smith for the economic evidence and ethical justifications.[16]

Adam Smith (1723–90), a prominent member of the Scottish enlightenment, applied the concepts "reason" and "liberty" to a wide range of endeavors, including philosophy, politics, economics, and law. Smith's University of Glasgow lectures served as the foundation for his two books, *Theory of Moral Sentiments* (1759) and *Wealth of Nations* (1776).[17] Smith had favored colonial representation in the British Parliament and was very critical of East India Company's market monopoly.

Living conditions for peasants in Scotland were harsh at the time of Smith's philosophizing, and their freedom was stifled. The famines of 1696–99 and 1739–40 resulted in the starvation of 5 percent to 10 percent of the Scottish population. Great Britain, which governed Scotland, had a majestic empire that expanded the globe, but, Smith maintained, "No society can surely be flourishing and happy, of which the far greater part of the members are poor and miserable."[18]

Utopian socialists blamed the selfishness of the wealthy for the misfortunes of the poor. Mercantilists blamed the poor for their own misfortunes. Smith took a more radical position. He blamed the British economic system and denounced the "wretched spirit of monopoly."[19] Smith recommended abandoning mercantilist policies that sanctioned monopolies, put quotas on imports, and regulated tradesmen. Key management positions were filled based on family and political connections rather than individual merit. The lack of competition under mercantilism, Smith argued, led to high prices, low-quality products, and shortages.

Smith formulated capitalism as an economic system ethically superior to government-controlled mercantilism.[20] He insisted that a successful economic system could be devised based on freedom and competition in both product and labor markets. Individuals naturally pursue their self-interests, Smith reasoned, and they do not have to be taught or ordered by government to do so. Individuals free to pursue their economic self-interests would flock to markets where demand is high and supply is low, which is where they are needed most. Some people will improve products to attract more buyers, enhance their skills to better serve customers, and create new markets to apply their skills and expertise. The benefits of a free and competitive market economy included more goods and services, lower prices, better-quality products, less inefficiency, and greater labor flexibility. As suggested by the title of Smith's economic treatise, these variables combine to enhance the wealth of nations.

Trained in Protestant theology, Smith was well aware that merchants might misuse their freedom and take advantage of customers or laborers. In *Theory of Moral Sentiments*, published 17 years prior to *Wealth of Nations,* Smith maintained that individuals typically exercise their free will within the confines of morality. The book's opening sentence states: "How selfish soever man may be supposed, there are evidently some principles in his nature, which interest him in the fortune of others, and render their happiness necessary to him, though he derives nothing from it, except the pleasure of seeing it."[21]

Smith differentiated between selfishness (concern only for self) and self-interest (concern for self in relation to others) and concluded that when granted freedom, a large majority of people would be motivated by self-interest, not selfishness. Individuals would form contracts for exchanging services and uphold them. Some individuals might be tempted to behave selfishly. But, Smith argued, individuals then are likely to self-regulate their behavior based on moral sentiments originating from one's conscience, belief in God, natural concern for the well-being of others, and reason. Even unethical bullies, who represent a small, though sometimes powerful, part of the population, can be persuaded by reason to take into consideration the interests of others. When these self-regulating moral mechanisms fail, a system of justice funded by, but independent of, government must punish the wrongdoer to protect the public from egregious immoral actions.

A strong system of justice, according to Smith, was essential for a free market system to perform well. The judicial system had to overcome the selfish desires of some powerful politicians and wealthy elites who shaped laws to benefit themselves. As Smith noted,

> Laws and government may be considered in this and indeed in every case as a combination of the rich to oppress the poor, and preserve to themselves the inequality of the goods which would otherwise be soon destroyed by the attacks of the poor, who if not hindered by the government would soon reduce the others to an equality with themselves by open violence.[22]

The broad scope of Adam Smith's ethical defense of capitalism is summarized in Exhibit 2.1.

Exhibit 2.1   Ethical Foundation of Capitalism

Adam Smith's ethical defense of capitalism rests on the following beliefs:
- Freedom and liberty are essential values.
- Free people naturally pursue their self-interests and respect the interests of others.
- People will choose to enter product and labor markets where there is the greatest need and opportunity.
- People morally self-regulate their actions based on their conscience, belief in God, concern for the well-being of others, and reason.
- A strong system of justice is essential to punish those who do not appropriately self-regulate their behaviors, and to enforce contracts.

Government intervention in the marketplace, Smith reasoned, is needed under only three conditions: (1) when contracts are violated; (2) when merchants abuse their freedom by committing injustices against others, such as in the case of slavery; and (3) when the pursuit of self-interest does not generate highly desired social welfare benefits, such as national defense and certain public works, such as roads.

Smith on Labor Issues

Freedom and self-interest play central roles in Smith's conception of capitalism. Laborers benefit from capitalism because economic growth generates more jobs and they are free to choose an occupation. Smith cautioned that there was a natural friction between the interests of owners and laborers. He highlighted three problems that could occur if owners, in pursuit of greater profits, did not rely on moral sentiments when dealing with laborers.

First, due to an overabundance of labor, owners could drive wages below subsistence amounts because of their ability to "hold out much longer" during wage conflicts.[23] It was much easier for a few owners in a similar field of commerce to remain united than it was for the laborers. Low-paid striking workers, needing money to feed their families, would quickly capitulate to the owner's superior bargaining position. Smith applied reason to persuade owners not to do this by noting "that men in general should work better when they are ill fed than when they are well fed, when they are disheartened than when they are in good spirits, when they are frequently sick than when they are generally in good health, seems not very probable."[24]

Second, excessive application of piece-rate incentives could increase productivity in the short term, but damage a worker's health in the long term. Laborers paid piece-rate, Smith argued, "are very apt to over-work themselves, and to ruin their health and constitution in a few years."[25]

Third, excessive application of division of labor could also increase productivity in the short term, but damage a worker's intellectual abilities in the long term. Smith reasoned that "the man whose whole life is spent in performing a few simple operations . . . generally becomes as stupid and ignorant as it is possible for a human creature to become."[26]

Economic Growth under Capitalism

Economic growth matters a great deal. Living in an expanding economy is more enjoyable—there are more jobs and disposable income available—than living in a contracting economy. Over the past 200 years, industrialized society has doubled life expectancy, eliminated famine, and developed a nonending list of technological innovations that enhance the quality of life.[27] Purchasing power increased tenfold during the twentieth century. If that is difficult to appreciate, imagine having only 10 percent of current income available to purchase goods and services.

The Industrial Revolution

The nation's founders adopted the basic guidelines of capitalism synthesized by Adam Smith. In slightly more than a century, the U.S. economy grew from family farms and general merchants offering a wide range of products into the world's largest economy. The United States has maintained its economic leadership through two world wars, a cold war against communism, the beginnings of a war on terrorism, and an economic global crisis. The nation's economic system uniquely blends entrepreneurial and large-firm capitalism.[28] Individuals are free to create or offer just about any product or service, and large-firms provide mechanisms for bringing new product and service innovations to a global market at affordable prices.

How did this economic evolution happen? After the Revolutionary War, political leaders believed the United States had a special mission to prove that a society grounded in liberty could flourish. The newly formed government permitted citizens to independently form businesses and choose places of employment. In addition, the

U.S. Constitution, Article I, Section 8, authorized Congress "to promote the progress of science and useful arts by securing for limited times to authors and inventors the exclusive right to their respective writings and discoveries." People could patent their inventions.

The economy boomed when the Industrial Revolution spread from Britain to the United States in the early 1800s.[29] Technological innovation and the division of labor significantly increased productivity and reduced the price of products. For instance, Elias Howe's sewing machine in 1846 made clothing affordable for more people. Sewing machines initially replaced laborers, but more laborers were eventually needed due to the increased demand generated by lower prices.

The growth in the number of factories attracted more European immigrants seeking an alternative to the poverty they had been experiencing. The nation's population increased from 3.9 million in 1790 to 17.1 million in 1840. The population growth coincided with the political philosophy of "manifest destiny," which entailed purchasing or conquering land from European nations, indigenous people, and Mexico until the U.S. territory reached from the Atlantic Ocean to the Pacific Ocean.[30]

Westward expansion required the transportation of goods to new markets and resulted in the creation of integrated industries, cheaper products, and job growth.[31] The new industries, built on new and modified technologies, included roadways, canals, steamboats, trains, railroads, automobiles, and airplanes, each providing faster means of transportation over greater distances to connect suppliers and buyers. Transportation systems needed iron and steel, and manufacturers of all these products needed coal, oil, and electricity as sources of cheap energy. Telegraphs, telephones, postal services, and computers provided faster means of communication over greater distances. Apartments and houses were needed to shelter people, schools and colleges to educate them, and movies and television to entertain them. Businesses needed accountants to document revenues and expenses, and lawyers to address legal issues.

These massive projects required large amounts of capital, which contributed to the growth of chartered corporations, banks, and the financial industry. The birth of each new industry led to the creation of more jobs, attracting immigrants from all over the world who would consume more products and services. A demand arose for professional managers to efficiently coordinate these activities.

New Laws: Antitrust, Charters, and Liabilities

Capitalism has an inherent contradiction. Competition is good in part because it forces companies to become more efficient and effective at providing quality goods at affordable prices. Successful companies increase market share and unsuccessful companies go bankrupt or are acquired by successful companies. As market share increases, some successful small businesses evolve into medium-sized businesses and then large corporations. The formerly highly competitive market becomes an oligopoly, in which a handful of large businesses compete against one another. The best competitor acquires more companies, runs less efficient competitors out of business, and evolves into an anticompetitive monopoly, an end result that is not good.

This inherent contradiction, and its associated problems, became more apparent in the second half of the 1800s as businesses continued to grow. By the turn of the century, over 50 industries were characterized by one corporation controlling at least 60 percent of market share.[32]

The federal government attempted to counteract these anticompetitive trends by creating the Interstate Commerce Commission in 1886, which determined reasonable railway rates. A few years later, Congress passed the Sherman Antitrust Act of 1890, which outlawed monopolies. Businesses could grow to a certain extent, and then any further growth was illegal. Large corporations wanting additional growth had to apply their skills and expertise in other industries.

Chartering laws changed in response to corporate growth, complexity, and political power, but not always as anticipated.[33] In the late 1800s, states competed against one another by simplifying rules for obtaining a corporate charter and eliminating restrictions to attract corporations that could increase a state's employment levels and tax revenues. In 1889, New Jersey, seeking to attract businesses away from neighboring New York City, lowered corporate tax rates and provided corporations the right to purchase stock in other corporations through a holding company, which led to corporate growth through mergers and acquisitions. When New Jersey raised corporate tax rates, Delaware became the most corporate-friendly state. Half of all publicly traded corporations are now incorporated in Delaware.

Corporate complexity made it necessary to hold corporations, rather than specific individuals, legally accountable. Who should be held accountable for the collapse of a bridge that kills people? Should the harmed parties sue the employees who built the bridge, the manager who established unreasonable work deadlines, or the product supplier? This change in law allowed those harmed to collect financial damages by suing the corporation in addition to, or instead of, a particular employee. As a result, corporations gained some obligations, and rights, previously limited to individuals.

The continual growth in corporate size led to the passage of shareholder "limited liability" laws. If a small business is sued or fails, the owner is responsible for paying off the lawsuit or debts. But potential purchasers of stock would not invest if personally held liable for paying off a large corporation's lawsuits or debt. The new law limited an individual shareholder's financial liability to the amount invested.

Labor Issues

U.S. capitalism has not experienced an ethically smooth march of progress. Contrary to Adam Smith's reasoned arguments, some people who benefitted the most from capitalism misused their dominant positions to the detriment of laborers. The most notable ethical problems included slavery, working conditions, and income and wage inequality.

Slavery

Slavery, the worst form of labor exploitation, predates capitalism and can be found in almost all ancient societies. Slavery is a system in which individuals are owned by other people and subject to the whims of their owners. Owners tortured slaves for not meeting work expectations and sexually abused slaves for their amusement. As discussed earlier, Christopher Columbus enslaved and tortured indigenous people upon his arrival. In the 1600s, slaves were imported from Africa to work on tobacco plantations. The number of slaves grew dramatically just prior to the Revolutionary War, from 120,000 in 1756 to 500,000 in 1776.[34]

The founders of the United States sidestepped the obvious contradiction between liberty and slavery. They wrote the Constitution in such a way to appease southern states, whose economies depended on slaves, into signing the document. Without this concession, the 13 colonies would not have formed the United States. George Washington, the nation's first president and a southern plantation owner, brought nine slaves with him to the Philadelphia White House. At the time of his wife's death in 1802, Washington still owned more than 300 slaves.[35]

Southern dependency on slavery continued to increase during the Industrial Revolution. Eli Whitney's cotton gin made it easier to separate seeds from cotton fibers, and the number of bales of cotton from southern plantations increased from 100,000 in 1800 to 5.4 million in 1859. Similarly, the number of slaves picking cotton and performing other tasks during the same time period grew to 4 million.[36] Shortly after the election of President Abraham Lincoln in 1860, 11 southern states seceded. More than 620,000 soldiers, and thousands more civilians, lost their lives in the ensuing Civil War fought to preserve the United States. The emancipation of slaves led to other ethical issues, such as just compensation, land rights, voting rights, and civil rights.

Strikes and Labor Unions

The failure of owners and managers to heed Adam Smith's appeal to treat laborers ethically led to the formation of unions.[37] A labor union is an association of employees that advances its members interests, such as wages, benefits, work rules, and other conditions of employment, through collective bargaining with an employer. Unions reduced power imbalances between owners and laborers by organizing employees to speak with a single voice against what they considered unethical treatment.

In the late 1700s, a free laboring class emerged in the seaport cities of Boston, Philadelphia, and New York. The first recorded strikes in the colonies were conducted by groups of journeymen tailors in New York City and shoemakers, printers, and carpenters in Philadelphia.[38] Philadelphia shoemakers formed the first local union in 1792, but 13 years later a jury composed of merchants found eight members of the shoemakers' union guilty of engaging in a criminal conspiracy to raise wages. Business owners claimed that unions violated their property rights and put their companies at a competitive disadvantage because paying higher than market wage rates forced them to charge higher prices for their products.

The first factory in the United States, built in 1815 in Waltham, Massachusetts, provided textile goods for stores in Boston. The labor force consisted of newly arriving immigrants, including boys and girls under the age of 12, who worked from 5 o'clock in the morning to 7 o'clock at night. In addition to long hours, features of factory life included low wages, poor ventilation, payment in scrip redeemable only in the factory store, and a severe fine system for the purpose of maintaining discipline.

In 1840, Philadelphia strikers won the right to work only 10 hours a day. This became the standard for federal employees. But 40 years later, approximately 80 percent of all laborers worked a minimum, rather than a maximum, of 10 hours a day.

Some union organizers in the United States were inspired by the writings of Europeans Karl Marx and Friedrich Engels.[39] Marx argued that history quickly proved Adam Smith's assumptions and predictions about the moral sentiments of business people incorrect. In the *Communist Manifesto,* published in 1848, Marx and Engels declared that the workers of the world should unite against greedy capitalists and take over ownership of the means of production.

Union leader Samuel Gompers opposed the radical action proposed by Marxists to secure worker rights in the United States. He also opposed affiliating the union movement with any particular political party. In 1881, Gompers helped found the Federation of Organized Trades and Labor Unions to unite independent labor unions. Five years later, the union became the American Federation of Labor (AFL).

On May 1, 1886, unions across the nation went on strike for the eight-hour workday. Proponents maintained that a day should be equally divided into three parts: eight hours for work, eight hours for personal interests, and eight hours for rest. In 1905, many laborers in the United States still worked 12-hour days. Henry Ford reduced his assembly line shifts to eight hours in 1914 and two years later the Adamson Act established an eight-hour day for railroad workers.

In 1933, the Great Depression resulted in the unemployment rate soaring to 25 percent. With millions of people looking for work, newly elected President Franklin Roosevelt developed a new set of laws for governing labor relations. The passage of the National Labor Relations Act (NLRA) of 1935 legally obligated employers to negotiate with duly elected unions and codified regulations governing the process for forming a union. Union membership rose from 7 percent to 36 percent by the end of World War II. When the war concluded, Congress feared that politically motivated strikes could ruin economic growth. The Taft Hartley Act of 1947 placed limits on strikes and prohibited Communist Party members from holding union offices.

The union movement has been hampered by the stigmas of violence and corruption.[40] Violence became a union strategy in response to some business owners hiring thugs to beat up union organizers. The International Brotherhood of Teamsters, which organized workers in the transportation industry, became the most notoriously corrupt union in the United States. People with criminal records rose to union leadership positions and extorted money from businesses in exchange for either not striking or striking a competitor.[41] Managers resisting the extortion were threatened with physical violence and nondelivery of goods.

Many union organizers, however, have lived very sacrificial lives for the well-being of others and emphasized non-violence when threatened by abusive business owners and strike-breakers (see Exhibit 2.2).

Exhibit 2.2 Profile of a Union Organizer*

Cesar Chavez, inspired by Gandhi's message of nonviolence and by Catholic social justice teaching, unionized immigrant farm workers in California and led a 10-year nationwide boycott against grapes picked by nonunion workers, until his death in 1993.

Chavez was born in Arizona in 1927, the son of illiterate Mexican immigrant parents. The poverty-stricken family lived in a tent and traveled throughout California picking grapes, strawberries, tomatoes, and cotton. Migrant farm workers received below-poverty wages, were charged for transportation to the fields and ice water, and had no bathroom facilities.

Chavez became a union organizer after serving in the United States Navy. He started an underground newspaper, held secret meetings, and eventually founded the National Farm Workers Association in 1962, later renamed the United Farm Workers, to represent the rights of farm workers.

(Continued)

Filipino grape workers went out on strike in 1965 for better wages and unemployment insurance. Chavez persuaded Mexican and Latino workers, fearful of being deported for immigration violations, to join the strike. Landowners accused Chavez of being a communist and imported Mexicans to work the fields. Local police sided with the landowners, threatened strikers with attack dogs and deportation, beat them up, sprayed the strikers with pesticides, and arrested them.

Chavez raised public awareness about these events by speaking at churches and universities. He called for a nationwide boycott of Schenley Industries, which purchased the farm worker–picked grapes for its liquor products. Influenced by the tactics of Gandhi and Martin Luther King Jr., Chavez led a 300-mile march to Sacramento, the capital of California, demanding political action. In 1966, Schenley Industries capitulated and recognized the union as the farm workers' bargaining agent. Chavez spent the rest of his life expanding the union, participating in collective bargaining negotiations, and conducting strikes and boycotts.

---

*Susan Ferriss and Ricardo Sandoval, *Cesar Chavez: The Fight in the Fields and the Farmworkers Movement* (New York: Harcourt Brace and Company, 1997).

Union membership steadily declined from 35 percent in 1955 to 12.3 percent in 2009.[42] The highest unionization rates are in the public sector (37 percent), namely employees in government, education, and protective services, such as firefighters and police officers. In the private sector, 7.2 percent of employees are union members.

Let's Build a Building

It's a Great Design That Fits Our Mission But . . .!

You are the executive director for a nonprofit environmental organization that has operated for years in an old industrial facility. The organization's operations have expanded in response to the "green revolution" taking place and the board of directors agrees to lead a fund-raising campaign for a new $3 million building on land with an option to buy ending August 2012.

Your architect receives 8 percent of overall building costs, which would amount to $240,000. Approximately 90 percent of the architect fee is paid out on a monthly basis prior to starting construction based on the amount of work completed.

You approve the architect's initial schematic design for the building layout and several months later he provides you with very impressive drawings that are 50 percent completed. Unfortunately,

the architect notes, this design would likely result in a building costing $3.2 million, which would be $200,000 over the budget. The economy is doing poorly and you are nervous about raising $3 million, no less $3.2 million. You make $200,000 worth of changes to the drawings to get the entire project back within budget.

The architect makes another presentation when the design is 80 percent completed. The architect then says: "It is not every day you get to build a building. Why don't you tell me what's on your wish list for an eco-friendly building and I'll see if I can make modifications in the final drawings to fit your dream within your $3 million budget."

This is very exciting. You examine other buildings, talk with people in new buildings similar to the one you're planning, read the latest building magazines, and come up with a wish list, much of it state-of-the-art eco-friendly designs. In July 2012, the architect amends the drawings to fit your dreams.

"So all this for $3 million, let's do it!" you say. "I'm sorry," the architect responds, "this beautiful building would actually cost $3.5 million." The architect would also earn an additional $40,000 at the 8 percent of cost fee.

You share this information with your board. Although they like the design, they are unable to contribute any additional money in the bad economy. But, they remind you, the final decision is up to you. If the option to buy the land expires, you risk losing the location. As far as you know, nobody else is looking at the property.

What would you do? Would you

1. Stay with the original $3 million building design, buy the land, and begin construction?

2. Approve the $3.5 million state-of-the-art eco-friendly building design, buy the land, and hope that somehow you can raise the extra $540,000?

3. Delay construction for one year, risk losing the land site, and see if you can raise the extra $500,000 before making a final decision on the building design?

Why?

Wages and Compensation

Income Inequality Income inequality is not unique to capitalist societies. Under feudalism and mercantilism, monarchs and their associates possessed tremendous wealth while some peasants died of starvation. Similarly, the ruling communist elite possessed most of their nation's wealth.

Capitalism's emphasis on liberty has increased national wealth more than any other economic system. In the United States, median family income, adjusted for inflation, increased from $47,400 in 1977 to $58,400 in 2005.[43] Median income declined during the 2007–10 financial crisis, dropping to $49,777 for 2009.[44]

But, as shown in Exhibit 2.3, economic inequality still remains.[45] The wealthiest 1 percent of the population possesses more wealth than the bottom 90 percent combined.[46] Following World War II, for three decades everyone's income increased by about 3 percent. But between 1976 and 2007, the share of total income going to the top 1 percent of earners increased from 8.9 percent to 23.5 percent, whereas the

Exhibit 2.3 Economic Class Structure in the United States

Class	Percentage of Population	Household Income	Class Characteristics
Upper Class	1%	$500,000 and higher	Top-level executives, celebrities, heirs; graduates of elite colleges and universities
Upper Middle Class	15%	$75,000 to $500,000	Professionals and managers; highly educated, often with graduate degrees
Lower Middle Class	32%	$35,000 to $75,000	Semiprofessionals and craftspeople; some college education
Working Class	32%	$16,000 to $35,000	Clerical, pink- and blue-collar workers; high school degree
Lower Class	20%	$16,000 and less	Poorly paid positions, rely on government assistance; some high school education

average inflation-adjusted hourly wage declined by more than 7 percent.[47] In 2008, Bill Gates had a net worth of $50 billion, and four Walmart heirs were worth an accumulated $80 billion.[48]

Education, which correlates with wealth, plays an important role in income inequality. As shown in Exhibit 2.4, the more education a person receives, the higher his or her income, with a slight decline occurring at the doctorate level.[49]

Exhibit 2.4 Median Personal Income by Educational Attainment		
Education Level	Percentage of Population	Annual Salary
Less than 9th Grade	5.5%	$21,960
Some High School	7.9%	$25,740
High School Graduate	31.2%	$33,801
Some College, no degree	17.2%	$39,665
Associate Degree	8.8%	$42,046
Bachelor's Degree	19.1%	$55,656
Master's Degree	7.5%	$67,337
Professional Degree	1.5%	$100,000
Doctorate Degree	1.3%	$91,020

Minimum and Living Wage The minimum wage refers to the lowest wage an employer can legally pay an employee, an amount higher than what the market would otherwise establish.[50] In response to high levels of unemployment and poverty during the Great Depression, the Roosevelt administration issued the Fair Labor Standards Act of 1938, which federally mandated a minimum wage.[51] The ethical principle guiding the legislation was "a fair day's pay for a fair day's work." The initial legislative bill proposed that certain industries pay a 40-cent hourly minimum wage ($6.05 modern equivalent adjusted for inflation).[52] Republicans and southern Democrats objected until the amount was reduced to 25 cents an hour, or $11 a week ($151.20 modern equivalent adjusted for inflation). The federal minimum wage has since been extended to public schools, nursing homes, farms, domestic workers, and small retail businesses and is periodically increased by congressional vote.

Some free market advocates claim that minimum wage laws violate the constitutional right of employers and employees to freely enter into contracts.[53] They argue that wages should be determined by labor market supply and demand, not by politicians, government bureaucrats, or voters. Artificially raising wages above free market rates, they claim, hurts those it is intended to benefit by increasing unemployment, contributing to inflation, and discouraging business investment and growth. The extra labor costs force employers to hire fewer low-skilled employees and/or increase their prices. Some employers offset minimum wage increases by reducing other employee benefits.

In the United States, both states and the federal government have the constitutional right to create a minimum wage. In 2008, approximately 2.2 million American wage earners were paid wages at or below (such as waiters/waitresses) the minimum wage.[54] This represents 3 percent of the nation's 75.3 million hourly wage earners age 16 and older, a significant decrease from 13.4 percent in 1979.

Congress does not index the minimum wage to inflation or a poverty threshold. The minimum wage's purchasing power peaked in the mid-to-late 1960s and has declined steadily since then. A full-time employee earning a minimum wage does not derive enough income to exceed the poverty threshold. A living wage refers to the amount of money a full-time employee needs to either afford the basic necessities in life or exceed the poverty threshold.[55] It is based on the principle that people working full time should earn enough money to financially support their families.[56]

Living wage proponents typically recommend indexing the minimum wage to the poverty threshold. In 2006, prior to the 2008 recession, more than 29 million employees earned wages below the official poverty threshold, defined as $9.91 an hour for a full-time employee.[57]

Most living wage initiatives are local municipal ordinances. Many, but not all, of them apply to private companies providing city services. Proponents argue that city government should not contract services from private employers who pay below poverty-level wages. In 2003, San Francisco mandated a living wage for all city businesses with at least 10 employees. By 2007, 134 municipalities had some type of living wage ordinance.

Executive Compensation Issues of fairness abound at the other end of the organizational hierarchy as well. Chief executive officers (CEOs) work long hours, sacrifice family life, experience tremendous amounts of stress, and are responsible for the livelihood of their employees. What is an appropriate level of compensation to them for bearing these burdens?

The average compensation for a Fortune 500 CEO in 2008 was $11 million, which includes stock options.[58] Assuming a CEO worked 12 hours a day, six days a week, and took a one-week vacation, that amounts to approximately $30,000 a day. Motorola's 45-year-old CEO Sanjay Jha's $104 million compensation in 2008 translates into $23,901 an hour, or $286,813 a day.[59]

At publicly held companies, the ratio of CEO pay to that of an average employee increased over a period of 50 years from 24:1 (the average employee worked 24 days to equal the daily wage of a CEO) to 275:1 (the average employee worked 275 days to equal the daily wage of a CEO). In the 1980s, Ben & Jerry's addressed the compensation fairness issue by establishing a five-to-one salary ratio between the highest and lowest paid employees. However, the compensation plan was abandoned in the 1990s due to difficulties Ben & Jerry's experienced trying to recruit skilled senior-level managers willing to accept this pay limitation.

John Mackey, CEO of Whole Foods Market, has struggled a great deal with trying to determine fair pay for his efforts relative to those of other employees. In 1978, at the age of 25, he opened a health food store in Austin, Texas, and two years later it evolved into Whole Foods Market, the start of a national chain of natural food supermarkets. Mackey instituted a salary ratio of 8:1, which grew to 19:1 in 2007.[60] The salary ratio did not include stock options and in 2005 he earned $2.7 million in compensation. In 2006, after poor organizational performance and media accusations of being hypocritical about his salary cap, Mackey reduced his salary to $1 a year and donated his stock portfolio to charity. In 2009, Mackey continued to earn a salary of $1 a year without any bonus or stock options. He received $653,670 in compensation from a previous incentive bonus plan, half of which he donated to charity.[61] In 2010, Mackey owned more than 82,000 shares in stock options earned during the intervening years.[62]

Other companies have tried to offset compensation disparities by offering employees an extensive benefits package. In 2010, for the 13th consecutive year, Recreational Equipment Incorporated (REI), the outdoor activity gear retail corporation, was ranked on *Fortune* magazine's "Best Companies to Work For" list. The previous year REI's turnover rate was 28.5 percent, significantly below the retail industry average of 47 percent. The "Best Practice in Use" exhibit highlights some of the company's employee benefit offerings.[63]

BEST PRACTICE IN USE

REI's Employee Benefits

- *Incentive Pay:* Incentive pay plan based on reaching individual, department, and company goals.
- *Salary, not Commission*: Allows salespeople to provide honest advice to customers without being biased due to commission factors.
- *Retirement and Profit Sharing:* Eligible employees guaranteed a contribution of 5% of eligible earnings and up to an additional 10% depending upon company profitability; employees are not required to contribute their own pay.
- *Part-Time Health Care Plan:* May enroll spouse, lifetime partner, and children; if medical is chosen, the employee receives a 60% subsidy of the cost from REI, and basic life and accidental death and dismemberment insurance is paid in full by REI.
- *Challenge Grant:* This program provides REI employees with an opportunity to determine a personal outdoor challenge and apply for a special grant to achieve their goals. Employees have received funds for a variety of challenges, from a 50-mile bike ride to a Mt. Everest expedition.
- *Employee Discounts:* 50% discounts on REI gear and apparel, free gear rentals for personal use, 30% off vendor merchandise, and 10% off sale items.
- *Culture and Work Environment at Headquarters:* Casual clothing, dog park and kennel, and bike trails for bike break during the day.
- *Sabbaticals:* After 15 years of service with REI, employees earn their first paid sabbatical—four consecutive weeks of time off; at every five-year anniversary thereafter, employees earn another sabbatical with one additional week added each time.

Why have the salaries of top executives increased exponentially compared to the salaries of average workers over the past 50 years? Typically, a compensation consultant presents the company's board of directors with compensation and benefits packages of other CEOs in the same industry. Board members, who are also highly paid executives and often handpicked by the CEO, choose a compensation package toward the high end of the scale so as not to lose the CEO to a competitor.

As a result, high-end pay packages quickly ratchet upward. Companies that do not match CEO compensation increases consider themselves at a bargaining disadvantage because the CEO could switch to a competitor and offer higher-paying jobs at their new companies to the best members of their former executive team.

In 2009, the federal government tried to determine "fair compensation" for the 25 top executives at any large financial firm that accepted some of the $700 billion federal bailout money. Rather than limiting the total amount of compensation, the government decided to regulate how compensation would be paid. Kenneth Feinberg, appointed by the U.S. Treasury Department, proposed a maximum of $500,000 base salary, no cash bonuses, and the remainder compensation in "salarized stock" payable in one-third installments between two to four years from when earned. For instance, a $9.5 million salary for 2010 is disbursed as $500,000 in cash and $9 million worth of company stock. One-third of the salarized stock becomes available for sale in 2012, one-third in 2013, and one-third in 2014. The extended payout period provides a disincentive for top executives to manipulate stock prices in the short term.

Further Expansion of Stakeholder Rights

Following World War II, the Soviet Union claimed that its form of economics, communism, was ethically superior to capitalism in terms of economic equality and distribution of goods. With communism spreading through Asia, Europe, Africa, and South and Central America, President John Kennedy responded by inspiring a new generation of leaders to create a fair and just society.[64] In the wake of Kennedy's 1963 assassination, President Lyndon Johnson led a "war on poverty."

Profit maximization and the rights of owners came under attack by social activists who believed American businesses were a detriment, rather than a contributor, to improving the quality of life. Student radicals, some sympathetic to communism, claimed corporate philanthropy was a public relations effort that hid business transgressions.[65] Political alliances formed to restrict business freedom by establishing legally binding rules through increased government regulation.

In relatively rapid succession, Congress, under a Democratic Party presidential administration, passed a slew of regulations protecting stakeholders against unethical business practices. Congress approved the Food, Drug, and Cosmetic Act Amendments (1962); Air Pollution Control Act (1962); Equal Pay Act (1963); Civil Rights Act (1964); Equal Employment Opportunity Commission (1964); Cigarette Labeling and Advertising Act (1965); Fair Packaging and Labeling Act (1966); Child Protection Act (1966); Traffic Safety Act (1966); Coal Mining Safety Amendments (1966); Flammable Fabrics Act (1967); Age Discrimination in Employment Act (1967); Consumer Credit Protection Act (1968); and Interstate Land Sales Full Disclosure Act (1968).[66]

These regulations challenged businesses to achieve economic growth and profits in a socially responsible manner that took into consideration the well-being of all stakeholders, not just shareholders. The expansion of stakeholder rights reflects a growing sense of entitlement among employees and citizens to be treated in an ethical manner. As a result, expectations that businesses should undertake greater social responsibilities have significantly increased while actual accomplishments lag behind, creating a social problem gap that fuels advocacy against businesses.[67]

Congress, under Richard Nixon and Gerald Ford's Republican Party presidential administrations, approved a similarly large number of regulations and federal agencies to protect consumers, employees, and communities from unethical business practices. These regulations and regulatory bodies included the Securities Investor Protection Act (1970), Poison Prevention Packaging Act (1970), Environmental Protection Agency (1970), Occupational Safety and Health Administration (1970), Consumer Product Safety Commission (1971), Employee Retirement Income Security Act (1974), and Toxic Substances Control Act (1976).

In the 1980s, Republican President Ronald Reagan argued that the high costs associated with the onslaught of government regulations outweighed the benefits. Excessive regulatory burdens put the United States at an economic competitive disadvantage not only with the still growing communist empire, but also Japan and other economically developing Asian nations. The Reagan and George H. W. Bush administrations began to deregulate the economy, as did the administrations of Democratic President Bill Clinton and Republican President George W. Bush.

In 2003, under George W. Bush's administration, the Office of Management and Budget (OMB) drafted a report for Congress summarizing the costs and benefits of federal government regulation.[68] Cost estimates ranged between $38 billion and $44 billion annually, while benefits were estimated between $135 billion and $218 billion. Others maintained that regulatory costs significantly exceeded OMB estimates. A report prepared for the Small Business Administration disputed OMB's results and estimated the cost of federal regulations in 2004 to be $1.1 trillion.[69]

Federal Sentencing Guidelines

The continued existence of free market capitalism depends on organizational employees behaving ethically. The more that organizational employees behave ethically, the more freedom managers and other employees can be granted. The more that organizational employees behave unethically, the more organizational decisions are regulated to protect stakeholders.

In 1991, President George H. W. Bush issued new Federal Sentencing Guidelines with the intention of encouraging, though not requiring, managers to implement policies and procedures that reinforce ethical behaviors. Discussions about the need for guidelines were initiated during President Jimmy Carter's administration and further developed during the Reagan presidency.

The sentencing guidelines are based on the best practices for ethics compliance programs, which, if implemented, could reduce the occurrence of unethical and criminal activities. The Ethics Resource Center tested this assumption and found that organizations with weak ethical cultures (few best practices) had twice as much unethical activity than organizations with strong ethical cultures.[70] The Federal Sentencing Guidelines are applicable to nonprofits, unions, partnerships, trusts, and universities as well as businesses.[71]

The 16 best practices suggested by the Federal Sentencing Guidelines, divided into six categories, appear in Exhibit 2.5.[72] The third column is available to indicate whether an organization has implemented the suggested best practice.

Guided by the principles of free market economics, the federal government wants managers to decide which, if any, of the best practices they should implement rather than impose a one-size-fits-all approach. An organization that behaves ethically

Exhibit 2.5 Best Practices for Compliance and Ethics Programs

Category	Best Practice	Implemented
Organizational Personnel Issue	Substantial authority is not given to any employee known to have engaged in illegal activities	
Compliance/Ethics Program Personnel	A specific high-level manager oversees the program	
	A specific individual is accountable for the program's day-to-day operations	
Content of the Compliance/Ethics Program	Code of Ethics	
	Procedures for preventing and detecting criminal misconduct or unethical behavior	
	Mechanism for employees to anonymously or confidentially seek guidance on, or report, criminal or unethical conduct without fear of retaliation	
Management of the Compliance/Ethics Program	Program training for all employees	
	Program content is communicated throughout the organization	
	Criminal risks common to the profession or industry are periodically assessed	
	Periodically assess the program's effectiveness	
Rewards and Punishments	Employees are provided incentives for performing in accordance with the program's provisions	
	Incentives for ethical behavior and legal compliance are consistently enforced	
	Employees violating the program's provisions, or who fail to take reasonable steps to prevent or detect criminal activity, are disciplined	
	Disciplinary measures for unethical behavior or criminal misconduct are consistently enforced	
After Criminal Conduct Detected	Reasonable steps are taken to respond appropriately to the criminal conduct	
	Reasonable steps are taken to prevent similar criminal misconduct in the future	
Number of Best Practices Implemented		

without any of the best practices could continue to operate as it has in the past. But if an employee commits a crime, the judge applies the best practices checklist to determine how much the organization should be punished for the employee's criminal behavior. The judge refers to a standardized chart listing fines for specific types of crime and organizational size and then adjusts the fine by a culpability multiplier of 0.05 to 4.0 based on the extent to which the organization has implemented the best practices.

Assume an employee commits a consumer fraud, and the corresponding fine listed in the judicial chart is $1.2 million. If an organization has not implemented any of the best practices, the initial $1.2 million fine can be assessed a culpability multiplier of 4.0, increasing the fine to $4.8 million. The organization is punished if it has a history of criminal activity, does not exhibit a "good faith" effort at minimizing unethical behaviors, or obstructs the government investigation.

If, on the other hand, the organization has exhibited a good faith effort by implementing the best practices, the initial $1.2 million fine could be assessed a culpability multiplier of 0.05, reducing the fine to $60,000. The judge rewards an organization for having a history of behaving ethically, implementing an effective ethics compliance program, and taking full responsibility for the employee's criminal activity.

If some, but not all, of the best practices have been implemented, the fine will be between these two amounts.

B Corporation

In 2007, B Lab, a nonprofit organization, initiated a third-party Benefit Corporation, known as a B Corporation, certification process for branding a business as being ethical, sustainable, and socially responsible.[73] The multi-stakeholder obligations of a B Corporation contrast with the typical C Corporation designation, with which managers have a primary obligation to act in ways that maximize shareholder wealth. The B Corporation designation is equivalent to branding businesses with the Good Housekeeping Seal of approval to attract socially concerned customers, investors, and employees.

The goal of B Lab's cofounders Jay Coen Gilbert, Bart Houlahan, and Andrew Kassoy is to create a new legal entity recognized by federal, state, and municipal governments that permits managers to consider the interest of employees, communities, and the environment, not just the owners, when making decisions. They envision the IRS eventually creating a class of tax benefits for B Corporations, such as taxing them at a 20 percent rate, which is between that of C Corporations (taxed at 40 percent) and nonprofits (not taxed). This would provide businesses a strong incentive to adopt best practices in the treatment of employees, customers, communities, and the natural environment.

In 2009, Philadelphia established the first favorable legislation by providing B Corporations with a $4,000 tax deduction.[74] One year later, Maryland became the first state to pass B Corporation legislation. The 2010 B Corporation state law allows directors to consider impacts to employees, community, and the environment, along with shareholder value, when making operating and liquidity decisions.[75]

B Lab staff members, business leaders, and other experts have developed a 160-question "B Impact Ratings System" survey that is graded on a 200-point scale to determine whether an organization meets the criteria of a B Corporation (see Exhibit 2.6).[76] Companies complete the survey with the assistance of a B Lab staff member. Applicants who obtain at least 80 points and amend governance documents to include stakeholder interests are granted a two-year B Corporation certification. Documentation must be provided for at least 20 percent of the survey responses. Every year, B Lab staff randomly audit 10 percent of the certified companies.

Exhibit 2.6 B Rating System for Manufacturing Firm: Version 1.0
Part I: Practices (100 points)
a. Governance: mission, transparency, reporting, accountability
b. Employees: communication, training, job flexibility, culture, accessibility, safety
c. Suppliers: accountability, partnership, quality assurance
d. Environmental Impact: accountability, facilities, energy inputs, design, transportation
e. Provide Opportunity to Previously Excluded Populations: leadership, diversity
f. Engage in Community Services: civic engagement policy and practices
Part II: Profits (50 points)
a. Compensate Employees Fairly: compensation, cash benefits
b. Distribute Wealth through Broad Ownership: employee ownership, investor base
c. Charitable Giving: philanthropy
Part III: Products (50 points)
a. Beneficial Products or Services: product or service benefits customers and society
b. Use Beneficial Methods of Production: fair trade suppliers, green building design
c. Target Underserved Populations: low-income or minority consumers

Within the first two years of formation, 205 companies achieved B Corporation certification. According to the 2009 B Corporation Annual Report, these businesses operated in 54 different industries and had $1.1 billion in annual revenue.[77] B Corporations are typically small or medium-sized companies. Many of them cater to socially concerned consumers, such as Seventh Generation and Numi Organic Tea.

B Corporations pay an annual certification fee based on size. Organizations with revenues under $10 million pay one-tenth of 1 percent of net sales. Larger companies pay one-twentieth of 1 percent of sales. The fee is waived if the B Corporation joins 1% for the Planet, an alliance of businesses that donate at least 1 percent of their annual revenues to environmental organizations.[78] Organizations can use the "B Impact Rating System" to benchmark their social and environmental performance even if they do not apply for certification.

The Optimal Ethics Systems Model

The Federal Sentencing Guidelines implemented in 1991 encourage businesses to voluntarily adopt some of the best practices in business ethics. The B Lab's rating system provides several other criteria associated with enhanced social performance. Business ethics scholars and consultants have also developed a variety of audits and surveys to help organizations account for ethical behaviors.[79]

The Optimal Ethics Systems Model, presented in Exhibit 2.7, synthesizes these various approaches into a systematic best practices framework for reinforcing ethical behaviors, and reducing ethical risks, throughout the workplace. Successful long-term organizational growth requires honesty, trust, integrity, and credibility, among other ethical values. Creating and sustaining a culture of trust can be achieved through the multiple support systems in the Optimal Ethics Systems Model.

Exhibit 2.7 Optimal Ethics Systems Model

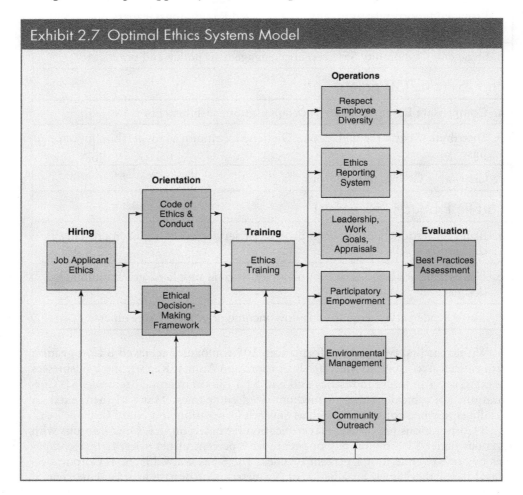

The best practices for each dimension in the model are explained in Chapters 3 through 12 of this textbook:

- Hiring Ethical People (Chapter 3)
- Codes of Ethics and Codes of Conduct (Chapter 4)
- Ethical Decision-Making Framework (Chapter 5)
- Ethics Training (Chapter 6)
- Respecting Employee Diversity (Chapter 7)
- Ethics Reporting Systems (Chapter 8)
- Ethical Leadership, Work Goals, and Appraisals (Chapter 9)
- Empowering Ethical Employees (Chapter 10)
- Environmental Management (Chapter 11)
- Community Outreach and Respect (Chapter 12)

Implementing the Optimal Ethics Systems Model can reduce unethical or illegal behaviors. Human beings, however, remain morally flawed and ethical problems can still arise.

When this happens, investigate the circumstances that led to the unethical or illegal behavior and, depending on the egregiousness of the unethical behavior, discipline or fire the employee. But such short-term solutions do not address the systematic root of the ethical problem. Why wasn't the employee's unethical proclivity detected earlier? Is there a problem with the hiring process, ethics training workshops, or performance evaluations?

Similar to Total Quality Management, the ultimate goal of the Optimal Ethics Systems Model is to reduce ethical risks as close to zero defects as possible. The Total Quality Management of Ethics process in "Tips and Techniques" provides a systematic approach for determining the root cause of an unethical behavior.

Tips and Techniques

The Total Quality Management of Ethics

1. Focus on the particular unethical activity the employee did.
2. Instead of merely blaming the particular employee, determine the systematic source that allowed the problem to occur. Did the problem originate from a(n)
   a. *Hiring Process Problem*: Was an unethical person hired?
   b. *Code of Ethics or Conduct Problem*: Do these codes inadequately address the issue?
   c. *Ethical Decision-Making Framework Problem*: Did the employee inadequately apply ethical reasoning to the situation?
   d. *Ethics Training Problem*: Does the training program inadequately address the issue?

(*Continued*)

Tips and Techniques (*Continued*)

    e. *Ethics Reporting System Problem*: Are the mechanisms for raising ethical issues and reporting unethical behaviors inadequate?

    f. *Manager Role Model Problem*: Is the employee's manager an inadequate role model?

    g. *Unrealistic Work Goal Problem*: Were the employee's work goals unattainable or misdirected?

    h. *Performance Evaluation Problem*: Are performance evaluation measures inadequate?

    i. *External Stakeholder Oversight Problem*: Did the regulator or professional association inadequately address the issue?

3. Seek input from affected constituents on how to strategically address the problem.

4. Develop an action plan that includes

    a. Clearly stated problem

    b. Initial solution to the problem

    c. Major obstacles against implementing the solution

    d. Recommendations for overcoming the obstacles

    e. Development and monitoring metrics to measure success

5. Make managers accountable for the results. Senior leaders should set unambiguous objectives and provide the necessary resources and appropriate incentives.

SUMMARY

Unethical business practices are not new, nor are they limited to capitalism. Business owners and managers have always had the freedom to choose to behave ethically or unethically. Unethical business practices existed at the time of Christopher Columbus, in colonial settlements on the American continent, and during the buildup to the Revolutionary War, all of which occurred prior to capitalism.

In the 1700s, Adam Smith outlined the ethical foundation of capitalism. He maintained that providing individuals with freedom and liberty to pursue their self-interests in the economic sector enhances the wealth of a nation. Minimal government intervention would be required, he argued, because people are concerned about the well-being of others and possess a conscience. These psychological mechanisms restrain people from exercising their liberty in a manner that harms others. If these restraints fail, then a system of justice must develop, and enforce, laws that punish those whose unethical behaviors harm others.

The vitality of free market capitalism depends on ethics. The more ethically business people behave, the more freedom and liberty government can allow in the economic system. Unethical behavior that reaches a critical level results in new government regulations and oversight mechanisms.

The remainder of this textbook describes how managers can implement the Optimal Ethics Systems Model to maximize the likelihood of ethical behaviors and minimize the likelihood of unethical behaviors.

KEY WORDS

Charters; Virginia Company of London; Plymouth Company; Boston Tea Party; Bill of Rights; Adam Smith; capitalism; mercantilist policies; Industrial Revolution; Sherman Antitrust Act of 1890; slavery; labor union; Karl Marx; minimum wage; living wage; government regulation; Federal Sentencing Guidelines; B Corporation; Optimal Ethics Systems Model

CHAPTER QUESTIONS

1. What are several salient business ethics issues in precapitalist America?

2. How did Adam Smith justify the ethics of capitalism?

3. Describe how the U.S. economy grew between the Revolutionary War and World War I.

4. What prominent labor issues challenged the fairness of free market capitalism?

5. Explain the Federal Sentencing Guidelines and how a judge would apply them.

In the Real World: Enron

Skilling's Innovative Gas Bank Idea—1990

Ken Lay accepted InterNorth's merger proposal. Following six months of astute political maneuvering, Lay became CEO, renamed the company Enron, and kept its headquarters in Houston.

In 1986, Enron reported $14 million in losses. The $4.3 billion debt nearly bankrupted Enron in 1987, and credit-rating agencies downgraded Enron's bonds to "junk" status. Lay hired McKinsey and Company, the world's most prestigious consulting firm, to develop innovative ideas for generating desperately needed revenue. One of the consultants, Jeff Skilling, proposed that Enron create a new type of business called a "Gas Bank."

The natural gas market consisted of public utilities signing short-term contracts, due to unpredictable price fluctuations, from natural gas suppliers. These short-term contracts made it impossible for either customers or suppliers to perform reliable long-term budgetary planning.

Skilling proposed a radically new business model. Enron could purchase natural gas from other suppliers by offering them long-term contracts at a premium price and then sell the natural gas to customers by offering them long-term contracts at a premium price. This would be appealing because both suppliers and customers would have predictable long-term cash flows.

However, the Gas Bank would need a tremendous amount of capital investment, something Enron did not have, to start purchasing natural gas from competitors. Many long-time Enron managers opposed Skilling's proposal, preferring that all new investments be directed toward traditional business operations, such as drilling for new sources of natural gas.

DECISION CHOICE. If you were the CEO of Enron, would you

1. Stay focused on what Enron already excels in, distributing natural gas through its own pipelines, and continue to search for more traditional solutions to Enron's growing debt problems?

2. Make a huge investment in creating a Gas Bank, a very risky financial endeavor never undertaken before?

Why?

ANCILLARY MATERIALS

Websites to Explore

- Government Statistics
  - Bureau of Labor Statistics, available at http://www.bls.gov/data/.
  - U.S. Census Bureau, Income Data, available at http://www.census.gov/hhes/www/income/income.html.
  - U.S. Census Bureau, Poverty Data, available at http://www.census.gov/hhes/www/poverty/poverty.html.
- Indexes and Calculators
  - Inequality Index, available at http://extremeinequality.org/?page_id=8.
  - "The Inflation Calculator," available at http://www.westegg.com/inflation/.
  - Economic Policy Institute, "Basic Family Budget Calculator," available at http://www.epi.org/content/budget_calculator/.
- "The 400 Richest Americans," *Forbes*, available at http://www.forbes.com/wealth/forbes-400.
- United States Sentencing Commission, "Organizational Guidelines," available at http://www.ussc.gov/orgguide.htm.
- B Corporation, available at www.bcorporation.net.

Best Place to Work Video

- Best Place to Work—REI, available at http://money.cnn.com/video/fortune/2010/01/20/f_bctwf_rei_outdoors.fortune/.

Business Ethics Issue Video

- "Inside the Meltdown," *Frontline,* about 2008 financial crisis; February 17, 2009, 57 minutes, available at http://www.pbs.org/wgbh/pages/frontline/meltdown/view/?utm_campaign=viewpage&utm_medium=grid&utm_source=grid.

TEDTalks Videos

- *Evolution of Compassion:* Robert Wright uses evolutionary biology and game theory to explain why we appreciate the Golden Rule ("Do unto others . . ."), why we sometimes ignore it, and why there's hope that, in the near future, we might all have the compassion to follow it; October 2009, 17 minutes, available at http://www.ted.com/talks/robert_wright_the_evolution_of_compassion.html.
- *Responding to Being Told You'll Die Soon:* Carnegie Mellon professor Randy Pausch, who was dying of pancreatic cancer, delivered a "last lecture" on how to really achieve your childhood dreams; September 2007, 76 minutes, available at http://www.ted.com/talks/randy_pausch_really_achieving_your_childhood_dreams.html.

Conversations with Charlie Rose

- A conversation about the indictment of Jeffrey Skilling, former CEO of Enron; February 19, 2004, 20 minutes, available at http://www.charlierose.com/view/interview/1567.
- A conversation with Kurt Eichenwald of the *New York Times* about the collapse of Enron in his book *Conspiracy of Fools*; March 17, 2005, 38 minutes, available at http://www.charlierose.com/view/interview/1003.

NOTES

[1] Arnold Joseph Toynee, *Civilization on Trial,* (Oxford: Oxford University Press, 1948).

[2] Naomi Klein, *The Shock Doctrine* (New York: Henry Holt and Company, 2007); David C. Korten, *When Corporations Rule the World* (San Francisco: Berrett-Koehler Publishers, 2001).

[3] John Keay, *The Spice Route: A History* (Berkley, CA: University of California Press, 2006).

[4] Jerry W. Markham, *A Financial History of the United States*, Vol. 1 (Armonk, NY: M. E. Sharpe, 2002), p. 3.

[5] John Noble Wilford, *The Mysterious History of Columbus: An Exploration of the Man, the Myth, the Legacy* (New York: Vintage, 1992); Howard Zinn, *A People's History of the United States 1492–Present* (New York: HarperCollins Publishers, 1995).

[6] Raleigh Trevelyan, *Sir Walter Raleigh* (New York: Holt Paperbacks, 2004); Karen Ordahl Kupperman, *Roanoke: The Abandoned Colony* (Totowa, NJ: Rowman & Littlefield, 1984).

[7] David A. Price, *Love and Hate in Jamestown: John Smith, Pocahontas, and the Heart of a New Nation* (New York: Alfred A. Knopf, 2003); Benjamin Woolley, *Savage Kingdom: The True Story of Jamestown, 1607, and the Settlement of America* (New York: Harper Collins, 2007).

[8] Ted Nace, *Gangs of America: The Rise of Corporate Power and the Disabling of Democracy* (San Francisco, CA: Berrett-Koehler Publishers, 2003); William R. Nester, *A Short History of American Industrial Policies* (New York: St. Martin's Press, 1998).

[9] Eugene Aubrey Stratton, *Plymouth Colony: Its History and People* (Provo, UT: Ancestry Publishing, 1986).

[10] Nathaniel Philbrick, *Mayflower: A Story of Courage, Community, and War* (New York: Viking, 2006).

[11] David McCullough, *1776* (New York: Simon & Schuster, 2005); Peter D. G. Thomas, *The Townshend Duties Crisis: The Second Phase of the American Revolution, 1767–1773* (Oxford, Eng.: Oxford University Press, 1987).

[12] Benjamin Woods Labaree, *The Boston Tea Party* (Boston, MA: Northeastern University Press, 1979).

[13] Philip Lawson, *The East India Company: A History* (London: Longman, 1993); Nace, *Gangs of America.*

[14] John K. Alexander, *Samuel Adams: America's Revolutionary Politician* (Lanham, MD: Rowman & Littlefield, 2002).

[15] Richard Labunski, *James Madison and the Struggle for the Bill of Rights* (New York: Oxford University Press, 2008).

[16] William H. Goetzmann, *Beyond the Revolution* (New York: Basic Books, 2009); Roy C. Smith, *Adam Smith and the Origins of American Enterprise* (New York: St. Martin's Griffin, 2004).

[17] Adam Smith, *The Theory of Moral Sentiments* (Indianapolis, IN: Liberty Classics, 1759/1976); Adam Smith, *The Wealth of Nations* (Chicago: University of Chicago Press, 1776/1976).

[18] Smith, *The Wealth of Nations*, Book I, Chapter VIII, p. 88.

[19] Ibid., Book IV, Chapter II, p. 483.

[20] Denis Collins, "Adam Smith's Social Contract," *Business and Professional Ethics*, 7, 3 (1988), 119–146; Ian Simpson Ross, *The Life of Adam Smith* (Oxford, Eng.: Clarendon Press, 1995); Patricia H. Werhane, *Adam Smith and His Legacy for Modern Capitalism* (New York: Oxford University Press, 1991).

[21] Smith, *The Theory of Moral Sentiments*, p. 9.

[22] Adam Smith, *Lectures on Jurisprudence,* in R. L. Meek, D. D. Raphael and P. G. Stein (Eds.) (Oxford, Eng.: Clarendon Press, 1978), pp. 208–209. Smith intended to publish these lecture notes prior to his death.

[23] Smith, *The Wealth of Nations*, Book I, Chapter VIII, p. 74.

[24] Ibid., p. 92.

[25] Ibid., p. 91.

[26] Ibid., Book V, Chapter I, pp. 302–303.

[27] William J. Baumol, Robert E. Litan, and Carl J. Schramm, *Good Capitalism, Bad Capitalism, and the Economics of Growth and Prosperity* (New Haven, CT: Yale University Press, 2007).

[28] Ibid.

[29] Joyce Appleby, *The Relentless Revolution: A History of Capitalism* (New York: W. W. Norton, 2009).

[30] Sam W. Haynes and Christopher Morris (Eds.), *Manifest Destiny and Empire: American Antebellum Expansionism* (College Station, TX: Texas A&M University Press, 1997).

[31] Alfred D. Chandler, *The Visible Hand: The Managerial Revolution in American Business* (Cambridge, MA: Harvard University Press, 1977); Ruth Schwartz Cowan, *A Social History of American Technology* (New York: Oxford University Press, 1997).

[32] William R. Nester, *A Short History of American Industrial Policies* (New York: St. Martin's Press, 1998).

[33] John Micklethwait and Adrian Wooldridge, *The Company: A Short History of a Revolutionary Idea* (New York: Modern Library, 2003).

[34] Jerry W. Markham, *A Financial History of the United States,* Vol. 1 (Armonk, NY: M. E. Sharpe, 2002).

[35] Nester, *A Short History of American Industrial Policies.*

[36] Zinn, *A People's History of the United States 1492–Present.*

[37] Melvyn Dubofsky and Foster Rhea Dulle, *Labor in America: A History* (Wheeling, IL: Harlan Davidson, 2004).

[38] Paul Le Blanc, *A Short History of the U.S. Working Class: From Colonial Times to the Twenty-First Century* (New York: Humanity Book, 1999); Martin Jay Levitt and Terry Conrow, *Confessions of a Union Buster* (New York: Crown Publishers, 1993); Nelson Lichtenstein, *State of the Union: A Century of American Labor* (Princeton, NJ: Princeton University Press, 2002); Zinn, *A People's History of the United States 1492–Present.*

[39] Karl Marx and Friedrich Engels, *The Communist Manifesto* (New York: Penguin, 1848/1998).

[40] Carl F. Horowitz, *Union Corruption* (Springfield, VA: National Institute for Labor Relations Research, 1999);Robert F. Kennedy, *The Enemy Within* (Westport, CT: Greenwood Press Publishers, 1960); David Witwer, *Corruption and Reform in the Teamsters Union* (Chicago, IL: University of Illinois Press, 2003).

[41] David Witwer, *Corruption and Reform in the Teamsters Union* (Chicago, IL: University of Illinois Press, 2003).

[42] Bureau of Labor Statistics, "Union Members Summary," January 22, 2010, available at http://www.bls.gov/news.release/union2.nr0.htm, accessed 10/15/10.

[43] David Leonhardt, "Income Inequality," *New York Times,* August 21, 2009.

[44] U.S. Census Bureau, "Income, Poverty and Health Insurance Coverage in the United States: 2009," September 16, 2010, available at http://www.census.gov/newsroom/releases/archives/income_wealth/cb10-144.html, accessed 10/15/10.

[45] William Thompson and Joseph Hickey, *Society in Focus* (Boston, MA: Pearson, Allyn & Bacon, 2005).

[46] Lawrence Michel, Jared Bernstein, and Sylvia Alegretto, *The State of Working America 2006/2007* (Ithaca, NY: ILR Press, 2007).

[47] Inequality Index available at http://extremeinequality.org/?page_id=8, accessed 10/15/10.

[48] "The 400 Richest Americans 2009," *Forbes,* September 30, 2009, available at http://www.forbes.com/lists/2009/54/rich-list-09_The-400-Richest-Americans_Rank.html, accessed 10/15/10.

[49] U.S. Census Bureau, *Annual Social and Economic (ASEC) Supplement,* salary data available at http://www.census.gov/hhes/www/cpstables/032009/perinc/new03_010.htm, accessed 10/15/10; U.S. Census Bureau, "Educational Attainment," available at http://www.census.gov/population/www/socdemo/education/cps2008.html, accessed 10/15/10.

[50] Jonathan Grossman, "Fair Labor Standards Act of 1938: Maximum Struggle for a Minimum Wage," *Monthly Labor Review,* 101, 6 (1978), 22–30; Jerald Waltman, *The Politics of the Minimum Wage* (Chicago, IL: University of Illinois Press, 2000).

[51] Jason Scott Smith, *Building New Deal Liberalism* (New York: Cambridge University Press, 2005).

[52] "The Inflation Calculator" available at http://www.westegg.com/inflation/, accessed 10/15/10.

[53] David Card and Alan B. Krueger, *Myth and Measurement: The New Economics of the Minimum Wage* (Princeton, NJ: Princeton University Press, 1995); Marvin H. Kosters, *The Effects of the Minimum Wage on Employment* (Washington, DC: AEI Press, 1996); Paul A. Samuelson and William D. Nordhaus, *Economics,* 18th ed. (New York: McGraw-Hill/Irwin, 2004).

[54] Bureau of Labor Statistics, "Characteristics of Minimum Wage Workers: 2008," Labor Force Statistics from the Current Population Survey, available at http://www.bls.gov/cps/minwage2008.htm, accessed 10/15/10.

[55] Robert Pollin and Stephanie Luce, *The Living Wage: Building a Fair Economy* (New York: The New Press, 1998); William P. Quigley, *Ending Poverty as We Know It: Guaranteeing a Right to a Job at a Living Wage* (Philadelphia, PA: Temple University Press, 2003); Jerold L. Waltman, *The Case for the Living Wage* (New York: Algora Publishing, 2004).

[56] Economic Policy Institute, "Basic Family Budget Calculator," available at http://www.epi.org/content/budget_calculator/, accessed 10/15/10.

[57] Brandon Roberts and Deborah Povich, *Still Working Hard, Still Falling Short* (Working Poor Families Project, 2008), available at http://www.workingpoorfamilies.org/pdfs/NatReport08.pdf, accessed 10/15/10.

58 Steven Brill, "What's a Banker Really Worth?" *New York Times Magazine,* January 3, 2010, 32+.

59 "10 Biggest CEO Paychecks: 2008," *CNNMoney. com,* available at http://money.cnn.com/galleries/2009/news/0904/gallery.biggest_ceo_paychecks/index.html, accessed 10/15/10.

60 Phred Dvorak, "Limits on Executive Pay: Easy to Set, Hard to Keep," *Wall Street Journal*, April 20, 2007.

61 Courtney Rubin, "Whole Foods CEO Donates Half of Pay to Charity," *Inc.*, January 26, 2010.

62 "Executive Profile: John P. Mackey," *Bloomberg Businessweek,* available at http://investing.businessweek.com/businessweek/research/stocks/people/person.asp?personId=196899&ticker=WFMI:US, accessed 10/15/10.

63 REI, "People," available at http://www.rei.com/aboutrei/stewardship_people.html, accessed 10/10/10; REI, "Pay & Benefits" available at http://www.rei.com/jobs/pay.html, accessed 10/10/10.

64 Richard Pipes, *Communism: A History* (New York: Modern Library, 2003).

65 Max Elbaum, *Revolution in the Air: Sixties Radicals Turn to Lenin, Mao and Che* (New York: Verso, 2002).

66 Murray L. Weidenbaum, *Business, Government, and the Public,* 4th ed. (Englewood Cliffs, NJ: Prentice Hall, 1990).

67 Archie B. Carroll and Ann K. Buchholz, *Business & Society: Ethics and Stakeholder Management,* 7th ed. (Mason, OH: South-Western Cengage Learning, 2009).

68 "Costs and Benefits of Government Regulation," available at http://usgovinfo.about.com/library/weekly/aacost-benefit.htm, accessed 10/15/10.

69 W. Mark Crain, "The Impact of Regulatory Costs on Small Firms," *Small Business Research Summary*, September 2005, No. 264, available at http://www.sba.gov/advo/research/rs264tot.pdf, accessed 10/15/10.

70 Ethics Resource Center, *2005 National Business Ethics Survey,* available at http://www.ethics.org/resource/2005-national-business-ethics-survey, accessed 10/15/10.

71 United States Sentencing Commission, "Organizational Guidelines," available at http://www.ussc.gov/orgguide.htm, accessed 10/15/10.

72 "Sentencing Organizations," *2005 Federal Sentencing Guideline Manual* available at www.ussc.gov/2005guid/tabconchapt8.htm, accessed 10/15/10.

73 B Corporation website available at www.bcorporation.net, accessed 10/15/10.

74 "B Corporations Gain Tax Advantage in Philly," December 23, 2009, available at www.bcorporation.net/index.cfm/fuseaction/news.detail/id/82a6a3ea-6efc-40c0-b4f7-bd13700d0970, accessed 10/15/10.

75 John Tozzi, "Maryland Passes 'Benefit Corp.' Law for Social Entrepreneurs," *Bloomberg Businessweek,* April 13, 2010.

76 *The B Ratings System: Version 1.0* available at http://www.bcorporation.net/resources/bcorp/documents/B%20Ratings%20System%20-%2030+%20Emp%20Mfg.pdf, accessed 10/15/10.

77 *2009 B Corporation Annual Report* available at http://www.bcorporation.net/resources/bcorp/documents/B%20Corp_2009AnnualReport.pdf, accessed 10/15/10.

78 1% for the Planet website available at www.onepercentfortheplanet.org/en/, accessed 10/15/10.

79 Terry Leap and Misty L. Loughry, "The Stakeholder-Friendly Firm," *Business Horizons*, 47, 2 (2004), 27–32; James Weber and Virginia W. Gerde, "A Model to Audit a Company's Ethics and Compliance Program: Part I," *Ethikos*, 23, 1 (2009), 8+; James Weber and Virginia W. Gerde, "A Model to Audit a Company's Ethics and Compliance Program: Part II," *Ethikos*, 23, 2 (2009), 8+.

PART II

Getting Everyone on Board

CHAPTER OUTLINE

3

HIRING ETHICAL PEOPLE

What would you do?

Resume Information

Upon graduation, you obtain a job on the staff of a Human Resource Department at a growing health care company. Your first assignment is to recruit a new marketing employee. After an extensive job search process, you are very impressed by Tim, a recent college graduate, and one other job applicant. You perform income tax verification for the jobs listed on Tim's resume, which include several part-time and summer positions in the area of sales and marketing. Everything is fine except there is no tax record for a three-month retail store marketing job. When you call Tim to clarify the situation, he tells you that it was an unpaid internship.

You hire Tim because of his excellent grades, relevant work experience in marketing, involvement in student organizations, and high personal integrity. You are immediately impressed by Tim's knowledge, hard work, and conscientiousness.

Three weeks into the new job, an emotionally upset Tim comes into your office. "I feel really terrible about something," Tim says. "You know that retail marketing position that appeared on my resume. That was a lie. You see, my friend had an excellent resume format. I copied his resume and then changed everything based on my own accomplishments and activities. But I forgot to delete his retail store job. That was his job, not mine. Everything else on the resume is absolutely true. When you asked me about the job, I froze and realized what happened. This is my dream job and I was afraid you wouldn't hire me if I told you about the mistake. But this really bothers me and I'm having trouble sleeping knowing that I lied to you."

Tim committed a fraud and was hired based on false information.

What would you do? Would you

1) Fire Tim for providing false information on the resume and lying about it; then hire the second job finalist, who also had impressive credentials?
2) Forgive Tim and give him a second chance to earn your trust?
   Why?

Chapter Objectives

After reading this chapter, you will be able to

- Screen job candidates for their ethics
- Understand which job candidate factors are illegal to consider when hiring
- Obtain accurate behavior information from resumes, reference checks, background checks, and integrity tests

- Use personality test scales that measure ethics
- Ask interview questions that address ethical issues
- Understand when drug and polygraph tests can be administered

Sometimes, after dismissing an employee for an ethical breach, a manager might wonder: How did this person get through the hiring process? There are millions of good-hearted and well-intentioned people, but this person was not one of them. The best safeguard against unethical activities at work is hiring people of high integrity.

This chapter provides a six-step process for determining the ethics of job candidates. Notify job candidates about the ethics job screen and then diligently gather information in a way that does not violate the Civil Rights Act of 1964. Potential sources of ethics information about job candidates include resumes, reference checks, background checks, personality tests, interview questions, and drug tests.

Importance of an Ethics Screen

The most important factor for developing and reinforcing a high-integrity work culture is hiring ethical job applicants. Employing someone whose ethics does not match that of a high-integrity work culture can contaminate an organization. The inappropriate hire may attract like-minded employees, who previously restrained themselves, and lead them in directions detrimental to organizational operations.

For instance, an organization may have a strongly stated policy forbidding employees to use email for personal reasons during work hours. The new employee, during regular working hours, decides to send out several personal emails. A few organizational members, who had previously never broken the "no personal email" policy despite pressing personal demands, may now believe it is permissible to do likewise.

Ethical borderlines can be a slippery slope. Personal email use during work hours can lead to doing other personal tasks during work hours. If a customer emergency arises, a former diligent employee may delay responding until completing a personal task, a problem that never arose prior to hiring the new employee.

Maximizing ethical work behaviors begins with the hiring process. Hiring someone is inviting the person into your home, if your organization is small, or your community, if the organization is large. Some people are kind, helpful, trustworthy, and friendly, while others are mean-spirited, irritating, dishonest, and annoying. One bad hire can make the daily life of many employees miserable.

The typical hiring process consists of reviewing resumes and job application forms for knowledge, skills, and abilities necessary to perform the job task.[1] Ethics is often assumed or overlooked. Task ability and passion matter a great deal. But the prospective employee's knowledge, skills, and abilities need to be complemented with moral values, such as respect for other people and rules. Personal integrity and high ethical standards are indispensible attributes to possess.

The Six-Step Ethics Job Screen Process

Assume you are responsible for hiring a new employee. Two highly qualified job candidates have the requisite knowledge, skills, and abilities. How can you determine which of the two is more ethical?

A wide range of methods are available to help managers determine a job candidate's ethics. The six-step Ethics Job Screen Process outlined in Exhibit 3.1 integrates the best practices into a systematic, chronologic framework that complements an organization's job-recruiting process.

The first step is a notification that attracts ethical job candidates and discourages people who tend to behave unethically from applying. The second step is a cautionary one, ensuring that any method used by the employer to determine ethics does not violate federal law. The next four steps are information sources.

Exhibit 3.1 Six-Step Ethics Job Screen Process

Step	Explanation
1. Ethics Screen Notice	Inform potential job applicants about the organization's ethics job screen.
2. Legal Ground Rules	Gather and use information in a way that does not discriminate against job candidates based on their race, color, religion, gender, national origin, age, or disability.
3. Behavioral Information	Review behavioral information from resumes, reference checks, background checks, and integrity tests.
4. Personality Traits and Related Characteristics	Obtain scores for personality traits and related characteristics such as conscientiousness, Organizational Citizenship Behavior, Social Dominance Orientation, and bullying.
5. Interview Questions	Interview job finalists about their responses to ethical dilemmas experienced at previous workplaces and how they would respond to ethical dilemmas experienced by current employees. In addition, clarify inconsistencies and ambiguities that arose during the previous two steps.
6. Post-Interview Tests	Where appropriate, conduct drug and polygraph tests.

Step 1: Ethics Screen Notice

Industrial psychologist Benjamin Schneider's Attraction-Selection-Attrition cycle (ASA) highlights how individuals are attracted to organizations that reflect their values and goals, organizations select applicants with personal attributes that "fit" the work culture, and then individuals depart if the fit is inappropriate.[2]

Notifying potential job candidates about the organization's ethics screen attracts ethical applicants and discourages morally egregious people from applying. Include a sentence in the job announcement noting that background and reference checks will be conducted and ethics is part of annual performance appraisals.[3]

People who behave ethically want to be members of ethical organizations. Ethical people employed by another organization with questionable ethics are usually searching for employment with other organizations where there is greater congruence between their ethics and those of their employer and coworkers. Notifying job applicants that ethics matters provides ethical people with additional job-related information they find appealing. Ethical people want to report to ethical managers, work with ethical colleagues, manage ethical subordinates, and represent ethical organizations in the broader community.

People who behave unethically, on the other hand, are not likely to apply for jobs with organizations that advertise the strength of their ethics job-screening process. The ethics notice informs unethical people that previous unethical behaviors will be revealed, which puts them at a significant disadvantage with equally skilled applicants who behaved ethically at previous places of employment.

Some job applicants may be concerned that the ethics screen is an invasion of privacy. Clarify that the ethics screen focuses on job-related issues and not activities unrelated to work. Inform job candidates that the information gathered will be used to assess the applicant's workplace ethics and remain confidential between the applicant and employer.

Ben & Jerry's takes an extra step by broadcasting the organization's progressive social mission throughout its website in hopes of attracting like-minded people. The company's three-part corporate mission focuses employees on achieving profit and growth (economic mission) by making high-quality ice cream (product mission) while improving the quality of life for all stakeholders (social mission). The "Best Practice in Use" exhibit highlights 2009 accomplishments related to these three social mission goals.[4]

BEST PRACTICE IN USE

Ben & Jerry's Social Mission Goals

1. *Use our company to further the cause of Peace and Justice:*

- **Fair Trade**—All global flavors will be sourced from fair trade suppliers by year-end 2013.
- **Civil Rights**—Lobbied Vermont (headquarters state) legislators to support a bill allowing same-sex marriage.

- **Peace Partnerships**—Financially supported "Peace One Day" (the NGO sponsors September 21 as an annual day of global cease fire and non-violence in conjunction with the UN International Day of Peace).
- **Ben & Jerry's Foundation**—Contributed $2 million in small grants to nonprofit, grassroots organizations working for progressive social change.
- **Community Action**—Franchisees directly contributed $600,000 in time, ice cream, and scholarships in support of community projects.

2. *Harmonize our global supply chain and ensure its alignment with our values:*

- **Cage-free and free-range eggs**—Sourced 83 percent of the eggs used in U.S. production from cage-free farms; plan to use only Certified Humane cage-free eggs in the U.S. by year-end 2010.
- **Sustainable Packaging**—Phased in Forest Stewardship Council certified paperboard for U.S. pint containers; the paperboard comes from forests that are managed for the protection of wildlife habitat, maintenance of biodiversity, avoidance of genetically modified tree species, and protection of traditional and civil rights.
- **Climate Change**—Completed a carbon inventory of U.S. business operations; offset all emissions associated with Vermont manufacturing facilities and employee air travel with the help of Vermont-based *Native*Energy, a provider of high quality carbon offsets.

3. *Take the lead promoting global sustainable dairy practices:*

- **Caring Dairy™**—Program helped many farmers in Vermont and the Netherlands improve their social, economic, and environmental performance, including reducing their climate impacts.
- **rBGH**—Opposed the use of rBGH, a genetically engineered hormone given to cows used to increase milk production.

Step 2: Legal Ground Rules

For nearly two centuries, employers could use any hiring selection criteria they desired. Explicit discrimination was widespread. Some employers displayed signs that read: "'X' Need Not Apply" with "X" being anyone of a different gender (usually women), religion (usually Jews, atheists, and Catholics), race (usually African Americans and Asians), or ethnicity (usually the latest group of immigrants). During the 1950s, classified advertisements in newspapers were often segregated according to "Male" and "Female" jobs. Secretarial and airline stewardess job openings noted preference would be given to young and attractive women applicants, who were then questioned about their child-rearing plans and spousal jobs.

Many federal and state laws now govern the types of information an employer can gather on job candidates and the reasons an employer can invoke for selecting one job candidate over another. Gather and use information in a way that does not discriminate among job candidates based on their race, color, religion, gender, national origin, age, or disability. Employers signal good ethics to job candidates by respecting the law when recruiting and selecting employees.

Title VII of the Civil Rights Act

In 1964, President Lyndon Johnson pressured Congress to pass the far-reaching Civil Rights Act. Title VII of the Civil Rights Act of 1964 prohibits businesses from discriminating among job applicants based on the person's race, color, religion, gender, or national origin.[5] These groups of previously discriminated people are referred to as protected classes. Title VII has been expanded to prohibit employers from discriminating based on age and physical or mental disabilities. Some states and municipalities have passed legislation that includes "sexual orientation" as a protected class, but not at the federal level.

The Equal Employment Opportunity Commission (EEOC) was created in 1965 to oversee provisions of the Civil Rights Act. The EEOC's scope extended with the passage of the Age Discrimination in Employment Act of 1967 and the Americans with Disabilities Act of 1990. The federal agency investigates discrimination complaints, seeks negotiated solutions to violations, and litigates when conciliation does not occur.

Three major exemptions to Title VII are:

- If an organization employs fewer than 15 people—small businesses are exempted from many regulations so as not to overwhelm them with regulatory compliance burdens
- If an organization serves a religious purpose
- If it is a bona fide occupational qualification for which the discrimination relates to the "essence" or "central mission" of the employer's business (i.e., preference for a Chinese person as a waiter in a Chinese restaurant)

Managers can refuse to hire people they do not like, but the dislike cannot be based on the job candidate being a member of a protected class.

Disparate Impacts

Unlawful discrimination can occur on the *front end* or the *back end* of the hiring process. *Front-end* job discrimination occurs when members of protected classes are excluded from the job candidate pool. This can happen intentionally, when organizations target only men or Caucasians, or unintentionally. Word-of-mouth recruiting, such as recommendations from other employees or colleagues, is often a very effective means of attracting high-quality employees. But if the organization has a homogenous workforce consisting of Caucasian males, this could result in a job application pool of only Caucasian males.

Back-end job discrimination can be intentional or unintentional. Intentional job discrimination would occur if a male manager decides not to hire a woman finalist because the other men in the office are sexist and would not follow orders from a woman.

Other times the discrimination could be unintended. A job selection rule that does not explicitly discriminate against a protected class but results in a disparate impact, may violate the Civil Rights Act. Disparate impacts occur when members of a protected class rarely make it through all the job-screening filters, suggesting that one of the decision rules could be unintentionally discriminatory.[6] Most disparate impact challenges are associated with written tests, height and weight requirements, educational requirements, and subjective procedures that are not associated with the specific tasks required to perform the job.

An organization's gender, racial, and ethnic employee profile should reflect the gender, racial, and ethnic profile of people living in the geographical region qualified to perform the job task. The EEOC recommends applying a four-fifths rule to determine whether an apparently nondiscriminatory selection process may result in disparate impacts.[7] The method consists of determining the acceptance rate for two groups of job applicants and, if nondiscriminatory, the acceptance rates would be within 80 percent of each other. This is calculated by dividing the percentage of protected class acceptances by the percentage of majority group (Caucasian or male) acceptances. A disparate impact calculator is available online.[8]

For instance, assume that over a seven-year period, a company hired 5 women and 15 men for 20 entry-level marketing job openings requiring a college degree. During the same seven-year period, 50 women and 60 men with marketing degrees applied for the jobs. The company hired 10 percent of the female (5/50) and 25 percent of the male (15/60) applicants. This violates the four-fifths rule (using the formula: 0.10/0.25 = 40 percent), suggesting that the selection process might be discriminatory. If sued, the company would have to provide a compelling reason that its job-screening process does not discriminate based on gender. For instance, a large percentage of the women applicants may have chosen employment at regional competitors offering better pay and benefits.

Some personality tests and background checks may also result in disparate impacts, eliminating highly qualified job applicants from further consideration because their non-job-related personality traits or previous life experiences differ from those of the Caucasian males making the hiring decisions.

Affirmative Action

An organization may implement an affirmative action plan if its gender or racial profile does not reflect the gender or racial profile of people living in the geographical region qualified to perform the job task. Affirmative action plans remedy past discriminatory behaviors by actively seeking, hiring, and promoting minority group members and women to equalize opportunities previously limited to Caucasian males. People with disabilities and certain veterans of the armed forces are also targeted recipients of affirmative action plans.[9]

The EEOC requires federal contractors and subcontractors to have an affirmative action plan that demonstrates commitment to the government's goal of equal employment opportunities. The requirement usually targets companies with at least 50 employees and contracts in excess of $50,000. Some states and municipalities have similar requirements.

Affirmative action plans remain controversial.[10] Some people claim that affirmative action plans are an unconstitutional form of "reverse discrimination," whereby Caucasian males are discriminated against based solely on their race and gender. Others oppose affirmative action plans on the grounds that they are no longer necessary because historical forms of racial and gender discrimination have been eliminated, or remediation for discrimination can be addressed through the justice system.[11]

Some employers try to avoid litigation by instituting a protected class quota system. For instance, an organization may need 10 African Americans to meet the community's racial profile because qualified African Americans are applying for job openings elsewhere. But employing 10 unqualified African Americans sets protected class quota recipients up for failure, reinforces negative stereotyping, and damages employee morale.

Other Legal Issues

Title VII of the Civil Rights Act has been supplemented with legislation prohibiting discrimination based on age, pregnancy, and disability. The Age Discrimination in Employment Act of 1967, amended in 1978 and 1986, prohibits organizations from not hiring someone because he or she is over the age of 40. The Pregnancy Discrimination Act of 1978 clarified that unlawful sex discrimination included not hiring a woman because of a visible pregnancy or the likelihood of her becoming pregnant. The Americans with Disabilities Act of 1990 extended civil rights protections to qualified job applicants with disabilities (defined as "a physical or mental impairment that substantially limits a major life activity").[12] Employers are expected to select the applicant who can most successfully perform the job, regardless of age, pregnancy status, or disability.

The National Council on Alcoholism and Drug Dependence reports that 6.6 percent of full-time employees are heavy drinkers.[13] Alcohol use is responsible for $33 billion to $68 billion in workplace losses. Alcoholics and problem drinkers are absent from work four to eight times more often than other employees.[14] If job related, employers can ask applicants about drunken driving arrests. Questions about being an alcoholic, however, are illegal under the Americans with Disabilities Act because alcoholism is categorized as a disability.[15]

An increasing number of immigrants from a variety of nations illegally enter the United States because of immigration quota restrictions. Experts estimate that 25 percent of the 47 million Latinos living in the United States are undocumented, having crossed the border illegally.[16] Hiring an illegal immigrant violates federal law. Employers must carefully approach this topic because asking only Latino job applicants if they are illegal immigrants discriminates based on national origin. Employment lawyers recommend that all job applicants be asked if they are legally authorized to work in the United States on a full-time basis.[17]

Exhibit 3.2 provides a checklist for determining the viability of a job selection rule. A "Yes" response to any of the three rules could result in a discrimination lawsuit. Require integrity and personality test vendors to affirm in writing that, based on use by other clients, the instrument has been proven not to violate any of the rules.

Exhibit 3.2 Job Selection Rule Checklist

Rule	Explanation
1.	Does the selection rule discriminate against job candidates based on their race, color, religion, gender, national origin, or age?
2.	Does the selection rule discriminate against job candidates with physical or mental disabilities?
3.	Does the selection rule result in outcomes whereby members of protected classes, who live in the geographic region and possess the basic level of education and experience required, are disproportionately underrepresented?

The legal system is equally demanding about the obligations job candidates owe the employer. Job candidates are legally required to respond truthfully to all job-related questions on application forms and submitted materials, such as resumes. Highlight this obligation by inserting a sentence directly above the job candidate's signature line stating that[18]

1. All answers provided by the job candidate are truthful.

2. Any false or purposely omitted information will lead to the job candidate's disqualification.

3. Any false or purposely omitted information that becomes known after employment will lead to job termination.

Step 3: Behavioral Information

Behavioral information about a job candidate's ethics is more reliable than attitudinal survey results or responses to hypothetical dilemmas. Four recruiting tools provide useful behavioral information about a job candidate's ethics: resumes, reference checks, background checks, and integrity tests. Each of these has strengths and weaknesses.

Resumes

The best predictor of future performance is past performance. A job candidate's previous accomplishments are encapsulated on a resume or job application. Typically, resumes contain valuable information about previous work experience and educational attainment, as well as committee responsibilities and community service activities. Serving on high-profile committees at work suggests that a job candidate is trustworthy, dependable, and well respected. Volunteer activities in the community suggest that the individual is concerned about the welfare of others.

Some job candidates stretch the truth, or lie outright, on resumes. Researchers estimate that 20 percent to 44 percent of all resumes—more than one in five—contain lies. ADP Screening and Selection Services conducted 2.6 million background checks on job application and resume information. The study found that 44 percent of the reviewed resumes had lies about work histories, 41 percent had lies about educational background, and 23 percent had fabricated licenses or other credentials.[19] Of 1,000 resumes uploaded on the ResumeDoctor.com website, 42.7 percent contained significant inaccuracies.[20]

College students seeking jobs upon graduation are prone to exaggeration on their resumes (see Exhibit 3.3). Reid Psychological Systems reported that 40 percent of college students pursuing jobs had lied on their resumes and job applications, and 95 percent were willing to make at least one false statement to obtain a job.[21] Even facts easy to verify are fabricated. Twenty percent of the students who submitted resumes to the Rutgers University Career Services inflated their grade point averages.[22]

The same problem is apparent among those applying for the highest-level job openings. Jude W. Werra, owner of a head-hunting company, publishes a Liar's Index twice a year. Werra reviews the resumes his firm receives for CEO and vice president job openings and calculates the percentage that contain false educational information. The Liar's Index usually ranges between 10 percent and 20 percent.[23]

Exhibit 3.3 College Student Job Application Lies

Researchers surveyed 390 college students who applied for at least one job within the past year whether they misrepresented themselves during the job application process.* Below are the misrepresentations and percentage of respondents who admitted doing so.

When applying for the job:

- I overemphasized or exaggerated my positive attributes (characteristics or traits such as hardworking, prompt, thorough) on my job application: 51%
- I exaggerated my work experience to make myself look more impressive than I really am: 38%
- I inflated a past pay rate to get a larger starting salary/pay at the new job: 27%
- I claimed to have experience that I didn't actually have: 16%
- I listed awards or distinctions on my resume or application form that I did not actually receive: 8%

---

* John J. Donovan, Stephen A. Dwight, and Gregory M. Hurtz, "An Assessment of the Prevalence, Severity and Verifiability of Entry-Level Applicant Faking Using the Randomized Response Technique," *Human Performance*, 16, 1 (2003): 81–106.

Marilee Jones, dean of student admissions at Massachusetts Institute of Technology, whose job duties included reviewing student resumes, was fired in 2007 after school officials learned her resume contained lies about her academic degrees. The misinformation first appeared on her resume 28 years earlier when she applied for a secretarial job in the Admissions Office.[24] The false information remained on her resume while she was promoted up the chain of command based on her job performance. A colleague not chosen for the dean position reviewed Jones's resume and anonymously informed school officials about the lies.

False information or inconsistencies on resumes and job applications suggest a lack of ethics and trustworthiness. If detected, notify the job candidate and ask for an explanation of the discrepancy. Correct and forgive innocent mistakes or misunderstandings, but carefully monitor the new hire to ensure that the mistake is not part of a larger pattern. More serious infractions indicate a job candidate's willingness to circumvent the truth to gain a competitive advantage.

Reference Checks

Reference checks play an important role in helping prospective employers learn more about the ethics of job candidates. Job candidates usually list references predisposed to sharing favorable information. The previous supervisor's perspective of the job candidate's strengths and weaknesses is probably the most relevant information source. Behavioral indicators of the job candidate's ethics include the applicant's attendance record, ability to follow directions, assistance to coworkers, timeliness, and disciplinary record.[25] If the previous supervisor is not listed among the references, ask the job candidate why. Maybe the supervisor is upset the job candidate quit or the job candidate had accused the supervisor of unethical behaviors.[26]

For management positions, request the names of previous subordinates as references. An excellent manager would welcome the opportunity to do so. Ask the previous subordinate whether he or she would want to work for this manager again. If it is not possible to contact the subordinate, ask the candidate how a previous subordinate would classify the applicant's strengths and weaknesses.

The reference check legal pendulum has swung from favoring a former employer's right to share information to a former employee's privacy rights. For many years, former employers were protected by a "qualified privilege" to openly share information about job candidates, including a negative employee appraisal. But then defamation lawsuits skyrocketed because some unscrupulous employers abused this privilege by slandering and libeling former employees, and some unscrupulous employees threatened litigation to prevent sharing unfavorable information.[27] As a result, some former employers will only verify dates of employment.

The legal pendulum is swinging back toward a reasonable middle ground due to some recent tragedies.[28] During a reference check, American Eagle Airlines was not informed that a pilot resigned from his previous job because he failed a critical flight test. The newly hired pilot then crashed a plane, killing 15 people. In another case, a previous employer attributed a job candidate's discharge to downsizing even though the discharge was due to violent tendencies, including carrying a gun to work. The job candidate was hired and later murdered three executives.

If a former employer or supervisor will only confirm dates of employment, then quickly ask: "Would you hire this person again?" Supervisors are usually willing to share positive information about a former employee, even if their organization has a strict policy not to divulge anything beyond the basic employment facts. A favorable supervisor response might be all the information needed. If the supervisor hesitates or refuses to answer, then ask the candidate follow-up questions during the interview session.

References are legally protected from a defamation lawsuit as long as the information being conveyed is truthful. A signed release statement by the job candidate provides the reference with greater confidence of legal protection against a defamation lawsuit.

Tips and Techniques

Legal Protections for Contacting References*

Include a statement on the job application form for the candidate to sign that

1. Authorizes you to investigate the truthfulness of the information provided
2. Authorizes references, former employers, and educators to respond truthfully about the person's qualifications and character
3. Promises not to hold any of the references liable for conveying truthful information

* C. Backer Bradden, Kim E. Patterson, and Robert K. Scholl, *Hiring and Firing in Wisconsin* (Madison, WI: State Bar of Wisconsin CLE Books, 1996), section 2.22.

Background Checks

A background check is more objective than a reference check, integrity test, or personality test. Conduct background checks to verify a job candidate's academic accomplishments, prior work responsibilities, and other work-related issues. Extensive background checks are legally required for certain high-security jobs, such as those in the financial securities, law enforcement, or health care industries. Background checks are also highly recommended when the job entails interacting with the public.[29]

A survey conducted by the Society for Human Resource Management found that between 1996 and 2003, companies using background checks increased from 51 percent to 80 percent.[30] Cost estimates for background checks range from a free search on Google to $10,000 or more.[31] Some online background check service providers are untrustworthy. A test of these providers showed that many were unable to recognize that a job candidate had criminal and civil records because their databases were outdated or incorrect.[32]

Academic Accomplishments Academic accomplishments are a common resume problem. A background check could reveal that a workshop attended at a local college or university has been inflated to the status of coursework taken toward an advanced degree, or whether the listed higher education institution is an unaccredited diploma mill that provides credentials to people without taking courses.[33]

Diploma mills are a billion-dollar industry. The General Accounting Office (GAO) examined 450,000 resumes in a government database and found 1,200 resumes listing degrees from 14 different diploma mills.[34] The recipients included the assistant secretary of defense and individuals working in nearly every federal agency. As part of the investigation, the GAO purchased two Lexington University degrees from Degrees-R-Us for Senator Susan Collins, a master's of science in medical technology and a bachelor's of science in biology, for $1,515 each.

Criminal Records and Credit Checks Other sources of information are criminal records, motor vehicle reports, Social Security verification, and credit checks. McDonald's paid $200,000 in damages for hiring a janitor who sexually assaulted a three-year-old customer.[35] McDonald's had conducted a reference check, but a state agency did not mention the individual's criminal history, which included a prison term for child molestation. The court ruled against McDonald's because it would have been relatively easy for the company to search a public criminal records database.

Access to a nationwide list of district court, circuit court, and bankruptcy court records is available on the Internet.[36] States also administer their own public records databases. Wisconsin maintains a Consolidated Court Automation Programs (CCAP) case management system for all public records required by state and federal records laws.[37] The CCAP system searches through felony cases, civil cases, tax warrants, small claims cases, unemployment compensation cases, workers' compensation cases, and traffic cases. The U.S. Department of Justice requires all states to maintain a sex offender registry.[38] Advocacy groups, such as Family Watchdog, provide free Internet searches on sex offenders that are updated daily.[39]

Companies using credit checks as part of the job-screening process rose from 19 percent in 1996 to 60 percent in 2010.[40] According to the Association of Certified Fraud Examiners, two key indicators of an employee engaged in fraud are living beyond his or her means and difficulty meeting financial obligations.[41] As a result, credit checks have taken on greater importance.

Creditworthiness and previous arrests must be job related if used as a determining factor for denying someone employment. Speeding tickets and drunken driving citations may be relevant for travelling salespeople but not retail clerks. Creditworthiness may be relevant for bank employees but not professors. Efforts are underway to pass legislation prohibiting the use of credit checks.[42] Legislation advocates argue that credit checks violate Title VII of the Civil Rights Act because blacks and Hispanics have significantly lower credit scores than Caucasians and Asians.

Notify the job candidate that a credit check will be conducted, and provide an opportunity for applicants to explain any information that raises questions about the individual's credibility. The Fair Credit Reporting Act requires that job applicants be informed if their rejection is based on credit report information.[43]

Facebook The Internet makes life more transparent. Approximately half of human resource managers surveyed perform due diligence by inserting a job candidate's name in an Internet search engine.[44] These searches can result in a list of websites highlighting a potential employee's ethical, or unethical, activities. Be careful when reviewing this information. The Internet is easy to abuse and may contain false information about an individual.

Facebook is a popular social networking website on which individuals submit personal information, photos, and videos about themselves.[45] Facebook, founded in 2004, was originally developed for teenagers and young adults, but now spans all generations. By 2009, more than half of Facebook's users were age 25 and older.[46] In 2010, after just six years of operation, more than 500 million people were active Facebook users, one out of every 14 people in the world.[47]

Searching these sites raises invasion of privacy concerns. Some sites are available for anyone to view, while others require entry approval. Personal profiles may highlight involvement in community service or contain embarrassing pictures and highly opinionated statements. Due diligence dictates asking a job candidate who writes about having urges to hurt elderly people about these sentiments before hiring him or her to assist elderly people with disabilities.

Provide job candidates an opportunity to respond to any questionable background check information during the interview process.

Integrity Tests

Integrity tests, also referred to as honesty tests, typically gather information about the job candidate's behaviors and attitudes toward unethical workplace activities, such as theft. Three popular integrity tests are portions of the Reid Report, the Stanton Survey, and the Personnel Selection Inventory (PSI). These computerized tests consist of a list of statements job candidates evaluate using Likert scale measures ranging from "Strongly Agree" to "Strongly Disagree." The answers can be quickly tabulated.

Integrity tests may take any of the following four approaches:[48]

1. *Direct admission of performing an illegal or questionable activity:* "I stole money from my previous employer."

2. *Opinions regarding illegal or questionable behavior:* "It is okay for people to steal from employers."

3. *Personality traits related to dishonesty:* "I constantly think about stealing from my employer."

4. *Reaction to a hypothetical situation featuring dishonest behavior:* "If I saw an employee steal money, I would ignore the situation and wait for the boss to find out."

Integrity tests have been used as a preemployment assessment tool since the late 1940s. Their popularity grew in 1988 when Congress passed the Employee Polygraph Protection Act, which significantly restricted nongovernment organizations from using lie detector machines as part of the job-hiring process.

In 1990, with more than 5,000 businesses using integrity tests, the federal government's Office of Technology Assessment (OTA) published a report summarizing research on the validity (did the tests really measure integrity or something other than integrity?) and reliability (would the same person taking the test twice receive similar scores?) of integrity tests.[49] The findings noted that 94 percent to 99 percent of the individuals who passed an integrity test (and thus classified as honest) did not later steal from their employer. However, 73 percent to 97 percent of the individuals who were hired despite being classified by test results as dishonest also did not steal. The OTA report concluded that research neither proved nor disproved whether integrity tests measured an individual's propensity to steal.

More recent research, however, has found that individuals with low integrity test scores at the time of employment, compared to those with higher scores, are more likely to later engage in theft, have high absenteeism, break rules, cheat, and become disciplinary problems.[50] One company used integrity tests to screen job candidates in 600 of its 1,900 stores and then compared inventory theft and employee turnover between

Let's Build a Building

Bid Shopping

You are a hospital administrator responsible for building a 10,000-square-foot clinic. A developer offers to design and build the new clinic to meet your specifications and then lease the clinic to you for approximately $19 a square foot over a 10-year period. Leasing the building is a very attractive alternative due to the economic recession. You tell the developer that you have an excellent relationship with a general contractor you've worked with in the past and would like to use your general contractor to help design and ultimately construct the clinic. The developer agrees.

Over the next four months, you work closely with your general contractor to design the space and select the materials for your new clinic. As is the norm in the industry, your general contractor does not charge you for this planning work. He has also turned down some other potential job offers in anticipation of building the hospital clinic. You keep the developer up to date during the design phase. Once the design is complete, your contractor provides you with a $2.3 million construction estimate.

The developer responds that your general contractor's costs are too high. If you insist on using your general contractor, the developer would have to increase your rental rate from $19 a square foot to $22 a square foot, which would amount to an extra $30,000 a year over the course of your 10-year lease, which totals $300,000.

The developer shops the general contractor's bid to several of his contacts. A general contractor the developer has worked with before offers to construct the building for $2.1 million, which is the construction cost the developer needs to meet your $19 a square foot lease budget. You share this information with your general contractor and he says there is no way he can construct the building at that cost. If he did he would not make any profit.

What would you do? Would you

1. Accept the lower bid from your developer's general contractor?
2. Tell the developer to hire your friend who has done all the planning and design work for you, and pay the extra $300,000 over the 10-year lease? Why?

the two groups of stores.[51] The outcome differences were dramatic. After one year, the group of stores using integrity tests experienced a 35 percent *decline* in inventory loss and 13 percent *decline* in employee turnover, while the stores not using integrity tests experienced a 10 percent *increase* in theft and a 14 percent *increase* in turnover.

Despite these impressive findings, using self-report integrity tests as the sole criterion for hiring ethical people may deny organizations the services of some very honest individuals. Tutorials and coaches are available to help individuals score high on integrity tests. In addition, these tests are prone to social desirability measurement problems in which the test taker provides a socially appropriate answer rather than an honest answer. The "best" integrity test answer is often obvious and, as a result, dishonest individuals who lie by providing the socially appropriate answer an employer wants can score higher than honest individuals.[52]

For example, a common integrity test statement is: "I am a trustworthy person." A dishonest person wanting the job would lie by choosing "Strongly Agree." An individual of high integrity, fully aware of personal moral shortcomings, might choose "Agree" rather than "Strongly Agree," resulting in a lower score. As a result, corroborate integrity test scores with other ethics measures and discuss the results during the job interview.

Step 4: Personality Traits and Related Characteristics

Integrity tests are primarily concerned about an individual's experience and attitudes about theft and other unethical activities. Personality tests, on the other hand, offer a much broader psychological understanding of the job candidate and can identify characteristics associated with ethical or unethical behaviors.

Of the hundreds of possible personality measures, "conscientiousness"—which measures responsibility, dependability, and work ethic—is the best predictor of ethics and job performance. Social Dominance Orientation and bullying measures predict a propensity for racial and gender discrimination and can result in hostile work environments. Organizational Citizenship Behavior is a related behavioral characteristic, rather than a psychological trait, that measures an individual's propensity to help others. Exhibit 3.4 diagrams the relationship these four measures have with ethical behavior.

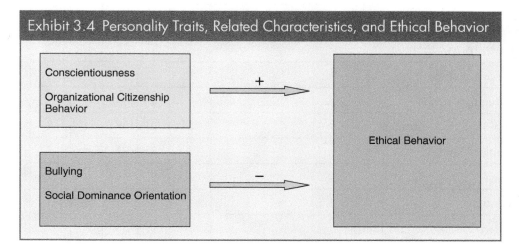

Exhibit 3.4 Personality Traits, Related Characteristics, and Ethical Behavior

Conscientiousness

Organizational Citizenship Behavior

+

Bullying

Social Dominance Orientation

−

Ethical Behavior

Other personality measures associated with ethics, such as locus of control and Machiavellianism, are discussed in Chapter 6 as potential ethics training workshop topics.

Conscientiousness

Personality theorists and researchers have reached a general consensus on a "Big Five Model" consisting of five broad dimensions or factors that describe human personality: extraversion (talkative, assertive, energetic, ambitious), agreeableness (likeable, friendly, easy to get along with), conscientiousness (responsible, dependable, hard working), emotional stability (calm, low anxiety, secure), and openness to experience (curious, independent minded, imaginative).[53] Scores on three of the Big Five personality factors—agreeableness, conscientiousness, and emotional stability—correspond to integrity test scores.[54]

Of these three factors, conscientiousness is the strongest predictor of ethical behavior.[55] Individuals who behave ethically are also responsible, dependable, and hard working. This is particularly noteworthy because conscientiousness is also a strong predictor of job performance.[56] In terms of the two nonrelated Big Five personality factors, ethical behavior is not related to being extroverted or introverted, nor is it related to being imaginative or pragmatic.

Researchers have also found a high correlation among conscientiousness, trustworthiness, and integrity.[57] Many ethical problems begin as minor deceptions and then escalate. Conscientious people are more likely to feel dissatisfied or guilty about deceiving others and less likely to participate in escalating deceptions or cover-ups.

Exhibit 3.5 lists survey statements used to measure conscientiousness.[58] Survey respondents report to what extent each item describes their behaviors using a 1 to 5 Likert scale ranging from "Strongly Disagree" to "Strongly Agree."

Exhibit 3.5 Conscientiousness Scale

Instructions: Please use the 1 to 5 scale below to assess how well each of the following statements describes yourself. The more honest you are the more helpful the information we will receive.

1=Strongly Disagree; 2=Disagree; 3=Neither Agree nor Disagree; 4=Agree; 5=Strongly Agree

	SD	D	N	A	SA
Positively Stated Items					
Accomplish my work on time	1	2	3	4	5
Do things according to a plan	1	2	3	4	5
Am careful to avoid making mistakes	1	2	3	4	5
Keep my checkbook balanced	1	2	3	4	5
Like to plan ahead	1	2	3	4	5
Return borrowed items	1	2	3	4	5
Positively Stated Items—Add the six scores:					

Negatively Stated Items					
Often forget to put things back in their proper place	1	2	3	4	5
Neglect my duties	1	2	3	4	5
Take tasks too lightly	1	2	3	4	5
Leave my work undone	1	2	3	4	5
Do not plan ahead	1	2	3	4	5
Put off unpleasant tasks	1	2	3	4	5
Am often late for work	1	2	3	4	5
Negatively Stated Items—Add the seven scores:					
Total Score—Subtract Negatively Stated Item Score from Positively Stated Item Score:					

As with integrity tests, personality tests can be prone to eliciting socially desirable answers because the character trait being measured is somewhat obvious. For example, individuals may report that they are careful not to make mistakes when that is not the case.[59] This can be verified when a reference check is conducted.

Organizational Citizenship Behavior

Organizational Citizenship Behavior (OCB) refers to work-related helping behaviors that go beyond normal job requirements, such as aiding others with job-related problems. Researchers report that individuals who score high on OCB also score high for performance quantity, performance quality, and customer service.[60]

OCB is typically measured based on seven factors:

- *Helping Behavior*: Voluntarily helping others with, or preventing the occurrence of, work-related problems.
- *Organizational Compliance*: Internalizing and accepting the organization's rules, regulations, and procedures.
- *Individual Initiative*: Voluntarily going above and beyond what is minimally required or generally expected by one's job description.
- *Organizational Loyalty*: Promoting the organization to outsiders, protecting and defending it against external threats, and remaining committed to it even under adverse conditions.
- *Civic Virtue*: Willingness to engage in organizational governance activities, monitoring the environment for threats and opportunities, and looking out for the best interests of the organization.
- *Self Development*: Voluntarily improving one's knowledge, skills, and abilities.
- *Sportsmanship*: Maintaining a positive attitude even when things do not directly benefit the person, and willing to sacrifice personal interest for the good of the work group.

Researchers have developed shorter OCB scales that tap into some of these factors. Exhibit 3.6 provides a five-item overall OCB scale[61] and Exhibit 3.7 provides a seven-item "Helping Behavior" scale, which is a prominent OCB factor.[62] Both surveys apply a 1 to 5 Likert scale ranging from "Strongly Disagree" to "Strongly Agree" and can be asked of job references.

Exhibit 3.6 Organizational Citizenship Behavior Scale

Instructions: Please use the 1 to 5 scale below to assess how well each of the following statements describes the job applicant. The more honest you are the more helpful the information we will receive.
1=Strongly Disagree; 2=Disagree; 3=Neither Agree nor Disagree; 4=Agree; 5=Strongly Agree

	SD	D	N	A	SA
The employee works to exceed each customer's expectations (conscientiousness)	1	2	3	4	5
The employee can be counted on when help is needed (altruism)	1	2	3	4	5
The employee feels responsible for the organization's success (civic virtue)	1	2	3	4	5
The employee has a "can do" attitude (sportsmanship)	1	2	3	4	5
The employee treats other people with respect (courtesy)	1	2	3	4	5

Add the five scores:

Exhibit 3.7 Helping Behavior Scale

Instructions: Please use the 1 to 5 scale below to assess how well each of the following statements describes the job applicant. The more honest you are the more helpful the information we will receive.
1=Strongly Disagree; 2=Disagree; 3=Neither Agree nor Disagree; 4=Agree; 5=Strongly Agree

	SD	D	N	A	SA
The employee helps others if someone falls behind in his/her work	1	2	3	4	5
The employee willingly shares his/her expertise with others	1	2	3	4	5
The employee acts like a peacemaker when other employees have disagreements	1	2	3	4	5
The employee takes steps to prevent problems with other employees	1	2	3	4	5
The employee willingly gives his/her time to help other employees who have work-related problems	1	2	3	4	5
The employee "touches base" with other employees before initiating actions that might affect them	1	2	3	4	5
The employee encourages others when another employee feels emotionally down	1	2	3	4	5

Add the seven scores:

Social Dominance Orientation and Bullying

Ethics demands sincere, open-minded, respectful conversations with a wide variety of people about alternative actions under consideration. Social Dominance Orientation (SDO) is the belief that an individual's particular group membership (defined in terms of race, gender, religion, or ethnicity) is superior to membership in other groups. Researchers have found that high SDO scores are associated with racism and sexism.

Exhibit 3.8 provides survey items for Social Dominance Orientation.[63] The scale items are measured with a 1 to 5 Likert scale ranging from "Strongly Disagree" to "Strongly Agree." Individuals expressing these sentiments can damage employee morale and diversity efforts in high-integrity organizations.

Exhibit 3.8 Social Dominance Orientation Scale

Instructions: Please use the 1 to 5 scale below to assess how well each of the following statements describes yourself. The more honest you are the more helpful the information we will receive.

1=Strongly Disagree; 2=Disagree; 3=Neither Agree nor Disagree; 4=Agree; 5=Strongly Agree

	SD	D	N	A	SA
Strong Social Dominance Items					
Some groups of people are simply inferior to other groups.	1	2	3	4	5
In getting what you want, it is sometimes necessary to use force against other groups.	1	2	3	4	5
It's OK if some groups have more of a chance in life than others.	1	2	3	4	5
To get ahead in life, it is sometimes necessary to step on other groups.	1	2	3	4	5
If certain groups stayed in their place, we would have fewer problems.	1	2	3	4	5
It's probably a good thing that certain groups are at the top and other groups are at the bottom.	1	2	3	4	5
Inferior groups should stay in their place.	1	2	3	4	5
Sometimes other groups must be kept in their place.	1	2	3	4	5
Strong Social Dominance Items—Add the eight scores:					
Weak Social Dominance Items					
It would be good if groups could be equal.	1	2	3	4	5
Group equality should be our ideal.	1	2	3	4	5
All groups should be given an equal chance in life.	1	2	3	4	5

(Continued)

Exhibit 3.8 Social Dominance Orientation Scale *(Continued)*					
We should do what we can to equalize conditions for different groups.	1	2	3	4	5
Increased social equality is beneficial to society.	1	2	3	4	5
We would have fewer problems if we treated people more equally.	1	2	3	4	5
We should strive to make incomes as equal as possible.	1	2	3	4	5
No group should dominate in society.	1	2	3	4	5
Weak Social Dominance Items—Add the eight scores:					
Total Score—Subtract Weak Social Dominance Score from Strong Social Dominance Score:					

A survey of U.S. workers found that approximately 30 percent were bullied by a boss or coworker.[64] The two most common forms of bullying were having information withheld that affected job performance and being exposed to an unmanageable workload. According to research studies, a predisposition to bullying others is also associated with racial and gender discrimination.

Researchers have developed a 22-item bullying scale, but it measures whether an employee has been bullied rather than whether a job applicant has bullying tendencies.[65] Information about a person's bullying tendencies can be obtained through a reference check. Questions from the bullying scale that could be asked include has the job applicant

- Purposely withheld information from others that negatively affected his or her performance
- Assigned unmanageable workloads
- Ordered subordinates to do work beyond their competence level
- Gave tasks with unreasonable/impossible targets/deadlines
- Excessively monitored the work of subordinates
- Humiliated and ridiculed subordinates

Mental Disability Tests

For legal reasons, tests that measure general personality traits must be differentiated from those that diagnose personality disorders or mental disabilities, such as the Minnesota Multiphasic Personality Inventory (MMPI).[66] MMPI, the most frequently used instrument for diagnosing personality disorders, includes scales for hysteria, paranoia, schizophrenia, and depression.[67]

Mental and physical disabilities have protected class status under the Americans with Disabilities Act. According to the EEOC, do not ask job applicants whether they have been treated for any mental health conditions or certain diseases. Instead, ask applicants if they are able to perform all job functions and meet the job's attendance requirements.[68] With proper medication, people diagnosed with manic depression or other mental health disabilities can be excellent employees.

Mental health and other medical tests for job candidates can be administered after a bona fide job offer has been made. Mental health tests are recommended, and at times mandated by law, for jobs involving high levels of stress, personal risk, and responsibility, such as nuclear power plant operators, armed security guards, or air traffic controllers.[69] If a mental health test reveals a disability, the company must provide accommodations unless doing so is burdensome.

Mental health tests such as the MMPI are not a valid way to determine the ethics of job candidates. A person with a manic depression disorder who takes the appropriate medication is likely to behave as ethically as anyone else in the general population.

Step 5: Interview Questions

The in-person interview provides another opportunity to obtain relevant information about a job candidate's ethics. The interviewer can ask for clarifications on the ethics-related information already gathered and probe information gaps and inconsistencies. In addition, question job applicants about how they responded to previous ethical dilemmas, be sensitive to false cues that might indicate the candidate is lying, and provide a realistic preview of the job environment.

Previous Ethical Dilemmas

Asking job candidates to describe how they managed an ethical dilemma at a previous employer can be very useful. Human beings are creatures of habit, and the job candidate will bring these response patterns to work.

Some individuals do not know what is meant by the words "ethics" or "ethical dilemma." Ask probing questions that highlight specific ethical issues—such as observing theft, sexual harassment, and legal violations. If the individual has not experienced any ethical dilemmas, then transform the issue into a hypothetical situation: "Would you accept a free lunch from a client wanting to do business with the organization?"

Sensitize job candidates to real-life ethical dilemmas current employees have experienced and ask how they would respond. The job interviewer can develop ethical dilemmas based on his or her own experience or have current employees compose them as an ethics training workshop activity (see Chapter 6). Develop three distinct responses to the ethical dilemma scenario, rank them according to being the "most ethical," "moderately ethical," and "least ethical" response, and evaluate how well the job applicant responded.

Ethics questions about previous work experiences must be job related, and a standardized format followed, to avoid protected class biases. Questions to ask include the following:

- Tell me about a time when you observed an employee or customer stealing product. How did you respond?
- Tell me about a time when you observed an employee sexually harassing another employee or customer. How did you respond?
- Tell me about a time when you observed anything at work, or did anything at work, that violated industry standards or the law. How did you respond?

- Tell me about a time when you were asked by a boss, coworker, customer, or supplier to do something unethical. How did you respond?
- Tell me about a time when you observed anything at work, or did anything at work, that bothered your conscience. How did you respond?

Visual Lie Detection

Interview questions may generate dishonest responses from the job candidate if the most ethical answer is obvious: "Of course I would report a boss or coworker embezzling money!" There is no particular "Pinocchio effect," whereby, similar to the Walt Disney character, an individual's nose grows whenever he or she tells a lie. Researchers examined 1,338 estimates of 158 different bodily and verbal cues for lying and found no single cue compelling.[70] Behavioral responses assumed to be cues for detecting a lie include the following:[71]

- *Bodily Tendencies:* Less eye contact, increased blinking, pupil dilation, fidgeting, shaking knee, tapping fingers, sweating, pressing lips together, displaying fewer gestures (tightly wound), deep breaths, gulps, and less pleasant facial features.
- *Verbal Tendencies:* Hesitancy in responding, frequent speech disturbances ("um," "ah," "da"), sighs, higher pitch, longer response before answering (trying to figure out a consistent lie), providing fewer details, and less certain in responses.

There is some truth that these bodily and verbal tendencies, or a combination of them, may suggest lying, but not enough truth to generalize to the specific person being interviewed. Sometimes honest individuals exhibit the assumed tendencies of liars. For instance, a person might avoid eye contact with the interviewer because she or he is shy, nervous about not getting the highly desired job, or lost in thought. On the other end of the interviewee behavior spectrum, a confident person looking directly into the interviewer's eyes might be a well-trained liar trying to deceive the interviewer.[72]

Realistic Job Previews

Present finalists with a realistic job preview, an honest description of daily work activities that highlights both the exciting and tedious aspects of the job.[73] If only the most exciting aspects of the job are discussed, the new employee will experience "entry shock" regarding the tedious aspects of work and conclude that he or she has been misled or managers cannot be trusted.

Researchers have found that an honest and balanced presentation of the actual job experience does not reduce acceptance rates, which is what interviewers fear. Instead, realistic job previews lead to higher levels of employee satisfaction and lower levels of turnover because the new employee's expectations are more aligned with reality.[74]

Step 6: Post-Interview Tests

After interviewing the finalists, some organizations make the job offer contingent on passing a drug test or a polygraph test. When appropriate, conduct drug and polygraph tests as a final test of the job finalist's integrity. Some jobs, such as those at a nuclear reactor facility, require these tests.

Drug Testing

According to the U.S. Department of Health and Human Services, 9.4 million working Americans use illicit drugs. The typical illegal drug user is a low-paid Caucasian male between the ages of 18 and 25.[75] Industries with the highest rates of illicit drug use are food preparation, restaurants and bars, construction, and transportation.

Workplace substance abuse is estimated to cost employers $120 billion a year. Drugs impair an individual's judgment, which puts the life of other employees or customers at risk. Research studies have found that substance abuse lowers productivity; causes accidents and injuries at work; and increases absenteeism, turnover, workers' compensation claims, and medical costs. Drug abusers are also more likely to sell drugs to coworkers and steal from employers to pay for their expensive drug habits.

Millions of Americans are tested for drug use as a preemployment screen or condition of continued employment. Some companies in the transportation industry, and those with large federal contracts, are required by law to conduct drug tests. Drug tests are easy to administer and relatively inexpensive.[76]

Drug use can be determined by an analysis of blood, urine, hair, or saliva. Marijuana, the most commonly tested-for drug, can be detected in the blood system for 2 days, in urine from 2 to 14 days, and in hair follicles for up to 90 days. Each method has its own set of strengths and weaknesses.

Urinalysis is the most often used method for preemployment drug testing. It is also the most personally invasive. A closely observed urine collection process can be a degrading experience. But if not closely observed, job candidates can switch samples or change the composition of the urine through detox products.

Hair testing is less invasive than urinalysis and has greater validity. A strand of hair contains an individual's drug history during the lifetime of that hair. However, it takes longer to obtain laboratory results from hair tests.

Analyzing saliva is noninvasive, easy to collect, and results can be obtained in a few minutes. But saliva is useful only for determining drug use during the previous two days, after which drug traces are no longer contained in saliva.

Polygraphs

Polygraphs, also known as lie detectors, can be used as a job screen by federal, state, and local government agencies, as well as businesses, engaged in national security issues.[77]

The complex history of lie detector tests is worth understanding because using a polygraph to detect lies remains controversial. Significant efforts have been made to improve the accuracy of these tests. The Department of Defense has an annual polygraph budget of $200 million, with $3 million allocated to the Polygraph Institute for instruction and research.[78]

The first lie detector machine, designed in 1917 by a Harvard-trained psychologist, measured an individual's blood pressure. The machine's capabilities were expanded to simultaneously measure three physiological factors—blood pressure, pulse rate, and skin changes. These measures were graphed on a piece of paper, thus the formal name of the machine, a polygraph.[79] But the results were unreliable, with accuracy rates only in the 40 percent to 55 percent range, on par with flipping a coin.

The scientific community concluded that polygraphs detected anxieties, not lies. The court system agreed with the scientific community in *United States v. Frye* (1923) and ruled that polygraph results could not be presented in a court of law.[80] Nonetheless, the lie detector market expanded from police departments to private employers wanting to determine the source of employee theft,[81] and then as a job-screening tool. Exhibit 3.9 provides a list of standard job screening polygraph questions. [82]

Exhibit 3.9 Standard Job Screening Polygraph Questions

1. Have you deliberately falsified or withheld information from your job application?
2. Have you ever been fired from a job?
3. In the last five years did you steal any merchandise from previous employers?
4. In the last five years did you steal any money from previous employers?
5. In the last ten years did you take part in or commit any serious crime?
6. During the past year, have you used marijuana more than (X times)?
7. Have you used any other narcotic illegally in the past five years?
8. Have you ever used a system to cheat one of your employers?
9. Have you deliberately lied in your response to any of these questions?

The heightened use of polygraphs by private employers in the 1980s, due to escalation in cold war espionage, created a backlash. Research reviews conducted by the federal government's Office of Technology Assessment and the American Psychological Association both concluded that the research results were mixed, with most polygraph tests prone to errors.[83] These findings led to the passage of the Employee Polygraph Protection Act of 1988, which prohibits most companies from using polygraph testing as a preemployment tool.

The prohibition does not apply to federal, state, and local governments. Private sector exemptions to the law include pharmaceutical and related firms that manufacture and distribute controlled substances, and armored car and other security industry firms. In addition, the federal government can require private subcontractors engaged in national security issues to include polygraph tests as part of the job-screening process.[84]

Polygraph testing has improved since the 1980s and, with a skilled operator, accuracy rates range from 81 percent to 98 percent. The modern polygraph collects data on at least three physiological systems associated with honesty and lying: respiration, sweat gland activity, and blood pressure. But, as these measures suggest, the polygraph still only detects nervousness, not lying.

A new type of polygraph test being developed by brain researchers uses functional magnetic resonance imaging (fMRI) scanners.[85] Researchers have isolated the section of the brain where lying occurs. When an individual answers truthfully, the brain image is consistent. When an individual lies, neurological activities can be detected because the person is deciding not to tell the truth and then thinking about what would be a believable lie to tell. The initial research results suggest that fMRIs are more accurate than traditional polygraph tests for detecting lies. The cost of using fMRIs for lie detection, however, is exorbitant, and lawsuits will likely be filed by the American Civil Liberties Union for invasion of privacy.

Given polygraph inaccuracies, provide job candidates who contest the findings an opportunity to explain any questionable result.

Exhibit 3.10 summarizes the strengths and concerns for the six types of behavioral information sources discussed in this chapter.

Exhibit 3.10 Behavioral Information Sources: Strengths and Concerns

Type	Strengths	Concerns
Resumes	Documents pervious work experience and accomplishments. Documents educational experience and accomplishments.	44% contain lies about work histories. 41% contain lies about education. 41% contain lies about licenses or other credentials.
Reference Checks	References have personal experience working with the job applicant. References are legally protected from a defamation lawsuit as long as the information being conveyed is truthful.	Many references listed have a favorable bias toward job applicant. Some references are unwilling to share negative information due to lawsuit concerns.
Background Checks	Wide range of information is easily available on Internet. Can verify that information on resumes is accurate.	Internet information can be inaccurate. Information obtained that is not related to job performance can create a negative bias.
Integrity Tests	Documents applicant's previous illegal actions and opinions about ethics issues.	Test takers can easily guess at the socially desired answer. Liars can provide false information and score higher than conscientious applicants.
Personality Tests	Scores for conscientiousness and Organizational Citizenship Behavior are strongly associated with both ethical behavior and employee performance. Scores for Social Dominance Orientation and bullying are strongly associated with sexism and racism.	Test takers can easily guess at the socially desired answer. Tests not performance related can lead to lawsuits.

(*Continued*)

Exhibit 3.10 Behavioral Information Sources: Strengths and Concerns (*Continued*)

Interview Questions	Sensitizes job candidates to real-life ethical dilemmas. Helps clarify questionable information gained from other methods.	Difficult to determine whether applicant is telling the truth or lying.
Drug and Polygraph Tests	Scientifically valid approaches for gathering important information.	Invasion of privacy. Legal action can be taken by a falsely accused job applicant.

Exhibit 3.11 But What If I'm a Small Business?

Including ethics as part of the job-screening process is even more important for small businesses. By ensuring that new employees are ethical, small business owners can confidently delegate tasks without having to worry about monitoring for theft or other unethical behaviors.

Similar to large company managers, a small business owner can obtain ethical behavior data from well-designed job applications and a reference check, ideally from the job applicant's previous supervisor. Background checks can be easily conducted via Internet searches. Then ask the job applicant how he or she has responded, or would respond, to common ethical issues, such as a friend demanding free products or services. Inform job applicants that unethical behaviors will not be tolerated and will result in termination.

SUMMARY

Employing ethical job candidates is the most important way to ensure ethical behavior at work. This chapter provides a six-step ethics job screen to help managers determine the ethics of job candidates. These methods include the following:

- Behavioral information obtained from resumes, reference checks, background checks, and integrity tests
- Survey instruments measuring conscientiousness, Organizational Citizenship Behavior, Social Dominance Orientation, and bullying
- Interview questions that explore previous ethical dilemmas at work
- Drug and polygraph tests when appropriate

Applying the six-step ethics job-screening process demonstrates a significant organizational effort to evaluate the ethics of job candidates and sends a strong message to both job candidates and current employees that ethics matter.

KEY WORDS

Attraction-Selection-Attrition cycle; Title VII of the Civil Rights Act of 1964; protected classes; Equal Employment Opportunity Commission (EEOC); disparate impact; four-fifths rule; affirmative action; unaccredited diploma mill; integrity tests; conscientiousness; Organizational Citizenship Behavior; Social Dominance Orientation; realistic job preview; polygraphs

CHAPTER QUESTIONS

1. What are the six steps of an ethics job-screening process?

2. Describe the importance of Title VII of the Civil Rights Act and how to determine if an organization's job-screening process results in disparate impacts.

3. What are six sources of behavioral information about a job candidate's ethics? What are the strengths and weaknesses of each information source?

4. Which of the Big Five personality factors are the most relevant for understanding a job candidate's ethics?

5. What types of questions would you ask job candidates during an interview to understand their ethics? How would you know if the candidates are responding truthfully?

6. Under what conditions can a job candidate be given a polygraph test?

In the Real World: Enron

Mark-to-Market Accounting—1991

Ken Lay approved Jeff Skilling's innovative proposal, created a Gas Bank Division, and hired Skilling to be the new division's CEO. The Gas Bank was immediately successful. By the end of 1990, Enron's annual revenue rocketed up to $13.2 billion, a 40 percent increase from the previous year. But the value of Enron's stock did not reflect this change.

The Gas Bank division operated more like a financial institution than a traditional gas pipeline company. Skilling maintained that stock market investors failed to realize the Gas Bank's true economic value because the division had to use the traditional oil-and-gas accounting system. Instead, he wanted to use the financial industry's mark-to-market accounting system. Mark-to-market would allow the Gas Bank to immediately claim anticipated long-term revenue when a public utility contract was signed, rather than waiting until the revenue was actually received during the length of the contract. Skilling insisted that these contracts were guaranteed income because governments would not allow public utilities to go bankrupt. The financial difference would be huge.

Changing the accounting system required approval from the Securities and Exchange Commission (SEC). The SEC rejected Enron's initial proposal because of potential pricing manipulations. Skilling countered that diligent auditor oversight would prevent price manipulations. Enron's auditor was Arthur Andersen, one of the most prestigious accounting firms in the world. Arthur Andersen agreed to write a letter to the SEC supporting the Gas Bank's use of a mark-to-market accounting system. The final decision to appeal the SEC ruling was up to Ken Lay.

DECISION CHOICE. If you were the CEO of Enron, would you

1. Keep the traditional oil-and-gas accounting system for Skilling's Gas Bank division?

2. Appeal the SEC rejection and resubmit a proposal for adopting a mark-to-market accounting system for the Gas Bank division?

Why?

ANCILLARY MATERIALS

Websites to Explore

- U.S. Department of Labor, Employment Law Guide, available at http://www.dol.gov/compliance/guide/index.htm.

- DisparateImpactCalculator,availableatwww .hr-software.net/EmploymentStatistics/ DisparateImpact.htm.

- Diploma mills, available at http://www.thecb .state.tx.us/apps/consumerinfo/notx.cfm; Accreditation verification, available at: http://ope.ed.gov/accreditation/Search.aspx.
- Personality Measures
  - Five-Factor Personality Model, available at http://ipip.ori.org/newBigFive5broadKey .htm.
  - Other personality scales, available at http:// ipip.ori.org/newBroadbandAppAB5CKey .htm.
  - MMPI, "Questions to Ask," available at http://www.falseallegations.com/mmpibw .htm.
- Sex Offender Websites
  - U.S. Department of Justice, available at http://www.nsopw.gov/Core/Conditions .aspx.
  - Family Watchdog, available at www .familywatchdog.us.

Best Place to Work Video

- The Ben & Jerry's Story told by co-founders Ben Cohen and Jerry Greenfield, 10 minutes, available at http://www.youtube.com/ watch?v=FU0Eg0sv3Lk.

Business Ethics Issue Video

- "The Madoff Affair," *Frontline*, about Bernie Madoff $65 billion ponzi scheme; May 12,

2009, 55 minutes, available at http://www.pbs .org/wgbh/pages/frontline/madoff/view/.

TEDTalks Videos

- *Nice People Becoming Bad:* Philip Zimbardo shares insights on how easy it is for nice people to turn bad and how easy it is to be a hero; February 2008, 24 minutes, available at http://www.ted.com/talks/philip_zimbardo_ on_the_psychology_of_evil.html.
- *Human Commonality:* Geneticist Spencer Wells talks about how his Genographic Project will use this shared DNA to figure out how we are—in all our diversity—truly connected; June 2007, 21 minutes, available at http://www.ted.com/talks/spencer_ wells_is_building_a_family_tree_for_all_ humanity.html.

Conversations with Charlie Rose

- A conversation about WorldCom and business ethics in corporate America, 60 minutes, June 27, 2002, available at http:// www.charlierose.com/view/interview/2484.
- A conversation with Arthur Levitt, the former chairman of the Securities and Exchange Commission, about reform in the accounting profession and greater fiscal accountability in corporate America, 60 minutes, October 18, 2002, available at http:// www.charlierose.com/view/interview/2326.

NOTES

[1] Centers for Disease Control and Prevention, "The Importance of KSA's (Knowledge, Skills and Abilities) in the Federal Application Process," available at http://www.cdc.gov/hrmo/ksahowto.htm, accessed 10/15/10.

[2] Benjamin Schneider, "The People Make the Place," *Personnel Psychology*, 40, 3 (1987), 437–453.

[3] Robert J. Grossman, "The Five-Finger Bonus," *HR Magazine*, 48, 10 (October 2003), 38–44.

[4] Ben & Jerry's, "2009 Social Environmental Assessment Report," available at http://www benjerry.com/company/sear/2009/sear09_9.0.cfm,

accessed 10/10/10; Ben & Jerry's, "Mission," available at http://www.benjerry.com/activism/ mission-statement/, accessed 10/10/10.

[5] Bernard Grofman (Ed.), *Legacies of the 1964 Civil Rights Act* (Charlottesville, VA: University of Virginia Press, 2000).

[6] "Disparate Impact Analysis," available at www.hr-software.net/EmploymentStatistics/ DisparateImpact.htm, accessed 10/15/10.

[7] Equal Employment Opportunity Commission, *Uniform Guidelines on Employee Selection Procedures,* Section 4.D. (1978), available at http://

www.uniformguidelines.com/uniformguidelines
.html#129, accessed 10/15/10.

8 "Disparate Impact Analysis."

9 U.S. Department of Labor website available at
http://www.dol.gov/dol/topic/hiring/affirmativeact
.htm, accessed 10/15/10.

10 Terry H. Anderson, *The Pursuit of Fairness: A
History of Affirmative Action* (New York: Oxford
University Press, 2005).

11 National Leadership Network of Black Conservatives, Project 21 website available at http://www
.nationalcenter.org/AA.html, accessed 10/15/10.

12 U.S. Equal Employment Opportunity Commission,
"Americans with Disabilities Act Questions and Answers," available at http://www.ada.gov/q&aeng02
.htm, accessed 10/15/10.

13 The National Council on Alcoholism and Drug
Dependence, "Alcohol and Other Drugs in the
Workplace," available at www.ncadd.org/facts/
workplac.html, accessed 10/15/10; a heavy drinker
is defined as drinking five or more drinks per occasion on five or more days in the past 30 days.

14 The National Council on Alcoholism and Drug
Dependence, "Alcohol and Other Drugs in the
Workplace"; M. Bernstein and J. J. Mahoney,
"Management Perspectives on Alcoholism: The
Employer's Stake in Alcoholism Treatment,"
Occupational Medicine, 4, 2 (1989), 223–232.

15 The U.S. Equal Employment Opportunity Commission, "ADA Enforcement Guidance," available
at htt p://www.eeoc.gov/policy/docs/preemp.html,
p. 10, accessed 10/15/10.

16 Jeffrey Passel and D'Vera Cohn, "A Portrait of Unauthorized Immigrants to the United States," April
2009, available at http://pewhispanic.org/reports/
report.php?ReportID=107, accessed 10/15/10;
also "Demographics and Socio-Economic Status
of Unauthorized Immigrants in the United States,
2000–2006," available at http://immigration
.procon.org/viewresource.asp?resourceID=845#In
troduction, accessed 10/15/10.

17 Lisa Guerin and Amy DelPo, *Everyday Employment Law* (Berkeley, CA: Nolo, 2001).

18 Bradden C. Backer, Kim E. Patterson, and Robert
K. Scholl, *Hiring and Firing in Wisconsin* (Madison, WI: State Bar of Wisconsin CLE Books, 1996),
section 2.20.

19 Susan Bowles, "Background Checks: Beware and
Be Prepared," *USA Today,* April 10, 2002.

20 Robert Strauss, "When the Resume Is Not to Be
Believed," *New York Times*, September 12, 2006.

21 Elaine McShulskis, "Beware College Grads Willing to Lie for a Job," *HR Magazine*, 42, 8 (1996),
22–24.

22 Strauss, "When the Resume Is Not to Be Believed."

23 Joe Dresang, "Just the Facts," *Milwaukee Journal
Sentinel*, April 5, 2007.

24 Michael Kinsley, "MIT Dean Marilee Jones Flunks
Out," *Time*, May 7, 2007.

25 New York University, "Reference Check Form,"
available at http://www.nyu.edu/hr/pdf/hrforms/
erefchk.pdf, accessed 10/15/10; Alison Doyle, "Questions Employers Ask When Conducting a Reference
Check," available at http://jobsearch.about.com/
od/referencesrecommendations/a/refercheck.htm,
accessed 10/15/10.

26 Paul Falcone, *The Hiring and Firing Question
and Answer Book* (New York: Amacom, 2002),
p. 114.

27 Robert S. Adler and Ellen R. Peirce, "Encouraging
Employers to Abandon Their "No Comment" Policies Regarding Job References: A Reform Proposal," *Washington & Lee Law Review*, 53 (1996),
1381–1397.

28 Ibid.

29 Falcone, *The Hiring and Firing Question and
Answer Book*.

30 Kris Frieswick, "Background Checks," *CFO*, 21,
11 (August 2005), 63–65.

31 Shari Caudron, "Who Are You Really Hiring?"
Workforce, November 2002, 28–32.

32 Consumer-Guide.to, available at http://consumer-
guide.to/Background.Checks/, accessed 10/15/10.

33 U. S. Department of Education, "The Database of Accredited Postsecondary Institutions
and Programs," available at http://ope.ed.gov/
accreditation/Search.aspx, accessed 10/15/10;
Texas Higher Education Coordinating Board,
"Institutions Whose Degrees Are Illegal to Use in
Texas," available at http://www.thecb.state.tx.us/
apps/consumerinfo/notx.cfm, accessed 10/15/10.

34 Committee on Governmental Affairs United States
Senate. *Bogus Degrees and Unmet Expectations:
Are Taxpayer Dollars Subsidizing Diploma Mills?*
(Washington, DC: U.S. Government Printing
Office, 2004).

35 Adler and Peirce, "Encouraging Employers to
Abandon Their "No Comment" Policies Regarding Job References."

36 Mary Lynn Wagner, "Extras—Federal Court Records on the Web," December 1, 1999, available at http://www.llrx.com/extras/webpacers.htm, accessed 10/15/10.

37 Wisconsin Court System, "Access to the Public Records of the Consolidated Court Automation Programs (CCAP)," available at http://wcca.wicourts .gov/index.xsl, accessed 10/15/10.

38 U.S. Department of Justice, "National Sex Offender Public Website," available at http://www.nsopw .gov/Core/Conditions.aspx, accessed 10/15/10.

39 Family Watchdog website available at www.family watchdog.us, accessed 10/15/10.

40 Anonymous, "States Consider Banning Credit Checks on Job Applicants," Associated Press, March 1, 2010.

41 Association of Certified Fraud Examiners, 2008 Report to the Nation on Occupational Fraud & Abuse, available at www.acfe.com/documents/2008-rttn .pdf, accessed 10/15/10.

42 Allen Smith, "EEOC Urges Caution on Unnecessary Credit Checks," HR News March 29, 2007, available at http://www.shrm.org/Publications/HRNews/ Pages/CMS_020975.aspx, accessed 10/15/10.

43 Fair Credit Reporting Act available at http://www.ftc .gov/os/statutes/fcradoc.pdf, accessed 10/15/10.

44 Rita Zeidner, "How Deep Can You Probe?" HR Magazine, October 2007.

45 Facebook website available at www.facebook .com, accessed 10/15/10.

46 Justin Smith, "Number of US Facebook Users Over 35 Nearly Doubles in Last 60 Days," Inside Facebook, available at http://www.insidefacebook .com/2009/03/25/number-of-us-facebook-users-over-35-nearly-doubles-in-last-60-days/, accessed 10/15/10.

47 Facebook, "Statistics," available at http:// www.facebook.com/press/info.php?statistics, accessed 10/15/10.

48 Kevin R. Murphy, Honesty in the Workplace (Pacific Grove, CA: Brooks/Cole, 1993).

49 Office of Technology Assessment, The Use of Integrity Tests for Pre-Employment Screening (Washington, DC: U.S. Government Printing Office, 1990).

50 H. John Bernardin and Donna K. Cooke, "Validity of an Honesty Test in Predicting Theft Among Convenience Store Employees," Academy of Management Journal, 36, 5 (1993), 1097–1108; Christopher M. Berry, Paul R. Sackett, and Shelly

Wiemann, "A Review of Recent Developments in Integrity Test Research," Personnel Psychology, 60, 2 (2007), 271–301; Deniz S. Ones, Chockalingam Viswesvaran, and Frank L. Schmidt, "Comprehensive Meta-Analysis of Integrity Test Validities: Findings and Implications for Personnel Selection and Theories of Job Performance," Journal of Applied Psychology, 78, 4 (1993), 679–703.

51 James Krohe Jr., "Are Workplace Tests Worth Taking?" Across the Board, 43, 4 (July-August, 2006), 16–23.

52 John J. Donovan, Stephen A. Dwight, and Gregory M. Hurtz, "An Assessment of the Prevalence, Severity and Verifiability of Entry-Level Applicant Faking Using the Randomized Response Technique," Human Performance, 16, 1 (2003), 81–106.

53 Robert R. McCrae and Paul T. Costa Jr., "Validation of the Five-Factor Model across Instruments and Observers," Journal of Personality and Social Psychology, 52, 1 (1087), 80–92. Survey scales for these factors are available at http://ipip.ori.org/ newBigFive5broadKey.htm, accessed 10/15/10.

54 Berry, Sackett, and Wiemann, "A Review of Recent Developments in Integrity Test Research."

55 Michael Mount, Remus Ilies, and Erin Kraut Johnson, "Relationship of Personality Traits and Counterproductive Work Behaviors: The Mediating Effects of Job Satisfaction," Personnel Psychology, 59, 3 (2006): 591–622.

56 Stephen P. Robbins and Timothy A. Judge, Essentials of Organizational Behavior, 9th ed. (Upper Saddle River, NJ: Pearson Prentice Hall, 2008), p. 35.

57 Christopher M. Berry, Deniz S. Ones, and Paul R. Sackett, "Interpersonal Deviance, Organizational Deviance, and Their Common Correlates: A Review and Meta-Analysis," Journal of Applied Psychology, 92, 2 (2007), 410–424.

58 "The Items in the 45 Preliminary IPIP Scales Measuring the 45 AB5C Facets," available at http:// ipip.ori.org/newBroadbandAppAB5CKey.htm, accessed 10/15/10.

59 Gregory M. Hurtz and George M. Alliger, "Influence of Coaching on Integrity Test Performance and Unlikely Virtues Scale Scores," Human Performance, 15, 3 (2002), 255–273.

60 Philip M. Podsakoff, Scott B. MacKenzie, Julie Beth Paine, and Daniel G. Bachrach, "Organizational Citizenship Behaviors: A Critical Review of the Theoretical and Empirical Literature and Suggestions

for Future Research," *Journal of Management,* 26, 3 (2000), 513–563.

61 Daniel J. Koys, "The Effects of Employee Satisfaction, Organizational Citizenship Behavior, and Turnover on Organizational Effectiveness: A Unit-Level, Longitudinal Study, *Personnel Psychology,* 54, 1 (2001), 101–114; some item wordings have been slightly modified.

62 Philip M. Podsakoff, Michael Aheame, and Scott B. MacKenzie, "Organizational Citizenship Behavior and the Quantity and Quality of Work Group Performance," *Journal of Applied Psychology,* 82, 2 (1997), 262–270; some item wordings have been slightly modified.

63 Jim Sidanius and Felicia Pratto, *Social Dominance: An Intergroup Theory of Social Hierarchy and Oppression* (New York: Cambridge University Press, 2001).

64 Pamela Lutgen-Sandvik, Sarah J. Tracy, and Jess K. Alberts, "Burned by Bullying in the American Workplace: Prevalence, Perception, Degree and Impact," *Journal of Management Studies,* 44, 6 (2007), 837–862.

65 Ibid.

66 Paul A. Murphy, *The Cult of Personality* (New York: Free Press, 2004).

67 Cheryl L. Karp and Leonard Karp, "MMPI: Questions to Ask," available at http://www.falseallegations .com/mmpi-bw.htm, accessed 10/15/10.

68 Guerin and DelPo, *Everyday Employment Law.*

69 David W. Arnold and John W. Jones, "Who the Devil's Applying Now?" *Security Management,* 46 (March 2002), 85+.

70 Bella M. DePaulo, James J. Lindsay, Brian E. Malone, Laura Muhlenbruck, Kelly Charlton, and Harris Cooper, "Cues to Deception," *Psychological Bulletin,* 129, 1 (2003), 74–118.

71 Miron Zuckerman, Bella M. DePaulo, and Robert Rosenthal, "Verbal and Nonverbal Communication of Deception," in L. Berkowitz (Ed.), *Advances in Experimental Social Psychology* (New York: Academic Press, 1981), pp. 1–57.

72 Letizia Caso, Augusto Gnisci, Aldert Vrij, and Samantha Mann, "Processes Underlying Deception: An Empirical Analysis of Truth and Lies When Manipulating the Stakes," *Journal of*

Investigative Psychology and Offender Profiling, 2 (2005), 195–202.

73 Ramon J. Aldag and Lauren W. Kuzuhara, *Mastering Management Skills: A Manager's Toolkit—Modular edition* (Mason, OH: Thomson South-Western, 2005), pp. 12–7.

74 Ibid.

75 Substance Abuse and Mental Health Services Administration (SAMHSA), "Workplace Substance Use: Quick Facts to Inform Managers," available at http://workplace.samhsa.gov/Work places/pdf/WorkplaceDrugUseFactSheet.pdf, accessed 10/15/10.

76 Falcone, *The Hiring and Firing Question and Answer Book,* p. 124.

77 Committee to Review the Scientific Evidence on the Polygraph, *The Polygraph and Lie Detection* (Washington, DC: The National Academies Press, 2003).

78 Defense Security Services, *Fiscal Year (FY) 2003 Budget Estimates,* available at www.defenselink.mil/ comptroller/defbudget/fy2003/budget_justification/ pdfs/operation/fy03_DSS.pdf, accessed 10/15/10.

79 Ken Alder, *The Lie Detectors* (New York: Free Press, 2007).

80 Office of Technology Assessment, *Validity of Polygraph Testing: A Research Review and Evaluation* (Washington, DC: U.S. Congress, 1983), Chapter 3, available at http://fas.org/sgp/othergov/ polygraph/ota/, accessed 10/15/10.

81 Kerry Segrave, *Lie Detectors: A Social History* (Jefferson, NC: McFarland & Company, 2004), p. 31.

82 Office of Technology Assessment, *Validity of Polygraph Testing.*

83 Ibid.; Committee to Review the Scientific Evidence on the Polygraph, *The Polygraph and Lie Detection* (Washington, DC: The National Academies Press, 2003).

84 U.S. Department of Labor, "The Employee Polygraph Protection Act," available at http:// www.dol.gov/compliance/laws/comp-eppa.htm, accessed 10/15/10.

85 Steve Silberman, "Don't Even Think About Lying," *Wired,* January 2006, 14, 1, available at http://www.wired.com/wired/archive/14.01/lying .html, accessed 10/15/10.

CHAPTER OUTLINE

4

CODES OF ETHICS AND CODES OF CONDUCT

What would you do?

Code Violation

After graduation, you obtain a supervisory position at a bank. Mary, one of your 12 tellers, is your best employee. She has worked at the bank for 10 years and is trusted and admired by both coworkers and customers. Her annual performance reviews are excellent. She shows up on time and works hard. Mary is conscientious and a good team player, and she has a wonderful personality.

Every day, each teller is required to accurately count his or her cash drawer, report any cash variances, and sign a balance sheet. The Cash Balancing Department is responsible for checking the tellers' work to make sure they balance their cash correctly and report any irregularities. Another department reviews the tellers' work (deposit slips, checks, payment tickets, etc.) for transaction processing errors. Together, these two departments verify whether any variance is a cash shortage or a transaction processing error, which is more often the case. Slight cash variances occasionally happen. Not reporting a cash variance and falsifying a balance sheet are grounds for immediate termination.

Under your management, Mary receives the "Teller of the Year" award for two consecutive years. So you are shocked one morning when the Cash Balancing Department informs you that Mary's balanced cash drawer was short $100 and she apparently falsified a $100 transaction to make the drawer appear balanced.

You meet with Mary as soon as she arrives at work and audit the cash drawer in her presence prior to any transactions. The drawer is $100 short.

"I have no idea how the mistake happened," Mary nervously says. "I've been up all night trying to figure out how the error occurred. This has never happened to me before. I can only guess that I must have given a customer $100 too much cash, but I can't believe a customer wouldn't return the money, particularly since it could cost me my job. I was hoping the customer would come back today and return the money. If that didn't happen, I was going to put $100 of my own money in the drawer at the end of the day. See, I have the money right here." Mary shows you five $20 bills. "I know this violates our Code of Ethics about always being honest, and our Code of Conduct about reporting shortages. But I just freaked out and didn't report the shortage right away."

Mary's record has been spotless up to this point. Your gut feeling is that she wasn't trying to steal money. Mary simply, and unwisely, responded to the $100 shortage by falsifying the balance sheets. She is now a nervous wreck and you're sure she would never do this again. You can allow Mary to put $100 in the drawer and declare everything legitimate.

According to bank policy, however, you must begin the termination process by informing the bank manager. Despite Mary's previous stellar performance, you know the bank manager will abide by current bank policy and not make any exception to the rule. You would lose your best teller and ruin Mary's career in the banking industry.

What would you do? Would you

1) Tell the bank manager and pursue termination?
2) Let Mary replace the missing $100 with her own money and put Mary on notice that the next time this happens she will be terminated?

Why?

Chapter Objectives

After reading this chapter, you will be able to:

- Understand the difference between a Code of Ethics and a Code of Conduct
- Explain the importance of code awareness and expectations
- Describe the content found in most Codes of Ethics and Codes of Conduct
- Create and implement an effective Code of Ethics communication strategy
- Conduct an annual employee assessment of the Code of Ethics

The perfect job candidate has been hired—the person is experienced, energetic, and intelligent and has high integrity. People of high integrity, however, do not necessarily share the same ethical viewpoints. Each person develops a unique ethical viewpoint, a perspective shaped by parents, siblings, friends, teachers, religious leaders, political leaders, other moral role models, and culture.

Ethical dilemmas arise because situations are ambiguous. What bothers one person's conscience may not bother another person's conscience. A rule one high-integrity person considers essential another high-integrity person might consider too rigid. Two managers of high integrity, for instance, may disagree on the appropriate discipline for a subordinate's misbehavior, such as an excellent bank teller who violated a bank's policy.

An organization's Code of Ethics and Code of Conduct minimize ethical ambiguities by communicating clear ethical guidelines for employees to apply when making decisions. These codes serve as the organization's conscience. This chapter explains the differences between a Code of Ethics and a Code of Conduct, summarizes the purpose and content of codes, and describes how to use a Code of Ethics as an assessment tool for improving ethical performance.

Difference between a Code of Ethics and a Code of Conduct

The terms "Code of Ethics" and "Code of Conduct" are often mistakenly used interchangeably. They are two unique documents. A Code of Ethics briefly describes broad ethical aspirations. A Code of Conduct more extensively describes acceptable behaviors for specific situations that are likely to arise.

A Code of Ethics, sometimes referred to as a Values Statement, is similar to the Ten Commandments, a few general principles to guide behavior that could fit on a business card. The general principles embodied in a Code of Ethics—such as respecting all owners, customers, employees, suppliers, community members, and the natural environment—represent aspirations. These principles describe the kind of people we want to be—someone who treats others as he or she wants to be treated. When faced with an ethical dilemma or ambiguous situation, principles articulated in the Code of Ethics can help guide the decision maker.

A Code of Conduct, often developed by an employee with legal expertise, provides substance to the Code of Ethics and is usually several pages long. A Code of Conduct applies the Code of Ethics to a host of relevant situations. Whereas one principle in the Code of Ethics might state that all employees will obey the law, a Code of Conduct might list several specific laws relevant to different areas of organizational operations that employees will obey.

The Code of Ethics of the National Association of Social Workers (NASW), for example, lists six ethical principles to guide behavior: service, social justice, dignity and worth of the person, importance of human relationships, integrity, and competence.[1] The more detailed NASW Code of Conduct provides specific examples, such as stating that social workers will obtain informed consent from clients regarding the purpose of services provided, relevant costs, and treatment alternatives. The NASW Code of Conduct also addresses situations involving conflicts of interest, confidentiality, records access, sexual relationships, sexual harassment, derogatory language, and termination of services.

Purpose and Importance of Codes

A Code of Ethics is usually the first step in formalizing an ethics program. The extent of an organization's ethics program is often related to its size.[2] In small organizations, the ethics code is embodied within the owner, who serves as a very observable role model. A formal ethics code is unnecessary because employees typically interact with one another on a regular basis. Begin drafting a Code of Ethics when the number of employees reaches about 10, a point when employees may not interact with one another or the owner as much. Ethical hazards and risks increase as organizations grow in complexity. Assign responsibility for managing organizational ethics to a specific individual at the 50-employee level and begin developing some ethics training sessions. Exhibit 4.1 provides guidelines for expanding ethics programming based on employee growth.

Exhibit 4.1 Ethics Program Growth and Organizational Size	
Number of Employees	Type of Ethics Program
1–9 Employees	Orient employees to relevant laws and regulation; share stories about ethical decisions
10–49 Employees	Develop and review a Code of Ethics and Code of Conduct
50–199 Employees	Appoint an ethics officer, create an ethics steering committee, and develop formal annual ethics training sessions
200–999 Employees	Develop ethics monitoring and reporting systems
1,000–4,999	Implement an ethics assist line and whistle-blowing procedures
More than 5,000	Create an Ethics Office

In the 1960s, only 15 percent of surveyed companies had a Code of Ethics. Now, nearly all Fortune 1000 companies have a Code of Ethics, as do many other organizations.[3] A 2008 survey of the International Association of Administrative Professionals reported that 85 percent of respondent organizations had an official written ethics policy, although only 56 percent believed all employees knew the policy existed.[4]

Why should an organization develop a Code of Ethics and a Code of Conduct? These codes fulfill multiple purposes including the following:

- Demonstrate managerial concern for ethics
- Convey a particular set of values and obligations
- Meet legal requirements and industry trends
- Positively impact employee behaviors

Demonstrate Managerial Concern for Ethics

First impressions matter a great deal. Discuss the organization's Codes of Ethics and Conduct with new employees to establish ethical expectations. Begin the meeting by demonstrating awareness of job-related ethical issues and public perceptions about business ethics. An array of job-related ethical issues appears in Chapters 1 and 2 and can be found on industry websites. The Gallup Poll regularly conducts surveys on public perceptions of honesty and ethical standards for a wide range of professions and industries. The results for 2009 appear in Exhibit 4.2.[5]

Exhibit 4.2 Honesty and Ethical Standards of Professions			
	Very High or High	Average	Low or Very Low
Nurses	83%	14%	2%
Druggists or Pharmacists	66%	29%	5%
Police Officers	63%	26%	10%
College Teachers	54%	33%	11%
Clergy	50%	36%	10%
Journalists	23%	45%	31%
Bankers	19%	46%	33%
Lawyers	13%	45%	40%
Advertising Practitioners	11%	46%	38%
Insurance Salespeople	10%	47%	42%
Stockbrokers	9%	40%	46%
Members of Congress	9%	35%	55%
Car Salespeople	6%	40%	51%

New employees play a pivotal role in helping an organization achieve the highest standards for honesty and ethical behaviors. By discussing the organization's Code of Ethics and Conduct, managers demonstrate concern that ethical issues will be appropriately addressed, establish an expectation that new employees will behave ethically, and highlight the importance of discussing ethical issues when they arise with supervisory personnel.

Convey a Particular Set of Values and Obligations

Codes convey a set of values and obligations that clarify appropriate behaviors and provide employees with clear and consistent moral guidance. For instance, assume five potential suppliers are competing for a $75,000 contract. One potential supplier offers the organization's key decision maker two all-expenses-paid vouchers for a Hawaiian vacation. Should the employee accept the gracious offer?

Factors that might influence an employee's decision include whether such behavior is typical within the employee's culture or industry, the employee's current economic situation, and the supplier's likelihood of being chosen. An employee might be unaware that accepting the offer creates an appearance that the contract decision is being influenced by a factor not associated with performance quality, service, or price. A clearly articulated Code of Ethics highlighting the importance of respecting all suppliers, and a Code of Conduct stating that an employee should not accept gifts from potential suppliers, eliminates any doubt as to the appropriate response to this situation.

Codes of Ethics articulate and reinforce a moral consensus, rather than just one person's opinion, and legitimize dialogue about ethical issues when challenging situations arise. Codes are typically welcomed and embraced by employees with strong moral identities and convictions. The organization becomes a place where an employee's moral identity and job identity can exist in harmony. There are not two sets of ethics, one set of ethical principles to be applied outside work and a different set at work. Instead, morality is integrated throughout the daily work experience. Codes also signal that employees will be held personally accountable for their ethical choices, and they provide an additional safeguard against pressures from managers, peers, or external constituents to behave unethically.

Employees need a reliable source of information to guide them when ethical issues arise. From a practical perspective, a manager might not be available when an ethical issue arises among subordinates. The previously mentioned Hawaiian vacation offer from a supplier to the organization's buyer is likely to happen away from the office. In addition, a peer responding immediately that a sexist comment violated the Code of Ethics sends a much stronger message than delaying a response until the issue reaches managerial awareness.

Meet Legal Requirements and Industry Trends

Codes are sometimes required by law. In 2002, Congress quickly passed the Sarbanes-Oxley Act following high-profile corporate accounting scandals involving Enron, WorldCom, Arthur Andersen, and other businesses. The legislation required all publicly traded companies to disclose whether they had a Code of Ethics for senior financial officers. The New York Stock Exchange (NYSE) and the National Association of Securities Dealers Automated Quotations (NASDAQ) went one step further. To gain renewed investor confidence in the stock market, NYSE and NASDAQ required that all listed firms must have a Code of Ethics for directors, officers, and employees.[6] Banks, health care firms, and organizations doing business with municipal, state, and federal governments are also required to have an ethics code.

As discussed in Chapter 2, the 1991 Federal Sentencing Guidelines provide financial benefits to organizations that have Codes of Ethics. Organizations are held accountable for employees breaking the law. Judges can reduce fines if an organization has implemented a Code of Ethics.

Many industry associations and professional organizations develop codes as a self-regulating strategy that deflects government regulation. Professional codes buffer their members from organizational, managerial, and work unit pressures to behave unethically. Lawyers, accountants, teachers, and social workers who violate their professional code can lose their license. This provides an additional safeguard for professionals not to accept an unethical directive from a company executive.

Many professional codes are available on the Internet. The Society for Human Resource Management Code of Ethics addresses six core areas, such as professional responsibility and development.[7] The National Association of Legal Professionals lists four general principles followed by 10 canons.[8] The Chartered Property Casualty Underwriters (CPCU) society provides a list of specific unethical practices that would result in disciplinary action.[9] The Pew Research Center's Project for Excellence in Journalism offers a collection of ethics guidelines developed by news organizations.[10] Similarly, the Online Ethics Center for Engineering and Research provides ethics codes for a host of engineering associations.[11]

Positive Impact on Employee Behaviors

Lastly, organizations implement Codes of Ethics and review them on an annual basis because of the many positive impacts they have on employee behaviors. Researchers report that organizations with Codes of Ethics have higher levels of employee commitment and greater tolerance for diversity.[12] Employees are proud to be associated with ethical organizations and desire to work for honest and trustworthy managers. The relationship is reciprocal. Whereas trustworthy managers attract trustworthy employees, trustworthy employees are recruited by trustworthy managers. Within an organization culture of trust, employees are more likely to trust managerial decisions, and managers are more likely to trust employee decisions.[13] This cycle of trust contributes to higher levels of employee morale and job satisfaction.[14]

Code of Ethics Content

A Code of Ethics expresses the principles that define an organization's ideal moral essence. Keep the language simple and avoid legalese or professional jargon. The best codes are easy to understand and inspirational; they unite employees regardless of their particular religion, ethnicity, gender, or geographical location.

The tone of an ethics code is very important. Providing employees with a list of prohibitions—things they *should not* do—can feel oppressive rather than inspirational. Make the Code of Ethics an affirmative statement of how employees *should* act, not how they should not act. Declaring that employees will not lie is restrictive language, whereas declaring that employees will always tell the truth appeals to people's more positive essence. The difference can have a profound effect on organizational culture. It's similar to the difference between a coach telling an athlete not to play badly versus a coach telling an athlete she is playing well and can do even better.

What values are stated in ethics codes? An extensive scholarly review of corporate Codes of Ethics, global Codes of Ethics, and the business ethics literature found the following six values continually expressed:[15]

1. *Trustworthiness*
2. *Respect*
3. *Responsibility*
4. *Fairness*
5. *Caring*
6. *Citizenship*

Many other values can be added to this list. For instance, in addition to honesty and respect, Microsoft's values statement includes the following:[16]

- Passion for customers, partners, and technology
- Willingness to take on big challenges and see them through

- Self-critical, questioning, and committed to personal excellence and self-improvments
- Accountable for commitments, results, and quality to customers, shareholders, partners, and employees

Exhibit 4.3 provides an example of a Fortune 100 corporate Code of Ethics that highlights four guiding principles using short and concise statements.[17]

Exhibit 4.3 Fortune 100 Code of Ethics

OUR VALUES

Communication

We have an obligation to communicate. Here, we take the time to talk with one another . . . and to listen. We believe that information is meant to move and that information moves people.

Respect

We treat others as we would like to be treated ourselves. We do not tolerate abusive or disrespectful treatment. Ruthlessness, callousness and arrogance don't belong here.

Integrity

We work with customers and prospects openly, honestly, and sincerely. When we say we will do something, we will do it; when we say we cannot or will not do something, then we won't do it.

Excellence

We are satisfied with nothing less than the very best in everything we do. We will continue to raise the bar for everyone. The great fun here will be for all of us to discover just how good we can really be.

International Codes

We live in a highly integrated global society. Should a multinational business apply one set of ethics in the United States and another in Italy, Russia, El Salvador, or Egypt, nations whose cultures and laws vary significantly from those of the United States?

In the 1970s, the integrity of capitalism was called into question when a U.S. Senate investigation found that more than 400 companies based in the United States secured business by bribing foreign government officials. Lockheed, a leading aerospace corporation, was among the most prominent.[18] For more than 20 years, Lockheed corporate executives approved the payment of bribes to guarantee military aircraft contracts, including $22 million for just one international deal. In 1977, Congress responded to these anticompetitive practices by passing the Foreign Corrupt Practices Act (FCPA), making it illegal for U.S. businesses to directly pay bribes in other nations or through intermediaries, such as joint venture partners or agents.[19] In addition, under the FCPA, foreign corporations whose securities are listed in the United States must maintain accounting ledgers that reflect these transactions.

The FCPA differentiates bribery from facilitating payments. A bribe is typically defined as providing someone with a monetary incentive or object of value to do something contrary to his or her job description. Facilitating payments, which are legal, expedite performance of "routine governmental action," such as obtaining permits, processing governmental papers, loading and unloading cargo, and scheduling inspections to transit goods across borders. Facilitating payments do not include being awarded new business or continuing business with a particular government official.

Some businesses headquartered in the United States argued that the FCPA puts them at a competitive disadvantage because businesses headquartered in other nations continue to pay bribes as a cost of doing business. As a result, the U.S. government pressured other nations to adopt similar anti-bribery legislation. In 1999, the Organization for Economic Co-operation and Development (OECD), representing 30 developed nations, ratified the Anti-Bribery Convention, which requires member nations to enact legislation criminalizing the payment of bribes in developing nations. These guidelines were modified in 2009 to ensure that member nations adopted the best practices for making companies liable for foreign bribes.[20] A growing number of non-OECD members have signed this agreement, including Brazil, Estonia, Israel, and South Africa.

Some business executives maintain that it is inappropriate and arrogant for the United States to impose its moral values on other nations. "When in Rome, do as the Romans" is their preferred guideline. This philosophy fosters adopting the lower ethical business standards found in many undeveloped nations, which solidifies corruption and political oppression in the host nation.

But that is not how U.S. law operates. American businesses are obligated to obey both U.S. laws and host nation laws, with the higher ethical standard taking precedence. If those in "Rome" pay bribes to obtain business or regulatory approval, American managers conducting business as those in Rome do will likely end up in a U.S. jail.

Attempts have been made to create a level moral playing field worldwide through an International Code of Ethics, in which principles such as integrity and honesty are adopted by all organizations conducting business, independent of locale. The Caux Round Table, an international network of business leaders from a variety of nations and cultures, spearheaded a collaborative effort to develop the Caux Principles for Responsible Business for conducting business worldwide. The result of their collaborative efforts appears in Exhibit 4.4.[21]

Exhibit 4.4 Caux Principles for Responsible Business	
Principle 1: Respect Stakeholders Beyond Shareholders	• A responsible business acknowledges its duty to contribute value to society through the wealth and employment it creates and the products and services it provides to consumers. • A responsible business maintains its economic health and viability not just for shareholders, but also for other stakeholders. • A responsible business respects the interests of, and acts with honesty and fairness towards, its customers, employees, suppliers, competitors, and the broader community.

(Continued)

Exhibit 4.4 Caux Principles for Responsible Business (*Continued*)

Principle 2: Contribute to Economic, Social, and Environmental Development	• A responsible business recognizes that business cannot sustainably prosper in societies that are failing or lacking in economic development. • A responsible business therefore contributes to the economic, social and environmental development of the communities in which it operates, in order to sustain its essential 'operating' capital—financial, social, environmental, and all forms of goodwill. • A responsible business enhances society through effective and prudent use of resources, free and fair competition, and innovation in technology and business practices.
Principle 3: Respect the Letter and the Spirit of the Law	• A responsible business recognizes that some business behaviors, although legal, can nevertheless have adverse consequences for stakeholders. • A responsible business therefore adheres to the spirit and intent behind the law, as well as the letter of the law, which requires conduct that goes beyond minimum legal obligations. • A responsible business always operates with candor, truthfulness, and transparency, and keeps its promises.
Principle 4: Respect Rules and Conventions	• A responsible business respects the local cultures and traditions in the communities in which it operates, consistent with fundamental principles of fairness and equality. • A responsible business, everywhere it operates, respects all applicable national and international laws, regulations and conventions, while trading fairly and competitively.
Principle 5: Support Responsible Globalization	• A responsible business, as a participant in the global marketplace, supports open and fair multilateral trade. • A responsible business supports reform of domestic rules and regulations where they unreasonably hinder global commerce.
Principle 6: Respect the Environment	• A responsible business protects and, where possible, improves the environment, and avoids wasteful use of resources. • A responsible business ensures that its operations comply with best environmental management practices consistent with meeting the needs of today without compromising the needs of future generations.
Principle 7: Avoid Illicit Activities	• A responsible business does not participate in, or condone, corrupt practices, bribery, money laundering, or other illicit activities. • A responsible business does not participate in or facilitate transactions linked to or supporting terrorist activities, drug trafficking or any other illicit activity. • A responsible business actively supports the reduction and prevention of all such illegal and illicit activities.

The Caux Principles advocate for socially responsible free market capitalism. The seven principles are grounded in two ethical ideals: human dignity (the sacredness of each person) and living and working together for the common good (mutual prosperity and fair competition). In supplemental material, the Caux Round Table provides specific standards for interactions with customers, employees, owners/investors, suppliers, communities, and competitors. Businesses are encouraged to be positive forces for justice in all nations that respect the interests of all stakeholders.

Creating a Code of Ethics

Many small businesses do not have a Code of Ethics. That is to their detriment based on all the preceding reasons. An ethics code serves as a constant reminder, particularly when the owner is not present, and sends a positive message to customers and suppliers, as well as employees.

It is relatively easy to copy another organization's Code of Ethics. After all, how many different ways can one say treat all stakeholders with utmost respect and integrity? But this would be a missed opportunity to enhance employee ownership of the Code of Ethics. Instead, have employees construct the code.

The Ethics Resource Center offers a "Code of Ethics Toolkit" that guides organizations and industry associations in developing a Code of Ethics.[22] The toolkit includes an ethics glossary, definition of values, recommended format, common provisions, and writing tips. The Society for Human Resource Managers modified the toolkit for its membership chapters, and it is available on the Internet.[23] The toolkit is particularly helpful in creating a Code of Ethics for specific business and work units that is aligned with the organization-wide ethics code.

Following are 13 steps for creating a Code of Ethics as a team-building exercise:

Step 1 – *Obtain approval.* Introduce the idea of writing a code to the executive team and board of directors. Organizational leaders maintain the right to accept, reject, or modify the code developed by employees.

Step 2 – *Create a code-writing team.* If the work unit is less than 20 employees, include all employees in this process. If more than 20 employees, it may be necessary to select a group of well-respected employees to represent everyone in the work unit.

Step 3 – *Gather list of ethical issues from relevant stakeholders.* Obtain general information on the types of ethical issues relevant to the work unit. Hold separate interviews or focus group sessions with key constituents, such as customers, suppliers, and owners, about their interactions with the work unit. Some stakeholders, particularly suppliers who do not want to lose business, may be hesitant to share their concerns. Gather additional information about ethical issues from the industry association or through an Internet search.

Step 4 – *Define a "Code of Ethics."* Differentiate the nature and purpose of a Code of Ethics (one or two sentences that express broad ethical aspirations for guiding employee behavior) from that of a mission statement (organization's purpose), vision statement (organization's future aspiration), and Code of Conduct (acceptable behaviors for specific situations).

Step 5 – *Gather a list of ethical behaviors from participants.* Have each participant independently write answers to the following four prompts:

1. Describe a situation when *you observed someone* in the organization behave very ethically toward a *customer.*
2. Describe a situation when *you behaved* very ethically toward a *customer.*
3. Describe a situation when *you observed someone* in the organization behave very ethically toward an *employee.*
4. Describe a situation when *you behaved* very ethically toward an *employee.*

Having employees independently respond generates more examples and engages more people. Writing down examples focuses participants on one memorable situation. The four prompts focus on admirable behaviors employees observed or did. This way the organization honors and reinforces already existing ethical behaviors.

Step 6 – *Determine common themes.* Form small teams of three or four employees to determine the essential elements of ethical behaviors related to customers and employees by doing the following two activities:

1. In a round robin format, each group member shares a story about the observed ethical behavior toward a *customer.* Next, each group member shares a story about how she or he has behaved ethically toward a customer. Determine the common themes embedded in these stories about the ethical treatment of customers (e.g., "The common themes in these stories are x and y.").
2. Continuing with the round robin format, each group member shares a story about the observed ethical behavior toward an *employee.* Next, each group member shares a story about how he or she has behaved ethically toward another employee. Determine the common themes embedded in these stories about the ethical treatment of employees (e.g., "The common themes in these stories are x and y.").

Step 7 – *Draft a Code of Ethics.* Create a code that emphasizes the common themes discussed during the previous step. The code may be one or two sentences, or several key words, each of which is described so others will understand what the word means. Keep the language clear and simple.

Step 8 – *Compare to other codes and modify.* Distribute codes from other organizations, including competitors and industry associations. Do this after, not before, each group drafts a code. The goal is to adopt a code employees created. If these codes are distributed first, a group might be tempted to just copy a preexisting code. Modify the previous draft as desired.

Step 9 – *Compare to other groups.* Each group presents its ethics code to the other groups. Groups compare their finished products and reach consensus on one particular code. Modify as desired.

Step 10 – *Code alignment.* Compare the agreed upon ethics code to that of the larger organization or to the relevant industry or association. Modify as desired.

Step 11 – *Code review.* Present the code to legal counsel, executives, and the board of directors for their approval. Modify as desired.

Step 12 – *Code communication strategy.* Create a strategy for communicating the code to all employees and key constituents.

Step 13 – *Code revision.* Annually assess code awareness, discuss code relevance with employee groups, and revise as needed.

Let's Build a Building

Competing Bids from General Contractors

Your organization is in a growth mode and, as a promising mid-level manager, you are assigned a special project overseeing the construction of a new building. After hiring an architect, and approving the building's design, it is time to obtain bids from general contractors to build the building. You employ a consultant to help you manage the building process. She and the architect agree that the new building will cost about $6 million to construct.

The architect, who is paid 8 percent of the total cost of the building, recommends that you obtain bids from three local high-quality general contractors he has worked with on previous jobs, one of whom worked on your organization's last building expansion. The consultant, who is paid a percentage of the final cost savings below the $6 million estimate, reviewed the work of your last building project and pointed out that the local contractor had substantially overcharged you for labor and equipment. As a result, the consultant recommends that you obtain bids from three additional high-quality general contractors who work primarily in other parts of the state.

You send out the complete building blueprints and specifications to these six general contractors. The three lowest bids—$5.6 million, $5.9 million, and $6.0 million—are from the outside general contractors recommended by the consultant. Their bids are accompanied by glowing reference letters from previous customers and assurances that they will use local suppliers whenever possible. The three local general contractors recommended by the architect submitted bids for $6.4 million, $6.7 million, and $6.9 million.

You narrow the choice between the $5.6 million low bid from the outside contractor and the $6.4 million bid from the local contractor who had worked on your last building expansion. The $6.4 million bidder is a member of your country club and rotary. At a social event, you ask the local contractor if he can match the outside contractor's $5.6 million low bid. The local contractor and architect tell you that there is no way the building can be built to your quality expectations for $5.6 million. You point out that the bids were based on complete blueprints and specifications, and all of their budget items had been double-checked as being reasonable. The local contractor responds that he is not looking forward to telling other Rotarian and country club members that you chose a general contractor from outside the region, which could cost you future local business.

What would you do? Would you

1. Accept the $5.6 million low bid from the outside general contractor who was recommended by the consultant?
2. Accept the $6.4 million bid from the local general contractor who was recommended by the architect and with whom your company has worked in the past?

Why?

Connecting Code of Ethics to Strategic Planning

The Code of Ethics can be a key aspect of an organization's strategic plan. Strategic planning integrates an organization's mission with its vision and provides clear direction on how the organization will progress from its current situation to a highly desired future situation. Connecting the code to an organization's mission and vision, rather than keeping it separate, establishes credibility and visibility for the Code of Ethics.

Mission statements, vision statements, and Codes of Ethics serve unique purposes. Combined, these documents define the organization to internal and external constituents.

An organization's mission statement describes what an organization does and for whom.[24] For instance: "Studio67 is a medium-sized restaurant focusing on organic foods and an intriguing atmosphere, in a prime neighborhood of Portland."[25]

A vision statement describes what an organization aspires to become in the future. General Motors' vision statement reads: "GM's vision is to be the world leader in transportation products and related services. We will earn our customers' enthusiasm through continuous improvement driven by the integrity, teamwork, and innovation of GM people."[26]

The word "integrity" in the General Motors' vision statement provides a link to elaborate and advertise the company's ethics code. The shared values embodied in a Code of Ethics provide relationship consistency between the organization and its stakeholders in the present and future. General Motors' mission and vision may fluctuate, but the way the company treats stakeholders will be consistent.

Strategic plans are communication devices. Ideally, an organization's mission statement, vision statement, and Code of Ethics communicate a "cause" that employees and other stakeholders can rally around, and potential customers want to be a part of. Jim Armstrong, who creates socially responsible messages for a wide range of organizations, provides a 10-step process for developing a cause-based communication strategy.[27] The "Questions to Address" in Exhibit 4.5 pushes those crafting the strategic message to delve into the core truth behind the organization's products or services to frame its communication strategy.

Exhibit 4.5 Crafting a Cause-Based Strategic Message

Step	Aspect	Questions to Address
1.	Your True Cause	"Why" does your organization do "what" it does?
2.	Why Tell Your Truth	What will communicating your cause accomplish for your organization?
3.	Tell "Me" the Truth	Who are your audiences?
4.	What's Stopping You from Telling the Truth	What are the emotional, psychological, political, and economic obstacles in your way?
5.	What's Truly in It for Them	What is the key benefit you can provide to your key audience?
6.	True to One's Word	What single word captures your benefit and primary idea?
7.	A Matter of Facts	Why should people believe you? What facts and evidence validate your claim?

8.	Cause for Action	What do you want your audience to do upon hearing your story?
9.	Your True Voice	What is the character and personality of your cause?
10.	True to Form	What types of communication mechanisms do you need to tell your story?

William George, the former chairman and CEO of Medtronic, outlines the chain of events connecting an organization's mission and values to increased profits and shareholder value (see Exhibit 4.6).[28] An organization's cause-based mission and vision, supported by its Code of Ethics, attract talented and ethical employees. These highly motivated employees provide product innovations and superior customer service. The ensuing increased customer satisfaction drives revenue, profits, and shareholder value.

Exhibit 4.6 The Power of a Mission-Driven Organization

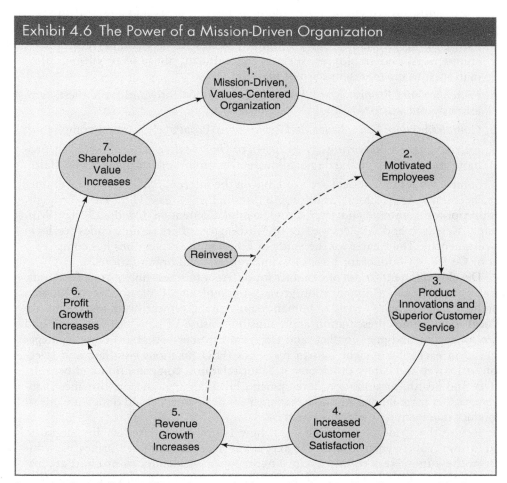

Source: Adapted from William George, *Authentic Leadership* (San Francisco, CA: Jossey-Bass, 2003), p. 65.

Code of Conduct Content

A Code of Conduct expands on the moral principles embodied in a Code of Ethics. A Code of Ethics principle such as "We will treat everyone fairly," for example, can be clarified in a Code of Conduct as "All information about an employee is considered confidential and is to be released only to authorized personnel."

Creating a Code of Conduct requires input from top-level executives, corporate lawyers, and human resource personnel. A Code of Conduct addresses the wide range of legal expectations and ethical risks unique to an organization or job title. The New York Stock Exchange recommends that a Code of Conduct address the following seven topics:[29]

1. *Conflicts of Interest:* Avoid conflict or potential conflict between an individual's personal interests and those of the organization.

2. *Corporate Opportunities:* Do not use corporate information or assets for personal gain.

3. *Confidentiality:* Do not disclose nonpublic information that could benefit competitors or harm the organization.

4. *Fair Dealing:* Abstain from any unfair treatment of customers, suppliers, competitors, and employees, such as concealment, abuse of privileged information, and misrepresentation of material facts.

5. *Protection and Proper Use of Assets:* Use assets efficiently and avoid theft, carelessness, and waste.

6. *Compliance with Laws, Rules, and Regulations:* Proactively promote compliance.

7. *Encouraging the Reporting of Any Illegal or Unethical Behavior:* Proactively promote ethical behavior and do not allow retaliation for reports made in good faith.

Sample Codes of Conduct are available on the Internet.[30] The Code of Conduct for Facebook users is a long list of prohibitions in three areas: Third Party Content, Inappropriate Content, and Useful or Harmful Content or Conduct.[31] The Municipal Research and Services Center of Washington offers sample codes for local governments.[32] The Center for the Study of Ethics in the Professions has compiled a list of Codes of Conduct for businesses and professional organizations.[33]

Develop different Codes of Conduct for different business units, work functions, or stakeholders as an organization grows in complexity. Professor Kevin Wooten conducted an extensive review of human resource management issues and found five ethical issues—misrepresentation and collusion, misuse of data, manipulation and coercion, value and goal conflict, and technical ineptness—that are uniquely experienced in each of the eight human resources (HR) functions—staffing and selection, employee and career development, labor relations, compensation and benefits, safety and health, organization development, HR planning, and performance management.[34] A large human resource management department could design a Code of Conduct statement that addresses each issue.

Revise the Code of Conduct when new issues arise. After an investigation found that Volkswagen and BMW executives accepted supplier bribes for contracts, the automakers revised their anticorruption guidelines to prohibit accepting gifts beyond a minimal financial threshold and required supervisor approval to accept invitations to sports and cultural events.[36]

Tips and Techniques

A Code of Conduct for Suppliers

Some organizations create codes of conduct for external stakeholders. Starbucks' suppliers must sign a Code of Conduct pledging that the supplier:[35]

- Demonstrates commitment to the welfare, economic improvement, and sustainability of the people and places that produce Starbucks' products and services
- Adheres to local laws and international standards regarding human rights, workplace safety, and worker compensation and treatment
- Meets or exceeds national laws and international standards for environmental protection
- Commits to measuring, monitoring, reporting, and verifying compliance
- Pursues continuous improvement of these social and environmental principles

Codes of Conduct are based on shifting moral expectations and legal obligations. New technologies create new ethical dilemmas requiring new ethical guidelines. Facebook is a social networking Internet system on which users invite "friends" into their web of cyberspace relationships. Is it ethical for a judge and a lawyer to be "friends" on Facebook? A Judicial Ethics Advisory Committee in Florida determined the answer to be "no."[37] Such a relationship creates a conflict of interest whereby clients could reasonably conclude that certain lawyers may receive favorable treatment from a judge. As highlighted in Exhibit 4.7, the same Facebook friend conflict of interest problem may exist between teachers and students.

Exhibit 4.7 Facebook Friendships between Students and Teachers

A Judicial Ethics Advisory Committee in Florida ruled that judges and lawyers linked as "friends" on Facebook creates an appearance of impropriety. Is it ethical for a student and a college professor to be friends on Facebook while the student is enrolled in the professor's (a) class or (b) school? Why?

Code of Conduct Relevancy

Use Codes of Conduct to highlight specific issues of major importance. Two problem areas many organizations have in common are the giving and receiving of gratuities[38] and email use.[39] The former pertains primarily to relationships with external stakeholders and the latter with internal stakeholders.

Business Gratuities

A business gratuity is a

> present, gift, hospitality, or favor for which fair market value is not paid by the recipient, . . . including such items as gifts, meals, drinks, entertainment (including tickets and passes), recreation (including golf course and tennis court fees), door prizes, honoraria, transportation, discounts, [or] promotional items.[40]

A fine line exists between a business gratuity/courtesy and a bribe. Did the buyer purchase the product because of its quality or had the buyer changed his or her mind after receiving an expensive gift?

Gratuities can be problematic when received from suppliers or given to customers. Instructing buyers not to accept gratuities from suppliers, and then encouraging salespeople to offer gratuities to customers, sends mixed messages that damage managerial credibility and create moral confusion. Organizations need consistent policies to avoid the negative impacts of employees claiming hypocrisy.

The general guideline for when a gratuity evolves into a bribe is when the object of value unduly influences buying decisions. But general guidelines are insufficient. Assume that a salesperson finds out that a potential customer is an avid golfer and wants to provide a gratuity to solidify the sales relationship. Which of the following intended gratuities might be considered a bribe: a $15 book about golf putting, a dozen golf balls costing $50, golf clothing valued at $150, a round of golf for two people at an exclusive golf club for $280, or two tickets and traveling expenses for the upcoming Masters golf tournament valued at $2,500?

Even if not a bribe, a business gratuity can cause problems for an organization if it creates an appearance of impropriety or could embarrass the organization if the transaction became public knowledge.

Create a Code of Conduct on business gratuities that describes clear examples of when salespeople can offer gratuities to potential and existing customers and purchasers can accept gratuities from suppliers.[41] The "Best Practice in Use" exhibit provides key portions of the Gap's Code of Conduct policy for gratuities.[42] The Gap's policy extends to family members; states specific monetary amounts; and clarifies exceptions to the rule, such as business meals and noncash holiday gifts.

An employee might accept a gratuity that is later determined to violate the Code of Conduct. In this situation, first attempt to return the gratuity. If that is too awkward, then donate the gratuity to charity.

Email

Electronic mail (email) is one of the most prominent forms of communication within and outside organizations. Many organizations have policies for email use. A 2009 survey reported that approximately half of all organizations monitor email use.[43] A 2007 survey conducted by the American Management Association found that 28 percent of the organizations had terminated an employee for inappropriate email use.

Typically, email use during work hours is limited to company business only. Organizations are concerned that employees will use email for non-work-related purposes, thus creating a drain on workplace productivity, and confidential information might be sent to unintended recipients.

BEST PRACTICE IN USE

Gap Inc. Code of Conduct: Gratuities

It's important to avoid even the appearance of making business decisions based on inappropriate or unethical influences. To prevent this situation, we discourage you and your family members from giving, soliciting or receiving gifts and entertainment from anyone doing business with (or wishing to do business with) Gap Inc.

Gift examples include cash or cash equivalents (gift cards), samples, discounts, event tickets, personal favors, recreation and transportation. Entertainment could include tickets to sporting events, concerts, golf and other events you attend or participate in with the outside individual.

The following types of gifts and entertainment are absolutely prohibited:

- Gifts exceeding $50 USD (or equivalent)
- Entertainment exceeding $100 USD (or equivalent)
- Any solicited gift
- Gifts exchanged in the form of cash or cash equivalents (gift cards)
- Entertainment that would violate other provisions of the Code

A few exceptions when it comes to gifts:

Business meals: As long as they are infrequent and not extravagant, business meals are not considered gifts or entertainment, and may be accepted. However, it is critical that any business meal not create a sense of obligation or result in favored treatment with a vendor or business partner.

Non-cash holiday gifts: As long as you share them with your department, you are allowed to accept holiday gift items such as gift baskets, cookies, chocolates, flowers, or other such non-cash gifts, even if they exceed the $50 USD (or equivalent) gift limit.

Third-party trainings: Some conferences or training by third parties may also be accepted with prior approval from the Global Integrity and Compliance Department.

Chinese communities: During Chinese New Year, you may accept a cash gift in the form of "Lai See," but only for a nominal amount valued up to HK$100 (or equivalent).

Some employees mistakenly assume that they have a "reasonable expectation of privacy" to the content of their workplace email communications.[44] Judges continually rule in favor of employers who own and maintain the computer and network systems. A humorous sexual or racist comment contained in an email communication between two colleagues at work can be grounds for dismissal.

Managers are responsible for protecting organizational assets, resources, and investments. Clearly note in the Code of Conduct that the employer's right to monitor email communications on company-owned computers and network systems supersedes employee privacy rights. The Association of Consulting Engineers Australia (ACEA) recommends a Code of Conduct policy for email use that prohibits recreational use of email during work hours, allows personal use during nonwork hours, and establishes disciplinary procedures for violations. Eight key provisions of the model ACEA Code of Conduct policy appear in Exhibit 4.8.[5]

Exhibit 4.8 Code of Conduct for Internet and Email Use

1. Only use the Internet and email for legitimate business purposes related to your job. However, permission from your manager may be sought to use the Internet in non-work time for study, research or other reasonable purposes. 'Legitimate business purposes' does not include social club, trade union or employment relations matters unless the specific permission of [insert relevant managerial position(s)] has been obtained.

2. Do not use the Internet or email to send defamatory, threatening or obscene messages to other employees or to anyone outside the company.

3. Do not use the Internet or email to send racially and or sexually harassing messages or other illegal communications to other employees or to anyone outside the company.

4. Do not download, retrieve or send sexually explicit, racist or otherwise discriminatory or illegal material from the Internet or from email at any time while you are on work premises, or while using company computers outside of work premises. This behavior is considered serious misconduct and will result in the instant dismissal of the employee(s) involved unless the employee is able to reasonably explain the occurrence as accidental or unintended.

5. Do not, without express authority, access (hack) any computer, whether owned by the company or by any other organization. This behavior is illegal, leaving employees liable to criminal prosecution as well as disciplinary action by the company.

6. Do not use another employee's computer or access to gain unauthorized access to the Internet or on-line services.

7. When you send mail on the Internet, do not include confidential information.

8. Do not connect to personal (i.e. employee subscribed accounts) Internet or on-line services during working hours using personal or company equipment.

Implementing an Effective Code Communication Strategy

The benefits of having a meaningful Code of Ethics are innumerable. Yet, researchers report that many companies do not effectively communicate their Codes of Ethics and Conduct to employees.[46] Codes cannot be effective if employees are unaware they exist or if rumors spread that the code was created merely to appease legal or regulatory authorities.[47]

The Code of Ethics in Exhibit 4.3 highlights how words are meaningless unless they correspond with actions. The code was developed by Enron, a decade prior to the company's financial collapse.[48] Enron also had a 60-page Code of Conduct, a list of prohibitions ignored by some traders and high level executives.

Ethical hypocrisy, the gap between an organization's formal ethical proclamations and its actual behavior, damages employee morale. Moral confusion arises when the Code of Ethics declares employees must be honest while a supervisor expects an employee to lie to a customer about a missed delivery deadline. Researchers report that people working for a supervisor who encouraged employees to lie about delivery information to clients, in violation of the organization's ethics code, had less job and organizational satisfaction, less organizational commitment, greater role conflict, and greater intention to quit.[49]

As highlighted earlier in Step 12 for Creating a Code of Ethics, develop a strategy for communicating the Codes of Ethics and Conduct to all employees and key constituents. Assign the responsibility to a particular person who can champion the cause. Elements of the communication strategy include the following:

- Connect the code to the organization's strategy
- Mention the Code of Ethics in job announcements
- Introduce the codes during employee orientation
- Annually distribute the Code of Ethics with a letter signed by a high-level executive emphasizing the importance of applying the code on a daily basis
- Display the Code of Ethics in newsletters, highly traveled areas, and on stationary and websites
- Discuss the codes during ethics training workshops
- Mention the Code of Ethics in correspondences with suppliers and customers
- Evaluate employees on code adherence in performance appraisals
- Link code adherence to promotions and merit raises
- Annually assess how well the organization embodies the code

Social pressure can be a major obstacle to code effectiveness. Employees are hesitant to report code violations committed by their friends, peers, or manager. Unethical employees accuse peers who enforce the code of being "tattletales" to discourage them from reporting violations. Employees are more likely to report a code violation if others in the organization disapprove of the violation, they do not fear retribution for reporting, or the person committing the violation has been given a previous warning.[50]

Codes are particularly essential during periods of market and organizational turbulence. Turbulence creates uncertainty and employees can shift into a survival of the fittest mindset. Saving one's job and organization rises to the top of the agenda and a "do whatever it takes" mentality can be invoked to justify behaviors that, under normal circumstances, would not be pursued. Managers who have a relativistic ethical orientation may behave in ways that, after the turmoil subsides, could cause the organization harm if reported in the media.[51]

Annual Code of Ethics Assessment

The last phase of implementation is probably the most important—use the code as an organizational assessment tool. Make the Code of Ethics a living document by annually assessing how well the organization and its employees live up to it. Then use the employee feedback as the basis for continuous improvement changes in organizational policies and practices.

Exhibit 4.9 provides a 10-step process for assessing an organization's ethical performance based on its Code of Ethics. The employee activity can be accomplished within 60 to 90 minutes.

Exhibit 4.9 Code of Ethics Employee Assessment

Step 1: Form small groups around common job tasks and have participants read the organization's Code of Ethics. If none exists, inform participants that organizational members are expected to treat owners, company property, employees, customers, suppliers, the government, and the natural environment with utmost respect and integrity.

Step 2: Each group member independently evaluates how well the organization meets each of its ethical aspirations using a five-point Likert scale.

Step 3: Each group member independently highlights one weak area and writes down strategies and action steps that can be taken to improve that score.

Step 4: Group members share their survey scores with one another and determine similarities and differences.

Step 5: Each group member shares a story about the survey item with the highest score. What happened during the past year that exemplifies why the organization is doing so well in that category?

Step 6: Each group member shares a story about a survey item with a low score.

Step 7: Each group member shares a strategy and action steps that would improve the low score and integrates ideas and suggestions from other group members to develop a more detailed continuous improvement plan.

Step 8: The group summarizes its scores and suggestions for improvement and submits the information to the facilitator for the purpose of continuous improvement follow-up.

Step 9: The facilitator forwards the information to the responsible manager.

Step 10: Management or the facilitator updates employees about progress made regarding the suggested improvements.

It is relatively easy to transform a Code of Ethics into a five-point Likert scale survey for employee assessment purposes. Exhibit 4.10 is a Code of Ethics that describes National Specialty Insurance's five core values.[52]

Exhibit 4.10 Code of Ethics

CORE VALUES

Operate with integrity and respect

Integrity means acting in an ethical and honest manner. Respect requires showing patience and acknowledging differences with civility. We expect you to act respectfully and with integrity in all business situations, whether inside or outside the office.

Provide, promote, and celebrate Legendary Service

You are responsible for providing products and services that meet or exceed the expectations of our business partners.

Use superior communications

All of your communications must be professional, courteous, and prompt.

Embrace continuous improvement

Change being constant and necessary, you must embrace opportunities to become more efficient and productive.

Actively engage in self-management

Assume responsibility for self-management at work by assessing your own performance daily, advance your professional growth, and improve your confidence in your ability to provide Legendary Service.

Exhibit 4.11 transforms the Code of Ethics into a Likert scale survey instrument that examines whether managers and nonmanagement employees embody each core value. The survey differentiates the evaluation of managers from nonmanagement employees because of their different responsibilities and activities. The six assessment prompts gather specific praiseworthy and blameworthy examples and suggestions for improvement.

Exhibit 4.11 Code of Ethics Survey

LIVING UP TO THE VALUES STATEMENT

Instructions: Please use the 1 to 5 scale below to assess how well each of the following statements exemplifies managers and nonmanagement employees. The more honest you are the more helpful the information we will receive. First assess the behavior of managers, and then the nonmanagement employees.

1=Strongly Disagree; 2=Disagree; 3=Neither Agree nor Disagree; 4=Agree; 5=Strongly Agree

	SD	D	N	A	SA
Managers					
Operate with integrity and respect	1	2	3	4	5
Provide and promote Legendary Service (meet and exceed customer expectations)	1	2	3	4	5
Use superior communications (are professional, courteous, and prompt)	1	2	3	4	5
Embrace continuous improvement (become more productive and efficient)	1	2	3	4	5

(Continued)

Exhibit 4.11 Code of Ethics Survey (Continued)					
Actively engage in self-management (assess their performance daily)	1	2	3	4	5
Managers Subtotal—Add the five scores and divide by five:					
Nonmanagement Employees					
Operate with integrity and respect	1	2	3	4	5
Provide and promote Legendary Service (meet and exceed customer expectations)	1	2	3	4	5
Use superior communications (are professional, courteous, and prompt)	1	2	3	4	5
Embrace continuous improvement (become more productive and efficient)	1	2	3	4	5
Actively engage in self-management (assess their performance daily)	1	2	3	4	5
Nonmanagement Employees Subtotal—Add the five scores and divide by five:					

Assessment of Managers
1. Provide an example of how *managers* live up to the company's Values Statement.
2. Provide an example of how *managers* fall short of living up to the company's Values Statement.
3. How can the company improve the shortcoming noted in #2?

Assessment of Nonmanagement Employees
4. Provide an example of how *nonmanagement employees* live up to the company's Values Statement.
5. Provide an example of how *nonmanagement employees* fall short of living up to the company's Values Statement.
6. How can the company improve the shortcoming noted in #5?

SUMMARY

Employees arrive at the organization possessing a wide variety of ethical perspectives. They need a common ethical reference point. Aligning personal values with those expressed in an ethics code creates a unique bonding experience that crosses hierarchal levels and minimizes organizational politics.

This chapter described the importance of a Code of Ethics consisting of several general moral principles and a more detailed Code of Conduct applied to specific situations. These codes serve as the organization's conscience. They demonstrate managerial concern about ethics and positively impact employee behaviors.

Make these codes meaningful and effective by using them as assessment tools. Have employees annually evaluate how well organizational members live up to these codes. In the spirit of continuous improvement, gather employee suggestions for addressing weak areas and then make appropriate changes in organizational policies and practices to improve ethical performance.

KEY WORDS

Code of Ethics; Code of Conduct; bribe; facilitating payments; Caux Principles for Responsible Business; strategic planning; mission statement; vision statement; business gratuity; ethical hypocrisy.

CHAPTER QUESTIONS

1. What is the difference between a Code of Ethics and a Code of Conduct?
2. Why are Codes of Ethics and Conduct important? What purposes do they fulfill?
3. What values are contained in most Codes of Ethics?
4. How would you create a Code of Ethics for an organization?
5. What topics should be addressed in a Code of Conduct?
6. How would you implement an effective Code of Ethics and Code of Conduct communication strategy?

In the Real World: Enron

The SPE Revenue Solution—1993

Ken Lay chose to appeal the SEC's decision to reject the Gas Bank Division's use of mark-to-market accounting techniques. The appeal was successful. Beginning in 1993, this new accounting technique contributed to a cash flow problem for the Gas Bank because reported revenue was mostly projected, not actual. In addition, Wall Street analysts increased Enron's revenue expectations based on the previous year's reported revenue, which created a need for bigger revenue deals.

Jeff Skilling hired Andy Fastow, a finance expert, to help Enron manage this revenue problem. One of Fastow's revenue ideas was to bundle the Gas Bank's loans and sell them at a discounted price to third parties. This had two benefits: it reduced Enron's debt and increased reported revenue.

Fastow targeted special purpose entities (SPEs) as potential purchasers of the Gas Bank's bundled loans. In the energy industry, SPEs are created to reduce risk associated with natural gas exploration. SPEs have two very important accounting regulations: first, at least 3 percent of an SPE's funding must come from an external partner; second, the SPE must be managed by an independent management team.

Fastow planned to finance these SPEs primarily with Enron stock and, when needed, meet Enron's financial targets by selling Gas Bank loans to the SPE. Enron's stock would become more attractive to investors because revenue targets were met and the company's debt-to-equity ratio improved. An increase in Enron's stock price would directly increase the SPE's economic value because the SPE owned substantial amounts of Enron stock. Fastow would promise to repurchase the loans from the SPE at a guaranteed profit if the SPE could not resell the loans to other parties. All Fastow needed were some compliant outside SPE investors and managers.

(Continued)

Many investment banks profited from funding Enron's Gas Bank activities and planned on funding Enron's future acquisitions. Fastow ranked investment banks according to Tier 1, Tier 2, and Tier 3 status, with Tier 1 being the banks that received the largest fees from doing business with the Gas Bank. Fastow told Tier 1 investment bankers that they had to invest in and manage his SPEs or they would no longer be considered when the Gas Bank needed more capital.

DECISION CHOICE. If you were a Tier 1 investment banker earning large fees by doing business with Enron's Gas Bank, and Andy Fastow asked you to invest in an SPE that would purchase bundled Gas Banks loans at a guaranteed profit, would you

1. Accept the offer?
2. Reject the offer and lose future fees from Enron?
3. Notify Arthur Andersen auditors about these secret side agreements?

Why?

ANCILLARY MATERIALS

Websites to Explore

- Codes of Ethics
  - Corporate Code of Ethics examples, available at http://www.ethicsweb.ca/resources/business/codes.html and http://web-miner.com/busethics.htm (scroll down to "Corporate Codes of Ethics" for examples).
  - Society for Human Resource Management, available at http://www.shrm.org/about/Pages/code-of-ethics.aspx.
  - Journalism, available at http://www.journalism.org/resources/ethics_codes.
  - Engineers, available at http://www.onlineethics.org/Resources/ethcodes/21733.aspx.
  - City and county government, available at http://www.mrsc.org/Subjects/Personnel/ethics.aspx.
- Code of Conduct
  - Microsoft, available at http://www.microsoft.com/About/Legal/EN/US/Compliance/Buscond/Default.aspx.
  - Gap, Inc. available at http://www.gapinc.com/public/documents/Code_English.pdf.
- Caux Round Table "Principles for Business," available at http://www.cauxroundtable.org/index.cfm?&menuid=8.
- Ethics Resource Center, "Ethics Toolkit," available at http://www.ethics.org/page/ethics-toolkit.
- Vision and Mission Statement Examples, available at http://www.samples-help.org.uk/mission-statements/corporate-vision-statements.htm.

Best Place to Work Video

- Best Place to Work—Build-A-Bear Workshop, available at http://money.cnn.com/video/fortune/2010/01/20/f_bctwf_build_a_bear.fortune/.

Business Ethics Issue Video

- "The Card Game," *Frontline*, about trying to reform the credit card industry, November 24, 2009, 57 minutes, available at http://www.pbs.org/wgbh/pages/frontline/creditcards/view/?utm_campaign=viewpage&utm_medium=grid&utm_source=grid.

TEDTalks Videos

- *Predictable Irrationality:* Behavioral economist Dan Ariely explains studies examining the hidden reasons we think it's sometimes OK to cheat or steal, and why we're predictably irrational; February 2009, 17 minutes, available at http://www.ted.com/talks/dan_ariely_on_our_buggy_moral_code.html.
- *Purpose of Life:* Pastor Rick Warren, author of *The Purpose-Driven Life,* reflects on his own crisis of purpose and his belief that God's intention is for each of us to use our talents and influence to do good; February 2006, 21 minutes, available at http://www.ted.com/talks/rick_warren_on_a_life_of_purpose.html.

Conversations with Charlie Rose

- A conversation with Jon Huntsman, U.S. Ambassador to China, about China; December 17, 2010, 30 minutes, available at http://www.charlierose.com/view/interview/11357.

- A conversation about the ramifications of the BP Oil spill; May 14, 2010, 30 minutes, available at http://www.charlierose.com/view/interview/11014.

NOTES

[1] "Code of Ethics" of the National Association of Social Workers available at www.socialworkers.org/pubs/code/code.asp, accessed 10/15/10.

[2] Steven R. Barth, *Corporate Ethics: The Business Code of Conduct for Ethical Employees* (Boston, MA: Aspatore Books, 2003).

[3] Deborah L. Rhode (Ed.), *Moral Leadership* (San Francisco, CA: Jossey-Bass, 2006).

[4] "Office Ethics," available at http://www.office-ethics.com/columns/survey08.html, accessed 10/15/10.

[5] Lydia Saad, "Honesty and Ethics Poll Finds Congress' Image Tarnished," *Gallup*, December 9, 2009, available at http://www.gallup.com/poll/124625/Honesty-Ethics-Poll-Finds-Congress-Image-Tarnished.aspx, accessed 2/10/10.

[6] Randy Myers, "Ensuring Ethical Effectiveness," *Journal of Accountancy*, 195, 2 (2003), 28–33.

[7] SHRM Code of Ethics, available at http://www.shrm.org/about/Pages/code-of-ethics.aspx, accessed 10/15/10.

[8] NALS Code of Ethics & Professional Responsibility, available at http://www.nals.org/aboutnals/Code/Index.html, accessed 10/15/10.

[9] CPCU Society Ethics Code, available at http://www.cpcusociety.org/page/65790/, accessed 10/15/10.

[10] "Ethics Codes," Journalism.org, available at http://www.journalism.org/resources/ethics_codes, accessed 10/15/10.

[11] "Codes of Ethics," Online Ethics Center for Engineering and Research, available at http://www.onlineethics.org/Resources/ethcodes/21733.aspx, accessed 10/15/10.

[12] Dayton Fandray, "The Ethical Company," *Workforce*, 79, 12 (December 2000), 74–78; Sean Valentine and Tim Barnett, "Ethics Code Awareness, Perceived Ethical Values, and Organizational Commitment," *Journal of Personal Selling & Sales Management*, 23, 4 (2003), 359–367; Sean Valentine and Gary Fleischman, "Ethics Codes and Professionals' Tolerance of Societal Diversity," *Journal of Business Ethics*, 40, 4 (2002), 301–313.

[13] Jay Prakash Mulki, Fernando Jaramillo, and William B. Locander, "Effects of Ethical Climate and Supervisory Trust on Salesperson's Job Attitudes and Intentions to Quit," *Journal of Personal Selling & Sales Management*, 26, 1 (2006), 19–26.

[14] Randi L. Sims, "The Relationship Between Employee Attitudes and Conflicting Expectations for Lying Behavior," *The Journal of Psychology*, 134, 6 (2000), 619–633.

[15] Mark S. Schwartz, "Universal Moral Values for Corporate Codes of Ethics," *Journal of Business Ethics*, 59, 1 (2005), 27–44.

[16] Microsoft Standards of Business Conduct, available at http://www.microsoft.com/About/Legal/EN/US/Compliance/Buscond/Default.aspx, accessed 10/15/10.

[17] *Enron Annual Report 1998* (Houston, TX: Enron, 1998), p. 71, available at http://picker.uchicago.edu/Enron/EnronAnnualReport1998.pdf, accessed 10/15/10.

[18] Walter J. Boyne, *Beyond the Horizons: The Lockheed Story* (New York: St. Martin's Press, 1998).

[19] United Stated Department of Justice, "Foreign Corrupt Practices Act," available at http://www.justice.gov/criminal/fraud/fcpa/, accessed 10/15/10.

[20] OECD, "About the New Recommendation for Further Combating Bribery of Foreign Public Officials in International Business," available at http://www.oecd.org/dataoecd/34/15/44281002.pdf, accessed 10/15/10.

[21] Caux Round Table, "Principles for Business," available at http://www.cauxroundtable.org/index.cfm?&menuid=8, accessed 10/15/10.

[22] Ethics Resource Center, "Ethics Toolkit," available at http://www.ethics.org/page/ethics-toolkit, accessed 10/15/10.

[23] Ethics Resource Center, "A Guide to Developing Your SHRM Chapter's Code of Ethics," available at http://www.shrm.org/about/Documents/chapter-coe.pdf, accessed 10/15/10.

[24] Patricia Jones and Larry Kahaner, *Say It and Live It: The 50 Corporate Mission Statements that Hit the Mark* (New York: Currency Doubleday, 1995).

[25] Tim Berry, "Writing a Mission Statement," available at http://articles.bplans.com/writing-a-business-plan/writing-a-mission-statement, accessed 10/15/10.

[26] "Examples and Sample Vision Statements," available at http://www.samples-help.org.uk/mission-statements/sample-vision-statements.htm, accessed 10/15/10.

[27] Jim Armstrong, *Beyond the Mission Statement* (Ithaca, NY: Paramount Market Publishing, 2006).

[28] William George, *Authentic Leadership* (San Francisco, CA: Jossey-Bass, 2003), p. 65.

[29] Curtis C. Verschoor, "The Ethical Climate Barometer," *Internal Auditor,* 61, 5 (2004), 48–53.

[30] "Code of Business Conduct—Sample," available at http://www.knowledgeleader.com/Knowledge Leader/content.nsf/Web+Content/Checklists GuidesCodeofBusinessConduct! OpenDocument, accessed 10/15/10.

[31] Facebook, "Content Code of Conduct," available at http://www.facebook.com/codeofconduct.php, accessed 10/15/10.

[32] Municipal Research and Services Center of Washington, "Sample Codes of Ethics," available at http://www.mrsc.org/Subjects/Personnel/ethics.aspx, accessed 10/15/10.

[33] Center for the Study of Ethics in the Professions, "Codes of Ethics Print and Electronic Archive," available at http://ethics.iit.edu/index1.php/library/Print%20Collections/Code%20of%20Ethics%20Print%20Archive, accessed 10/15/10.

[34] Kevin C. Wooten, "Ethical Dilemmas in Human Resource Management: An Application of a Multidimensional Framework, a Unifying Taxonomy, and Applicable Codes," *Human Resource Management Review*, 11, 1 (2001), 159–176.

[35] Sandra Waddock, *Leading Corporate Citizens: Vision, Values, Value Added* (New York: McGraw-Hill Irwin, 2006), p. 22.

[36] Tony Lewin, Jason Stein, and Jens Meiers, "VW, BMW Change Ethics Codes in Wake of Scandal," *Automotive News Europe*, 11, 17 (August 21, 2006), 4.

[37] John Schwartz, "For Judges on Facebook, Friendship Has Limits," *New York Times,* December 11, 2009.

[38] Gregory B. Turner, G. Stephen Taylor, and Mark F. Hartley, "Ethics, Gratuities and Professionalization of the Purchasing Function," *Journal of Business Ethics*, 14, 9 (1995), 751–760.

[39] Thomas J. Hodson, Fred Englander, and Valerie Englander, "Ethical, Legal and Economic Aspects of Employer Monitoring of Employee Electronic Mail," *Journal of Business Ethics*, 19, 1 (1999), 99–108.

[40] Steven R. Barth, *Corporate Ethics: The Business Code of Conduct for Ethical Employees* (Boston, MA: Aspatore Books, 2003), p. 35.

[41] Ibid.

[42] Gap, Inc., "Our Code of Business Conduct," available at http://www.gapinc.com/public/documents/Code_English.pdf, accessed 10/15/10.

[43] William P. Smith and Filiz Tabak, "Monitoring Employee E-mails: Is There Any Room for Privacy?" *Academy of Management Perspectives*, November, 23, 4 (2009), 33-48.

[44] Ibid.

[45] Consult Australia, available at http://www.consultaustralia.com.au/ and www.emailbackup.com.au/EIUP.doc, accessed 10/15/10.

[46] Denis Collins, "The Quest to Improve the Human Condition: The First 1,500 Articles in the *Journal of Business Ethics*," *Journal of Business Ethics*, 26, 1 (2000), 1–73.

[47] Valentine and Barnett, "Ethics Code Awareness, Perceived Ethical Values, and Organizational Commitment."

[48] *Enron Annual Report 1998.*

[49] Randi L. Sims, "The Relationship Between Employee Attitudes and Conflicting Expectations for Lying Behavior," *The Journal of Psychology*, 134, 6 (2000), 619–633.

[50] Mark S. Schwartz, "Effective Corporate Codes of Ethics: Perceptions of Code Users," *Journal of Business Ethics*, 55, 4 (2004): 323–343.

[51] Lawrence B. Chonko, Thomas R. Wotruba, and Terry W. Loe, "Ethics Code Familiarity and Usefulness: Views of Idealist and Relativist Managers Under Varying Conditions of Turbulence," *Journal of Business Ethics*, 42, 3 (2003), 237–252.

[52] National Specialty Insurance (NSI), a division of West Bend Mutual Insurance Company, "Core Value Statement," available at www.national-specialty.com/Common/ASPDocuments/default.asp, accessed 10/15/10.

CHAPTER OUTLINE

5

ETHICAL DECISION MAKING

What would you do?

The Leadership Seminar

Upon graduation, you obtain a research position for a local brewing company. Nine employees work in the office, including the company president Deborah, and Emily, who has the co-titles of human resource manager and office manager.

One year later, Emily enrolls herself and four other employees, including you, in an all-day leadership seminar to be held on a Monday, about three hours from work. You are the newest employee attending, the other participants include Emily's close friend Cherri, a seven-year employee, and two others who have been employed for two years. Emily's plan is for everyone to meet at the office Sunday afternoon, drive together in her SUV, eat dinner at a fancy restaurant, and have the remainder of the evening as free time.

At dinner Sunday night, Emily orders three bottles of wine for the five employees. On the way back to the hotel, Emily stops at a grocery store to pick up some snacks. Emily and Cherri purchase an array of hard liquor. Emily then invites everyone to a party in her hotel room.

The next morning everyone was scheduled to meet in the hotel lobby at 7:30 and then leave for the leadership seminar. You arrive at 7:20 and wait. At 7:40, Cherri is the next one to arrive and she says, "We decided to go home instead of attend the seminar because Emily is very sick. I think she has the flu. The new plan is to meet in the lobby at 8:30 to leave."

Emily arrives at 9:00 and immediately apologizes for being sick. "And," Emily adds, "don't tell any of the other employees in our office that we missed the seminar. This trip is costing the company about $5,000 for registrations and travel expenses. If anyone asks, just tell them it was very interesting. Are we all agreed on this? Don't forget that I'm your boss!" You know from past experience that loyalty to Emily is essential if you are going to be successful in the company. Everyone nods in agreement.

After leaving the hotel, Emily treats everyone to a late breakfast and jokes about her nagging hangover. Then she pulls into a mall parking lot near the seminar so everyone can shop for several hours. "We can't get back to town until early evening," Emily notes, "otherwise people will get suspicious."

The very next morning Deborah, the president, calls you into her office to discuss a new project she wants you to work on. As soon as you enter her office, Deborah asks, "So how was the leadership seminar yesterday?"

What would you do? Would you

1) Tell Deborah it was "very interesting" as instructed by Emily, which contributes to hiding the $5,000 misallocation of funds and lost workday?

2) Tell Deborah you never attended the leadership seminar, which could get Emily and the other employees in trouble and angry at you?
Why?

Chapter Objectives

After reading this chapter, you will be able to:

- Describe individual characteristics that impact ethical beliefs, sensitivities, intentions, and behaviors
- Analyze the processes by which general ethical beliefs and sensitivities lead to the formation of specific ethical intentions

- Apply a systematic rational ethical decision-making framework to arrive at a moral conclusion
- Facilitate a negotiation between competing ethical perspectives
- Recognize warning signs that an unethical decision is approaching

Codes of Ethics and Conduct are very useful tools for encouraging ethical behavior at work. Codes of Ethics provide general guidelines for responding to ethical dilemmas, and Codes of Conduct provide specific instructions for addressing common ethical issues. But Codes of Conduct cannot address every issue and in many circumstances employees respond instantaneously to ethical issues when they arise. Reliance on ethical intuitions can generate beneficial results, but sometimes they can be problematic.

This chapter explores a variety of factors that influence whether a person decides to behave ethically or unethically, beginning with how ethical intentions are formed quickly, initially defended, and then may be revised through a rational ethical decision-making process.

The first part of this chapter helps managers understand factors that shape ethical intuitions, intentions, and behaviors. The second part summarizes two common ethical decision-making frameworks and then offers a systemic seven-question rational ethical decision-making framework grounded in moral philosophy. The framework enables employees to independently derive a moral answer to ethical dilemmas. A process for persuading people who approach a decision from a different ethical perspective and warning signs that an unethical situation is arising are also provided.

Ethical Behavior Model

Ethical dilemmas tend to be complicated and involve trade-offs based on competing values and interests. Sometimes the trade-offs are between doing what in the ideal sense is the right thing to do, yet in the specific situation there is a strong temptation to do what is wrong. Employees know that they should not cheat on their expense accounts, but some do anyway.

But sometimes the trade-offs are between competing conceptions about what is the right thing to do. It is right to keep a promise, and it is right to tell the truth. Should a subordinate maintain a promised loyalty to the boss by covering up for a missed seminar or truthfully tell the company president that the boss did not attend the seminar?

As noted by business ethicist Marvin Brown, "Most people do what they think is right, considering the world they think they live in."[1]

When a person says "I know this is wrong but I'm going to do it anyway," the person is quickly translating the apparent wrong behavior as the right thing to do in the moment. An employee who cheats on expense accounts, for example, tends to initially justify the obvious wrong behavior as the right thing to do—the falsified receipts may make up for previous unclaimed expenses due to lost receipts or provide what the person assumes to be deserved supplemental income for being overworked or underpaid.

Managers need to understand the complexity of decision-making influences and processes that an individual goes through when deciding whether to engage in an ethical or unethical behavior. The terms "ethical" and "moral" are commonly interchangeable and will be throughout this chapter and textbook.

James Rest, an educational psychologist, has developed a four-component model sequentially showing that an individual is likely to behave morally if he or she (1) is aware that an ethical dilemma has arisen, (2) forms a moral judgment, (3) develops motivation to do something about it, and (4) is a person of high moral character.[2]

All four factors are essential. The first phase in the process requires an individual understanding that a particular situation poses an ethical dilemma. Identification of the problem usually entails empathy for someone who may be harmed by the decision. But even if the individual is aware that a situation poses an ethical dilemma, no moral action will be taken if the next three phases fail to occur—the person must form a moral judgment, be motivated to do something about it, and possess the moral courage to actually take the appropriate action.

In general, *ethical beliefs* generate *ethical intentions* and result in *ethical behaviors*. But there is typically a drop off going from one step to the next. Many people may agree on what ethical action "should" be done, but fewer people "would" actually do the right thing, and even fewer actually "did" what they think they should or would do.

Consider your own reaction to observing a coworker or customer stealing. As shown in Exhibit 5.1, many people believe that stealing is wrong. But then obstacles arise that prevent employees from taking action to stop this unethical behavior.

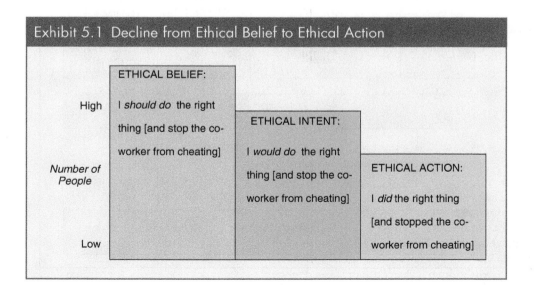

Exhibit 5.1 Decline from Ethical Belief to Ethical Action

Number of People (High to Low)

ETHICAL BELIEF:
I *should do* the right thing [and stop the coworker from cheating]

ETHICAL INTENT:
I *would do* the right thing [and stop the coworker from cheating]

ETHICAL ACTION:
I *did* the right thing [and stopped the coworker from cheating]

Researchers James Weber and Janet Gillespie tested this model by surveying the moral beliefs, intentions, and behaviors regarding cheating at work or in the classroom of 370 managers enrolled in an MBA program.[3] Approximately 84 percent of the respondents replied that people who cheat should be reported [Belief]. Next, a big gap exists between "should" and "would." Only 64 percent of the respondents stated that they personally would report a cheater [Intention]. The gap between ethical belief and ethical intent in Exhibit 5.1 can be caused by not wanting to create a negative relationship with the coworker or fear of becoming known as a "squealer."

Lastly, another big gap exists between "would" and "did." Only 40 percent of the managers surveyed who actually observed someone cheating at work or in school reported the unethical behavior [Action]. Why did a large percentage of managers who claimed they would report the cheater not follow up on the ethical intention? Maybe the manager decided to wait for someone else to take action, or the manager planned to report the incident to the person in authority but the appropriate situation for doing so never arose, or the manager decided that the costs associated with reporting the wrongdoing exceeded the benefit of doing so.

The complex and intricate paths linking individual characteristics to ethical beliefs, intentions, and behaviors are diagrammed in Exhibit 5.2 and discussed in the following sections.

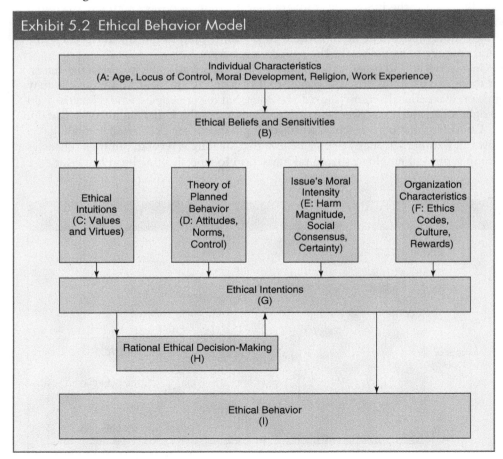

Exhibit 5.2 Ethical Behavior Model

Individual Characteristics (A)

Why are some individuals sensitive to ethical issues or concerned about how their actions impact the welfare of others, while others seem oblivious to ethical issues going on around them or how their actions impact others?

Researchers have examined a wide range of factors that may be associated with ethical beliefs, ethical sensitivities, ethical intentions, and ethical behaviors. Michael O'Fallon and Kenneth Butterfield reviewed 174 ethical decision-making research studies published between 1996 and 2003 and compared their findings with two previous studies that examined decision-making studies published between 1961 and 1997.[4] Exhibit 5.3 reports O'Fallon and Butterfield's primary findings regarding individual factors such as age, education level, gender, and work experience. The authors use the term "ethical decision making" to capture ethical beliefs, sensitivities, intentions, and behaviors.

According to the information in Exhibit 5.3, the individual factors that have the largest impact on ethical decision making are (1) more education; (2) more work experience;(3) religion; (4) reasoning at a higher level of moral development;

Exhibit 5.3 Individual Characteristics	
Variable	Results
Age	Mixed and inconsistent results: some studies report that those older tend to be better ethical decision makers, some report those younger tend to be better ethical decision makers, and some report no relationship between age and ethical decision making.
Education Level	People with more education tend to be better ethical decision makers.
Gender	There are often no differences in ethical decision making between males and females; when differences are found, females tend to be better ethical decision makers than males.
Locus of Control (do you control events [internal], or do events control you [external])	Mixed results: some studies report no effect; other studies report that people with high internal locus of control or low external locus of control tend to be better ethical decision makers.
Machiavellianism (belief that "the ends justify the means")	People classified as low Machs tend to be better ethical decision makers.
Moral Development	People who reason at a higher level of moral development tend to be better ethical decision makers.
Nationality	Mixed results: some studies suggest that U.S. respondents are better ethical decision makers; other studies report that they are not.

(Continued)

Exhibit 5.3 Individual Characteristics (*Continued*)	
Philosophy/Value Orientation	People classified as high for "idealism" or "deontology" (respect everyone all the time) tend to be better ethical decision makers compared to those classified as low for "idealism" or "deontology" or high for "relativism" (no absolute right or wrong) or "economic orientation."
Religion	People who score high for "religious" tend to be better ethical decision makers.
Work Experience	People with more work experience tend to be better ethical decision makers.

(5) a higher score for deontology or idealism; and (6) a lower score for relativism, teleology, economic orientation, or Machiavellianism. Some evidence suggests that being a woman, having a high internal locus of control, and being a U.S. citizen are positively related to ethical decision making as well.

Ethical Beliefs and Sensitivities (B)

A belief is a mental state that guides behaviors. Some people believe working hard is good because it is a contractual obligation, generates positive feelings and emotions, or will result in a financial bonus. Others may believe that working hard is not good because they prefer a leisurely lifestyle or they will not be appropriately rewarded for working hard.

Ethical sensitivity refers to an individual's awareness that a particular situation raises ethical concerns. How much effort an employee exerts at work is an ethical issue. Not working hard can add to the work burdens of other employees, which is not fair. But not everyone is sensitive to that dynamic.

Ethical sensitivities are essential because they impact behavior and the lives of other people. Some owners pay adult employees minimum wages because that is what the law requires. An ethically sensitive manager may pay a higher "living wage" because the minimum wage is not sufficient income to pay for food, rent, medical, and transportation expenses. Or, an ethically insensitive manager may believe it is appropriate to make sexual jokes around employees and display sexually explicit pictures on office walls. Becoming more aware of how others interpret or experience our decisions and behaviors expands a person's ethical sensitivities.

As discussed in the previous section, ethical beliefs and sensitivities are the result of a host of individual characteristics, such as age, education, moral development level, or work experience. Being sensitive to the ethical dynamics of a situation is an essential step in forming ethical intentions and ultimately ethical behaviors. People cannot intend to behave ethically if they do not think there is an ethical issue at stake.

Ethical Intuitions (C)

People usually have a very short time to respond to an ethical issue. If a customer calls about a product delivery time schedule, and a manager tells the employee answering the call to falsely claim that the product will be delivered on time, the employee has a second to decide what to tell the customer. People in these situations follow their intuition. Ethical intuition is a quick insight independent of any reasoning process about right and wrong. Ambiguous situations, in which there is high uncertainty regarding people's motivations or the consequences of their actions, also tap into the decision maker's intuition.

Professor Jonathan Haidt of the University of Virginia takes a social psychological approach to understanding ethical decisions and behavior. He concludes that many ethical decisions are the result of intuitive reactions rather than deep reflection.[5] These gut reactions flow out of a person's deeply embedded value system. The employee who is instructed by a manager to lie to a customer about product delivery will either immediately tell the lie and justify the behavior as ethical based on following orders, or just as quickly refuse to lie. Time is not available for a long ethical deliberation. Both the customer and manager are waiting for an immediate reply. Later a decision maker might say: "At the time it seemed the right thing to do, but now that I've thought about it . . ." or "I had to decide right away, I had no time to think about it." In these instances, the person has relied on ethical intuition.

Scott Sonenshein offers a three-phase Sensemaking Intuition Model for events that contain a great deal of uncertainty and multiple interpretations.[6] An individual quickly constructs the issue in a sensible manner and makes an intuitive judgment. In an ambiguous situation, the decision maker quickly makes an analogy to a similar situation and then acts. When responding to a verbally abusive customer, for instance, the decision maker might quickly consider how he or she successfully responded to a verbally abusive acquaintance and repeat that action.

According to Haidt, our quick intuitive ethical judgments are the result of habituated patterns, emotions, and internalized teachings. A person observes an elderly woman struggling to put a heavy product in her shopping cart and immediately stops to help. This intuitive response happens because the person is acting out an internalized script influenced by parents, the individual's social network, or the broader culture, or the person has done this many times before, or an emotional connection was made with the elderly woman's situation.

To understand the nature of ethical intuitions, Haidt and his colleagues researched the apparent large difference in ethical intuitions liberals and conservatives have to public policy issues.[7] They found that liberals interpret the ethics of a situation based primarily on two value sets: harm/care and fairness/reciprocity. Liberals respond when someone frames an issue in terms of harms or fairness and favor outcomes that minimize harms or are determined to be the most fair. Conservatives, on the other hand, interpret the ethics of a situation based primarily on three different value sets: ingroup/loyalty, authority/respect, and purity/sanctity. Conservatives respond when someone frames an issue in terms of group loyalty, respect for authority, or moral purity/sanctity, and they favor outcomes that reinforce loyalty, authority, or moral purity/sanctity.

The ethical intuition value sets for liberals and conservatives appear in Exhibit 5.4. An affirmative response to any question under each value set is likely to generate moral indignation from people of that political persuasion. This does not mean liberals and conservatives ignore the other political group's values. They just care more about their own political group's values.

Exhibit 5.4 Liberal and Conservative Ethical Intuitions—What Matters Most	
Liberals	Conservatives
Harm/Care: • Did someone get harmed? • Did someone emotionally suffer? • Did someone act violently?	Ingroup/Loyalty: • Did someone betray his or her group? • Did someone behave disloyally? • Did someone put his or her interests above that of his or her group?
Fairness/Reciprocity: • Did someone treat some people differently than others? • Did someone act unfairly? • Did someone profit more than others?	Authority/Respect: • Did someone fail to fulfill the duties of his or her role? • Did someone show a lack of respect for legitimate authority? • Did someone in authority fail to protect subordinates?
	Purity/Sanctity: • Did someone do something morally disgusting? • Did someone violate standards of purity and decency? • Did someone do something unnatural or degrading?

Theory of Planned Behavior (D)

Icek Ajzen highlights other factors that contribute to forming an ethical intention. According to Ajzen's theory of planned behavior, formulating an intention to act ethically is a function of a person's attitudes toward the behavior, subjective norms, and perceived behavioral control.[8] Each of the three factors has two dimensions. The factor dimensions are explained below in terms of whether a person should prevent a coworker from stealing:

- Attitude toward the behavior dimensions:
  - *The strength of the belief:* I strongly believe that stealing is wrong.
  - *The evaluation of the outcome:* I strongly believe that my stopping the stealing would be a good thing to do.
- Subjective norms dimensions:
  - *The strength of the normative belief:* Other individuals and groups I respect believe that stealing is wrong.
  - *The motivation to comply with the referent group:* I really want to comply with the desires of individuals and groups I respect.

- Perceived behavioral control dimensions:
  - *The strength of the control belief:* I strongly believe that I have the ability, resources, and opportunity to stop the stealing.
  - *The perceived power of the control belief:* Given my ability, resources, and opportunity, it would be relatively easy for me to stop the stealing.

The theory of planned behavior is useful for understanding precursors to ethical behavior. Employees will behave ethically if the desired behavior fits their belief system, they personally have a strong desire to behave ethically, others at work desire the ethical behavior, and the employee has the ability and resources available to follow through on the ethical behavior. If any of these factors is weak, ethical intentions become weak and the desired ethical behavior may not happen.

The influence of peer groups is of particular importance. People adjust their beliefs and actions to fit that of the work group. If work unit leaders and colleagues share a particular ethical perspective, then individuals are likely to adopt them so as not to be marginalized or "rock the boat." If peers respect management and work diligently, a new member to the work unit will likely respect management and work diligently. But if peers continually criticize managers and perform only at adequate levels, a new member will likely do so as well. In the latter situation, to act contrary to existing norms requires a tremendous amount of moral courage.

Issue's Moral Intensity (E)

Ethical intentions and behaviors are also shaped by an issue's moral intensity.[9] Taking computer paper home from the office for personal use is not morally equivalent to selling stolen trade secrets from a competitor. Moral intensity refers to issue-related factors, rather than individual or organizational factors, that are likely to determine the magnitude of a person's moral approval or disapproval.

Moral intensity is among the most researched topics within the field of ethical decision making. The judicial system punishes some unethical business activities more than others. Factors that influence the decision making of judges and juries include the nature of the harm (physical, economic, or psychological) and the nature of those harmed (person or nonperson).[10] The legal system holds managers most blameworthy for physical harms to people. Less blameworthy are psychological harms to people and physical harms to animals.

According to business ethics scholar Tom Jones, an issue's moral intensity is likely to vary based on six factors:[11]

1. *Magnitude of consequences* refers to the total sum of harms and benefits generated by an act, such as the number of people who may be harmed (2 versus 100 people) or whether the harm is a minor injury or a death. Harmful acts with severe consequences have high moral intensity.

2. *Social consensus* refers to the degree of social agreement that an act is good or bad. There is strong social consensus that dumping toxic wastes into rivers is wrong. Consensus can occur at two levels, on the broad societal level or within a localized group of people. The strongest consensus occurs when both levels are in agreement.[12] For instance, there may be a general abstract consensus in society that bribery is wrong, but if everyone locally participates in bribery then bribery is more morally acceptable.[13] Situations that violate social consensus have high moral intensity.

3. *Probability of effect* refers to the probability that an act's effect will actually occur or cause the predicted harm. Cigarette smoking causes cancer. Acts with a high likelihood of causing harm have high moral intensity.

4. *Temporal immediacy* refers to the length of time between an act and the onset of consequences. A manager could immediately terminate 90 employees or provide a 60-day prenotification. Acts that immediately cause harm have high moral intensity.

5. *Proximity* refers to the nearness of an act to its victims and beneficiaries. People are more concerned with the burying of hazardous waste near their homes than in the uninhabited mountains of Nevada. Harmful acts that are nearby have high moral intensity.

6. *Concentration of effect* refers to the amount of harm an act will create in a concentrated area. Two thousand units of pollution can be disbursed locally or nationally. Harmful acts concentrated in a particular area have high moral intensity.

Therefore, the most morally intense acts are those with a high likelihood of causing severe harm to many people in a short period of time within a close and concentrated area, and where there is strong social consensus that the act is wrong. If such an act occurs, the manager and organization face public outrage and strong legal condemnation.

Organization Characteristics (F)

Ethical intentions and behaviors are also shaped by organizational factors. As discussed in the first chapter, the most prominent reasons for unethical behavior within organizations were following the boss's directives, meeting overly aggressive business or financial objectives, helping the organization to survive, meeting schedule pressures, and wanting to be a team player.[14]

O'Fallon and Butterfield, in their extensive review of the business ethics research literature, found four organizational characteristics associated with ethical behaviors:[15]

- *Codes of Ethics:* The existence of a Code of Ethics is positively related to ethical decision making.
- *Ethical Climate/Culture:* Ethical climates and culture have a positive influence on ethical decision making.
- *Organization Size:* Smaller organizations have a tendency to make better ethical decisions.
- *Rewards and Sanctions:* Organizations that reward ethical behaviors and punish unethical behaviors have a positive impact on ethical decision making.

Therefore, employees of organizations with a Code of Ethics, an ethical climate, and whose managers reward ethical behavior and punish unethical behaviors are more likely to make better ethical decisions.

Ethical Intentions (G)

The preceding factors contribute to the formation of an intention to behave ethically. An ethical intention is determining mentally to take some action that is morally appropriate. In general, individual characteristics shape a person's ethical beliefs and sensitivities, which influence, and are also influenced by, an individual's ethical intuitions, values, virtues, subjective norms, behavioral controls, the issue's moral intensity, and factors unique to the organization. One of these factors, or a combination of them, may generate an ethical intention.

But even if an intention to act ethically is solidified, an individual still may not follow through on the ethical intention. An employee can announce his or her sincere intention to work harder or treat others with more respect, yet not do so when the time to act arrives or decide to act on the opposite intention instead. Obstacles that divert someone from not acting on an ethical intention include second doubts, weakness of will, lack of moral courage, and old habits.

When second doubts arise, the decision maker reanalyzes the importance or anticipated outcomes of some of the previous mediating factors between ethical beliefs and intentions. Maybe stopping the coworker from stealing will generate worse outcomes (moral intensity), such as ostracism from work peers (an organization characteristic). If these new beliefs outweigh the initial ethical belief, the previous strong ethical intention may fade away.

A weakness of will or lack of moral courage may also dilute the initial ethical intention.[16] People are particularly prone to weakness of will when the moral duty to act is weak.[17] Yet it also happens when initial intentions are strong. For instance, the individual may sincerely want to prevent a coworker from stealing, but too much moral courage might be needed to intervene. Confronting a coworker about stealing may require too much effort for the individual stepping out of his or her comfort zone.

Lastly, breaking old habits can be formidable. An employee who has never spoken out against unethical behaviors at work may initially intend to change that habit after observing the coworker's theft. But then the usual list of fears arises, and it is easier for the employee to respond as he or she always has, which is to remain quiet and let someone else do something about it.

Rational Ethical Decision Making (H)

Employees arrive at organizations with a set of preconceived ideas about right and wrong. As discussed in pervious sections, people develop ethical intentions based on ethical intuitions and other extenuating concerns. After an initial intention is formed, some people pause and apply a more rational approach to ethical decision making. Others trust their initial intentions and only apply a rational analysis when their behavior is called into question, either by their own conscience or by others.

Assume you are a bartender. A very pregnant 35-year-old woman and her group of friends, previously served by another bartender, request another beer. Being a well-educated and ethically sensitive person, you realize this is an ethical dilemma. You learned in school that the Centers for Disease Control and Prevention has determined that "There is no safe level of alcohol use during pregnancy," which is when the baby's brain is being developed.[18] According to the Mayo Clinic, approximately 40,000 babies are born annually with some type of alcohol-related damage.[19] Alcohol consumption can cause miscarriage, stillbirth, and a range of fetal alcohol spectrum disorders (FASDs) following birth, which includes physical, behavioral, and learning problems.

But the woman is an adult capable of making her own decisions and has already been served by another bartender, which has happened before. Amid the loud bar noises, you find yourself pouring her another beer. Then you stop and reflect for a moment. Is it ethical to serve her a beer?

Rational ethical decision-making frameworks help individuals analyze the ethical basis of their decisions and actions. The simplest question to ask is the following: How would my mother (or any person of high integrity you respect) feel if what I'm planning to do appeared on the front page of a newspaper?

This section summarizes two common ethical decision-making frameworks and then offers a systematic seven-question rational ethical decision-making framework grounded in moral philosophy.

Rotary International's Four-Way Test

The Rotary International's Four-Way Test provides a simple framework for analyzing the ethical dimension of a decision. More than 1.2 million business, professional, and community leaders are members of 32,000 Rotary International clubs around the world. Many of these clubs recite the Four-Way Test at their weekly meetings.

The Four-Way Test was created in 1932, when Chicago businessman Herbert Taylor met with four of his managers, each practicing a different religion, to develop a set of ethical principles to guide managerial decisions and ensure business success. Taylor encouraged members of his local rotary to use these four principles. In 1943, the national Rotary organization adopted Taylor's Four-Way Test:[20]

Of the things we think, say, or do,

1. Is it the TRUTH?
2. Is it FAIR to all concerned?
3. Will it build GOODWILL and BETTER FRIENDSHIPS?
4. Will it be BENEFICIAL to all concerned?

Raytheon's Ethics Quick Test

Raytheon, a defense industry technology company, provides its 75,000 employees with an Ethics Quick Test consisting of the following questions to consider when facing an ethical dilemma:[21]

- Is the action legal?
- Is it right?
- Who will be affected?
- Does it fit Raytheon's values?
- How will I feel afterwards?
- How would it look in the newspaper?
- Will it reflect poorly on the company?

Raytheon redeveloped these questions as part of an ACTION decision-making model for employees, which appears in the "Best Practice in Use" exhibit.[22] The company reminds employees that not taking an action is itself an action that can have serious consequences.

BEST PRACTICE IN USE

Raytheon ACTION Decision-Making Model

Act Responsibly
- Has someone taken responsibility?
- Do you have all the information you need?
- Has the information been clarified?

Consider Our Ethical Principles
- Does the action foster respect and trust?
- Does it reflect integrity?
- Does it promote teamwork?
- Does it demonstrate quality, innovation, and citizenship?

Trust Your Judgment
- Is the action fair?
- Does it feel comfortable?
- Is it the "right" thing to do?
- Could it be shared publicly?

Identify Impact on Stakeholders
- Does the action positively impact the employee, team, supplier, customer, company, shareholders, and public?

Obey the Rules
- Does the action comply with the law, company policy, regulatory agency requirements, and customer requirements?

Notify Appropriate Persons
- Has communication been open and honest?
- Have potential problems been disclosed?

A Systematic Rational Ethical Decision-Making Framework

The Rotary's Four-Way Test and Raytheon's Ethics Quick Test and ACTION model are helpful lists of questions. But they are not philosophically systematic.

The moral philosophy literature provides a more systematic approach for deriving moral conclusions. Ethical reasoning is just like any other managerial problem-solving process. When confronting a problem, managers typically list the available options, prioritize them, and determine which alternative makes the most sense. The same decision-making process can be applied to ethical analysis.

Strong consensus, though not absolute agreement, exists among philosophers that some ethical reasons are more morally acceptable than others. For example, it has been long established that the Golden Rule ("do to others as you would want done to you") takes precedence over an individual's self-interests when these two ethical theories are in conflict, although some hard-core libertarians might object.

Exhibit 5.5 provides a systematic rational ethical decision-making framework that can help management and nonmanagement employees reveal the ethical dimension of any decision being made. A similar ranking of the ethical principles can be found in many cultures.

> ## Exhibit 5.5 A Systematic Rational Ethical Decision-Making Framework
>
> *Instructions:* Answer Questions 1 through 7 to gather the information necessary for performing an ethical analysis. Based on this information, develop a decision that has the strongest ethical basis.
>
> 1. Who are all the people affected by the action? [Stakeholder Analysis]
> 2. Is the action beneficial to me? [Egoism]
> 3. Is the action supported by my social group? [Social Group Relativism]
> 4. Is the action supported by national laws? [Cultural Relativism]
> 5. Is the action for the greatest good of the greatest number of people affected by it? [Utilitarianism]
> 6. Does the action treat every stakeholder with respect and dignity, and is the act something that everyone should do? [Deontology]
> 7. Is this how a virtuous person would act? [Virtue Ethics]
>   - *If answers to Questions 2 through 7 are all "yes,"* then do it.
>   - *If answers to Questions 2 through 7 are all "no,"* then do not do it.
>   - *If answers to Questions 2 through 7 are mixed,* then modify your decision.
>   - *If answers to Questions 5, 6, and 7 are "yes,"* this action is the *most* ethical. You may need to modify this decision in consideration of any "no" answers to Questions 2 through 4.
>   - *If answers to Questions 5, 6, and 7 are "no,"* this action is the *least* ethical. Modify this decision in consideration of these objections.
>   - *If answers to Questions 5, 6, and 7 are mixed,* this action is *moderately* ethical. Modify this decision in consideration of objections raised by Questions 5, 6, or 7. You may need to further modify this decision in consideration of any "no" answers to Questions 2, 3, or 4.

The seven-question framework can help managers reach a moral conclusion regarding the rightness or wrongness of any decision. The answers to questions 5, 6, and 7 point managers in the direction of the most moral decision. Doing something because the action is to the greatest good of the greatest number of people affected by it, treats all stakeholders with respect and integrity, and is something a virtuous person would do provides a tremendous amount of moral certitude. This is how we hope our leaders behave. But if that action might also result in the decision maker being fired (Question 2), more reflection might be needed to determine how to do what is right without being fired.

Note how the "legal" answer is not the highest ethical theory (Question 4). Laws are not created out of thin air; they are justified by concerns about the greatest good for the greatest number, respect for everyone, and virtuous behavior. Laws that fail to meet these three fundamental ethical concerns are usually an issue of public and political concern, debated, and sometimes changed.

The following sections describe the ethical foundation behind the seven questions that appear in Exhibit 5.5. Understanding the ethical foundation provides employees with greater confidence when applying the decision-making framework. In addition, the ethical theories enable employees to understand why they reach different moral conclusions for a particular decision.

The Six Ethical Theories

Questions 2 through 7 of the rational ethical decision-making framework each represent one of the six major ethical theories. The first question—"Who are all the people affected by the action?"—is referred to as stakeholder analysis and is not considered an ethical theory. Identifying all the people affected by a decision, nonetheless, helps inform the ethical analysis.

The six ethical theories are ordered in Exhibits 5.5 and 5.6 beginning with the most basic ethical theory (egoism) and ending with the most important and demanding ones (deontology and virtue ethics). Exhibit 5.6 elaborates on the meaning of each ethical theory that appears in Exhibit 5.5. View these six ethical theories as sequential steps on a moral ladder, and the first step is egoism.

Exhibit 5.6 Six Ethical Theories

EGOISM: How does the action relate to me? If the action furthers my interests, then it is right. If it conflicts with my interests, then it is wrong.

SOCIAL GROUP RELATIVISM: How does the action relate to my social group (peers, friends, etc.)? If the action conforms to the social group's norms, then it is right. If it is contrary to the social group's norms, then it is wrong.

CULTURAL RELATIVISM: How does the action relate to the national culture, particularly its laws? If the action conforms to the law, then it is right. If it is contrary to the law, then it is wrong.

UTILITARIANISM: How does the action relate to everyone who is affected by it? If the action is beneficial to the greatest number of people affected by it, then it is right. If it is detrimental to the greatest number, then it is wrong.

DEONTOLOGY: Does the action treat *every stakeholder* with respect and dignity in all situations? Is the action something that everyone should do? If yes, then it is right. If no, then it is wrong.

VIRTUE ETHICS: How would a virtuous person act in this situation? If the act strengthens moral character, then it is right. If it is contrary to moral character building, then it is wrong.

Egoism When faced with a decision, an egoist asks: "How does the action relate to me? If the action conforms to my interests, it is right. If it is contrary to my interests, it is wrong." Egoists tend to reason as follows: "I strongly believe that x is the best decision, because that is my personal preference."

In *Theory of Moral Sentiments* and *Wealth of Nations*, Adam Smith emphasizes that people by nature are egoists.[23] Each person thinks about himself or herself more than anyone else and is often more upset about a slight cut to his or her finger than an earthquake that might kill thousands of people in a distant land. The slight cut causes continual direct bodily pain, whereas the earthquake tragedy enters a person's consciousness, causes sadness, and is then replaced by more personal concerns.

People naturally make decisions based on self-interest (concern for self in relation to others). Individuals tend to be very concerned about how their actions and the actions of others impact their own well-being. People have a strong preference for actions that improve their financial condition, and an aversion for actions that worsen their financial condition.

Similarly, when an organizational policy change is under consideration, people naturally wonder if the policy change will make their work lives more or less burdensome. Individuals tend to prefer policy changes that ease their burdens and oppose those that worsen their burdens. Burdens include having a guilty conscience, which can cause high levels of anxiety. Being concerned about one's own interests doesn't necessarily mean that a person is selfish. Instead, egoists recognize that decisions and actions impact their lives and that their interests matter.

Ayn Rand's novels *The Fountainhead* and *Atlas Shrugged* are among the most engaging articulations of the importance of egoism.[24] In both novels, individual liberty and self-interest matter a great deal. According to Rand, the best thing for the common good is to become an individual of high integrity willing to pursue one's self-interests at all costs. Rand is critical of people who cave in to the perspective of the masses for the sake of communal harmony, and she rebels against a paternalistic government whose leaders and bureaucrats assume they know what is best for everyone. Rand proposes an ethic of rugged individualism, whereby individuals stand up for what they believe and learn from their mistakes. Society improves when each person improves his or her own life circumstances and does what is individually meaningful and fulfilling.

Let's Build a Building

Subcontractor Bids

You have chosen the general contractor to build the building and bids have been put out for subcontractors to perform the specific aspects of the work.

Three of your accounting clients bid in a different subcontractor category—dry walling, plumbing, and HVAC (heating, ventilation, and air conditioning). Your clients are the lowest bidders in dry walling and plumbing, but a high bid in HVAC. As is common practice, after the bid deadline subcontractors ask the contractor for the amount of the lowest bid submitted.

The general contractor reviews the client bids with you.

He informs you that the low-bid dry waller does high-quality work, but the low-bid plumber is known for substandard work. The general contractor strongly recommends the plumber with the second lowest bid, whom he has worked with on previous projects. This is problematic because the low-bid plumber has been a very loyal customer over the years and has suggested that he might change accounting firms if not chosen for this building project.

The general contractor has high regard for your HVAC client, but that bid was nearly double the amount of the low-bid HVAC. This is also problematic because the low-bid HVAC, if not chosen, could complain to others in the community about your bidding manipulations because he knows he's the lowest bid.

What would you do? Would you

1. Use a *"low-bid hired"* rule that would result in your HVAC client not being chosen, and choosing your plumber client who performs substandard work?

2. Use an *"all clients hired"* rule that would result in the two high-quality dry waller and HVAC clients being chosen, though the HVAC client is at twice the low bid, and choosing your substandard plumber client?

3. Use a *"high-quality hired"* rule that results in choosing two of your three clients—the low-bid dry waller client and high-bid HVAC client, but not the low-bid substandard plumber, thus risk losing the plumber as a loyal client? Why?

Organizations need individuals who look after their own interests to ensure that they receive the resources needed to perform their job tasks. As the predominant ethical theory, however, egoism can be problematic for organizations.

Whose interests matter the most when two people have conflicting interests? In highly politicized organizations, individuals fight for scarce resources, such as budgets or office space, even though it is clearly more beneficial to the organization if one particular person receives the scarce resource. If egoism is the predominant ethical theory, then the more politically powerful or astute employee gets the scarce resource, possibly to the determinant of organizational performance.

Egoists seeking a reasonable solution to conflicts that arise between their interests and the interests of others will usually broaden their understanding to include the interests of larger social groups, therefore taking the next step up the moral reasoning ladder.

Social Group Relativism When faced with a decision, a social group relativist asks: "How does the action relate to my social group? If the action conforms to my social group's norms, it is right. If it is contrary to my social group's norms, it is wrong." Social group relativists tend to reason as follows: "I strongly believe that x is the best decision, because that is what my social group supports."

Associating oneself with the ethical standards of a group is often considered to be a higher stage of moral reasoning than egoism. Social group relativists are concerned about what their social group thinks about an issue because they share common interests. Wealthy people identify with what is best for the wealthy; poor people identify with what is best for the poor. Associations are formed to more efficiently and effectively represent social group interests. The Chamber of Commerce represents the interests of the business community. The Better Business Bureau ensures that consumers are treated ethically by businesses. Mothers Against Drunk Driving lobby for alcohol restrictions that are opposed by the National Beer Wholesalers lobby. Each lobbying group monitors government decision making to make sure that public policies favor, or do not damage, member interests.

Social group relativism is a common ethical theory. Managers usually feel a strong affinity for the interests of other managers. When problems arise, a manager might ask other managers what they have done in the past when faced with a similar problem. The decision maker wants to do what a good manager would do in the particular situation.

Similarly, nonmanagement employees usually feel a strong affinity for the interests of other nonmanagement employees, customers tend to view things from a customer's perspective, suppliers tend to view things from a supplier's perspective, and community members tend to view things from a community member's perspective.

The tendency to interpret situations from a social group's perspective is particularly evident in partisan sports and politics. Fans of a particular team tend to interpret every ambiguous game situation in a way that benefits their team. Close calls ruled in favor of the opposition are met with groans and shouts of umpire incompetence. A key play performed by the favored team exemplifies superior skills, whereas the same play performed by the opposition is attributed to luck.

In politics, individual Democrats and Republicans occasionally vote against their personal policy preference and conscience in the name of party unity and future political victories. A Democrat politician who filibusters Congress is considered a hero among Democrats, but if a Republican politician performs the same maneuver, the Democrats claim the behavior is unpatriotic and contrary to the will of the people. A Republican politician who sponsors a misleading advertisement against an opponent is considered strategic among Republicans, but if a Democrat sponsors a misleading advertisement against an opponent, the Republicans claim the advertisement is another example of lies and dirty politics.

Organizations need marketing managers who look after the interests of the marketing department, and accounting managers who look after the interests of the accounting department. As the predominant ethical theory, however, social group relativism can be problematic for organizations.

Which social group's interests matter the most when the two social groups involved in a situation have conflicting interests? In highly politicized organizations, departments fight for scarce resources even though it is clearly more beneficial to the organization if one particular department receives the scarce resource. If social group relativism is the predominant ethical theory, then the more politically powerful or astute department gets the scarce resource, possibly to the detriment of organizational performance.

Social group relativists seeking a reasonable solution to this dilemma will usually broaden their understanding to include the interests of the entire organization or larger society, therefore taking the next step up the moral reasoning ladder.

Cultural Relativism When faced with a decision a cultural relativist asks: "How does the action relate to my national culture, particularly the law? If the action conforms to the law, it is right. If it is contrary to the law, it is wrong." Cultural relativists tend to reason as follows: "I strongly believe that x is the right thing to do, because the law says so."

Associating oneself with the ethical standards embodied within a nation's set of laws is often considered to be a higher stage of moral reasoning than social group relativism. The person perceives herself or himself as a member of a larger society that has some common interests. A common saying among cultural relativists is "When in Rome do as the Romans do." This demonstrates tolerance and respect for the practices and policies of the host nation or community.

Cultural relativists are concerned about what the legal system thinks about an issue. Laws are established through two distinct processes, Congress and the judicial system, that cultural relativists respect. Political legislation is the result of politicians presenting competing perspectives (liberal versus conservative, Democrats versus Republicans) and reaching a conclusion by voting on the issue. Judicial laws are the result of lawyers presenting competing perspectives, and a conclusion is reached by a judge hearing the case.

Cultural relativism is also a rather common ethical theory. Many managers do not want to break the law, even when doing so might personally benefit them or their company. When problems arise, they review the law or ask company lawyers to provide a legal opinion. They want to do what is right in the eyes of the legal establishment. A cultural relativist is likely to implement a compliance-based ethics program to ensure that the organization does not violate the law, rather than an integrity-based ethics program that aims at a standard superior to legal compliance.[25]

Organizations need managers who are cultural relativists adamant that local, state, and federal laws be obeyed. As a predominant ethical theory, however, cultural relativism can be problematic for organizations. Sometimes laws conflict with one another, or following the law endangers the lives of others. Just because something is legal does not mean that it is ethical. Until midway through the Civil War, businesses could legally use slave labor in the United States, but doing so was unethical because it violated individual liberty. Similarly, just because an organization has the legal right to pollute up to a certain amount does not mean it should, particularly if available pollution controls are not burdensome.

Cultural relativists seeking a reasonable solution to these dilemmas will usually broaden their understanding to include determining the greatest good for the greatest number of people affected, individual rights, or virtuous behavior, therefore taking the next step up the moral reasoning ladder. These three highest theories are aimed at minimizing the most common human biases—a preference for self-interests, group interests, and national interests.

Utilitarianism   When faced with a decision, a utilitarian asks: "How does the action relate to everyone who is affected by it? If it is beneficial to the majority, then it is right. If it is detrimental to the majority, then it is wrong." Utilitarians tend to reason as follows: "I strongly believe that x is the best decision, because the consequences benefit the greatest number of people."

Concern about an action's consequences on the general welfare is often considered to be a higher stage of moral reasoning than cultural relativism. In this sense, the person is not just concerned about national laws, but whether the law is morally justified when the well-being of others is taken into consideration.

Utilitarians emphasize the consequences of an action on *all* those affected by it. During the Middle Ages, political and economic policies were legislated that primarily served the interests of the ruling monarch's family. The philosophers Jeremy Bentham[26] and John Stuart Mill[27] countered that what mattered most was the greatest good for the greatest number of people. In *On Liberty*, Mill argued that the greatest good for political arrangements entailed respecting every person's liberty, not just that of the monarchy or parliament.[28] Ethical conduct is that which creates the most good in the world, provided that the liberty of others is not violated.

Utilitarianism serves as the foundational ethic for the political, economic, and business systems in the United States. Democracy is utilitarian in the sense that everyone can state his or her preference and the best public policy is that which the majority desires. The ethics of capitalism is based on utilitarian logic—the economic pursuit of self-interest improves national wealth more than other economic systems. Cost-benefit analysis is based on utilitarian logic—determine a project's total benefits and total costs, and if the benefits outweigh the costs the project receives a favorable review.

Everyone counts equally under utilitarianism. There can be no favoritism based on status or power. Utilitarian-thinking managers would centrally locate a scarce piece of equipment needed by everyone, rather than giving preference to the employee or department with the most political power. Whatever is best for the organization determines the action taken.

Organizations need managers who are utilitarians, always looking after what is best for the organization and broader society. As a predominant ethical theory, however, utilitarianism can be problematic for organizations.

Managers of an organization composed of white males might decide that the organization would perform at optimal efficiency and improve gross national product (GNP) if it did not employ any women or African Americans. Or, to avoid bankruptcy that would result in everyone being unemployed, managers might decide to eliminate costly safety protections that benefit only a few maintenance workers.

Utilitarians seeking a reasonable solution to these issues will usually broaden their conceptualization of "greater good" to include human rights or undertake actions that they would want everyone to do, thereby taking the next step up the moral reasoning ladder.

Deontology When faced with a decision, a deontologist asks: "Does the action treat *every stakeholder* with respect and dignity? Is the action something that everyone should do? If yes, then it is right. If no, then it is wrong." Deontologists tend to reason as follows: "I strongly believe that *x* is the best decision, because everyone has a duty to treat everyone else with respect in all situations."

Respecting all stakeholders is often considered to be a higher stage of moral reasoning than utilitarianism. In this sense, the individual is not just concerned about the will of the majority, but whether every person is treated fairly in all situations. Deontologists emphasize the motives behind an action and individual rights, rather than the consequences. They have a duty to follow "moral rules" applicable to all people in all situations, such as the Ten Commandments.

Simply following the Golden Rule ("do to others as you want done to you") is helpful, but insufficient because what the decision maker might want done to him or her is unethical, such as not wanting to know about a regulatory violation. The philosopher Immanuel Kant prevents this faulty reasoning based on a categorical imperative, which is a rule that applies to all situations. Kant's primary categorical imperative maintains that one must "Act according to the maxim whereby you can at the same time will that it should become a universal law."[29] In other words, what would happen if everyone did what you were planning to do? If lying to avoid imprisonment is permissible in one situation, then it must be permissible by all people in all situations, a universal rule that rational people would reject.

People who want others to respect them have a duty to respect others. For a deontologist, the appropriate action is to *always* be honest, keep promises, provide mutual aid when needed, and respect people and property. Universal human rights, which respect the dignity and autonomy of every human being, are based on deontology logic. Deontology can be difficult for managers to apply because the ethical theory demands that the organization respect every stakeholder all the time.

The "Trolley Problem" in Exhibit 5.7 is a series of three ethical dilemmas developed by moral philosophers that highlight the tension between utilitarianism and deontology, and explore contextual factors that might influence a person to change his or her acion.[30]

Organizations need managers who are deontologists, ensuring that every stakeholder is respected all the time. As a predominant ethical theory, however, deontology can be problematic.

Focusing solely on respecting the interests of every stakeholder is not always achievable, practical, or desirable. Assume that given time and budget limitations, employees must choose whether to provide preferential service to the largest revenue-generating customer or give all customers an equal amount of service. The 80/20 Rule suggests that 20 percent of an organization's customer base provides

Exhibit 5.7 The Trolley Problem

Scenario 1

Assume an out-of-control trolley car is hurtling down a street. Five people working on the track are in its path and about to be killed. You can save five lives by pulling a lever that will divert the trolley to an alternative track. Unfortunately, one worker is on the alternative track and pulling the lever would kill him. Is it ethical to pull the lever?
[Utilitarian response: Yes; Deontology response: No]

Scenario 2

Assume the one worker is a member of your family. Is it ethical to pull the lever?
[Utilitarian response: Yes; Deontology response: No]

Scenario 3

Assume that you are standing on a bridge when the runaway trolley takes aim at the five people working on the track. Unfortunately, the only nearby heavy object, besides yourself, is the stranger standing next to you. You are strong and throwing the stranger over the bridge will stop the trolley. Is it ethical to throw the stranger in the path of the trolley?
[Utilitarian response: Yes; Deontology response: No]

80 percent of its revenue.[31] Deontology would demand that all customers be equally respected. But if the top revenue-generating customers are not given preference, they might take their business elsewhere, which could bankrupt the organization and cause everyone to be unemployed.

Deontologists seeking a reasonable solution to these issues will usually broaden their understanding to include a wider arrangement of virtues, therefore taking the final step up the moral ladder.

Virtue Ethics When faced with a decision, a virtue ethicist asks: "How would a virtuous person act in this situation? If the act strengthens moral character, then it is right. If it is contrary to moral character building, then it is wrong." Virtue ethicists tend to reason as follows: "I strongly believe that x is the best decision, because that is what a person of high moral character would do."

Virtue refers to achieving excellence in morals. The list of virtues is quite extensive. Business ethicist Robert Solomon catalogued 45 virtues related to business activities.[32] The most common grouping of virtues includes justice, empathy, passion, piety, reliability, respect, and incorruptibility.[33]

Practicing the virtues is often considered to be a higher stage of moral reasoning than utilitarianism and deontology.[34] Utilitarianism is an "ends-based" ethical theory in which right action is defined by the consequences. Deontology is a "rules-based" ethical theory in which right action is defined by following a set of moral rules that should be applied by everyone in all situations.

Virtue ethics, on the other hand, is based on cultivating good habits. Humans are creatures of habit. Kindness and fairness must be practiced daily to become virtuous habits. A person becomes kind and fair by being kind and fair. A kind person should act with kindness and fairness in a variety of situations and toward a variety of people over an extended period of time, particularly when it is most difficult to do so. Through constant choice, being kind and fair becomes a virtuous habt.

Aristotle noted that the purpose of life is to be happy, and the greatest happiness is achieved when a person excels in virtue.[35] Someone who habitually practices the virtues lives a proper human life. A virtuous manager is a person who not only exercises the virtues, but also helps make everyone else in the organization a better person by providing them with the resources to excel.[36]

There are many virtues people can practice.[37] As shown in Exhibit 5.8, some virtues are more meaningful for an individual living as a member of the broader society. Individuals should practice fairness, kindness, compassion, and generosity in their interactions with others. The primary virtues for managers, however, include other virtues because they have a fiduciary duty to manage organizational resources on behalf of owners. Managers must practice fairness in their dealings with all stakeholders, transparency (openness and candidness) so stakeholders can trust managerial words and actions, accountability for achieving organizational goals, and two-way communication to fully understand and respect the interests and perspective of others.

Exhibit 5.8 Virtues and Vices

Individual Virtues	Managerial Virtues	Individual and Managerial Vices
• Fairness	• Fairness	• Greed
• Kindness	• Transparency	• Anger
• Compassion	• Accountability	• Ignorance
• Generosity	• Two-way Communication	• Lust

Vices represent either a lack of virtue or an excess of virtue. For instance, courage is a virtue. Cowardice is a lack of courage, and recklessness is an excess of courage. Common vices that are detrimental to both individuals and managers include greed (excessive desire for possessions and material wealth), anger (excessive desire to express hate), ignorance (lack of possessing appropriate information), and lust (excessive desire for sex). In terms of lust, adulterous affairs and inappropriate sexual relationships with colleagues, subordinates, customers, and suppliers damage trust and morale at the workplace.

Organizations need managers who are virtue ethicists, constantly practicing virtuous behaviors. As a predominant ethical theory, however, virtue ethics can be problematic.

Different virtues generate different requirements and sometimes the requirements conflict with one another. Practicing honesty can result in telling a hurtful truth, which conflicts with practicing kindness. For these reasons, the decision maker must reflect on information generated by all six ethical theories.

The six ethical theories parallel Lawrence Kohlberg's six levels of moral reasoning discussed in Chapter 1.[38] As shown in Exhibit 5.9, moral reasoning in Stages 1 and 2 reflects egoism, Stage 3 moral reasoning reflects social group relativism, Stage 4 moral reasoning reflects cultural relativism, Stage 5 reflects utilitarianism and deontology, and Stage 6 reflects deontology and virtue ethics.

Exhibit 5.9 Kohlberg's Stages of Moral Development and Ethical Theories		
Age Group	**Stage of Moral Development**	**Ethical theory**
Mature Adulthood	**Stage 6: Universal Ethical Principles**—Justice, equality, fairness for everyone, universal human rights	**Virtue Ethics** (How would a virtuous person act?) and **Deontology** (Does the action treat every stakeholder with respect?)
Mature Adulthood	**Stage 5: Prior Rights, Social Contract, Utilities**—Human rights	**Deontology** (Does the action treat every stakeholder with respect?) and **Utilitarianism** (Is the action the greatest good for the greatest number?)
Adulthood	**Stage 4: Social System**—Duty to society's customs, traditions, laws	**Cultural Relativism** (Does the action maintain laws and customs?)
Early Adulthood, Adolescence	**Stage 3: Mutual Interpersonal Expectations**—Well-being of friends and coworkers	**Social Group Relativism** (Is the action supported by my peers?)
Adolescence, Youth	**Stage 2: Reward Seeking**—Self-interest, fairness to me, reciprocity	**Egoism** (Does the action benefit me?)
Childhood	**Stage 1: Punishment Avoidance**—Obedience to rules due to fear of authority	**Egoism** (Does the action hurt me?)

Do all individuals in the world share these same ethical principles and values, or are they simply those that Americans honor? According to the Council for a Parliament on the World's Religions, there is significant agreement among the major world religions on five principles that should govern human behavior in all realms of life, including business: (1) "Do unto others as you would have them do to you," (2) "Thou shall not commit sexual impropriety," (3) "Thou shall not steal," (4) "Thou shall not lie," and (5) "Thou shall not kill."[39] These deontology-based guidelines are universal.

Rushworth Kidder and the Institute for Global Ethics have surveyed people from around the world about the ethical values that matter the most to them. Similar to the Council for a Parliament on the World's Religions, Kidder and his colleagues have found strong consensus among five values, or virtues, that are common worldwide. They are responsibility, fairness, respect, compassion, and honesty (see Exhibit 5.10).[40] Cultures may weigh each of these five shared virtues differently, but they are all consistently among the top five. No matter where in the world a person may be, people in that nation value individuals who are responsible, fair, respectful, compassionate, and honest.

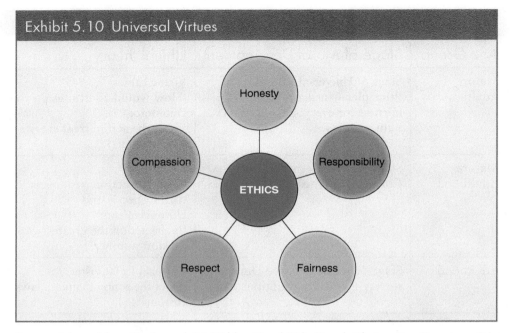

Exhibit 5.10 Universal Virtues

Source: Adapted from Rushworth M. Kidder, *Good Kids, Tough Choices* (San Francisco, CA: Jossey-Bass, 2010), pp. 47–48.

Reaching a Moral Conclusion

Each ethical theory raises important issues for the decision maker to consider, and each theory has strengths and weaknesses. Exhibit 5.11 provides a critical thinking process based on the systematic rational ethical decision-making framework in Exhibit 5.5.

Applying the seven questions to the most salient ethical dilemmas will likely reveal that each decision option has strengths and weaknesses, and ethical trade-offs might be required. The systematic rational ethical decision-making section began with a situation in which a 35-year-old pregnant woman, previously served by a different bartender, requests another beer. The bartender knows alcohol consumption can cause physical, behavioral, and learning problems to the baby following birth. Nonetheless, the bartender's ethical intuition was to serve the beer because the woman is an adult capable of making her own decisions and has already been served. The bartender forms an intention to serve the beer. But then the bartender might stop and rethink the ethical intention.

In using the Critical Thinking Table in Exhibit 5.11, the decision maker's first step is to list the decision options under consideration. The bartender has three decision options: (1) serve the beer, (2) educate the woman about the harms alcohol causes a fetus and let her decide, or (3) refuse to serve the beer.

The second step of the systematic rational ethical decision-making process is to apply the seven questions to the decision to obtain relevant information. Begin by listing the stakeholders affected by the decision. Stakeholders directly affected are the woman, the fetus, the bartender, and the other bartenders. Stakeholders

Exhibit 5.11 Critical Thinking Decision-Making Process Table		
Step 1: Write the decision options in the appropriate column below.		
Step 2: Apply the seven "Applying Ethical Theories to Decision Making" questions to the decision to obtain relevant ethical information.		
Step 3: Insert the ethical strength and weakness revealed by each of the seven ethical questions in the appropriate column below.		
Step 4: Review the option strengths and insert in the options column the "value" that supports the option (i.e., honesty, loyalty, efficiency, respect, job security, profits)		
Step 5: Given the strengths and weaknesses, choose a decision option, explain why that option and value were chosen rather than the alternative options, and determine how to manage the weaknesses associated with the option chosen.		
1. Who are all the people affected by the action?		
2. What option benefits me the most?		
3. What option does my social group support?		
4. What option is legal?		
5. What option is the greatest good for the greatest number of people affected?		
6. What option is based on truthfulness and respect/integrity toward each stakeholder?		
7. What option would a virtuous person do?		
Option	Option *Strengths* Based on Application of Ethical Theories	Option *Weaknesses* Based on Application of Ethical Theories
#1:		
#2:		
#3:		
Option and Value Chosen		
Chosen Because		
How Will You Manage Chosen Option Weaknesses?		

indirectly affected include the men and women at the bar observing the interaction. Then determine which option meets the ethical theory requirements.

Which option benefits the bartender the most? All three can meet the criteria depending on the how the bartender defines self-interest. Serving the beer can earn the bartender a tip, educating the woman can make the bartender feel purposeful, and refusing to serve the woman can be pleasing to the bartender's conscience. The social group would support serving the woman because that is what the other bartenders do. All three options are legal. The greatest good is to not serve the beer given the life expectancy of the fetus. The results for being truthful and respecting each stakeholder are mixed. Not serving the beer and educating the woman are based on being truthful, and they respect the fetus. But they do not respect the woman's right to choose. A virtuous person would not serve the beer to the pregnant woman given the harm that can be done to the fetus. This is a difficult ethical dilemma because no one option generates a positive response from all six ethical theories.

Given the mixed results, the third step entails further clarifying the strengths and weaknesses of each option based on the ethical theories. The *first option* is to serve the pregnant woman the requested beer. Serving the beer creates no customer hassles and may earn you a tip (egoism strengths). On the other hand, it may bother your conscience that she is probably making an uninformed decision (egoism weakness). Another bartender has already served her a beer (social group relativism strength) and the pregnant woman has the legal right to drink alcohol (cultural relativism strength). But alcohol consumption by pregnant women can cause fetal alcohol syndrome, the effects of which are irreversible (utilitarianism and deontology weaknesses). This negatively impacts the baby's future and can be a tremendous health care cost (utilitarianism weakness). Serving the pregnant woman beer respects her rights (deontology strength) but does not respect the rights of the future baby (deontology weakness). Lastly, serving the beer does not practice compassion on behalf of the future baby, which is in the most vulnerable position (virtue ethics weakness). The woman might be happy in the moment but would feel guilty if the child were born with fetal alcohol syndrome (virtue ethics weakness).

The *second option* is to educate the woman about the harms alcohol causes a fetus and let her decide. Educating the woman about the dangers and letting her decide reduce your anxiety about the woman not making an informed decision (egoism strength), though your coworkers might get upset that you are not efficiently serving other customers (social group relativism weakness). You have the legal right to educate her about fetal alcohol syndrome (cultural relativism strength) and sharing this information with her may benefit other people (utilitarianism strength). If the woman ignores your education efforts, the fetus may be harmed (utilitarianism and deontology weaknesses). By allowing the woman to decide, you are respecting her autonomy (deontology strength) though not respecting the fetus (deontology weakness). Educating the woman practices compassion for the woman (virtue ethics strength), but if she ignores your advice, then the fetus may be harmed (virtue ethics weakness).

The *third option* is to refuse to serve the pregnant woman a beer. Doing so eases your conscience because the fetus is being protected (egoism strength), but it can lead to the woman and her friends making a scene (egoism weakness), and your coworkers might get upset (social group relativism weakness). Bartenders have the legal right to not serve people if doing so will cause harm to the person or others (cultural relativism strength), but she has the legal right to be served (cultural relativism weakness). Not serving the beer is the greatest good for the greatest number of people affected by it (utilitarianism strength) and respects the future baby (deontology strength) but does not respect the woman (deontology weakness). Lastly, the fetus is in the most vulnerable position, and this is an opportunity for the bartender to practice personal responsibility and moral courage (virtue ethics strength).

The fourth step requires reviewing the ethical strengths of each option and determining its underlying value. In this case, serving the beer is based on earning a tip and respecting the woman's right to choose. Educating the woman is based on respecting the woman's right to choose. Refusing to serve the beer is based on the greatest good, respecting the fetus, and behaving like a virtuous person.

The fifth step of the decision-making process entails reviewing the strengths and weaknesses associated with each option, choosing a decision option, explaining why this option and value were chosen, and then determining how to manage the weaknesses associated with the chosen option. As noted earlier, answers to Questions 5, 6, and 7 point the decision maker in the direction of the most moral decision. But if that action also might result in the decision maker being fired (Question 2), more reflection might be needed to determine how to do what is right without being fired.

For this particular situation, a very strong moral choice is to refuse to serve the pregnant woman alcohol. It is what a virtuous person would do (Question 7) and is the greatest good for the greatest number of people (Question 5). The choice respects the future baby (Question 6) and eases your conscience (Question 2). But there are several weaknesses to this decision option. Refusing to serve the beer does not respect the woman's right to choose (Question 6) and violates her legal right to be served a beer (Question 4). Other weaknesses include criticism from other bartenders (Question 3), the potential scene she can cause at the bar (Question 2), and a loss of a tip (Question 2).

The bartender must carefully explain the rationale for not serving the woman, which could be extremely difficult to do in a crowded and noisy bar. Given the concerns raised by virtue ethics, deontology, and utilitarianism, do not serve her another beer and briefly express your health concerns. If she insists on a beer, she can ask another bartender. To prevent this situation from arising again, the bartender could speak with the owner about posting a sign that says pregnant women will be refused service because of concern for fetal alcohol syndrome.

Utilitarianism, deontology, and virtue ethics matter a great deal. In many situations, the three highest ethical theories arrive at similar conclusions, providing the decision maker with a tremendous amount of moral certitude. Sometimes they may conflict. When this happens, respecting everyone and doing what a virtuous person would do are considered the two most important ethical responses. When this is not a practical solution, serving the greatest good or concerns raised by the other ethical theories take on greater moral weight.

Persuading Others

After applying the systematic rational ethical decision-making framework, two employees may still sincerely disagree about what is the appropriate ethical action. Reasonable people can strongly disagree whether it is ethical or unethical for a manager to demand that everyone on the project team work through a weekend just prior to a holiday. Most managers are primarily social group relativists (Question 3), wanting to do what a good manager would do, and cultural relativists (Question 4) who want to obey the law. But some managers are primarily egoists (Question 2), utilitarians (Question 5), deontologists (Question 6), or virtue ethicists (Question 7). Their ethical intuition is grounded in one of these six theories.

Most people are very comfortable with the ethical theory they intuitively rely on, and they may feel annoyed when others question their decisions. When ethical conflicts arise in organizations, the person with higher status tends to get his or her way. This conflict resolution approach assumes that the higher-status person is applying the higher ethical theory, an assumption that has been proven false innumerable times. A manager's failure to engage employees who apply different ethical theories can damage employee morale and result in unethical behaviors and lawsuits.

A healthier approach is for a manager to listen carefully to people who disagree, categorize the other person's response in terms of one of the six ethical theories, and then reframe the analysis using the other person's ethical theory to address the employee's concern. This is hard work. It requires a great deal of patience and practice because we are more accustomed to reasoning based on our preferred ethical theory, which we consider to be the most appropriate one.

Each ethical theory is similar to a different foreign language. Assume that egoism (self-interests) is equivalent to speaking English and utilitarianism (greatest good) is equivalent to speaking Spanish. If an English speaker wants to persuade a Spanish speaker, the English speaker must communicate in Spanish; otherwise, no progress will be made. The same logic applies to using the ethical theories as a persuasion tool.

Assume that two people are having a disagreement, one is an egoist and the other a utilitarian, and each person wants to persuade the other. The egoist believes the right thing to do is "x" and the utilitarian believes the right thing is "y." For the egoist to persuasively reason with the utilitarian, the egoist must realize that the utilitarian does not care what is in his or her self-interest, so appealing to the utilitarian's self-interest will fall on deaf ears. What utilitarians do care about is the greatest good for the greatest number of people. To be persuasive, the egoist must communicate using utilitarian reasoning and demonstrate how a greatest good analysis results in doing x rather than y.

Similarly, egoists do not care about the greatest good for the greatest number of people, so appealing to the egoist's sense of the greatest good will fall on deaf ears. What egoists do care about is their self-interest. To be persuasive, the utilitarian must communicate using egoistic reasoning and demonstrate how it is in the egoist's self-interest to do y rather than x.

Tips and Techniques

Achieving Ethical Consensus

Many ethical disagreements can be solved. Use the following steps to help people achieve ethical consensus and win-win ethical outcomes.*

Step 1: Both parties state their position on the issue.

Step 2: Both parties reveal the values and ethical reasoning that underlie their position.

Step 3: Both parties paraphrase each other's position.

Step 4: Both parties paraphrase each other's underlying values and ethical reasoning.

Step 5: Both parties, working together, craft a resolution to the conflict over the issue.

Step 6: Both parties check that the resolution does not conflict with their own values or ethical reasoning, or those of the other party.

---

*Warren French, "Business Ethics Training: Face-to-Face and at a Distance," *Journal of Business Ethics*, 66, 1 (2006): 117–126.

After hearing all of these different ethical perspectives during an employee meeting, consensus still might not be achieved, and the decision maker has to reach a decision unilaterally. By going through this process, the decision maker is able to respond to the concerns raised by competing ethical theories. The other employees may not agree with the manager's final conclusion, but they will understand the manager's ethical reasoning and be able to convey that reasoning to other organizational members.

Ten "Ethical Hazard Approaching" Signs

How can a manager know when moral intuition needs to be complemented with rational analysis? Employees in a manufacturing facility with toxic chemicals are visually warned when entering hazardous areas by flashing red lights, loud sirens, and large signs with skulls and crossbones. Unfortunately, warning lights do not flash when employees enter an ethical hazard zone.

Michael Josephson describes 10 common rationalizations for unethical acts that appear in Exhibit 5.12 as "ethical hazard approaching" signs.[41] Pause and reflect on the thought, "It's ethical because it's legal." As discussed earlier in this chapter, ethics is more than just the law. Laws change all the time, often because an individual, or group of people, strongly believes that an existing law, such as slavery in the nineteenth century, is unethical.

Exhibit 5.12 Ten "Ethical Hazard Approaching" Signs

Beware when someone says:

1. It may seem unethical . . . but it is legal and permissible
2. It may seem unethical . . . but it is necessary
3. It may seem unethical . . . but it is just part of the job
4. It may seem unethical . . . but it is all for a good cause
5. It may seem unethical . . . but I am just doing it for you
6. It may seem unethical . . . but I am just fighting fire with fire
7. It may seem unethical . . . but it doesn't hurt anyone
8. It may seem unethical . . . but everyone else is doing it
9. It may seem unethical . . . but I don't gain personally
10. It may seem unethical . . . but I've got it coming

Train employees to recognize these rationalizations. When spoken, pause for additional ethical reflection. Some of this training can occur in a reflective workshop setting. Have the workshop facilitator read the list of 10 justifications; after each one, ask participants to share stories about when they heard this rationalization given. Then attendees can apply the systematic rational ethical decision-making framework and propose a more ethical course of action for the next time the situation occurs.

SUMMARY

This chapter explored how to generate decisions that result in ethical behaviors. Two models were presented, an ethical behavior model (Exhibit 5.2) and a rational ethical decision-making framework (Exhibit 5.5). Ethical intentions are influenced by the decision maker's individual characteristics, ethical beliefs and sensitivities, ethical intuitions, organizational norms and control mechanisms, and the issue's moral intensity. A person's ethical intentions can result in ethical behavior, or the person may pause and reconsider the intention using a systematic rational ethical decision-making framework.

The systematic rational ethical decision-making framework enables decision makers to derive well-grounded moral conclusions to work-related issues. The framework takes into consideration the perspectives of six major ethical theories and rank-orders their concerns in a useful manner. Using this framework helps employees understand the ethical ramifications of workplace issues.

KEY WORDS

Belief; ethical sensitivity; ethical intuition; theory of planned behavior; moral intensity; ethical intention; egoism; social group relativism; cultural relativism; utilitarianism; deontology; categorical imperative; virtue ethics

CHAPTER QUESTIONS

1. Which individual characteristics impact ethical beliefs, sensitivities, intentions, and behaviors?

2. How are ethical intuitions formed? How do the value sets of liberals and conservatives differ?

3. Describe Icek Ajzen's theory of planned behavior.

4. Which seven questions are the bases for a systematic rational ethical decision-making framework? Which three questions point the decision making in the direction of the most moral decision?

5. Discuss some of the warning signs that an unethical decision is approaching.

In the Real World: Enron

Transferring Managerial Power—1996

Investment bankers participated in Andy Fastow's SPE arrangements, and Enron reported record revenue and profit levels. With the help of mergers and acquisitions, Enron became the world's largest natural gas company, and its stock price continued to perform well. In 1996, *Fortune* magazine named Enron "America's Most Innovative Company."

Ken Lay, having saved the company, was now ready to train his successor. Enron's future CEO would first have to learn how to manage the Fortune 100 firm's day-to-day operations as chief operating officer (COO). Lay's plan called for the COO to be promoted to CEO by 2001.

The three internal candidates for COO were the CEO of Enron's traditional natural gas pipeline division, the CEO of the highly successful Gas Bank division (Jeff Skilling), and the CEO of the growing international business division (Rebecca Mark). A fourth possibility was to hire a highly qualified outsider.

Skilling strongly advocated for the position and threatened to quit if not promoted to COO. Skilling accused Rebecca Mark, the international division's CEO, of mismanagement and incompetence. He also opposed the natural gas pipeline division CEO, arguing that the new economy valued intellectual skills and market transactions more highly than traditional brick-and-mortar assets. Only he, Skilling argued, possessed the appropriate vision for Enron.

Meanwhile, Skilling's weaknesses included a lack of hands-on cash management experience, taking extreme risks, impatience with those who did not quickly grasp his intellectual and visionary insights, competitiveness with other executives, and arrogance.

DECISION CHOICE. If you were the CEO of Enron, who would you promote to COO:

1. CEO of the traditional natural gas pipeline division?
2. Jeff Skilling, the CEO of the highly successful Gas Bank division?
3. Rebecca Mark, the CEO of the growing international division?
4. A highly qualified outsider?

Why?

ANCILLARY MATERIALS

Websites to Explore

- Ethical dilemmas reported in newspapers, available at http://deniscollins.tumblr.com/.
- Examples of ethical decision-making models, available at http://www.ethicsweb.ca/resources/decision-making/index.html.
- Josephson Institute, available at http://josephsoninstitute.org/MED/index.html.
- Ayn Rand Institute, available at http://www.aynrand.org/.

Best Place to Work Video

- Best Place to Work—Stew Leonard's, available at http://money.cnn.com/video/fortune/2010/01/20/f_bctwf_stew_leonards.fortune/.

Business Ethics Issue Video

- "Black Money," *Frontline*, about international bribery; April 7, 2009, 57 minutes, available at http://www.pbs.org/wgbh/pages/frontline/blackmoney/view/?utm_campaign=viewpage&utm_medium=grid&utm_source=grid.

TEDTalks Videos

- Moral Roots of Liberals and Conservatives: Psychologist Jonathan Haidt explains the five moral values that form the basis of our political choices, whether we're left, right or center, and he pinpoints the moral values that liberals and conservatives tend to honor most; March 2008, 19 minutes, available at http://www.ted.com/talks/jonathan_haidt_on_the_moral_mind.html.
- Justice and Ethical Decision Making: Harvard professor Michael Sandel probes: Is torture ever justified? Would you steal a drug that your child needs to survive? Is it sometimes wrong to tell the truth? How much is one human life worth?; September 2005, 55 minutes, available at http://www.ted.com/talks/michael_sandel_what_s_the_right_thing_to_do.html._

Conversations with Charlie Rose

- A conversation with David Brooks, *New York Times* columnist and author, about the unconscious mind, emotions, decision making, and social behaviors; September 16, 2010, 60 minutes, available at http://www.charlierose.com/view/interview/11206.
- A conversation with Jeff Bezos, founder, president, chief executive officer, and chairman of the board of Amazon.com; February 26, 2009, 60 minutes, available at http://www.charlierose.com/view/interview/10105.

NOTES

1. Marvin T. Brown, *The Ethical Process* (Upper Saddle River, NJ: Prentice Hall, 2003), p. 6.

2. James R. Rest and Darcia Naravaez (Eds.), *Moral Development in the Professions: Psychology and Applied Ethics* (Hillsdale, NJ: Lawrence Erlbaum Associates, 1994).

3. James Weber and Janet Gillespie, "Differences in Ethical Beliefs, Intentions, and Behaviors," *Business and Society*, 37, 4 (1998), 447–467.

4. Michael J. O'Fallon and Kenneth D. Butterfield, "A Review of the Empirical Ethical Decision-Making Literature: 1996–2003," *Journal of Business Ethics*, 59, 4 (2005), 375–413; Robert C. Ford and Woodrow D. Richardson, "Ethical Decision Making: A Review of the Empirical Literature," *Journal of Business Ethics*, 13, 3 (1994), 205–221; Terry W. Loe, Linda Ferrell, and Phylis Mansfield, "A Review of Empirical Studies Assessing Ethical Decision Making in Business," *Journal of Business Ethics* 25, 3 (2000), 185–204.

5. Jonathan Haidt, "The Emotional Dog and Its Rational Tail: A Social Intuitionist Approach to Moral Judgment," *Psychological Review*, 108, 4 (2001), 814–834.

6. Scott Sonenshein, "The Role of Construction, Intuition, and Justification in Responding to Ethical Issues at Work: The Sensemaking-Intuition Model," *Academy of Management Review*, 32, 4 (2007), 1022–1040.

7. Jesse Graham, Jonathan Haidt, and Brian A. Nosek, "Liberals and Conservatives Rely on Different Sets of Moral Foundations," *Journal of Personality & Social Psychology*, 96, 5 (2009), 1029–1046.

8. Icek Ajzen, "The Theory of Planned Behavior," *Organization Behavior & Human Decision Processes*, 50, 2 (1991), 179–211.

9. Eric Stein and Norita Ahmad, "Using the Analytical Hierarchy Process (AHP) to Construct a Measure of the Magnitude of Consequences Component of Moral Intensity," *Journal of Business Ethics*, 89, 3 (2009), 391–407.

10. Denis Collins, "Organizational Harm, Legal Condemnation and Stakeholder Retaliation: A Typology, Research Agenda and Application," *Journal of Business Ethics*, 8, 1 (1989), 1–13.

11. Thomas M. Jones, "Ethical Decision Making by Individuals in Organizations: An Issue-Contingent Model," *Academy of Management Review*; 16, 2 (1991), 366–395.

12. Thomas Donaldson and Thomas W. Dunfee, "Toward a Unified Conception of Business Ethics: Integrative Social Contracts Theory," *Academy of Management Review*, 19, 2 (1994), 252–284.

13. Thomas Donaldson and Thomas W. Dunfee, "When Ethics Travel: The Promise and Peril of Global Business Ethics," *California Management Review*, 41, 4 (1999), 45–63.

14. Anonymous, "How to Help Reinvigorate Your Organization's Ethics Program," *HR Focus*, June 2003, 7–8.

15. O'Fallon and Butterfield, "A Review of the Empirical Ethical Decision-Making Literature: 1996–2003."

16. Tobia Hoffman (Ed.), *Weakness of Will from Plato to the Present* (Washington, DC: Catholic University of America Press, 2008).

17. Allen Buchanan, "Perfecting Imperfect Duties: Collective Action to Create Moral Obligations," *Business Ethics Quarterly*, 6, 1 (1996), 27–42.

18. Centers for Disease Control and Prevention, "Alcohol and Public Health Frequently Asked Questions," available at http://www.cdc.gov/alcohol/faqs.htm#drinkPreg, accessed 10/15/10.

19. Mayo Clinic Staff, "Fetal Alcohol Syndrome," available at http://www.mayoclinic.com/health/fetal-alcohol-syndrome/ds00184, accessed 10/15/10.

20. Paul Engleman, "Is It the Truth?" *The Rotarian*, August 2009, 46–51.

21. Dayton Fandray, "The Ethical Company," *Workforce*, 79, 12 (2000), 74–78.

22. Ratheon, "ACTION Decision-Making Model," available at http://www.raytheon.com/ourcompany/static/cms01_023634.pdf, accessed 10/15/10.

23. Adam Smith, *The Theory of Moral Sentiments* (Indianapolis, IN: Liberty Classics, 1759/1976); Adam Smith, *The Wealth of Nations* (Chicago, IL: University of Chicago Press, 1776/1976).

24. Ayn Rand, *The Fountainhead* (Indianapolis, IN: Bobbs-Merrill Company, 1943); Ayn Rand, *Atlas Shrugged* (New York: Random House, 1957).

25. Lynn Sharp Paine, "Managing for Organizational Integrity," *Harvard Business Review*, 106, 2 (1994), 110–111.

26. Jeremy Bentham, *An Introduction to the Principles of Morals and Legislation* (Oxford, Eng.: Clarendon Press, 1789/1907).

[27] John Stuart Mill, *Utilitarianism and Other Essays* (New York: Penguin Classics, 1863/1987).

[28] John Stuart Mill, *On Liberty* (New York: Penguin Classics, 1859/1974).

[29] Immanuel Kant, *Groundwork for the Metaphysics of Morals* (New York: Harper Torchbooks, 1788/1964).

[30] Judith Jarvis Thomson, "The Trolley Problem," *The Yale Law Journal*, 94, 6 (1985), 1395–"1415.

[31] Richard Koch, *The 80/20 Principle* (New York: Currency Books, 1999).

[32] Robert Solomon, *A Better Way to Think About Business,* (Oxford University Press: New York, 1999).

[33] Kevin J. Shanahan and Michael R. Hyman, "The Development of a Virtue Ethics Scale," *Journal of Business Ethics*, 42, 2 (2003), 197–208.

[34] Alasdair MacIntyre, *After Virtue* (London: Duckworth, 1985).

[35] Aristotle, *Nichomachean Ethics* (New York: Oxford University Press, 1925).

[36] Alexander Bertland, "Virtue Ethics in Business and the Capabilities Approach," *Journal of Business Ethics*, 84, 1 (2009), 25–32; Robert Solomon, *Ethics and Excellence: Cooperation and Integrity in Business* (Oxford, Eng.: Oxford University Press, 1992).

[37] His Holiness the Dalai Lama and Howard C. Cutler, *The Art of Happiness: A Handbook for Living* (New York: Riverhead Books, 1998); Solomon, *Ethics and Excellence.*

[38] Denis Collins and Laura Page, "A Socrates/Ted Koppel Paradigm for Integrating the Teaching of Business Ethics in the Curriculum," in Sandra Waddock (Ed.), *Research in Corporate Social Performance and Policy*, 15, 2, special issue on "Teaching Business and Society Courses with Reflective and Active Learning Strategies" (Greenwich, CT: JAI Press, 1997), pp. 221–242.

[39] Daniel J. Koys, "Integrating Religious Principles and Human Resource Management Activities," *Teaching Business Ethics*, 5, 2 (2001), 121–139.

[40] Rushworth M. Kidder, *Good Kids, Tough Choices* (San Francisco, CA: Jossey-Bass, 2010), pp. 47–48.

[41] Josephson Institute, "What Are the 10 Myths of Ethics?" available at http://josephsoninstitute.org/business/overview/faq.html#10, accessed 10/15/10.

CHAPTER OUTLINE

6

ETHICS TRAINING

What would you do?

The Taped Signature

Upon graduation, you obtain an underwriting manager position for the branch office of a wholesale mortgage company in a highly competitive market. A person purchasing a house typically contacts a mortgage broker to obtain the lowest possible mortgage loan rate. The mortgage broker then shops the potential loan to several mortgage companies. The mortgage broker gathers and processes paperwork associated with the mortgage loan and sends the paperwork to the wholesale mortgage company for final approval. The mortgage broker is licensed by the state and personally liable for fraud for the life of the loan.

Real estate sales are sluggish regionally because of an economic recession. On Friday morning, one of your underwriters brings you a document she just received from a mortgage broker who is one of the branch office's biggest clients. The document is a copy of a disclosure form that requires a signature from both borrowers, in this case a married couple. The borrowers must close on their new home Friday afternoon, or they will lose the house to another buyer.

The husband signed the original document but, in the spot that requires the wife's signature, there is a small piece of paper taped to the document, apparently a cutout of the wife's signature from the copy of a different document. It is taped in such a way that if you put the document through a photocopy machine, the signature would appear original. If the broker meant for the wife to sign it later, a post-it note with an arrow pointing where to sign would have been used. Most likely, the mortgage broker meant to photocopy this form and then send the photocopy to you as if the wife had signed it. Instead, the mortgage broker mistakenly sent you the original copy with the taped signature.

The husband is the primary source of family income and very credit worthy. Nonetheless, it is illegal for the husband or a mortgage broker to forge the wife's signature. The married couple will be signing other documents at the time of the closing. You have done a lot of business with this mortgage broker without any previous problems, and your wholesale mortgage company branch needs the business.

What would you do? Would you

1) Pretend you didn't see the document and hope no one else will notice it among the many other documents in the file?
2) Put the forged document through a copy machine and shred the one you received

from the mortgage broker that has the piece of tape on it?

3) Call the mortgage broker, explain the situation, refuse to finance the loan, and never do business with the broker again because of the forged document?

4) Call the mortgage broker, request that the broker immediately obtain the wife's signature, and indicate that the next time something like this happens you would refuse to do business with the broker.

Why?

Chapter Objectives

After reading this chapter, you will be able to:

- Discuss the importance of organizational trust
- Describe the extent of ethics training nationwide
- Understand the shortcomings of web-based ethics training programs

- Develop 10 types of ethics training workshops
- Create business ethics scenarios for workshop discussion
- Administer ethics personality surveys
- Assess the ethics training workshop

ndividuals are more likely to discuss work-related ethical issues with family and friends than coworkers or executives. A managerial challenge is to design workshops in which employees can discuss ethical issues at work. Ethics training can initiate dialogue around contentious ethical issues. A well-facilitated ethics training workshop has greater impact on employee behaviors than the presence of an ethics code or memos from the boss. Researchers report that people employed in organizations with formalized ethics training have more positive perceptions about their organization's ethics and greater job satisfaction.[1]

This chapter emphasizes the importance of creating a culture of trust, reviews the extent of ethics training nationwide, recommends ethics training for everyone in the organization, highlights providing web-based and facilitator-guided ethics training programs, and examines choosing the workshop facilitator. Ten different types of ethics training workshops are presented.

Building Trust and an Ethical Culture

Ethics training helps create a culture of trust at work. According to the management theorist W. Edwards Deming, "Trust is mandatory for optimization of a system. . . . Without trust, each component will protect its own immediate interests to its own long-term detriment, and to the detriment of the entire system."[2]

Organizational trust refers to having a positive attitude that another member of the organization will be fair and not take advantage of one's vulnerability or dependency in a risky situation.[3] Trust has cognitive and emotional dimensions. Cognitively, trust is developed based on careful reflection of past experiences with organizational members and practices. A trusting relationship forms through repeated social exchanges between two people, in which each person makes decisions and acts in a way that takes into consideration the other person's interests and well-being. Trust also has an emotional dimension. Trust is linked to an individual's feelings and intuition, and it creates a positive emotional bond between two people.

A high degree of trust has many organizational benefits. Trust eliminates psychological barriers separating employers and employees. The other person's goodwill and reliability are assumed in a trusting relationship, which allows for greater flexibility to respond as needed without burdensome oversight or approval process. When things go wrong at work, the information is shared with the trusted party, rather than hidden from view or ignored.

Trust creates economic benefits through enhanced individual and organizational performance. Trusting and cooperative relationships play a critical role in effective communications and teamwork, which impacts employee commitment, employee loyalty, productivity, and profits.[4]

As highlighted in the opening chapter, ethical organizations, which have high levels of trust, attract and sustain high-quality employees, customers, and suppliers. They also have low levels of office politics and employee cynicism.[5] Ethical work cultures lead to greater accountability through clearly defined standards and shared expectations. The two-way communication reinforces policy compliance and reduces organizational risks.

Hard-earned trust can quickly disappear when violated, which can hamper organizational performance. Managers and other employees lose credibility and legitimacy when their promises are broken and their words are no longer believed. Employees may refrain from providing essential critical comments out of fear of being punished. Ethics training, if well done, holds both managers and nonmanagement employees accountable for their ethical behaviors and provides an opportunity for misunderstandings to be addressed.[6]

Extent of Ethics Training

Ethics training is becoming more common in all types of organizations and professions. A 2004 survey of publicly traded companies found that 68 percent provided ethics training.[7] More than 80 percent of city governments provide ethics training for employees.[8]

Members of some professions are required to take ethics training as part of obtaining or renewing their professional license to protect the public from incompetent practitioners. Many states mandate that continuing education courses for licensed accountants and lawyers include an ethics component.[9] All members of the National Association of Realtors must also complete ethics training courses.[10] Professional organizations, such as the American Institute of CPAs (AICPA), provide ethics resources on their websites, including a list of disciplinary actions.[11] Some employee unions offer ethics training at all levels of union membership to enhance effectiveness and build legitimacy.[12]

Organizations may be tempted to eliminate ethics training as an extraneous expense when budgets are tight, but this is exactly when ethics training is needed most. Employees who tend toward the relativistic belief that cutting ethical corners may be necessary to "save the organization" might sound heroic in the short term, but these actions can come back to haunt the organization in the long term. Misleading a major customer to meet one month's difficult goal can damage organizational performance for many months.

Who to Train

Conduct ethics training throughout the organization. Ethics permeates all organizational operations. An organization's integrity and reputation are based on the performance of every employee. All employees, ranging from the CEO and board of directors to the janitor, experience ethical dilemmas on a daily basis. An inappropriate comment by someone answering the telephone or responding to an email can cause lost business. Best Buy recognized the importance of organization-wide ethics training when, shortly after officially adopting a Code of Ethics, all 140,000 employees in the United States and Canada received ethics training.[13]

The late 1990s and early 2000s accounting scandals, epitomized by Enron and WorldCom, highlight the importance of ethics training at the highest levels of an organization. Upper-level managers participated in the scandals, and board members failed to take appropriate disciplinary action. The Conference Board, a not-for-profit corporate educational and networking organization, reports that in 1987 only 21 percent of its members provided ethics training at the board level, but by 2005 the number had risen to 96 percent.[14]

Upper-level managers establish the overall ethics tone that is then filtered throughout an organization. Ethics training can help organizational leaders achieve consensus on how to address difficult situations they encounter and how they will hold other employees accountable for their behaviors.

Middle managers and supervisors deserve special attention for ethics training. Direct supervisors have the most immediate impact on the ethics of subordinates. They model acceptable behaviors and determine which performance behaviors to praise and blame. As their job classification suggests, middle-level managers are often stuck in the middle of hierarchical pressures. They are responsible for achieving challenging goals established by upper-level managers using the organization's often limited day-to-day resources. Middle-level managers and supervisors must be receptive to subordinates sharing delicate information about organizational operations and provide feedback that unethical decisions or behaviors will not be tolerated.

Both new and long-term employees need ethics training. Making ethics training part of a new employee's orientation process demonstrates from the outset the importance of ethics to the organization. Conduct a follow-up session six months later to reinforce the crucial role of ethics and explore ethical issues they have experienced at work up to that point.

Long-term employees significantly shape the organization's ethical tone. One long-term employee's denigrating comments about the organization's ethical efforts can undo all the managerial effort at aligning a new employee with the organization's ethics. Train long-term employees to lead ethics training workshops and share stories about how the organization's Code of Ethics was upheld in difficult situations.

Web-Based Ethics Training

Online ethics training programs are easy to implement at minimal cost. According to one survey, companies conduct more than 90 percent of their ethics training through e-learning programs.[15] All new hires at Coors Brewing Company must complete a web-based training module within 90 days of employment.[16] In Illinois, all state employees are required to do web-based ethics training annually.[17]

Web-based training offers a simple method for making employees aware of the most common ethical issues. Software programs provide standardized information about legal requirements and moral expectations. The information can be studied at a pace that matches the employee's learning style. Question-and-answer test formats provide immediate feedback on the knowledge being learned. At EnPro, an industrial products company, employees retake the computerized ethics training program until they achieve a perfect score.

Web-based programs can cover a broad range of issues or focus on one particular topic. All staff members of the U.S. House of Representatives who file financial disclosure statements receive specialized training.[18] Essential ethics questions appear on the House of Representative's website under "Frequently Asked Questions."[19] The questions are organized according to nine general categories: gifts, travel, campaign activity, outside employment and income, financial disclosure, casework, official allowances, staff rights and duties, and official and outside organizations. Staff members working outside Washington, D.C., are also required to attend briefings held by legal counsel.

Complement web-based ethics training programs with facilitator-guided face-to-face interactions and group activities. Web-based training by itself does not address all the nuances and contextual issues associated with ethical dilemmas. Ethics training requires dialogue. The best response to even the most cut-and-dried ethical dilemma can be highly debatable.

For instance, WeComply, a web-based ethics training vendor, provides an ethics scenario in which an employee walks into a coworker's office to discuss a project and sees a sexually explicit image on her computer screen.[20] The only acceptable ethical response, according to WeComply's automated system, is to immediately report the incident to the coworker's supervisor. In an interactive workshop, attendees can discuss whether the WeComply answer is indeed the most ethical option to pursue. Within a culture of trust, some people might want to first address the ethical transgression directly with the coworker. Before bringing in a third party, the employee could ask the coworker if the images violate company policy. Oftentimes the guilty employee has to be told only once. If this does not work, then inform the coworker's supervisor. The WeComply web-based system does not allow room for such questioning or creative thinking.

Another weakness of web-based training is that employees are not pushed out of their ethics comfort zone. Skilled facilitators can guide the discussion to other relevant issues worthy of exploration, point out contradictions, and call on quiet participants to express their views in a safe learning environment. Interactive training workshops can also enhance team building and collegiality.

Similarly, complement facilitator-guided ethics training programs with web-based ethics training. Participants can deepen their understanding of ethical issues through web-based exercises such as researching ethical issues in a particular industry or profession, videos, online discussions, and other creative uses of technology.

The Workshop Facilitator

Facilitating an ethics discussion takes a particular skill. Some employees readily submit to authority and believe it is inappropriate to question those above them in the hierarchy. Other employees enjoy expressing concerns and may be insensitive to the negative impact their words can have. A good facilitator inspires self-learning among the participants by keeping everyone focused on the main issues while being flexible to new issues as they arise.[21] The facilitator can encourage participants to form opinions, analyze and modify their own views, and engage in civil disagreements without offending people holding the opposing view or stifling discussion.

An ideal workshop facilitator is someone the participants trust and has the requisite skills to create a safe learning environment. Initially consider a human resources department staff person. But some employees will not speak honestly in front of a human resources employee, particularly about ethical issues, because they fear that their comments might have a negative impact on performance evaluations and lead to termination.

If this is the case, assign the facilitator role to someone both the direct supervisor and employees trust. Possibilities include an informal leader from within the work unit, someone everyone respects who works in another department, or an outside consultant. The best option may be to train an informal leader from within the work unit who has management potential. This person already has a sense of key ethical issues and can ensure that the discussion is realistic and relevant.

Framing the Training Workshop

Some organizations do not provide ethics training workshops because they believe doing so suggests that their employees are unethical or that the organization has ethical problems. This obstacle can be avoided by recognizing that every person is morally imperfect and that every organization has ethical risks. Present the ethics training in the spirit of ongoing continuous improvement efforts and part of a systematic effort to reinforce the organization's ethical culture.

There is no "one-size-fits-all" ethics training program, yet there are general trends and best practices found among organizations.[22] Offer at least one mandatory ethics training annually. Researchers report that the frequency of training has positive impacts on employee attitudes and behaviors.[23] If attendance is voluntary, the employees who need the training the most may not attend.

Some organizations only want to sponsor one ethics training workshop a year. If this is the case, first consider conducting the "Code of Ethics Employee Assessment" outlined in Exhibit 4.9. Some organizations might find the approach too challenging to undertake for its first ethics training workshop because of the many issues that may be raised. Exhibit 6.1 outlines a more moderate initial ethics training workshop for addressing an important issue during a 90-minute session.

Many employees believe that ethics is "self-evident" until asked to explore a classical ethical dilemma that pits truth versus loyalty, the individual versus community, short term versus long term, or justice versus mercy.[24] Workshop relevancy can be created at the beginning of the workshop with a short quiz about a complex issue—such as what the Code of Conduct says about conflicts of interest—and the results can serve as benchmark data to measure achieving workshop learning objectives.[25] Make the ethics training program content as specific as possible.[26] Target specific behaviors and provide specific examples, but present the material in general terms so as not to offend any specific employee.

Use cases that are relevant to the greatest number of participants. If the attendees are sales personnel, use sales examples; if they are mid-level managers, use mid-level manager examples. Ask participants how they would respond to the situation, and have

---

Exhibit 6.1 Ethics Training Workshop Outline

- CEO or supervisor expresses support for the activity
- Clarify workshop rationale, goals, and objectives
- Present competitive advantages of maintaining an ethical work culture (see Chapter 1)
- Foster awareness of industry, organizational, or work unit ethical issues
- Introduce the organization's Codes of Ethics and Conduct (see Chapter 4)
- Focus on a salient issue or behavior that challenges the Codes of Ethics and Conduct
- Legitimize an ethical decision-making process (see Chapter 5)
- Individually apply the decision-making process to a specific relevant situation
- Discuss the issue in small groups
- Debrief
- Assess and evaluate the workshop for continuous improvement

---

them discuss their answers in small groups. Praise divergent thinking and creative problem solving, but make sure the suggestions are ethically sound. Train participants on how to respond when these particular situations arise in the future.

Ethics Training Options

A wide variety of ethics training workshops can be designed to address ethical issues at the workplace. Exhibit 6.2 summarizes 10 very useful ethics training workshop options. Each workshop option will be discussed in greater detail.

Exhibit 6.2 Ethics Training Workshop Options

1.	*Ethical Culture Assessment*—Assess the extent to which ethics permeates organizational operations, including how well the organization is living up to its Code of Ethics. Praise areas of strength and develop strategies for improving the lowest scoring areas.
2.	*Code of Conduct Analysis*—Create a *Who Wants to be a Millionaire?* or *Jeopardy* quiz show, or dialogue sessions, to raise awareness of Code of Conduct content, code application, and code violation outcomes. Present actual cases of employees, or people in the industry, violating a Code of Conduct, and the punishments they received.
3.	*Typical Behaviors Experience*—Introduce employees to common industry or work task ethical issues.
4.	*Apply the Systematic Rational Ethical Decision-Making Framework*—Provide several real-life situations, along with the seven-question systematic rational ethical decision-making framework, and have participants apply the framework to arrive at a moral conclusion.

(Continued)

	Exhibit 6.2 Ethics Training Workshop Options (*Continued*)
5.	*Create Business Ethics Scenarios for Discussion*—Have employees create ethical scenarios based on their own experiences and discuss them.
6.	*Fraud and Theft Exploration*—Educate employees on how to detect fraud and theft. Brainstorm how these crimes could be committed and recommend preventive control mechanisms.
7.	*Level of Moral Development Analysis*—Measure employee level of moral development using an ethical dilemma and survey instrument.
8.	*Ethics Personality Measures*—Administer surveys that measure personality factors and moral attributes associated with ethical behaviors, such as idealism/relativism, ethical ideology, moral identity, Machiavellianism, and locus of control.
9.	*Benchmark to an Ideal Employee*—Develop a profile of an "ideal employee" and put into a survey format. Then have employees assess themselves to this ideal, praise the good, analyze shortcomings, and develop strategies for capitalizing on the strengths and transforming weaknesses into strengths.
10.	*Work as a Calling*—Reflect on making job tasks enjoyable and meaningful experiences.

Ethical Culture Assessment

Organizations are complex entities. Managers can obtain an overall ethics pulse in an ethics workshop by using ethical culture assessment tools that elicit employee feedback on the ethics of organizational operations.

Annually assessing the organization's ethical performance based on its Code of Ethics offers an opportunity for employees to discuss relevant ethical issues related to work activities. Exhibit 4.9 provides a 10-step process for conducting this workshop. Each employee assesses the organization's ethical performance based on its Code of Ethics. Results are then shared in small groups, successes recognized, and strategies developed for ethical weaknesses.

A different approach is to have employees complete an "ethical culture" survey and discuss the results. Business ethics researchers have designed several surveys that measure an organization's ethical culture. The three most popular measures are the "Corporate Ethical Values," "Ethical Culture," and "Ethical Climate" surveys. For each of these surveys, employees assess descriptive statements about organizational operations using a Likert scale (usually ranging from Strongly Disagree to Strongly Agree). Similar to the Code of Ethics workshop format, have employees independently rate the organization, share results in small groups, and suggest improvement strategies.

The "Corporate Ethical Values" survey is the shortest of these three measurement instruments and focuses on the behavior of managers.[27] The survey consists of five items, such as "Top Management has let it be known that unethical behaviors will not be tolerated" and "In order to succeed in this company it is often necessary to compromise one's ethics."

The "Ethical Culture" survey consists of nine descriptive items (see Exhibit 6.3). Most, but not all, of the survey items are concerned about the behaviors of top managers.[28]

Exhibit 6.3 Ethical Culture Survey

Instructions: Please use the 1 to 5 scale below to assess how well each of the following statements describes your organization. The more honest you are the more helpful the information we will receive.

1=Strongly Disagree; 2=Disagree; 3=Neither Agree nor Disagree; 4=Agree; 5=Strongly Agree

	SD	D	N	A	SA
Management in this organization disciplines unethical behavior when it occurs.	1	2	3	4	5
Penalties for unethical behavior are strictly enforced in this organization.	1	2	3	4	5
Unethical behavior is punished in this organization.	1	2	3	4	5
The top managers of this organization represent high ethical standards.	1	2	3	4	5
People of integrity are rewarded in this organization.	1	2	3	4	5
Top managers of this organization regularly show that they care about ethics.	1	2	3	4	5
Ethical behavior is the norm in this organization.	1	2	3	4	5
Top managers of this organization guide decision making in an ethical direction.	1	2	3	4	5
Ethical behavior is rewarded in this organization.	1	2	3	4	5
Add the nine scores:					

The "Ethical Climate" survey offers a broad-based assessment of ethical behavior within the organization.[29] The 37-item survey measures ethics code awareness, ethical decision-making processes, ethical resources, informal ethical norms, and ethical leadership. Items include "I have read the organization's ethics code," "When faced with making a decision that has an ethical implication, I feel I can discuss the matter with my immediate supervisor," and the reverse score item "If I reported a colleague for an ethical violation, there would be retaliation against me."

Two other organization-wide ethical assessment survey instruments can be very helpful. The SAIP Institute at the University of St. Thomas developed a survey instrument based on the Caux Round Table Principles for Business and modeled after the Baldrige National Quality Program.[30] The "Self-Assessment and Improvement Process (SAIP)" is available in three versions, each with additional assessment items. An eInsight Ethics quiz using the SAIP survey is available online.[31] Survey scores are compared against industry peers and improvement suggestions offered. Sample items include "Does your organization have an identified set of core values?" "How honest and respectful are you with your customers?" and "How do you treat your suppliers/vendors?"

The Institute for Local Government and the International City/County Management Association (ICMA) developed an ethical culture assessment tool for municipal and county governments.[32] The assessment instrument measures employee expectations, management attitudes and behaviors, and elected officials' attitudes and behaviors. Sample items are "I am expected to treat everyone who comes before the agency equally, regardless of personal or political connections" and "Executives (or elected officials) refuse to accept gifts and/or special treatment from those with business before my agency."

Code of Conduct Analysis

Many employees are not familiar with the intricate details found in most Codes of Conduct. New hires, in particular, are unlikely to know the complexities associated with using company assets, conflicts of interest, regulatory laws, and implications of failing to report unethical behavior. Workshops can be designed to raise awareness about code content, how to apply the code in specific situations, and the personal ramifications of code violations.

Code of Conduct Content

A Code of Conduct can be long and complicated. Enron's Code of Ethics fit on a business card, but its Code of Conduct exceeded 60 pages.[33] The ethics training workshop facilitator can use a game format to engage the minds of employees when educating them about Code of Conduct content. *Jeopardy* and *Who Wants to Be a Millionaire?* offer two television game show formats that are a fun way to raise awareness.

In *Jeopardy*, three contestants compete to be the first person to provide the correct response.[34] The game board consists of six columns, each representing a different topic. The five rows contain answers that escalate in difficulty and monetary value. If the contestant provides the wrong question, the monetary amount is deducted from previous winnings. Whoever has the highest monetary earnings at the end of the game wins a prize. In this modified version of *Jeopardy*, insert questions about the Code of Conduct at the intersection of each row and column and challenge the workshop participants to provide the correct answer. Allow attendees time to discuss each answer as needed.

Lubrizol, a specialty chemical manufacturer, developed an ethics training game modeled after *Who Wants to Be a Millionaire?* to address different employee learning styles.[35] In *Who Wants to Be a Millionaire?*, teams of workshop participants compete to answer successively difficult questions.[36] The questions can be either "fill in the blank" or multiple choice. Begin with a simple question, such as:

Who is the organization's ethics officer?

Then for the next round have the facilitator ask a more difficult question of higher monetary value, such as:

Which one of the following is an appropriate reason for rejecting a job applicant: (A) age, (B) religion, (C) gender, (D) physical disability, or (E) inability to perform the required task?

Applying the Code of Conduct to Specific Situations

Coca-Cola's ethics training includes reviewing the company's Code of Business Conduct and determining whether several real-life scenarios are in accordance with, or violate, the code.[37] Employees doing this exercise realize the complexity, difficulty, and necessity of applying the code.

Coca-Cola's Code of Business Conduct, and one scenario and correct answer, appear in the "Best Practice in Use" exhibit. This format teaches employees about previous disciplinary actions taken by the organization. These types of training activities reinforce the serious ramifications of unethical behaviors.

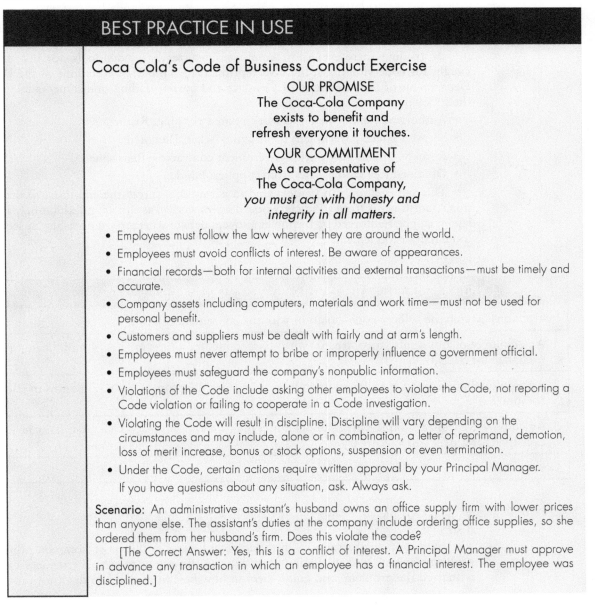

BEST PRACTICE IN USE

Coca Cola's Code of Business Conduct Exercise

OUR PROMISE
The Coca-Cola Company
exists to benefit and
refresh everyone it touches.

YOUR COMMITMENT
As a representative of
The Coca-Cola Company,
*you must act with honesty and
integrity in all matters.*

- Employees must follow the law wherever they are around the world.
- Employees must avoid conflicts of interest. Be aware of appearances.
- Financial records—both for internal activities and external transactions—must be timely and accurate.
- Company assets including computers, materials and work time—must not be used for personal benefit.
- Customers and suppliers must be dealt with fairly and at arm's length.
- Employees must never attempt to bribe or improperly influence a government official.
- Employees must safeguard the company's nonpublic information.
- Violations of the Code include asking other employees to violate the Code, not reporting a Code violation or failing to cooperate in a Code investigation.
- Violating the Code will result in discipline. Discipline will vary depending on the circumstances and may include, alone or in combination, a letter of reprimand, demotion, loss of merit increase, bonus or stock options, suspension or even termination.
- Under the Code, certain actions require written approval by your Principal Manager.

  If you have questions about any situation, ask. Always ask.

Scenario: An administrative assistant's husband owns an office supply firm with lower prices than anyone else. The assistant's duties at the company include ordering office supplies, so she ordered them from her husband's firm. Does this violate the code?

[The Correct Answer: Yes, this is a conflict of interest. A Principal Manager must approve in advance any transaction in which an employee has a financial interest. The employee was disciplined.]

Outcome of Code of Conduct Violations

Employees may cynically believe that people who violate the organization's Codes of Ethics and Conduct are neither caught nor punished. The facilitator can design a workshop educating employees about the types of unethical activities that have previously occurred within the organization or industry, and how the guilty person was punished.

The U.S. Department of Defense maintains an ongoing list of ethical violations and corresponding punishments for use in an ethics training program.[38] A short description of the unethical behavior is followed by the specific code being violated and the assessed punishment. Categories in the September 2007 report include abuse of position, bribery, credit card abuse, fraud, gifts, travel violations, and misuse of government resources and personnel.

By reading these scenarios, employees realize that individuals are not only caught for code violations, but also reprimanded. Employee violations of the U.S. Department of Defense Code of Conduct and corresponding punishments include the following:

- Authorized purchase of non-work-related clothing: Reassigned
- Showed police government ID to avoid ticket: Demoted
- Romantic relationship with government contractor: Reassigned
- Obtained free auto repairs from supplier: Fired

This information can be delivered in a way that forces the employee to determine punishments from a judiciary board's perspective, as shown in Exhibit 6.4. The lesson can be reinforced by having employees debate whether the punishment seems too harsh or too lenient.

Exhibit 6.4 Match the Bribe to the Penalty Exercise	
Instructions: Match the bribery code violation with the jail sentence	
1. An employee recommended a contractor who charged inflated prices in exchange for $115,000.	A. 4 months in jail
2. An employee approved a supplier contract in exchange for a laptop computer.	B. 7 months in jail
3. An employee enrolled several Korean pilots into a flight school in exchange for a paid trip to Korea.	C. 46 months in jail
Correct Answers: 1: C 2: B 3: A	

Typical Behaviors Experienced

The workshop facilitator can introduce employees to the most common ethical problems experienced in the industry, explore the extent to which attendees have witnessed the problem, and guide them in how best to respond to the most prominent issues.

Lying to managers, employee theft, discrimination, and sexual harassment have long been ethical problems at the workplace. New products and technologies, such as derivatives, may raise new ethical issues. Nonetheless, the general pattern of unethical behavior—a seller privy to inside information misleads customers—remains similar.

For instance, in 1989 property and casualty insurance underwriters rated 32 issues in terms of the extent that they were a problem.[39] The same survey was conducted in 1999. During the course of a decade, the top two issues remained the same: (1) lack of knowledge or skills to competently perform one's duties and (2) failure to identify the customer's needs and recommend products and services that meet those needs. Two of the next three issues were also the same.

Lists of common ethical issues that can be used in a workshop are available on many industry association websites or in academic textbooks and relevant journal/magazine articles. Among the ethics resources on the AICPA website is a short quiz on auditor independence, a common problem that challenges personal integrity.[40] As discussed in Chapter 4, Professor Kevin Wooten developed a typology of human resource ethical issues based on five ethical issues that can occur in eight different functions (staffing, compensation, appraisals, etc.).[41] HR personnel can rate how often they or their coworkers experienced, or have been pressured to perform, the unethical behavior.

Let's Build a Building

Union Subcontractors

Your company is involved in two major construction projects, one for renovating a building in a large metropolitan area and the other for a new building in a rural area. The construction industry in the metropolitan area is dominated by unions, and all of your renovation labor is being performed by union workers.

You have chosen a general contractor for your new building in the rural area based on competitive bids. The general contractor uses primarily nonunion subcontractors, which substantially lowers costs because nonunion workers have lower labor rates and fewer employee benefits.

The president of the plumbers union working on the renovation project in the metropolitan area has been closely following the evolution of your new rural project. He strongly suggests that you use a union plumber on your new rural area building. This will provide more jobs for union workers.

When the general contractor receives the plumbing bids for the new rural building, the lowest bid from a union plumbing subcontractor is $120,000. The lowest bid from a nonunion plumbing subcontractor is $70,000, which is $50,000 lower than the union plumber bid. The general contractor shares this information with you and recommends using the nonunion plumbing subcontractor because it was a fair and open bidding process.

You share the bid information with the president of the plumbers union. He offers to split the difference and have the union write you a $25,000 check, and not a penny more, to help offset the difference between the union and nonunion subcontractor bids if you agree to hire the union plumbing subcontractor.

In addition, the union president threatens to initiate a work slowdown on the metropolitan area building renovation project, and to picket your new rural building job site with signs claiming you are un-American for not employing union plumbers on the new job. These are not empty threats. His union has successfully used these tactics on some companies.

What would you do? Would you

1. Insist that the rural building general contractor hire unionized plumbers?

2. Insist that the rural building general contractor accept the low bid from the nonunionized plumbers?

Why?

Apply the Systematic Rational Ethical Decision-Making Framework

This training workshop teaches employees how to apply the systematic rational ethical decision-making framework to particular situations. As discussed in Chapter 5, people usually rely on their moral intuitions when ethical issues arise. Sometimes ethical intuitions are inadequate or incorrect and a more rational and systematic approach is necessary. The six-step facilitation process in Exhibit 6.5 is aimed at maximizing interactive dialogue.

Exhibit 6.5 Facilitating an Ethics Dialogue Workshop
Step 1: Distribute the seven-question systematic rational ethical decision-making framework and review it using a sample business problem.
Step 2: Distribute a real-life situation to workshop participants, read it out loud, and have participants apply the systematic rational ethical decision-making framework to derive a moral conclusion that supports one of the decision options.
Step 3: Count the votes for each recommendation.
Step 4: Develop position rationale in small groups.
Step 5: Empower the minority position and challenge the majority position.
Step 6: Reach a conclusion.

Have the facilitator distribute and review the critical thinking decision-making process table that appears in Chapter 5 (see Exhibit 5.11). Next, distribute a real-life ethical dilemma and read it out loud. Some participants will want to choose a response that is not provided. For the sake of conciseness, provide a reason why the newly proposed option is not possible. Then have workshop participants write answers to the seven systematic rational ethical decision-making framework questions, summarize the strengths and weaknesses of each option, circle the decision option they would choose, write one sentence describing why that option is the best answer, and then explain how the weaknesses associated with the chosen option could be managed.

Tips and Techniques
Requiring Written Response to Ethical Dilemmas A written answer to an ethical dilemma typically fosters greater reflection than simply stating a verbal opinion. A written answer • Commits the person to a particular decision option • Prevents employees from changing their decision based on how others vote • Provides the facilitator with a hook to involve a quiet participant ("Could you please read your written answer to the workshop?") • Establishes an initial data point that can be compared to an employee's belief at the end of the workshop

Two people choosing the same option may disagree as to why that is the right choice. With ethics, why an option is chosen is more revealing than which action is chosen.

As noted in Step 3, have the facilitator record how many employees voted for each decision option. By publicly tallying the votes, employees quickly learn that not everyone agrees with them. An evenly divided vote is a sign of a well-written ethical dilemma.

Next, put workshop attendees on teams based on common responses. Enhance the learning experience and discussion by forming teams consisting of three to five employees. If six people choose the same option, divide them into two teams of three employees each. Have each person read his or her one-sentence "Why?" answer to the other team members. If different justifications are provided, have the team prioritize them. Then have the team discuss why the options chosen by the other teams are less desirable. Assign one team member the role of a devil's advocate who argues on behalf of the other options. This enables the team to develop more thoughtful responses as to what is wrong with the opposing views.

Choose the team with the minority viewpoint to come to the front of the workshop and present its perspective first. If a team with the majority opinion speaks first, those holding a minority view may be so overwhelmed that they do not want to express a contrary opinion, particularly if members of the majority view team have organizational authority. Any team can present first if workshop teams are evenly divided among the available options.

Then have participants go back into their respective teams and develop an answer that addresses all of the concerns expressed. The team can develop a win-win situation that integrates all views expressed or choose one option over another, but this time with a more thorough understanding and response to opposing perspectives. Choose one team to share its final decision and poll the other workshop participants to see how many agree.

The business ethics literature and Internet websites have many vignettes participants can examine. Some vignettes are just one or two sentences long and open ended, such as the following: What would you do if a manager promoted a loyal, but incompetent, friend over a better qualified person with whom he had no close ties?[42] Many vignettes, such as those available on the Institute for Global Ethics website, ask participants to choose between two or three likely responses.[43] Some vignettes offer three potential responses and rank them according to ethical preferences,[44] and others recommend an appropriate ethical response.[45]

Vignettes are available for specific professions, such as information technology,[46] accounting,[47] sports management,[48] and government employees[49] or are directly linked to Code of Conduct issues.[50] John Weber has produced a set of sales personnel vignettes for each of the 10 stages in the "selling model" (identifying opportunities, stimulating interest, negotiations, etc.).[51] Each vignette is followed by a series of questions, such as the following: Discuss whether the amount of a gift, or the timing of a gift, can influence whether a gift from a supplier compromises integrity.

Cisco Systems, the electronic technology multinational corporation, offers an approach for encouraging discussion and reaction to an ethical dilemma based on the popular television show *American Idol*.[52] Several workshop participants provide their answers to a panel of judges. Each judge critiques each answer. The judges praise what they like best about the answer and offer constructive criticisms for improvement. After hearing the panel of experts, the remaining workshop participants vote on which of the contestants provided the best answer.

Create Business Ethics Scenarios for Discussion

The most meaningful ethical issues to explore are those employees observe, experience, or hear about while employed either in their current organization or for a previous employer. The facilitator can help employees develop written scenarios about these ethical issues using the instructions in Exhibit 6.6 and share them with others. Another source for real-life ethical dilemmas occurs when an employee hears one of the 10 common rationalizations for ethical hazards in Exhibit 5.12. Emphasize the importance of anonymity when writing the dilemma. The point of writing the dilemma is to highlight difficult issues that arise at work, not to embarrass anyone.

Exhibit 6.6 Ethical Dilemma Narrative Exercise

As employees, you have experienced or observed many ethical dilemmas. Write a *one- or two-paragraph* ethical dilemma about an experience that challenged your understanding about business ethics. Three ways that can help you arrive at an issue follow:

1. Describe an incident at work that challenged your conscience.

2. Describe an incident at work that seemed disrespectful toward owners, customers, managers, employees, suppliers, community or the natural environment (violated a code of ethics).

3. Describe an incident at work that seemed to be a conflict of interest, misuse of assets, violated confidentiality, or violated a law/regulation (violated a code of conduct).

In order to preserve anonymity, *change references to specific people and places.*

• Begin the first sentence with "You are the (state the job title of the key person facing the ethical dilemma, i.e. accounting manager)."

• Describe the dilemma (context, concerns, conflict) and clarify both sides of the issue (other people need to understand why the unethical option was a reasonable thing for the decision maker to pursue).

• Reach the key decision point, and then ask "What would you do?" followed by several possible action options, such as (a) notify X or (b) do nothing.

You will then read your dilemma in a small group and ask others what action option they would pursue if they were the decision maker facing the dilemma.

Limit the write-up to one page, and the decision options to two or three responses. Otherwise, the ensuing discussion can become difficult to manage. Participants can further explore these dilemmas using the directions outlined in Exhibit 6.5, beginning with each participant independently choosing among the available response options. This workshop can also serve as a team-building activity.

Provide an example of an ethical dilemma narrative to help participants with the writing process, one that contains an ethical lesson the manager wants the workshop participants to learn or reinforce. The "sick leave" scenario in Exhibit 6.7 is worthwhile because it represents an issue common across industries.

Exhibit 6.7 "Sick Leave" Ethical Dilemma Narrative

Sick Leave?

You supervise 10 employees. Kim, the best performer, called in sick today with a very high fever. You learn from a very trustworthy subordinate whom Kim is meeting for lunch that Kim is not actually sick. Instead, Kim is taking a "mental health" day and just wanted some unscheduled time off from work. The company's sick leave policy does not allow for mental health days. You suspect that Kim might do this once or twice a year, within the allowable sick day allocation. Allowing Kim to take a "mental health" day off when not sick can damage employee morale by creating a double standard, one for Kim and one for everyone else.

What would you do? Would you

1. Demand that Kim work an extra day without pay to make up for the missed workday?

2. Just give Kim a warning?

3. Do nothing?

Why?

The employee-created real-life scenarios can be used in future "Apply the Systematic Rational Ethical Decision-Making Framework" workshops and by the human resources department as part of the interview process to determine the ethics of potential job candidates (see Chapter 3).

Fraud and Theft Exploration

As discussed in Chapter 1, approximately 60 percent of employees have stolen from their employers.[53] According to the Association of Certified Fraud Examiners (ACFE), companies lose an estimated 5 percent of their annual revenue to fraud.[54]

The terms *theft*, *fraud*, and *embezzlement* are interrelated. Theft refers to taking someone's property without their permission. Fraud is the use of one's occupation for personal enrichment through the deliberate misuse or misapplication of the employing organization's resources or assets. Embezzlement is a particular type of theft and fraud whereby an employee steals money from his or her employer.

Frauds occur in many types of organizations, including small businesses, large corporations, nonprofits, government agencies, and churches. Amounts can range from a few dollars stolen from the petty cash drawer to the $50 billion Bernie Madoff stole from investors. The three most common forms of embezzlement are employees writing fraudulent checks that they or their friends cash, taking money from cash revenues, and processing fraudulent invoices.[55]

Accounting frauds by public companies are very troubling because investors rely on auditors to convey truthful information. The Government Accounting Office (GAO) identified 919 financial statement restatements announced by 845 public companies between January 1, 1997, and June 30, 2002, to correct previous material misstatements of financial results.[56] These companies represented approximately 10 percent of all public companies listed on the New York Stock Exchange, Amex, and NASDAQ. There are legitimate reasons for restating financial statements, though sometimes this is necessary due to accountants and executives manipulating earnings. In either case, the restatement announcements resulted in a $100 billion loss in market capitalization borne by shareholders.

Some employee frauds can be simple—submitting falsified receipts—whereas others are more complex. For instance, one case involved cooperation among a real estate agent, home buyers, a tax preparer, and a bank loan officer. A potential home buyer contacted the real estate agent about home availabilities. The real estate agent contacted the bank loan officer to determine how much income the borrower needed to obtain a loan. If the potential buyer's income was insufficient, the tax preparer falsified the buyer's tax return by inflating income to make up the necessary difference. The borrower got the home, the real estate agent earned a commission for selling the home, the bank loan officer earned a commission for selling the loan, and the tax return preparer received payment from the borrower for the fake tax return. Fifty fraudulent mortgage loans worth more than $8 million over a two-year period were disbursed before the scam was discovered.[57]

According to the ACFE 2008 survey, the average fraud lasts 18 months before being detected. The three most common sources of fraud detection are tips (46 percent), accidental findings (20 percent), and internal audits (19 percent).[58] Employees are by far the primary source of tips (57 percent) followed by customers (17 percent).

Employee workshops on fraud detection are a disincentive for those considering committing a fraud and can help detect frauds as soon as they occur. Exhibit 6.8 outlines a fraud workshop.[59] Participants explore specific cases of fraud and review best practices in fraud and embezzlement detection.[60]

Exhibit 6.8 Antifraud Education Program

- Introduction to fraud—a short primer on fraud and why it is important for employees to learn about it
- Common ways that fraud can be committed at a company's place of business
- Discuss organization areas particularly vulnerable to fraud
- How fraud is detected—what to look for and what constitutes suspicious behavior
- How to report fraud—whom to report the information to, anonymous reporting methods
- What is done with tips and frauds—how tips are evaluated and the follow-up steps
- How the identity of the person who reported the suspected fraud is protected

---

Employees may know easy ways frauds can be committed. The workshop facilitator can also have employees independently respond to the following two questions, discuss their answers in small groups, and then submit recommendations to managers:

1. How can an employee steal money, products, or property from the organization?
2. What control mechanisms can be put in place to make sure this does not happen?

Level of Moral Development Analysis

Ethics training can help employees better understand their own ethical profile. One of the most important ethics measures—level of moral development—remains an elusive concept to measure. Lawrence Kohlberg and his colleagues developed a "Moral Judgment Interview" (MJI) instrument, a 45-minute semi-structured interview that involves coding responses to an individual's verbal response to three hypothetical ethical dilemmas. A major virtue of MJI is that respondents express their own moral reasons for justifying a particular action. MJI, however, is not practical for an HR department because of the complicated, and time consuming, 24-step coding procedure. Kohlberg's scoring manual numbers more than 800 pages.[61]

James Rest, a professor of educational psychology, simplified the scoring process tremendously by developing the Defining Issues Test (DIT), a multiple-choice moral reasoning survey instrument, consisting of 6 one-paragraph hypothetical ethical dilemmas that can be group administered and computer scored.[62] The respondent chooses a preferred behavior and then evaluates a list of already provided reasons for justifying such action.[63] Multiple ethical dilemmas are provided to determine consistency or trends in the individual's reasoning process. The copyrighted DIT-2 dilemmas and scoring system are available through the Center for the Study of Ethical Development.[64]

William Boyce and Larry Jensen developed a Moral Content Test (MCT) based on Kohlberg's ethical dilemmas.[65] Their questionnaire consists of six dilemmas followed by ten reasons justifying the action. Each reason is rated on a 1 to 5 scale in terms of importance and then the four most important reasons are ranked. Each reason represents egoism, utilitarianism, or deontology. The ranking of each ethical theory is inserted into a chart and then the totals are accumulated for the six ethical dilemmas to determine a pattern in moral reasoning.

Other moral reasoning instruments workshop facilitators can use include Linda Thorne's four auditing dilemmas,[66] a Managerial Moral Judgment Test (MMJT) created by Greg Loviscky, Linda Trevino, and Rick Jacobs consisting of six business-related ethical dilemmas,[67] and the Moral Reasoning Inventory (MRI) developed by James Weber and Elaine McGivern consisting of two ethical dilemmas about responding to an unethical boss.[68]

Ethics Personality Measures

A variety of ethics and personality measures linked with ethical attitudes, decision making, and behaviors can serve as the focus of an ethics training workshop. Three of these measures—conscientiousness, organizational citizenship behavior, and social dominance orientation—were summarized in Chapter 3 for their usefulness during the hiring phase.

Following are descriptions of 11 other personality measures associated with ethics. For instance, researchers report that moral identity scores are related to prosocial behaviors at work,[69] and expedient ethical ideology scores are related to antisocial activities.[70] People with a strong internal, compared to external, locus of control exhibit more ethical behavior and are better able to resist coercion, thus less susceptible to pressure from unethical bullies.[71]

The workshop facilitator can distribute any of the surveys described next—along with the surveys measuring conscientiousness, organizational citizenship behavior, and social dominance orientation. Most of the surveys are assessed with a Likert scale that indicates the extent to which the person agrees or disagrees with a set of descriptive statements. After employees complete and score the survey, the results can be discussed in terms of employee self-understanding, benchmarking continuous improvement, or enhancing understanding among coworkers.

Idealism/Relativism measures whether a person tends to be an "idealist" or "relativist" when responding to an ethical dilemma.[72] The 20-item survey consists of two 10-item factors (idealism and relativism). Sample items are "A person should make certain that his/her actions never intentionally harm another person, even to a small degree" and "What is ethical varies from one situation and society to another."

Ethical Ideology measures whether a person tends to be "principled" (deontology) or "expedient" (relativism) when responding to an ethical dilemma.[73] The 18-item survey includes statements such as "Integrity is more important than financial gain," and "Lying is sometimes necessary to accomplish important, worthwhile goals" (reverse scored). Higher scores represent a greater degree of principled ideology and lower scores a greater degree of an expedient ideology.

Moral Identity measures whether a person internalizes moral character traits (internationalization) and projects them to others (symbolization).[74] Survey participants read a list of 9 moral character traits (e.g., caring, compassionate, fair) and then answer a 10-item survey consisting of two 5-item factors (internalization and symbolization). Sample items are "Being someone who has these characteristics is an important part of who I am," and "I am actively involved in activites that communicate to others that I have these characteristics."

Moral Courage measures whether a person exercises moral principles.[75] The 15-item survey consists of five 3-item factors (moral agency, multiple values, endurance of threats, going beyond compliance, and moral goals). Sample items are "I am the type of person who is unfailing when it comes to doing the right thing at work," and "I think about my motives when achieving the mission to ensure they are based upon moral ends."

Empathy measures a person's emotional reaction to the experiences of another person.[76] The 28-item survey consists of four 7-item factors (perspective taking, emphatic concern, personal distress, fantasy). Sample items are "Before criticizing somebody, I try to imagine how I would feel if I were in their place," and "When I see someone being taken advantage of, I feel kind of protective toward them."

Altruism measures whether a person engages in altruistic behaviors.[77] Survey participants evaluate the extent to which they have performed a list of 20 behaviors. Sample items are "I have donated blood," "I have done volunteer work for a charity," and "I have offered to help a handicapped or elderly stranger across a street."

Trust measures whether a person is willing to be vulnerable in supervisor interactions.[78] A 7-item survey consist of items such as "If my supervisor asked why a problem occurred, I would speak freely even if I were partly to blame," and "My supervisor keeps my interests in mind when making decisions."

Ethical Self-Efficacy measures whether a person believes he or she can successfully perform an ethical behavior.[79] A 12-item survey consists of three factors (uses and keeps computer self-efficacy, distribution self-efficacy, and persuasion self-efficacy). Sample items are "When you badly need a computer program but do not have time to purchase a copy, how confident are you to refuse to use an illegal copy of that software," and "If you see colleagues using an illegal copy of a computer software program, how confident are you to try to dissuade them from using it."[80]

Machiavellianism measures whether a person identifies with "the ends justify the means" moral thinking.[81] The 20-item survey consists of items such as "It is hard to get ahead without cutting corners here and there," "It is wise to flatter important people," and "Most people are brave."

Locus of Control measures whether a person believes she or he controls (internal), or is controled by (extenal), events in life.[82] The 30-item survey consists of two 15-item factors (internal and external locus of control). Sample items are "If somebody works hard he or she will be successful," and "When I do something wrong there is very little I can do afterwards to make it right."

Life Regard measures whether a person values living a meaningful life (framework) and whether this desire is being fulfilled (fulfillment).[83] The 28-item survey consists of two 14-item factors (framework and fulfillment). Sample items are "I have a clear idea of what I'd like to do with my life," and "When I look at my life I feel the satisfaction of really having worked to accomplish something."

Benchmark to an Ideal Employee

Employees need to know in advance what managers expect of them. Managers usually have an image about how an ideal subordinate behaves. The manager's image might not match the image subordinates possess.

Have each manager independently develop a list of behavioral attributes an ideal employee would possess, such as keeping promises or continually learning best practices. Share these lists with other managers in small groups and combine similar items under the same heading, such as customer relations. Each manager can choose the categories and behavioral items of an ideal employee that are most relevant to the manager's work unit.

Then present the composite profile of an ideal employee to subordinates for the purposes of self-assessment feedback. Subordinates can benchmark themselves to the ideal employee, praise their strongest qualities, analyze shortcomings, and develop strategies for capitalizing on strengths and transforming weaknesses into strengths. This can be done individually or as a small group activity with constructive feedback and suggestions. The ideal employee profile can become part of the annual performance appraisal analysis and tied to merit raises.

Exhibit 6.9 provides an example of an ideal employee self-assessment survey developed and conducted by National Specialty Insurance.[84]

Exhibit 6.9 Qualities of an Ideal Employee Self-Assessment

Instructions: Please use the 1 to 5 scale below to assess how well each of the following statements exemplifies your work performance. The more honest you are the more helpful the information you will receive.

1=*Strongly Disagree;* 2=*Disagree;* 3=*Neither Agree nor Disagree;* 4=*Agree;* 5=*Strongly Agree*

	SD	D	N	A	SA
General Character					
I treat all employees, agents and other business contacts with respect	1	2	3	4	5
I keep my promises	1	2	3	4	5
I hold myself accountable for my actions	1	2	3	4	5
I abide by organizational policies and procedures	1	2	3	4	5
General Character Subtotal: Add the four scores and divide by four:					
Customer Relations					
I know what my customers need and expect	1	2	3	4	5
I have rapport with my customers	1	2	3	4	5
I understand and meet service expectations	1	2	3	4	5
I inform customers when I am not available, when I will return, and to whom their communications can be directed in my absence	1	2	3	4	5
Customer Relations Subtotal: Add the four scores and divide by four:					
Colleague Relations					
I am an active member of my team	1	2	3	4	5
I provide constructive criticism	1	2	3	4	5
I learn best practices from other employees	1	2	3	4	5
I help other employees	1	2	3	4	5
Colleague Relations Subtotal: Add the four scores and divide by four:					
Communication Skills					
I listen actively by providing appropriate and timely responses	1	2	3	4	5
I keep written communications concise and grammatically correct	1	2	3	4	5
I date correspondence and include my name and contact information	1	2	3	4	5

I return telephone messages on the day they are received	1	2	3	4	5
I use the most effective form of communication for specific situations	1	2	3	4	5
Communication Skills Subtotal: Add the five scores and divide by five:					

Work Task Skills

I do my assigned work	1	2	3	4	5
I organize my work and work space for efficient use of my time	1	2	3	4	5
I ask my colleagues for help when I need it	1	2	3	4	5
I am responsive to questions about my work	1	2	3	4	5
I ask for and use feedback	1	2	3	4	5
Work Task Skills Subtotal: Add the five scores and divide by five:					

Continuous Improvement

I am receptive to change	1	2	3	4	5
I identify opportunities to improve my job	1	2	3	4	5
I incorporate improvements into my daily work	1	2	3	4	5
I communication and collaborate with my team to implement improvements	1	2	3	4	5
I disagree when it is likely to promote constructive change	1	2	3	4	5
I set objectives to enhance my professional growth	1	2	3	4	5
I enroll and actively participate in professional development opportunities	1	2	3	4	5
I am prepared to explain how I contribute to the organization	1	2	3	4	5
Continuous Improvement Skills Subtotal: Add the eight scores and divide by eight:					

Company Pride

I actively promote the accomplishments of the organization	1	2	3	4	5
I celebrate my successes and those of the organization	1	2	3	4	5
I volunteer and participate annually in at least one organization activity, function, group outing, etc., that is not directly related to my job	1	2	3	4	5
I volunteer annually for at least one community activity	1	2	3	4	5
Company Pride Skills Subtotal: Add the four scores and divide by four:					

Work as a Calling

Every job can be framed in terms of a calling or vocation.[85] A calling cannot be projected onto subordinates; it must be determined from within each employee. Some people feel called to market products that improve the quality of life; others feel called to be administrative assistants whose service improves the work unit's performance. No matter what the job task, the end result can be meaningful interactions with customers or coworkers.

In a workshop setting, have employees individually answer the sets of questions in Exhibit 6.10 and discuss their responses in small groups. These discussions can either help employees frame their daily job tasks as something that has a positive impact on the lives of others or remind them of their original purpose for choosing a particular career or job path.

Exhibit 6.10 Work as a Calling
When did you first feel drawn to the kind of work you are doing? • What did it feel like? • Has this feeling increased or decreased over the years? • How can this feeling be regenerated?
Do you experience joy in your work? • When and under what circumstances? • How often do you experience this? • How does this joy relate to difficulties associated with your work?
Do others experience joy as a result of your work? • Directly? • Indirectly? • How can this experience of joy be increased?
What do you learn at work? • In what ways is work a learning experience for you? • In what ways is work a learning experience for others?
How is your work a benefit to future generations?
If you were to quit work today, what difference would it make to • Your personal or spiritual growth? • The personal or spiritual growth of your work colleagues?

Assessing the Ethics Training Workshops

How do you know if the ethics training has been effective? Similar to all types of workplace training, managers need to assess the effectiveness of ethics training workshops. Assessment is a systemic collection, review, and use of information to determine workshop effectiveness. Three primary purposes of assessment are (1) evaluating if the ethics training workshop material presented has been learned by the participants; (2) evaluating if the workshop participant's objectives have been met, and based on this information; (3) providing more effective instruction in the future by building on what worked previously and modifying what didn't work.

In the spirit of continuous improvement, assess the training session at its conclusion to determine if workshop goals and objectives were accomplished. Many ethics training workshops address knowledge, skills, and discussion issues. Participants can be tested at the end of a workshop to ensure that the knowledge has been successfully conveyed. Ethical skills take longer to develop, but specific aspects of the techniques taught in a training workshop can be tested, such as applying the rational ethical decision-making framework to a real-life work-related dilemma.

Keep the assessment tool simple and short for employees and the facilitator. Following are questions that could be asked after a variety of ethics training sessions.[86] The first three questions can be applied to any type of workshop, while the last two questions are workshop specific.

- Were specific real-life situations addressed?
- Were questions raised by participants?
- Did the trainer serve as a coach and facilitator, rather than a lecturer?
- Were participants shown how to address, report, or correct ethical problems?
- Were the situations raised linked back to the Code of Ethics, Code of Conduct, or organizational strategy?

Measuring participant reaction at the workshop's conclusion provides managers with immediate feedback. If important content has been supplied, have participants complete a follow-up test several weeks after the workshop to determine information retention. This can be done with a web-based exam.

Follow-up interviews with the participants and their supervisors can also verify that new skills are being applied. Did the participants implement any action plans developed during the workshop? Did supervisors support, encourage, and reward the participants for applying new skills?

Some workshop topics lend themselves to return-on-investment calculations. For instance, a manager can benchmark the level of employee theft prior to a workshop about employee theft and then gather similar information one year later to determine if any financial benefits can be attributed to the ethics training.

SUMMARY

Many organizations recognize the need to conduct ethics training for employees at all levels of the organization. Web-based ethics training is appealing because of its homogeneity and low costs. However, the best ethics training involves employee dialogue regarding real-life situations experienced at work.

This chapter recommended 10 different ethics training workshops. Offer at least one workshop annually. Employees can contribute to continually improving the organization's ethical performance by praising the good, developing and implementing strategies to overcome weaknesses, and assessing the results.

KEY WORDS

Organizational trust; web-based training; theft; fraud; embezzlement; assessment

CHAPTER QUESTIONS

1. Why is organizational trust so important?

2. How would you design an ethics training program? Who should serve as facilitator?

3. Describe 10 types of ethics training workshop options. Which of these workshop options would you recommend? Why?

4. What are the recommended six steps for facilitating an ethics dialogue workshop?

5. Which personality surveys can employees take to gain a better understanding of ethics at work?

6. How would you assess the success of an ethics training workshop?

In the Real World: Enron

SPE Investments—1997

Ken Lay decided to promote Jeff Skilling to COO, beginning in March 1997. Skilling quickly began planning to succeed Lay as CEO in 2001. With his power extended to other divisions, Skilling inserted loyalists in key executive positions throughout Enron.

Skilling promoted Andy Fastow to vice president of treasury and business funding, with a goal of raising $20 billion a year in capital. All people needing capital would have to cooperate with Fastow's group. If they didn't, Fastow reminded them, he could ruin their careers.

During 1997, Enron still had too much debt on its books and needed cash. Fastow created a new SPE called RADR. The SPE would borrow money to pay Enron $17 million cash for an ownership stake in one of Enron's wind farms. This sale would remove the wind farm's debt from Enron's balance sheet.

Outside investors had profited nicely in Fastow-structured SPEs. Fastow now wanted to invest in the RADR SPE so he could profit too. Enron's Code of Conduct, however, prohibited senior executives from having a financial stake in any organization doing business with Enron. Such business transactions would create a major conflict of interest—would the executive be more concerned about Enron's economic interests or the other business's economic interest?

Fastow approached Michael Kopper, his assistant and protégé, with a way to get around this legally binding stipulation. Fastow's wife could loan Kopper $419,000 to give to his domestic partner to create an investment group called "Friends of Enron," which could then invest in RADR as the independent outside third party. Kopper, in turn, could pay back the loan and distribute RADR profits, by managing the "Friends of Enron" investment group. Kopper could write multiple "gift" checks to Fastow family members below the minimum amount required by the IRS to be reported for tax purposes. Kopper could also donate money to the Fastow Foundation, a tax-exempt Houston charitable organization created and controlled by Andy.

DECISION CHOICE. If your boss, an Enron vice president, instructed you to participate in this plan, would you

1. Support the plan?

2. Risk getting fired for refusing to participate in the plan?

3. Inform CEO Ken Lay about the plan?

4. Notify Arthur Andersen auditors about the plan?

5. Notify the SEC about the plan?

   Why?

ANCILLARY MATERIALS

Websites to Explore

- Ethical Dilemmas for Training
  - Institute for Global Ethics, Ethical Dilemmas, available at http://www.globalethics.org/dilemmas.php.
  - Thomsett International, "Crossing the Line" vignettes, available at http://www.thomsettinternational.com/main/articles/hot/hot_ethics.htm.
- SAIP Institute, eInsight Ethics Quiz, available at http://ethics.jjhill.org/eQuiz_Start.cfm.
- Government Ethics Training
  - Institute for Local Self Government, Ethics Training Materials, available at http://www.cacities.org/resource_files/20383.completeguide.pdf.
  - United States House of Representatives, Code of Conduct training, available at http://ethics.house.gov/Advice/Default.aspx.
  - U.S. Department of Defense, "Encyclopedia of Ethical Failure," September 2007, available at www.dod.mil/dodgc/defense_ethics/dod_oge/Encyclopedia_of_Ethical_Failures_2007_Full_Version.doc.
- Moral Development—Center for the Student of Ethical Development, available at http://www.centerforthestudyofethicaldevelopment.net/.

Best Place to Work Video

- Best Place to Work—Dreamworks, available at http://money.cnn.com/video/fortune/2009/01/21/fortune.bctwf.dreamworks.fortune/.

Business Ethics Issue Video

- "A Dangerous Business," *Frontline,* about worker safety and environmental violations at McWane, Inc.; January 9, 2003, 54 minutes, available at http://www.pbs.org/wgbh/pages/frontline/shows/workplace/view/?utm_campaign=viewpage&utm_medium=grid&utm_source=grid.

TEDTalks Videos

- *Difficult Negotiations:* William Ury, author of *Getting to Yes,* offers a way to create agreement in even the most difficult situations—from family conflict to, perhaps, the Middle East; October 2010, 19 minutes, available at http://www.ted.com/talks/william_ury.html.
- *Democracy and Public Policy Debates:* Democracy thrives on civil debate, Michael Sandel says, and leads a debate over a Supreme Court case (*PGA Tour, Inc. v. Martin*) whose outcome reveals the critical ingredient in justice; February 2010, 20 minutes, available at http://www.ted.com/talks/michael_sandel_the_lost_art_of_democratic_debate.html.

Conversations with Charlie Rose

- A conversation with James Wolfensohn about the World Bank, the future of the world economy and what it means to lead a global life; December 22, 2010, 20 minutes, available at http://www.charlierose.com/view/interview/11370.
- A conversation with John Wood, author of *Leaving Microsoft to Change the World;* December 9, 2010, 15 minutes, available at http://www.charlierose.com/view/interview/11342.

NOTES

1 Sean Valentine and Gary Fleischman, "Ethics Training and Businesspersons' Perceptions of Organizational Ethics," *Journal of Business Ethics,* 52, 4 (2004), 381–390.

2 W. Edwards Deming, "Forward" in John O. Whitney (Ed.), *The Trust Factor* (New York: McGraw-Hill, 1994), p. viii.

3 J. David Lewis and Andrew Weigert, "Trust as a Social Reality," *Social Forces,* 63, 4 (1985), 967–985.

4 F. David Schoorman, Roger C. Mayer, and James H. Davis, "An Integrative Model of Organizational Trust: Past, Present, and Future," *Academy of Management Review,* 32, 2 (2007), 344–354.

5 M. Ronald Buckley, "Ethical Issues in Human Resource Systems," *Human Resource Management Review,* 11, 1/2 (2001), 11–30.

6 Deloise A. Frisque and Judith A. Kolb, "The Effects of an Ethics Training Program on Attitude, Knowledge, and Transfer of Training of Office Professionals: A Treatment- and Control-Group Design," *Human Resource Development Quarterly,* 19, 1 (2008), 35–53.

7 David Salierno, "Ethics Survey Offers Mixed Messages," *Internal Auditor,* 61, 3 (2004), 23–24; Deloitte and *Corporate Board Member Magazine,* "Business Ethics and Compliance in the Sarbanes-Oxley Era," available at www.globalcompliance.com/pdf/BusinessEthicsandComplianceSurvey.pdf, accessed 10/15/10.

8 Jonathan West and Evan M. Berman, "Ethics Training in U.S. Cities," *Public Integrity,* 6, 3 (2004), 189–206.

9 Jane B. Romal and Arlene M. Hibschweiler, "Improving Professional Ethics," *CPA Journal,* 74, 6 (2004), 58–63.

10 Barry Spizer, "Log On for Free Ethics Course," *Commercial Investment Real Estate Journal,* 22, 3 (2004), 4.

11 American Institute of CPAs, "Tools and Aids," available at http://www.aicpa.org/InterestAreas/ProfessionalEthics/Resources/Tools/Pages/default.aspx, accessed 10/15/10.

12 Maggie Cohen, "Union Ethics Training: Building the Legitimacy and Effectiveness of Organized Labor," *WorkingUSA,* 11, 3 (2008), 363–382.

13 Jean Thilmany, "Supporting Ethical Employees," *HRMagazine,* 52, 9 (2007), 105–112.

14 Ronald E. Berenbeim, *Universal Conduct—An Ethics and Compliance Benchmarking Survey,* The Conference Board Report 1393-06-RR (New York: The Conference Board, 2006).

15 Ibid.

16 Samuel Greengard, "Golden Values at Coors," *Workforce Management,* March 2005, 52–53.

17 Thilmany, "Supporting Ethical Employees."

18 Anonymous, "House Offices Must Certify Ethics Training Compliance," *PA Times,* 31, 1 (2008), 13.

19 U.S. House of Representatives, Committee on Standards of Official Conduct, "Frequently Asked Questions," available at http://ethics.house.gov/Advice/Default.aspx, accessed 10/15/10.

20 Vadim Liberman, "How Ethical Are You?" *Across the Board,* 40, 6 (2003), 49–50.

21 John A. Weber, "Business Ethics Training: Insights from Learning Theory," *Journal of Business Ethics,* 70, 1 (2007), 61–85.

22 Leslie E. Sekerka, "Organizational Ethics Education and Training: A Review of Best Practices and Their Application," *International Journal of Training & Development,* 13, 2 (2009), 77–95.

23 Sean Valentine, "Ethics Training, Ethical Context, and Sales and Marketing Professionals' Satisfaction with Supervisors and Coworkers," *Journal of Personal Selling & Sales Management,* 29, 3 (2009), 227–242.

24 Rushworth M. Kidder, *How Good People Make Tough Choices* (New York: William Morrow and Company, 1995), p. 18.

25 Weber, "Business Ethics Training: Insights from Learning Theory."

26 Walter O. Baggett, "7 Criteria for Ethics Assessments," *Internal Auditor,* 64, 1 (2007), 65–69.

27 Shelby D. Hunt, Van R. Wood, and Lawrence B. Chonko, "Corporate Ethical Values and Organizational Commitment in Marketing," *Journal of Marketing,* 53, 3 (1989), 79–90.

28 Linda Klebe Trevino, Kenneth Butterfield, and Donald McCabe, "The Ethical Context in Organizations: Influences on Employee Attitudes and Behaviors," *Business Ethics Quarterly,* 8, 3 (1998), 447–476.

[29] Kathie L. Pelletier and Michelle C. Bligh, "Rebounding from Corruption: Perceptions of Ethics Program Effectiveness in a Public Sector Organization," *Journal of Business Ethics,* 67, 4 (2006), 359–374.

[30] The SAIP Institute, University of St. Thomas, available at http://www.stthomas.edu/business/centers/saip/, accessed 10/15/10.

[31] The Hill Center for Ethical Business Leadership, "eInsight Ethics Quiz," available at http://ethics.jjhill.org/eQuiz_Start.cfm, accessed 10/15/10.

[32] Institute for Local Government, "Ethics," available at http://www.ca-ilg.org/trust, accessed 10/15/10.

[33] Joseph Weber, "The New Ethics Enforcers," *Business Week,* February 13, 2006, 76–77.

[34] Jeopardy website available at www.jeopardy.com, accessed 10/15/10.

[35] Thilmany, "Supporting Ethical Employees."

[36] Who Wants to Be a Millionaire website available at www.millionairetv.com/, accessed 10/15/10.

[37] Steven R. Barth, *Corporate Ethics* (Boston, MA: Aspatore Books, 2003), pp. 102–119.

[38] U.S. Department of Defense, "Encyclopedia of Ethical Failure," September 2007, available at www.dod.mil/dodgc/defense_ethics/dod_oge/Encyclopedia_of_Ethical_Failures_2007_Full_Version.doc, accessed 10/15/10.

[39] Robert W. Cooper and Garry L. Frank, "Key Ethical Issues Facing the Property and Casualty Insurance Industry: Has a Decade Made a Difference?" *CPCU Journal,* 54, 2 (2001), 99–112.

[40] Ellen T. Goria and Edie Yaffe, "Test Your Knowledge of Professional Ethics," *Journal of Accountancy,* October 2002.

[41] Kevin C. Wooten, "Ethical Dilemmas in Human Resource Management: An Application of a Multidimensional Framework, a Unifying Taxonomy, and Applicable Codes," *Human Resource Management Review,* 11, 1 (2001), 159–176.

[42] Justin G. Longenecker, Carlos W. Moore, J. William Petty, Leslie E. Palich, and Joseph A. McKinney, "Ethical Attitudes in Small Businesses and Large Corporations: Theory and Empirical Findings from a Tracking Study Spanning Three Decades," *Journal of Small Business Management,* 44, 2 (2006), 167–183.

[43] Institute for Global Ethics, Ethical Dilemmas, "Right vs. Right," available at http://www.globalethics.org/dilemmas.php, accessed 10/15/10.

[44] Valentine and Fleischman, "Ethics Training and Businesspersons' Perceptions of Organizational Ethics."

[45] Tara Shawyer and John Sennetti, "Measuring Ethical Sensitivity and Evaluation," *Journal of Business Ethics,* 88, 4 (2009), 663–678.

[46] Thomsett International, "Crossing the Line," available at http://www.thomsettinternational.com/main/articles/hot/hot_ethics.htm, accessed 10/15/10.

[47] Linda Thorne, "The Development of Two Measures to Assess Accountants' Prescriptive and Deliberative Moral Reasoning," *Behavioral Research in Accounting,* 12, 1 (2000), 139–169.

[48] Andrew Rudd, Susan Mullane, and Sharon Stoll, "Development of an Instrument to Measure the Moral Judgments of Sport Managers," *Journal of Sport Management,* 24, 1 (2010), 59–82.

[49] Institute for Local Self Government, "Of Cookie Jars and Fishbowls: A Public Official's Guide to Use of Public Resources," available at http://www.cacities.org/resource_files/20383.completeguide.pdf, accessed 10/15/10.

[50] Obeua Persons, "Using a Corporate Code of Ethics to Assess Students' Ethicality: Implications for Business Education," *Journal of Education for Business,* 84, 6 (2009), 357–366.

[51] Weber, "Business Ethics Training."

[52] Luis Ramos, "Outside-the-Box Ethics," *Leadership Excellence,* 26, 4 (2009), 19.

[53] Luis R. Gomez-Mejia, David B. Balkin, and Robert L. Cardy, *Managing Human Resources,* 5th ed. (Upper Saddle River, NJ: Pearson Prentice Hall, 2007).

[54] Association of Certified Fraud Examiners, *ACFE 2008 Report to the Nation on Occupational Fraud & Abuse,* available at www.acfe.com/documents/2008-rttn.pdf, accessed 10/15/10.

[55] W. Steve Albrecht, Conan C. Albrecht, and Chad O. Albrecht, *Fraud Examination,* 2nd ed. (Mason, OH: Thomson Southwestern Publishing, 2006).

[56] U.S. Government Accountability Office (GAO), *Financial Statement Restatements: Trends, Market Impacts, Regulatory Responses, and Remaining Challenges,* October 4, 2002, available at http://www.gao.gov/new.items/d03138.pdf, accessed 10/15/10.

[57] Ed Treleven, "Bank Fraud Case Expanded," *Wisconsin State Journal,* April 9, 2010.

58 Association of Certified Fraud Examiners, *ACFE 2008 Report to the Nation on Occupational Fraud & Abuse*, available at www.acfe.com/documents/2008-rttn.pdf, accessed 10/15/10.

59 Tracy L. Coenen, *Essentials of Corporate Fraud* (Hoboken, NJ: John Wiley & Sons, 2008).

60 Edward J. McMillan, *Policies and Procedures to Prevent Fraud and Embezzlement: Guidance, Internal Controls, and Investigation* (Hoboken, NJ: John Wiley & Sons, 2006).

61 Anne Colby and Lawrence Kohlberg, *The Measurement of Moral Judgment* (New York: Cambridge University Press, 1987).

62 James Rest, *Development in Judging Moral Issues* (Minneapolis: University of Minnesota Press, 1979); James Rest, Darcia Narvaez, Muriel J. Bebeau, and Stephen J. Thoma, *Postconventional Moral Thinking: A Neo-Kohlbergian Approach* (Mahwah, NJ: Lawrence Erlbaum Associates, 1999).

63 Center for the Study of Ethical Development, "Heinz and the Drug," available at http://www.centerforthestudyofethicaldevelopment.net/DIT%20—Sample%20Dilemma.htm, accessed 10/15/10.

64 Center for the Student of Ethical Development website available at http://www.centerforthestudyofethicaldevelopment.net/, accessed 10/15/10.

65 William D. Boyce and Larry Cyril Jensen, *Moral Reasoning: A Psychological-Philosophical Integration* (Lincoln: University of Nebraska Press, 1978).

66 Thorne, "The Development of Two Measures to Assess Accountants' Prescriptive and Deliberative Moral Reasoning."

67 Greg E. Loviscky, Linda K. Trevino, and Rick R. Jacobs, "Assessing Managers' Ethical Decision-Making: An Objective Measure of Managerial Moral Judgment," *Journal of Business Ethics*, 73, 3 (2007), 263–285.

68 James Weber and Elaine McGivern, "A New Methodological Approach for Studying Moral Reasoning Among Managers in Business Settings," *Journal of Business Ethics*, 92, 1 (2010), 149–166.

69 Ruodan Shao, Karl Aquino, and Dan Freeman, "Beyond Moral Reasoning: A Review of Moral Identity Research and Its Implications for Business Ethics," *Business Ethics Quarterly*, 18, 4 (2008), 513–540.

70 Barry R. Schlenker, "Integrity and Character: Implications of Principled and Expedient Ethical Ideologies," *Journal of Social and Clinical Psychology*, 27, 10 (2008), 1078–1125.

71 Linda Klebe Trevino and Stuart A. Youngblood, "Bad Apples in Bad Barrels: A Causal Analysis of Ethical Decision-Making Behavior," *Journal of Applied Psychology*, 75, 4 (1990), 378–385.

72 Donald R. Forsyth, "A Taxonomy of Ethical Ideologies," *Journal of Personality and Social Psychology*, 39, 1 (1980), 175–184.

73 Barry R. Schlenker, Michael F. Weigold, and Kristine A. Schlenker, "What Makes a Hero? The Impact of Integrity on Admiration and Interpersonal Judgment," *Journal of Personality*, 76, 2 (2008), 323–355.

74 Karl Aquino and Americus Reed II, "The Self-Importance of Moral Identity," *Journal of Personality & Social Psychology*, 83, 6 (2002), 1423–1440.

75 Leslie E. Sekerka, Richard P. Bagozzi, and Richard Charnigo, "Facing Ethical Challenges in the Workplace: Conceptualizing and Measuring Professional Moral Courage," *Journal of Business Ethics*, 89, 4 (2009), 565–579.

76 Mark H. Davis, "Measuring Individual Differences in Empathy: Evidence for a Multidimensional Approach," *Journal of Personality and Social Psychology*, 44, 1 (1983), 113–126.

77 J. Philippe Rushton, Roland D. Chrisjohn, and G. Cynthia Fekken, "The Altruistic Personality and the Self-Report Altruism Scale," *Personality and Individual Differences*, 2, 4 (1981), 293–302.

78 F. David Schoorman, Roger C. Mayer, and James H. Davis, "An Integrative Model of Organizational Trust: Past, Present, and Future," *Academy of Management Review*, 32, 2 (2007), 344–354.

79 Albert Bandura, *Self-Efficacy: The Exercise of Control* (New York: Freeman, 1997).

80 Feng-Yang Kuo and Meng-Hsiang Hsu, "Development and Validation of Ethical Computer Self-Efficacy Measure: The Case of Softlifting," *Journal of Business Ethics*, 32, 4 (2001), 299–315.

81 Richard Christie and Florence I. Geis, *Studies in Machiavellianism* (New York: Academic Press, 1970).

82 Julian Rotter, "Generalized Expectancies for Internal Versus External Control of Reinforcements,"

Psychological Monographs, 80, 609 (1966), 1–28; Dorothy Marcic, Joe Seltzer, and Peter Vaill, *Organization Behavior: Experiences and Cases,* 6th ed. (Cincinnati, OH: South-Western, 2001), pp. 17–20.

[83] John Battista and Richard Almond, "The Development of Meaning in Life," *Psychiatry,* 36, 4 (1973), 409–427.

[84] National Specialty Insurance (NSI), a division of West Bend Mutual Insurance Company.

[85] Matthew Fox, *The Reinvention of Work* (San Francisco, CA: HarperCollins, 1995).

[86] Baggett, "7 Criteria for Ethics Assessments."

CHAPTER OUTLINE

7
RESPECTING EMPLOYEE DIVERSITY

What would you do?

Diverse Food Smells

After graduation, you obtain an information technology supervisory position. The six employees in your diversified work unit, four men and two women, work very well together. They enjoy being around one another and teach one another the latest technological changes.

One impressive IT team activity is the shared lunch period. Every noon, for the past two years, the six employees meet in the lunch area, which includes a microwave and stove, to relax and discuss the technology problems encountered earlier in the day. At least twice a week, they cook meals for the group.

You consider yourself lucky when Simar accepts your job offer to join the IT team. He's creative, excelled at the local university, and is fun to be around. Simar, originally from India, initially brings his lunch from home, an assortment of curries consisting of vegetables and onions seasoned with various spices. The other employees occasionally tease Simar about the unique smells of the curry seasonings.

A few weeks ago, Simar began cooking lunch on the communal stove. Late one afternoon, Tom complains to you about what he considers the "foul" smells of the

Indian spices. "It's so bad we're thinking of not eating here anymore," he says. "But then why should we have to eat somewhere else just because of Simar?" You mention the importance of respecting diversity and being tolerant, and Tom walks away feeling awkward.

The next day, Tom, Henry, and Mandy enter your office. "We had so much fun at lunch until you hired Simar," Mandy reminisces. "This used to be such a great place to work. Don't get me wrong. Simar's a great guy and he knows his stuff, but I can't stand the smell of those spices. We're thinking about eating out tomorrow and letting him have the lunch area to himself." Mandy pauses before continuing, "You know that rubs me the wrong way because I don't think we should exclude him. And besides, as I told Tom, even if we did eat out those spice smells will still be in the air when we get back."

You delicately raise the issue with Simar. He gets defensive and accuses the other IT team members of being racist. "Everyone in India loves this food," Simar says. "I'm merely eating what I've always eaten for lunch. And besides, I think some of their food stinks."

What would you do? Would you

1) Allow Simar to continue to cook his curries in the lunch area?

2) Develop a policy stating that certain "smelly" foods cannot be cooked in the lunch area?

3) Ban all cooking in the lunch area?

Why?

Chapter Objectives

After reading this chapter, you will be able to:

- Describe competitive advantages of diversity
- Explain the most common types of workplace discrimination
- Adopt best operational practices for managing diversity
- Successfully implement a diversity initiative
- Facilitate a variety of diversity workshops

Within the mind of each person is a unique set of assumptions about right and wrong behaviors. Also within the mind of each person is a unique set of assumptions about other employees, customers, and suppliers based on their gender, race, ethnicity, religion, or disability. This chapter provides a brief history of population diversity in the United States. Harmful discriminatory employment practices and behaviors led to the need for Title VII of the Civil Rights Act of 1964 and the Equal Employment Opportunity Commission (EEOC). Title VII defines, and the EEOC monitors, illegal types of workplace discrimination.

There are many competitive advantages of appropriately managing diversity. The chapter examines the most common types of workplace discrimination and the best operational practices for enhancing and managing diversity, including a 10-step process for implementing a diversity initiative. Diversity training problems and solutions are examined, and instructions offered for conducting a series of diversity training workshops that increase social group self-awareness, explore specific issues, and help employees manage different communication styles.

Four Dimensions of Diversity

Diversity is a complex concept. Respecting the diverse aspects of people goes beyond the factors that fall under the purview of the EEOC. Every person is diverse in multiple ways. Each aspect of diversity can contribute to improving organizational performance or be the source of detrimental prejudices and stereotypes.

Upon meeting a stranger, it is normal to form opinions about the person based on a multitude of factors, including the person's appearance. Prejudging, stereotyping, and categorizing others are common mechanisms by which people make sense of the world. We are continually inundated by external stimuli and internal thoughts. Patterns emerge, based on our limited experiences, that link particular sets of external stimuli with internal thoughts.

If our experiences with young employees, for instance, demonstrate that they are quick learners but lack practical workplace knowledge, then it is reasonable to prejudge a new young employee as someone who probably is a quick learner and lacks practical workplace knowledge. Nonetheless, each new young employee is different. Our incorrect prejudices could offend a new young employee with appropriate workplace knowledge and result in an inefficient allocation of organizational resources.

Our prejudgments are usually a reaction to a diversity factor. Diversity can be conceptualized in terms of four unique dimensions: permanent, evolving, personality, and organizational (see Exhibit 7.1). Each diversity dimension adds complexity to who we are, how others perceive us, and how we perceive others. The EEOC primarily focuses on permanent dimensions, yet valuing diversity means valuing all four diversity dimensions.

Permanent Dimension

The permanent dimension refers to physical attributes or inclinations people are born with that do not naturally change over time. Human characteristics that are

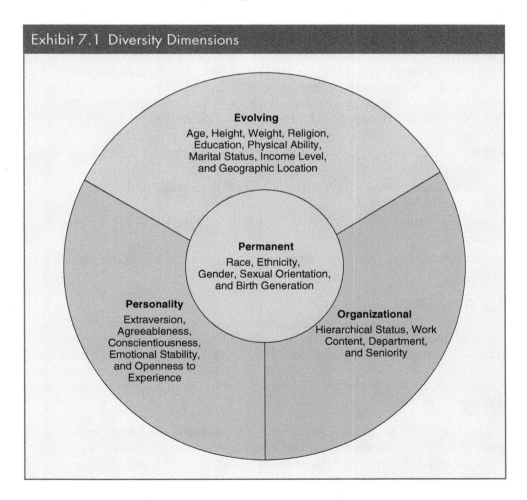

Exhibit 7.1 Diversity Dimensions

Evolving
Age, Height, Weight, Religion, Education, Physical Ability, Marital Status, Income Level, and Geographic Location

Permanent
Race, Ethnicity, Gender, Sexual Orientation, and Birth Generation

Personality
Extraversion, Agreeableness, Conscientiousness, Emotional Stability, and Openness to Experience

Organizational
Hierarchical Status, Work Content, Department, and Seniority

permanent and beyond a person's control include race, ethnicity, gender, sexual orientation, and birth generation. A person born a Caucasian, Italian American, male, heterosexual, baby boomer remains so throughout life. Any of these factors can significantly influence a person's identity and life experiences.

Evolving Dimension

Individuals can be categorized according to evolving characteristics as well as permanent ones. Evolving dimensions include age, height, weight, religion, education, physical ability, marital status, income level, and geographic location. At one point in life, an employee is a young person, and this characteristic may influence how others treat the individual. Later in life, the same person is an older person, and the individual may be treated very differently by others because of the change in age.

Personality Dimension

People can be categorized according to their personality. As discussed in Chapter 3, personality theorists and researchers have reached a general consensus on a "Big Five Personality Model" consisting of five different personality aspects: extraversion, agreeableness, conscientiousness, emotional stability, and openness to experience.[1]

The Myers-Briggs Type Indicator (MBTI) is probably the most popular personality assessment tool used by employers.[2] MBTI provides individual employees, as well as their colleagues and managers, with a better understanding of the employee's personal preferences. MBTI is based on four dimensions, each with a paired continuum:[3]

- Where you get your energy: Introvert (internally) or Extrovert (relationship with others)
- How you learn: Sensor (by understanding procedures) or Intuitive (by understanding the big picture)
- How you make decisions: Thinking (by following logic) or Feeling (by ensuring harmony)
- How you organize your time: Judger (rigidly organized) or Perceiver (flexible)

Organizational Dimension

Employees can also be categorized according to their organizational status. These defining characteristics—which can be either unchanging or evolving—include hierarchical status, work content, department, and seniority. We may prejudge others based on their being a senior manager or a recently hired nonmanagement employee. Others may prejudge us based on our being an accountant, financial analyst, or salesperson.

Every individual can be uniquely characterized according to these four dimensions. Aspects of these four dimensions can unify people based on commonalities or cause friction based on differences. Both unity and division occur in organizations and the broader society.

History of Ethnic and Religious Diversity and Discrimination

When Christopher Columbus arrived on the shores of the Dominican Republic in 1492, the landmass eventually named the United States served as home to an estimated 10 million indigenous people.[4] Population demographics changed dramatically over the next 500 years. In 2008, 307 million people lived in the United States, of which 65.6 percent were Caucasian, 15.4 percent Hispanic, 12.8 percent African American, 4.5 percent Asian, and 1.5 percent two or more races.[5] Only 1.0 percent were indigenous Native Americans.

Population Diversity Growth

The transformation from an indigenous to a nonindigenous population occurred through waves of new immigrants seeking to improve their living conditions, except for African Americans who arrived prior to the Civil War through captivity and enslavement. Each newly arriving immigrant group was met with prejudice and fear from many among the existing population, a new "other" or group of strangers often speaking a different language, with whom inhabitants had to interact.[6]

As discussed in Chapter 5, social group relativism is a predominant ethical theory in society whereby preferences about right and wrong are based on the interests of a person's social group. Columbus's arrival led to a confrontation between social groups. Indigenous people did not welcome Christopher Columbus with open arms, or vice versa. Differences in race, ethnicity, religion, and language contributed to mistrust. Trading goods between the two groups was soon followed by European conquest and enslavement of the indigenous inhabitants with the aid of more powerful military technology.

The success of Italian and Spanish explorers in the "New World" attracted explorers from England, the Netherlands, and France. Each European nationality ruthlessly competed against one another for the best trading posts and settlements, which were hospitable only to settlers from their own country. African slaves arrived to work on plantations, and accounted for 20 percent of the new nation's 3.9 million inhabitants by the time President George Washington gave the first State of the Union address in 1790.

Beginning 1830, the federal government welcomed more British, German, and French immigrants to help settle the expanding nation. These new arrivals were joined by three-quarters of a million poor Irish fleeing the potato famine (1845–1849) and looking for employment and better land. Irish immigrants were discriminated against not only because of their nationality, language, and economic status, but also because of their religion: Roman Catholicism.

Chinese people began arriving in the mid-1800s, drawn by the allure of getting rich from the California Gold Rush and jobs building the transcontinental railroad. They were followed by poverty-stricken Swedes, Norwegians, and Italians. Each ethnic group lived in separate ghettos, clinging to their different languages, religious beliefs, and cultural traditions. The religious mix became more salient with the arrival of more than 2 million Jewish people fleeing religious persecution in Russia and Europe, followed by Muslim Lebanese and Syrians.

The annexation of Texas, New Mexico, and Arizona added many Mexicans to the American ethnic mosaic, and they were joined by Latin Americans, Asians, and Middle Easterners seeking work and political freedom. With the continued increase in Hispanic immigration and low birth rates among Caucasians, the U.S. Census Bureau projects that Caucasians will dip below 50 percent of the population by 2042.[7]

Discriminatory Employment Practices

For nearly two centuries, from 1776 until 1964, Caucasian males primarily employed and serviced people from their own national heritage and religious group, a pattern followed by other racial and ethnic groups. Job openings were filled by family members, relatives, and friends, people who shared a common language. German Protestants, for instance, trusted hiring only German Protestants, and Irish Catholics trusted only Irish Catholics. African Americans and Asian Americans did likewise.

Businesses began to diversify as they grew in size and expanded their markets. Nonetheless, managers tended to hire and promote those employees who shared a common gender, race, ethnicity, or religious heritage. Businesses operated under the employment-at-will doctrine; which allowed employers and employees to end an employment relationship for any reason, or "at will," so long as it did not violate contractual agreements or federal, state, and municipal laws. This doctrine was widely accepted during the industrial revolution and legally codified in an 1884 Tennessee Supreme Court ruling clarifying that an employer can "discharge or retain employees at will for good cause, for no cause, or even for cause morally wrong, without being thereby guilty of legal wrong."[8] As a result, during layoffs, employee dismissals were often predicated on an employee's gender, race, ethnicity, or religious heritage. Title VII of the Civil Rights Act of 1964 made many of these discriminatory hiring, promotion, and firing practices illegal.

The United States has evolved to the point where Barack Obama, an African American born to a Caucasian mother and Kenyan father, won the presidency in 2008, a diversity accomplishment many believed impossible to achieve just a few decades earlier during the late 1960s race riots. Obama's most notable contender for the Democratic Party nomination was a woman, Hilary Clinton, as was the Republican Party's vice presidential nominee, Sarah Palin, then the governor of Alaska.

Illegal (Undocumented) Immigrants

Nonetheless, problems remain. A contentious aspect of local, state, and national law is the treatment of undocumented, or illegal, immigrants. For the working poor and politically oppressed born in other nations, the United States has always represented a land of opportunity and freedom. But when the number of laborers exceeds job availability, anti-immigration sentiments rise due to the decline in wages.

In 1921, the Emergency Quota Act placed limits on the number of immigrants admitted into the United States, which often fluctuates due to labor needs. Ever since then, immigrants have entered the nation illegally to seek employment or unite with their legally immigrated family members. In 2008, an estimated 12 million illegal, sometimes referred to as undocumented, immigrants lived in the United States.[9] Approximately 76 percent of illegal immigrants are Hispanic, mostly from Mexico and Central America.

Illegal immigrants account for 5.4 percent of the national labor force. They typically perform low-skilled and low-paid jobs. California, Arizona, and Nevada have the highest percentage of undocumented laborers, whose children and families have overwhelmed some schools and state and local social services.

The government defines an "alien" as someone belonging to another country who has not acquired United States citizenship. Federal law requires aliens who are 14 years old or older and in the United States for more than 30 days to register with the federal government and maintain registration documents in their possession at all times. In 2010, the Arizona legislature passed a more restrictive state law requiring police who stop aliens for a traffic violation or some other crime to ask for a driver's license or some other state ID. Those without proof of legal status on them may be detained and eventually deported if no legal proof exists.[10]

Self-Categorization

Every employee should feel comfortable at work, and every customer and supplier should feel comfortable doing business with any organization. But that is not always the case. Despite the diversity progress made, discrimination remains a problem requiring managerial attention. Like attracts like, and individuals relate more comfortably with people similar to themselves. Individuals still tend to communicate, collaborate, and associate with those who share some similar feature or characteristic important to the person.

According to self-categorization theory, individuals define themselves in relation to others based on a "self-identity" or "social identity" factor and form binding relationships with people who categorize themselves similarly. Individuals typically self-identify in terms of race, ethnicity, or gender, though a wide range of other categories could take precedence, such as being left-handed or rooting for a particular sports team.[11] Within groups, members may further self-identify based on some factor that differentiates group members.

People usually form group coalitions based on race and ethnicity—characteristics that reflect their family and neighborhood demographics—and then by gender within the race/ethnicity grouping. Caucasians, for instance, tend to associate with Caucasians. Among Caucasians, males tend to associate with males whereas females tend to associate with females. The same is true for African Americans, Hispanics, or Koreans.

Workplace Discrimination

Individuals discriminate all the time. To discriminate means to make a distinction among possible options. Problems arise, however, when dissimilar people are treated as inferior or excluded. Customers and employees who differ from others according to some prominent characteristic—race, gender, ethnicity, age, or religion—often report not being respected by the dominant social group. The first woman, African American, or Muslim hired by an organization must typically overcome negative stereotypes. Workplace segregation can reinforce prejudices toward members of other groups, which contributes to communication breakdowns, high conflict, low morale, reduced productivity, and potential lawsuits.[12] As shown in Exhibit 1.1 in Chapter 1, there were more than 100,000 discrimination cases filed with the EEOC in 2009, and settlements exceeded $440 million.[13]

Two prominent ethical principles must guide decision making when making distinctions among people at the workplace: fairness and respect for others. Fairness refers to making decisions according to rules not based on personal biases, and respect for others refers to treating everyone with dignity.

Managers, for instance, must discriminate among hundreds of job applicants when deciding which person to hire. The decision-making rule used to discriminate among the applicants could be ethical, unethical, legal, or illegal. When differentiating among job candidates or choosing which employee to assign a job task or promote, make sure that the decision-making rule being applied is fair and respectful.

When hiring, it is ethical and legal to discriminate based on previous job experience, potential productivity, and educational level. It is unethical and illegal, however, to discriminate based on "protected class" status, defined as a person's race, color, religion, gender, national origin, age, pregnancy, and physical or mental disabilities. Some state and municipal laws also include sexual orientation—lesbian, gay, bisexual, and transgender people (LGBT)—as a protected class.

Key workplace issues related to gender, race, ethnicity, religion, age, disability, and sexual orientation discrimination are summarized in the following sections. As shown in Exhibit 7.2, the ethics of discriminating against people wearing tattoos has been brought to the attention of both the EEOC and the judicial system.

Exhibit 7.2 Tattoo Discrimination

Decision-making rules that raise ethical concerns are often subject to lawsuits. For instance, approximately 40 percent of people between the ages of 18 and 40 have at least one tattoo.[14] In 2010, Benjamin Amos, a Starbucks store manager, sued the company after the regional office fired him for wearing a tattoo.[15] Amos had the tattoo when hired, and several female employees working in the store had tattoos. Is it ethical to fire an employee for wearing a tattoo, body art, or body piercings? Does an employer have a legal right to do so?

According to the EEOC, employers can impose appearance policies and dress codes that apply to all employees, or employees within certain job categories, as long as the policy does not treat someone less favorably because of his or her religion or ethnicity.

Gender Discrimination Issues

Gender discrimination refers to treating an employee differently because of his or her gender. In 2001, six female Walmart employees filed a gender discrimination class action lawsuit representing more than 1 million women. At the time of the lawsuit filing, women employees constituted 72 percent of Walmart's sales staff but just 33 percent of its managers, significantly lower than the 56 percent of women store managers at comparable retailers.[16] An investigation requested by Walmart executives six years earlier found that men were 5.5 times more likely than women to be promoted into salaried management positions, and women in salaried jobs earned 19 percent less than men.[17]

Women are sometimes discriminated against in job assignments based on physical and personality characteristics. Stereotypes of women include being too physically weak, too sensitive, or too polite to perform certain job tasks. Men, on the other hand, are sometimes stereotyped as being aggressive, less emotionally vulnerable, and task focused rather than relationship focused, qualities assumed to be needed for executive leadership. The stereotype that men should be leaders and women support staff is attributed to people growing up in a family and neighborhood where women were subservient to male authorities. Compounding the problem, researchers report that women who behave contrary to stereotype are evaluated negatively.[18] Thus, women are sometimes denied jobs requiring assertive behaviors, and woman who exhibit assertive behaviors are sometimes penalized for doing so.

Pay Inequality The Equal Pay Act of 1963 prohibits pay discrimination based solely on gender considerations.[19] Men and women must receive equal pay for equal work. Previously, different wages for the same job tasks were justified on the grounds that men were the head of household whereas women were earning supplemental family income.

Assigning one job title to a male employee and another title to a female employee does not necessarily signify that the work being performed is, or that the pay linked to the job titles should be, different. The work being performed is considered equal if the two jobs entail equal skill, effort, responsibility, and working conditions. Different wages for performing the same type of work are justified only if related to an employer's seniority system, merit system, quantity or quality of productivity, or a factor other than gender.

On average, females earn approximately 69 percent of male salaries. In 2008, the mean salary for all males age 25 and older working full time was $64,283.[20] Females age 25 and older working full time earned a mean salary of $44,595.[21] The Bureau of Labor Statistics, which includes wages for 16-year-olds, reports a higher comparable wage rate of 80 percent.[22] The pay gap increases, rather than decreases, when education is taken into consideration. Males with at least a college degree working full time earned an average of $95,326, whereas their female counterparts earned an average of $61,319, or 64 percent of male salaries.

A variety of explanations other than gender discrimination may explain these earning differentials:

- *Career pattern choices*: Women, in general, choose less-prestigious careers that have lower market wage rates, such as nursing, secretarial work, sales associates, and child care services, whereas men choose higher wage professions, such as doctors, engineers, information technology, and production operators.[23] Even within the same field, such as medicine, women tend to choose lower wage occupations (family practice) compared to men (surgeons).

- *Seniority factor*: Large numbers of women have only recently entered some highly paid occupations, so they are not yet earning the highest wage scale.[24]

- *Job demand choices*: Women choose less demanding jobs that allow for more workplace flexibility to care for family and household needs, and pay less.

- *Organization size choices*: Women prefer working for small firms, which pay less than larger firms.

- *Salary negotiation issues*: Women are less likely to negotiate for higher wages. In one study, researchers report that only 13 percent of women MBA graduates negotiated for a higher initial salary, whereas 52 percent of their male counterparts did.[25]

- *Customer preferences*: Customers perceive male employees as more competent and providing better service than female employees, thus justifying a higher wage based on customer satisfaction evaluations.[26]

Pregnancy Many talented and highly educated women become pregnant between the ages of 20 and 40. In 1978, Congress passed the Pregnancy Discrimination Act (PDA) to protect the civil rights of pregnant women. The PDA classified discrimination based on pregnancy, childbirth, or related medical condition as a form of gender discrimination.[27]

Prior to the federal legislation, employers used a woman's pregnancy as a reason for promotion denials and job terminations. Employers also denied pregnant women health insurance and other fringe benefits when on maternity leave. The PDA ensured that women experiencing pregnancy, childbirth, or related medical conditions would be treated the same as an employee with an illness or temporary disability.

The PDA requires that employers provide appropriate job accommodations for pregnant women that do not cause undue hardship to the employer, such as temporarily modifying tasks and assignments. An undue hardship refers to the cost and difficulty associated with making the accommodation.

Employee health insurance policies must include coverage for pregnancy-related conditions, and sick or unpaid leave policies must include morning sickness and childbirth recovery. Upon returning to work, women are entitled to the same or equivalent job, much like any employee returning after sick or disability leave.

The PDA did not require that any specific amount of leave be extended to childbearing women beyond existing company policies. Congress passed the Family and Medical Leave Act (FMLA) of 1993 in part to address this issue and expanded its provisions to include any employee needing time off to address health-related problems.[28]

The FMLA ensures a total of 12 workweeks of unpaid leave during any 12-month period, and the continuation of health care and other fringe benefits during this period, for

- the care of a newborn baby, a newly adopted child, or a new foster child
- the care for an immediate family member (spouse, child, or parent) with a serious health condition
- an employee's serious health condition

The FMLA applies to all state, local, and federal employers, as well as private sector firms that employ 50 or more workers. An employee must have worked at least 1,250 hours during the previous 12 months to be eligible for coverage. With the employer's approval, an employee can substitute paid medical leave for unpaid time off. The FMLA exempts highly compensated employees, defined as managers in the top 10 percent of the company's pay scale, whose absence could not be filled and would cause an undue hardship on the employer. These unanticipated leaves of absences encourage managers to cross-train employees; otherwise, they may need to employ temporary workers.

Glass Ceiling Glass ceiling refers to situations in which the hierarchical advancement of a qualified woman or minority group member is prematurely stopped at a lower level because of gender, racial, or ethnic discrimination.[29]

In 2008, women represented 46.5 percent of the entire civilian labor force.[30] Assuming women and men are generally equally competent, a similar percentage of women should hold managerial jobs. But, according to the Bureau of Labor Statistics, in 2009, women accounted for only 25 percent of all CEOs, and 30 percent of all general and operations managers.[31] There seems to be an invisible barrier preventing women from climbing to the top of some organizational hierarchies, which is why the phenomenon is called a "glass" ceiling.

To understand glass ceiling dynamics, researchers examined the career paths of more than 50 male-female paired senior executives employed by the same organization.[32] Female executives, compared to their paired male counterparts, were much more likely to report exclusion from informal networking, difficulty getting developmental assignments, difficulty undertaking job relocations, and a lack of culture fit. In another study, researchers examined the performance ratings of upper-level managers and found that promoted women had received higher performance ratings than the promoted men, suggesting that more accomplishments were required from women than from men who are being considered for promotion.[33]

Reverse Gender Discrimination Reverse discrimination refers to discriminating against a dominant or majority group member, such as Caucasian males, in favor of a historically disadvantaged or minority group member. Organizations that put in place an affirmative action plan to promote more women to management positions discriminate against equally qualified men based solely on gender. If it is unfair for women to have been historically discriminated against based on gender, isn't it also unfair to deny men a job, promotion, or assignment based on gender?

A growing number of reverse discrimination lawsuits are being filed. Vision Quest National, located in a high-crime neighborhood, operated day and night shifts. When several women night shift employees threatened to quit, the company implemented a policy for women to be given a preference for day shift work. A male night shift employee making the same request was fired. He sued for gender discrimination and won the lawsuit.[34]

In another case, a male cosmetics employee at Dillard's department store in Florida filed a gender discrimination lawsuit for several instances of being treated less favorably by management based solely on his gender. Dillard's provided store uniforms to women, not to men, and offered only women-oriented sales contest prizes. He also claimed that he was being passed over for promotions because of his gender and sued for gender discrimination.[35]

Race and Ethnicity Discrimination Issues

In 2008, approximately 73 percent of the civilian labor force was Caucasian, compared to 13 percent being Hispanic and 10 percent African American.[36] Racial and ethnic discrimination refers to treating an employee differently because of his or her race or ethnicity. It is illegal to discriminate in job assignments and promotions based on an individual's race or ethnicity, even if customers or other employees express a preference for Caucasians.

National origin prohibitions include discrimination based on a person's birthplace, ancestry, culture, and native language. A potential or current employee can be discriminated against based on his or her accent if it affects the individual's ability to perform the job, such as in communicating with customers. Employees may be required to speak English during work-related interactions, but not during lunch or breaks.

The formation of racial and ethnic stereotypes is usually the result of segregation. Most Caucasians, African Americans, and Hispanics are born and raised in segregated neighborhoods. The lack of daily social interactions among races and ethnicities fosters stereotypes and prejudices. These trends are changing. In a 2008 survey, two-thirds of Caucasians reported that they interacted with African Americans either often or daily.[37]

Yet progress remains hampered. Racial and ethnic minorities are much more likely to perceive discrimination as a problem than the Caucasians wielding managerial power. African Americans, compared to Caucasians, are four times more likely to report that racial discrimination is a serious problem and three times more likely to attribute racial discrimination as a cause for differences in jobs and income.[38]

Religious Discrimination Issues

In 2008, approximately 76 percent of the population age 18 and older were Christians—51 percent were Protestant and 25 percent Catholic—down from 86 percent in 1990.[39] The remainder included 1.2 percent Jewish, 0.9 percent Eastern religions, 0.6 percent Muslim, 0.5 percent Buddhist, and 15 percent no religion.

Religious discrimination refers to treating an employee differently because of his or her religious beliefs.[40] Job assignments, promotions, and terminations cannot be determined based on religious reasons.

Employees can practice a religious belief at work if the employee is sincere and the practice is not harmful to others. Employers must provide religious accommodations that are reasonable and do not cause an undue burden to the employer. Undue employer hardships include the accommodation being costly, causing a decrease in workplace efficiency, compromising workplace safety or sanitation, harming employee morale, or infringing on the rights of other employees. Claiming that another employee or customer would be upset or uncomfortable because of an employee's religion or religious practice is not an undue hardship.

Employers are also expected to provide flexible scheduling for religious holidays and respect religious clothing and grooming policies. An employer cannot forbid an employee from wearing a Jewish yarmulke, Sikh turban, or a Muslim headscarf, or a religious hairstyle, unless the clothing or hairstyle negatively impacts job performance. If one employee is allowed to decorate office space for a religious holiday, all employees must be allowed to do likewise regardless of their specific religion. An employer cannot force an employee to participate in a particular religious activity.

Age Discrimination Issues

Age discrimination refers to treating an employee differently because of his or her age. The Age Discrimination in Employment Act (ADEA) of 1967 prohibits dismissing, or not promoting, anyone age 40 or older because the individual is considered "too old" for the job.[41] Job assignments, promotions, and terminations must be based on productivity, skills, abilities, or any factor other than protected class status, including age. Initially, the ADEA protected employees between the ages of 40 and 65. In 1987, the upper age limit was removed.

Exemptions to the law require a bona fide occupational qualification, such as not rehiring an aging actor for a young role, or matters of public safety, such as requirements for airplane pilots or bus drivers. The exemption is job specific. An airline, for instance, can require that airplane pilots retire at age 60, but the retirement rule cannot be extended to other employees, such as engineers. Wanting to maintain a "youthful environment" is not an acceptable reason for age discrimination.

Common age-related stereotypes include older employees being less productive, less physically and technologically capable, and less motivated to work hard. Thomas Ng and Daniel Feldman conducted a meta-analysis of research studies that explored the relationship between age and various job performance factors.[42] They found that age was not related to core task performance or creativity. In other words, older employees were just as productive and creative as younger employees. The researchers, however, found three age-related differences: older employees were more likely to demonstrate organizational citizenship behavior and to comply with safety rules, and less likely to engage in counterproductive work behaviors.

Due to longevity and accomplishments, older employees in some organizations have higher salaries. If an organization seeks to reduce labor costs, salaries can be a deciding criterion, but not age. According to the Older Workers Benefit Protection Act of 1990, older employees must be eligible for the same employee benefits as all other employees and cannot be forced to retire earlier than stated in existing policies. Employers can provide employees incentives to voluntarily take early retirement, but not require early retirement.

Disability Discrimination Issues

Approximately 50 million Americans have a physical or mental disability, of which 55 percent are employed.[43] Historically, citizens with physical and mental disabilities had been discriminated against in areas such as employment, housing, and education.[44] Congress passed the Americans with Disabilities Act of 1990 (ADA) to prohibit discrimination against a qualified worker with a disability who can perform the job task with or without reasonable accommodation. The legislation defines a disability as "a physical or mental impairment that substantially limits one or more major life activities of such individual." Examples include impairments associated with seeing, hearing, walking, standing, speaking, learning, and breathing.

The ADA requires employers to provide reasonable accommodations for the disability, such as modifying a job assignment, work schedule, facilities, and equipment. A requested modification is unreasonable if it causes an undue hardship on the employer. According to the ADA, factors that an employer can take into account to determine the reasonableness of an accommodation include the following:

- The nature and cost of the accommodation
- The overall size and financial resources of the facility or business
- The impact of the accommodation on business operations

An employer is expected to modify a desk so a person in a wheelchair can have computer access or modify phone equipment for someone with a hearing impairment.

Discrimination against people with disabilities must be task related, not disability related, unless the person with the disability posses a direct threat to other employees or customers. In 1999, a jury rewarded a terminated employee with a mental disability $13 million in punitive damages, later reduced to $230,000 because of a statutory cap placed on punitive damages. The local manager and staff were willing to make reasonable accommodations for the employee, but a regional manager overruled them because he didn't think the company should employ "those kinds of people."[45]

Alcoholism is a disability under the ADA. An employer cannot discipline or fire an individual because he or she is an alcoholic. The employer, however, can prohibit alcohol consumption during work hours for all employees, including alcoholics, and discipline or fire an employee for productivity or performance-related factors.

Sexual Orientation Discrimination Issues

Homosexuality has existed in all cultures and throughout history.[46] As of 2010, there were an estimated 40,000 legal same-sex marriages in the United States.[47] Gays and lesbians are estimated to be between 1.5 and 4.1 percent of the U.S. adult population, which translates to 3.2 million to 8.8 million people.[48] The percentages of men who are gay and women who are lesbian are very similar. Researchers maintain that the overall percentages are low estimates due to how narrowly homosexuality is defined and confidentiality concerns of survey respondents.

Although there has been a long history of workplace discrimination against lesbian, gay, bisexual, and transgender (LGBT) people, sexual orientation discrimination is not covered by Title VII of the Civil Rights Act. Nonetheless, more than 15 states and 150 municipalities have passed laws prohibiting sexual orientation discrimination.[49] In 1982, Wisconsin became the first state to pass such a law, which prohibited sexual orientation discrimination in employment, housing, public education, credit, and public accommodations.

Researchers report that 15 percent to 43 percent of LGBT employees have experienced workplace discrimination. Approximately 8 percent to 17 percent report being fired or denied employment because of their sexual orientation and 7 percent to 41 percent were either verbally or physically abused or had their workplace vandalized.[50] LGBT youth are much more likely than the general population to experience homelessness, rejection by family members, physical abuse, emotional abuse, and sexual abuse, which can impact future job prospects and workplace behaviors.[51]

The Employment Non-Discrimination Act (ENDA), federal legislation under consideration to protect LGBT people from job discrimination, is modeled after the Civil Rights Act.[52] The legislation is spearheaded by the National Gay and Lesbian Task Force, whose first major victory was getting the American Psychiatric Association to declassify homosexuality as a mental illness in 1973.

In 1994, the U.S. military implemented a contentious "Don't Ask, Don't Tell" policy, a compromise developed by the Clinton administration to address the military's ban on homosexuals. Military leaders opposed to gay and lesbian soldiers maintained that homosexuality threatened troop cohesiveness in combat units.[53] Under the Clinton administration's policy, military recruiters would not ask about an applicant's sexual orientation, and applicants would not reveal their sexual orientation. Between 1994 and 2010, however, more than 10,000 military personnel were discharged for declaring their sexual orientation. In 2010, Congress passed legislation prohibiting the military from discriminating against gay, lesbian, and bisexual people.[54]

Some companies provide "domestic partnership" benefits to same-sex or different-sex couples, although they are not required to do so by federal or state law. In 1982, the *Village Voice*, an alternative newsweekly based in New York City, became the first employer to offer domestic partner benefits to lesbian and gay employees. By 2009, 57 percent of the Fortune 500 companies provided domestic partner health insurance benefits, including nine of the top ten largest corporations, and 85 percent prohibited sexual orientation discrimination.[55] In 2010, the federal government developed policies that granted hospital visiting rights to same-sex partners and extended the Family Medical Leave Act to care for sick or newborn children of same-sex partners.[56]

Harassment

Harassment is defined as "unwelcome conduct that is based on race, color, religion, sex (including pregnancy), national origin, age (40 or older), disability or genetic information" from a supervisor, coworker, or nonemployee, such as a customer or supplier.[57] Examples of offensive conduct include offensive jokes, slurs, name-calling, physical assaults or threats, intimidation, ridicule, insults, offensive objects, pictures, and interference with work performance.

Harassment becomes unlawful when the conduct is severe or pervasive enough to create a work environment that a reasonable person would consider intimidating, hostile, or abusive. A one-time minor isolated incident does not qualify as harassment. Nonetheless, minor incidents should be brought to an employer's attention for further investigation to determine if a pattern is being established.

Dating, Sexual Harassment, and Hostile Work Environment

Office romances and dating coworkers are increasingly common with more women in the workforce and the considerable amount of time employees spend at work. According to one survey, 41 percent of the respondents between the ages of 25 and 40 have had office romances.[58] Discourage employees who are dating each other from exhibiting public signs of affection at work because doing so damages morale and suggests signs of favoritism.[59]

Dating is based on mutual consent; sexual harassment is not. The same survey reported that 26 percent of the respondents had been sexually harassed at work. Sexual harassment occurs when (1) an unwelcomed sexual favor is a quid-pro-quo condition of employment, promotion, pay increase, continued employment, or desired assignment or (2) offensive comments about a person's gender or physical harassment of a sexual nature results in a hostile work environment.[60]

Sexual harassment includes unwelcomed sexual comments, jokes, leering, pictures, or physical touching. Prohibit these unwelcomed behaviors in all work-related settings, such as private offices, public work areas, off-property meetings, and business trips. Sexual harassment results in lower levels of job satisfaction for both the victims and those observing the behavior, and lower levels of organizational commitment.[61]

Let's Build a Building

Billing for Cranes

Five months into the construction of your new building, you stop by the jobsite and count two cranes, one of which is not being used. When you get back to the office, you review the general contractor's construction contract and notice that the original agreement was for one crane. You review the most recent bills and realize that for the previous two months, you were billed for two cranes. The cost per crane is $9,600 a month, which amounts to $19,200 for the second crane.

You mention the crane billing discrepancy to a business associate familiar with the construction industry. "Oh, that's rather typical," she tells you. "A major revenue source for general contractors is rental income from their equipment. I heard that this particular general contractor owns more than $50 million worth of equipment. In order to make the payments and generate a return on investment, the general contractor needs to bill that equipment to as many projects as possible for as long as possible."

At the next jobsite meeting, you ask the project manager why there are two cranes instead of the agreed-upon one crane. He says two cranes are required to improve productivity and keep on schedule for your grand opening. You point out that only one crane is being used; the other crane just seems to be parked there. "Oh, we use both cranes," he responds, "but sometimes not at the same time."

The following day you drive by the jobsite and see that, once again, only one crane is being used. You mention this to your business associate again. "They're scamming you," she insists. "The only way these guys respect you is if you play hardball. On your next bill, only pay for one crane, not two, and if they make a big deal of it, tell them you want to be reimbursed $19,200 for the previous months when you were charged for two cranes even though the contract clearly states only one crane would be used. I can find you a low-cost construction consultant who will put in writing that only one crane is needed."

You realize that if you refuse to pay for the additional crane, the general contractor could issue a work slowdown to prove that two cranes were really needed. The building is scheduled to open in seven months, and the use of a crane is projected for another three months, which would cost $28,800 for the extra crane.

What would you do? Would you

1. Play it safe and pay $28,800 for the additional crane until the project ends?
2. Demand that the original contract for just one crane be upheld and request a $19,200 refund for the previous two months?
3. Refuse to pay for the additional crane from now until the end of the project?

   Why?

When quid-pro-quo sexual harassment or a hostile environment occurs, the employer must immediately notify the accused person to stop the offensive behavior. An employer is legally liable for an employee sexually harassing another employee if the employer either knows, or should have known, of the harassment and failed to take prompt and reasonable corrective action. Employers must be proactive in the matter because many men and some women interpret sexual comments in a flattering, rather than derogatory, manner.[62]

Harassing attitudes and behaviors are usually developed and reinforced in subgroups during teenage years and young adulthood and carried over into the workplace. The most common target of sexual harassment is a woman employee in a male-dominated occupation.[63] Researchers report that women are also susceptible to being sexually harassed by professional clients or customers in the service industry. Provocatively dressed women are particularly prone to being sexually harassed.

Males are also subjected to sexual harassment, which accounted for 16 percent of the EEOC filings in 2009.[64] Most of these cases reflect two types of scenarios.

One situation involves males harassed by females in female-dominated occupations, such as nursing. The other situation involves males harassed as being too feminine by other males in male-dominated occupations, such as construction.

The same power dynamic occurs when employees are illegally harassed based on their race, ethnicity, or religion. The victim, often an isolated workplace minority group member in a highly segregated workforce, is harassed by someone in the dominant group.

Retaliation for Discrimination Claim

All EEO laws carry a stipulation that it is illegal to take retaliatory adverse action against someone who complains to an employer, manager, or law official about a discrimination issue.[65]

Typical forms of retaliation include termination, demotion, promotion denial, increased surveillance, unjustified negative performance evaluations, and harassment.[66] Employees who speak up for, or testify on behalf of, the alleged victim or cooperate with an investigation are also protected against adverse retaliatory action. Even if an employer is found innocent of the original discrimination charge, an employer can be found guilty if retaliatory action was taken against an employee associated with the initial claim or subsequent investigation.

Competitive Advantages of Diversity Management

The U.S. population continues to diversify, as does the employee and customer base of organizations. For more than two centuries, Caucasian males dominated the American workforce. This is no longer the case. In 2008, Caucasian males made up only 39 percent of the entire civilian labor force.[67] Caucasian females comprised 34 percent of the workforce, followed by all Hispanics (13 percent), African Americans (10 percent), and Asians (4 percent).

The purchasing power of minorities continues to escalate as well. In 2007, the combined buying power of African Americans, Asian Americans, and Native Americans was $1.4 trillion, triple that from two decades earlier.[68] Hispanic disposable income accounts for 10 percent of all spending.

The avoidance of lawsuits and increased government regulation are fear-based incentives for managing diversity. Expand legal compliance initiatives to values-based initiatives that embrace and promote employee diversity. Five positive bottom-line reasons why respecting diversity creates a competitive advantage for organizations follow:

1. *To attract and retain diverse customers:* Customers tend to feel more comfortable doing business with people who respect them. Customers from diverse social groups who feel unwelcomed by insensitive salespeople from a different social group will take their business elsewhere.

2. *To attract and retain diverse employees:* As an organization's reputation for appropriately managing diversity issues increases, so does the diversity of the organization's job applicant pool.

3. *To achieve cost reductions:* Cost reductions associated with diversity management include fewer employee grievances, absences, turnover, and litigation. Responding to claims that an employee is being discriminated against requires time and resources to resolve.

4. *To enhance decision making, problem solving, and creativity:* Due to different life experiences, different cultural groups perceive the world in different ways, enhancing organizational decision making, problem solving, and creativity. A multicultural workforce is likely to make more informed decisions regarding its own cultural groups and examine an issue from multiple perspectives.

5. *To increase stakeholder goodwill:* Organizations that are diversity leaders earn goodwill from the media, government, socially conscious consumers, and job candidates wanting to contribute to a broad social mission. This translates into free advertising from the media and consumers, and from high-profile government and industry task forces.

Best Operational Practices for Managing Diversity

Create workplaces that respect diverse people by implementing the best practices for diversity management. In 1998, the EEOC Task Force published examples of the "best" diversity policies, programs, and practices in the private sector (see following list).[69] Integrating these best practices in diversity management throughout organizational operations can ensure long-term continuous success.

- *Diversity officer/committee/office*: Assign organizational responsibility for diversity to a diversity officer, committee, or office. This establishes a particular person as being accountable for diversity issues.

- *Recruiting and hiring*: Develop a list of highly qualified diverse job candidates whom employees know, and personally invite them to apply. Sources include previous business dealings, professional associations, civic organizations, minority job fairs, and internship programs for colleges and high schools with high minority populations.

- *Personnel policies*: Provide flexible personnel policies reflecting the needs of diverse populations. Areas for flexibility include the use of personal days, cafeteria-style benefits plans, and work schedules.

- *Dispute resolution mechanisms*: Be receptive to diversity-related grievances and investigate every claim. Presume everyone innocent until proven otherwise. The most efficient dispute resolution system is a direct dialogue between both parties. If unsuccessful, have a supervisor or diversity officer serve as mediator. If unsuccessful, have a peer review panel arbitrate a binding resolution.

- *Retention and promotions*: Diversity retention techniques that lead to promotions include job training and rotation, challenging assignments, holistic performance appraisals, career counseling, mentoring, focus group feedback, and promotion from within.

- *Performance appraisals*: Link bonuses to achieving diversity goals. Include a performance appraisal scale measuring behaviors that demonstrate respect for diverse coworkers and customers.

- *Termination and downsizing*: The two best criteria for determining layoffs are job requirements and past performance. When organizations use seniority as a layoff criterion, newly hired diverse employees are the first to be terminated, undoing years of concerted effort to diversify the workforce. Conduct an adverse impact analysis to determine if the list of employees to be laid off adversely affects the percentage of women and racial and ethnic minorities employed by the organization. If it does, then consider modifying the layoff criteria to avoid the undesired result.

Many industry groups and magazines award organizations for their diversity accomplishments. In 2009, *Working Mother*'s Diversity Leadership Awards winners included Ariel Investments, Cisco Systems, the *New York Times,* Office Max, and Trinity Health.[70]

Wells Fargo is one of the nation's largest financial services corporations. In 2010, its 278,000 employees included 60 percent women and 34 percent minorities. Among officers and managers, 49 percent were women and 23 percent minorities. Wells Fargo has received diversity awards and recognitions for diversity management by *DiversityInc, Hispanic Business Magazine, Working Mother Magazine,* the Human Rights Campaign Foundation, and the American Foundation for the Blind (see "Best Practice in Use" exhibit).

BEST PRACTICE IN USE

Wells Fargo Diversity Imperative

Wells Fargo defines diversity as a "business imperative." Key features of the company's diversity program include the following:

- *Enterprise Diversity Council:* Makes recommendations to the executive management team regarding progress in diversity education, recruiting and placement of diverse employees (including company executives), and other leadership best practices.

- *Diverse Growth Segments Group:* Creates and executes business strategies for serving, and marketing to, Latino, Asian American, African American, and Native American communities.

- *Business Line Diversity Councils:* More than fifty business line diversity councils advise managers on policies, programs, culture, and leadership.

- *Team Member Networks:* Special employee networking groups for women, Asians, Blacks and African Americans, Hispanics, Native Americans, and People with Disabilities.

- *Supplier Diversity:* Supplier base reflects the diversity of the customers and employees in the community. Opportunities are available to businesses that qualify for the company's first-tier supplier diversity database (provide a beneficial service and certified as a minority, woman, or disadvantaged-owned enterprise). Second-tier supplier status consists of minority subcontractors employed by Wells Fargo suppliers.

The Human Rights Campaign, which advocates on behalf of equality for LGBTs, has developed a "Corporate Equality Index." In 2010, 337 major U.S. businesses earned the top rating of 100 percent.[71] Criteria include a nondiscrimination (or equal employment opportunity) policy statement that mentions sexual orientation or gender identity, domestic partner benefits, diversity awareness training, a diversity council, and target marketing and recruiting to the LGBT community.

Implementing a Diversity Initiative

Creating an organizational culture that respects diversity requires planning and effort. The following 10-step process describes how to successfully implement diversity initiatives based on a traditional organizational change model.[72]

1. *Present a business case for the diversity initiative:* Determine which of the five competitive advantages of diversity discussed earlier is most important for achieving superior organizational performance. Use this reason as the key motivator for undertaking the diversity initiative. Support the rationale with demographic trends, competitive analysis, and adoption of best practices in the industry.

2. *Create a shared vision statement:* Employees implementing the diversity initiative must be committed to achieving the desired results. Achieve commitment by involving them in the crafting of a vision statement emphasizing fair treatment of all stakeholders. Clearly link the diversity vision to the competitive advantage.

3. *Respectfully build from the past:* A diversity initiative is one step along the continuous improvement path. Praise previous diversity successes and use past success as the foundation for new initiatives.

4. *Create a sense of urgency:* Emphasize the importance of undertaking the change right now, ahead of the competition, not later when the competition has already staked its claim in the diverse markets and talent pools.

5. *Empower a change agent:* All organizational changes require a point person ultimately accountable for achieving the desired results. Give a particular "go-to" person authority to manage the change process.

6. *Gather political support:* Success depends on all work units supporting the diversity initiative. Educate all formal and informal leaders about the importance of the change initiative. Establish a diversity committee composed of key supporting people to oversee the initiative.

7. *Craft an implementation plan:* Gather input from those directly affected by the changes. Anticipate, and overcome, obstacles by inviting representatives from the affected organizational units and diversity groups to comment on the implementation plan. Link action plan strategies to reasonable long-term and short-term goals.

8. *Develop enabling processes:* Train key participants to manage the change process. Establish multiple communication channels for input and feedback on the quality and quantity of changes being made. Share feedback and results with key constituents, and revise the plan as needed.

9. *Evaluate the progress:* Gather relevant historical data to benchmark and measure progress toward achieving the stated goals and objectives. Recognize all positive changes. In the spirit of continuous improvement, explore unmet goals with key constituents.

10. *Reinforce the change:* Link the accomplishment of diversity objectives to performance evaluations and compensation. Spotlight diversity champions and share their best practices. Rewards and visibility reinforce credibility.

Diversity Training

By mirroring the increasingly diverse marketplace, a diverse workforce makes communication and relationships with diverse customers more comfortable and congenial. Yet within an organization, diverse people may possess negative stereotypes and prejudices about members of other groups, which damages morale and performance. Diversity necessitates expanding an employee's comfort level beyond his or her own race, ethnicity, or gender.

Helping employees overcome their biases against diverse people requires training. Corporations began diversity training initiatives during the 1960s to ensure compliance with the Civil Rights Act and avoid costly lawsuits and negative publicity.[73] These initial training sessions focused on learning about Title VII, particularly regarding the treatment of women and African Americans. Workshop leaders presented policies and situations that could prevent or generate legal action against the organization.

In the 1980s, projections about the decline of Caucasian males as a percentage of the U.S. workforce resulted in a training focus shift from how to comply with the law to how to better assimilate diverse people into the workplace. A decade later, prejudicial statements about, and discrimination against, Caucasian males resulted in expanding sensitivity training to address the feelings and concerns of all employees, not just minorities. By the 2000s, with the further globalization of the world's economy, developing a multicultural competent workforce became part of strategic planning, which made diversity training an even more prominent issue.

Exhibit 7.3 highlights some common diversity training problems that can arise from within, or between, dominant and subordinate workplace groups, along with recommended solutions. The dominant group refers to the diverse characteristic that is held in common by a large number of employees, typically Caucasian males. The subordinate group refers to the diversity characteristic held by a small minority of organizational members.

Carefully frame diversity training workshops so they will be well received by employees. Begin the diversity training workshop by discussing the five competitive advantages of diversity presented earlier. The purpose of diversity training is to improve organizational performance and profitability.

Next, provide some national and industry examples of diversity problems and their associated costs, such as the number of EEOC cases filed and financial penalties shown in Exhibit 1.1. Employees need to understand that discrimination is a national and industry-wide problem; it is not unique to any particular organization.

Exhibit 7.3 Diversity Training Problems and Solutions	
Problem	**Solution**
The trainer lacks credibility with either the dominant group or subordinate group.	Use workshop coleaders, one from the dominant group and one from the subordinate group; they can model positive behaviors through their interactions managing the workshop.
The organization's diversity problems are portrayed too negatively.	Begin the workshop by recognizing the efforts of diversity champions so that others may rally around them. Then discuss organizational shortcomings.
Employees from the dominant group are portrayed too negatively.	Begin the workshop by recognizing how particular members of the dominant group have successfully managed diversity issues. Then challenge everyone to do even more.
Training is limited to the dominant group.	Prejudices are not unique to any one particular demographic group. Explore everyone's prejudices, those of both the dominant group and the subordinate group.
Training exercises are not relevant.	Address real work-related interactions among diverse people.
Training emphasizes employee differences to the exclusion of common ground.	Despite our differences, diverse groups of people share many things in common with other diverse groups. Highlight these commonalities.
Training emphasizes knowledge and attitudes to the exclusion of behaviors.	Address behavioral changes that need to occur. Clearly articulate and discuss specific acceptable and unacceptable behaviors. Practice rules of civil behavior.

Then educate employees about the best operational practices, presented earlier in this chapter, so they can see what leading-edge organizations are doing to manage diversity. Praise previous diversity efforts the organization and particular managers have undertaken, and acknowledge the need for continuous improvement. Lastly, design workshops that foster greater personal awareness of diversity issues, and develop action plans to improve diversity management.

Diversity Discussion Guidelines

Many employees are not comfortable discussing diversity issues. Diversity topics can feel threatening and an invasion of privacy. Some people may unintentionally offend others or not be aware that their attitudes are racist or sexist. Others fear having their views misinterpreted or misjudged as being naïve or bigoted.

Initial employee tension and resistance can be defused by a warm-up activity in which participants agree on discussion guidelines. Begin by reviewing the organization's Code of Ethics and highlight the importance of applying relevant aspects of the code, such as respect for others, during workshop discussions. If discussion guidelines already exist, have attendees review them and make modifications as needed.

If the organization lacks discussion guidelines, have participants independently develop a set of rules governing how participants should treat one another during the discussion. Then have each person share his or her guidelines with the entire group. Reach consensus on three to seven guidelines that would foster honest and respectful communication. Discussion guidelines typically include one person speaking at a time without interruption, being open and honest, participating fully at one's own comfort level, listening respectfully, asking questions (why do you believe that?) rather than making accusatory statements (that's a sexist comment!), supporting the expression of dissent in a harassment-free environment, focusing on issues rather than the person making the statement, and maintaining confidentiality.[74]

Maintaining discussion confidentiality is particularly important. Remind participants that personal views and stories shared during the workshop are not to be repeated or shared outside the workshop without the person's consent. Explain that gossip following the workshop violates the organization's Code of Ethics, damages trust, and prevents other employees from sincerely participating in future diversity workshops. Reinforce the discussion guidelines by distributing a confidentiality agreement to be signed by workshop participants, with a stipulation that violating the confidentiality agreement will negatively impact performance appraisals.

Tips and Techniques

Diversity Training Goals

It takes time and effort to develop a safe and supportive work environment that respects diverse people. All employees need to be trained to appropriately interact with diverse populations of customers and coworkers.

Two important goals of diversity training goals are to

1. Eliminate values, stereotypes, and managerial practices that inhibit the personal and professional development of diverse employees.

2. Allow diverse employees to contribute their best efforts for achieving superior organizational performance.

Diversity Training Exercises

The following sections summarize diversity workshop exercises that are informative, relevant, and useful. The first four diversity exercises foster self-awareness: Who Are You?, Dominant Group and Subordinate Group Awareness, The Dominant Group's Status, and Implicit Attitude Test. The next two diversity exercises explore what it is like being prejudged, and how everyone is unique, yet shares things in common with others. The seventh diversity exercise focuses on generating discussion about sexual harassment. The last exercise highlights a diversity factor that is easily overlooked, yet is at the core of daily work interactions—differences in communication styles.

Who Are You?

No two people are alike. The "Who Are You?" exercise in Exhibit 7.4 helps work-shop participants understand their unique diversity dimensions. Employees describe themselves according to the four diversity dimensions and then discuss how these factors impact their attitudes and behaviors at work.

Exhibit 7.4 Who Are You? Exercise
Describe yourself according to the four diversity dimensions and discuss how these dimensions impact who you are. • Describe your permanent dimensions (i.e., race, ethnicity, gender, sexual orientation, and birth generation). • Describe your evolving dimensions (i.e., age, height, weight, religion, education, physical ability, marital status, income level, and geographic location). • Describe your personality dimensions (i.e., Big Five Personality Model or Myers-Briggs Type Indicators). • Describe your organizational dimensions (i.e., hierarchical status, work content, department, and seniority). • Which of these dimensions most strongly define who you are? Why? • Which of these dimensions impact how others treat you at work? How?

Dominant Group and Subordinate Group Awareness

Members of the dominant group tend to possess more power and influence over decisions and the shaping of organizational culture than do subordinate group members. For instance, if all managers are Caucasian males (the dominant group), then Caucasian males have special status and their values shape organizational culture. This impact is much more obvious to subordinate group members than to dominant group members, who tend to take their special status for granted. Membership in a dominant group can foster a sense of superiority over subordinate group members, which can lead to organizational efficiency and effectiveness problems.

Exhibit 7.5 describes how the dominant and subordinate groups differ relative to several key workplace issues.

Exhibit 7.5 Dominant/Subordinate Group Dynamics		
Category	Dominant Group Members	Subordinate Group Members
Power	Have access to power	Need access to power
Rules	Make the rules	Abide by the rules or try to fit in
Resources	Control resources	Need access to resources
Culture	Define the culture	Struggle to "fit in"

Truth	Define the truth	Have their truth and experiences questioned and often invalidated
Normal	Seen as normal	Seen as inferior or as an exception to their group
Capable	Assumed to be capable (qualified)	Often assumed to be deficient (unqualified)
Benefit of Doubt	Given the benefit of doubt	Have to earn the benefit of doubt or "prove" they are qualified
Awareness of Group Membership	Unaware of group membership	Very aware of group membership
Sense of Worth	See their group as the "best"	Internalize dominant groups' beliefs as reflected in lack of worth, low self-esteem or self-confidence
Behavior	Encourage subordinate group members to assimilate	Adapt by developing behaviors pleasing or acceptable to dominant group members and cannot "show up" too authentic or genuine
Discrimination	See incidents of discrimination as individual actions that have little to do with group membership	See patterns of group level behavior based on repetitive nature

Source: © 2008 Elsie Y. Cross Associates, Inc., www.eyca.com, with permission to adapt.

Have workshop attendees define their group membership as either the dominant group or the subordinate group. Then use the categories in Exhibit 7.5 to examine how membership in this group impacts workplace performance. Which categories, if any, are problematic for the organization? How can these problems be rectified?

The Dominant Group's Status

Members of the dominant group are often unaware of the special status they have over subordinate group members. Peggy McIntosh's "White Privilege" experiential exercise emphasizes many subtle aspects of dominant group privilege in American society.[75] In this workshop, participants line up with their backs to a wall. The facilitator reads descriptive statements that highlight dominant group privileges. After each statement, participants who answer affirmatively take one step forward. Sample statements include the following:

1. I can turn on the television or open to the front page of the newspaper and see people of my race or gender widely represented in a positive manner.

2. I can do well in a challenging situation without being called a credit to my race or gender.

3. I can be pretty sure that if I ask to talk to the "person in charge," I will be facing a person of my race or gender.

Typically, after the last statement is read, dominant group members are several steps ahead of subordinate group members. Participants turn to face each other and express their thoughts and feelings about the results of the exercise. This exercise can be modified to fit whichever race, ethnicity, gender, or religion describes the dominant group in an organization. Be sensitive when facilitating the postexercise discussion because dominant group members can become defensive or subordinate group members antagonized when the gap is exposed.

Implicit Attitude Test (IAT)

The Implicit Attitude Test (IAT) helps employees understand unconscious prejudices they might hold toward people belonging to other groups.[76] The IAT is a 10-minute reaction time test that uses computer images to measure a person's association between (1) a paired diversity characteristic (i.e., male versus female) and (2) a paired set of descriptors (i.e., pleasant versus unpleasant). An IAT score suggests the strength of association between the diversity characteristic and the descriptor.

For instance, the employee is shown a picture of a Caucasian male. The words "pleasant" and "unpleasant" flash on the computer screen and the test taker is instructed to click the word that best describes the picture. The amount of time it takes to choose one of the two descriptors is recorded. An instantaneous "Caucasian male—pleasant" response suggests that the employee has a pleasant association with Caucasian males. An instantaneous "Caucasian male—unpleasant" response suggests the opposite. Subsequent images flashed on the screen include an African American male with the same two descriptors and a woman's face with the descriptors "executive" and "housework." Once again, the amount of time it takes a participant to choose one of the two descriptors is recorded.

People respond quicker to strongly paired associations, which may suggest a stereotype or bias the person possesses. The more rapid the person's response to the pairing, the more compatible the two concepts are in the person's mind. The time gap is greater for concepts that are not strongly paired in a person's mind.

If the amount of time it takes an employee to choose "executive" rather than "housework" after seeing a man's face is the same as it takes to choose "executive" after seeing a woman's face, then the employee associates both genders with being business executives. If it takes longer to choose "executive" after seeing a woman's face or if the employee chooses "housework" instead of "executive," then the employee does not strongly associate women with being business executives.

An IAT score that suggests a bias in favor of Caucasian males does not mean the employee will behave in a sexist or racist manner. Instead, the employee is simply being made aware that these associations are going on in his or her mind and may lead to discriminatory behaviors.

Millions of people have anonymously taken the IAT. Researchers report that 88 percent of Caucasians taking the test have implicit biases for Caucasians over African Americans, and 83 percent of heterosexuals have implicit biases for heterosexuals over gays and lesbians.[77]

Experiences Being Prejudged

Every individual has been prejudged because of some notable characteristic—age, profession, geography, race, gender, religion, and so on. Exhibit 7.6 provides some prompt questions for workshop participants to answer on their own and then discuss in small groups.[78]

Exhibit 7.6 Experiences Being Prejudged Exercise
1. Describe how you have been stereotyped in a positive way. When did the incident occur? Where did the incident occur? Who said what to whom? Was the stereotype accurate?
2. Describe how you have been stereotyped in a negative way. When did the incident occur? Where did the incident occur? Who said what to whom? Was the stereotype accurate?
3. What were your reactions when the negative incident occurred? How did you feel? What did you think? What did you do?
4. What were the overall consequences of the negative incident? How did the incident affect you in the future? Did it change your expectations of yourself? Did it change your expectations of others?

Individual Uniqueness and Commonalities

People want to be treated as individuals, rather than as representatives of a social group. The exercise in Exhibit 7.7 helps employees understand how each of them is unique, and also how each of them shares some common traits with members of other diverse groups.[79]

Exhibit 7.7 Individual Uniqueness and Commonalities Exercise
Step 1: Write down five experiences, activities, accomplishments, or attributes that make you unique from others. For example: I was a vice president of my university student government, had season tickets to the New York Giants, played center field on my baseball team, was a missionary, and came in second place for an 880-yard run in grade school.
Step 2: Share your items with other participants and circle those that are still unique.
Step 3: Have an informal discussion with other participants and find five things you have in common with them.

Sexual Harassment

As discussed earlier, the EEOC differentiates between two types of sexual harassment—quid-pro-quo and hostile environment. In small groups, discuss whether each of the following four scenarios constitutes sexual harassment. Do they create a "hostile environment" at work? Are there differences of opinions among, or between, the responses of male and female participants? Other scenarios can be developed by employees who have been sexually harassed or have been accused of sexual harassment.

Scenario One: Mary is Tom's administrative assistant. Every morning Tom makes flattering comments about Mary's appearance.

Scenario Two: Mary is Tom's administrative assistant. Tom invites Mary out for drinks to a singles bar after work. Mary claims not to be available. One week later Tom invites Mary out for drinks after work again.

Scenario Three: Mary is Tom's administrative assistant. Tom is an affectionate person and gently touches the arms of both male and female workers while engaged in conversation. Tom gently touches Mary's arms two or three times a day during conversations.

Scenario Four: Mary is Tom's administrative assistant. Tom receives several unsolicited junk emails a day, including those about improving sexual performance. Tom believes one of these unsolicited sexual performance emails is quite humorous, and he forwards the email to Mary.

Communication Style

Communication style is an often overlooked aspect of employee diversity. People tend to express themselves in a way that feels normal to them and assume that others like to communicate in the same manner. But this disrespects the uniqueness of the person receiving the information, can result in misunderstandings, and can negatively impact employee performance.

Some people, for example, tend to get right to the point and typically assume that the people they communicate with want to get right to the point. They also prefer that others communicating with them get right to the point. If the other person does not, then that other person is judged to be distracted or wasting time.

Some people, however, tend to first ask about the other person's family situation. People who first make a personal connection assume that the people they communicate with want to first make a personal connection. They also prefer that others communicating with them first make a personal connection. If the other person does not, then that other person is considered rude or uncaring.

Treating others with respect means understanding how other people prefer to communicate. This can be a very difficult and strenuous process because the communication initiator must convey information in a way that the other person prefers to receive information, rather than in the way that feels normal to the communication initiator.

In *Success Signals*, Rhonda Hilyer, president and CEO of Agreement Dynamics, has developed a useful tool of four communication styles, each symbolized by a different color.[80] Individuals can exhibit all four styles to some extent, but most likely one or two styles dominate. The four communication styles are summarized in Exhibit 7.8.

Have workshop participants identify which of the four colors best represents

• Their own communication style

• Their boss's communication style

• Their subordinate's communication style

Exhibit 7.8 Communication Styles	
Brown	**Green**
• Direct, brief, and decisive • Focus on tasks and results • Assertive • Desire "yes/no or black/white" answers • Doesn't want a lot of detail • Stays on point • Impatient if things move too slowly	• Logical, sequential, and focused on details • Desires historical data • Literal and factual • Appears reserved and avoids emotions • Needs time to process information • A planner, precise and organized
Blue	**Red**
• Concerned with how others feel and will be affected • Supportive and agreeable • Includes others in the decision-making process • Likes to chat and form a personal connection before getting on task • Good listener	• Flamboyant, dramatic, and energetic • Fast paced • Frequently tells jokes or stories • Tends to overgeneralize for effect • Likes humor and creative ideas • Spontaneous, innovative, and enthusiastic

Source: Adapted from Rhonda Hilyer, Agreement Dynamics, Inc.

- A peer's communication style
- The communication style of the person they struggle with the most at work

Next, help employees understand how coworkers perceive their communication style. For instance, request that all participants with a brown communication style stand in front of the workshop. Then ask coworkers who struggle with browns to express what they appreciate about the brown style and how they are sometimes frustrated or confused by the brown style. This process helps browns understand how others react to their communication style. In addition, coworkers realize that their struggles with the browns might be a result of the communication style differences rather than with the person.

Then follow the same procedures for the other three communication styles.

If an employee wants to influence a coworker, the employee can practice conveying information using the coworker's communication style. Doing so results in a more harmonious communication experience and successful conveyance of information:

- If the employee wants to influence a brown, practice communicating in a direct manner with a brown.
- If the employee wants to influence a blue, practice discussing a blue's life situation prior to asking the blue to do something.

- If the employee wants to influence a green, practice providing a green with a great deal of detail relevant to the issue being discussed.
- If the person wants to influence a red, practice communicating with a red in a fun and expressive manner.

SUMMARY

Ethical organizations respect diverse employees and customers. Doing so creates many competitive advantages over other organizations. This chapter summarized the competitive advantages of diversity management, the history of population diversity in the United States, workplace discrimination, best operational practices for managing diversity, and how to implement a diversity initiative.

Common diversity training problems were highlighted and addressed. A wide variety of diversity workshop exercises were reviewed, ranging from self-awareness to enhancing organizational performance by understanding different communication styles. All of these diversity activities directly impact an organization's operational and financial performance.

KEY WORDS

Employment at-will doctrine; self-categorization theory; fairness; respect for others; Equal Pay Act; Pregnancy Discrimination Act; undue hardship; Family and Medical Leave Act; glass ceiling; reverse discrimina-

tion; Age Discrimination in Employment Act; Americans with Disabilities Act; Employment Non-Discrimination Act; harassment; sexual harassment; dominant group; subordinate group

CHAPTER QUESTIONS

1. What are the four diversity dimensions?
2. What is the evolution of ethnic and religious diversity in the United States beginning with Christopher Columbus?
3. Describe several workplace discrimination issues. What laws govern these issues?
4. Discuss five competitive advantages of diversity management.

5. What are some of the best operational practices for managing diversity?
6. What are the recommended 10 steps for implementing a diversity initiative?
7. Describe several diversity training workshops. How would you address the typical problems associated with diversity training?

ANCILLARY MATERIALS

Websites to Explore

- Government Statistics for Diversity
  - U.S. Census Bureau, Quick Facts, available at http://quickfacts.census.gov/qfd/states/00000.html.
  - U.S. Census Bureau, National Population Projections, available at http://www

.census.gov/population/www/projections/summarytables.html.
  - Bureau of Labor Statistics, "Household Data Annual Averages," available at http://www.bls.gov/cps/cpsaat11.pdf.
- Diversity Laws and Topics

In the Real World: Enron

Checks and Balances—1997

Michael Kopper agreed to Andy Fastow's plan for funding the RADR SPE, and everyone involved profited.

In early 1997, David Duncan, a relatively young rising star and Arthur Andersen partner at age 38, became Andersen's lead auditor on the Enron account. He would be reviewing the work of his former boss at Andersen, Rick Causey, now Enron's chief accounting officer (CAO). Duncan was a strong client advocate, someone who helped clients achieve desired accounting objectives. His annual bonus and advancement within Andersen depended on increasing client fees by 20 percent. Enron was Duncan's only customer. Critically questioning Enron's accounting transactions and financial arrangements could mean career suicide, something Fastow and Skilling pointed out to Duncan and his subordinates.

Fastow's creative SPE schemes saved Enron's fourth-quarter 1997 financial performance. Cash flow went from a negative $588 million at the end of September to a positive $501 million at the end of December, a $1 billion change for a company not dependent on Christmas sales.

Carl Bass, a senior Andersen accountant on Duncan's audit team, objected to Enron's aggressive accounting methods. Bass, having worked on the Enron account for two years, had developed a low regard for both Fastow and Causey. Bass concluded that Enron was inappropriately booking income and that Duncan should not sign off on the 1997 fourth-quarter audited statements until the company applied more rigorous accounting methods. This action would be interpreted negatively by Wall Street investors.

Fastow threatened to change accounting firms if Duncan did not sign the audited statements. Duncan, as the lead engagement partner, had the final say in the matter.

DECISION CHOICE. If you were lead external auditor engagement partner on the Enron account, would you

1. Risk losing the Enron account, which is the basis for your career path within Andersen, by demanding that Fastow and Causey follow more rigorous accounting methods?

2. Risk your professional license by allowing Fastow and Causey to use aggressive accounting methods?

Why?

- U.S. Equal Employment Opportunity Commission, "Laws and Guidance," available at http://www.eeoc.gov/laws/.
- United States Department of Labor, Compliance Topics, available at http://www.dol.gov/compliance/topics/.
- Pew Hispanic Center, available at http://pewhispanic.org/.
- Sexual Orientation Issues
  - "Best Places to Work for LGBT Equality," available at http://www.hrc.org/issues/workplace/11832.htm.
  - Williams Institute, sexual orientation law, available at http://www.law.ucla.edu/williamsinstitute/home.html.
  - Lambda Legal, list of states and municipalities prohibiting sexual orientation discrimination, available at http://www.lambdalegal.org/states-regions/.
- National Gay and Lesbian Taskforce, available at www.thetaskforce.org.
- White Privilege Questionnaire, available at http://husky1.stmarys.ca/~evanderveen/wvdv/Race_relations/white_privilege.htm.
- The Implicit Attitude Test, available at https://implicit.harvard.edu/implicit/demo/.

Best Place to Work Video

- Best Place to Work—Google, available at http://money.cnn.com/video/fortune/2008/01/22/bpw.google.fortune/.

Business Ethics Issue Video

- "Digital Nation," *Frontline*, about people immersed in a "wired" life; February 2, 2010, 90 minutes, available at http://www

.pbs.org/wgbh/pages/frontline/digitalna
tion/view/?utm_campaign=viewpage&utm_
medium=grid&utm_source=grid.

TEDTalks Videos

- *Diversity Empowerment of Women:* Hanna
  Rosin reviews new data that shows women
  actually surpassing men in several important measures, such as college graduation
  rates; December 2010, 17 minutes, available
  at http://www.ted.com/talks/hanna_rosin_
  new_data_on_the_rise_of_women.html.

- *Gender Diversity:* Tony Porter shares stories
  from his own life about how the "act like
  a man" mentality, drummed into so many
  men and boys, can lead men to disrespect,
  mistreat and abuse women and each other;

December 2010, 12 minutes, available at
http://www.ted.com/talks/tony_porter_a_
call_to_men.html.

Conversations with Charlie Rose

- A conversation about the repeal of "Don't
  Ask Don't Tell" with Al Hunt of Bloomberg
  News and David Ignatius of the *Washington Post*; December 22, 2010, 20 minutes,
  available at http://www.charlierose.com/
  view/interview/11369.

- A conversation with Paul Volcker, former
  chairman of the Federal Reserve, about
  the 2008–2009 global economic crisis;
  September 29, 2009, 60 minutes, available at http://www.charlierose.com/view/
  interview/10631.

NOTES

1. Robert R. McCrae and Paul T. Costa Jr., "Validation of the Five-Factor Model across Instruments
   and Observers," *Journal of Personality and Social
   Psychology*, 52, 1 (1087): 80–92. Survey scales for
   these factors are available at http://ipip.ori.org/
   newBigFive5broadKey.htm, accessed 10/30/10.

2. James Krohe Jr., "Are Workplace Tests Worth Taking?" *Across the Board*, 43, 4 (2006), 16–23.

3. The Myers & Briggs Foundation, available at
   www.myersbriggs.org, accessed 10/30/10.

4. Howard Zinn, *A People's History of the United
   States 1492–Present* (New York: HarperCollins
   Publishers, 1995), p. 16.

5. U.S. Census Bureau, "Quickfacts," available at
   http://quickfacts.census.gov/qfd/states/00000
   .html, accessed 10/30/10. Total exceeds 100 percent because some Hispanics may be of any race, so
   they are also included in applicable race categories.

6. Elliott Robert Barkan, *And Still They Come: Im-
   migrants and American Society, 1920 to the 1990s*
   (Wheeling, IL: Harlan Davidson, 1996); Michael
   Barone, *The New Americans: How the Melting Pot
   Can Work Again* (Washington, DC: Regnery Pub-
   lishing, 2006).

7. U.S. Census Bureau, "2008 National Population
   Projections," http://www.census.gov/population/
   www/projections/2008projections.html, accessed
   10/30/10.

8. *Payne v. Western & A.R.R.*, 81 Tenn. 507, 519–
   520 (1884).

9. Jeffrey Passel and D'Vera Cohn, April
   2009, "A Portrait of Unauthorized Immigrants to the United States," available at
   http://pewhispanic.org/reports/report.php?
   ReportID=107, accessed 10/30/10; see also "Demographics and Socio-Economic Status of Unauthorized Immigrants in the United States, 2000–
   2006," available at http://immigration.procon.org/
   viewresource.asp?resourceID=845#Introduction,
   accessed 10/30/10.

10. Randal C. Archibold, "Arizona Enacts Stringent
    Law on Immigration," *New York Times*, April 23,
    2010.

11. John C. Turner, *Rediscovering the Social Group:
    A Self-Categorization Theory* (Oxford, Eng.:
    Blackwell, 1987).

12. Ellen Ernst Kossek, Sharon A. Lobel, and Jennifer
    Brown, "Human Resource Strategies to Manage
    Workforce Diversity," in Alison M. Konrad, Push-
    kala Prasa, and Judith K. Pringle (Eds.), *Handbook
    of Workplace Diversity* (Thousand Oaks, CA:
    Sage, 2005), pp. 53–74.

13. U.S. Equal Employment Opportunity Commis-
    sion, "Discrimination by Type," available at http://
    www.eeoc.gov/laws/types/index.cfm, accessed
    10/30/10.

[14] Guy Trebay, "Tattoos Gain Even More Visibility," *New York Times,* September 24, 2006.

[15] Laura Fishman, "Employee's Tattoos Lead to Title VII Suit Against Starbucks," *Houston Employment Law Blog,* February 16, 2010, available at http://houstonemploymentlawsblog.com/2010/02/employees-tattoos-lead-to-suit-against-starbucks.html, accessed 10/30/10.

[16] Michelle Conlin, "Is Wal-Mart Hostile to Women?" *Business Week,* July 16, 2001.

[17] Steven Greenhouse, "Report Warned Wal-Mart of Risks Before Bias Suit," *New York Times,* June 3, 2010.

[18] Linda L. Carli, Suzanne J. LaFleur, and Christopher C. Loeber, "Nonverbal Behavior, Gender, and Influence," *Journal of Personality and Social Psychology,* 68, 6 (1995), 1030–1041.

[19] U.S. Equal Employment Opportunity Commission, "Equal Pay Act of 1963," available at http://www.eeoc.gov/laws/statutes/epa.cfm, accessed 6/3/10.

[20] U.S. Census Bureau, "PINC-03. Educational Attainment--People 25 Years Old and Over, by Total Money Earnings in 2008, Work Experience in 2008, Age, Race, Hispanic Origin, and Sex [Males]," available at http://www.census.gov/hhes/www/cpstables/032009/perinc/new03_136.htm, accessed 10/30/10.

[21] U.S. Census Bureau, "PINC-03. Educational Attainment--People 25 Years Old and Over, by Total Money Earnings in 2008, Work Experience in 2008, Age, Race, Hispanic Origin, and Sex [Females]," http://www.census.gov/hhes/www/cpstables/032009/perinc/new03_262.htm, accessed 10/30/10.

[22] U.S. Department of Labor, "Quick Stats on Women Workers, 2009," see item 9, available at http://www.dol.gov/wb/stats/main.htm, accessed 10/30/10.

[23] Bureau of Labor Statistics, "Household Data Annual Averages," available at http://www.bls.gov/cps/cpsaat11.pdf, accessed 6/3/10.

[24] Sharlene N. Hesse-Biber and Gregg L. Carter, *Working Women in America* (New York: Oxford University Press, 2005).

[25] Linda Babcock and Sara Laschever, *Women Don't Ask: Negotiation and the Gender Divide* (Princeton, NJ: Princeton University Press, 2003).

[26] David R. Hekman, Karl Aquino, Brad P. Owens, Terence R. Mitchell, Pauline Schilpzand, and Keith Leavitt, "An Examination of Whether and How Racial and Gender Biases Influence Customer Satisfaction," *Academy of Management Journal,* 53, 2 (2010), 238–264.

[27] U.S. Equal Employment Opportunity Commission, "Pregnancy Discrimination," available at http://www.eeoc.gov/laws/types/pregnancy.cfm, accessed 10/30/10.

[28] U.S. Department of Labor, "Family and Medical Leave," available at http://www.dol.gov/compliance/topics/benefits-leave-FMLA.htm, accessed 10/30/10.

[29] Federal Glass Ceiling Commission, *Good for Business: Making Full Use of the Nation's Human Capital.* Washington, DC: U.S. Government Printing Office, 1995.

[30] U.S. Bureau of Labor Statistics, "Labor Force Characteristics by Race and Ethnicity, 2008," available at http://data.bls.gov/cgi-bin/print.pl/cps/race_ethnicity_2008_1.htm, accessed 10/30/10.

[31] Bureau of Labor Statistics, "Household Data Annual Averages."

[32] Karen S. Lyness and Donna E. Thompson, "Climbing the Corporate Ladder: Do Female and Male Executives Follow the Same Route?" *Journal of Applied Psychology,* 85, 1 (2000), 86–101.

[33] Karen S. Lyness and Madeline E. Heilman, "When Fit Is Fundamental: Performance Evaluations and Promotions of Upper-Level Female and Male Managers," *Journal of Applied Psychology,* 91, 4 (2006), 777–785.

[34] "Gender Discriminations," *Inc.,* available at http://www.inc.com/encyclopedia/gender-discriminations_pagen_3.html, accessed 10/30/10.

[35] "Gender Discrimination," *Encyclopedia of Business,* 2nd Edition, available at http://www.referenceforbusiness.com/small/Eq-Inc/Gender-Discrimination.html, accessed 10/30/10.

[36] U.S. Bureau of Labor Statistics, "Labor Force Characteristics by Race and Ethnicity, 2008."

[37] Jonathan Kaufman, "Rethinking Racial Progress," *Wall Street Journal,* August 28, 2008.

[38] CNN/Opinion Research Corporation Poll, January 14–17, 2008, www.pollingreport.com/race.htm, accessed 10/30/10.

[39] Barry A. Kosmin and Ariela Keysar, *American Religious Identification Survey* (Hartford, CT: Trinity College, 2008), available at http://b27.cc.trincoll

.edu/weblogs/AmericanReligionSurvey-ARIS/reports/ARIS_Report_2008.pdf, accessed 10/30/10.

[40] U.S. Equal Employment Opportunity Commission, "Religious Discrimination," available at http://www.eeoc.gov/laws/types/religion.cfm, accessed 10/30/10.

[41] U.S. Equal Employment Opportunity Commission, "The Age Discrimination in Employment Act of 1967," available at http://www.eeoc.gov/laws/statutes/adea.cfm, accessed 10/30/10.

[42] Thomas W. H. Ng and Daniel C. Feldman, "The Relationship of Age to Ten Dimensions of Job Performance," *Journal of Applied Psychology*, 93, 2 (2008), 392–423.

[43] U.S. Department of Labor, Office of Disability Employment Policy, "Frequently Asked Questions," available at http://www.dol.gov/odep/faqs/, accessed 10/30/10.

[44] U.S. Equal Employment Opportunity Commission, "Titles I and V of the Americans with Disabilities Act of 1990 (ADA)," available at http://www.eeoc.gov/laws/statutes/ada.cfm, accessed 10/30/10.

[45] U.S. Equal Employment Opportunity Commission, "The Americans with Disabilities Act of 1990," available at http://www.eeoc.gov/eeoc/history/35th/1990s/ada.html, accessed 10/30/10.

[46] Francis Mark Mondimore, *A Natural History of Homosexuality* (Baltimore, MD: John Hopkins University Press, 1996).

[47] Kevin Sack, "When the Bride Takes a Bride, Businesses Respond," *New York Times,* July 15, 2010.

[48] Edward O. Laumann, Robert T. Michael, and John H. Gagnon, *The Social Organization of Sexuality: Sexual Practices in the United States* (Chicago, IL: University of Chicago Press, 1994) has the lower 1.5 percent estimate based on the National Health and Social Life Survey (NHSLS). The higher 3 percent estimates is from Gary J. Gates, *Same-Sex Couples and the Gay, Lesbian, Bisexual Population: New Estimates from the American Community Survey* (Los Angeles, CA: The Williams Institute, 2006), available at http://www.law.ucla

.edu/williamsinstitute/publications/SameSexCouplesandGLBpopACS.pdf, accessed 10/30/10.

[49] Lambda Legal website provides a list of states and municipalities prohibiting sexual orientation discrimination at http://www.lambdalegal.org/states-regions/, accessed 10/30/10.

[50] Lee Badgett, Deborah Ho, and Brad Sears, *Bias in the Workplace: Consistent Evidence of Sexual Orientation and Gender Identity Discrimination* (Los Angeles, CA: The Williams Institute, 2007), available at: http://www.law.ucla.edu/williamsinstitute/publications/Bias%20in%20the%20Workplace.pdf, accessed 10/30/10.

[51] National Gay and Lesbian Taskforce, *Lesbian, Gay, Bisexual and Transgender Youth: An Epidemic of Homelessness,* available at http://www.thetaskforce.org/reports_and_research/homeless_youth, accessed 10/30/10.

[52] National Gay and Lesbian Taskforce, "Employment Non-Discrimination Act (ENDA)," available at http://www.thetaskforce.org/issues/nondiscrimination/ENDA_main_page, accessed 10/30/10.

[53] Merrill A. McPeak, "Don't Ask, Don't Tell, Don't Change," *New York Times,* March 4, 2010.

[54] David M. Herszenhorn and Carl Hulse, "House Votes to Allow Repeal of 'Don't Ask, Don't Tell' Law," *New York Times,* May 27, 2010.

[55] Human Rights Campaign, "LGBT Equality at the Fortune 500," available at http://www.hrc.org/issues/fortune500.htm, accessed 10/30/10.

[56] Robert Pear, "Gay Workers Will Get Time to Care for Partner's Sick Child," *New York Times,* June 21, 2010.

[57] U.S. Equal Employment Opportunity Commission, "Harassment," available at http://www.eeoc.gov/laws/practices/harassment.cfm, accessed 10/30/10.

[58] Alan Kopit, "Research Reveals Rise in Interoffice Romance," *Lawyers.com,* available at http://research.lawyers.com/Research-Reveals-Rise-in-Interoffice-Romance.html?SPC-CNN, accessed 10/30/10.

59 Susan M. Heathfield, "Tips About Dating and Sex and Romance at Work," About.com: Human Resources, available at: http://humanresources.about.com/cs/workrelationships/a/workromance.htm, accessed 10/30/10.

60 U.S. Equal Employment Opportunity Commission, "Sexual Harassment," available at http://www.eeoc.gov/laws/types/sexual_harassment.cfm, accessed 10/30/10.

61 Chelsea R. Willness, Piers Steel, and Kibeom Lee, "A Meta-Analysis of the Antecedents and Consequences of Workplace Sexual Harassment," *Personnel Psychology*, 60, 1 (2007), 127–162.

62 Jennifer L. Berdahl and Karl Aquino, "Sexual Behavior at Work: Fun or Folly?" *Journal of Applied Psychology*, 94, 1 (2009), 34–47.

63 Hilary J. Gettman and Michele J. Gelfand, "When the Customer Shouldn't be King: Antecedents and Consequences of Sexual Harassment by Clients and Customers," *Journal of Applied Psychology,* 92, 3 (2007), 757–770.

64 U.S. Equal Employment Opportunity Commission, "Sexual Harassment Charges, EEOC & FEPAs Combined: FY 1997–FY 2009," available at http://www.eeoc.gov/eeoc/statistics/enforcement/sexual_harassment.cfm, accessed 10/30/10.

65 U.S. Equal Employment Opportunity Commission, "Retaliation," available at http://www.eeoc.gov/laws/types/retaliation.cfm, accessed 10/30/10.

66 U.S. Equal Employment Opportunity Commission, "Facts About Retaliation," available at http://www.eeoc.gov/laws/types/facts-retal.cfm, accessed 10/30/10.

67 U.S. Bureau of Labor Statistics, "Labor Force Characteristics by Race and Ethnicity, 2008." Percentages are estimates due to controlling for double counting of Hispanics in the government database.

68 Kathryn A. Canas and Harris Sondak, *Opportunities and Challenges of Workplace Diversity* (Upper Saddle River, NJ: Pearson Prentice Hall, 2008), p. 6.

69 Equal Employment Opportunity Commission, *Best Practices of Private Sector Employers* (Washington, DC: Equal Employment Opportunity Commission, 1997), report available at http://www.eeoc.gov/eeoc/task_reports/best_practices.cfm, accessed 10/30/10.

70 *Working Mother,* "2009 and Past CEO Diversity Leadership Honorees," available at http://www.diversitybestpractices.com/node/746, accessed 10/30/10.

71 Human Rights Campaign, "Corporate Equality Index," available at http://www.hrc.org/cei2011/index.html, accessed 10/30/10.

72 Rosabeth Kanter, Barry Stein, and Todd Jick (Eds.), *The Challenge of Organizational Change* (New York: Free Press, 1992).

73 Rohini Anand and Mary-Frances Winters, "A Retrospective View of Corporate Diversity Training From 1964 to the Present," *Academy of Management Learning & Education*, 7, 3 (2008), 356–372.

74 Parker J. Palmer, *A Hidden Wholeness: The Journey Toward an Undivided Life* (San Francisco, CA: Jossey-Bass, 2004).

75 Peggy McIntosh, "White Privilege and Male Privilege: A Personal Account of Coming to See Correspondences through Work in Women's Studies," *Peace and Freedom*, July/August 1989.

76 The Implicit Attitude Test is available at https://implicit.harvard.edu/implicit/demo/, accessed 10/30/10.

77 Shankar Vedantam, "See No Bias," *Washington Post*, January 23, 2005.

78 Anne McKee and Susan Schor, "Confronting Prejudice and Stereotypes: A Teaching Model," *Journal of Management Education*, 18, 4 (1994), 447–467.

79 Ibid.

80 Rhonda Hilyer, *Success Signals,* 7th ed. (Seattle, WA: Agreement Dynamics, 2006). For more information, contact Agreement Dynamics at 1-800-97-AGREE or HQ@agreementdynamics.com.

PART III

Daily Internal
Operations

CHAPTER OUTLINE

8

ETHICS REPORTING SYSTEMS

What would you do?

Double Standard

After graduation, you obtain a staff position in the Human Resource Department of a medium-size company. Your job duties include conducting ethics training workshops and monitoring the organization's ethics assist line.

The organization's Code of Ethics emphasizes four values—truth, respect, honest communications, and integrity. This month's workshop is about integrity. The 50 participants engage in several small group activities and you are pleased with their discussions.

The following day you notice a message on the ethics assist line. "I wanted to point out some possible hypocrisy with our Code of Ethics during yesterday's workshop," the message begins, "but I didn't want to offend Sally, our vice president of sales. According to our Code of Ethics, it is a violation for any of our purchasing agents to receive a gift from a supplier. But our salespeople are allowed to offer entertainment gifts to potential customers. The sales department can give the same gifts that our purchasers cannot receive. That's not integrity; that's a hypocritical double standard. The company doesn't trust our purchasing agents to receive the gifts that our salespeople give to their clients."

You review company records and note that the organization's Code of Ethics for buyers is a standard adopted from the Institute for Supply Management, the trade association for purchasers and supply managers.

Next you approach Sally about this concern. "You bet I encourage our salespeople to give clients free tickets to sporting events and art performances at the Civic Center," Sally informs you. "These gifts work. That's how we get a lot of new business and take care of our existing customers. Plus we're supporting community activities. Our major competitors do the same thing. None of our employees personally gains from this. If my sales employees can't give gifts, we would lose a lot of business. Lost sales mean lost commissions. Before you know it, our best salespeople would quit and get jobs with our competitors. If our revenues decline, it would be your fault!"

Despite Sally's adamant policy defense, the ethics assist line issue still bothers you because the company does seem to have a double standard, one for purchasing agents and another for salespeople. If it is ethical for your salespeople to give these gifts, then shouldn't it be ethical for your purchasing agents to receive them from their suppliers? But then again, the industry association, which encourages best practices, opposes gift giving.

What would you do? Would you

1. Maintain the double standard?
2. Change the policy and not let salespeople give these gifts?
3. Change the policy and allow purchasing agents to receive these gifts?

Why?

Chapter Objectives

After reading this chapter, you will be able to:

- Understand why some employees do not report ethical misconduct
- Describe how to engage employees in discussing ethical misconduct
- Administer an internal reporting system for ethical issues

- Create an Ethics & Compliance Officer and ombudsperson positions
- Manage an assist line to receive employee complaints by telephone or Internet
- Describe the negative outcomes whistle-blowing has on both the whistle-blower and the organization

Situation 1: "As my colleague (or manager), I don't think you should be sexually harassing Jill."

Situation 2: "As the owner, I thought you might want to know that my manager seems to have understated our costs by $10,000 in this month's financial report and is overstating our product capabilities to our customers."

These two statements are truthful and simple, yet for many people the statements are very difficult to say. High-performance organizations depend on employees speaking honestly with their colleagues, managers, and company owners when ethical problems arise. Situation 1 demonstrates an ideal reaction, whereby the employee raises concerns directly with the colleague or manager engaged in the ethical misconduct. The next best option is for the employee to inform the superior of a person engaged in an unethical activity, as demonstrated in Situation 2.

This chapter examines why employees maintain silence when they observe ethical misconduct and what management behaviors and internal mechanisms can elicit such essential information. Excellent managers are the type of people colleagues and subordinates can trust and confide in with such personally sensitive information. But some employees remain uncomfortable sharing ethical issues with their direct supervisors. The chapter explores three alternative internal communication mechanisms for obtaining information about unethical behavior: an Ethics & Compliance Officer, an ombudsperson, and an assist line. A failure in these internal communication systems can result in external whistle-blowing, which is damaging for both the organization and the whistle-blower.

Employee Silence on Ethical Misconduct

A manager's knowledge about how well the organization performs is generally limited to his or her immediate experiences and information sources, such as specific metrics and feedback from employees and customers. When problems arise, managers depend on employees to take immediate corrective action or inform them so the managers can address the problem before the situation worsens. Managers need to know as soon as possible if an employee has observed a supplier bribing the organization's purchasing agent, coworkers not performing their duties, or a major customer sexually harassing salespeople.

Sometimes, however, employees are hesitant to share personally sensitive issues with their manager. Employee silence refers to an employee who observes ethical misconduct at work but does not discuss the matter with the person engaged in the ethical misconduct or someone else in the organization with authority. After the damage occurs or escalates, managers are left wondering why nobody told them about salespeople lying to customers, employee theft, sexual harassment, or the use of questionable accounting techniques.

Extent of Employee Silence

According to the 2009 Ethics Resource Center (ERC) biannual survey, 37 percent of the respondents who observed ethical misconduct did not report it.[1] The ERC research differentiates between two potential beneficiaries of ethical misconduct—the organization and an employee. Some ethical misconduct furthers the company's financial performance agenda, such as bribing customers to purchase the company's products or services. Other ethical misconducts are undertaken for personal benefits, such as stealing product from the company.

Exhibit 8.1 highlights how often an observed ethical misconduct that benefitted the organization or an employee is unreported. For instance, among those employees who observed a bribe, less than half report the bribe to management. Similarly, less than half of the respondents who observed improper hiring practices, discrimination, Internet abuse, lying to stakeholders, lying to employees, and sexual harassment reported the ethical misconduct.

Exhibit 8.1 Unreported Observed Ethical Misconducts	
Ethical Misconducts Undertaken to Benefit the Company	**Ethical Misconducts Undertaken to Benefit the Individual**
• Bribes (Unreported 64% of the time) • Using Inside Information about a Competitor (46%) • Environmental Violations (45%) • Alteration of Documents (45%) • Alteration of Financial Records (43%) • Safety Violations (37%)	• Improper Hiring Practices (Unreported 67% of the time) • Discrimination (65%) • Internet Abuse (62%) • Lying to Stakeholders (59%) • Lying to Employees (58%) • Sexual Harassment (51%)

The ERC study also differentiates "red-flag" financial reporting misconduct—falsifying or manipulating financial information, overriding routine procedures, or creating fictitious vendors or invoices—from other types of ethical misconducts. During the previous 12 months, approximately 14 percent of the ERC respondents observed one or more "red-flag" financial reporting misconducts. Among these, 30 percent of the observers did not report the financial misconduct, which put their organizations at significant legal risk.

Research on the extent of employee silence on other issues sheds additional light on this problem.[2] As reported in Chapter 1, researchers Frances Milliken, Elizabeth Morrison, and Patricia Hewlin conducted 40 in-depth interviews with employees representing a wide range of industries. The participants worked between six months and 16 years with their current employers, and 70 percent had been previously employed in a different organization. Thirty-four of the 40 participants (85 percent) described at least one story in which they intentionally did not speak openly to a superior about a workplace situation that really concerned them. This research strongly suggests that many people simply do not feel comfortable speaking with their bosses about certain types of problems.

Reasons for Employee Silence

Why don't employees intervene when colleagues and managers ethically misbehave? Why don't employees at least inform the person's superior? Eventually, some Enron employees, investment bankers, and accountants knew that Andy Fastow had engineered a massive financial and accounting fraud. But nobody spoke out until very late in the process.

A wide range of reasons for maintaining silence about an observed ethical misconduct can be attributed to organizational factors, observer factors, and anticipated negative outcomes (see Exhibit 8.2).[3]

Exhibit 8.2 Reasons for Employee Silence

Organizational Factors	Observer Factors	Anticipated Negative Outcomes
• Work culture discourages conveying negative information or dissent • Loyalty to employees, manager, organization, and profession is not aligned with ethics • No established reporting system beyond chain of command • Lack of anonymity for reporting misconduct	• Habituated not to share sensitive information • Low moral intensity • Lack of evidence • Lack of empowerment • Lack of seniority • Low hierarchical position • Lack of personal relationship with the person or person's supervisor • Lack of moral courage	• Being labeled or viewed negatively (e.g., troublemaker, complainer, tattletale) • Damaging a relationship (e.g., loss of trust, respect, acceptance) • Retaliation or punishment (e.g., loss of job or promotion) • Negatively impacting others (e.g., don't want to upset or embarrass someone, or get someone in trouble) • Being blamed for the problem • No corrective action will be taken

Organizational Factors   Many people are uncomfortable conveying negative information to organizational leaders who dislike criticism or dissent. Authoritarian leaders rule according to the saying: "My way or the highway." They expect absolute loyalty from subordinates to their position and commands, and they consider taking suggestions or advice from subordinates, no matter how essential, as a leadership weakness. Some leaders tell subordinates they don't want to hear about problems, just solutions. Advising employees to develop solutions is well intended, but the perceived lack of receptiveness to hearing about problems reinforces the normal hesitancy subordinates have approaching a supervisor, which delays the time it takes an important concern to reach the manager's attention.

Within an authoritarian work culture, it is safer for an observer of ethical misconduct to remain silent. Speaking out or taking action can result in accusations of disloyalty and insubordination, being blamed for the problem, reassignment, or dismissal. Reporting the problem to the manager's superior demonstrates stepping outside the chain of command, another sign of disrespect toward following rules and procedures.

Ethical misconduct observers will often remain silent when loyalty to employees, managers, and the organization outweighs loyalty to ethics or professional obligations. When this misalignment occurs, being ethical often refers only to personal loyalty, which ignores the concerns raised by the higher-level ethical theories discussed in Chapter 5, such as utilitarianism, deontology, and virtue ethics. An employee loyal to ethics or a professional code is characterized as being disloyal to organizational managers and employees, even in situations when the ethical misconduct is detrimental to organizational operations. Researchers report, for instance, that at critical moments, accountants often consider the trade-off between loyalty to a colleague and the organization versus loyalty to professional rules and codes when deciding whether to follow an order to misreport financial information.[4]

Two related organizational factors that contribute to employee silence about ethical misconduct are the lack of a reporting system beyond the chain of command and reporting anonymity. If a supervisor commits the ethical misconduct or is not open to employee input, employee silence is solidified when the chain of command is the only reporting system available. In addition, it is difficult for an observer to report ethical misconduct when the person behaving unethically can readily identify the information source.

Observer Factors   Individuals are creatures of habit. As discussed in Chapter 1, a child's reaction to an ethical dilemma is initially influenced by parents, siblings, and friends, which generates a pattern of responses to moral issues. At a young age, individuals form a habit of speaking out or remaining silent about observed ethical misconduct. Some parents and teachers pressure children not to question authority. Some siblings and friends pressure children not to squeal. These deeply engrained habits are then brought into the workplace.

The moral intensity of an issue (see Chapter 5) influences whether an observer will speak out or maintain silence. Based on the moral intensity factors, observers are likely to remain silent if the ethical misconduct causes minimal negative consequences to the recipient or organization, occurs in a physically distant part of the organization, or there is a lack of consensus in the organization that the misconduct is actually unethical. Each of these factors reduces the moral intensity of the wrongdoing. Silence is also likely if the observer lacks sufficient evidence that the alleged person committed the ethical misconduct.

Job-related factors influence employee silence as well. Employee empowerment refers to employees possessing the authority to make decisions affecting themselves and their work. The observer may not be empowered to act, believing that it is the supervisor's responsibility to respond to the ethical misconduct or that the supervisor is indifferent about ethics. If an observer of ethical misconduct is a new employee, or low in the hierarchy, the person may lack the legitimacy to be taken seriously by others in the organization. The observer may also lack a personal relationship with the person engaged in the misconduct or that person's superior. For each of these situations, an observer may remain silent until employed long enough to accumulate the power, formal authority, or respect necessary to successfully intervene.

Lastly, observers who lack moral courage will remain silent about ethical misconducts even if the appropriate reporting systems are available and the previously mentioned individual factors are not a hindrance. An observer with clear evidence, seniority, and organizational authority may still remain silent about ethical misconducts due to a lack of courage or self-esteem. Speaking out against ethical misconduct requires confidence in one's ability to survive the variety of anticipated negative outcomes discussed in the following section.

Anticipated Negative Outcomes   "Will this be worth the hassle?" is a reasonable question for an observer to address prior to speaking out against an ethical misconduct. Rather than framing the issue of speaking out in positive language and the higher ethical theories, such as doing what is right or wanting to benefit the organization or society, some people frame the issue in terms of the anticipated negative outcomes to self and others and wonder whether it is worth the effort to incur the wrath of others.

Anticipated negative outcomes that influence whether an observer approaches the person engaged in misconduct or the person's superior include being viewed negatively by others, damaging work relationships, negatively impacting the lives of others, and being blamed for the problem. For some employees, their deepest friendships are with people they work with on a daily basis. Informing a superior about a colleague's ethical misconduct could result in the colleague being disciplined or terminated. Being the cause of another employee's dismissal can damage family relationships outside of work.

In addition, informing a supervisor about ethical misconduct committed by a colleague could create traumatic daily experiences, such as colleagues accusing the employee of being a "squealer" or disloyal. The employee reporting the misconduct could be ostracized by colleagues. Once labeled a squealer, coming to work could become psychologically unbearable.

Fear of retaliation from colleagues and supervisors is a realistic concern. In the 2009 ERC survey, 15 percent of the respondents reported being retaliated against for reporting an observed ethical misconduct. More than half of this group were excluded from decisions and work activities, verbally abused by their supervisor or another manager, or distanced from their peers. Other forms of retaliation the respondents experienced included being denied promotions or raises (43 percent), relocated or reassigned (27 percent), and demoted (18 percent).

A "nothing will get done" belief is also a major contributor to employee silence. It can be extremely disheartening for an observer to develop the moral courage to speak out against an ethical misconduct, only to have nobody in authority take corrective action. This detrimental belief is often developed when managers fail to act on previously reported ethical misconduct.

For instance, from 2003 to 2005, Dell production and sales managers were under tremendous pressure to produce and sell desktop personal computers. Dell knowingly sold millions of faulty computers to corporations and small businesses.[5] Service employees were told by managers that when customers complain, blame the customers for misusing the product. If the customer persists, then replace the faulty motherboard with another faulty motherboard. In this situation, informing a Dell salesperson or supervisor about the ethical misconduct would not make a difference. Supervisors already knew about the faulty wiring and chemical leaks, but they had no slack resources to adequately address the problem. Why would a Dell employee report the ethical misconduct when managers not only encouraged the misbehavior, but also rewarded subordinates who engaged in ethical misconduct?

Ethically Approachable Managers

The best ethics reporting system is a manager who welcomes ethical discussions with employees and input on ethical misconduct. A diverse set of managerial techniques and attributes can help employees become comfortable sharing sensitive ethical information. Managers who are honest and responsible, and provide opportunities for sharing information as part of normal operations, are easier for employees to approach.

Ethical discussions need to be an ongoing dialogue. Employees are more likely to discuss an ethical concern with a manager if these types of discussions occur on a regular basis rather than only during dire circumstances. If it is normal to have conversations about ethics, then discussing instances of potential ethical misconduct becomes part of the workplace culture. Managers can demonstrate familiarity with the types of ethical issues the organization experiences by staying abreast of the ethics and diversity training workshop topics and discussions, and ensuring the implementation of action plans supporting existing strengths and addressing ethical weaknesses.

Previous chapters highlighted the importance of introducing the organization's Code of Ethics and the ethical decision-making framework during employee orientation. Refer to these documents as often as possible and relate them directly to specific decisions and actions. Emphasize how good decisions and actions were rooted in ethics. Describe how managers took into consideration the impact a decision had on affected stakeholders, and that the good consequences were generated by good motives.

Becoming an "approachable" manager is an important managerial skill for helping employees overcome fears about discussing any workplace problem, including ethical misconduct. Approachability begins with managerial honesty and transparency. A manager must be willing to discuss his or her own ethical mistakes in a manner that humanizes the manager without losing authority. Every human being is morally imperfect, which includes every manager.

Honest managers attract honest reactions, such as in the statement: "Since you're being honest with me, I might as well be honest with you." Managers who honestly share their ethical challenges tend to attract employees wanting to discuss their own ethical challenges or observations about ethical misconduct. Managers pretending moral infallibility tend to alienate employees seeking moral guidance.

Approachability also means having frequent interactions with subordinates. Highly visible managers who circulate among their subordinates foster trust and authenticity because less is hidden from view. Being receptive to employee concerns generally requires an open door policy whereby subordinates feel welcome to enter a manager's office and engage in a discussion. Schedule short check-in meetings with employees on a regular basis to address continuous improvement issues. This establishes a meeting time when other issues, including ethical dilemmas, can be addressed.

An open door policy does not mean the door remains open during every conversation. Closing the office door after a subordinate enters allows for a free-ranging discussion of workplace issues without worrying about who might overhear. Sharing concerns about a colleague or manager can be emotionally draining. The information deserves to be kept private and confidential. During these meetings, send a clear message that nothing matters more in the moment than this discussion. Good listening skills include allowing the subordinate time to frame the issue, not interrupting the conversation to answer a cell phone or email request, and verbally summarizing what the subordinate said to make sure the shared information has been appropriately understood.

Managers must trust their ethical intuitions and engage the subordinate in further conversation if there is a sense that the employee is hesitant to discuss something. Near the conclusion of any one-on-one meeting, ask the subordinate if there have been any situations lately when living up to the Code of Ethics has been challenging. Share examples that may be of concern to deepen managerial understanding of workplace dynamics.

Overcoming the "nothing will get done" obstacle requires demonstrating a strong sense of managerial responsibility. Individuals have often been told "trust me, I care," only to have their trust violated. Observers of ethical misconduct must believe that the manager not only understands and cares, but also will act on the knowledge and make appropriate changes. Provide the observer with progress feedback to keep the communication channel open for other relevant information.

In general, ethically approachable managers embody virtuous behaviors. An approachable manager, like a virtuous one, exhibits empathy, sympathy, compassion, justice, integrity, and kindness in a nonjudgmental manner. Subordinates will not share their observations of ethical misconduct if a manager judges them for not having already intervened. Forgive the observer for not acting in the moment and praise the employee for exhibiting moral courage by sharing the information. Subordinates conveying personally sensitive information expect managers to reason at the highest levels of moral development and follow through on their commitments. By doing so, the manager further increases his or her approachability and the likelihood of gathering additional essential information about organizational performance before situations worsen.

In large organizations, an Ethics & Compliance Officer, ombudsperson, chaplains, and assist lines are other internal mechanisms for eliciting and discussing ethical issues. These options are discussed in the following sections. Small organizations can simply assign the duties of an Ethics & Compliance Officer to a high-level manager.

Ethics & Compliance Officer

The Federal Sentencing Guidelines (see Chapter 2) provide a judicial incentive for assigning a high-level employee the responsibility of managing ethical performance. Giving ethics high visibility demonstrates a good faith effort to enhance ethics within the organization, which may reduce judicial penalties.

A growing number of organizations assign this responsibility to an Ethics & Compliance Officer (ECO). The position enables sensitive information to be shared without being diluted or stymied by the chain of command. There are more than 4,000 ECOs nationwide. The number will continue to grow, because new laws, such as the Sarbanes-Oxley Act, require greater institutional support for monitoring ethical behavior.[6]

The Ethics & Compliance Officer Association (ECOA), a professional organization for managers of ethics and compliance programs founded in 1992, has more than 1,100 members from a wide range of industries. The nonprofit organization is a support network for ECOs, as exemplified by its four values: integrity, confidentiality, collegiality, and cooperation. Members can share common problems and best practices with those having similar responsibilities.

Some organizations create a separate ECO position focused solely on enhancing ethical performance.[7] Many organizations, however, add the title and job responsibilities to an existing position, such as legal counsel, ombudsperson, regulatory compliance manager, internal auditor, or human resources manager. In small organizations, some of the duties discussed below can be assigned to a high-level manager or taken on by the owner.

Organizations also differ according to the nature and scope of ECO activities. Some organizations are highly centralized and one person or office determines ethics activities and standards for the entire organization. Other organizations are highly decentralized; the ECO provides oversight and the different locations or markets create their own ethics activities and standards, allowing for greater flexibility.

ECO Duties and Skills

What does an ECO do? ECO duties and responsibilities include the following:[8]

- Manage internal reporting systems
- Assess areas for ethical risks
- Offer guidance
- Monitor the organization's adherence to its Code of Ethics and Code of Conduct
- Oversee the ethics communication strategy
- Develop and interpret ethics policies
- Oversee the ethics training program
- Receive information about potential wrongdoings
- Collect and analyze relevant data
- Ensure that decisions are made and enforced
- Inform employees about outcomes

As suggested by the list of responsibilities and attributes, an ECO plays a key networking role and must be able to converse with various constituencies. Not all ethical issues have equal standing. The ECO needs to differentiate between material and immaterial issues. Faulty product on the market has greater weight than a personal slight, and knowingly selling faulty product with a high likelihood of causing considerable consumer damage has greater weight than an overlooked design requirement that is unlikely to harm anyone.

Tips and Techniques

Ethics & Compliance Officer Attributes*

An ECO receives very sensitive information about organizational behaviors that must be managed in a delicate manner.

An ECO should be someone who has

- Insider status and is well networked with business unit managers
- A high position that exemplifies authority
- The trust and respect of organizational executives
- Independence from senior staff and freedom from internal political pressure
- Operational experience
- Knowledge of organizational issues and activities
- Access to internal information as needed
- Knowledge of ethical theories
- Counseling and communication skills
- Problem-solving skills

* Dove Izraeli and Anat BarNir, "Promoting Ethics through Ethics Officers: A Proposed Profile and an Application," *Journal of Business Ethics*, 17, 11 (1998), 1189–1196.

Ethics-related information can come from suppliers and customers, in addition to employees. The ECO needs to work within the organization's tradition and work culture, gather the perspectives of multiple people associated with the issue, and then present a balanced perspective to the appropriate manager with suggested solutions. An ECO perceived as an ethics police officer is unlikely to be well received by managers responsible for implementing any change recommendations.

Every inquiry an ECO receives is essential because it takes only one unethical activity to severely damage an organization's operations. ECOs respond to a wide variety of practical questions, such as gift giving with suppliers and customers or personal use of organizational property. Employees often need clarity on these types of questions because of situational nuances. Many organizations, for instance, have an ethics policy stating that employees should not receive substantial gifts from vendors. But how much money is a substantial amount, and what if the gift is the result of winning a raffle at an industry conference? The ECO can provide the employee with immediate feedback on these matters.

Managing an Internal Reporting System

The ECO's primary duty is to manage the organization's internal reporting system. The process model in Exhibit 8.3 provides guidance on how to accomplish this.[9] As discussed in Chapter 4 (see Exhibit 4.1), most organizations do not begin considering appointing an ethics officer until they have at least 50 employees. But even smaller organizations can benefit from a clearly articulated internal reporting system and following these steps, particularly the process for investigating and resolving disputes.

	Exhibit 8.3 Internal Reporting System Process
Step	**Activity**
1.	Develop the ethics reporting policy in partnership with those in upper management positions to establish their buy-in.
2.	Communicate the ethics reporting policy to all employees through multiple media, such as the employee handbook, email, the company intranet site, department meetings, and training sessions.
3.	Emphasize the importance of reporting concerns about unethical and illegal conduct. Management cannot act on what it does not know.
4.	Assure people that any form of retaliation against an employee who raises an ethical concern is prohibited.
5.	If appropriate, the employee should first attempt to resolve the issue by directly approaching the individual engaged in the questionable activity.
6.	If direct discussion or resolution is not possible, then the employee should confidentially meet with the ECO to discuss the issue.
7.	If the employee prefers not to reveal his or her identity, then the employee should anonymously submit the concern to the ECO through the organization's intranet reporting system or in a sealed box. Establish a means of communication if the issue becomes a high-priority item needing additional information from the employee.
8.	Assure the employee that his or her identity will not be revealed without consent.
9.	Interview the employee and discuss clarifying questions.
10.	Develop a plan for investigating the case in a manner that honors the employee's confidentiality or anonymity.
11.	Conduct the investigation in a fair and confidential manner.
12.	If the investigation reveals that the employee's allegations are accurate, take prompt action to correct the wrongdoing.
13.	Inform the employee about the outcome of the investigation.
14.	Establish an appeals process for employees dissatisfied with the outcome of the initial investigation. Provide an advocate, probably from the Human Resources Department, to assist an employee who wishes to appeal an outcome.

Ombudsperson

Another internal channel for communicating information about potential ethical and legal violations is an organizational ombudsperson. The ombudsperson concept originated in government and has spread to other types of organizations, including corporations, hospitals, newspapers, universities, and nonprofits.[10]

An ombudsperson's job scope is typically much narrower than that of an ECO, and some organizations contract out for this service. An ombudsperson guarantees the employee anonymity; asks permission to contact key people; develops a plan for gathering information without revealing the identity of the complainant; investigates the claim outside the regular chain of command; reaches a conclusion; and, if so concluded, advocates for implementing the appropriate change. By providing employees with an institutional voice, the ombudsperson serves as a deterrent against managerial abuse of power and other unethical activities. The ombudsperson is granted access to all employees, including board members, when investigating a complaint.

The Office of the Ombudsman for the National Institutes for Health, within the U.S. Department of Health and Human Services, receives a range of inquiries, including those about interactions between staff members and managers, discrimination, harassment, and authorship and scientific collaboration issues.[11] The ombudsperson provides employees with an alternative formal grievance and complaint process independent of the federal agency. Reporting a discrimination or harassment problem to an ombudsperson does not preclude filing a formal complaint with the EEOC, although obtaining a solution to the problem within the organization could be quicker and less traumatic. The ombudsperson's annual report helps identify trends and patterns within the agency.

An ombudsperson, similar to an accountant or lawyer, is held legally accountable to a professional Code of Ethics. The International Ombudsman Association's Code of Ethics highlights four ethical principles and corresponding policies:[12]

1. *Independence:* The ombudsperson is independent in structure, function, and appearance to the highest degree possible within the organization.

2. *Neutrality and impartiality:* The ombudsperson remains unaligned and impartial and does not engage in any situation that could create a conflict of interest.

3. *Confidentiality:* The ombudsperson holds all communications in strict confidence and does not disclose confidential communications unless given permission to do so. The only exception to this privilege of confidentiality is when there is an imminent risk of serious harm.

4. *Informality:* The ombudsperson does not participate in any formal adjudicative or administrative procedure related to concerns brought to his or her attention.

Putnam Investments, a money management investment company, employs an ombudsperson as a resource to help employees address ethical and legal workplace concerns. *Barron's* magazine rated Putnam as the highest ranked equity and bond fund for 2009, a year when the financial community received massive government bailouts for risky investments.[13] As shown in the "Best Practice in Use" exhibit, Putnam employees are encouraged to contact the ombudsperson for a wide range of issues.[14] These same issues can help frame the type of concerns employees submit via an assist line.

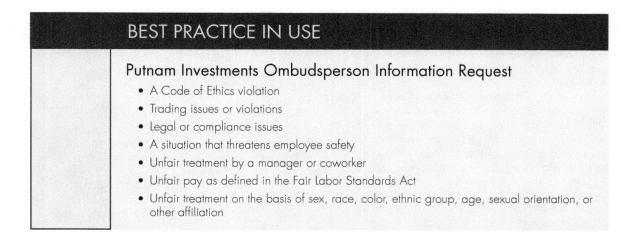

BEST PRACTICE IN USE

Putnam Investments Ombudsperson Information Request

- A Code of Ethics violation
- Trading issues or violations
- Legal or compliance issues
- A situation that threatens employee safety
- Unfair treatment by a manager or coworker
- Unfair pay as defined in the Fair Labor Standards Act
- Unfair treatment on the basis of sex, race, color, ethnic group, age, sexual orientation, or other affiliation

Chaplains

Some businesses have contracted out with chaplain consulting organizations as a mechanism for employees to confidentially share their personal and ethical concerns. Chaplains are members of a religious clergy trained in providing spiritual advice. Dating back to the 1940s, corporate chaplains originally provided, upon request, pastoral care for employees and their families dealing with illnesses, death, addictions, or other personal issues, and they were part of a company's employee benefits package. Over time, their list of services expanded to include helping employees manage ethical dilemmas and interactions with other employees. Most corporate chaplains have seminary degrees and are trained counselors.

The two most prominent providers of chaplains are Marketplace Chaplains[15] and Corporate Chaplains of America.[16] Marketplace Chaplains offers a team consisting of male, female, and ethnically diverse chaplains who regularly visit the worksite. The organization's more than 2,500 chaplains represent more than 80 different religious denominations. Marketplace Chaplains serves 418 clients with 500,000 employees and family members and operates in more than 43 states and 70 industries. Client size ranges from a single-person business to a corporation with more than 37,000 employees.

The chaplains are on call 24 hours a day, seven days a week. Workplace interactions between a chaplain and an employee are kept to a minimum. Most meetings are arranged for nonworking hours, except in times of crisis. Conversations with chaplains are confidential, although an employee can request the chaplain to discuss a matter with corporate managers. According to Psychology Professor Kelly Williams, organizations using employee assistance programs such as corporate chaplains reduce turnover and costs by "forging a psychological contract with their employees that really says 'we care about you' . . . a message that goes a long way."[17]

Let's Build a Building

Undocumented Workers

You put out a bid request for general contractors to renovate a retail store for a grand reopening. The entire project should take only three months. Three bids are submitted and one bid is substantially lower than the other two.

You speak with the low-bid general contractor to verify that he hasn't overlooked any costs. "No, I have low labor rates and my crews are just extremely efficient," he tells you. You hire the low-bid general contractor. The project will begin in mid-May and will be completed by mid-August, in plenty of time for the Labor Day grand reopening.

During the fourth week of renovation, you drive by the jobsite and are impressed with how much progress has been made. You get out of the car to praise the foreman, who appears a little nervous upon your arrival. The foreman, who looks Mexican, speaks very limited English, as do the other workers on the jobsite.

When you get back to the office, you have a message waiting from one of the original higher-bid general contractors. "How's the project coming along?" he asks. You mention that progress is excellent; however, the workers are unable to communicate with you. "What do you expect; they're a bunch of illegal immigrants," he tells you.

Next, you call the general contractor and ask him to provide you with worker documentation. "You're best off not asking," he tells you. "These are extremely hard-working men. They have family members here and elsewhere to care for. Yeah, fines can be high, but the government hardly ever enforces the law. There are more than 11 million undocumented immigrants in the United States. You think the government can't find them? For goodness sakes, just walk into the kitchen of just about any restaurant!"

Nonetheless, you fear that the general contractor who did not get the winning bid might inform government officials about undocumented workers on the jobsite, as well as the negative political backlash that would follow.

Your general contractor argues that he can finish the project on time only by using his current work crew. They are well-trained hard workers willing to work long hours for low pay. It would take several weeks for him to replace them, which would delay the grand reopening at least one month. In addition, the costs would substantially increase.

What would you do? Would you

1. Remain quite about the undocumented immigrants to complete the project on time and on budget?

2. Demand that the undocumented immigrants be replaced, miss the grand opening deadline, and incur substantial cost overruns?

Why?

Assist Lines

Assist lines; previously referred to as "ethics hotlines," have long been popular with organizations as a method of obtaining information about situations that may be unethical or illegal. Nearly all Fortune 500 companies provide toll-free assist lines for employees from all over the world to share their concerns. Small organizations can contract out to an assist line managed by a third party. Scripted questions are delivered live by calling a particular phone number or through a computerized system that gathers the appropriate information. Employees reporting to the assist line are assured anonymity and privacy, and the information provided goes directly to the appropriate person within the employee's organization.

Professional organizations also provide assist lines for members who prefer to confidentially address issues with someone not employed by their organization. The

American Institute of CPAs (AICPA) offers members two types of confidential assist lines, one by telephone and the other by email.[18]

Types of Inquiries

Many organizations now refer to this communication channel as an assist line rather than an ethics hotline. First, the phrase "ethics hotline" makes it seem as though the employee is snitching or squealing on someone, an impression that managers want to avoid. Second, "assist" more accurately describes most of the calls that are received.

Sears, whose assist line receives 16,000 to 18,000 calls a year from its 300,000 employees, reports that only a very small percentage of the calls are about potential law violations.[19] Instead, the largest group of assist line callers consists of employees asking for help solving a human resources issue, such as how to respond to an unfavorable performance evaluation or lack of work breaks. Receiving these types of inquiries was not the original intention of an ethics hotline. Organizations welcomed these types of comments in the spirit of continuous improvement and because employees could express their frustrations.

The second largest group of assist line callers consists of employees asking for ethics policy clarifications. This is a good sign. Employees are asking for clarification before the fact, rather than being reported for committing a violation after the fact.

Effective Assist Lines

Confidentiality and false accusations are two central issues addressed by effective assist lines.

Assist line success requires honoring confidentiality at all times. Some employees may doubt that the assist line is really confidential or that their identity will remain anonymous. Any confidentiality breaches without the employee's permission will quickly spread throughout the organization and prevent other employees from using the system.

Some employees may fear that the assist line will generate false accusations from a spiteful person, someone seeking revenge for a bad performance appraisal or competing for an internal job opening. Clearly state that all assist line submissions must be offered in good faith and anyone purposely submitting a false accusation will be disciplined.

Assist lines can be designed to uniquely address professional issues or to ensure that assist line contractors adequately address specific concerns. Exhibit 8.4 provides a list of items the AICPA recommends for assessing the effectiveness of an audit committee assist line. [20]

Exhibit 8.4 AICPA Audit Committee Assist Line Checklist

_____ Does the assist line have a dedicated hotline number, fax number, website, email address, and regular mail or post office box address to expedite reports of suspected incidents of misconduct?

_____ Does the assist line demonstrate confidentiality, including showing how caller ID, email tracking, and other technologies cannot be used to identify the whistle-blower?

(Continued)

Exhibit 8.4 AICPA Audit Committee Assist Line Checklist (*Continued*)

_____ Does the assist line use independent and trained interviewers to handle calls rather than a voice mail system?

_____ Is the assist line available 24 hours a day, 365 days a year?

_____ Does the assist line have multilingual capability to address callers with different ethnic backgrounds or who are calling from different countries?

_____ Are callers provided with a unique identification number that enables them to call back later anonymously to receive feedback or follow-up on questions from investigators?

_____ Does the assist line have a case management tracking system to log all calls and their follow-ups and to facilitate management of the resolution process?

_____ Does the assist line have established protocols for the timely distribution of each type of complaint to appropriate individuals within the company and to the audit committee and board of directors when appropriate?

_____ Are complaints of any kind involving senior management automatically and directly submitted to the audit committee without filtering by management or other entity personnel?

_____ Does the assist line effectively distribute comprehensive multilingual educational materials and training programs to raise awareness among potential users?

_____ Does the assist line support outreach to potential stakeholders other than employees?

How an Assist Line Works

EthicsPoint, founded in 1999 by a group of certified fraud examiners, is an assist line used by many corporations, universities, nonprofits, and government agencies.[21] The EthicsPoint format is similar to many other assist lines. An employee anonymously contacts EthicsPoint by email or telephone and receives a confidential case identification number. Employees comfortable with the system can provide their names, but this is not required.

The response system is scripted to gather as much information as possible from an anonymous employee. The information is categorized based on the type of issue and operations area and then anonymously routed to the appropriate manager at the employee's organization. The submission is not routed to any person named in the inquiry.

For colleges and universities, the EthicsPoint system highlights four categories of wrongdoing. An "other" category is available for issues that do not fit any of these four options:

1. Unethical financial abuse, such as fraud

2. Unethical personal conduct, such as discrimination

3. Unethical treatment of college property, such as theft

4. Unethical use of information technology, such as data privacy abuse

The manager who receives the information responds to the EthicsPoint system using the case identification number. The manager can submit additional questions for the employee to anonymously answer or clarify any misunderstandings about the organization's policy on the issue. The anonymous employee can trace the case's progress using the identification number. These communications are filtered through EthicsPoint unless the employee submitting the inquiry is willing to contact the manager directly.

Whistle-blowing

This book attempts to help students create organizations of high integrity and superior performance. Many avenues for ethics communication have already been discussed: annual Code of Ethics assessments, ethics training workshops, diversity training workshops, developing ethically approachable management skills, an ECO or ombudsperson, and the installation of assist lines. Implementing these reporting systems provides managers and subordinates an opportunity to express their concerns about ethical misconduct within the organizational system so they can be appropriately addressed. If necessary, an employee can push a particular concern up to the top of the chain of command.

But sometimes an individual concerned about ethics works for an organization that refuses to take action against unethical or illegal activities. When this happens, an employee is faced with a major conflict of values—should the employee remain loyal to the organization or inform someone outside the organization who can take appropriate action?

Contacting someone outside the organization about potential or actual nontrivial misconduct inside the organization is referred to as whistle-blowing. If nobody within the organization is willing to take appropriate action, then the employee can inform a regulator, lawyer, reporter, law enforcement official, or a watchdog group. Whistle-blowers have provided the public with valuable information, such as falsified financial reports, unsafe products, and environmental violations.[22]

The federal government encourages its employees to blow the whistle. The U.S. Office of Special Counsel (OSC), an independent federal investigative and prosecutorial agency with jurisdiction over current and former federal employees, investigates and prosecutes cases supplied by whistle-blowers that violate personnel policies.[23] The OSC guarantees whistle-blower confidentiality and submits investigative reports to congressional oversight committees that include the whistle-blower's comments. The OSC also obtains remedies for whistle-blower retaliation as appropriate, such as back pay and job reinstatement.

When to Blow the Whistle

Public perception of whistle-blowers has shifted over time. Initially, whistle-blowers were perceived as disgruntled employees seeking revenge against a boss or employer. Whistle-blowers are now more likely to be appreciated for providing a public service. Nonetheless, blowing the whistle on an employer can be detrimental to the whistle-blower as well as the organization. After failing to pursue change within the organization, potential whistle-blowers must cautiously explore the ramifications of blowing the whistle prior to formally informing the public about ethical misconduct.

Begin by consulting with an attorney. Legal advisors recommend that the following four conditions be met before an employee informs an external authority:[24]

1. Serious harm is involved.

2. The whistle-blower has already expressed his or her concerns to an immediate superior.

3. The whistle-blower has exhausted other communication channels within the organization.

4. The whistle-blower has convincing, documented evidence.

Several organizations offer guidance and legal assistance to whistle-blowers. The Government Accountability Project, created in 1977, is a nonprofit advocacy and lobbying organization whose high-profile whistle-blowing cases and program areas include financial institutions, the environment, food integrity, homeland security, and public health misconduct.[25] Taxpayers Against Fraud focuses on government fraud by either government officials or those doing business with the government.[26] The Project on Government Oversight (POGO) is a nonprofit organization created in 1981 to expose corruption in the military procurement system and has since expanded its scope to include any fraud or mismanagement associated with the federal government.[27] The National Whistleblowers Center provides information and services to potential or actual whistle-blowers; offers a helpline, attorney referrals, and financial support; and lobbies Congress on whistle-blowing issues.[28]

The False Claims Act

Researchers estimate that 10 percent of federal government spending is lost to fraud.[29] The U.S. Department of Justice encourages whistle-blowing on fraud issues by offering financial rewards for information that leads to successful recovery of funds. As of 2010, the federal government has paid whistle-blowers approximately $3 billion, with an average award of $1.5 million.

The False Claims Act was initially passed in 1863 during the Civil War to prevent defense contractors from fraudulently selling the Union Army rifles, ammunition, and horses. The False Claims Act includes a qui tam provision whereby citizens can sue the fraudulent supplier on behalf of the government and receive a percentage of the financial recovery. Qui tam is a Latin term originating in thirteenth-century England that means suing on behalf of the king and yourself. The 1863 law passed by Congress allowed citizens suing for false claims to receive up to 10 percent of the recovered funds.

President Ronald Reagan's administration strengthened the False Claims Act in 1986 following a series of defense industry frauds against the federal government. An employee who independently sues his or her employer for fraud can now receive between 15 percent and 30 percent of the total recovery amount plus attorney fees and related costs and expenses for successful lawsuits. If the government joins the lawsuit, the employee can receive up to 25 percent of the total recovery. The lawsuit must be filed within six years of the date of the fraud.

Between 1986 and 2009, whistle-blowers received $340 million in qui tam payments.[30] During those 23 years, the government recovered $12 billion, with the top 100 cases accounting for $8.2 billion in recovered money.[31] Among the top 100 cases, 56 were health care corporations and 23 defense industry contractors. The whistle-blower in each of these cases received at least $1 million. Exhibit 8.5 lists the seven highest settlements, all in the health care industry, as of September 2009.[32]

Exhibit 8.5 Top Seven False Claims Acts Cases (as of September 2009)		
Settlement Amount	Company	Case
$1 billion	Pfizer, 2009	Fraudulent marketing and kickbacks to health care providers prescribing the drug
$900 million	Tenet Healthcare, 2006	Manipulating Medicare payments, kickbacks, and bill padding
$731.4 million	HCA (The Health Care Company), 2000	Billing for unnecessary lab tests not doctor ordered, upcoding medical problems to get higher reimbursements, and billing for nonreimbursable items
$650 million	Merck, 2008	Overbilling Medicaid for popular medicines
$631 million	HCA, 2003	Kickbacks to physicians and cost-reporting fraud
$567 million	Serono Group, 2005	Kickbacks to physicians for prescribing drug, kickbacks to pharmacies for recommending drug, and illegal marketing of drug
$559.4 million	Taketa-Abbott Pharmaceutical Products, 2001	Fraudulent drug pricing and marketing, gave doctors kickbacks by proving free samples with knowledge physicians would bill Medicare and Medicaid for them

According to the False Claims Act Legal Center, a potential whistle-blower should consider the following prior to filing under the False Claims Act:[33]

- The whistle-blower must have actual knowledge of the fraud, not just a suspicion, and the evidence cannot come from a publicly disclosed source, such as a newspaper or court record.
- The fraud cannot be a tax fraud; tax fraud is specifically exempt from prosecution under the False Claims Act.
- Federal money must be involved, or, in a state with its own False Claims Act, state money must be involved.
- Most lawyers work on a contingency fee basis and will pursue a case only if the financial amount of the fraud is sizable, and the entity to be sued is able to pay back the stolen money and associated fine.

Reporting Tax Fraud

All individuals with gross income above a certain level and all businesses that earned income during the year must file income taxes. In 2006, with estimates of U.S tax evasion as high as $350 billion, the IRS created a Whistleblower Office to receive information about possible individual or corporate tax frauds.[34] Tax fraud occurs in many forms, such as omitting earned income, bogus income tax shelters, hiding or transferring assets or income outside the United States, overstating deductions, and keeping two sets of books.[35]

The IRS Whistleblower Office modeled a Whistleblower Reward Program after the False Claims Act, paying whistle-blowers 15 percent to 30 percent of the unpaid taxes recovered.[36] To be eligible for a reward, the tax fraud and assessed penalties must exceed $2 million. If the tax cheat is an individual, rather than a corporation, the fraudulent person must have gross income above $200,000 for a reward to be disbursed.[37]

During the program's first full year of operation, $65 billion in alleged tax frauds were reported.[38] Unlike the Justice Department's False Claim Act, the IRS Whistleblower Reward Program attempts to keep the informant's identity anonymous by handling the matter as a routine audit. The Dodd-Frank Wall Street Reform and Consumer Protection Act of 2010, developed in response to the 2008 to 2010 financial crisis, offers the same reward program for information about securities violations successfully enforced by the Securities and Exchange Commission.[39]

Whistle-blower Protection Laws

An employee, customer, supplier, or other informed person can blow the whistle to a government official or the media on any organization. Typically, though, the most informed person about an organization's illegal activities is an employee of the organization.

Fear of retaliation is one of the primary reasons why employees do not blow the whistle on illegal activities. Exhibit 8.6 summarizes key federal laws that protect all, or major groups of, employees from retaliation for whistle-blowing. Retaliation protection clauses are common for new federal laws. Many states have also passed whistle-blower protection laws, but they are primarily aimed at state employees rather than private employers.

Exhibit 8.6 Whistle-blower Protection Laws

Year	Law	Description
1935	National Labor Relations Act	Forbids employers from retaliating against any employee who files a charge with the National Labor Relations Board
1964	Civil Rights Act	Protects employees who file a discrimination charge and participate in an investigation
1970	Occupational Safety and Health Act	Prohibits retaliation against any employee who files an OSHA complaint or testifies

2002	Sarbanes-Oxley Act	Prohibits retaliation against any employee of a publicly traded company who provides a law enforcement officer with truthful information relating to the commission or possible commission of any federal offense
2010	Dodd-Frank Wall Street Reform and Consumer Protection Act	Establishes a "whistle-blower bounty program" that rewards people who provide information that leads to a successful SEC enforcement between 10% and 30% of the monetary sanctions over $1 million.

Sarbanes-Oxley Act of 2002 (SOX)

Whistle-blower protection laws were strengthened following the high-profile accounting scandals involving Enron, WorldCom, Tyco, and other companies that cost investors billions of dollars during the early 2000s. Congress quickly passed the Sarbanes-Oxley Act of 2002 (SOX) to ensure additional confidence in the stock market and the financial statements of publicly held companies.[40] According to SOX, no publicly traded company or subcontractor of that company can discharge, demote, suspend, threaten, harass, or in any other manner discriminate against a whistle-blower.[41] It also establishes criminal penalties for retaliation against whistle-blowers of fines and imprisonment up to 10 years.

The number of whistle-blower reports grew substantially after this legislation became law. In 2001, prior to the passage of SOX, the SEC averaged 6,400 whistle-blowing reports a month. Two years later, the monthly average escalated to 40,000.[42]

In addition to strengthening of whistle-blowing protection laws, major features of SOX include the following:

- Creation of a Public Company Accounting Oversight Board, a private, not-for-profit entity that reports to the SEC and registers and inspects public accounting firms and sets quality and ethical standards for the issuers of audit reports.

- Disclosure of whether a Code of Ethics has been established for executives and making it available to the public.

- Prohibition against making personal loans to executive officers and directors.

- Establishment of an "anonymous reporting mechanism" for employees to report fraud.

- Managerial assessment of the effectiveness of their company's internal control structure for financial reporting and auditor comments about management's assessment.

- Outside, independent directors chosen for the board of directors, and a "financial expert" on the board's audit committees

- Auditors cannot engage in consulting work for the companies they are auditing without approval of the client's audit committee.

- The same senior auditors cannot work on the same account for more than five years, and other auditors for more than seven years.

Negative Outcomes for Whistle-blowers

The decision to blow the whistle on an employer requires careful consideration. Whistle-blowing can have many negative impacts on an employee's life. Researchers report that soon after blowing the whistle, many whistle-blowers experience[43]

1. Negative performance evaluations
2. Undesired job transfers
3. Demotions
4. Criticism or avoidance by coworkers
5. Physical, psychological, and family problems
6. Loss of job or forced retirement
7. Blacklisting impeding employment
8. Protracted legal battles waged at personal expense

The employee's manager or other high-level managers initiate most of these mistreatments. But sometimes trusted colleagues also change their relationship with whistle-blowers to avoid being associated with the negative publicity.

Laws prohibit all of these retaliatory actions. Nonetheless, the legal process can take years to settle the issue, during which time the whistle-blower might be unemployed and without any guarantees that the outcome will be favorable. Judges and juries can attempt to financially compensate whistle-blowers for psychological stress and family problems, but the negative impacts on the lives of whistle-blowers and family members are difficult to reverse. As a result of being ostracized, a recipient of insults and mistreatment creates memories and feelings that cannot be simply forgotten.

Cynthia Cooper, for instance, was one of three whistle-blowers awarded *Time* magazine's 2002 "Persons of the Year" for her courageous role in telling external authorities about WorldCom's massive accounting fraud. As WorldCom's vice president of the Internal Audit Department, Cooper attempted to address the illegal accounting issues internally.[44] But key executives refused to make changes after she contacted them. Her life became a living nightmare just prior to, and after, blowing the whistle. Cooper experienced trouble sleeping during her secret internal audit investigation, knowing that the evidence meant some of her friends might go to jail. Her peers, who blamed Cooper for job losses they experienced due to a massive corporate restructuring after the scandal became public, ostracized her. Cooper suffered long bouts of depression, unable to do much beyond crying in bed all day. She left WorldCom and started her own consulting firm.

SUMMARY

Employees need multiple internal communication channels to discuss potentially illegal or ethical misconduct. The most reliable and effective communication method is an ethically approachable manager who welcomes, in a nonjudgmental manner, information about ethi-

cal misconduct. The manager needs to be someone an observer of ethical misconduct can feel comfortable having sensitive discussions with and who would then take corrective action. Ethics & Compliance Officers, ombudspersons, and assist lines provide employees with other institutional mechanisms for reporting unethical or illegal behaviors. These internal reporting systems must be carefully managed. If an appropriate ethics reporting system is not available, employees are left with two op-

tions, both damaging to the organization. The observer can either remain quiet as the situation worsens or damage the organization's reputation by blowing the whistle to a public authority.

KEY WORDS

Employee silence; authoritarian leaders; employee empowerment; Ethics & Compliance Officer; ombudsman; chaplain; assist lines;

whistle-blowing; False Claims Act; qui tam; Whistleblower Reward Program

CHAPTER QUESTIONS

1. Why do some employees refuse to report ethical misconduct?
2. What skills must a manager develop for employees to feel comfortable to discuss potential unethical behaviors?
3. Discuss the typical duties and skills of an Ethics & Compliance Officer. How can

these activities be managed in a small organization?
4. Describe the 14 steps for developing and managing an internal reporting system process.
5. What are some of negative outcomes that many whistle-blowers have experienced?

In the Real World: Enron

Code of Ethics Exemption Request—June 1999

David Duncan, the lead Arthur Andersen auditor on the Enron account, ignored his colleague's concerns and supported Andy Fastow's and CAO Rick Causey's aggressive interpretation of accounting rules. As a result, Enron nearly doubled its annual profits for 1997, from $54 million to $105 million.

Beginning in 1999, with Wall Street experiencing a bull market and Enron's stock continually rising, Lay and Skilling expanded into new trading markets, including minerals, by acquiring an average of two companies a month. Under Skilling's direction, Enron evolved from a natural gas pipeline company to a trading company, with traders accounting for a third of its 15,000 employees.

Ken Lay and Jeff Skilling were now on center stage in a global economy, providing for people's heating, electricity, and water needs across the Earth. Revenue shot up accordingly, from $13.3 billion in 1996 to $31 billion in 1998.

Skilling promoted Fastow to CFO of Enron. Fastow structured an SPE named LJM1 to support a network of financially troubled SPEs doing business with, or on behalf of, Enron. If this network of SPEs failed, Enron would experience tremendous financial strain.

Fastow told Skilling that outsiders would invest in the risky LJM1 only if Fastow were its managing partner. Enron's Code of Ethics prohibited executives from participating in a company doing business with Enron, so Fastow would need to be exempted from this policy. Skilling approved the exemption and Lay did likewise. The final step in the exemption approval process required approval by Enron's Board of Directors.

Lay, Skilling, and Duncan attended the June 28, 1999, Board of Directors meeting. Fastow explained why it was essential for him to serve as a managing partner of LJM1 and, thus, be exempt from the relevant Code of Ethics policy. To safeguard against any potential conflict of interest, every deal between Enron and LJM1 would be presented to the Board of Directors for final approval. As an additional safeguard, the public accounting firm KPMG, rather than Arthur Andersen, would audit LJM1's financial statements, so

(Continued)

two accounting firms would be reviewing the fairness of all LJM1 transactions with Enron.

DECISION CHOICE. If you were on Enron's Board of Directors would you

1. Exempt Fastow from Enron's Code of Ethics, given the established accounting safeguards?

2. Refuse to exempt Fastow and cause the financial failure of an entire set of SPEs heavily invested in by Enron?

Why?

ANCILLARY MATERIALS

Websites to Explore

- Ethics & Compliance Officer Association, available at www.theecoa.org.
- International Ombudsman Association, available at www.ombudsassociation.org.
- Marketplace Chaplains USA, available at http://mchapusa.com/.
- EthicsPoint, available at www.ethicspoint.com.
- Whistleblowing
  - U.S. Office of Special Counsel (OSC), available at www.osc.gov/wbdisc.htm.
  - National Whistleblowers Center, available at http://www.whistleblower.org/.
  - The False Claims Act Legal Center, available at http://www.taf.org/.
  - Project on Government Oversight, available at http://www.pogo.org/.
  - IRS Tax Fraud Whistleblower, available at http://www.irs.gov/compliance/article/0,,id=180171,00.html.

Best Place to Work Video

- Best Place to Work—NetApp, available at http://money.cnn.com/video/fortune/2009/01/21/fortune-bctwf-netapp.fortune/.

Business Ethics Issue Video

- "Flying Cheap," *Frontline*, about the impact of airlines outsourcing flights to regional carriers; February 9, 2010, 57 minutes, available at http://www.pbs.org/wgbh/pages/frontline/flyingcheap/view/?utm_campaign=viewpage&utm_medium=grid&utm_source=grid.

TEDTalks Videos

- *Happiness:* Dan Gilbert, author of *Stumbling on Happiness*, challenges the idea that we'll be miserable if we don't get what we want and how our "psychological immune system" lets us feel truly happy even when things don't go as planned; February 2004, 22 minutes, available at http://www.ted.com/talks/dan_gilbert_asks_why_are_we_happy.html.
- *Lessons Learned from Presidents:* Historian Doris Kearns Goodwin talks about what we can learn from American presidents, including Abraham Lincoln and Lyndon Johnson; February 2008, 19 minutes, available at http://www.ted.com/talks/doris_kearns_goodwin_on_learning_from_past_presidents.html.

Conversations with Charlie Rose

- A conversation with journalist Rick Stengel on WikiLeaks; November 3, 2010, 25 minutes, available at http://www.charlierose.com/view/interview/11325.
- A conversation with Brian Ross about his book *The Madoff Chronicles: Inside the Secret World of Bernie and Ruth*; October 27, 2009, 60 minutes, available at http://www.charlierose.com/view/interview/10692.

NOTES

1. "Ethics Resource Center Publishes 2009 National Ethics Survey," available at http://www.ethics world.org/ethicsandemployees/nbes.php#new09, accessed 10/30/10; *2009 National Business Ethics Survey* is available at http://www.ethics.org/nbes/downloadnbes.html, accessed 10/30/10.

2. Frances J. Milliken, Elizabeth W. Morrison, and Patricia F. Hewlin, "An Exploratory Study of Employee Silence: What Employees Do Not Say to Their Bosses and Why," *Journal of Management Studies*, 40, 6 (2003), 1453–1476.

3. Ethics Resource Center, *How Employees View Ethics in Their Organizations 1994–2005* (Washington DC: Ethics Resource Center, 2005), p. 29, available at http://www.ethics.org/files/u5/2005NBESsummary.pdf, accessed 10/30/10; Milliken, Morrison, and Hewlin, "An Exploratory Study of Employee Silence."

4. Eileen Z. Taylor and Mary B. Curtis, "An Examination of the Layers of Workplace Influences in Ethical Judgments: Whistleblowing Likelihood and Perseverance in Public Accounting," *Journal of Business Ethics*, 93, 1 (2010), 21–37

5. Ashlee Vance, "In Faulty-Computer Suit, Window to Dell Decline," *New York Times*, June 28, 2010.

6. Ethics & Compliance Officer Association website available at www.theecoa.org, accessed 10/30/10.

7. Duffy A. Morf, Michael G. Schumacher, and Scott J. Vitell, "A Survey of Ethics Officers in Large Organizations," *Journal of Business Ethics*, 20, 3 (1999), 265–271.

8. Edward Petry, "Appointing an Ethics Officer," Healthcare Executive, 13, 6 (1998), 35; Bruce Rubenstein, "Ethics and Compliance Officers Meet to Share Information and Best Practices," *Corporate Legal Times*, 10, 99 (2000), 72.

9. Luis R. Gomez-Mejia, David B. Balkin, and Robert L. Cardy, "Developing an Effective Whistle-Blowing Policy," included in *Managing Human Resources*, 5th ed. (Upper Saddle River, NJ: Pearson Prentice Hall, 2007), p. 451.

10. Larry B. Hill, "The Ombudsman Revisited: Thirty Years of Hawaiian Experience," *Public Administration Review*, 62, (2002), 24–41.

11. NIH Ombudsman, "FAQ," available at http://ombudsman.nih.gov/faq.html, accessed 10/30/10.

12. International Ombudsman Association website available at www.ombudsassociation.org, accessed 10/30/10.

13. *Barron's* "Special Report: Best Mutual Fund Families," *Barron's*, February 1, 2010.

14. Putnam, "Corporate Ombudsman," available at www.putnam.com/ombudsman, accessed 10/30/10.

15. Marketplace Chaplains USA website available at http://mchapusa.com/, accessed 10/30/10.

16. Corporate Chaplains of America website available at www.chaplain.org, accessed 10/30/10.

17. Gena Kittner, "Chaplains Help Stressed Workers," *Wisconsin State Journal*, February 11, 2009.

18. American Institute of CPAs, "Professional Ethics," available at http://www.aicpa.org/InterestAreas/ProfessionalEthics/Pages/ProfessionalEthics.aspx, accessed 10/30/10.

19. Anonymous, "Extolling the Virtues of Hot Lines," *Workforce*, 77, 6 (1998), 125–126.

20. AICPA Antifraud Programs and Controls Task Force, "Audit Committee Considerations for Whistleblower Hotlines," *Journal of Accountancy*, 209, 6 (2010), 24.

21. EthicsPoint website available at www.ethicspoint.com, accessed 10/30/10.

22. Roberta Ann Johnson, *Whistleblowing: When It Works—And Why* (Boulder, CO: Lynne Rienner Publishers, 2003).

23. U.S. Office of Special Counsel (OSC), "Whistleblower Disclosures," available at www.osc.gov/wbdisc.htm, accessed 10/30/10.

24. Richard De George, "Ethical Responsibilities of Engineers in Large Organizations," *Business & Professional Ethics Journal*, 1, 1 (1981), 1–14.

25. Government Accountability Project website available at http://www.whistleblower.org/, accessed 10/30/10.

26. The False Claims Act Legal Center, "Taxpayers Against Fraud," available at http://www.taf.org/abouttaf.htm, accessed 10/30/10.

27. Project on Government Oversight website available at http://www.pogo.org/, accessed 10/30/10.

28. National Whistleblowers Center website available at http://www.whistleblowers.org/, accessed 10/30/10.

29 Joel D. Hesch, *Whistleblowing: A Guide to Government Reward Programs* (Lynchburg, VA: Goshen Press, 2010).

30 Robin Page West, "Employment Law: How a Qui Tam Whistleblower Case Works," July 1999, available at www.expertlaw.com/library/employment/qui-tam.html, accessed 10/30/10; Qui Tam Online Network website available at www.QuiTamOnline.com, accessed 10/30/10.

31 Corporate Crime Reporter, "The Top 100 False Claims Act Settlements," December 30, 2003, available at http://www.corporatecrimereporter.com/fraudrep.pdf, accessed 10/30/10.

32 The False Claims Act Legal Center, "Top 100 False Claims Cases by Amount Awards," available at www.taf.org/top100fca.htm, accessed 10/30/10; The False Claims Act Legal Center, "Statistics,"

33 The False Claims Act Legal Center, "Information for Whistleblowers," available at www.taf.org/whistleblower.htm, accessed 10/30/10.

34 Joel D. Hesch, *Reward: Collecting Millions for Reporting Tax Evasion* (Lynchburg, VA: Liberty University Press, 2009).

35 Whistleblowing and Reporting Government Fraud, "12 Most Common Tax Fraud Schemes," available at http://www.governmentfraud.us/pages/tax-irs-fraud/common-tax-fraud-schemes.php, accessed 10/30/10.

36 IRS.gov, "Procedure Unveiled for Reporting Violations of the Tax Law, Making Reward Claims," available at http://www.irs.gov/newsroom/article/0,,id=176632,00.html, accessed 10/30/10.

available at http://www.taf.org/statistics.htm, accessed 10/30/10.

[37] IRS.gov, "Claims Submitted to the IRS Whistle-blower Office under Section 7623," available at http://www.irs.gov/pub/irs-drop/n-08-04.pdf, accessed 10/30/10.

[38] Janet Novack and William P. Barrett, "Tax Informants Are on the Loose," *Forbes,* December 14, 2009.

[39] U.S. Senate Committee on Banking, Housing & Urban Affairs, "Brief Summary of the Dodd-Frank Wall Street Reform and Consumer Protection Act," available at http://banking.senate.gov/public/_files/070110_Dodd_Frank_Wall_Street_Reform_comprehensive_summary_Final.pdf, accessed 10/30/10; Dodd-Frank Wall Street Reform and Consumer Protection Act, "Bill Summary and Status," available at http://thomas.loc.gov/cgi-bin/bdquery/z?d111:H.R.4173, accessed 10/30/10.

[40] Sanjay Anand, *Essentials of Sarbanes-Oxley* (Hoboken, NJ: John Wiley & Sons, 2007).

[41] Sarbanes-Oxley Act of 2002, "Protection for Employees of Publicly Traded Companies Who Provide Evidence of Fraud," H.R. 3763, Section 806: 58-60; available at http://fl1.findlaw.com/news.findlaw.com/hdocs/docs/gwbush/sarbanesoxley072302.pdf, accessed 10/30/10.

[42] Stephen Taub, "SEC: 1300 'Whistles' Blow Each Day: Most Tips Concerning Accounting Problems at Public Companies," *CFO.com,* August 3, 2004.

[43] Thomas L. Carson, Mary Ellen Verdu, and Richard E. Wokutch, "Whistle-Blowing for Profit: An Ethical Analysis of the Federal False Claims Act," *Journal of Business Ethics,* 77, 3 (2008), 361–376.

[44] Cynthia Cooper, *Extraordinary Circumstances* (Hoboken, NJ: John Wiley & Sons, 2008).

CHAPTER OUTLINE

9

MANAGERS AS ETHICAL LEADERS AND ROLE MODELS

What would you do?

A Successful New Product But ...

After graduation, you are hired as a salesperson for a national chemical company with 10 primary products. The company has seven sales regions. During your first two years, you have worked in two of them and met salespeople from the other five regions at training sessions and national meetings. The company has a unique salary compensation system, rather than a commission-based compensation system. The salary compensation system is considered more professional and encourages cooperation instead of competition among salespeople within a region and between regions.

You notice that a significant number of salespeople do not work as hard as they could because of the guaranteed salary. You suggest to your boss and the sales vice president that a minimum guaranteed salary with a commission-based compensation system would increase sales productivity. When your sales manager leaves the company, the sales vice president approaches you and says: "You've been one of our top producers the past two years, and I found your commission compensation idea interesting. I'm going to promote you to sales manager, and you'll be reporting directly to me. I want you to change the

compensation system as you suggested. You have high integrity and are respected by the other salespeople. I think they will accept the compensation change under your leadership."

In order to be fair to everyone and minimize resistance to change, you create a compensation system whereby, if in place the previous year, a salesperson would have earned about the same annual income. This way nobody has to worry about losing income. You took each salesperson's total sales per product, factored in the product's contribution to profits, and determined a commission amount per product until the numbers balanced. The commissions range from $15 to $25 per product, with the higher commission for the more profitable products.

The new minimum salary with a commission compensation agreement is a formal contract. Despite some initial hesitancy, all salespeople sign the contract. They trust you based on the ethical leadership abilities you demonstrated the past two years.

Before starting the new sales program, the vice president of sales informs you that the company is rolling out a new product that the executive team wants the salespeople to push. The new product will be sold in two regions for the upcoming year, and the other five regions the following year. To encourage sales of the new product, you and the VP agree on a $35 commission per new product sold.

The new product is a huge success. After the first quarter operating under the new compensation system, salespeople selling the new product have doubled their income compared to the same quarter the previous year. However, salespeople in the five regions not selling the new product begin complaining that the new commission system is unfair because they do not have the opportunity to sell the new product. They are earning about the same income as the first quarter the previous year, but the salespeople in the two regions with the new product have doubled their income. If this trend continues, the year-end discrepancy between the two regions with the new product and the five regions without will be significant.

You are concerned that employee morale in the five regions without the new product will dramatically decline. On the other hand, if you change the commission plan right now, it might ruin morale among the salespeople selling the new product and thus have a negative impact on potential profits. You think you can convince the employees selling the new product to void the original contract, but then again, you're not sure and maybe some of them will seek legal representation.

What would you do? Would you

1) Honor the original contract agreement between the company and salespeople for this year? Next year all salespeople will be selling the same products so there is no need to make any changes in the compensation system.
2) With the aid of company lawyers persuade the salespeople in the two regions selling the new product to void their current commission contract? Then recalculate a new commission plan so that both groups will earn approximately the same amount of commissions at the end of the year, although this can damage the morale of the new product salespeople and constrain profits.

Why?

Chapter Objectives

After reading this chapter, you will be able to:

- Describe how managers can be ethical leaders and role models
- Explain different leadership styles and assess ethical leadership
- Set SMART work goals and implement management-by-objectives
- Design and conduct employee performance appraisals that encourage ethical behavior
- Effectively and fairly discipline employees for work rule violations

W hy might a usually ethical employee decide to suddenly mislead a manager or customer about meeting an end-of-the-month product delivery deadline? When questioned, one might expect to hear the employee claim that he or she was under pressure and rationalize that

. . . my boss sometimes does it!

. . . I had to meet my monthly work goal!

. . . it counts a lot in my monthly performance review!

Accordingly, three aspects of daily organizational life significantly impact an employee's ethical performance:

1. The behaviors of organizational executives, managers, and direct supervisors

2. Work goals

3. Employee performance appraisals

This chapter explores how managers are ethical role models; the ethics of exercising power in an organization; and different leadership styles, including that of being an ethical leader. Ethical leaders develop great places to work by reinforcing ethical behavior among employees through work goals and performance appraisals that encourage and reward ethical behaviors. Several surveys are provided to help managers evaluate themselves and others in terms of ethical leadership and behaviors.

Managers as Ethical Role Models

Long-term organizational success requires managing continual changes in the business, political, and social environments. Managers must respond to new competitors, new strategies, new laws and regulations, and new generations of employees. The way managers respond to these issues sets the general ethical tone of an organization.

Role Modeling

Subordinates are constantly evaluating the ethics of a manager's decisions and behaviors. Actions speak louder than words. The way a manager treats owners, customers, and employees sets the standard for acceptable behavior within the manager's work unit. A manager's behavioral commitment, or lack thereof, to ethical principles filters down to subordinates and other employees. Managers have already been promoted, so their daily workplace actions are indicators to subordinates of what it takes to be promoted.

Direct supervisors have the greatest impact on an employee's ethical performance. Hard-working, conscientious, caring, and ethical managers who generate high-quality performance outcomes tend to attract, develop, and promote hard-working, conscientious, caring, and ethical employees who generate high-quality performance outcomes. On the other hand, if a manager comes in late, leaves early, performs shoddy work, violates confidentiality, and cuts ethical corners to achieve work goals, then so will the manager's subordinates, particularly when the manager is not around.

A 2007 survey of employees suggests that a rather large percentage of managers are ethically challenged:[1]

- 39 percent reported that their managers failed to keep promises.
- 37 percent reported that their managers failed to give credit when due.
- 24 percent reported that their managers violated employee privacy.
- 23 percent reported that their managers blamed others to cover up mistakes or to minimize embarrassment.

These managerial misbehaviors contradict the attribute employees most want their leaders and supervisors to exhibit—honesty.[2] Honesty is a mutually reinforcing ethical bond between managers and their subordinates. Dishonesty by either the manager or employees punctures the ethics bond between them. A highly ethical employee receiving daily direction from a dishonest supervisor can deal with the psychological stress this generates by loyally aligning with the supervisor's dishonest methods, disloyally reporting the supervisor's misconduct to the supervisor's boss, or quitting.

Stage of Moral Development and Ethical Role Models

Many managers are very ethical and honest, and of high integrity. But not all of them, nor all the time, as suggested by survey results that appear throughout this book.

The ethical variance among managers can be quite broad. Chapter 1 described six unique stages of moral development on a continuum from obedience-and-punishment orientation (Stage 1) through universal ethical principles orientation (Stage 6). Researchers report that managers typically reason according to Stage 3 (do what a good manager would do) and Stage 4 (obey the law).[3]

The type of ethical role model a manager chooses to be will reflect his or her level of moral development. For instance, can you always trust a manager with confidential information? It depends on the situation and a manager's level of moral development. A manager reasoning at Stage 2 may break confidentiality if doing so is rewarded. A manager reasoning at Stage 6 would break confidentiality only if justice demanded it.

William Torbert has developed a management role model typology based on Lawrence Kohlberg's six stages of moral development:[4]

Stages 1 and 2 – *Opportunist*: An opportunist is strongly influenced by rewards and punishments and will exhibit ethical behaviors when ethical behaviors are rewarded and unethical behaviors are punished, or exhibit unethical behaviors when the reverse factors occur.

Stage 3 – *Diplomat*: A diplomat is strongly influenced by social group norms and supports decisions agreed to by other managers. Diplomats want to be good team players, seek group consensus, and avoid group conflict. When other managers agree to ethical behaviors, then the diplomat will behave ethically. If they agree to unethical behaviors, the diplomat will behave unethically.

Stage 4 – *Technician*: A technician is strongly influenced by technical logic and determines the right thing to do based on data and organizational interests. Technicians arrange organizational pieces so that the job can be performed well. Technician managers will behave ethically when rational analysis recommends a solution that is ethical. If rational analysis recommends an unethical behavior, then the technician manager will behave unethically.

Stage 5 – *Achiever*: An achiever is goal oriented and strongly influenced by organizational success. An achiever sets high personal goals and is oriented toward implementing the strategy with the highest likelihood of generating successful organizational outcomes. Obstacles are to be navigated and conquered. Achiever managers will behave ethically when ethical behaviors result in goal accomplishment. If ethical behaviors prevent the accomplishment of goals, then achiever managers will behave unethically.

Stage 6 – *Strategist and Magician*: Torbert invokes two different Stage 6 management role models. A strategist is a systems thinker who welcomes ambiguity and multiple perspectives, analyzes the strengths and differences of different approaches, and then applies one overarching organizing principle appropriate for all people in all situations to generate the best solutions. Magicians add to this a commitment to personal, employee, and organizational transformation, and a willingness to change based on a vision of the good. Strategist and magician managers strive to behave according to an ideal conceptualization of ethical behavior and fulfillment.

In research studies, Torbert and his colleagues found that supervisors tend to be technicians, middle-level and upper-level managers tend to be technicians and achievers, and professionals tend to be achievers and strategists. Each of these role models determines ethical behavior using an analytical framework associated with its corresponding stage of moral development.

Personal Integrity

Personal integrity has long been recognized as an essential component of successful leadership. Back in 1954, Peter Drucker, the "father of modern management," noted that, "The final proof of [management's] sincerity and seriousness is uncompromising emphasis on integrity of character. For it is character through which leadership is exercised, it is character that sets the example and is imitated in turn."[5]

Half a century later, researchers conducted interviews with 1,040 managers in more than 100 organizations about why managers fail.[6] Among the top reasons were failure to practice effective communications, failure to nurture effective working relationships, failure to care for employees, and failure to demonstrate personal integrity and foster trust. According to the interviewees, successful managers embodied high standards of integrity, humility, and genuine concern for others.

But what would you do if you agreed to sell 40 percent of an oil company for $54 million and then six months later, prior to closing the deal, 40 percent of the company was now worth $250 million? Would you abide by the original $54 million selling price, request the full $250 million current value, or settle somewhere between the two amounts?

Jon Huntsman, the chairman and founder of Huntsman Chemical, insisted that personal integrity and his conscience required that he abide by the original $54 million agreement. According to Huntsman, who later became governor of Utah and U.S. ambassador to China, "There are, basically, three kinds of people: the unsuccessful, the temporarily successful, and those who become and remain successful. The difference, I am convinced, is character."[7]

Managerial Power and Leadership Styles

A manager's general leadership style also influences organizational ethics. Managers possess power for the purpose of achieving organizational objectives. This section explains the concept of power and explores different leadership styles managers can adopt when exercising their power.

Exercise of Power

Ethical managers need to be concerned with how they exercise power within the organization. Power refers to the ability to act, create an effect, or wield force. Social psychologists John French and Bertram Raven differentiated among five types of power bases individuals can have in relationship to others:[8]

1. *Legitimate Power:* Power that is formally assigned to an individual, such as a title or position; "I'm going to do what that person says because the person is my boss!"
2. *Reward Power:* Power obtained by being a person distributing rewards; "I'm going to do what that person says because I want to get a bonus and be promoted!"
3. *Coercive Power:* Power obtained by enforcing punishments; "I'm going to do what that person says because I don't want to get fired!"
4. *Referent Power:* Power obtained because people want to be like you; "I'm going to do what that person says because I really admire the person!"
5. *Expert Power:* Power obtained by being a source of desired knowledge or skills; "I'm going to do what that person says because the person is an expert on the issue!"

Some managers operate based on all five power bases—they have an official job title, reward desirable behaviors, punish undesirable behaviors, gather loyalists, and possess expert knowledge. As ethical role models, managers must make sure that they exercise these power levers in an ethical manner. Power begets responsibility. Ethical decision making and responsible behaviors reinforce a manager's power base. Managers who do not behave responsibly eventually lose their power base.

In 2007, for instance, Randy Michaels was hired as executive vice president for the *Chicago Tribune* and soon promoted to CEO. Within three years, the board of directors fired him for creating an unethical work culture characterized by offensive and sexual misbehaviors.[9]

Authoritarian Leadership Style

Historically, the dominant view on how to manage an organization and its employees consisted of managers organizing work and directing people. An authoritarian leadership style refers to demanding blind submission to someone in authority. Authoritarian managerial power has a long history that includes the institution of slavery in ancient Greece and Rome and in the pre–Civil War United States.

Social Darwinists such as Andrew Carnegie maintained that executives earn authoritarian power by successfully climbing the organizational ladder.[10] Through a competitive promotion system, managers who mastered administrative skills at one level of operations are promoted to the next higher level of management, equipping them with the knowledge and skills needed to successfully command an organization and tell subordinates what to do.

In the early 1900s, Frederick Winslow Taylor encapsulated the authoritarian leadership style by scientifically studying every worker motion necessary to perform a task at peak efficiency and effectiveness.[11] He used a stopwatch to calculate each worker's maximum output capacity and then determined the one most efficient and effective method for performing the job. Taylor's attitude toward leading subordinates was the following: "Here's what needs to be done and here's how to do it; now just do it and I'll pay you."

An authoritarian management style raises several ethical issues. Employees are tightly controlled and their opinions are not respected. These restrictions inhibit individual creativity and contribute to a culture of dependency. Researchers report that rigid, one-way communication from supervisor to subordinate constrains an employee's moral development.[12] Authoritarian leadership is also associated with abusive supervision, whereby subordinates are verbally abused, intimidated, degraded, and treated with hostility to achieve desired organizational outcomes.[13]

Participatory Leadership Style

During the 1950s, Douglas McGregor differentiated between two different management approaches, referred to as "Theory X" and "Theory Y," based on a different set of beliefs about employees.[14] Theory X represented the traditional perspective—people were lazy, disliked work, avoided responsibilities, and did as little as possible unless induced by monetary incentives to provide their best effort. As a result, Theory X managers adopted an authoritarian management style whereby employees were coerced, controlled, directed, or threatened to perform the task necessary to achieve productivity goals.

But not all managers operated according to Theory X beliefs. Theory Y managers assumed people usually enjoyed mental and physical activities, were self-directed, desired challenging and interesting work, and welcomed additional work-related responsibilities. As a result, Theory Y managers could get the most out of employees by demonstrating greater respect for them through a participative management style that involved subordinates in the decision-making process.[15] Rensis Likert's research led him to conclude that a participative management system resulted in higher levels of employee productivity, loyalty, and motivation, all of which contributed to higher profits.[16]

Paul Hersey and Ken Blanchard fine-tuned the differences between authoritarian and participative leadership styles by noting that there is no one best way to manage everybody.[17] A manager's leadership style needs to fit the type of employee being managed. Blanchard further developed a Situational Leadership II Model that categorizes four leadership styles—directing, coaching, supporting, and delegating—according to an employee's level of competence and commitment or confidence.[18]

Directing: If an employee has low competence and high commitment, such as an enthusiastic beginner, the manager needs to clearly direct the employee through one-way communication.

Coaching: If an employee has either low or some competence and lacks commitment, such as a disillusioned learner, the manager needs to provide direction, guide the employee using two-way communication that stresses accountability, and provide feedback.

Supporting: If an employee has moderate to high competence and variable commitment, such as a capable but cautious performer, the manager needs to listen to the employee's concerns and suggestions and then provide support and encouragement.

Delegating: If an employee has high competence and high commitment, such as a self-reliant achiever, the manager needs to delegate responsibilities, provide resources, and monitor progress.

From an ethics perspective, situational leadership sensitizes managers to focus on employee needs and providing the style of leadership the employee's needs dictate. Similar to McGregor and Likert, Hersey and Blanchard have an ultimate preference that uses the greatest human capacity, in this case, delegating. But delegation will work only if an employee has the appropriate competencies and confidence. Delegating work to an employee with low competence or low commitment will result in failure. Nonetheless, managers need to provide an employee with low competence the appropriate training and development, and an employee with low confidence the appropriate support, so that the employee can succeed if delegated tasks.

Ethical Leadership

Whether a situation calls for an authoritarian or participatory leadership style, one aspect is constant in all situations, the need for an ethical leadership style.

In a series of articles, Michael Brown, Linda Trevino, and their colleagues provide an expansive understanding of what it means to be an ethical leader.[19] Their analysis is built on both leadership theory and business ethics research. They maintain that a manager's reputation for being an ethical leader is based on two factors: (1) being a moral person and (2) being a moral manager.

As a *moral person*, managers must exhibit ethical traits in their personal lives, such as honesty, integrity and trustworthiness, as well as treating people with respect. As a *moral manager*, managers must be aware of ethical issues, encourage others at work to behave ethically, and hold employees accountable for ethical behavior.

A manager's private life affects the way employees and other key stakeholders perceive the manager's ethics. A manager who encourages and reinforces ethical behaviors at work but engages in drunken behaviors, adulterous affairs, drug addictions, or excessive profanity loses the respect of others. Likewise, a manager who is personally ethical but does not encourage and reinforce ethical behaviors among subordinates also falls short as an ethical leader.

Within this analytical framework, Brown, Trevino and David Harrison define ethical leadership as "the demonstration of normatively appropriate conduct through personal actions and interpersonal relationships, and the promotion of such conduct to followers through two-way communication, reinforcement, and decision-making."[20] Some managers may not understand what "normatively appropriate conduct" means within the context of their organization. Normatively appropriate conduct stipulations are embodied in an organization's Codes of Ethics and Conduct.

Ethical Leadership Survey

Brown, Trevino, and Harrison developed an Ethical Leadership Survey consisting of 10 statements that describe attributes of being a moral person and a moral manager (see Exhibit 9.1).

Exhibit 9.1 Ethical Leadership Survey

Instructions: Please use the 1 to 5 scale below to assess the following 10 statements. The more honest you are the more helpful the information we will receive.

1=Strongly Disagree; 2=Disagree; 3=Neither Agree nor Disagree; 4=Agree; 5=Strongly Agree

	SD	D	N	A	SA
My manager conducts his or her personal life in an ethical manner.	1	2	3	4	5
My manager defines success not just by results but also the way that they are obtained.	1	2	3	4	5
My manager listens to what employees have to say.	1	2	3	4	5
My manager disciplines employees who violate ethical standards.	1	2	3	4	5
My manager makes fair and balanced decisions.	1	2	3	4	5
My manager can be trusted.	1	2	3	4	5
My manager discusses business ethics or values with employees.	1	2	3	4	5
My manager sets an example of how to do things the right way in terms of ethics.	1	2	3	4	5
My manager has the best interests of employees in mind.	1	2	3	4	5
When making decisions, my manager asks, "What is the right thing to do?"	1	2	3	4	5
Add the 10 scores:					

Use the Ethical Leadership Scale to assess a specific manager. The survey can also be used to assess top management in general by substituting "top management" for "my manager."

A wide range of highly desirable outcomes is associated with ethical leadership. Researchers have found strong associations between ethical leadership and satisfaction with leaders, perceived leader effectiveness, willingness to give extra effort, willingness to report problems to management, job satisfaction, and organizational commitment.[21] Researchers also report that the highly desirable outcomes associated with ethical leadership result from a "trickle-down" effect whereby ethical managers at the top of the organization positively impact their direct reports, a process that cascades through ethical role modeling down the organizational hierarchy. Abusive behaviors at the top of the organization can trickle down as well.[22] When managed appropriately, organization citizenship behaviors flow throughout the organization and deviant behaviors are minimized.[23]

Some supervisors may resist top management efforts to inculcate ethical behaviors. A specific supervisor, for instance, may believe ethical behavior is a hindrance to achieving a short-term goal or may feel pressured by difficult goals to cut ethical corners. If top managers reinforce ethical behaviors but supervisors do not, ethical communications from top management are less likely to be embodied by employees lower in the organizational hierarchy. A direct supervisor who behaves unethically creates obstacles for subordinates who report to the supervisor to behave ethically.

Tips and Techniques

Common Decencies at Work

Ethical leaders extend basic common decencies that demonstrate respect to subordinates. According to Steve Harrison, small managerial gestures contribute to the creation and maintenance of great organizations. Examples of common decencies include the following:

- Calling employees by name and remembering their names
- Referring to employees as "associates" and "colleagues"
- Respecting confidences and avoiding gossip
- Sending out a handwritten thank-you note every day
- Not asking questions to which you already have the answer
- For meetings you convene, being the first to sit down and the last to get up
- Conveying bad news in person
- Giving away recognition when things go well and hoarding responsibility when they don't

Virtue Ethics Survey

Ethical leaders are transparent and authentic. Ethical leaders mean what they say and practice virtuous behaviors. As discussed in Chapter 5, the list of virtuous traits is extensive. The most common grouping of virtues includes justice (fairness), empathy, passion, reliability, honesty, integrity, and respect.[24] Researchers have found the personality traits agreeableness (likeable, friendly, and easy to get along with) and conscientiousness (responsible, dependable, and hard working) to be strongly associated with ethical leadership.[25]

Ronald Riggio, Weichun Zhu, Christopher Reina, and James Maroosis developed a survey that focuses on the four cardinal virtues emphasized by Aristotle: justice, fortitude, prudent, and temperance.[26] Justice refers to fairness, fortitude to courage and perseverance, prudence to practical wisdom, and temperance to controlling one's emotions. Exhibit 9.2 provides a survey instrument for measuring these key virtues. Managers can use the survey instrument as a self-assessment and compare their responses with those of subordinates.

Exhibit 9.2 Virtue Ethics Survey

Instructions: Please use the 1 to 5 scale below to assess the following 19 statements. Assess the extent to which each statement describes your manager. The more honest you are the more helpful the information we will receive.

1=Not at All; 2=Once in a While; 3=Sometimes; 4=Fairly Often; 5=Frequently, if Not Always

	N	O	S	F	A
Justice					
Gives credit to others when credit is due	1	2	3	4	5
Demonstrates respect for all people	1	2	3	4	5
Credits others for their accomplishments	1	2	3	4	5
Respects the rights and integrity of others	1	2	3	4	5
Makes promotion decisions based on a candidate's merit	1	2	3	4	5
Treats others as he or she would like to be treated	1	2	3	4	5
Justice—Add the six scores:					
Fortitude					
Would rather risk his or her job than do something that was unjust	1	2	3	4	5
Stands up for his or her beliefs among friends who do not share the same views	1	2	3	4	5
Makes the morally best decision in a given situation	1	2	3	4	5
Enforces ethical standards when dealing with a close friend	1	2	3	4	5
Listens to his or her "inner ethical voice" when deciding how to proceed	1	2	3	4	5
Fortitude—Add the five scores:					
Prudence					
Does as he or she ought to do in a given situation	1	2	3	4	5
Carefully considers all the information available before making an important decision that impacts others	1	2	3	4	5
Reflects on the consequences of his or her actions before making a decision	1	2	3	4	5
Seeks out information from a variety of sources so the best decision can be made	1	2	3	4	5

(Continued)

Exhibit 9.2 Virtue Ethics Survey (*Continued*)					
Considers a problem from all angles and reaches the best decision for all parties involved	1	2	3	4	5
Prudence—Add the five scores:					
Temperance					
Is not overly concerned with his or her personal power	1	2	3	4	5
Does not brag about his or her own accomplishments	1	2	3	4	5
Does not micromanage other people's work	1	2	3	4	5
Temperance—Add the three scores:					

Servant Leadership

Many of the virtues noted here are encapsulated under the concept of *servant leadership*. Robert Greenleaf, an American Telephone & Telegraph executive responsible for management development, based the concept of servant leadership on biblical ideals and used Jesus as an ethical role model.[27] Greenleaf referred to servant leadership as achieving organizational results by humbly caring for and serving the needs of superiors, colleagues, and subordinates. Theorists and researchers have determined the following five characteristics as representing those of a servant leader:[28]

1. *Altruistic Calling:* A servant leader has a deep-rooted desire to make a positive difference in other people's lives, putting others' interests and needs ahead of his or her own.

2. *Emotional Healing:* A servant leader is a great listener who uses empathy to foster spiritual recovery from work-related hardships and trauma.

3. *Wisdom:* A servant leader is aware of one's surroundings, is sensitive to environmental cues, and anticipates consequences of decisions and actions, thus enabling the integration of ideals with pragmatism.

4. *Persuasive Mapping:* A servant leader can map issues within the organizational context and use sound reasoning to articulate new possibilities and opportunities aligned with the organization's vision.

5. *Organizational Stewardship:* A servant leader links the organization's activities with the development of community well-being through programs and outreach, making the community a better place to live because of the organization's existence.

From a servant leadership perspective, any occupation, profession, job title, or job task is a call to serve. A servant leader is one who ensures that all employees have the requisite support systems to perform at their greatest capabilities to meet customer needs. Rather than expecting employees to serve the needs of the manager, a servant leader serves the needs of his or her employees in alignment with the organization's vision or mission.

When Max DePree was CEO of the office furniture manufacturer Herman Miller, he emphasized the importance of recognizing human diversity, nurturing relationships, and building community at work by making full use of each employee's talents through participatory management techniques.[29] As summarized in the "Best Practice in Use" exhibit, CEO Aaron Feuerstein demonstrated servant leadership and the exercise of moral virtues when a tragic fire threatened the jobs of 3,000 employees.[30]

BEST PRACTICE IN USE

Aaron Feuerstein at Malden Mills

On December 11, 1995, a tragic fire destroyed three of Malden Mills' main manufacturing facilities. Thirty-six people were injured but, fortunately, nobody died. The fire's impact also devastated the Lawrence, Massachusetts, community. With unemployment already very high, Malden Mills, a privately owned fabric mill, was one of the few remaining large employers in the area.

Malden Mills had been manufacturing textiles since 1906. At the time of the fire, it had sales of $380 million and employed approximately 3,000 people, most of them union members earning wages 20 percent above the industry average.

Aaron Feuerstein, the 70-year-old third-generation owner and CEO, could call it quits, take the $300 million insurance payout, and enjoy a well-deserved retirement. Or, he could follow the lead of many other companies in the industrial Northeast who were relocating operations either overseas or to southern states offering generous tax incentives and a nonunion employee base.

But that is not what he decided to do. Instead, he invested the insurance money, along with an additional $100 million from a loan, to rebuild an environmentally friendly manufacturing facility in Lawrence.

Even more remarkable, he guaranteed full salaries and benefits for all unemployed union workers for two months as the factory was being rebuilt, and he continued paying health benefits for those still unemployed because the factory was not fully operational. The additional cost: approximately $25 million.

According to Feuerstein: "It's true that the decision to rebuild right here in the pocket of unemployment in Lawrence was my decision. I'm very proud I made that decision. There was no way I was going to take 3,000 people and throw them into the street. There was no way I was going to be the one to condemn Lawrence and Methuen to economic oblivion."

In 1997, just two years after the fire, Malden Mills earned $400 million in revenue.

Employee Feedback

Being ethical, without being perceived by others as ethical, is problematic. The trust and employee commitment that accompany ethical managers will not be generated if employees do not perceive that their manager is indeed ethical. Sometimes the fault lies with managers who may be unaware that some of their actions are being interpreted as unethical. Sometimes the fault lies with employees who are uninformed about a manager's ethical efforts or remain cynical about managerial intentions.

Creating employee feedback systems that gather information about ethical perceptions symbolizes the importance of ethics to the organization, and these systems are an essential information source. The feedback process can be very simple. On a monthly basis, employees of Physicians Plus Insurance Corporation, a health insurance provider headquartered in Madison, Wisconsin, logged on an Intranet website to complete an eight-item "PULSE Survey" about management performance. Survey items included the following: "In the past month, I felt respected by my manager" and "In the past month, our department's customers received superior service every time."

Other relevant survey items can be taken from the Employee Leadership Survey and Virtue Ethics Survey presented earlier in this chapter. Share the survey results with members of the executive team and other managers. Provide summaries to the employees completing the surveys to reinforce that their input is being listened to, appreciated, and acted upon. Answers to survey items that are repeated in future surveys can be tracked over time.

A Great Place to Work

An organization composed of ethical leaders and managers would be a great place to work. The Great Place to Work® Institute has developed a model of best management practices for creating a work culture that achieves superior performance. The institute surveys employees and encourages organizations to benchmark against one another and their own previous performances.[31] The Great Place to Work® survey results form the basis of *Fortune* magazine's annual list of "100 Best Companies to Work For."

A great place to work is defined by the institute as a place where people "trust the people they work for, have pride in what they do, and enjoy the people they work with."[32] Such an organization has high levels of credibility, respect, fairness, pride, and camaraderie, all of which are associated with ethical leadership. Exhibit 9.3 summarizes how the model's five dimensions are exemplified.[33]

Exhibit 9.3 Great Place to Work® Dimensions

Dimension	How it Plays Out in the Workplace
Credibility	• Communications are open and accessible • Competence in coordinating human and material resources • Integrity in carrying out vision with consistency
Respect	• Supporting professional development and showing appreciation • Collaboration with employees on relevant decisions • Caring for employees as individuals with personal lives
Fairness	• Equity: balanced treatment for all in terms of rewards • Impartiality: absence of favoritism in hiring and promotions • Justice: lack of discrimination and process for appeals
Pride	• In personal job, individual contributions • In work produced by one's team or workgroup • In the organization's products and standing in the community
Camaraderie	• Ability to be oneself • Socially friendly and welcoming atmosphere • Sense of "family" or "team"

Similar to the results of research on ethical organizations, researchers report that organizations that meet the Great Place to Work® standards receive more qualified job applicants; have lower levels of turnover and health care costs; and have higher levels of customer satisfaction, productivity, and profitability. Publically traded "100 Best Companies to Work For" outperformed the stock market by 10.3 percent from 1998 to 2009, which was also three times greater than the Standard and Poor's 500 index performance.[34]

A great place to work is not one that tolerates incompetence or unethical behavior. As noted by Brown and Trevino, a moral manager encourages others at work to behave ethically and holds employees accountable for doing so. Managers control two important levers for ensuring high-quality and ethical performance: work goals and employee performance appraisals. These two essential control mechanisms, and ethical issues related to them, are explored during the remainder of this chapter.

Let's Build a Building

Lien Waivers

You work for the local public library and are responsible for overseeing the construction of a new library. You run into a small subcontractor working on the new library project at a community meeting and thank her for the timely progress being made. The subcontractor pulls you aside and mentions that she has not been paid by the general contractor the past three months, which surprises you because the title company has not mentioned any payment issues.

Typically, a title company is responsible for disbursing monthly payments to the general contractor for services rendered. Subcontractors submit their bills and a signed lien waiver agreement to the general contractor on the 25th day of the month to be paid on the 25th day of the following month. By signing a lien waiver, a subcontractor certifies full payment for previous work and waives the right to later sue for nonpayment. Then the general contractor submits monthly bills and copies of the signed subcontractor lien waiver forms to the title company for the next monthly payment.

When the subcontractor did not receive her first outstanding monthly payment, she contacted the general contractor and was told there had been a computer malfunction with the accounting software. After the subcontractor did not receive her second outstanding monthly payment, she continued to submit bills but refused to sign a lien waiver agreement.

The subcontractor does not want to litigate against the politically well-connected general contractor. But she is now running into a cash flow problem. Her banker has threatened to shut off her line of credit if a sizable deposit is not made within the next 30 days. As a small contractor, she has not bid on any other projects because this job was expected to last eight months. There are no other short-term revenue sources available.

Back at the office, you contact the title company about the lien waiver forms. You are told that there are no outstanding lien waivers. To their knowledge, all subcontractors have been paid in full. Apparently, the general contractor has been forging the subcontractor's signature on the lien waivers.

You wonder what the general contractor has done with your money. Replacing the untrustworthy general contractor, which you would have to do if you initiate legal action based on the fraud, could delay the building project another six months.

What would you do? Would you

1. Trust that the general contractor will soon pay the subcontractors for the work they already performed? Then tell the title company and the general contractor that from now on the title company will pay the subcontractors directly.

2. Initiate legal action against the general contractor for the fraudulent lien waivers and replace with another general contractor, which would cause significant project delays?

   Why?

Organization and Work Goals

Organization and work goals clarify expectations for both managers and employees. Conscientious employees desire goals that establish clear measurable targets that can quantify and validate their accomplishments. Well-designed goals hold managers, coworkers, and subordinates accountable to one another. Ill-conceived goals, on the other hand, can generate unethical behaviors. Unreasonable profit expectations, for instance, can lead some managers to falsify accounting records to increase revenue, approve extremely risky loans they normally would reject, or deny subordinates earned wages and benefits to meet labor cost goals.[35]

Holistic Organizational Goals

Traditionally, managers focus on influencing employees to accomplish the twin goals of increasing productivity and profitability. Managers attempt to get as much productivity from employees as possible while minimizing costs to enhance profits. In 2009, organization theorists James O'Toole and Warren Bennis stated the following: "It's clear we need a better way to evaluate business leaders [than creating wealth for investors]. Moving forward, it appears that the new metric of corporate leadership will be closer to this: the extent to which executives create organizations that are economically, ethically, and socially sustainable."[36]

The Balanced Scorecard is a technique that provides ethical leaders with more holistic goals and measurements for evaluating organizational performance. In addition to relevant financial performance numbers, the Balanced Scorecard contains quantifiable non-financial performance measures in terms of the customer, internal business processes, employee learning, and employee growth.[37] Managers determine five or six meaningful measures from each of these four Balanced Scoreboard categories. Common indicators include measures for customer satisfaction, product quality, employee satisfaction, employee training, and employee development. Many types of organizations have adopted the Balanced Scorecard approach, including nonprofits, schools, government agencies, as well as businesses.

Another popular holistic goal approach available to ethical leaders is the Triple Bottom Line. Sustainability theorist John Elkington conceived of the Triple Bottom Line in 1994 as a comprehensive measure that takes into account an organization's ecological performance, social performance, and financial performance.[38] The Triple Bottom Line approach extends managerial focus from shareholders to other stakeholders. The United Nations has adopted the Triple Bottom Line as an accounting standard for communities, where the success of organizations is based on how their decisions impact "people, planet, and profit."[39] A growing number of innovative businesses are also adopting the Triple Bottom Line approach.[40]

Stretch Goals

Many organizations establish "stretch goals" that challenge employees to perform at peak efficiency and effectiveness.[41] A stretch goal, contrasted to an incremental goal, is one that appears to be just a little out of the employee's reach, thus the need to stretch to accomplish the goal. Employees are more likely to accomplish something that seems impossible if a goal is established that focuses the employee's attention on the task.

An employee who averages $100,000 a month in sales may need a stretch goal of $150,000 to overcome complacency and adopt more creative and innovative methods.

Researchers report, however, that stretch goals sometimes tempt employees to stretch the truth and behave unethically if that is the only way they can achieve the goal by the specified deadline.[42] Sales performance stretch goals are a particularly troublesome area, and they contribute to sales. people being ranked among the most unethical professions in annual public opinion polls. Researchers report that 79 percent of surveyed managers have heard salespeople make an unrealistic promise on sales calls.[43] Some salespeople paid on a commission basis will recommend unnecessary services, such as repairing products that are operating well, and then overcharge for the services rendered.

In *The Force*, David Dorsey shadowed the top salesperson at Xerox.[44] To be rewarded for accomplishing 120 percent of his sales goal, this otherwise relatively nice salesperson regularly lied about product price and capabilities, his negotiating authority, his work schedule, the availability of customer perks, and product delivery capabilities. He did whatever it took to close a deal, which usually meant lying and being manipulative. Meanwhile, he and his colleagues considered themselves ethical and were well rewarded for their service to the company.

A similar phenomenon occurred at both Enron and Arthur Andersen. Wall Street analysts and investors continually expected Enron to increase revenue by 20 percent annually, and Arthur Andersen partners expected field partners to increase client revenue by 20 percent annually. The pressure to accomplish these very difficult goals generated unethical behaviors that led to the collapse of both companies.

Goal Setting

Establishing appropriate work goals is a complex process. Goals that are too specific, or whose time spans are too short, can result in employees not being observant about other opportunities to improve performance.[45] Too many goals can divert an employee's attention from other high-priority issues.

Depending on the nature of the job task, establish daily, weekly, monthly, and yearly goals. In addition, establish and review interim goals, and reward employees for achieving them.

SMART goals have five attributes. The SMART acronym stands for goals that are[46]

1. *Specific:* The outcome is clearly identifiable.

2. *Measurable:* The outcome can be measured.

3. *Aligned:* The outcome contributes to organizational strategy.

4. *Reachable:* The outcome is challenging, but realistically attainable.

5. *Time-Bound:* The outcome is to be achieved by a specific point in time.

"Doing Your Best" is an inadequate employee goal. "Best" needs to be clearly defined, such as increasing sales 5 percent by December 31. A clearly defined goal statement that meets the five SMART criteria minimizes ambiguity about employee performance expectations.

Obtain employee input to ensure that work goals are attainable. Often, if asked to determine a "fair" goal, employees offer goals that are equal to, or more difficult than, goals managers would initially propose. Employees' participation in the goal-setting process increases their commitment and accountability to the goal.

Establishing feedback sessions to review goal progress also increases the likelihood of success.

Align employee goals with organizational goals. Management-by-objectives (MBO) is a goal-setting technique in which managers and their subordinates jointly determine work unit and individual goals in alignment with organizational goals. Support staff, for instance, can determine individual objectives and objectives that link their work to the superior performance of other employees and work units.

The MBO process begins with executives defining the organization's strategic goals in ways that are specific and measurable. These goals are then cascaded downward through the organization. The next level of managers, be it a division or department, meets to establish goals that are in alignment with the organization's strategic goals. Then members of the manager's work unit meet to establish goals that are in alignment with department goals.

Lastly, employees meet with their supervisor to develop individual goals in alignment with the work unit's goals. Jointly review the employee's previous performance, as well as the performances of others with similar job tasks, to determine a goal range. Then have the employee propose a challenging, yet attainable, goal within this range, along with strategies that will lead to goal achievement. The employee's supervisor can accept the goal, note that the goal is too difficult, or challenge the employee to propose a more difficult goal. If one of the latter two cases occurs, jointly develop a more appropriate goal and discuss strategies for goal achievement.

Stress Management

Goals require deadlines, and deadlines can create stress through psychological and physical tension. High levels of stress, inappropriately managed, can lead to health problems, low productivity, accidents, absenteeism, turnover, and unethical employee behaviors.[47]

Work goals are just one source of workplace stress. Other causes of stress include conflicts at work, rapid change, unfavorable working conditions, authoritarian or incompetent supervisors, and personal problems at home. The U.S. Department of Health and Human Services estimates that job stress costs organizations $200 billion annually.[48]

Organizations can help employees manage stress through health-related wellness programs and employee assistance programs (EAPs). Delegation training helps employees with unreasonable burdens to assign tasks to others. Some organizations have established a "quiet time" that eliminates interruptions during a specified time period.[49]

Meditation can be an excellent form of stress reduction. Meditation helps a person self-regulate his or her mind by focusing on the present moment and not engaging random thoughts, many of which are about past regrets or anxieties about future events. Meditation helps individuals develop clarity of mind, patience, compassion, and sustained attention, all attributes of ethical leadership.[50] Researchers also report that meditation is associated with high levels of self-esteem and satisfaction with life, characteristics beneficial to high-performance organizations.[51]

With practice, meditation can be successfully conducted within 12 minutes. Organizations such as Apple Computer, McKinsey Consulting, Hughes Aircraft, and Google offer meditation as an employee benefit.

Managers can meditate on their own or lead members of their work unit in a meditation session held in a conference room. The process is rather simple:[52]

Step 1 – Find a quiet place where you will not be disturbed.

Step 2 – Set a timer with a soft bell for the desired length of the session.

Step 3 – Sit up straight on the floor with legs crossed in a lotus position or on a chair with your feet firmly on the ground.

Step 4 – Slowly relax your muscles.

Step 5 – Close your eyes and breathe slowly in a regular rhythm. If a beginner, start by counting breaths. Inhale, momentarily hold the breath, and then count the exhale as "one." Continue counting upward to a specific number, such as 40. If the number of a particular breath is forgotten, just begin counting again. More experienced meditators usually chant or focus on the blank space within their consciousness. A poetic Buddhist chant is the following:

Inhale #1: "Breathe in, I calm my body."

Exhale #1: "Breathe out, I smile."

Inhale #2: "Dwelling in the present moment,"

Exhale #2: "I know that it is a wonderful moment."

Step 6 – Breathe each breath slightly deeper and hold slightly longer.

Step 7 – Distracting thoughts will enter your mind. Don't engage the thought; let it go. If you fear losing a vital thought, just write it down on a nearby piece of paper and then resume the meditation process.

Step 8 – Continue the process until the alarm gently sounds. Slowly become aware of where you are, open your eyes, and get up gradually.

Employee Performance Appraisals

Ethical leaders can hold followers accountable through performance appraisals. An employee performance appraisal evaluates factors that are directly or indirectly related to achieving organizational and employee goals. An appraisal can be conducted solely for the sake of employee development or linked to merit raises and used to determine promotions and dismissals. Gather information about the employee's strengths and weaknesses relative to key performance criteria, and then work with the employee to develop new work goals in the spirit of continuous improvement.

A performance appraisal is similar to the Balanced Scorecard concept, a holistic approach that measures the most important aspects of an employee's job task. The performance appraisal scorecard clarifies what the employee will be held accountable for accomplishing. Employees are more likely to pay attention to an issue if it is included in a performance appraisal. Without performance appraisals, employees are left guessing as to how superiors are interpreting their efforts. The measures need to be objective, not subjective, to minimize biases associated with favoritism.

Include an ethics component in employee performance appraisals. In 2003, the Ethics Resource Center asked survey respondents whether ethical behavior was rewarded by their organization. Only half reported this was the case.[53] Not including ethical behavior among the performance appraisal variables signifies that ethical behaviors are not of major importance.

At Moody's credit rating service, for instance, rewarding unethical behavior severely damaged the company's reputation and the U.S. economy. In 2008, after the U.S. housing market collapse led to a worldwide recession, Moody's was criticized for overstating the creditworthiness of companies it rated.[54] A follow-up government investigation revealed that some rating analysts at Moody's assigned undeserved good credit ratings to some companies to ensure future business with them. The false information misled investors about the company's credit worthiness. Employees of Moody's who cooperated with this scam received positive performance appraisals, bonuses, and promotions. Analysts who ethically maintained more rigorous credit rating standards were dismissed for being uncooperative.

Link employee performance appraisal results to merit raises and promotions to ensure that employees who behave ethically and achieve goals in alignment with organizational objectives are appropriately rewarded. Employees will behave more ethically when ethical behaviors are recognized and rewarded.

Design performance appraisals and gather relevant data that address four prominent ethical performance issues:

1. Does the employee behave unethically?
2. Does the employee live up to the Code of Ethics?
3. Does the employee embody the attitudes and behaviors of an ideal employee?
4. Does the employee achieve and support ethics-based initiatives?

These performance appraisal measures are discussed in the following sections.

Unethical Behaviors

William Shakespeare said, "To thine own self be true." Nobody is ethically perfect, yet people tend to resist sharing their imperfections with others. Have employees hypothetically conduct an honest and confidential self-assessment of their own struggles to behave ethically at work. This makes them more aware of areas needing improvement to become a more ethical individual and employee.

The seven-item survey in Exhibit 9.4 highlights unethical behaviors that might publicly embarrass an employee.[55] Modify the items to fit the context of the organization or work unit. Completing the survey—honestly and confidentially—reinforces that these unethical behaviors are wrong and provides the employee with ethical performance goals for the next performance appraisal period.

Exhibit 9.4 Practicing Unethical Behaviors Survey

Instructions: Following are seven unethical behaviors. Read each statement and then circle the letter that best describes the frequency of the behavior. The more honest you are the more helpful the information you will receive.

1=Never; 2=Sometimes; 3=Frequently; 4=Always

	N	S	F	A
I misrepresent the facts about my job activities or those of a coworker.	1	2	3	4

I divulge personal or confidential information to coworkers, customers, competitors, friends, or the general public.	1	2	3	4
I permit, or fail to report, violations of federal, state, or municipal laws or regulations.	1	2	3	4
I protect unethical coworkers from corrective discipline.	1	2	3	4
I permit, or fail to report, theft or misuse of company property.	1	2	3	4
I cover up on-the-job accidents and fail to report health and safety hazards.	1	2	3	4
I take credit for ideas that are actually those of a coworker.	1	2	3	4
Add the seven scores (the higher the score the more unethical is your behavior):				
Which of the unethical behaviors do you want to change between now and the next performance review? What specifically do you need to do to reduce your unethical behavior score for that item?				

Living Up to the Code of Ethics Performance Appraisals

Annually appraise how well employees perform according to the organization's Code of Ethics. In Chapter 4, an organization's five-item Code of Ethics (see Exhibit 4.10) was transformed into an organizational assessment survey to benchmark progress (see Exhibit 4.11). The survey has been modified in Exhibit 9.5 for the purpose of conducting an individualized employee performance appraisal.

Exhibit 9.5 Employee Code of Ethics Performance Appraisal

Instructions: Please use the 1 to 5 scale below to assess how well each of the following statements exemplifies the employee's performance. The more honest you are the more helpful the information you will receive.

1=Strongly Disagree; 2=Disagree; 3=Neither Agree nor Disagree; 4=Agree; 5=Strongly Agree

	SD	D	N	A	SA
Operates with integrity and respect	1	2	3	4	5
Provides and promotes legendary service (meets and exceeds customer expectations)	1	2	3	4	5
Uses superior communications (is professional, courteous, and prompt)	1	2	3	4	5

(Continued)

Exhibit 9.5 Employee Code of Ethics Performance Appraisal (*Continued*)					
Embraces continuous improvement (becomes more productive and efficient)	1	2	3	4	5
Actively engages in self-management (assesses performance daily)	1	2	3	4	5
Add the five scores above:					
Which of these items should the employee improve upon between now and the next performance review? How can the employee score higher on that item?					

Also appraise employee performance for all ethics-based initiatives. These items can be added to regular performance appraisals. Measures for ethics-based initiatives may include accomplishing affirmative action hiring and promotion goals, work unit ethics scores, percentage of employees participating in ethics and diversity training workshops, theft reductions, and number of employee grievances.

Ideal Employee Attitudes and Behaviors Performance Appraisals

Employee performance appraisals can be used to benchmark the distance an employee still needs to travel in the direction of becoming an ideal employee. Annually appraise employee performance based on the qualities of an ideal employee.

Chapter 6 provides a "Qualities of an Ideal Employee" survey (see Exhibit 6.9) developed by a team of managers for their subordinates. The seven factors, each operationalized with behavioral descriptors, are general character, customer relations, colleague relations, communication skills, work task skills, continuous improvement, and company pride. Develop ideal profiles for every category of employee—executives, managers, supervisors, and subordinates—based on the seven factors. Exhibit 9.6 provides a survey based on a profile for an ideal leader.[56]

Exhibit 9.6 Leadership Skills Performance Appraisal				
Instructions: Please use the 1 to 4 scale below to assess how well each of the following statements exemplifies the employee's performance. The more honest you are the more helpful the information you will receive. *4=Always; 3=Frequently; 2=Sometimes; 1=Never*				
	A	F	S	N
Is positive	4	3	2	1
Listens well	4	3	2	1
Is comfortable giving feedback	4	3	2	1

Is trusted by others	4	3	2	1
Is easy to approach	4	3	2	1
Is available to others when needed	4	3	2	1
Communicates clearly	4	3	2	1
Seeks input from others	4	3	2	1
Praises others	4	3	2	1
Is patient	4	3	2	1
Follows through on commitments	4	3	2	1
Is supportive	4	3	2	1
Provides clear expectations	4	3	2	1
Knows others well	4	3	2	1
Add the 14 scores above:				
Which of these items should the employee improve upon between now and the next performance review? How can the employee score higher on that item?				

Collection and Evaluation Issues

How employee performance appraisal information is collected and evaluated raises ethical issues. Poorly managed performance appraisals are detrimental to employee development, morale, and productivity. Conduct employee performance evaluations in a timely manner, at least once a year. Some organizations conduct quarterly appraisals to provide employees with more regular feedback. More frequent appraisals minimize damages because managers become aware of problems needing correction soon after they appear.

In addition, fairness dictates that employees receive evaluation scores that are related to their actual job performance. Some managers give poor performers average ratings to avoid difficult discussions and conflict, and they give excellent performers average ratings out of fear that other managers looking for star performers will recruit their excellent employees. These justifications result in a false sense of security among poor performers and can undermine employee confidence among the excellent performers. An underappreciated star performer may soon seek employment elsewhere.

Collect performance information from a wide range of people who interact with the employee being evaluated. Many direct supervisors observe only a small portion of an employee's performance. An employee may behave admirably in the presence of the direct supervisor, but inadequately when not closely monitored. Or, an employee may behave admirably in response to a powerful manager but inadequately to less powerful colleagues requesting information.

A more authentic and holistic picture of an employee's performance can be determined based on 360-degree performance evaluations.[57] The phrase "360 degrees" refers to a circle with the person being evaluated in the nucleus position. Collecting information from multiple perspectives provides a more comprehensive understanding of employee performance. Develop a list of people who interact with the employee and choose a representative sample of people hierarchically above the employee, below the employee, and on the same level. When appropriate, include feedback evaluations from customers and suppliers. Enhance self-awareness by having the employee perform a self-assessment and then compare the self-assessment results with how others evaluate the employee.

Employees can be rated in comparison to an absolute standard of performance or ranked in comparison to one another. A rating system is more ethical than a ranking system in that an employee earns a rating based on his or her job task efforts and accomplishments, whereas a ranking system may not adequately describe an employee's value to the work unit.

Some executives prefer a ranking system because it forces managers to determine which employees are the top performers and worst performers relative to other employees. While Jack Welch was CEO at General Electric, he initiated a three-tier 20-70-10 ranking system: 20 percent top performers, 70 percent middle performers, and 10 percent low performers.[58] Star performers were well rewarded through recognition and high bonuses, middle performers received extensive feedback and opportunities to further enhance their skills through additional training, and low performers were either dismissed or provided a second chance to improve performance within agreed-upon timelines.

Ranking people can create unhealthy competition among employees. If only one employee in a work unit can receive the top ranking, for instance, employees in the work unit will be tempted to compete, rather than cooperate, with one another to achieve the highest rank. Why help a colleague if doing so might result in the colleague being ranked higher than you?

Conversely, one employee must receive the lowest rank in a work unit composed of highly talented and well-trained employees. Technically, the employee is the worst performer in the work group. But, the employee can still be a very good performer. Falsely labeling a very good performer as the worst performer can damage work unit morale and be detrimental to the employee's career.

Performance Appraisal Feedback

The purpose of a performance appraisal feedback session is to praise an employee's good behaviors and accomplishments and develop strategies for improving weaknesses.[59] Performance appraisal feedback sessions can be tense. Carefully manage the feedback session because employees may feel anxious about giving or receiving critical information.

On a regular basis, provide positive feedback immediately after a praiseworthy behavior and constructive feedback immediately after a blameworthy behavior. Employees who informally receive feedback on a regular basis are less surprised by the annual formal performance appraisal results and better prepared to discuss improvement issues.

As an ethical leader, demonstrate respect for employees by meeting personally with each direct report to discuss the performance appraisal results. Hold performance appraisal feedback sessions in a neutral setting, such as a conference room. Conducting appraisal feedback sessions in the supervisor's office, particularly if the feedback is critical, creates an uncomfortable office environment. Employees may avoid visiting a supervisor's office because of the negative memories associated with performance evaluations.

Prior to the meeting, compare the employee's self-assessment with the 360-degree performance appraisal results. Begin the meeting by discussing areas that both the employee and the raters highlighted as strengths. Praise these behaviors and accomplishments. Employees are much more receptive to positive feedback than negative feedback, which people tend to deny or block out.

Then discuss any areas raters highlighted as strengths but the employee did not. Make the employee aware that others are impressed with these behaviors and outcomes. Next, discuss any areas the employee highlighted as strengths but the raters did not. Explore with the employee why this perceptual gap exists. Avoid generalities by highlighting a specific example and provide documentary evidence to minimize ambiguities. One meaningful example is usually sufficient. Otherwise, the employee may feel attacked and leave the feedback session feeling hopeless.

Lastly, discuss those areas that both the employee and raters highlighted as weaknesses. Focus on solving specific shortcomings and how to improve the weakness. Jointly establish goals and strategies that will lead to better results. From an ethics perspective, these efforts help employees become better people.

Disciplining Work Rule Violations

Ethical leadership does not mean never disciplining or firing anyone. Poor performers who fail to improve need to be dismissed for the benefit of the work unit and organization, and sometimes downsizing is unavoidable. Ethics, however, suggests that a poor performer be given an opportunity to improve within a certain timeline prior to dismissal, or that care and concern be extended when downsizing occurs by providing outplacement services.

Fairness is an extremely important ethical value. The 360-degree performance appraisal process may reveal some previously unknown employee work rule violations. How managers respond to allegations that a subordinate has behaved unethically significantly influences how employees evaluate a manager's fairness. Everyone is innocent until proven guilty. Investigate the situation prior to imposing disciplinary action. Maybe the employee's behavior was misunderstood by the respondent or justifiable given additional contextual information.

Major Infractions

Employees define major and minor ethical infractions based on the type of punishment determined by managers. Any behavior punished harshly is typically considered a major infraction and gets the attention of employees. Employee theft and drug and alcohol violations are usually treated as major ethical infractions.

Polygraph tests can be used for employee theft. Managers must have good cause before submitting an employee to a polygraph test. Otherwise, trust is being violated and employee morale will suffer. Exhibit 9.7 summarizes some of key rules governing employee polygraph tests.[60]

Exhibit 9.7 Employee Polygraph Protection Act of 1988

Key factors of the legislation include the following:

- Random polygraph testing of employees is prohibited.
- Polygraphs can be used on employees who are reasonably suspected of involvement in a specific workplace incident resulting in economic loss to the employer.
- An employee can refuse to take the polygraph test or terminate a polygraph test at any time; refusal to participate in a polygraph test cannot be used as a reason for discipline or job termination.
- If an employee fails the polygraph test, the employee cannot be fired without other corroborating evidence.

Violations of drug and alcohol rules are also major ethical infractions. Randomly test employees whose activities continually put public safety at risk due to their drug use or alcohol abuse. Chapter 3 summarizes the key elements of drug testing. A new type of test measures chronic alcoholism by using biological indicators called "biomarkers" that remain elevated for several days after drinking has stopped.[61] These tests are considered 20 times better at detecting heavy drinking than urine analysis.

Minor Infractions

Many workplace violations are relatively minor, such as being late for work or playing solitaire on the computer during work time. Constructively address minor infractions before they escalate into bigger problems.

The following is a continuum of potential punishments, beginning with the most lenient and ending with the harshest, for managing workplace violations:[62]

1. Talk to, and coach, the employee about the problem
2. Oral warning
3. Written warning
4. Provide special in-house services to help employee
5. Send employee to formal training for help
6. Explore transferring employee to a different department
7. Put the employee on probation

8. Fine the employee or withhold a portion of merit pay

9. Suspend without pay

10. Termination

The severity of the violation dictates where on the continuum to begin. An employee caught bringing home office computer paper for personal use might just need to be spoken with, or given an oral warning. A manager might issue a written warning to an employee caught lying to a customer. An employee caught embezzling funds is usually terminated immediately.

The goal of discipline is to rehabilitate employees who violate work rules, not to fire them. Guilty parties need to acknowledge the wrongdoing, apologize, and then change their behavior. Effective rehabilitation also requires that the employee being disciplined accept the fairness of the disciplinary process. Termination is appropriate if rehabilitation fails or the violation is severe.

Forgiveness

Management and nonmanagement employees will make technical and human interaction mistakes, and their words and behaviors may deeply harm others. Disclosing mistakes is challenging because doing so can damage the person's reputation and make the person vulnerable to criticisms and punishment. But corrective actions cannot be taken until the mistake is acknowledged. The longer the mistake is ignored or covered up, the greater the likelihood of the mistake escalating.

Violated trust needs repair. Similar to the rehabilitation process for work rule violations, apply the "AAA" method—admit, apologize, and make amends. Once the mistake is admitted, deeper understanding can occur that will prevent the mistake from happening again. Apologizing develops empathy and sympathy in the person harmed by the action. Making amends demonstrates sincerity.

The other half of the harm equation involves the person being harmed forgiving the initiator of the harm. Managers must exemplify the value of forgiveness and coach employees on how to forgive. This is particularly important if the work group is recovering from a dishonest or abusive manager because employee resentment will be projected onto the manager's replacement. The new manager needs to acknowledge, and heal, the harm caused by the previous manager, rather than ignore it, and workgroup members need to forgive their previously morally imperfect manager.

Robert Enright of the International Forgiveness Institute defines forgiveness as a gift freely given in the face of moral wrong, without denying the wrong itself.[63] Forgiveness recognizes the inherent worth of the wrongdoer and replaces the resentment a violated person may feel with goodwill, a process that increases the forgiver's self-esteem.

Enright offers a four-phase model that ethical managers can apply to guide employees through the forgiveness process. The process begins with personal awareness of the negative impacts stemming from the harm-generating behavior:

Phase 1 – *Uncovering Phase*. The violated person recognizes that the unjust situation has created unhealthy anger and emotional pain.

Phase 2 – *Decision Phase*. The violated person explores the personal pain or damage that would continue by not forgiving the wrongdoer, compared to the positive changes that could occur by forgiving.

Phase 3 – *Work Phase*. The violated person grieves over the unfairness of the wrong-doing; reframes the wrongdoer as a person of inherent human worth deserving of forgiveness; and practices the virtues of goodness, service, mercy, and generosity by forgiving the wrongdoer.

Phase 4 – *Outcome Phase*. The forgiving person experiences the emotionally healing benefits of forgiveness and finds meaning in the previous suffering.

SUMMARY

Managers must clearly signal on a daily basis that ethical behaviors are expected, and unethical behaviors are unacceptable. Employees learn more about what types of behaviors are acceptable by observing the actions of their direct supervisors, rather than from listening to inspirational words coming out of the executive suite or reading widely distributed memos on the topic.

A manager earns a reputation for being an ethical leader by being a moral role model, setting high ethical expectations for others, and establishing systems that encourage employees to behave ethically. Managers become moral role models by exhibiting virtuous behaviors, such as being honest and fair.

Two essential management tools that encourage ethical behavior are work goals and performance evaluations. Establish work goals that inspire ethical behavior. Beware of stretch goals that may tempt employees to stretch the truth about performance. Formally appraise the ethical performance of employees on a regular basis and link these scores to merit raises and promotions. Address any work rule violations immediately and fairly. If the wrongdoer is terminated, psychologically heal the workforce and redevelop a culture of trust by helping employees forgive the wrongdoer.

KEY WORDS

Power; authoritarian; Theory X; Theory Y; ethical leadership; servant leadership; Balanced Scorecard; Triple Bottom Line; stretch goal; SMART goals; management-by-objectives; employee performance appraisal; 360-degree performance evaluations; forgiveness

CHAPTER QUESTIONS

1. What are William Torbert's six management role models, which are associated with the different stages of moral development?

2. Discuss the five sources of power available to managers, and the ethical issues related to authoritarian and participatory leadership styles.

3. What is ethical leadership and how can it be measured?

4. How can work goals and performance appraisals influence ethical and unethical behaviors?

5. Why is it important to forgive managers and coworkers? Describe Robert Enright's four phases of forgiveness.

In the Real World: Enron

Auditor Oversight Problems—Spring 2001

Enron's Board of Directors decided to exempt Andy Fastow from the Code of Ethics policy. LJM1, however, violated Generally Accepted Accounting Principles because the SPE's management team was not independent of Enron. This technicality was lost amongst the flurry of mergers and acquisitions demanding the Board's attention. Fastow's management of LJM1, and its well-hidden purchases of Enron's assets, enabled Enron to meet quarterly financial targets.

Fastow's creative financing efforts were widely acclaimed in the business media, earning him *CFO Magazine's* 1999 CFO Excellence Award. Enron's 1999 revenue reached $40 billion, a very impressive 28 percent increase from the previous year, and $100 billion for 2000. Enron climbed to #7 on the Fortune 500 list and was now the nation's largest supplier of electricity, as well as natural gas.

Enron became the hottest stock on Wall Street. Stock purchased in March 1997 for $40, when Jeff Skilling became COO, achieved a stock-split adjusted value of $181 a share in August 2000. In 2000, Enron won *Fortune* magazine's most innovative company award for the fifth consecutive year and was ranked #25 for "Most Admired Company in the World."

In the midst of these accolades, Ken Lay triumphantly retired as Enron's CEO in February 2001, passing the reins on to Skilling, his protégé. The succession plan included Skilling taking over for Lay as Enron's chairman of the Board of Directors at the end of 2001.

Meanwhile, within Arthur Andersen, Carl Bass was promoted to the company's Professional Standards Group (PSG), an oversight team composed of experienced senior partners who provide independent rulings on contentious accounting issues for audit teams. The Enron account fell under Bass's jurisdiction. In the spring of 2001, Bass refused to sign off on a questionable financial structure for a series of Fastow-created SPEs. Bass instructed David Duncan, the Andersen audit team's lead accountant, to inform Enron's Board of Directors about the SPE accounting problem.

Duncan ignored Bass's order and shared the problem with Rick Causey, Enron's CAO and former Andersen partner. Causey, incensed by what he considered to be Bass's unfair treatment, complained bitterly to senior Arthur Andersen partners. Causey and other Enron executives threatened to change audit companies if Bass was not removed from the Enron account and replaced by a different PSG member. The Enron account earned a remarkable $50 million in fees for Arthur Andersen's Houston office.

DECISION CHOICE. If you were a senior Arthur Andersen partner and Enron strongly requested that Carl Bass be replaced by a different PSG member to review Duncan's audit team's work, would you

1. Defend Bass and risk losing the $50 million Enron account?
2. Remove Bass from the Enron account and replace him with another highly qualified PSG member?
   Why?

ANCILLARY MATERIALS

Websites to Explore

- Theory X and Theory Y survey, available at http://www.businessballs.com/mcgregor.htm.
- GreatPlacetoWorkInstitute,availableatwww.greatplacetowork.com.
- The American Institute of Stress, available at www.stress.org.
- International Forgiveness Institute, available at www.forgiveness-institute.org.

Best Place to Work Video

- CBS News *60 Minutes* on Aaron Feuerstein, available at http://www.youtube.com/watch?v=9YcWLXBXaD8.

Business Ethics Issue Video

- "The Storm," *Frontline,* about government response to Hurricane Katrina; November 22, 2005, 55 minutes, available at http://www.pbs.org/wgbh/pages/frontline/storm/view/?utm_campaign=viewpage&utm_medium=grid&utm_source=grid.

TEDTalks Videos

- Inspirational Leadership: Simon Sinek discusses a powerful model for inspirational leadership starting with a golden circle and the question "Why?" using Apple, Martin Luther King, and the Wright brothers as examples; September 2009, 18 minutes, available at http://www.ted.com/talks/simon_sinek_how_great_leaders_inspire_action.html.

- Leadership: Richard Branson describes the ups and the downs of his career, from his multibillionaire success to his multiple near-death experiences; March 2007, 30 minutes, available at http://www.ted.com/talks/richard_branson_s_life_at_30_000_feet.html.

Conversations with Charlie Rose

- A conversation with Michael Lewis, author of "The Big Short," about the 2008–2010 financial crisis; March 16, 2010, 60 minutes, available at http://www.charlierose.com/view/interview/10911.

- A conversation with Lloyd Blankfein, chief executive officer and chairman of Goldman Sachs; April 30, 2010, 60 minutes, available at http://www.charlierose.com/view/interview/10989.

NOTES

1 Paul Harvey, Jason Stoner, Wayne Hochwater, and Charles Kacmar, "Coping with Abusive Supervision: The Neutralizing Effects of Ingratiation and Positive Affect on Negative Employee Outcomes," *Leadership Quarterly,* 18, 3 (2007), 264–280.

2 James M. Kouzes and Barry Z. Posner, *The Leadership Challenge,* 4th ed. (Hoboken, NJ: John Wiley & Sons, 2007).

3 James Weber, "Managers' Moral Reasoning: Assessing Their Responses to Three Moral Dilemmas," *Human Relations,* 43, 7 (1990), 687–702.

4 Benyamin M. Lichtenstein, Beverly A. Smith, and William R. Torbert, "Leadership and Ethical Development: Balancing Light and Shadow," *Business Ethics Quarterly,* 5, 1 (1991), 97–116.

5 Peter Drucker, *The Practice of Management* (New York: HarperCollins, 1954/2006), p. 157.

6 Clinton O. Longenecker, Mitchell J. Neubert, and Laurence S. Fink, "Causes and Consequences of Managerial Failure in Rapidly Changing Organizations," *Business Horizons,* 50, 2 (2007), 145–155.

7 Jon M. Huntsman, *Winners Never Cheat: Even in Difficult Times* (Upper Saddle River, NJ: Pearson Education, 2008), pp. 52 and 89–91.

8 John R. P. French and Bertram Raven, "The Bases of Social Power," in Dorwin Cartwright (Ed.), *Studies in Social Power* (Ann Arbor, MI: University of Michigan Press, 1959), pp. 150–167.

9 David Carr, "At Flagging Tribune, Tales of a Bankrupt Culture," *New York Times,* October 5, 2010; David Carr and Tim Arango, "Tribune Chief Accepts Advice and Backs Out," *New York Times,* October 22, 2010.

10 Andrew Carnegie, *The Gospel of Wealth* (Cambridge MA: The Belknap Press of Harvard University Press, 1900/1962).

11 Frederick Winslow Taylor, *The Principles of Scientific Management* (New York: Harper & Row, 1912/1947).

12 Richard D. White, "Organizational Design and Ethics: The Effects of Rigid Hierarchy on Moral Reasoning," *International Journal of Organization Theory & Behavior,* 2, 3&4 (1999), 431–456.

13 Samuel Aryee, Zhen Xiong Chen, Li-Yun Sun, and Yaw A. Debrah, "Antecedents and Outcomes of Abusive Supervision: Test of a Trickle-Down Model," *Journal of Applied Psychology,* 92, 1 (2007), 191–201.

[14] Douglas McGregor, *The Human Side of Enterprise* (New York: McGraw Hill, 1960).

[15] For a free Theory X and Theory Y survey, see "Douglas McGregor—Theory X Y," available at http://www.businessballs.com/mcgregor.htm, accessed 10/30/10.

[16] Rensis Likert, *The Human Organization* (New York: McGraw Hill, 1967).

[17] Paul Hersey and Kenneth Blanchard, *Management of Organizational Behavior—Utilizing Human Resources* (Englewood Cliffs, NJ: Prentice Hall, 1969); Paul Hersey, *The Situational Leader* (New York: Warner Books, 1985).

[18] Ken Blanchard, *Leading at a Higher Level* (Upper Saddle River, NJ: Blanchard Management Corporation, 2009).

[19] Linda Klebe Trevino, Laura Pincus Hartman, and Michael Brown, "Moral Person and Moral Manager: How Executives Develop a Reputation for Ethical Leadership," *California Management Review*, 42, 4 (2000), 128–142; Linda Klebe Trevino, Michael Brown, and Laura Pincus Hartman, "A Qualitative Investigation of Perceived Executive Ethical Leadership: Perceptions from Inside and Outside the Executive Suite," *Human Relations*, 56, 1 (2003), 5–37; Michael E. Brown and Linda K. Trevino, "Ethical Leadership: A Review and Future Directions," *Leadership Quarterly*, 17, 6 (2006), 595–616; Michael E. Brown, Linda K. Trevino, and David A. Harrison, "Ethical Leadership: A Social Learning Theory Perspective for Construct Development," *Organizational Behavior and Human Decision Processes*, 97, 2 (2005), 117–134.

[20] Brown, Trevino, and Harrison, "Ethical Leadership," p. 120.

[21] Ibid., pp. 117–134; Mitchell Neubert, Dawn Carlson, K. Kacmar, James Roberts, and Lawrence Chonko, "The Virtuous Influence of Ethical Leadership Behavior: Evidence from the Field," *Journal of Business Ethics*, 90, 2 (2009), 157–170.

[22] Aryee, Chen, Sun, and Debrah, "Antecedents and Outcomes of Abusive Supervision."

[23] David M. Mayer, Maribeth Kuenzi, Rebecca Greenbaum, Mary Bardes, and Rommel Salvador, "How Low Does Ethical Leadership Flow? Test of a Trickle-Down Model," *Organizational Behavior & Human Decision Processes*, 108, 1 (2009), 1–13.

[24] Kevin J. Shanahan and Michael R. Hyman, "The Development of a Virtue Ethics Scale," *Journal of Business Ethics*, 42, 2 (2003), 197–208.

[25] Fred O. Walumbwa and John Schaubroeck, "Leader Personality Traits and Employee Voice Behavior: Mediating Roles of Ethical Leadership and Work Group Psychological Safety," *Journal of Applied Psychology*, 94, 5 (2009), 1275–1286.

[26] Ronald E. Riggio, Weichun Zhu, Christopher Reina, and James Maroosis, "A Virtue-Based Measure of Ethical Leadership," paper presented at the 2009 Academy of Management meeting, Chicago; original reverse score items have been reworded to positive statement for ease of survey completion.

[27] Robert K. Greenleaf, *Servant Leadership* (New York: Paulist Press, 1977/2002).

[28] John E. Barbuto Jr. and Daniel W. Wheeler, "Scale Development and Construct Clarification of Servant Leadership," *Group & Organization Management*, 31, 3 (2006), 300. These characteristics also appear as key concepts in the growing "spiritual leadership" literature; see Fahri Karakas, "Spirituality and Performance in Organizations: A Literature Review," *Journal of Business Ethics*, 94, 1 (2010), 89–106.

[29] Max DePree, *Leadership as an Art* (New York: Doubleday, 1987/2004).

[30] Rebecca Leung, "The Mensch of Malden Mills," *CBS News*, July 6, 2003, available at http://www.cbsnews.com/stories/2003/07/03/60minutes/main561656.shtml, accessed 10/30/10; John W. McCurry, "TW's 1997 Leader of the Year: Aaron Feuerstein," *Textile World,* 147, 10 (October 1997); Matthew W. Seeger and Robert R. Ulmer, "Virtuous Responses to Organizational Crisis: Aaron Feuerstein and Milt Cole," *Journal of Business Ethics,* 31, 4 (2001), 368–376.

[31] Great Place to Work Institute website available at www.greatplacetowork.com, accessed 10/30/10.

[32] Great Place to Work Institute, "Our Model," available at www.greatplacetowork.com/great/model.php, accessed 10/30/10.

[33] Great Place to Work Institute, "The Dimensions of a Great Place to Work," available at www.greatplacetowork.com/great/dimensions.php, accessed 10/30/10.

[34] Great Place to Work Institute, "Financial Results," available at http://www.greatplacetowork.com/what_we_believe/graphs.php, accessed 10/30/10.

[35] Steven Greenhouse, *The Big Squeeze: Tough Times for American Workers* (New York: Alfred Knopf, 2008).

36 James O'Toole and Warren Bennis, "What's Needed Next: A Culture of Candor," *Harvard Business Review*, 87, 6 (2009), p. 56.

37 Robert S. Kaplan and David P. Norton, *The Balanced Scorecard* (Boston, MA: Harvard Business School Press, 1996); Mohan Nair, *Essentials of Balanced Scorecard* (Hoboken, NJ: John Wiley & Sons, 2004).

38 John Elkington, "Towards the Sustainable Corporation: Win-Win-Win Business Strategies for Sustainable Development," *California Management Review*, 36, 2 (1994), 90–100.

39 Yara C. Cintra, L. Nelson Carvalho, and Bruna Perlingeiro, "The 'Triple Bottom Line' Approach on Social and Environmental Reporting: Should Financial Accounting Standard Setters Step In?" *European Journal of Management*, Winter (2008), available at http://findarticles.com/p/articles/mi_6772/is_4_8/ai_n31160436/, accessed 10/30/10.

40 Andrew W. Savitz and Karl Weber, *The Triple Bottom Line* (San Francisco, CA: Jossey-Bass, 2006); Bob Willard, *The Sustainability Advantage: Seven Business Case Benefits of a Triple Bottom Line* (British Columbia, Canada: New Society Publishers, 2002).

41 Steven Kerr and Steffen Landauer, "Using Stretch Goals to Promote Organizational Effectiveness and Personal Growth: General Electric and Goldman Sachs," *Academy of Management Executive*, 18, 4 (2004), 134–138.

42 Maurice E. Schweitzer, Lisa Ordonez, and Bambi Douma, "The Role of Goal Setting in Motivating Unethical Behavior," *Academy of Management Journal*, 47, 3 (2004), 422–432.

43 Erin Stout, "To Tell the Truth," *Sales & Marketing Management*, 154, 7 (2002): 40+.

44 David Dorsey, *The Force* (New York: Random House, 1994).

45 Lisa D. Ordóñez, Maurice E. Schweitzer, Adam D. Galinsky, and Max H. Bazerman, "Goals Gone Wild: The Systematic Side Effects of Overprescribing Goal Setting," *Academy of Management Perspectives*, 23, 1 (2009), 6–16.

46 Edwin A. Locke and Gary Latham, *A Theory of Goal Setting and Task Performance* (Upper Saddle River, NJ: Prentice Hall, 1990).

47 Wendell L. French, *Human Resources Management*, 6th ed. (New York: Houghton Mifflin Company, 2007), p. 512; see also American Institute of Stress, "Job Stress," available at www.stress.org/job.htm, accessed 10/30/10.

48 U.S. Department of Health and Human Services, *Healthy People 2000*, cited in Wendell L. French, *Human Resources Management*, 6th ed. (New York: Houghton Mifflin Company, 2007), p. 512; see also American Institute of Stress, "Job Stress," available at http://www.stress.org/job.htm and HumanNature@Work website available at http://www.humannatureatwork.com/serious.htm, accessed 10/30/10.

49 Kirk Ladendorf, "Intel Tries Out Some Quiet Time in Austin," *American Statesman*, July 21, 2008.

50 Katherine A. MacLean, Emilio Ferrer, Stephen R. Aichele, David A. Bridwell, Anthony P. Zanesco, Tonya L. Jacobs, Brandon G. King, Erika L. Rosenberg, Baljinder K. Sahdra, Phillip R. Shaver, B. Alan Wallace, George R. Mangun, and Clifford D. Saron, "Intensive Meditation Training Improves Perceptual Discrimination and Sustained Attention," *Psychological Science*, 21, 6 (2010), 829–839.

51 Kirk Warren Brown and Richard M. Ryan, "The Benefits of Being Present: Mindfulness and Its Role in Psychological Well-Being," *Journal of Personality and Social Psychology*, 84, 4 (2003), 822–848.

52 Sylvia Boorstein, *Don't Just Do Something, Sit There* (New York: HarperOne, 1996).

53 Anonymous, "How to Help Reinvigorate Your Organization's Ethics Program," *HR Focus*, 80, 6 (2003), 7–8.

54 David Segal, "Questions for Moody's and Buffett," *New York Times*, June 2, 2010.

55 Sharon Lund O'Neil and Elwood N. Chapman, *Your Attitude Is Showing*, 12th ed. (Upper Saddle River, NJ: Pearson Prentice Hall, 2008), p. 249.

56 Modified from Chris Clarke-Epstein, *78 Important Questions Every Leader Should Ask and Answer* (New York: Amacom, 2006).

57 Mary Carson, "Saying It Like It Isn't: The Pros and Cons of 360-Degree Feedback," *Business Horizons*, 49, 5 (2006), 395–402; Jeffrey I. Seglin, "Reviewing Your Boss," *Fortune*, June 11, 2001, p. 248.

58 Jack Welch, *Straight from the Gut* (New York: Warner Business Books, 2001).

59 Raymond A. Noe, John R. Hollenbeck, Barry Gerhart, and Patrick M. Wright, *Human Resource Management*, 5th ed. (New York: McGraw-Hill Irwin, 2006).

[60] Department of Labor, "Employee Polygraph Protection Act," available at http://www.dol.gov/whd/regs/statutes/poly01.pdf, accessed 10/30/10.

[61] Pamela Bean, "State of the Art: Contemporary Biomarkers of Alcohol Consumption," *Medical Laboratory Observer,* November 2005.

[62] Jerald Greenberg and Robert A. Baron, *Behavior in Organizations*, 9th ed. (Upper Saddle River, NJ: Pearson Prentice Hall, 2008), p. 124.

[63] Robert D. Enright, *Forgiveness Is a Choice* (Washington, D.C.: APA Books, 2001); see also International Forgiveness Institute website available at www.forgiveness-institute.org, accessed 10/30/10.

CHAPTER OUTLINE

10

ENGAGING AND EMPOWERING ETHICAL EMPLOYEES

What would you do?

A Unified Team

After graduation, you obtain employment as an engineer designer at a medium-sized company. You report to Tom, the Engineering Department manager. Tom is a very charismatic leader and is well liked by everyone in the department. He has a unique vision for the company and longs to become vice president of operations, to whom he reports directly.

Jenny, the current vice president of operations, assigns the Engineering Department a new project. Tom chooses you to be on the four-member team, which Tom is supervising. Tom begins the first team meeting with some disparaging words about Jenny. "Once again, Jenny is making a blunder," Tom says. "She wants us to leverage existing products to come up with a new product. What we need to do is build a new product from scratch. We have the talent right in this room to challenge the industry."

You ask about the vice president's idea. Tom explains the general outline and you think the idea has a great deal of merit. "Yeah, it could work," Tom declares, "but that's not the type of product we should be developing. We need to think big and become a transformative organization.

Everything Jenny assigns us is small incremental improvements. There's nothing creative or innovative coming out of Jenny's mind."

Tom pitches several innovative ideas for new products, which excites everyone on the team. Tom then proposes a project management schedule. At first, you are confused because Tom has assigned the team's most inadequate performer the responsibility of working on Jenny's idea of leveraging existing products, which will guarantee the project's failure. Tom assigns you and the other two team members to create an innovative new product.

A week later, you overhear the vice president bragging to other executives about how your team will be saving the company money by creating a new product that leverages existing systems. It dawns on you that Tom is setting up the vice president for failure.

You wonder if you should tell the vice president about what is happening on the team. If the vice president's product fails, Tom might get promoted to vice president, and he's likely to promote you as well, based on your accomplishments and loyalty. On the other hand, the vice president's idea is credible and would benefit the company. If the project fails and the vice president remains in power, she could take her anger out on the entire team.

What would you do? Would you

1. Remain silent and continue to follow Tom's directions?
2. Inform the vice president about the team's efforts?

Why?

Chapter Objectives

After reading this chapter, you will be able to:

- Describe how to engage employees at work
- Manage three types of employees: go-getters, fence-sitters, and adversarials
- Facilitate an Appreciative Inquiry workshop to achieve superior customer service

- Implement Open Book Management and a Scanlon-type gainsharing plan
- Distribute financial improvements to all employees through profit sharing, stock options, employee stock ownership plans, and cooperatives

A high-performing ethical organization is a community of people in which each employee has a sense of belongingness and ownership and feels respected and accountable. According to a 2007 study conducted by the Society of Human Resource Management, employees with the highest levels of emotional commitment to the organization perform 20 percent better than other employees, and are 87 percent less likely to leave the organization.[1]

Employees in high-performance organizations are engaged with their work tasks and committed to achieving work unit goals. They are provided information necessary to perform their job well, empowered to control their immediate surroundings, and have the authority to do what needs to get done. At Google, for instance, managers trust software engineers to use 20 percent of their time on unapproved projects.[2]

Some systems of management treat nonmanagement employees with greater respect than others by actively involving them in the decision-making process. Researchers report that top-down, one-way communication and decision-making processes make subordinates passive and reactive, rather than proactive.[3] Organizations with engaged and empowered employees emphasize two-way communication with participative management processes.

This chapter examines how to engage employees by meeting essential human needs, ensuring organizational justice, and providing meaningful work. The chapter also explores how to empower employees by giving them decision-making authority, providing relevant information about organizational operations, and sharing the financial benefits generated by their efforts.

Extent of Employee Engagement

Organizations need talented employees committed to task performance, organizational goals, and the organization itself. Employee engagement is an emotional bond or attachment an employee has to the work task, organization, and its members. For engaged employees, work is a meaningful experience they feel passionate about. Engaged employees perform at high levels and are less likely to quit due to high levels of job satisfaction.

A strong linkage exists between ethical organizations and employee engagement. Researchers at the Ethics Resource Center and Hay Group report that employees in organizations whose managers and supervisors have high ethical integrity, open and honest communications, and high levels of accountability are more engaged in performing work tasks.[4] Engaged employees are more likely to report ethical misconduct, which reduces the company's ethical risks.

Many people in the American workforce, unfortunately, claim that they have low levels of employee engagement. In 2009, the Gallup Organization reported that only 30 percent of American workers—less than one-third—are engaged in their jobs. Approximately 52 percent were not engaged, and 18 percent were actively disengaged.[5]

Similarly, many individuals are dissatisfied with their jobs and the trend is worsening. The Conference Board has been monitoring employee satisfaction since 1987. A 2009 survey of 5,000 households found that only 45 percent of Americans were satisfied with their work, the lowest level of satisfaction in the more than 22 years of conducting the survey.[6] Among the survey respondents, the main contributors to employee dissatisfaction included uninteresting jobs, income lagging behind inflation, and health insurance costs.

It is important to note that the relationship between job satisfaction and employee productivity is complex.[7] Intuitively, the relationship makes sense—happy employees will work hard to maintain their position. But, some employees may have high job satisfaction because they don't have to work hard, and some dissatisfied workers may be top performers because of a well-designed job or superior management and technological skills. Nonetheless, job satisfaction is an essential aspect of the work. Job dissatisfaction leads to turnover as dissatisfied employees search for more rewarding work elsewhere.

What do people want in a job? Of course people want a good salary and job security—everyone has bills to pay. In a 2009 survey conducted by the Society for Human Resource Management, job security (63 percent), benefits (60 percent), and compensation/pay (57 percent) were the three most important features employees wanted in a job.[8]

But is that all they want? No. Many other factors matter to employees. Also chosen as "very important" by survey respondents were opportunities to use skills and abilities (55 percent), relationship with immediate supervisor (52 percent), management recognition of employee job performance (52 percent), communication between employees and senior management (51 percent), the work itself (50 percent), autonomy and independence (47 percent), meaningfulness of job (45 percent), and relationship with coworkers (42 percent).

In the midst of the worldwide recession that began in 2008, Kelly Services surveyed 100,000 people in 34 countries about work-related issues. Approximately half of the survey respondents replied that they would be willing to sacrifice status and pay for more meaningful work.[9]

Engaging Employees

How can managers organize work so employees are more engaged with their job tasks and organizational goals? This section explores how to engage employees by meeting human needs, improving job satisfaction, ensuring organizational justice, responding to unethical bullies, and providing meaningful work.

Human Needs

Some developmental psychologists and organization theorists maintain that individual behaviors are driven by the desire to fulfill fundamental human needs. Respecting others requires that managers recognize and address fundamental human needs at the workplace.

Developmental psychologist Abraham Maslow differentiated five categories of needs every individual has: physiological, safety, social, self-esteem, and self-actualization.[10] Maslow maintained that these five needs exist in the form of a hierarchy in which individuals first seek to fulfill lower-level needs, beginning with physiological needs, and then incrementally progress up the hierarchy, culminating in fulfilling self-actualization needs. As shown in Exhibit 10.1, all of these needs can be addressed at the workplace.

Maslow's hierarchy of needs can be applied to life in organizations. An engaged employee, one who has an emotional bond to the work task and organization, is typically fulfilling the three highest-level needs—social, self-esteem, and self-actualization—at work. But, the higher-level needs that contribute to employee engagement are difficult to tap into unless the first two levels of needs—physiological and safety—are being fulfilled.

Employees, for instance, need lunch and rest breaks to replenish their body, and adequate wages to purchase essential goods. If the organization does not meet these basic needs, most employees will quit when a better-paying job becomes available at another organization. Once physiological needs are met, the employee becomes more concerned about safe working conditions, job security, and retirement benefits. For an employee to be fully engaged with the organization and job tasks, however, the three highest-level needs must be fulfilled. A fully engaged employee is someone who develops friendships at work, is recognized for personal achievements, and undertakes challenging and meaningful work.

A manager can create a sense of belonging for employees by welcoming them into the work unit, including them in desirable activities, recognizing individual work contributions, listening to their concerns, and providing appropriate resources.[11] Satisfying the need for self-esteem and meaningful work further engages employees and deepens an employee's identification with the job task, work unit, and organization.

The work of David McClelland complements Maslow's hierarchy of needs.[12] Similar to Maslow, McClelland emphasizes the importance of employees experiencing a need for affiliation (level 3) and a need for achievement (level 4). He complements these with a need for power or authority.

Unlike Maslow, McClelland does not organize the need for affiliation, achievement, and power in the form of a hierarchy. Instead, McClelland argues, individuals

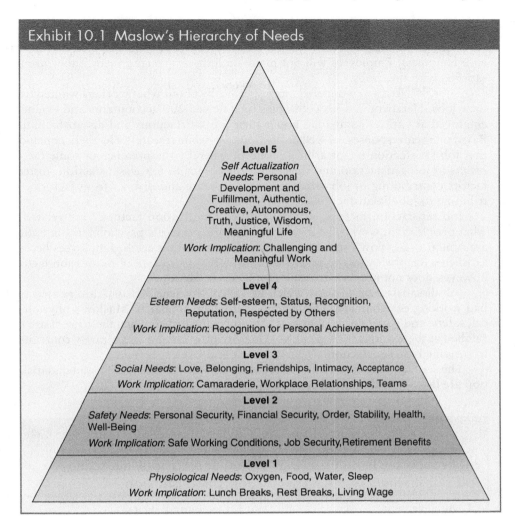

Exhibit 10.1 Maslow's Hierarchy of Needs

Level 5
Self Actualization Needs: Personal Development and Fulfillment, Authentic, Creative, Autonomous, Truth, Justice, Wisdom, Meaningful Life
Work Implication: Challenging and Meaningful Work

Level 4
Esteem Needs: Self-esteem, Status, Recognition, Reputation, Respected by Others
Work Implication: Recognition for Personal Achievements

Level 3
Social Needs: Love, Belonging, Friendships, Intimacy, Acceptance
Work Implication: Camaraderie, Workplace Relationships, Teams

Level 2
Safety Needs: Personal Security, Financial Security, Order, Stability, Health, Well-Being
Work Implication: Safe Working Conditions, Job Security, Retirement Benefits

Level 1
Physiological Needs: Oxygen, Food, Water, Sleep
Work Implication: Lunch Breaks, Rest Breaks, Living Wage

can be rated high, moderate, or low for each of the three needs. For instance, some people can have a high need for achievement and power and a low need for affiliation, whereas others can have a high need for power and affiliation and a low need for achievement.

Managers can best engage an employee by matching the individual's most dominant need with its associated motivating factor. Generally,

- Employees with a high need for achievement are motivated by challenging work.

- Employees with a high need for power are motivated by managing other people.

- Employees with a high need for affiliation are motivated by collegial work environments.

Job Satisfaction

As discussed in Chapter 1, human beings are pleasure seekers and desire to experience happiness. Employees will not maintain long-term engagement if they are not satisfied with their jobs.

Frederick Herzberg wondered more specifically about what workers wanted from their jobs. Herzberg and his colleagues interviewed 203 accountants and engineers employed at various companies about their job satisfactions and dissatisfactions.[13] Based on their responses, as well as previous academic research, Herzberg concluded that job satisfaction is not a linear concept whereby the presence of some factors results in job satisfaction and their lack contributes to job dissatisfaction. Instead, factors contributing to job satisfaction are separate and distinct from factors contributing to job dissatisfaction.

Job satisfaction factors, which he called "motivation factors," are related to what people do at work. The motivation factors, primarily psychological in nature, are similar to Maslow's self-esteem and self-actualization needs. Employees become satisfied when their jobs are psychologically enriching. A lack of motivation factors, however, does not necessarily result in job dissatisfaction.

Job dissatisfaction factors, which he called "hygiene factors," are related to a bad working environment. The hygiene factors are similar to Maslow's physiological, safety, and social needs. Employees become dissatisfied when these needs are not fulfilled at the workplace. A good working environment, however, rarely contributes to sustained job satisfaction.

The six factors that contribute the most to employee satisfaction and dissatisfaction are listed in order of importance in Exhibit 10.2.

Exhibit 10.2 Herzberg's Job Satisfaction-Dissatisfaction Theory	
Motivation Factors Impacting Job Satisfaction	**Hygiene Factors Impacting Job Dissatisfaction**
1. Achievement	1. Company Policies and Administration
2. Recognition	2. Quality of Supervision
3. Work Itself (doing a complete job)	3. Relationship with Boss
4. Responsibility	4. Working Conditions
5. Advancement	5. Base Wage or Salary
6. Growth	6. Relationship with Peers

Low wages, for instance, often contribute to employee dissatisfaction. Higher wages, on the other hand, do not lead to a more satisfied workforce. Employees appreciate higher pay, but the satisfaction associated with higher pay is typically of short duration. They become accustomed to the higher wages. Better wages do not motivate employees to work harder or smarter over an extended period of time; they just prevent employee dissatisfaction. Correcting this problem is ethical and eliminates the dissatisfaction. But, do not expect employees to become more fully engaged with their work as a result.

Achievement, recognition, advancement, and personal growth, on the other hand, contribute significantly to job satisfaction and employee engagement. Job enrichment programs, for instance, enhance employee satisfaction because the employee learns new work skills, participates in problem-solving activities, works on an entire project rather than just parts of the project, makes decisions, and receives feedback.[14] Job enrichment programs engage the employee's mental processes, thus improving the individual's psychological well-being and overall job satisfaction.

Yet many managers continue to falsely assume that the best way to motivate employees is through financial rewards and the threat of disciplinary action. In 2009, Daniel Pink reviewed behavior research over the past 50 years and concluded that the insights of Maslow, McClelland, and Herzberg are still valid.[15] High levels of employee performance and satisfaction, Pink argued, result from employees driven to meet three basic needs: autonomy (self-direction), mastery (continually learning and creating new things), and purpose (work is a personal cause or mission).

Organizations rated highly on *Fortune* magazine's "100 Best Companies to Work For" annual list are those that successfully address Maslow's lower- and higher-level needs, Herzberg's job dissatisfaction and job satisfaction factors, and Pink's conception of employee drive. In 2010, the top three companies were SAS, Edward Jones, and Wegmans.[16] These workplaces provide employees with good wages and a safe working environment, which eliminate dissatisfactions, and offer a nurturing work environment and psychologically rewarding jobs, which motivate employees to achieve superior performance.

Organizational Justice

Employee engagement is more likely when employees perceive justice, or fairness, in decisions associated with organizational policies, procedures, and outcomes.[17] As discussed in Chapter 5, justice is the most essential moral value. Unabated injustice results in the collapse of communities. Employees disengage from job tasks and the organization when injustice occurs at work and managers do not respond appropriately. Ethical managers must ensure that justice is a highly valued attribute of organizational operations.

Organizational justice is multidimensional. Scholars distinguish among four forms of organizational justice—procedural, informational, interactional, and distributive justice:[18]

- *Procedural Justice:* Decision-making procedures are fair. Employees can provide input, procedures are unbiased and applied consistently, and decisions can be appealed.

- *Informational Justice:* Information is conveyed fairly. Employees receive relevant and accurate information in a timely manner.

- *Interactional Justice:* Employees treat each other fairly. Employees are treated with dignity by supervisors, peers, and subordinates.

- *Distributive Justice:* The distribution of outcomes is fair. Pay, benefits, promotions, and workloads reflect individual capabilities and efforts.

Researchers report that organizational justice is highly associated with organizational citizenship behaviors and commitment to supervisors and the organization.[19] Employees are more willing to help coworkers who have heavy workloads or are struggling with work-related problems when they themselves have been treated fairly and with integrity.

Unjust managers, on the other hand, inspire deviant and retaliatory behaviors from employees, including production disruptions, theft, and violence. Employees treated unjustly claim that the organization no longer deserves their best efforts and disengage from organizational activities. For instance, employees become demotivated when managers give comparable or higher pay to those who do not work as hard or accomplish as much, or when they observe managers treating other employees or customers unjustly.

Unethical Bullies

Unethical bullies create a range of injustices at work. Employees usually cannot perform at peak productivity when they are being bullied by peers, subordinates, or supervisors. According to the Workplace Bullying Institute's 2007 survey, 37 percent of the respondents had been bullied at work and 13 percent were being bullied at the time of the survey.[20] Immediate supervisors were the most predominant group of bullies (72 percent).

Bullying is defined as repeated verbal abuse or abusive conduct that is threatening, humiliating, and intimidating and interferes with work.[21] Bullying can take many forms, including hostile and insulting remarks about appearance or lifestyle, hurtful jokes and pranks, taunting, excessive teasing and ridicule, continual false accusations, public criticisms, and angry tantrums.[22] Bill Gates, for instance, was prone to publicly calling Microsoft employees "stupid idiots," although some insisted the hostile name calling was an endearing term that inspired them to work harder.[23]

Bullying has many negative impacts on overall organizational performance. Bullying is associated with low levels of job satisfaction, organizational commitment, and morale, and high levels of absenteeism, psychological distress, and turnover.[24] Bullying can lead to illegal forms of harassment and discrimination, and it can threaten employee safety. Unethical bullies create stress among recipients and witnesses. Victims feel frustrated and anxious, which can lead to clinical depression.

Bullying behaviors often go unreported because bullies tend to be formal (if boss) or informal (if peer) leaders. Bully victims and witnesses usually remain silent because they fear being stigmatized as a squealer or retaliation from the bully. But their silence leads to employee disengagement because their passion for work is diluted due to anxieties and dissatisfaction. Managers must counsel bullies and hold them accountable through the ideal employee performance evaluations discussed in Chapter 9.

Workplace bullying legislation has been proposed in nearly one-third of all states, beginning with California in 2003. The legislation would allow employees to sue organizations for creating an "abusive work environment." [25] No state has yet passed the legislation.

Meaningful Work

Maslow, McClelland, Herzberg, and Pink emphasize the importance of meaningful work for engaging and motivating employees. Every job task and organization can be a meaningful experience.

What does meaningful work mean? Meaningful work is typically defined as spending time at work to achieve something that is personally desirable.[26] When work is personally meaningful, an employee passionately engages all his or her entire intellectual, physical, and emotional energies in the work that needs to be done because it is what he or she feels destined to do. Employees feel usefully alive in a way that benefits the organization and their own personal development.

Mihaly Csikszentmihalyi refers to this phenomenon as a person's "flow," wherein an employee can invest his or her entire self—mind, body, emotion, and spirit—in work.[27] Life makes emotional and logical sense, the individual feels at peace with the situation, and the employee's job fits his or her self-determined destiny. Harmony exists between "self-concept" and "job task."[28] Meaningfulness occurs when an employee exhibits passion for daily work activities and pride in accomplishments.

Imagine a manager, teacher, artisan, salesperson, secretary, or janitor so wrapped up in work that the job task becomes the core of his or her being. The job fits the employee's concept of self, and interpersonal work relationships are rewarding. Such meaningful work can be experienced in any job an employee finds enriching and at any level of organizatioal operations.

Organization scholars Marjolein Lips-Wiersma and Lani Morris provide a broad conceptualization of what makes work meaningful using a 2 x 2 matrix (see Exhibit 10.3).[29] These four distinct themes were derived from discussions with 214 employees working for a wide range of organizations.

According to Lips-Wiersma and Morris, the following are four sources of meaningful work:

1. *Serving others:* by making a difference in their lives and meeting the needs of humanity
2. *Unity with others:* by working together, sharing values, and having a sense of belonging
3. *Developing and becoming self:* through moral development and personal growth, and by being true to self
4. *Expressing one's full potential:* by creating things, achieving tasks, and influencing others

Combined, these four sources of meaningful work contribute to the development of a highly motivated and engaged workforce. As diagrammed in Exhibit 10.3, the four sources can be understood along two continuums: (1) being and doing and (2) self and others. A tension exists along each continuum that requires carefully balancing the two extreme positions.

In terms of being and doing, for instance, employees need time for reflection (being) and action (doing). In addition, employees must care for their own self-actualizing needs (self) and for the needs of coworkers and customers (others). Always acting for the benefit of others can contribute to employee burnout. Always reflecting about self can lead to employee isolation and disengagement. All four concerns are essential to experience a deep sense of meaning and purpose at work.

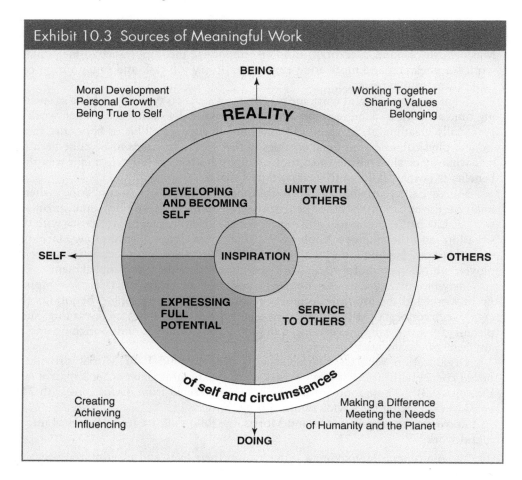

Exhibit 10.3 Sources of Meaningful Work

The four sources in Exhibit 10.3 are encircled by "Reality." As emphasized throughout this textbook, we do not live in an ideal world. Reality is such that every person and organization has a unique set of flaws and weaknesses. Many times managers cannot implement the ideal solution to a problem because of limitations in employee capabilities and organizational resources. The desire for a meaningful existence, however, motivates engaged employees to move the organization toward the direction of the ideal.

Measuring Employee Engagement

Over a period of 25 years, the Gallup Organization has conducted interviews about work with more than 1 million employees. Marcus Buckingham and Curt Coffman explored this database to determine what talented employees wanted most from the workplace. More than any other factor, what they desired most was to work for an excellent manager.[30] The relationship talented employees had with their immediate supervisor mattered more than anything else.

The Gallup researchers then analyzed the survey responses of more than 80,000 managers from 400 companies to determine the attributes that differentiated "excellent managers" from "average managers." According to the most talented employees, an excellent manager treated every employee as an individual, focused on an employee's strengths rather than weaknesses, and measured and rewarded outcomes. Excellent managers selected talented job applicants, established high expectations, and then developed their subordinates for advancement within the organization.

The researchers interviewed excellent managers about their techniques for managing people. They heard a common refrain about employees:[31]

People don't change that much.

Don't waste time trying to put in a person what was left out.

Try to draw out of a person what was left in.

That is hard enough.

According to Buckingham and Coffman, "excellent front-line managers had engaged their employees and these engaged employees had provided the foundation for top performance."[32] The researchers concluded that 12 core elements must be experienced at work to attract, engage, and retain talented employees. These elements appear in Exhibit 10.4 as an employee survey that can be administered to determine if a workplace fully engages its employees. The survey results can serve as a benchmark for continuous improvement.

Exhibit 10.4 12 Core Elements of Employee Engagement

Instructions: Please use the 1 to 5 scale below to assess the following 12 statements. The more honest you are the more helpful the information we will receive.

1=Strongly Disagree; 2=Disagree; 3=Neither Agree nor Disagree; 4=Agree; 5=Strongly Agree

	SD	D	N	A	SA
1. I know what is expected of me at work.	1	2	3	4	5
2. I have the materials and equipment needed to do my work right.	1	2	3	4	5
3. I have the opportunity to do what I do best every day.	1	2	3	4	5
4. In the last week, I have received recognition or praise for good work.	1	2	3	4	5
5. My supervisor, or someone at work, seems to care about me as a person.	1	2	3	4	5
6. Someone at work encourages my development.	1	2	3	4	5
7. My opinions seem to count at work.	1	2	3	4	5
8. The mission/purpose of my company makes me feel like my work is important.	1	2	3	4	5
9. My coworkers are committed to doing quality work.	1	2	3	4	5
10. I have a best friend at work.	1	2	3	4	5
11. During the past six months, I have talked with someone about my progress.	1	2	3	4	5
12. During the past year, I have had opportunities to learn and grow.	1	2	3	4	5
Add the 12 scores:					

Similar to the theorists discussed earlier in this section, the Gallup Organization researchers found that pay is not among the most important motivational factors contributing to employee engagement and productivity. Pay matters, but the most productive workers can usually obtain equivalent or higher pay elsewhere. Talented employees remain with an organization because they are fully engaged in their work tasks and workplace relationships.

Employee Empowerment

Employee engagement contributes to, but does not necessarily require, employee empowerment. Engagement is an emotional connection to the job task, work unit, or organization. Empowerment refers to giving employees decision-making authority, which can be further solidified with an ownership stake in the organization. The "Best Practice in Use" exhibit provides a list of empowerment mechanisms implemented by Whole Foods Market.[33]

BEST PRACTICE IN USE

Whole Foods Market Empowerment Mechanisms

Employee Autonomy and Teams

- Every employee is assigned to one of the store's eight work teams.
- Teams are responsible for operating decisions, including pricing, ordering, in-store promotions, and staffing.
- New employees must obtain a two-thirds majority vote from team members to become a full-time employee.
- Stores are encouraged to buy locally.
- Operating and financial data are available to all employees, including daily store sales, team sales, product costs, and store profit.
- Performance data on all employees are shared among the teams and compared to performance data at other Whole Foods stores.

Compensation Issues

- Salary cap limits executive pay by a specific multiplier of the average employee salary (no more than 19 times that of an average employee salary in 2007).
- Everyone knows one another's hourly pay or salary.
- Profit per labor hour is calculated for every team in the store, and then for every individual on the team; bonuses are earned by teams that exceed a certain threshold.
- Ninety-three percent of stock options are granted to nonexecutives.

Who to Empower?

Before deciding how to empower employees, managers must first decide which employees to empower. Not all employees want to be empowered, nor should all employees be empowered. Being ethical and fair does not mean that every employee must be empowered. Each employee has different capabilities and attitudes toward work. Being fair means providing all employees with the opportunity to be empowered based on meeting certain workplace criteria.

Some managers mistakenly design systems to control for under-performing employees and, in the name of fairness, impose the same control system on all employees. When this happens, some of the best performers quit for employment with an organization that will treat them with the respect they deserve. Managers need to treat their best performers differently, such as providing them with more autonomy and decision-making authority, than other employees— they have earned it. Provide greater decision-making authority to under-performing employees only after they meet or surpass expectations.

Many organizations have three types of employees in terms of workplace attitudes and behaviors:[34]

1. Go-getters, who are fully engaged with the work experience
2. Fence-sitters, who put in a good day's work for a good day's pay
3. Adversarials, who have an unfavorable attitude to both the nature of work and authority

Organizations of high integrity and superior performance are able to attract and retain a large number of go-getters. The average organization, however, typically consists of a handful of go-getters, many fence-sitters, and a handful of adversarial employees. Managers must treat the three employee groups differently.

Exhibit 10.5 summarizes these three types of employees.

Exhibit 10.5 Workplace Attitudes and Behaviors			
Type	Prevalence	Attitude & Behavior	How to Manage
Go-Getters	Some	Task oriented Can-do attitude Enjoy working	Freedom and autonomy New challenges Leadership positions Praise and extra rewards
Fence-Sitters	Many	A job is a job Meet performance expectations 9–5 then punch out	Increase performance expectations Team up with go-getters Separate from adversarials
Adversarials	Some	Managers are ignorant Work is a nuisance Convert fence-sitters	Confront and discipline Team up with go-getters Separate from fence-sitters

Go-Getters Go-getters are task-oriented employees with a "can-do" attitude. They enjoy working, are proactive, and appreciate new challenges. They tend to be exemplar organizational citizens. Go-getters are satisfied with their jobs, deeply engaged with their work, trust supervisors, and perceive fairness in organizational procedures and outcomes.[35] They have plenty of ideas for continuous improvement and want the freedom to implement their creative solutions.

Empower go-getters and groom them for managerial positions. Many go-getters prefer to work on their own or with other go-getters. They find fence-sitters uninspired and adversarial employees too negative. Empower go-getters to work with fence-sitters and adversarial employees. Go-getters can teach fence-sitters easier ways to perform their work tasks and offer adversarial employees a more constructive way to frame organizational events and apply their energy.

Fence-Sitters Fence-sitters meet managerial expectations and go no further. Unlike go-getters, fence-sitters do not try to self-actualize through work. They consider a job as a necessary burden to pay expenses. Enjoyment is to be experienced outside work hours, not during work hours. Fence-sitters put in a solid work effort and meet performance expectations because they do not want to be fired. Fence-sitters watch the clock and count down the minutes until departure.

Empower fence-sitters only under restricted conditions. Challenge fence-sitters by continually increasing performance expectations. The more that is expected of fence-sitters, the more they will accomplish. Go-getters can show fence-sitters how to effectively and efficiently achieve results. Separate fence-sitters from adversarial employees, who typically try to distract fence-sitters from putting in a good day's work.

Adversarial Employees Adversarial employees do not like work and possess negative attitudes toward others, particularly managers and go-getters. They often slack off when not under managerial observation and encourage fence-sitters to do likewise. They view managers as the enemy and criticize managers whenever possible. Adversarial employees find creative ways to not perform work tasks or leave work early and then brag about them to one another and the fence-sitters.

Do not empower adversarial employees. Instead, confront and discipline them. Otherwise, they will not change their attitudes or behaviors. Sometimes an employee is adversarial because the job fit is inappropriate. In this case, assign the adversarial employee to a different task, work group, or manager.

Closely supervise adversarial employees, because they cannot be trusted to act with the organization's best interests at heart. Document the behavioral impacts of their negative attitudes, such as failure to cooperate with managers or go-getters. Require that adversarial employees receive counseling through the organization's Employee Assistance Program to get at the root of their negative work attitude, which may be grounded in childhood experiences. Give adversarial employees an opportunity to change by a jointly determined deadline and dismiss them if the agreed-upon change does not occur. Some reformed adversarial employees are very grateful for being given another chance.

An adversarial employee can be rebelling against being overly controlled. Within clearly defined parameters, managers can experiment by giving an adversarial employee more responsibility and see what happens. If the adversarial employee does not respond as hoped for, quickly end the experiment. When adversarials do change, they can become go-getters. Adversarial employees have leadership skills, though they are currently directed toward the wrong ends.

Measuring a Manager's Empowerment Behaviors

Empowerment techniques go beyond just providing employees with the authority to make decisions. They also entail delegating specific tasks, providing access to relevant information, and allocating appropriate resources and funds. Empowered employees develop the mindset of a manager by taking on some managerial responsibilities and accountabilities.

A wide range of management behaviors that can foster employee empowerment appears in Exhibit 10.6 as a survey instrument for evaluating a direct supervisor's use of empowerment techniques.[36] The survey is applicable for all direct supervisors, from a first-line supervisor to the CEO.

Exhibit 10.6 Empowering Behaviors Survey

Instructions: Please use the 1 to 5 scale below to assess the following 14 statements about your supervisor.

The more honest you are the more helpful the information we will receive.

1=Strongly Disagree; 2=Disagree; 3=Neither Agree nor Disagree; 4=Agree; 5=Strongly Agree

	SD	D	N	A	SA
My Supervisor:					
1. involves me in decisions that affect my work	1	2	3	4	5
2. asks for my opinion	1	2	3	4	5
3. allows me to have a say in matters concerning my work	1	2	3	4	5
4. consults me regarding important changes in my task	1	2	3	4	5
5. offers me the possibility to bear responsibility	1	2	3	4	5
6. allows me to set my own goals	1	2	3	4	5
7. shows confidence in my ability to contribute to the goals of this unit	1	2	3	4	5
8. lets me have a strong hand in setting my own performance goals	1	2	3	4	5
9. demonstrates total confidence in me	1	2	3	4	5
10. listens to my problems and concerns	1	2	3	4	5
11. works with me individually, rather than treating me as just another member of the group	1	2	3	4	5
12. provides advice whenever I need it	1	2	3	4	5
13. is genuinely concerned about the growth and development of subordinates	1	2	3	4	5
14. looks out for my personal welfare	1	2	3	4	5
Add the 14 scores:					

Let's Build a Building

Flag People

You are the new director of a nonprofit low-income housing provider that is building a new 80-unit apartment building in an existing housing development you own. Your organization's financial reserves have dwindled over the past few years, and you are responsible for overseeing several cost-cutting initiatives.

You plan to obtain competitive bids, but your in-house construction project manager suggests that you use the same contractor that has worked on previous jobs during the past 10 years. It has come to your attention that the in-house project manager and general contractor have developed a very close friendship, which has resulted in the contractor donating more than $100,000 to your organization.

You ask your in-house project manager to provide your organization's chief financial officer with the general contractor's project cost estimate. After thoroughly analyzing the general contractor's initial bid, you and the CFO identify several questionable charges, including more than $120,000 for flag people. You know a local minority-owned business can provide flag people for $52,000 rather than $120,000.

After meeting with the general contractor, your in-house project manager tells you that the general contractor has concerns about the minority subcontractor's ability to perform the work. The general contractor suggests that you leave the $120,000 in the original contract, but he is confident that the final costs for flag people will probably be closer to $50,000. The general contractor would then refund you the difference upon completion of the project.

As the construction nears completion, you again review the job costs. Up until the last pay request, the contractor had billed only $50,000 for flag people. However, the contractor charged an additional $70,000 for flag people in the last bill. When questioned, the contractor argues that he had several substantial unexpected costs. The $70,000 will offset these additional costs. You ask for cost documentation. "My records are incomplete," the contractor says, "and your in-house project manager assured me months ago that the additional costs would be approved."

What would you do? Would you

1. Pay the extra $70,000 as an additional project expense?

2. Refuse to pay the additional $70,000 because the contractor has no documentation to prove his claim and risk losing future financial donations from the contractor?

Why?

Empowering Through Teams

Every work unit is a team or small community. Teams need to be engaged and empowered. Management consultant Gary Hamel asks: "When in life have *you* felt the most joyful and the most energized by work? . . . Whatever the particulars of that episode in your life, I bet it involved a group of people who were bound by their devotion to a common cause, who were undeterred by a lack of resources and undaunted by a lack of expertise, and who cared more about what they could accomplish together than how credit would be apportioned. In short, you were part of a community."[37]

Empowering Effective Teams

Some teams are very effective; some are not. According to Patrick Lencioni, ineffective teams suffer from five dysfunctions: absence of trust, fear of conflict, lack of commitment, avoidance of accountability, and inattention to collective results.[38]

Conversely, the most effective teams consist of members who (1) trust one another, (2) engage in constructive conflict, (3) personally commit to goal accomplishment, (4) are accountable for their behaviors, and (5) focus on collectively achieving their assigned tasks.

Lencioni maintains that each factor is a necessary condition to accomplish the succeeding factor. *Trust* serves as the foundation for effective team performance. Teams will not effectively accomplish the goal if members do not trust one another. Trustworthy team members are honest, capable, and caring. The team member's words are truthful and can be acted upon without concern about misrepresentation or a hidden agenda.

Trust building begins with the work unit's manager. Be open to other people's ideas and constructive criticism. Set the example by first expressing your own weaknesses and vulnerabilities, which is why the team is needed, in an uplifting manner. Employees need to be free to ask for help or admit shortcomings and deficiencies without it being held against them.

Employees who trust one another are psychologically safe to express differences of opinion. Engage employees in *constructive conflict* rather than artificial harmony. When disagreements arise, focus on the issue at hand rather than personalities or inconsequential concerns. The time to raise concerns about a decision is during the constructive conflict stage of team development, not after the decision has been made. Make sure that all concerns are addressed respectfully. Individual team members need to understand why their ideas or recommendations are being rejected.

Goal *commitment* occurs when team members believe that all of their concerns have been addressed. It is difficult for a team member to commit to a goal or strategy that he or she disagrees with. By expressing their disagreements, team members deepen their understanding. Otherwise, trust evaporates. If it becomes clear that the team decision is wrong, then raise the issue again at the next team meeting.

Team members committed to a goal can be held *accountable* for their behaviors and accomplish the collective results. It is difficult to hold people accountable if they have not fully committed to goal accomplishment. Once held accountable, the likelihood of achieving the *collective result* increases.

Conflict is normal in both simple and complex organizations. Highly engaged and committed employees will disagree about the best way to manage a situation. The pinch theory technique is a useful tool for preventing team conflicts from escalating.[39] A pinch situation is one where there is a difference between people regarding expectations, values, opinions, or goals. Both parties enter the following 10-step planned reconciliation process. The first six steps help clarify the conflict and the final four steps help to resolve the conflict.

Conflict Clarification

Step 1 – *Party calling the "pinch" goes first:* "I'm calling this pinch because you always give me your project work to review late in the afternoon. Sometimes I find things wrong in your analysis, but we all make mistakes so that is not why I'm calling this pinch. The problem is that when I find mistakes in your analysis, I end up having to work late to make corrections."

Step 2 – *Second party repeats the information:* "You said that I make mistakes in my project work, which makes you have to work late."

Step 3 – *First party confirms or clarifies the repeated information:* "That's close but not quite what I said. You always give me your project work at the end of the day. So when I find mistakes, I end up having to work late."

Step 4 – *Second party gives his or her side of the story:* "I don't mean to make you work late. I just have a very busy schedule. I usually wait until late in the day to complete our project work, which is why I give it you at the end of the day. Sorry about that"

Step 5 – *First party repeats the information:* "You said that you're a busy person and wait until the end of the day to do the project we're working on together."

Step 6 – *Second party confirms or clarifies the repeated information:* "Yes, and I also said that I was sorry about this causing you problems."

Conflict Solution

Step 7 – *First party proposes a solution:* "If you can give me your project work at 3:30 instead of 4:45, I wouldn't have to stay late to finish my portion of our project work."

Step 8 – *Second party accepts or offers a different solution:* "Getting the project work done by 3:30 is pushing it for me. It'll create extra anxiety and stress for me. I feel more confident about getting you the project work by 4:00 instead of 3:30."

Step 9 – *First party and second party continue to offer solutions until a resolution is reached.* "Here's what. If you know it's going to be later than 4:00, let me know by 3:45 so that I can reorder my own end of the day work tasks and still finish on time."

Step 10 – *Upon agreement, the parties write out the solution, sign the document, and keep it on file:* "Tom agrees to drop off his project work no later than 4:00. If running late, he will give Teresa a warning by 3:45."

Many work problems can be solved effectively and efficiently by a well-coached team of subordinates. Managers must obtain relevant ideas from all team members. Employees have diverse personalities (see Chapter 7). Some people are introverted and others extroverted. Extroverts are very willing to publicly share their ideas, while introverts are reticent to speak and tend to be more sensitive to criticism. If not appropriately managed, team discussions will be dominated by the viewpoints of extroverts.

The team problem-solving process discussed next helps access each member's unique knowledge—that of introverts as well as extroverts—and helps generate solutions with the highest likelihood of achieving superior performance.

1. *Present the problem:* Present the problem to all team members and address clarifying questions so all key issues are understood.

2. *Define individual solutions:* Each team member individually writes down possible solutions to the problem.

3. *Present individual solutions:* Each team member reads his or her solution to the entire team and the list of potential solutions is recorded. Team members listen carefully without responding.

4. *Clarify individual solutions:* Each team member explains his or her solution in greater detail and responds to clarifying questions. The solutions are not

judged as good or bad. Criticizing solutions during this step will inhibit introverted people from further participation.

5. *Brainstorm:* For three minutes, team members should spontaneously propose as many solutions as possible, no matter how odd or impractical they might initially seem. New ideas can amend solutions already mentioned. Do not critique these new solutions yet. This step is likely to be dominated by extroverts. Make sure that introverted people are given an opportunity to express their new ideas.

6. *Group and prioritize solutions:* As a team, organize the list of potential solutions according to common themes and prioritize them according to the greatest likelihood of success. Consider ease of implementation and costs when prioritizing the solutions. Develop action plans for implementing the best solutions.

7. *Play devil's advocate:* Assign one team member the role of devil's advocate. This person should state all the reasons why the highest-priority solution is likely to fail. Other team members should respond to these concerns and develop plans for how these obstacles and shortcomings could be managed.

8. *Implement and monitor:* Have teams implement high-priority solutions that fall within the boundaries of their authority, and monitor the outcomes. Team members should present complex and costly solutions or solutions that impact the operations of other work units to the appropriate manager for further analysis.

Open Book Management

Empowering employees requires giving them the information they need to make individual or team decisions. Transparency is an essential element of trust building. Open Book Management is a technique whereby managers share relevant financial and operational information with nonmanagement employees so they can better understand the organization's financial situation and operational issues and make better informed decisions.[40] "Open Book" means what the term implies—opening the financial books to all employees. The information shared could include balance sheets, revenue, profit, cost of goods, customer returns, on-time shipments, and so on.

Trusting nonmanagement employees with previously confidential financial and operational information enables them to behave more like managers. More than 10,000 companies use some form of Open Book Management, including units at Allstate Insurance, Sprint, and Amoco.[41] Of the 20 "Top Small Company Workplaces" chosen by Winning Workplaces for 2010, 83 percent practiced some form of Open Book Management.[42]

Determine which data are critical for the employees to know. Meet with teams to jointly establish challenging goals aligned with organizational goals for the key variables. Display scoreboards in public areas that measure progress toward targeted goals.

Open Book Management is particularly useful during recessionary periods or a slowdown in the business cycle. Greater access to planning and budgeting information enables employees to foresee the need for change. Employees usually assume

Tips and Techniques

Open Book Management

To optimize Open Book Management success, provide employees with

1. Relevant financial and operational information for decision-making purposes
2. Training to understand the numbers critical for tracking organizational performance
3. Training to understand how their daily activities impact the financial and operational targets
4. Authority to make decisions that will enable the work unit to reach the targets
5. A financial stake in the organization's success, such as a bonus tied to meeting targets or profit sharing

the organization is earning substantial profits and are often surprised when they see small profit margins or operating losses. At one company, employees were shocked to learn that heating a warehouse cost $5,000 a month and made changes that reduced the amount to $900 a month.[43]

Appreciative Inquiry

A key task for managers is to empower employees by aligning employee strengths with the organization's mission so that employee weaknesses become irrelevant. Appreciative Inquiry is a team-based management technique that focuses on the strengths of both the employee and the organization.[44] Appreciative Inquiry is a particularly powerful method for aligning fence-sitters and adversarial employees, as well as go-getters, with continuous improvement efforts and superior performance.

As a manager, appreciate each employee's strengths and determine how to link employee strengths to achieving superior performance, rather than dwelling on each employee's weaknesses. The same process can be applied at the organizational level—what are the organization's strengths, and how can these strengths be leveraged to achieve superior performance?

Appreciative Inquiry is a four-phase process: employees (1) identify organizational processes that work well (*discover*), (2) envision processes that would work well in the future (*dream*), (3) plan and prioritize processes that would work well (*design*), and (4) implement the proposals (*destiny*). Appreciative Inquiry has been applied in all types of organizations—large and small businesses, manufacturing facilities, retail stores, hospitals, churches, nonprofits, and government agencies.

The heart of an organization's mission is to serve customers. An Appreciative Inquiry workshop can be designed to empower employees to achieve superior customer service based on organizational strengths.

Step 1 – *Individually reflect on superior customer service [Discover]*. Each employee independently responds to the following prompts:

- Describe a situation when *you received* superior customer service.
- Describe a situation when *you provided* superior customer service.
- Describe a situation when *a coworker provided* superior customer service.
- Describe other ways *the organization has provided* superior customer service.
- Describe other ways *the organization can provide* superior customer service.
- What *changes* would have to be made in the organization to achieve this?

Step 2 – *With a small team, determine the essential elements of superior customer service*. Each team member presents situations when he or she received superior customer service, provided superior customer service, and observed others in the organization providing superior customer service. As a team, list the most important elements mentioned in these stories that enabled employees to achieve superior customer service (e.g., "The common themes in these stories are *x* and *y*."). Share these elements with the larger group.

Step 3 – *Develop a collective vision of what is needed to achieve superior customer service [Dream]*. Each team member describes other ways the organization can provide superior customer service and changes that would have to be made to accomplish this. For instance, "We could provide superior customer service if we did *x* and *y*." As a team, develop a compelling image of how the organization can achieve superior customer service in the future. Share this image with the larger group.

Step 4 – *Create a draft of a new organizational mission statement that emphasizes superior customer service at every level of operations*. Each team member independently composes a one-sentence mission statement and presents it to the team. As a team, achieve consensus on a one-sentence mission statement that meets the following four criteria, and share the mission statement with the larger group:

1. Is it desired? Would you want it?
2. Is it stated in affirmative and bold terms?
3. Is it clear and achievable?
4. Does it stretch and challenge the organization in a desired direction?

Step 5 – *Determine the organization's current "positive core."* Each team member independently determines two or three core aspects of the organization that already support the mission statement and superior customer service. For each aspect, provide an example. For instance, "We are already good at doing *x* and *y*." As a team, reach consensus on the core aspects. Share the core aspects, and examples, with the larger group.

Step 6 – *Make personal commitments [Design]*. Each team member independently lists what he or she will do more of, or do differently, to deliver superior customer service. For instance, "I promise to do *x* and *y*." Share this information with team members and hold each other accountable. Share these commitments with the larger group.

Step 7 – *Make organizational action recommendations*. Each team member recommends initiatives for how the organization can achieve superior customer service. How can the vision and image (Step 3), mission statement (Step 4), current strengths (Step 5), and personal commitments (Step 6) become a highly integrated reality? As a team, further develop these recommendations and share with the larger group.

Step 8 – *Have management follow up [Destiny]*. As an example of superior customer service and accountability, managers commit to providing feedback on this information within a reasonable time frame and support employee implementation of changes.

Daily Performance Reflections

Empowered team members not only address problems as they arise and participate in long-term planning, but they also share their daily accomplishments and lessons learned with other team members.

Set aside 10 to 15 minutes at the end of every day for teams to process the events that occurred during the day and make preparations for managing any ongoing problems the following day. Organize daily reflections during which each employee shares the information below about the workday. Have one employee address all five issues and then the next employee does likewise:

1. A performance accomplishment or satisfaction experienced
2. A problem that arose
3. How the problem was solved
4. A lesson learned from the accomplishment or problem that might benefit other team members
5. A problem that still needs to be addressed

Begin the daily performance reflections with a success story, and make others aware how each employee made a difference in organizational operations. Discussing how a problem was solved deepens employee empowerment. Conclude by discussing an ongoing problem and ask team members about potential solutions to the problem. This gives the employee hope that the situation can be resolved soon.

Empowering Through Group-Based Financial Incentives

Employees can also be empowered to behave as managers and owners by providing financial incentives that reward them as if they were managers and owners. Five possibilities are Scanlon-type gainsharing plans, profit sharing, stock option and stock purchase plans, employee stock option plans, and cooperatives.

Scanlon-Type Gainsharing Plans

Scanlon-type gainsharing plans empower employees by delegating institutional responsibility and accountability for improving operations to employee teams.[45] Gainsharing plans were initially implemented in manufacturing facilities and have been extended to restaurants, hospitals, and government offices. Work unit teams elicit, evaluate, and implement continuous improvement suggestions and receive financial rewards for surpassing historical performance standards. Cost savings are then shared between the organization and its employees based on an agreed-upon formula.

The five elements of a Scanlon-type gainsharing plan are a gainsharing coordinator, suggestion system, gainsharing team, review board, and group-based financial bonus.

1. *Gainsharing coordinator:* The gainsharing coordinator is responsible for managing the gainsharing system. The coordinator is typically a go-getter nonmanagement employee or human resources manager. Nonmanagement employees tend to trust the gainsharing system more if a member from their group is managing the system. Gainsharing coordinator duties include managing the suggestion system process, training team members, attending team meetings, and maintaining records. This can be a full-time position or amended to an employee's current job duties.

2. *Suggestion system:* Employees submit written suggestions to the gainsharing coordinator on how to improve efficiency, reduce costs, and increase revenue. The suggestions are listed in a logbook or computer file and sent to the appropriate work team.

3. *Gainsharing team:* A gainsharing team consists of either all nonmanagement employees in the work unit or work unit representatives voted to the team. Organizations with small work units tend to put everyone on a gainsharing team, whereas larger work units vote for representatives. The teams can be defined in terms of job tasks (nurses on one team, facilities employees on another team) or location (everyone on the third floor of a hospital). Teams meet weekly or monthly to review suggestions and brainstorm solutions. The teams have a monthly budget to implement suggestions that fall within their domain. Suggestions that exceed the team's monthly budget or that impact other work units are forwarded to a review board.

4. *Review board:* The review board consists of one representative from each gainsharing team, the gainsharing coordinator, and relevant managers. The nonmanagement representatives report on the changes their teams implemented and respond to questions. They also present suggestions that exceed their monthly budget allocations or impact other work units. Review board members reach a consensus on whether to implement these more costly or inter–work unit suggestions.

5. *Group-based financial bonus:* A group-based financial bonus calculation is devised that compares projected costs and actual costs for a given period of time, usually a month. The projected costs are based on historical performance, usually an average of the previous three years. The cost calculation can be broad (e.g., the total value of goods and services divided by labor costs) or narrow (e.g., electricity costs divided by labor costs). When actual costs are lower than the projected historical cost, the financial difference is shared between the employees and the organization, typically on a 50/50 ratio.

Half of the nonmanagement employees' share is then distributed as a bonus for that month. The other half of the nonmanagement employee share is set aside in a year-end reserve pool that accounts for months when actual costs exceed projected historical costs. Any amount remaining in the reserve pool at the end of the year is then distributed among the nonmanagement employees.

Profit Sharing

Providing employees with a share of company profits is also ethical, motivating, and empowering. When the company does well, the employees benefit financially. As a result, employees feel empowered to work as if they are owners. Researchers report that profit sharing has positive impacts on employee cooperation, turnover, productivity, costs, and profits.[46] Profit sharing also positively impacts organizational commitment, a research finding in all sizes of firms, although strongest in small firms.[47]

Profit sharing supplements, but does not replace, base pay. Employees earn wages based on skills and labor market conditions and then participate in the distribution of profits generated by their work efforts. Sharing profits with all employees is a natural extension of sharing financial information through Open Book Management and involving employees in the decision-making process.[48]

Profit-sharing companies set aside a percentage of profits beyond a targeted amount into a bonus pool. Some companies distribute profits as a percentage of compensation, under the assumption that higher-paid employees contribute more to the financial outcome. Other companies create a multifactor calculation that allows for bonus fluctuations based on team and individual accomplishments.

Profits are distributed in cash or stock at the end of the fiscal year, or as deferred compensation. The deferred compensation is not taxed until accessed by the employee, usually upon retirement, death, disability, or employment termination. Employees can borrow money against their profit-sharing account.

Profit-sharing plans are governed by the Employee Retirement Security Act (ERISA). Employer contributions cannot exceed an average of 15 percent of an employee's salary during any two-year period. Employers can deduct profit sharing as a business expense.

Profit-sharing plans enhance organizational loyalty by spreading out the length of time required for an employee to have full access to the funds. Typically, an employee is fully vested after three to six years. If an employee leaves the organization prior to being fully vested, the amount remaining in the employee's profit-sharing account is redistributed to the other plan participants.

Stock Option and Stock Purchase Plans

According to the 2006 General Social Survey, 20 million American workers own stock in their company through a 401(k) plan, employee stock option plans (ESOPs), direct stock grant, or similar plan, and 10.6 million hold stock options.[49] Stock options, historically reserved for executives, are now offered by many public and private companies to all employees.[50] More than 10,000 Microsoft employees have become millionaires through the company's stock option plan.

Stock options give an employee the right to purchase a specific number of company shares at a fixed price by a particular future date, typically 10 years. The number of stock options an employee receives is based on a formula, usually determined as percentage of compensation to total payroll and performance accomplishments.

Employees earning higher pay, who are more accountable for profitability, have access to, and can afford to purchase, more stock options. Design stock option plans to reward, and retain, the go-getters. Employees often have full vesting rights after three to five years and are taxed on the profits earned when they option to buy and sell their stock.

An *employee stock purchase plan* is slightly different from a stock option plan. Under an employee stock purchase plan, employees request to have deductions taken out of their pay and put into an account to purchase stock at a discount, usually 15 percent, by a specified date. Some companies will match a certain percentage of the employee deduction. If an employee decides to not purchase the company's stock by the expiration date, the employee gets his or her pay deductions back.

Some privately held companies, whose stocks are not sold on the open market, offer employees *phantom stock*. An independent appraiser determines the phantom stock value of privately owned companies. Publicly held companies that do not want to dilute the ownership rights of existing shareholders can also issue phantom stock.

Similar to stock options, phantom stock has a specified expiration date and can be structured in different ways. Many companies use the phantom stock as an employee bonus linked to firm profitability. Employees earn a cash bonus equal to the increase in the phantom stock's value between the day issued and the day exercised.

Employee Stock Option Plans (ESOPs)

Employee stock option plans, ESOPs, take stock options one step further in empowering employees. The company gives all full-time employees over the age of 21 a significant equity stake in the company.[51] Unlike stock option plans, all full-time employees must be included as ESOP members.

In 2008, approximately 11,500 ESOPs, most of them corporations, covered 10 million employees.[52] ESOPs were legally established in 1957. Most ESOPs have less than 1,000 employees. The 100 largest ESOPs range from 1,070 to 144,000 employees and include supermarkets, manufacturers, engineering firms, tree service businesses, construction businesses, motels, nursing homes, and drug stores.[53]

Although all full-time employees must be included to create an ESOP, an ESOP does not necessarily control the entire company. The United Airlines ESOP, for instance, was granted equity shares accounting for 55 percent of the firm's cash flow rights.[54] The average ESOP owns only 6 percent of a company's equity.

ESOPs are complex financial vehicles requiring legal assistance. ESOPs cost about $50,000 to $100,000 to set up and operate the first year, with annual maintenance fees ranging from $15,000 to $30,000 for firms with less than a few hundred employees. The initial legal costs may seem high, but it is typically equivalent to, or less than, what an owner would pay a broker to sell the business.[55]

Owners usually consider creating an ESOP when a change of ownership is being explored. Rather than selling the company to an outsider, the owner can sell the company to employees. To create an ESOP, the company borrows money from a bank to purchase company stock that is then placed into a trust fund. The loan interest is tax deductible and paid off through dividends. Loan principal payments are deductible up to 25 percent of payroll. Employees do not purchase the company;

the trust fund does. The stocks are then allocated into employee accounts according to a specific formula, typically based on compensation and seniority.

The company makes annual tax-deductible contributions into the fund to purchase stock employees then sell back to the company. Most of the money in the trust fund must be invested in company operations. The value of employee stock is independently appraised on an annual basis. The value of the stock increase is tax deferred until sold.

ESOPs provide employees with a right to purchase the stock, but employees are not obligated to do so. Employees can purchase their vested shares when they leave the organization—when they quit, are fired, retire, or die—and must sell the stock back to the company or other employees within one year at the appraised value.

Employees can vote their ESOP shares on major issues. A board of directors that employs professional managers governs the ESOP. In publicly held companies, ESOP participants have the same rights as other stockholders.

The best performing ESOPs provide employees with daily operational decision-making authority, but this is not required of an ESOP. A National Center for Employee Ownership study compared 45 ESOPs with 225 comparable non-ESOPs and found that companies with a combination of ESOP and participative management culture grew 8 percent to 11 percent faster than those without them.[56]

Cooperatives

Producer, consumer, and employee cooperatives are an alternative communal way to govern a business and raise capital. In a producer cooperative, such as an agricultural cooperative, producers pool their capital and resources for their mutual benefit. Consumer cooperatives are businesses owned by customers for their mutual benefit, such as credit unions and health care cooperatives. In both circumstances, profits are either reinvested in the cooperative or distributed among the owners (producers or consumers).

Employee cooperatives are organizations owned by the employees and democratically governed—one vote per employee-owner. Employee cooperatives can be found in a wide range of industries and organizations, including agriculture, banks, food stores, coffee, home health care, technology, and poultry.[57]

Each employee-owned cooperative creates its own unique rules. In some cooperatives, the employee-owners vote on board members, managers, capital investments, wages, and company policies. Large cooperatives tend to elect a board of directors that determines major strategic issues and hires managers. Profits are reinvested in the organization, set aside in reserves, or distributed to the employee-owners based on an agreed-upon formula.

Equal Exchange, founded in 1986, is one of the largest employee cooperatives in the United States.[58] All employees have the right to vote (one vote per employee, not per share), the right to serve as a manager or board director, the right to information (Open Book Management), and the right to freedom of speech within the organization. Of Equal Exchange's net profits, 7 percent is donated to nonprofit organizations and 3 percent is invested in other employee cooperatives. Of the remaining 90 percent net profit, two-thirds is reinvested in the organization and one-third is divided equally among the employee-owners.

SUMMARY

Superior-performing organizations place a high value on trust and responsibility. Employees are deeply engaged in work tasks, empowered to make decisions, and committed to the organization. Trust increases when employees are treated like managers or owners, and the barriers between management and nonmanagement employees have been minimized.

This chapter explored a wide variety of management systems and techniques for involving em-

ployees in the organization's decision-making processes and providing financial rewards for improved organizational performance. In an empowered organization, employees not only make and implement decisions on a daily basis that improve organizational operations, but also share in the cost savings and profits they help generate.

KEY WORDS

Employee engagement; Abraham Maslow; David McClelland; Frederick Herzberg; organizational justice; bullying; meaningful work; empowerment; pinch theory; team problem-solving process; Open Book Management; Appreciative Inquiry; Scanlon-type gainsharing plans; stock options; ESOPs; cooperatives

CHAPTER QUESTIONS

1. How can managers organize work so that employees are more engaged with job tasks and organizational goals?

2. Describe different techniques for managing go-getters, fence-sitters, and adversarials.

3. What is the team problem-solving process? What are its advantages?

4. How would you design an Appreciative Inquiry workshop to achieve superior customer service?

5. Describe how to implement a Scanlon-type gainsharing plan.

6. What are the benefits of offering profit sharing and stock options and creating an employee stock ownership plan and cooperatives? Describe each of these techniques for empowering employees.

In the Real World: Enron

Informing Ken Lay—August 2001

At Enron's request, Arthur Andersen's senior partners removed Carl Bass from reviewing the Enron account and reassigned him to SEC relations. Unfortunately, in 2000 the Internet economic bubble burst, the nation entered into a recession, and the stock market declined. For Enron, this meant losing many Internet customers and being financially overextended when the credit markets tightened. Negative publicity

associated with Enron traders manipulating the California electricity trading market didn't help.

Nonetheless, Enron claimed $100 billion in revenue for the first half of 2001, and stock analysts estimated that at this pace Enron would end the year as #1 on the Fortune 500 list.

But then a subset of Andy Fastow's network of SPEs began to collapse because they were funded primarily with Enron stock, which was declining in value with the rest of the stock market. Fastow's conflict of interest

(Continued)

between Enron and the SPEs became more apparent. Skilling ordered Fastow to resign either from Enron or as LJM's managing partner. Fastow decided to remain as Enron's CFO. Instead, Michael Kopper, Fastow's assistant and protégé, resigned from Enron and took over as LJM's managing partner.

The pressure was getting to Skilling as his dream job started to turn into a financial nightmare. If Enron's stock continued to decline in price, more Fastow-created SPEs would collapse. Skilling struggled with depression, alcohol consumption, and insomnia. On August 13, 2001, Skilling shocked the Board of Directors by submitting his resignation as Enron's CEO, citing family reasons. The public announcement resulted in a massive sell-off of Enron stock, and its price plummeted even more.

Ken Lay agreed to come out of semiretirement to serve as Enron's CEO again and reestablish stock market confidence. He announced an all-employee meeting to address a whirlwind of rumors surrounding Skilling's resignation. Sherron Watkins, a vice president who worked for Fastow, submitted an anonymous one-page letter that highlighted some of Fastow's SPE accounting manipulations for Lay to comment on at the all-employee meeting. Lay chose not to address Watkins's letter.

Watkins then claimed authorship of the letter, shared it with Enron's in-house lawyers, and scheduled a meeting with Lay for the following week to discuss the matter. The in-house lawyer strongly recommended that Watkins cancel her meeting with Lay until after Enron's chief legal counsel investigated her accusations about Fastow. After all, external auditors, external lawyers, and the Board of Directors had approved transactions between LJM and Enron.

DECISION CHOICE. If you were an Enron vice president, would you

1. Cancel your meeting with Lay and wait until hearing back from Enron's in-house lawyers?

2. Continue your own investigation and meet with Lay at the already scheduled time?

3. Confidentially notify Arthur Andersen about your suspicions?

4. Confidentially notify the SEC about your suspicions?

5. Confidentially notify *Wall Street Journal* reporters about your suspicions?

Why?

ANCILLARY MATERIALS

Websites to Explore

- "100 Best Companies to Work For" winners, *Fortune*, available at http://money.cnn.com/magazines/fortune/bestcompanies/.

- Top Small Company Workplaces, available at http://www.winningworkplaces.org/topsmallbiz/index.php#2010.

- Appreciative Inquiry, available at http://appreciativeinquiry.case.edu/default.cfm.

- The National Center for Employee Ownership, available at http://www.nceo.org/.

- U.S. Federation of Worker Cooperatives, available at www.usworker.coop.

- Workplace Bullying Institute, available at http://www.workplacebullying.org/; Stop Workplace Bullying, available at http://bullyfreeworkplace.org/.

Best Place to Work Video

- Whole Foods' CEO John Mackey on "Conscious Capitalism," available at http://www.youtube.com/watch?v=CYJl3DOMGM8&feature=related.

Business Ethics Issue Video

- "College,Inc.," *Frontline*, about for-profit universities; May 4, 2010, 55 minutes, available at http://www.pbs.org/wgbh/pages/frontline/collegeinc/view/?utm_campaign=viewpage&utm_medium=grid&utm_source=grid.

TEDTalks Videos

- *Motivation and Your Internal Drives:* Tony Robbins discusses the "invisible forces" that motivate everyone's actions; February 2006, 22 minutes, available at http://www.ted

.com/talks/tony_robbins_asks_why_we_ do_what_we_do.html.

- *Pursuing Your Dreams:* At his Stanford University commencement speech, Steve Jobs, CEO and co-founder of Apple and Pixar, urges us to pursue our dreams and see the opportunities in life's setbacks; June 2005, 15 minutes, available at http://www.ted.com/talks/steve_ jobs_how_to_live_before_you_die.html.

Conversations with Charlie Rose

- A conversation about President Obama's speech on Wall Street marking one year since the fall of Lehman Brothers and the global

economic recovery plan; September 14, 2009, 60 minutes, available at http://www .charlierose.com/view/interview/10604.

- A conversation with author Jonathan Zittrain about his book *The Future of the Internet and How to Stop It; May 13, 2008, 31 minutes, available at http://www .charlierose.com/view/interview/9081.*

NOTES

[1] Nancy Lockwood, "Leveraging Employee Empowerment for Competitive Advantage," *Society for Human Resource Management Research Quarterly*, March 2007.

[2] James Krohe Jr., "If You Love Your People, Set Them Free," *Conference Board Review,* 47, 5 (2010), 30–37.

[3] Richard D. White, "Organizational Design and Ethics: The Effects of Rigid Hierarchy on Moral Reasoning," *International Journal of Organization Theory & Behavior,* 2, 3&4 (1999), 431–456.

[4] Ethics Resource Center and Hay Group, *Ethics and Employee Engagement* (Washington, DC: Ethics Resource Center, 2009) available at http:// www.ethics.org/files/u5/NBESResearchBrief2.pdf, accessed 11/10/10.

[5] Jennifer Robison, "Engagement, Wellbeing, and the Downturn," *GALLUP Management Journal*, August 5, 2010, available at http://gmj .gallup.com/content/141722/Engagement-Wellbeing-Downturn.aspx, accessed 11/10/10.

[6] Jeannine Aversa, "Americans' Job Satisfaction Falls to Record Low," Associated Press, January 5, 2010.

[7] Timothy A. Judge, Carl J. Thoresen, Joyce E. Bono, and Gregory K. Patton, "The Job Satisfaction–Job Performance Relationship: A Qualitative and Quantitative Review," *Psychological Bulletin,* 127, 3 (2001), 376–407.

[8] Society for Human Resource Management, *2009 Employee Job Satisfaction: A Survey Report by SHRM* (Alexandria, VA: SHRM, 2009), available

at http://www.shrm.org/Research/SurveyFindings/ Articles/Documents/09-0282_Emp_Job_Sat_ Survey_FINAL.pdf, accessed 11/10/10.

[9] Anonymous, "Meaningful Work Is Still the Most Desired," *Work-Life Newsbrief & Trend Report*, May 2009, p. 5.

[10] Abraham H. Maslow, *Motivation and Personality,* 2nd ed. (New York: Harper & Row, 1970).

[11] John P. McClure and James M. Brown, "Belonging at Work," *Human Resource Development International,* 11, 1 (2008), 3–17.

[12] David C. McClelland, *The Achieving Society* (Princeton, NJ: Van Nostrand, 1961).

[13] Frederick Herzberg, Bernard Mausner, and Barbara Bloch Snyderman, *The Motivation to Work* (New York: John Wiley and Sons, 1959); Frederick Herzberg, *Work and the Nature of Man* (New York: World Publishing Company, 1966).

[14] J. Richard Hackman and Greg R. Oldham, *Work Redesign* (Reading, MA: Addison-Wesley, 1980).

[15] Daniel H. Pink, *Drive: The Surprising Truth About What Motivates Us* (New York: Riverhead Books, 2009).

[16] *Fortune,* "100 Best Companies to Work For," 2010 list, available at http://money.cnn.com/magazines/ fortune/bestcompanies/2010/full_list/, accessed 11/10/10.

[17] Robert Folger and Russell Cropanzano, *Organizational Justice and Human Resource Management* (Beverly Hills, CA: Sage, 1998).

[18] Jason A. Colquitt, "On the Dimensionality of Organizational Justice: A Construct Validation of a

Measure," *Journal of Applied Psychology*, 86, 3 (2001), 386–400.

[19] Jerald Greenberg and Jason A. Colquitt, *The Handbook of Organizational Justice* (Mahwah, NJ: Erlbaum, 2005); Mark G. Ehrhart, "Leadership and Procedural Justice Climate as Antecedents of Unit-Level Organizational Citizenship Behavior," *Personnel Psychology*, 57, 1 (2004), 61–94.

[20] Workplace Bullying Institute website available at http://www.workplacebullying.org/research/WBIZogby2007Survey.html, accessed 11/10/10.

[21] Gary Namie and Ruth Namie, *The Bully at Work: What You Can Do to Stop the Hurt and Reclaim Your Dignity on the Job* (Naperville, IL: Sourcebooks, Inc., 2009).

[22] Bennett J. Tepper, "Consequences of Abusive Supervision," *Academy of Management Journal*, 43, 2 (2000), 178–190.

[23] James Wallace and Jim Erickson, *Hard Drive: Bill Gates and the Making of the Microsoft Empire* (New York: HarperBusiness, 1992).

[24] Tepper, "Consequences of Abusive Supervision," Bennett J. Tepper, Christine A. Henle, Lisa Schurer, Robert Giacalone, and Michelle K. Duffy, "Abusive Supervision and Subordinates' Organization Deviance," *Journal of Applied Psychology*, 93, 4 (2008), 721–732.

[25] Stop Workplace Bullying website, "Results of 2007 Zogby Survey," available at http://bullyfreeworkplace.org/id27.html, accessed 11/10/10.

[26] Douglas R. May, Richard L. Gilson, and Lynn M. Harter, "The Psychological Conditions of Meaningfulness, Safety and Availability and the Engagement of the Human Spirit at Work," *Journal of Occupational and Organizational Psychology*, 77, 1 (2004), 11–37.

[27] Mihaly Csikszentmihalyi, *Flow: The Psychology of Optimal Experience* (New York: Harper Perennial, 1990).

[28] Scroggins, "Antecedents and Outcomes of Experienced Meaningful Work."

[29] Marjolein Lips-Wiersma and Lani Morris, "Discriminating Between 'Meaningful Work' and the 'Management of Meaning,'" *Journal of Business Ethics*, 88, 3 (2009), 491–511.

[30] Marcus Buckingham and Curt Coffman, *First, Break All the Rules: What the World's Greatest Managers Do Differently* (New York: Simon & Schuster, 1999).

[31] Ibid., p. 57.

[32] Ibid., p. 40.

[33] Gary Hamel, *The Future of Management* (Boston, MA: Harvard Business School Press, 2007), pp. 69–82.

[34] Denis Collins, *Gainsharing and Power: Lessons from Six Scanlon Plans* (Ithaca, NY: Cornell University Press, 1998).

[35] Mark C. Bolino and William H. Turnley, "Going the Extra Mile: Cultivating and Managing Employee Citizenship Behavior," *Academy of Management Executive*, 17, 3 (2003), 60–71.

[36] Deanne N. Den Hartog and Annebel H. B. De Hoogh, "Empowering Behaviour and Leader Fairness and Integrity: Studying Perceptions of Ethical Leader Behaviour from a Levels-of-Analysis Perspective," *European Journal of Work & Organizational Psychology*, 18, 2 (2009), 199–230.

[37] Hamel, *The Future of Management,* pp. 61–62.

[38] Patrick Lencioni, *Overcoming the Five Dysfunctions of a Team* (San Francisco: Jossey-Bass, 2005).

[39] Rudolph Hirzel, "PINCH! A Simple Model for Dealing with Conflict," *The Journal for Quality*

and Participation, Summer 2004, available at http://findarticles.com/p/articles/mi_qa3616/is_200407/ai_n9425836/, accessed 11/10/10.

40 John Case, *Open-Book Management: The Coming Business Revolution* (New York: Collins Business, 1996).

41 John Case, *The Open-Book Experience: Lessons from Over 100 Companies Who Successfully Transformed Themselves* (New York: Basic Book, 1998).

42 Leigh Buchanan, "Learning from the Best," *Inc.,* 32, 5 (2010), 85–96; Winning Workplaces website available at http://www.winningworkplaces.org/topsmallbiz/index.php#2010, accessed 11/10/10.

43 John Tozzi, "To Beat the Recession, Open Your Books," *Business Week Online,* July 8, 2009.

44 David L. Cooperrider and Diana Whitney, *Appreciative Inquiry: A Positive Revolution in Change* (San Francisco, CA: Berrett-Koehler, 2005); see Appreciative Inquiry Commons website available at http://appreciativeinquiry.case.edu/default.cfm, accessed 11/10/10.

45 Collins, *Gainsharing and Power.*

46 Raymond A. Noe, John R. Hollenbeck, Barry Gerhart, and Patrick M. Wright, *Human Resources Management,* 5th ed. (New York: McGraw-Hill Irwin, 2006).

47 Alberto Bayo-Moriones and Martin Larraza-Kintana, "Profit-Sharing Plans and Affective Commitment: Does the Context Matter?" *Human Resource Management,* 48, 2 (2009), 207–226.

48 Toni Jarimo and Harri I. Kulmala, "Incentive Profit-Sharing Rules Joined with Open-Book Accounting in SME Networks," *Production Planning & Control,* 19, 5 (2008), 508–517.

49 The National Center for Employee Ownership, "Data Show Widespread Employee Ownership in U.S.," available at http://www.nceo.org/main/article.php/id/10/, accessed 11/10/10.

50 National Center for Employee Ownership, *A Comprehensive Overview of Employee Ownership,* available at http://www.nceo.org/main/article.php/id/6/, accessed 11/10/10.

51 Joseph Blasi, Douglas Kruse, and Aaron Bernstein, *In the Company of Owners: The Truth about Stock Options* (New York: Basic Books, 2003).

52 John Koegel, "Is There an ESOP in Your Future?" *Community Banker,* 17, 1 (2008), 22–23.

53 Corey Rosen, "The Employee Ownership 100: America's Largest Majority Employee-Owned Companies," May 2010, available at http://www.nceo.org/main/article.php/id/11/, accessed 11/10/10.

54 E. Han Kim, "Corporate Governance and Labor Relations," *Journal of Applied Corporate Finance,* 21, 1 (2009), 57–66.

55 Mark Battersby, "Weighing the ESOP Option," *Landscape Management,* 47, 10 (2008), 140–144.

56 J. Robert Beyster, "Embracing Change Through Employee Ownership," *Benefits & Compensation Digest,* 45, 3 (2008), 28–31.

57 Frank Adams and Gary Hansen, *Putting Democracy to Work: A Practical Guide for Starting and Managing Worker-Owned Businesses* (San Francisco, CA: Berrett-Koehler Publishers, 1993); see also U.S. Federation of Worker Cooperatives website at www.usworker.coop, accessed 11/10/10.

58 Equal Exchange, "Worker Owned," available at www.equalexchange.com/worker-owned, accessed 11/10/10.

PART IV

Being a Good Citizen

CHAPTER OUTLINE

11

ENVIRONMENTAL MANAGEMENT

What would you do?

Environmentally Friendly Cabinets

Upon graduation, you are hired as a purchasing manager for a medium-sized company. You also chair the company's "Green Committee," which is responsible for implementing new environmentally friendly policies and procedures.

While participating in the annual United Way Day of Caring event, you find yourself painting the study room walls at the Boys & Girls Club with a purchasing manager from another company. You notice some interesting-looking filing cabinets. "Oh," Tamara says, "we donated those to the Boys & Girls Club. They're very cool looking aren't they. That's because everything about them is environmentally friendly. It's one of those new 'cradle to cradle' products where every piece of the product was previously used, and all the chemicals are nontoxic. When it's time to buy new cabinets, every piece comes apart easily and can be reused in other products. Nothing ends up in a landfill."

You're lucky to find this out because your company will soon purchase new filing cabinets for all the offices. Just a few months ago, the Green Committee approved a "sustainable products checklist" that lists 10 eco-friendly variables to consider when making a purchase, such as whether the product is recyclable, energy efficient,

nontoxic, and locally available. The committee's purchasing guidelines, signed by the president, states that if two product prices are within 5 percent of each other, depending on the size of the order, purchase the product with the higher sustainability score.

For the previous three decades, the company has purchased all office furniture from a local vendor. The vendor is community oriented, and you constantly run into him at community activities. He too had been volunteering that day at the Boys & Girls Club.

You use the sustainability checklist to do a product comparison between the local vendor's product and the product you saw at the Boys & Girls Club. The results aren't even close. The only item the local vendor scores high on is being locally available. The nine other items on the checklist favor the other product. The environmentally friendly cabinets are priced 4 percent higher.

"I wish I could get it for you," the local vendor says when you inquire about buying the environmentally friendly cabinets from him, "but the out-of-state company selling that product refuses to sell through other distributors. You know you've been doing business with us for about 30 years. We sell high-quality products and provide excellent service. With the recession going on, we can really use your business right now. Let me know as soon as possible when you want me to deliver our cabinets."

What would you do? Would you

1. Purchase the much more eco-friendly cabinets from the out-of-state supplier?
2. Purchase the slightly lower cost regular cabinets from the long-term local vendor? Why?

Chapter Objectives

After reading this chapter, you will be able to:

- Understand climate change and government responses to environmental problems
- Articulate the competitive advantages of being eco-friendly

- Manage the environmental change process
- Create an Environmental Management System plan
- Develop measureable environmental goals and objectives
- Assess environmental performance

Treating the Earth with respect is one of the greatest ethical and management challenges. For centuries, managers have treated the Earth as an unlimited resource to be exploited. The Earth is 4.5 billion years old. Beginning with the eighteenth-century Industrial Revolution, significant damage has been done to the atmosphere and ground because of business activities. Business response to environmental problems has evolved from denial up until the 1960s to regulatory compliance in the 1970s and 1980s, eco-efficiency in the 1990s, and sustainable management in the 2000s.[1]

A growing number of managers now realize that appropriately managing the relationship between organizational operations and the environment can enhance profits and long-term success, as well as quality of life for current and future generations.[2] Consumer spending for eco-friendly products has increased substantially. In 2008, consumers spent $500 billion on sustainable products and services, double that of the previous year.[3]

Environmentally friendly organizations have adopted a Triple Bottom Line approach that assesses three performance factors: economic performance, social performance, and environmental performance.[4] Profit, people, and the planet all matter for organizations seeking to ensure long-term viability.

But how "green" should an organization become—a little green, moderately green, or very green? Sometimes trade-offs are involved in the decision-making process. Should a company show preference for a community-minded local supplier selling high-quality, though not eco-friendly, filing cabinets or eco-friendly filing cabinets from a distant supplier? Should an organization build a new facility that achieves "basic" Leadership in Energy and Environmental Design (LEED) certification or the much more expensive top-of-the-line platinum LEED certification? Some environmental improvements provide long-term cost savings but require substantial up-front costs. At what point does the initial cost outlay matter more than the long-term savings?

This chapter summarizes environmental problems and the efforts of environmental organizations, government, and businesses to address them. Environmental management is a competitive advantage that can save the organization money, enhance its reputation, and attract and motivate employees. The chapter examines how superior environmental performance can be achieved by screening suppliers, adopting an Environmental Management System and The Natural Step framework, conducting environmental risk assessments, designing eco-friendly products, operating in green buildings, and monitoring environmental performance indicators.

Environmental Trends and Climate Change

Environmental Trends

The number of people consuming the Earth's scarce resources continues to rise. In 1900, there were 1.7 billion people on Earth. In 2010, the world's population exceeded 6.8 billion, a multiple of four in slightly more than a century.[5] During that same time period, the U.S. population also rose by a factor of four, from 76 million to 310 million people. The higher the population, the greater the number of organizations needed to meet ever increasing consumer needs.

Organizations not only meet the needs of consumers, but also are one of the largest consumers of the Earth's resources. Fossil fuels are used to light and heat buildings, operate machinery, and transport products from suppliers to consumers. The way managers have typically chosen to transform natural resources from inputs to outputs contributes to air, water, and land pollution, leaving the natural environment worse for future generations. A United Nations report estimates that in 2008, the 3,000 largest companies caused $2.2 trillion in environmental damage.[6]

Organizations can also cause tremendous environmental damage through negligent behaviors. Chevron, for instance, has been engaged in a nearly two-decade litigation battle for having dumped 18 billion gallons of toxic wastewater in a region of the Amazon rainforest inhabited by 30,000 people.[7] British Petroleum (BP) long had a reputation for being socially responsible, including being rated the #1 most environmentally accountable company in the world by *Fortune* in 2007.[8] The magazine recognized BP for its research and development of wind, solar, and other environmentally friendly technologies and replacing executives at facilities that experienced major accidents. Then, on April 20, 2010, an explosion on an oil rig in the Gulf of Mexico killed 11 workers. More than 5 million gallons of crude oil spilled into the gulf before BP could cap the oil well three months later. The worst offshore oil spill in the world caused extensive damage to marine life and the fishing and tourism industries. BP agreed to set up a $20 billion spill fund to compensate victims and will face years of litigation.[9]

Prior to the Industrial Revolution, greenhouse gases were minimal. Since then, billions of pounds of toxins have been released into the air, water, and soil every year.[10] American businesses have long been the worst culprits. The United States, with just 5 percent of the world's population, accounts for 20 percent of worldwide carbon dioxide (CO_2) emissions.[11] CO_2 is by far the most significant greenhouse gas, and it remains in the atmosphere for decades. In 2008, the United States ranked last among the largest industrialized democracies (the "Group of 8") for environmental performance, and 39th among 149 nations for a combination of the most important environmental measurements.[12] Rapidly industrializing China surpassed the United States as the world's largest emitter of greenhouse gases in 2006.[13] The other major emitters are Russia, India, and Japan.[14]

The type of energy a nation uses to fuel its economy is a political decision. Exhibit 11.1 summarizes the different energy sources for six industrialized nations to demonstrate the variety of choices.[15] China relies mostly on coal (66.2 percent), Japan on oil (42.7 percent), and France on nuclear power (42.8 percent). Neighboring Canada uses water significantly more than the United States (11.3 percent versus 0.9 percent). Geothermal and solar, which cause the least harm to nature, are minimally used, with Germany leading the way at just 1.2 percent.

Exhibit 11.1 Energy Sources per Nation							
Source	World	U.S.	Canada	Germany	France	Japan	China
Oil	34.3%	38.9%	37.1%	33.1%	30.8%	42.7%	17.5%
Coal	25.1%	23.7%	10.7%	25.4%	4.9%	23.1%	66.2%
Natural Gas	20.9%	23.0%	28.1%	23.1%	14.4%	16.8%	3.0%
Nuclear	6.5%	9.3%	8.7%	10.7%	42.8%	13.9%	0.8%
Combustibles/ Biomass	10.6%	3.5%	4.2%	6.6%	5.1%	1.5%	10.0%
Water (Hydro)	2.2%	0.9%	11.3%	0.5%	1.9%	1.3%	2.1%
Geothermal & Solar	0.4%	0.6%	0.9%	1.2%	0.2%	0.7%	0.3%

Climate Change

There is strong scientific consensus that climate change is occurring.[16] The Earth's temperature has increased by 1.4 degrees Fahrenheit since the Industrial Revolution. The National Aeronautics and Space Administration (NASA), which monitors weather patterns, reports that the 10 hottest years in recorded history have all occurred between 1998 and 2010.[17] The Intergovernmental Panel on Climate Change, composed of 2,500 scientists and risk experts, estimates an increase in the Earth's temperature of between 2.5 to 10.4 degrees Fahrenheit by 2100 if no major efforts are undertaken to reduce greenhouse gas emissions.

A small number of scientists maintain that continual record high temperatures do not prove that global warming is occurring.[18] Weather changes can be cyclical rather than accumulative. The extreme droughts and floods currently being experienced have occurred at other times in history. In addition, scientific knowledge about global warming is always incomplete and uncertain, and any projection into the future might be based on a series of invalid assumptions.

What causes global warming? According to the Union of Concerned Scientists, "the primary cause of global warming is from human activity, most significantly burning of fossil fuels to drive cars, generate electricity, and operate our homes and businesses."[19] Planets too close to the sun are too hot, and planets too distant are too cold, for human survival. The Earth is habitable because solar radiation travels through outer space, bounces off the Earth, and is captured by heat-trapping gases in the Earth's atmosphere that serve as an insulator. CO_2 is one of the heat-trapping gases. Driving a car, using electricity, and heating homes release additional CO_2 that is absorbed by the atmosphere. This creates an even thicker insulation shield around the Earth, which makes the Earth warmer.

For 10,000 years, the earth's atmosphere contained 280 CO_2 molecules per million of atmospheric gases. This changed shortly after the Industrial Revolution. By 2007, every million molecules of atmosphere gases contained 384 CO_2 molecules. Scientists predict that within 50 years, there will be 550 CO_2 molecules per million if laws and energy policies remain unchanged.[20]

Climate Change Impacts

Altered weather patterns have increased the frequency and severity of droughts and flooding in summer, and snowstorms in winter, which damage the economy. During the past 30 years, weather-related disasters have cost in excess of $700 billion.[21] In August 2005, Hurricane Katrina caused more than $133.8 billion in damages and 1,833 deaths. Other major weather disasters since then include Hurricane Ike ($27 billion, 82 deaths), Hurricane Rita ($17.1 billion, 119 deaths), Midwest floods in June 2008 ($15 billion, 24 deaths), and Western wildfires in 2007 ($10 billion, 12 deaths). Exhibit 11.2 highlights the extreme weather costs for 2009.

Exhibit 11.2 2009 U.S. Weather Disasters		
Date	Disaster	Damage
Entire 2009	Southwest/Great Plains Drought	$5.2 billion
February 2009	Southeast/Ohio Valley Thunderstorms	$1.4 billion; 10 deaths
March 2009	Midwest/Southwest Tornadoes	$1.0 billion
April 2009	South/Southwest Tornadoes	$1.2 billion; 6 deaths
June 2009	Midwest/South/East Thunderstorms	$1.1 billion
Summer–Fall 2009	Western Wildfires	$5.9 million; 10 deaths

The situation is likely to worsen internationally as populations continue to increase and underdeveloped nations industrialize. Journalist Thomas Friedman puts population growth impacts in perspective using an *Americum* unit of analysis. An Americum is any group of 350 million people living an American lifestyle. The world has recently evolved from two Americums (North America and Europe) to five (add China, India, and a combination of Southwest Asian nations, Australia, and New Zealand). Soon there will be four more Americums (another one in China, another one in India, one in a combined Russia/Central Europe, and one in a combination of South America and the Middle East). Two Americums have contributed to climate change. What nine Americums will cause, Friedman ponders, remains to be determined.

Environmental Organizations

The initial impetus to demand, or inspire, organizations to be more environmentally friendly came from citizens who possessed a strong environmental ethic.[22] As noted by the cultural anthropologist Margaret Mead, "Never doubt that a small group of thoughtful, committed citizens can change the world. Indeed, it is the only thing that ever has."

Social change often originates at the grassroots level where concerned citizens mobilize other citizens to take action. Social change organizations are not politically monolithic. Some are conservative, some libertarian, some liberal, and some cross political boundaries. Their efforts, when successful, lead to voluntary business adaptations or new government policies.

Environmentalism has a long history in the United States, dating back to the beginning of the Industrial Revolution. In 1836, essayist and public lecturer Ralph Waldo Emerson wrote about his deep appreciation of nature and inspired the formation of the Transcendentalist movement.[23] Transcendentalists emphasized the importance of individualism and that an ideal spiritual state transcended physical existence. They warned against the damage caused to nature by the Industrial Revolution and feared replicating the land, water, and air pollution many had seen in Europe. Henry David Thoreau, one of the best-known transcendentalists, conducted a two-year experiment in simple living on Emerson's property and published his reflections in *Walden*.[24]

A conservation movement gained strength in the late 1800s. In 1886, the Audubon Society was created to protect wildlife. In 1892, conservationist John Muir founded the Sierra Club to protect natural wildlife and forests in California and Nevada from timber industry loggers and farmers who overgrazed land with sheep. In the early 1900s, Republican President Theodore Roosevelt's administration created five national parks, 51 bird reserves, and 150 national forests.[25]

Aldo Leopold's *A Sand County Almanac*, published in 1949, gave further voice and direction to the environmental movement and wildlife preservation.[26] Leopold emphasized living in harmony with nature and opposed the setting aside of public land simply for purposes of hunting and other recreational activities. In *Silent Spring*, published in 1962, Rachel Carson documented how insecticides and pesticides, particularly chemical DDT, though helpful in reducing malaria and saving crop productions, could cause long-term harm to fish, wildlife, and humans.[27]

By the mid-1960s, water and air pollution caused by manufacturing facilities and other businesses became more visible. Concerns previously raised by conservationists and environmentalists dovetailed with a growing anti-corporation student movement engaged in public demonstrations and political lobbying. Using his own funds, Senator Gaylord Nelson organized the first Earth Day for April 22, 1970, to further educate students about the need to preserve natural resources and unite environmental organizations around a common cause.

Government and Market Responses

Government Regulation

In 1969, the Cuyahoga River in Ohio caught fire for at least the 13th time in a century due to the chemical toxins from industrial facilities contained in the water. The drama of social movement protests and the burning of the Cuyahoga River caught the attention of the media, lawyers, and politicians. The Environmental Defense Fund and the Natural Resources Defense Council, created in 1967 and 1970, focused on legal strategies to protect the environment and punish the most egregious environmental polluters. These events, lobbying, and legal pressures led to an onslaught of environmental regulations and policies signed into law by Republican President Richard Nixon (see Exhibit 11.3).

Exhibit 11.3 Key Environmental Regulations During Richard Nixon's Administration	
Clean Air Act (1970)	Amended Clean Air Act of 1963 by establishing national air quality standards and statutory deadlines for compliance
Environmental Protection Agency (1970)	Federal agency established to protect human health and safeguard the natural environment—air, water, and land; consolidated in one federal agency activities for researching, setting standards, monitoring, and enforcing environmental protection
National Environmental Policy Act (1970)	Required environmental impact studies for all federal government projects
Clean Water Act (1972)	Created a permit system to regulate water pollution point sources for industrial and agricultural facilities
Endangered Species Act (1973)	Protected species at risk of extinction, and the ecosystems they depend on, due to economic growth and development

Just because an environmental law is passed by government, however, does not mean organizations will comply. Reasons for noncompliance include not being aware of the law's requirements, disagreement with the law, low likelihood of authorities detecting noncompliance, and the benefits of noncompliance outweighing the costs. Government resources are often limited and an inability by government to monitor or enforce laws can lead to noncompliance.

The Environmental Protection Agency (EPA) has established a compliance assistance website and national compliance assistance centers that provide businesses access to compliance information, advice, and aid.[28] The EPA's Compliance Incentives and Auditing website lists available incentives and offers auditing protocols, Environmental Management Systems tools, and pollution prevention programs for both large and small businesses.[29] To enhance compliance, the EPA complements routine self-reporting with random and targeted on-site inspections.

As noted earlier, sometimes there are trade-offs between environmental performance and economic performance at both the firm and national levels. In the 1980s, President Ronald Reagan thought the pendulum had swung too far in favor of environmental protection at the expense of economic competitiveness. The Reagan administration sought a better balance between environmental interests and business interests through "cooperative regulation" rather than adversarial regulation. Burdensome and inefficient regulations that stymied businesses from competing in a global economy were eliminated or modified. Reagan reduced the EPA's budget and number of employees and explored free market solutions that motivated businesses to voluntarily reduce their environmental impacts.

International Agreements

Pollution knows no international boundaries. Pollutants released into the air or water travel to neighboring nations and can cross oceans, impacting the environmental well-being of distant nations. In 1987, President Reagan signed the Montreal Protocol, an international agreement to phase out chlorofluorocarbons (CFCs) that erode the ozone. A layer of ozone in the stratosphere prevents dangerous ultraviolet light from reaching the Earth's surface. Scientists had determined that the ozone layer was thinning due to increased amounts of chlorine, the primary ingredient in the chemical compound CFC, in the atmosphere. At the time, CFCs were being commonly used as a coolant in refrigerators and air conditioners. The following year, the EPA launched a Toxic Release Inventory (TRI) program to compile data on toxic chemicals released into the environment by certain industries and the federal government.[30] TRI data informed communities about local toxins and contributed to better decision making.

The warming of the Earth from greenhouse gases impacts people in every nation. In June 1992, the United Nations sponsored an "Earth Summit" in Rio de Janeiro, Brazil, to discuss greenhouse gases, alternative sources of energy, and water scarcity. Representatives of 172 governments, including 108 heads of state, and representatives from 2,400 nongovernmental organizations (NGOs) attended the event. One summit outcome was the Climate Change Convention, a non-binding treaty to stabilize atmospheric greenhouse gas concentrations by first establishing a national inventory of greenhouse gas emissions that could serve as a comparative benchmark. The U.S. Congress and President George H. W. Bush approved the treaty.

A follow-up climate change conference was held in Kyoto, Japan, in 1997. The Kyoto Protocol established a goal of reducing worldwide greenhouse gas emissions 5 percent below the 1990 level by 2012. The national goals would be binding for industrialized nations that signed the agreement, but not for developing nations. Nations that surpassed their goals could sell the excess capacity to nations who did not meet their goals. Ratified by more than 180 nations, the Kyoto Protocol went into effect in 2005 without the consent of the United States.

President George W. Bush withdrew from the Kyoto ratification process because achieving the emissions goal assigned to the United States—7 percent below the 1990 level—would seriously harm the national economy. American businesses would have to implement costly new technologies to reduce carbon emissions. The skyrocketing costs would result in higher-priced products. Fewer people could afford products, which would cause a reduction in sales and revenue, and a significant increase in unemployment. The Bush administration also argued that the treaty created unfair competition because developing nations, such as China and India, were exempt from treaty mandates. Although exempt, the Chinese government linked pay and promotions for local government officials to meeting environmental targets that would help reduce China's severe pollution problems.[31]

Cap and Trade and Climate Exchanges

For the most part, the climate change debate has shifted from whether it is occurring to what appropriate actions should be taken. In 2010, the U.S. Congress had not reached consensus on how to build a green economy: what are its key features, how fast should it be developed, what are its negative impacts on economic growth? Government policy mechanisms for greening the economy typically include implementing a Cap and Trade program, a pollution (carbon) tax, and incentives to develop green technologies.[32] In terms of implementation speed, some interest groups lobby Congress for more aggressive action in light of doomsday climate change projections, whereas others lobby for incremental action in light of estimated costs and projected damage to economic growth.

Cap and Trade, an emissions trading system, is one of the most prominent ideas under consideration. Cap and Trade combines federal controls that limit the amount of pollution permitted with the establishment of a market in which businesses can trade licenses to pollute. In 1990, Congress passed Clean Air Act amendments to address the problem of acid rain. Rainfall, snow, and fog had become more acidic from fossil fuels mostly originating from coal-fired power plants. Acid rain killed fish and damaged plants and buildings. Rather than fining public utilities for their acidic emissions, Congress created a Cap and Trade emissions trading program for public utilities.

Under Cap and Trade, the EPA established a goal of emitting 10 million tons of sulfur dioxide below 1980 levels by 2000, at which time a limit 8.95 million tons of sulfur dioxide emissions per year would become the standard. Emission permits were then allocated among public utility companies based on previous performance to meet long-term reduction goals. A company that exceeded its allocated sulfur dioxide emissions amount had to purchase an equivalent amount of unused permits from companies that polluted less than their allocated limits or pay a substantial fine.

In 2003, the Chicago Climate Exchange was created as a national market to manage a voluntary, yet legally binding, Cap and Trade program for CO_2 and five other greenhouse gas emissions.[33] Its 400 members—which included companies, municipalities, educational institutions, and farmers—agreed to reduce CO_2 emissions 6 percent by 2010. An independent third party verified performance. The exchange closed in 2010 when participants withdrew their membership because Congress failed to pass anticipated Cap and Trade legislation.[34] As of 2011, carbon trading on exchanges no longer takes place in the United States.

In 2005, a similar Climate Exchange Cap and Trade program was created in Europe.[35] The European Climate Exchange, which has more than 100 members, is now the leading emissions trading market in the world. Unlike its Chicago counterpart, the European Climate Exchange continues to operate because of mandatory carbon emissions caps imposed by the Kyoto Protocol on European nation signatories.

There is strong opposition to expanding Cap and Trade programs in the United States.[36] Cap and Trade critics argue that new technologies for capturing carbon emissions are expensive. Energy companies will pass this increased cost on to energy consumers through higher energy rates. As a result, businesses will increase product prices and municipal, state, and federal governments will increase taxes to offset higher energy costs. Low-income people will be disproportionately affected because they have the least amount of discretionary income.

Other Efforts

Some U.S. state and city governments have signed their own versions of the Kyoto Protocol. More than 850 mayors representing 80 million citizens have signed the U.S. Conference of Mayors Climate Protection Agreement, committing them to strive to meet or beat the Kyoto Protocol targets in their own communities.[37] In 2006, California passed the Global Warming Solutions Act, which commits the state to achieve a 25 percent reduction in emissions by 2020 to be in compliance with Kyoto Protocol provisions.

Ten northeastern states participate in the Regional Greenhouse Gas Initiative (RGGI), a Cap and Trade program designed to reduce power plant greenhouse gas emissions 10 percent by 2019.[38] Similarly, six midwestern governors and the premier of the Canadian province of Manitoba have signed the Midwestern Greenhouse Gas Accord.[39] An advisory group has recommended that the participants target 20 percent below 2005 levels by 2020, and 80 percent below 2005 levels by 2050.[40]

Some states have created unique incentives to encourage better environmental performance from organizations. Wisconsin's innovative Green Tier program, initiated in 2006, provides regulatory flexibility, permit streamlining, and other incentives for businesses that implement an Environmental Management System (EMS).[41] Certified Green Tier organizations submit annual reports documenting their environmental performance. Companies piloting the Green Tier program reduced hazardous air pollutant emissions by 30 percent, compared to the 12 percent statewide total.

More than 500 higher education presidents have signed the American College and University Presidents Climate Commitment.[42] Their goal is to reduce carbon emissions on campuses to zero. The schools agreed to complete an emissions inventory, set milestones and target dates, integrate sustainability into the curriculum, and share their action plans and inventory and progress reports with the public.

President Barack Obama's administration addressed some environmental problems through the Economic Stimulus Act of 2009. More than $80 billion in the legislation was allocated to companies generating renewable energy sources, developing clean energy technologies, and creating jobs retrofitting homes to conserve energy.[43] The Obama administration also established higher energy efficiency standards for appliances, cars, and trucks.

Environmental performance has also caught the attention of Wall Street investors and financial research analysts. The Dow Jones Sustainability Index (DJSI) was created in 1999 as a way to track the financial performance of leading sustainability-driven companies.[44] Companies are assessed according to Triple Bottom Line criteria: economic, environmental, and social performance.[45] In 2010, the DJSI World index consisted of the leading 318 sustainable development companies, among a population of 2,500 companies, in 57 industries. Changes are made annually to the index based on environmental performance. For instance, BP was removed from the index in 2010 because of the oil well tragedy in the Gulf of Mexico. Major brokerage houses are also developing measures to quantify environmental performance, compare companies, and predict future performance.[46]

A final market response is the increased availability of funding through venture capitalists, grants, and prizes. Some venture capital funds specifically target environmental markets, such as solar energy. In the first half of 2008, venture capitalists invested more than $2 billion in 139 green technology start-ups.[47] The federal government offers grants, loans, and tax incentives for companies to improve water quality, upgrade energy efficiency, develop green technology, or redevelop environmentally contaminated industrial or commercial (brownfield) sites.[48] Richard Branson, the CEO of Virgin Airlines, has offered a $25 million prize for new technology that can remove CO_2 from the earth's atmosphere.[49]

Competitive Advantages of Being Eco-Friendly

Whether or not global warming is occurring, there are many reasons and competitive advantages for being eco-friendly. Similar to the marketing of ethics and diversity programs within an organization, emphasize the business case when communicating the need for an organization to achieve superior environmental performance. Improving environmental performance is a long-term investment. Changes in organizational operations that improve environmental performance usually entail start-up costs, and sometimes these costs can be excessive. Managers must evaluate these investment costs in comparison to long-term benefits, which include future cost savings, innovative market opportunities, and enhanced employee and community relations that improve operational performance and profitability (see Exhibit 11.4).[50]

Exhibit 11.4 Competitive Advantages of Being Eco-Friendly

COST SAVINGS

- Reduction in escalating energy costs
- Lower insurance premiums for sustainable development initiatives
- Lower bank loan rates for acquisitions due to less environmental risk
- Reduction in costs associated with environmental clean-ups and property damage
- Avoidance of regulatory delays in bringing new products to market
- Greater regulatory flexibility for organizations with an Environmental Management System

INNOVATIVE MARKET OPPORTUNITIES

- Product differentiation through eco-labeling
- New markets for green products and producing green technologies
- Customers with higher environmental expectations develop greater loyalty to products
- Qualifying for green and socially responsible mutual funds provides easier access to capital

(Continued)

Exhibit 11.4 Competitive Advantages of Being Eco-Friendly (*Continued*)
EMPLOYEE RELATIONS BENEFITS
• Many young professionals consider environmental reputation when searching for jobs
• Employees are prouder to be associated with the organization
• Enhances employee commitment and performance
COMMUNITY RELATIONS
• Media outlets highlight the organization as a good citizen
• Community members are more accepting of organizational expansion
• Community activists are more willing to engage in discussions

A bottom-line approach to environmental management change increases the likelihood of other managers valuing being eco-friendly. Which competitive advantages in Exhibit 11.4 are relevant to organizational operations? Use these reasons to justify, and support, new environmental initiatives.

Going Green Examples

The media is particularly fond of highlighting the accomplishments of green companies. Many magazine, television, and radio websites provide Internet links to environmental exemplars, which results in free publicity for eco-friendly organizations. *Newsweek*[51] and *Inc.*[52] rank and spotlight the best green organizations. *Fortune* is among the many magazines with websites dedicated to environmental issues and eco-friendly businesses.[53] State and local media also provide free publicity for green business. For instance, WISC-TV's extensive "going green" website offers links to Wisconsin business profiles and websites.[54]

In addition, environmental advocacy groups direct consumers to green products and businesses. Green America's online *National Green Pages* sorts more than 10,000 eco-friendly products for consumer searches.[55] Green shopping websites make it easy for consumers to use eco-friendliness as a purchasing criterion.[56] Even mainstream magazines direct consumers to green products. In 2007, *National Geographic* acquired the "Green Guide," which reviews products and offers consumers help in making environmentally friendly buying decisions.[57]

Walmart

Walmart has long been disparaged by consumer activists for being environmentally insensitive and by community activists for contributing to the collapse of small downtown businesses. Walmart is now among the leading corporations to capitalize on the link between eco-friendliness and profits. The title of the company's 2010 Sustainability Report is "We Save People Money So They Can Live Better."[58] Walmart has developed a sustainability website to communicate its eco-friendly plans and accomplishments to a broad audience.[59]

Walmart is the nation's largest private user of electricity and owns the second-largest fleet of trucks. In 2005, Walmart developed short-term sustainability goals such as 25 percent efficiency increases in fleet vehicles, 30 percent reduction in store energy use, and 25 percent reduction in solid waste within three years. Surpassing these goals generated tremendous savings and revenue opportunities for Walmart. Eliminating excessive packaging on its private-label line of toys saved $2.4 million in annual shipping costs, installing auxiliary power units on trucks saved $26 million annually in fuel costs, and installing balers to recycle and sell plastics generated $28 million in extra revenue.[60] In 2009, Walmart reduced plastic bag waste by 66.5 million pounds. These goals have been expanded to (1) 100 percent renewable energy, (2) zero waste, and (3) increased sales of sustainable products.[61]

Walmart's environmental improvements impact the world's economy. It is now the nation's largest seller of organic products. By guaranteeing the lowest prices, it makes organic products more affordable for people with less discretionary income, which increases demand. Other companies are developing organic versions of their well-known products to fill Walmart shelf space allocated to green products.

Walmart is also impacting the global business carbon footprint by greening its supply chain. The company has more than 100,000 suppliers. Those wanting to do business with Walmart must themselves be environmentally friendly. In 2010, 93 percent of Walmart's direct sourcing merchandise originated in factories highly rated for their environmental and social practices.[62] Import suppliers must also source 95 percent of their production from factories that receive one of Walmart's top two highest audited ratings for environmental and social practices.

In 2010, the company announced a goal to eliminate 20 million metric tons of greenhouse gases from its supply chain by 2016, equivalent to removing 3.8 million automobiles from the road for a year.[63] Walmart is partnering with the Environmental Defense Fund, long known for suing corporations for their environmental misdeeds, on this effort.

Walmart is also developing a system for educating consumers through "eco-labels." In 2010, the company embarked on a five-year project to create a universal rating system for assessing the environmental and social sustainability of all products.[64] This information will appear on product labels in Walmart stores.

Green Business Parks

A central theme of eco-friendliness is waste equals food.[65] One organization's waste can be another organization's input. This theme has been operationalized within a business park in Umea, Sweden, where 100 percent of waste by-products are reused or recycled.

In 2000, the Umea business park's occupants included a Ford Motor Company dealership, a gas station, a car wash, a convenience store, and a McDonald's. The heat generated by the McDonald's cooking grills and the convenience store's refrigerator system was circulated through underground pipes to other businesses, as was runoff water from the car wash.[66] Other eco-friendly practices within the business park include green roofs, solar panels, building parts that can be disassembled and reused, electricity generated from a coastal windmill, and sewage converted to fertilizer.

Going Green Actions

The environmental literature overflows with lists of actions organizations can take to be more environmentally friendly. One of the most thorough lists is the "Green Masters Program Checklist" developed by the University of Wisconsin-Madison.[67] Exhibit 11.5 highlights two recommended actions for each of the 10 categories.

As discussed in Chapter 9, a moral manager is someone who not only puts into place organizational systems that reinforce ethical behaviors, but is also a moral person. The same consistency is required when inspiring subordinates to engage in

Exhibit 11.5 Green Actions	
Actions	**Examples**
Energy	• Measure energy used per dollar revenue or per square foot of building • Replace current light fixtures with energy efficient light bulbs
Climate Change	• Measure greenhouse gas emissions per dollar revenue or per unit of output • Identify and quantify sources of emissions
Water	• Measure gallons water consumed per dollar revenue • Retain and reuse storm water using managed water runoff techniques
Waste	• Measure pounds waste per dollar revenue or per unit of output • Set all copiers and printers to two-sided
Transportation	• Provide financial incentives for employees to use public transportation to work • Use teleconferences or web conferences rather than traveling for face-to-face meetings
Purchasing	• Purchase from environmentally friendly office suppliers • Replace distant vendors with more local vendors
Natural Resources	• Plant native, water-efficient plants on company grounds and near buildings for shade • Eliminate use of pesticides or synthetic chemical fertilizers
Educational Outreach	• Develop an annual sustainability report • Share your organization's experiences and best practices in a mentoring relationship with another business to replicate benefits
Social Stratification	• Ensure all employees have access to natural light and fresh air • Work with a local technical school on tailored training for future employees
Systematic Evaluation	• Complete a baseline audit that identifies all company actions, inputs, and outputs that affect the environment • Employ a system to prioritize environmental actions

Tips and Techniques

Office Depot's Advice on How to Save Money by Going Green*

- Energy Star–qualified office equipment saves up to 75% in electricity use.
- Compact fluorescent bulbs last 10 times longer than incandescent bulbs and save electricity.
- Power strips save electricity.
- Daylighting saves electricity.
- Remanufactured ink and toner cartridges cost an average of 15% less than national brands and come with a 100% money back quality guarantee.
- Recycle empty ink and toner cartridges for discounted prices.
- Use digital storage solutions.
- Donate unwanted products and furniture for tax deductions.
- Use reusable coffee mugs instead of disposable cups.

---

* Office Depot, "Top 20 Ways to Go Green at Work," available at www.community.officedepot.com/top20list.asp , accessed 12/3/10.

eco-friendly activities at work—managers must practice what they preach and adopt eco-friendly behaviors within their own lifestyles. The list of individual lifestyle going green actions typically includes buying a fuel-efficient car, recycling, reusing, energy and water conservation, and stopping junk mail.[68] *EnAct: Steps to Greener Living* provides more than 1,000 actions for conserving energy and living a green lifestyle that can be performed individually or with friends and neighbors.[69] Exhibit 11.6 lists 15 rather simple steps offered by the Natural Resources Defense Council for being a better environmental steward.[70]

Exhibit 11.6 15 Simple Steps for Greening Your Lifestyle

Unfriendly Environmental Action	Environmental Impact	Corrective Action
1. Using plastic and paper grocery bags	Twelve million barrels of oil are used to make the 88.5 billion plastic bags consumed annually. It takes four times more energy to make paper bags.	Use reusable bags made of cotton or nylon.
2. Buying bottled water, even if you plan to recycle	When recycling, it takes 26 bottles of water to produce the plastic for a one-liter bottle, and doing so pollutes 25 liters of groundwater.	Use reusable water bottles made from materials such as stainless steel or aluminum that are not likely to degrade over time.

(Continued)

Exhibit 11.6 15 Simple Steps for Greening Your Lifestyle (Continued)

3. Receiving unwanted catalogs	Each year, 19 billion catalogs are mailed to American consumers, which consume 53 million trees and 56 billion gallons of wastewater to produce.	Visit www.catalogchoice.org to stop unwanted catalogs.
4. Using conventional laundry detergents	Conventional laundry detergents contain many chemicals and pollutants that damage the environment and personal health.	Choose natural detergents and other laundry products that are plant-based, concentrated, and biodegradable.
5. Using hot water when washing clothes	About 90 percent of the energy used by a typical washing machine is used to heat the water.	Wash and rinse most clothes in cold water. Wash heavily soiled clothing in warm water.
6. Using a clothes dryer	The clothes dryer is the second biggest household energy user, after the refrigerator.	Hang wet clothes on a line in the sun and air or on a folding rack. When using the dryer, clear the lint filter after each load and dry only full loads of clothes.
7. Leaking toilets	One in every five toilets leak. A leaking toilet can waste anywhere between 30 and 500 gallons of water every day.	Repair old or poorly fitting toilet flapper valves.
8. Conventional toilet paper made from virgin fiber	If every household bought just one four-pack of 260-sheet recycled bath tissue, it would eliminate 60,600 pounds of chlorine pollution, preserve 356 million gallons of fresh water, and save nearly 1 million trees.	Use recycled toilet paper.
9. Disposable virgin fiber paper towels	If every household replaced just one roll of virgin fiber paper towels (70 sheets) with 100 percent recycled ones, 544,000 trees would be saved.	Use microfiber towels that can be washed and reused.
10. Washing dishes by hand and running a partially loaded dishwasher	Compared to washing dishes by hand, running a fully loaded dishwasher—without pre-rinsing the dishes—can use a third less water, saving 10 to 20 gallons of water a day.	For dirty dishes, scrape large pieces of food into a compost, do not pre-rinse dishes, and run a fully loaded dishwasher.

11. High-energy refrigerators	The typical refrigerator accounts for 10 percent to 15 percent of the average home energy bill each month.	Twice a year, clean condenser coils in the back of the refrigerator and set refrigerator temperature between 38 and 42 degrees.
12. Thermostat set too high in winter and too low in summer	Approximately 25% of the energy consumed in homes is attributed to heating and cooling. Lowering your thermostat one degree can reduce heating bills by as much as 10%.	Use an automated "smart" thermostat. During the winter, set thermostats to 68 degrees or less during the daytime and 55 degrees before going to sleep or when away for the day. During the summer, set thermostats to 78 degrees or more.
13. Traditional dry cleaning	Traditional dry cleaners use a cancer-causing chemical called perchloroethylene (perc). Traces of this toxic chemical remain on clothes after dry cleaning and evaporate into the air in your car or home.	When buying clothes, choose fabrics that do not require dry cleaning. If dry cleaning is required, use a perc-free dry cleaner.
14. Underinflated automobile tires	More than a quarter of all cars and nearly one-third of all SUVs, vans, and pickups have underinflated tires. If every American kept his or her tires properly inflated, 2.8 billion gallons of gasoline would be saved annually.	Check tire pressure and properly inflate.
15. Trash	The energy saved from recycling a single aluminum can operates a television for three hours.	Buy products in returnable and recyclable containers and recycle as much as you can.

Let's Build a Building

Soil Quality

You are responsible for overseeing the construction of an eight-unit student apartment building on land you own near a college. The bank requires that you have at least 50 percent of the apartments pre-leased to secure funding for construction. To your pleasant surprise, you quickly obtain signed leases with eight students for the $900 apartment rentals. Occupancy begins August 1 for the fall semester.

The architect and general contractor work together on designing the apartments. The previous owner of the land was a dry cleaner. According to the initial environmental evaluation that was completed when you purchased the land, there was no evidence of environmental contamination.

(Continued)

The general contractor begins excavation on February 1, six months prior to the building opening. On the third and final day of excavation, the general contractor finds a vein of soil running the length of the property that appears to be contaminated. The only way to know for sure is to conduct another soil test. If the soil is contaminated, it will cost $15,000 for soil remediation.

The project is already three weeks behind due to spring rains and the remediation will cause another delay. The extra delay means you will miss the August 1 opening and be in violation of the signed student leases. The students will then cancel their leases and rent elsewhere. As a result, you will lose $7,200 a month in rental income (eight apartments times $900), which amounts to $86,400 in revenue for the year. In addition, the extra costs will force you to increase rents to $1,100. That will make them difficult to rent in the price-competitive student market.

You are legally responsible for hiring an excavator to test the soil. But first you ask the general contractor if there is really any health risk from the potentially contaminated soil. The general contractor says, "No, it's simply another example of government overregulating business. The vein has been on the site for years and is near the bottom of the foundation. Nobody will be digging that deep again. If it is contaminated, the contamination is harmless and will not be a health risk to tenants. I'm willing to ignore the problem if you want me to." The general contractor is also willing to avoid the potential problem because the general contractor will lose business if you cancel the project.

What would you do? Would you

1. Have the soil tested and lose the student leases?
2. Not test the soil?
   Why?

Managing the Environmental Change Process

Becoming an eco-friendly organization requires leadership from the CEO or president and a values-based organizational culture that not only honors compliance with environmental regulations, but also emphasizes the benefits associated with exceeding them. Assign one manager primary responsibility for implementing environmental change initiatives. Depending on company size, the environmental champion could be the environmental health and safety director, an environmental manager, or a manager whose multiple duties include environmental performance.

Greening the organization is a concept that is well regarded by employees and relatively easy for them to rally behind. Make sure employees are well informed about the organization's environmental efforts. According to a Society for Human Resource Management survey, three-quarters of the employees in companies without an environmental program want to "go green."[71] Employees who score high on organizational citizenship behaviors can play an essential role in overseeing the implementation process, ensuring that appropriate tasks are completed and monitored.[72]

Environmental activities cut across departments and work units. Create a cross-functional Green Committee composed of go-getters to address common concerns, share knowledge, and ensure successful implementation of action plans. Committee duties can include acknowledging previous environmental accomplishments, gathering relevant data, engaging employees in small incremental changes, addressing interdepartmental issues, inspiring employees by taking on a large project that has a high likelihood of success, enhancing customer and supplier awareness of environmental efforts, and communicating environmental successes to other employees.

Exhibit 11.7 summarizes 10 aspects of the environmental change process, beginning with the importance of one environmental manager held accountable for initiatives. At Edgewood College, a small liberal arts college in Madison, Wisconsin, the environmental change process began with the creation of a Green Campus Task Force

Exhibit 11.7 Managing Environmental Change

Aspect	Focus/Objectives	Tools and Methodologies
Environmental Manager	One manager is accountable for environmental initiatives.	The environmental manager is a leadership position requiring political skills and broad knowledge of organizational operations.
Management Support	Obtain vocal and visible support from CEO, COO, and other executives.	Ask CEO and others about their environmental vision for firm; introduce top management to business case for sustainability; request they convey this message to rest of the organization.
Green Committee	Achieve buy-in from work units throughout the organization.	Choose go-getters from different work units to oversee environmental performance, elicit ideas, and manage the implementation of action plans.
Vision and Strategy	Develop the vision of a sustainable firm in a sustainable society.	Integrate eco-friendliness into vision, strategy, and financial models; link environmental action plans to the vision and strategy.
Training, Education, Coaching	Use coaching style to educate all employees about putting environmental principles into practice.	Adapt training materials to specific organizational context and employee work units; train the trainers and coaches; develop engaging training materials.
Employee Involvement	Foster team building activities, encourage suggestions, and continually reinforce.	Teams can focus on reducing wastes and resources used; follow through on employee suggestions; encourage friendly competition among employees and work units.
Practical Application & Innovation	Determine "low-hanging fruit," practical change ideas for immediate and long-term implementation.	Develop mechanisms for reviewing suggestions and innovations; provide resources to experiment and try new ideas; provide on-going coaching; share lessons learned.
Feedback and Measurement	Benchmark, track, measure, evaluate, provide feedback, and reward results.	Develop baseline measures, document, and post results; translate resource savings into financial language; recognize and communicate achievements.
Influence	Involve employees, suppliers, customers, competitors, shareholders, and community members.	Encourage all stakeholders to attend workshops; partner with other groups; educate suppliers and customers through booklets, product labels, annual reports, and website resources.
Integrate into All Business Functions	Make sustainability a normal business consideration.	Implement an Environmental Management System (EMS); address at all meetings and include in all reports; include in business plan, performance evaluations, and bonuses.

Source: Brian Nattrass and Mary Altomare, *The Natural Step for Business: Wealth, Ecology and the Evolutionary Corporation* (British Columbia, Canada: New Society Publishers): 152–153; copyright 1999, with permission to adapt from New Society Publishers.

to more directly encourage faculty, staff, and students in developing an eco-friendly campus. The committee catalogued previous green campus accomplishments and shared them with administrators and the campus community. Next, the committee developed a list of environmental indicators to serve as an annual benchmark to measure and report improvements. The committee, in partnership with key staff members, designed and implemented an Environmental Management System in accordance with international standards. These efforts contributed to the school's receiving Green Tier certification from Wisconsin's Department of Natural Resources for superior environmental performance.

Based on these successes, a wide range of environmental projects was undertaken with the support of the college administrators and monitored by the green committee. These included constructing the first LEED-certified residence hall in Wisconsin; implementing many energy-efficient building projects; constructing a 1,200-foot boardwalk on the campus' lakefront property that enabled college personnel, students, community groups, and neighbors to appreciate and manage the wetland; and developing a sustainability tour for visitors and prospective students that highlighted these accomplishments. The school's Planning and Budget Committee approved an energy savings fund into which 50 percent of the energy cost savings are deposited that the Green Campus Task Force, with college approval, can use to fund new environmentally friendly projects. Organization members are regularly informed about these accomplishments and they, in turn, supply ideas for continuous improvement.

Green Mission Statement

Some organizations create an "environmental mission statement" that clearly articulates its relationship with the natural environment. Similar to a Code of Ethics, use the environmental mission statement as a foundation for determining and assessing organizational actions. The Starbucks environmental mission statement in Exhibit 11.8 begins with the need to integrate concern for the environment in all aspects of operations and highlights the interrelationship between profits and environmental performance.[73]

Exhibit 11.8 Starbucks Environmental Mission Statement

Starbucks is committed to a role of environmental leadership in all facets of our business.

We will fulfill this mission by a commitment to:

Understanding of environmental issues and sharing information with our partners.

Developing innovative and flexible solutions to bring about change.

Striving to buy, sell and use environmentally friendly products.

Recognizing that fiscal responsibility is essential to our environmental future.

Instilling environmental responsibility as a corporate value.

Measuring and monitoring our progress for each project.

Encouraging all partners to share in our mission.

Green Suppliers

According to the open systems theory of management, organizations receive inputs from the external environment and transform them into outputs released back into the external environment. Going green entails making sure that the inputs being received are themselves environmentally friendly. Hold suppliers accountable for providing green products and operating in an eco-friendly manner.

As discussed earlier, many websites are available that highlight green products. Energy Star certification ensures that products are energy efficient. The government program, initiated by the Clinton administration in 1992, certifies that the product—such as a computer, heating and cooling system, lighting, and appliances—uses at least 10 percent, and usually around 30 percent, less energy than required by federal standards. Similarly, a coalition of apparel companies is developing an eco-friendly labeling system that allows consumers to compare the environmental performance of clothing and shoe supply chains.[74]

Darcy Hitchcock and Marsha Willard have developed a sustainable products checklist that organizations can use for comparative evaluation purposes when deciding which product to purchase.[75] Exhibit 11.9 lists five key factors that can be scored on a 1 to 5 scale. A 5 means the product meets the criteria at the highest level. Not all factors matter equally. The second column allows buyers to weight the importance of each factor (e.g., 10 equals highest importance). Multiply the weight assigned to a factor by the score to determine a multiplicative eco-friendly

Exhibit 11.9 Sustainable Products Checklist

Factor	Factor Weight (1–10 Value)	Product A Score (1–5 Value)	Product A Multiplicative Score	Product B Score (1–5 Value)	Product B Multiplicative Score
Reusable	10	2	20	3	30
Recyclable	8	3	24	2	16
Biodegradable	5	1	5	5	25
Energy Efficient	10	3	30	4	40
Nontoxic	8	3	24	4	32
Minimal Packaging	7	4	28	2	14
Locally Available	5	4	20	2	10
Total			151		167

score for each factor. Then add all the multiplicative scores for a final total and compare with final totals for other products under consideration. For this particular example, Product B is a more sustainable choice, 167 points versus 151 points for Product A.

Walmart goes deeper into the supply chain by making sure that its supplier operations meet high environmental standards. In Walmart's initial attempt to create a Supplier Sustainability Index—a universal rating system for assessing a supplier's environmental and social sustainability record—the company developed measures for four performance categories: (1) energy and climate, (2) material efficiency, (3) natural resources, and (4) people and community. Assessment questions for each category appear in the "Best Practice in Use" exhibit.[76] Walmart pushes best practices further down the supply chain by giving suppliers credit for applying similar eco-friendly standards on their suppliers.

BEST PRACTICE IN USE

Walmart's Supplier Sustainability Index Questions

Energy and Climate: *Reduce energy costs and greenhouse gas emissions*

1. Have you measured your corporate greenhouse gas emissions? (Y/N)
2. Have you opted to report your greenhouse gas emissions to the Carbon Disclosure Project (CDP)? (Y/N)
3. What are your total greenhouse gas emissions reported in your most recently completed report? (Enter total metric tons CO2, e.g. CDP6 Questionnaire, Section 2b—Scope 1 and 2 emissions)
4. Have you set publicly available greenhouse gas reduction targets? If yes, what are those targets? (Enter total metric tons and target date; 2 fields or leave blank)

Material Efficiency: *Reduce waste and enhance quality*
Scores will be automatically calculated based on your participation in the Packaging Scorecard in addition to the following:

5. If measured, please report total amount of solid waste generated from the facilities that produce your product(s) for Walmart Inc. for the most recent year measured. (Enter total lbs)
6. Have you set publicly available solid waste reduction targets? If yes, what are those targets? (Enter total lbs and target date; 2 fields or leave blank)
7. If measured, please report total water use from the facilities that produce your product(s) for Walmart Inc. for the most recent year measured. (Enter total gallons)
8. Have you set publicly available water use reduction targets? If yes, what are those targets? (Enter total gallons and target date; 2 fields or leave blank)

Natural Resources: *High-quality, responsibly sourced raw materials*

9. Have you established publicly available sustainability purchasing guidelines for your direct suppliers that address issues such as environmental compliance, employment practices, and product/ingredient safety? (Y/N)
10. Have you obtained 3rd party certifications for any of the products that you sell to Walmart? If so, from the list of certifications below, please select those for which any of your products are, or utilize materials that are, currently certified.

People and Community: *Responsible & ethical production*

11. Do you know the location of 100% of the facilities that produce your product(s)? (Y/N)

12. Before beginning a business relationship with a manufacturing facility, do you evaluate their quality of production and capacity for production? (Y/N)

13. Do you have a process for managing social compliance at the manufacturing level? (Y/N)

14. Do you work with your supply base to resolve issues found during social compliance evaluations and also document specific corrections and improvements? (Y/N)

15. Do you invest in community development activities in the markets you source from and/or operate within? (Y/N)

Environmental Management System (EMS)

The International Organization for Standardization (ISO), a nongovernmental organization, has worked closely with industries, technical experts, and other stakeholders to develop an Environmental Management System (EMS) plan for achieving superior environmental performance.[77] An EMS is the basic component of ISO 14001 certification, a competitive advantage in a marketplace in which more organizations are using a green screen to choose suppliers. This is a voluntary self-regulatory system not mandated by government regulation.[78] An EMS typically improves stakeholder relationships by reducing the environmental risk imposed on a community.[79]

The EMS plan is a document that describes how the organization conducts environmental policy development, environmental planning, environmental implementation, environmental monitoring and corrective actions, and management review. The document must contain sufficient detail for an employee to understand how these environmental processes operate.

Exhibit 11.10 highlights procedures to document each of the five sections of an EMS plan. An employee, after reviewing the EMS, should know exactly what to do if he or she wants to propose a new environmental policy or make an environmental performance recommendation. Audit the EMS annually to ensure that the procedures are operating effectively.

Exhibit 11.10 Environmental Management System (EMS) Plan

What are the procedures for:

ENVIRONMENTAL POLICY

- Developing environmental policies?

ENVIRONMENTAL PLANNING

- Identifying operations that impact the environment?
- Identifying environmental risks?
- Identifying applicable environmental laws and regulations?

(Continued)

Exhibit 11.10 Environmental Management System (EMS) Plan (*Continued*)

- Establishing short- and long-term environmental objectives and targets?
- Developing action plans aimed at achieving the environmental objectives and targets?

ENVIRONMENTAL IMPLEMENTATION AND OPERATION

- Determining who is responsible for specific aspects of environmental performance?
- Determining and developing environmental training activities?
- Developing environmental emergency plans?
- Communicating environmental issues and accomplishments to employees and external stakeholders?

ENVIRONMENTAL CHECKING AND CORRECTIVE ACTION

- Maintaining records related to environmental performance?
- Monitoring and assessing key environmental objectives and performance measures?
- Determining corrective actions?
- Auditing the Environmental Management System?

MANAGEMENT REVIEW

- Managerial review of environmental performance, including responses to environmental emergencies and the adequacy of environmental accomplishments?

Environmental Risk Assessment

A key aspect of an EMS is managing environmental risk. Each organization has a unique set of environmental input, throughput, and output risks. Assess the environmental performance of suppliers, because they can significantly disrupt organizational operations. Sony incurred negative publicity when illegal cadmium was found in PlayStation cables purchased from suppliers.[80]

Exhibit 11.11 provides a list of questions to consider when performing an environmental risk assessment. Answering these questions can help organizations identify environmental risks within the supplier–operations–customer value chain.[81]

Managers often make risk assumptions that are biased toward a favored outcome. The environmental risk assessment items in Exhibit 11.11 are, as much as possible, stated in a way that requires gathering objective information. Calculating risk is an art, not a science, and requires impartiality and rationality. Ignoring risks, such as Sony not examining its PlayStation cables for cadmium, can cause long-term damages that could have been averted.

Exhibit 11.11 Identifying Environmental Risks

Value Chain Phase	Sample Questions to Help Identify Environmental Risk
Suppliers	• What substances go into the products suppliers sell to us? Are they toxic?
	• What resources (energy, water, and materials) are our suppliers most dependent on? Are they abundant or constrained, now and in the near future?
	• Do our suppliers pollute? Do they meet all applicable laws? Will legal requirements get tighter for them?
Company Operations	• How big is our environmental footprint?
	• What resources are we most dependent on and how much do we use?
	• What emissions do we release into the air or water?
	• How do we dispose of waste?
	• How up-to-date is our Environmental Management System?
	• What are the chances of a spill, leak, or release of hazardous materials?
	• Have others in our industry had problems?
	• What local, state, federal, or international regulations apply to our business? Are we in full compliance? Are these regulations getting tighter?
Customers	• Are there hazardous substances in our products?
	• How much energy (or water or other resources) does our product require customers to use?
	• What do customers do with our products when they are done with them? What should happen if we are required to take the products back?

Source: Daniel C. Esty and Andrew S. Winston, *Green to Gold* (New Haven, CT: Yale University Press): 117; copyright 2006, with permission to adapt from Yale University Press.

The Natural Step (TNS) Framework and Cost Reductions

An increasing number of communities and businesses are using The Natural Step (TNS) framework as a conceptual tool for environmental analysis and action plan development.[82] The TNS framework attributes the root causes of environmental problems to four issues: removing too many substances from the Earth's crust, producing too many synthetic compounds that are difficult for nature to break down, manipulating the ecosystem, and inefficiently and unfairly meeting human needs worldwide.

TNS helps frame an organization's environmental management practices within a broad vision of sustainable development.[83] Many companies have used the framework, including IKEA, Nike, Interface, and Hot Lips Pizza.[84] The city government of Madison, Wisconsin, has adopted TNS as a common framework for fostering cooperation among 2,700 employees working for different divisions and agencies.[85]

TNS is a good beginning point for determining what changes in organizational operations could improve environmental performance. Have work units, total quality management teams, or gainsharing teams explore the following three TNS objectives to reduce the use of resources that damage environmental well-being.

Objective #1—Reduce Wasteful Dependence on Fossil Fuels and Underground Metals and Minerals

- What scarce minerals and materials does the organization use?
- How can the scarce minerals and materials be substituted with minerals and materials that are more abundant in nature?
- How can the organization use its mined materials more efficiently?

Objective #2—Reduce Wasteful Dependence on Chemicals and Synthetic Compounds

- What chemicals and synthetic compounds does the organization use?
- How can the chemicals and synthetic compounds be substituted with natural compounds or those that break down more easily in nature?
- How can the organization use its synthetic compounds more efficiently?

Objective #3—Reduce Encroachment on Nature

- What land, water, and wildlife resources does the organization use?
- Are any of the organization's uses of land, water, and wildlife resources unnecessary?
- How can the organization use its land, water, and wildlife resources more efficiently?

After applying the TNS analysis, create a list of issues the organization could address to improve its environmental performance and an action plan for doing so. Use the team problem-solving process described in Chapter 10 to develop and prioritize solutions. Then pick a "low-hanging fruit"—an inexpensive solution that is relatively easy to implement. Closely monitor the potential obstacles raised by the devil's advocate. Success in achieving the low-hanging fruit solution will help employees gain the confidence needed to successfully implement more complicated solutions.

Many organizations experience similar environmental problems. Attend local and industry meetings that discuss best practices in environmental management. Ask the local public utility to perform an energy audit and provide onsite consultation on how to save money by reducing energy use. Document organizational waste within each work unit and determine how to eliminate it. If the waste cannot be eliminated, then locate organizations willing to purchase or use the waste. Conduct communications through email, rather than using paper, and develop an online document storage system. Document the amount of business travel conducted during a particular time period. Determine which offsite meetings could have been conducted through teleconferencing, video conferencing, or interactive email communications.

Two other items with huge environmental impacts, and potentially high cost savings, that managers can explore are product packaging and design and building design. These issues are discussed in the next two sections.

Product Packaging and Design

The European Union's Packaging and Packaging Waste Directive, passed in 1994, provides a glimpse into a major environmental management trend that is likely to impact business operations in the United States.[86] The law originated in Germany, where product packages had accounted for approximately 25 percent to 30 percent of scarce landfill space. All businesses operating within the European Union (EU) are now responsible for directly recovering and recycling product packaging, or they have to pay a Green Dot licensing fee to a third party that collects and recycles the packaging.

Packaging refers to both the package immediately surrounding the product and the transportation container—everything except the product itself. The EU law covers cardboard, plastic, metals, wood, paper, crates, drums, pallets, and Styrofoam containers. The EU program licenses more than 130,000 companies and 460 billion packaging items.

Environmentalists anticipate legislating cradle to cradle laws that would regulate the product itself. These products are designed to achieve zero waste, which means no end to the product life cycle.[87] Every aspect of production waste is reused again in either operations or by another organization, as described earlier by the Umea, Sweden, business park occupants. After use, the product is broken down into its component parts and then reused or recycled, rather than disposed of in a landfill. Organizations can obtain cradle to cradle certification for products from an independent third party.[88]

In 2006, Walmart developed a sustainable packaging scorecard in association with its goal to be packaging neutral by 2025.[89] Walmart defines packaging neutral as "all packaging recovered or recycled at our stores and Clubs will be equal to the amount of packaging used by the products on our shelves." The actual scorecard consists of nine factors, each with an assigned weight.

Green Buildings

Employees spend a tremendous amount of their lives at the workplace. One of the most visible signs of caring for the environment and employees is operating in a green building. The greenness of a company's building or office says a lot about organizational values and quickly establishes the company as an environmental leader in the community. Green buildings improve employee health, reduce energy costs, and limit detrimental environmental impacts.

In the United States, buildings account for 38 percent of all CO_2 emissions, 72 percent of electricity use, 40 percent of raw materials use, 39 percent of energy use,

30 percent of waste output, and 14 percent of potable water consumption.[90] The United States Green Building Council's Leadership in Energy and Environmental Design (LEED) rating system provides eco-friendly measurement standards for certifying building construction and remodeling.[91]

The green building movement is growing rapidly. LEED building certification began in 1998. In November 2010, the amount of LEED-certified buildings surpassed 1 billion square feet, with another 6 billion square feet registered, accounting for 36,000 commercial projects.[92] Some organizations use LEED's building guidelines but do not apply for certification because of documentation cost issues or a lack of interest in being officially certified.

In the spirit of continuous improvement, LEED has evolved through different certification versions. Three common complaints have been that LEED requirements add to building costs, the point system can be manipulated, and the system seems very bureaucratic.[93] In 2009, version 3.0 became the new LEED guideline.[94] The four levels of LEED certification are Basic (40 points), Silver (50 points), Gold (60 points), and Platinum (80 points). Exhibit 11.12 provides examples of eco-friendly practices, and the number of points available, for each of the seven LEED 2009 new construction and major renovations categories.

Exhibit 11.12 The LEED Version 3.0 Rating System

Category	Points	Practice
Sustainable Sites	26	• Construction activity pollution prevention* • Appropriateness of selected site • Brownfield redevelopment • Alternative transportation availability • Stormwater design
Water Efficiency	10	• Water use reduction* • Water efficient landscaping • Innovative wastewater technologies
Energy & Atmosphere	35	• Fundamental commissioning of building energy systems* • Minimum energy performance* • Fundamental refrigerant management* • Optimize energy performance • Green power
Materials & Resources	14	• Storage and collection of recyclables* • Building reuse • Construction waste management • Materials reuse • Recycled content

Indoor Environmental Quality	15	• Minimum indoor air quality performance (IAQ)* • Environmental tobacco smoke control* • Increased ventilation • Low-emitting materials • Controllability of systems • Thermal comfort • Daylight and views
Innovation in Design	6	• Innovation in design (beyond LEED requirements) • LEED accredited professional
Regional Priority	4	• Environmental importance for project's region

*Indicates a required practice.

Environmental Performance Indicators and Sustainability Reporting

Continuous environmental improvement entails creating historical benchmark measurements documenting previous environmental performance, measuring current environmental performance, and developing goals and targets for future environmental performance.

Each organization has a unique set of environmental impacts. The Natural Step section of this chapter suggests areas for environmental impact reductions. Many measurable environmental impacts appear in Exhibit 11.5 (green actions) and Exhibit 11.11 (environmental risks). Gather information to measure these impacts and document continuous improvement.

Climate Care, owned by J. P. Morgan, provides a simple Internet-based carbon calculator for business use.[95] The calculator requires data for office CO_2 consumption, company travel mileage, freight mileage and weight, and additional carbon emissions.

Link the analysis of environmental performance measures to organizational strategy. If an organization is in a growth strategy, for instance, an increase in energy use could be a healthy sign because business is expanding. Therefore, rather than an accumulated amount, a more useful measure for growing companies is a ratio of energy use per revenue dollar.[96] Share the performance indicator results with all employees so they know whether improvement is occurring, and use the results as benchmarks for new goals and targets.

An environmental financial statement is another type of performance indicator. Baxter International's environmental financial statement quantifies the financial impact of its global environmental management program.[97] Baxter's environmental programs generated $82.6 million in cost savings from 2002 through 2007, triple the cost of the programs. From 2005 to 2009, Baxter's revenue grew more than 27 percent, but energy use increased by only 1 percent, greenhouse gas emissions decreased by 5 percent, and water usage declined by 9 percent. Environmental savings and costs avoidance for 2009 totaled $7.2 million.

Global Reporting Initiative (GRI), an international multi-stakeholder coalition, provides general guidelines for sustainability reporting that allow for some environmental performance comparisons between organizations.[98] The guidelines have been used by more than 1,500 organizations, including large corporations, small businesses, NGOs, and public agencies.

The GRI reporting framework was developed with input from businesses, investors, accountants, and activists, and it takes into account economic, environmental, and social performance measures. The environmental performance section discusses EMS variables and provides performance measures for environmental inputs (e.g., material, energy, water) and outputs (e.g., emissions, effluents, waste). In 2006, after extensive public review and feedback, GRI released the third generation of reporting guidelines.

Carbon Offsets and Green Philanthropy

Some organizations reduce the carbon waste on Earth by purchasing carbon offsets equivalent to their carbon footprint and participating in green philanthropy. Carbon offsets entail paying another organization to reduce greenhouse gas emissions on the company's behalf. Companies such as Dell, Google, and Nike calculate their current greenhouse gas emissions and then purchase an equivalent or proportional amount of carbon offsets.

The most common carbon offsets are investing in tree plantings and forestry projects, clean and renewable energy projects, and energy efficiency projects in other parts of the world. When making travel arrangements at Travelocity.com, consumers can make a financial contribution to the Conservation Fund's Go Zero program, which plants native trees that offset the carbon emissions associated with the trip.[99] Organizations can also purchase carbon credits from climate exchanges, which reduce the amount of carbon credits available to high-polluting organizations.

Many nonprofit organizations are dedicated to reducing detrimental environmental impacts. The nonprofit "One Percent for the Planet" consists of more than 1,400 companies committed to donating 1 percent of annual sales revenue to environmental groups.[100] In 2009, the nonprofit raised more than $15 million for 2,200 environmental groups.

SUMMARY

Ethical organizations place a high value on appropriately managing the Earth's scarce resources and creating environmentally healthy workplaces for their employees. Eco-friendly organizations tend to have lower energy costs and find it easier to attract and maintain high-quality employees.

This chapter explored a wide variety of environmental management techniques. Organizations can achieve superior environmental performance by

- Managing the environmental change process
- Creating an EMS plan that documents relevant organizational procedures
- Conducting an environmental risk assessment
- Using The Natural Step objectives to develop action plans
- Redesigning the product to achieve zero waste
- Operating in green buildings
- Developing performance indicators to measure continuous improvement
- Reporting the results of these efforts

Organizations adopting these procedures will reduce costs, be a step ahead of regulatory trends, and contribute to the environmental well-being of future generations.

KEY WORDS

Triple Bottom Line; climate change; Americum; Transcendentalists; Earth Day; Montreal Protocol; Kyoto Protocol; Cap and Trade; Green Tier; Dow Jones Sustainability Index; waste equals food; sustainable products checklist; Environmental Management System (EMS); The Natural Step (TNS) framework; European Union's Packaging and Packaging Waste Directive; Leadership in Energy and Environmental Design (LEED); Global Reporting Initiative (GRI); carbon offsets

CHAPTER QUESTIONS

1. Describe the nature of climate change and its impacts.

2. How have federal, state, and municipal governments responded to environmental problems?

3. What are the competitive advantages of being eco-friendly?

4. What specific actions can businesses take to improve their environmental performance?

5. Describe how to manage the environmental change process within an organization.

6. What are the key features of an Environmental Management System?

7. How can an organization assess environmental risk and apply The Natural Step framework?

In the Real World: Enron

Announcing Third-Quarter Results— October 2001

Sherron Watkins, refusing to be bullied by corporate lawyers, met with Ken Lay in late August to discuss Fastow's accounting manipulations. Lay did not seem to fully grasp the depth of the accounting problems Watkins described, though he promised to look more deeply into the matter. Watkins also informed a contact at Arthur Andersen, who then sent a memo summarizing his conversation with Watkins to David Duncan, Andersen's lead auditor on the Enron account.

In late August 2001, Enron's Chief Accounting Officer Richard Causey informed Lay that he and Fastow, with Skilling's knowledge, had hidden losses totaling nearly $7 billion the past few years. As CEO, Lay was responsible for these numbers, but he simply hadn't been paying close attention. Lay had always let others he trusted, such as Skilling, Causey, and Fastow, manage the details while he lobbied politicians and potential customers around the world.

On September 11, 2001, shortly after Lay found out about the hidden losses, terrorists hijacked four airplanes and crashed two of them into the World Trade Center towers, brutally killing more than 3,000 innocent people. When the stock market reopened, many stocks nosedived, including Enron's.

Causey was responsible for preparing Enron's third-quarter financial statements, scheduled for release on October 16. Lay now faced a decision that would directly impact 20,000 Enron employees—how honest should he be with investors about Enron's hidden losses? CEOs have a fiduciary duty to honestly convey financial information to shareholders. But Enron's accounting books were a mess, and nobody was absolutely sure as to the exact amount of financial losses Enron had sustained the past few years.

Wall Street analysts predicted that Enron had third-quarter losses totaling $2 billion due to the nationwide recession, Internet business collapse, and terrorist attack.

(Continued)

Lay met with several trusted Enron executives to brainstorm his options. They recommended that Lay report only $1.2 billion of the estimated $7 billion in losses, because that amount could be reasonably explained without damaging Enron's already falling stock price too much. In addition, beating Wall Street expectations might attract new investors.

The executives also pointed out that if Lay reported all $7 billion in losses on October 16, Enron's stock price would collapse from a massive stock sell off, causing Enron to default on its loans. A resultant government investigation could quickly bankrupt the company. Many Enron employees, who had loaded their pension funds with Enron's

soaring stock the past few years despite being told to diversify, would lose their entire life savings.

DECISION CHOICE. If you were the CEO of Enron, how much of the hidden losses would you report to the public when announcing third-quarter results on October 16:

1. $7 billion in losses, and risk financial collapse?
2. $2 billion in losses, to match Wall Street expectations?
3. $1.2 billion in losses, as recommended by some Enron executives?

Why?

ANCILLARY MATERIALS

Websites to Explore

- *Newsweek* "Green Rankings," available at http://www.newsweek.com/feature/2010/green-rankings.html.
- *Fortune,* "The Business of Green," available at http://money.cnn.com/magazines/fortune/greenbiz/.
- White House, Energy and the Environment, available at http://www.whitehouse.gov/issues/energy-and-environment.
- Union of Concerned Scientists, available at http://www.ucsusa.org/.
- Climate Crisis (Al Gore), available at http://www.climatecrisis.net/.
- Business and Sustainable Development: A Global Guide, available at http://www.iisd.org/business/.
- Environmental Statistics
  - International Energy Agency, available at http://www.iea.org/stats/index.asp.
  - U.S. Energy Information Administration statistics, available at http://www.eia.gov/.
  - U.S. Department of Commerce, National Climatic Data Center, available at http://www.ncdc.noaa.gov/oa/ncdc.html.
- Green Tier, Wisconsin Department of Natural Resources, available at http://dnr.wi.gov/org/caer/cea/environmental.

- Dow Jones Sustainability Index, available at http://www.sustainability-index.com/.
- Green Guide, available at www.thegreenguide.com.
- Walmart Sustainability, available at http://walmartstores.com/Sustainability/.
- The Natural Step, available at http://www.naturalstep.org/.
- U.S. Green Building Council, available at: http://www.usgbc.org/.
- Global Reporting Initiative, available at: http://www.globalreporting.org/Home.

Best Place to Work Video

- Best Place to Work—Mayo Clinic, available at http://money.cnn.com/video/fortune/2008/01/22/bpw.mayo.fortune/.

Business Ethics Issue Video

- "Heat," *Frontline,* about America's energy landscape; October 21, 2008, 120 minutes, available at http://www.pbs.org/wgbh/pages/frontline/heat/view/?utm_campaign=viewpage&utm_medium=grid&utm_source=grid.

TEDTalks Videos

- Cradle-to-Cradle Eco-Friendly Design: Green-minded architect and designer William McDonough asks what our buildings and products would look like if designers took into account "all children, all species, for all time"; February 2005, 20 minutes, available at http://www.ted.com/talks/william_mcdonough_on_cradle_to_cradle_design.html.

- Climate Change: Al Gore presents evidence that the pace of climate change may be even worse than scientists recently predicted; March 2008, 28 minutes, available at http://www.ted.com/talks/al_gore_s_new_thinking_on_the_climate_crisis.html.

Conversations with Charlie Rose

- A conversation with Shai Agassi, CEO of Better Place about his plans for an electric car infrastructure; December 1, 2010, 25 minutes, available at http://www.charlierose.com/view/interview/11323.

- A conversation with author Thomas L. Friedman about his book *Hot, Flat, and Crowded: Why We Need a Green Revolution—and How It Can Renew America*; September 9, 2008, 53 minutes, available at http://www.charlierose.com/view/interview/9249.

NOTES

[1] Brian Nattrass and Mary Altomare, *The Natural Step for Business: Wealth, Ecology and the Evolutionary Corporation* (British Columbia, Canada: New Society Publishers, 1999); Andrew J. Hoffman, From Heresy to Dogma: An Institutional History of Corporate Environmentalism (Stanford, CA: Stanford Business Books, 2001).

[2] Dana Mattioli, "How Going Green Draws Talent, Cuts Costs," *Wall Street Journal*, November 13, 2007.

[3] Sindya N. Bhanoo, "Products That Are Earth-and-Profit Friendly," *New York Times*, June 11, 2010.

[4] John Elkington, "Towards the Sustainable Corporation: Win Win Win Business Strategies for Sustainable Development," *California Management Review*, 36, 2 (1994): 90–100; John Elkington, *Cannibals with Forks: The Triple Bottom Line of 21st Century Business* (Oxford, Eng.: Capstone, 1997).

[5] U.S. Census Bureau, U.S. & World Population Clocks, available at www.census.gov/main/www/popcld.html, accessed 12/3/10.

[6] Juliette Jowit, "World's Top Firms Cause $2.2 tn of Environmental Damage, Report Estimates," guardian.co.uk, February 18, 2010, available at http://www.guardian.co.uk/environment/2010/feb/18/worlds-top-firms-environmental-damage, accessed 12/3/10.

[7] Jonathan Stempel, "Chevron Urges Arbitration in $27 Billion Ecuador Case," *Reuters*, August 5, 2010.

[8] *Fortune*, "Most Accountable Companies" 2007 list, available at http://money.cnn.com/magazines/fortune/global500/2007/accountability/full_list.html, accessed 12/3/10.

[9] Jonathan Weisman and Guy Chazan, "BP Halts Dividend, Agrees to $20 Billion Fund for Victims," *Wall Street Journal*, June 16, 2010.

[10] William McDonough and Michael Braungart, *Cradle to Cradle* (New York: North Point Press, 2002).

[11] United Nations Statistics Division, Millennium Development Goals Indicators, available at http://mdgs.un.org/unsd/mdg/SeriesDetail.aspx?srid=749&crid=, accessed 12/3/10.

[12] Felicity Barringer, "U.S. Given Poor Marks on Environment," *New York Times*, January 23, 2008; Yale Center for Environmental Law and Policy and Center for International Earth Science Information Network, 2008 *Economic Performance Index*, available at www.yale.edu/epi/files/2008EPI_PolicymakerSummary_final.pdf , accessed 12/3/10.

[13] Anonymous, "China Overtakes U.S. in Greenhouse Gas Emissions," *New York Times*, June 20, 2007.

[14] Union of Concerned Scientists, "Each Country's Share of CO_2 Emissions," available at http://www.ucsusa.org/global_warming/science_and_impacts/science/each-countrys-share-of-co2.html, accessed 12/3/10.

15. International Energy Agency of the Organization for Economic Co-operation and Development (OECD), *Renewables in Global Energy Supply: An IEA Facts Sheet* (Paris, France: IEA Publications, 2007) available at http://www.iea.org/papers/2006/renewable_factsheet.pdf, accessed 12/3/10. National statistics available by clicking on the individual nation at http://www.iea.org/stats/index.asp, accessed 12/3/10.

16. National Climatic Data Center, "Globally Average Temperature Abnormality for Land and Sea Surfaces for 1880–2010" time series graph at http://www1.ncdc.noaa.gov/pub/data/cmb/GCAG/images/timeseries/global_merged.png, accessed 12/3/10.

17. Climate Progress, "NASA: First Half of 2010 Breaks the Thermometer," available at http://climateprogress.org/2010/07/10/nasa-hottest-year-solar-minimum/, accessed 12/3/10; David Leonhardt, "Overcome by Heat and Inertia," *New York Time*, July 10, 2010.

18. Mike Hulme, *Why We Disagree About Climate Change* (New York: Cambridge University Press, 2009); Lawrence Solomon, *The Deniers: The World-Renowned Scientists Who Stood Up Against Global Warming Hysteria, Political Persecution and Fraud* (Minneapolis, MN: Richard Vigilante Books, 2008); Roy W. Spencer, *Climate Confusion: How Global Warming Hysteria Leads to Bad Science, Pandering Politicians and Misguided Policies That Hurt the Poor* (New York: Encounter Books, 2010); S. Fred Singer and Dennis T. Avery, *Unstoppable Global Warming: Every 1500 Years* (Lanham, MD: Rowman & Littlefield, 2007).

19. Union of Concerned Scientists, "Global Warming 101," available at http://www.ucsusa.org/global_warming/global_warming_101/, accessed 12/3/10.

20. Thomas L. Friedman, *Hot, Flat, and Crowded* (New York: Farrar, Straus and Giroux, 2008), p. 36; see also "Figure 2. World Marketed Energy Use By Fuel Type, 1990–2035," available at http://www.eia.doe.gov/oiaf/ieo/graphic_data_highlights.html, accessed 12/3/10; U.S. Energy Information Administration, "International Energy Outlook 2010," July 10, 2010, available at http://www.eia.doe.gov/oiaf/ieo/pdf/0484(2010).pdf, accessed 12/3/10.

21. U.S. Department of Commerce, National Climatic Data Center, "Billion Dollar U.S. Weather Disasters," available at http://www.ncdc.noaa.gov/oa/reports/billionz.html#chron, accessed 12/3/10.

22. Paul Hawken, *Blessed Unrest: How the Largest Movement in the World Came Into Being* (New York: Viking, 2007).

23. Ralph Waldo Emerson, *Essays and Lectures* (New York: Library of America, 1841/1983).

24. Henry David Thoreau, *Walden* (Boston: Beacon Press, 1854/2004).

25. W. Todd Benson, *President Theodore Roosevelt's Conservations Legacy* (West Conchohocken, PA: Infinity Publishing, 2003).

26. Aldo Leopold, *A Sand County Almanac* (New York: Oxford University Press, 1949/2001).

27. Rachel Carson, *Silent Spring* (New York: Mariner Books, 1962/2002).

28. U.S. Environmental Protection Agency, "Compliance Assistance," available at http://www.epa.gov/compliance/assistance/index.html, accessed 12/3/10; U.S. Environmental Protection Agency, "Compliance Assistance Centers," available at http://www.assistancecenters.net/, accessed 12/3/10.

29. U.S. Environmental Protection Agency, "Compliance Incentives and Auditing," available at http://www.epa.gov/compliance/incentives/index.html, accessed 12/3/10.

30. U.S. Environmental Protection Agency, "Toxics Release Inventory (TRI) Program," available at http://www.epa.gov/tri/, accessed 12/3/10.

31. Robert Collier, "China About to Pass U.S. as World's Top Generator of Greenhouse Gases," *San Francisco Chronicle*, May 5, 2007.

32. Paul Krugman, "Building a Green Economy," *New York Times Magazine*, April 11, 2010.

33. Chicago Climate Exchange website, available at www.chicagoclimatex.com, accessed 12/3/10.

34. John Collins Rudolf, "Cap-and-Trade Exchange Calls It Quits," *New York Times*, November 17, 2010.

35. European Climate Exchange website, available at www.europeanclimateexchange.com, accessed 12/3/10.

36. FreedomWorks, "Top 10 Reasons to Oppose Cap and Trade," March 6, 2009, available at http://www.freedomworks.org/publications/top-10-reasons-to-oppose-cap-and-trade, accessed 12/3/10.

37. Mayors Climate Protection Center, "U.S. Conference of Mayors Climate Protection Agreement," available at www.usmayors.org/climateprotection/agreement.htm, accessed 12/3/10.

38 Regional Greenhouse Gas Initiative, available at www.rggi.org, accessed 12/3/10.

39 Midwestern Greenhouse Gas Reduction Accord, available at www.midwesternaccord.org, accessed 12/3/10.

40 *Midwestern Greenhouse Gas Reduction Accord: Advisory Group Final Recommendation*, May 2010, available at http://www.midwesternaccord.org/Accord_Final_Recommendations.pdf, accessed 12/3/10.

41 Wisconsin Department of Natural Resources, "Green Tier," available at http://dnr.wi.gov/org/caer/cea/environmental, accessed 12/3/10.

42 American College & University President's Climate Commitment, available at www.presidentsclimatecommitment.org, accessed 12/3/10.

43 White House, "Energy & Environment," available at http://www.whitehouse.gov/issues/energy-and-environment, accessed 12/3/10.

44 Dow Jones Sustainability Index website, available at http://www.sustainability-index.com/, accessed 12/3/10.

45 Dow Jones Sustainability Index, "Criteria and Weightings," available at http://www.sustainability-index.com/07_htmle/assessment/criteria.html, accessed 12/3/10.

46 Pete Engardio, "Beyond the Green Corporation," *Business Week*, January 29, 2007.

47 Claire Cain Miller, "Venture Firm's 'Green' Funds Top $1 Billion," *New York Times*, September 1, 2009.

48 U.S. Environmental Protection Agency, "Grants and Fellowship Information," www.epa.gov/epahome/grants.htm, accessed 12/3/10; Business.Gov, "Environmental Grants, Loan and Incentives," www.business.gov/guides/environment/grants-and-loans/index.html, accessed 12/3/10.

49 James Kanter, "$25 Million to Encourage Cleaner Air," *New York Times*, February 10, 2007; see also "Earth Challenge," www.virginearth.com, accessed 12/3/10.

50 Michael E. Porter and Claas Van Der Linde, "Green and Competitive: Ending the Stalemate," *Harvard Business Review*, 73, 5(1995), 120–134; Amory B. Lovins, L. Hunter Lovins, Paul Hawken, Jonathan Lash, Fred Wellington, Kimberly O'Neill Packard, and Forest L. Reinhardt, "Going Green, Profitably," *Harvard Business Review OnPoint Collection*, July 1, 2007; Stefan Ambec and Paul Lanoie, "Does It Pay to Be Green? A Systematic Overview," *Academy of Management Perspectives*, 22, 4 (2008), 45–62; Nattrass and Altomare, *The Natural Step for Business*.

51 Kathleen Deveny, "The 100 Greenest Companies in America," *Newsweek*, October 25, 2010. The list is available at http://www.newsweek.com/feature/2010/green-rankings.html, accessed 12/3/10.

52 Larry Kanter, "The Eco-Advantage," *Inc.*, November 1, 2006.

53 *Fortune*, "The Business of Green," available at http://money.cnn.com/magazines/fortune/greenbiz/, accessed 12/3/10.

54 Channel 3000, "Going Green Wisconsin," available at www.channel3000.com/goinggreen/index.html, accessed 12/3/10.

55 Green America, "National Green Pages," available at http://www.greenamericatoday.org/pubs/greenpages/, accessed 12/3/10.

56 Green Choices website, available at www.greenchoices.org, accessed 12/3/10; Natural Collection website, available at www.naturalcollection.com, accessed 12/3/10; Greenfibers website, available at www.greenfibres.com, accessed 12/3/10.

57 National Geographic Green Guide website, available at www.thegreenguide.com, accessed 12/3/10.

58 Walmart, *Global Sustainability Report: 2010 Progress Update*, available at http://cdn.walmartstores.com/sites/sustainabilityreport/2010/WMT2010GlobalSustainabilityReport.pdf, accessed 12/3/10.

59 Walmart Corporate, "Sustainability," available at http://walmartstores.com/sustainability/, accessed 12/3/10.

60 Bill Clinton, *Giving* (New York: Alfred A. Knopf, 2007); Marc Gunther, "The Green Machine," *Fortune*, July 27, 2006.

61 Walmart Corporate, "Sustainability," available at http://walmartstores.com/sustainability/, accessed 12/3/10.

62 Walmart, *Global Sustainability Report*.

63 Stephanie Rosenbloom, "Wal-Mart Unveils Plan to Make Supply Chain Greener," *New York Times*, February 25, 2010.

64 Stephanie Rosenbloom, "At Wal-Mart, Labeling to Reflect Green Intent," *New York Times*, July 16, 2009.

65 McDonough and Braungart, *Cradle to Cradle*.

66 Sarah James and Torbjorn Lahti, *The Natural Step for Communities: How Cities and Towns Can Change to Sustainable Practices* (British Columbia, Canada: New Society Publisher, 2004).

67 Wisconsin School of Business, "Green Masters Program Checklist," available at http://www.bus.wisc.edu/sustainability/green_masters_checklist_2010.pdf, accessed 12/3/10.

68 Yahoo! Green, "Living Green," available at http://green.yahoo.com/living-green/, accessed 12/3/10.

69 Sonya Newenhouse, *EnAct: Steps to Greener Living* (Madison, WI: Madison Environmental Group, 2008) is available for free online at http://www.enactwi.org/index.php?page=download-the-pdfs, accessed 12/3/10.

70 MSN, "15 Simple Steps That Actually Make a Difference for the Environment," available at http://lifestyle.msn.com/your-life/living-green/staticslideshowdg.aspx?cp-documentid=23719792, accessed 12/3/10; National Resources Defense Council, "Simple Steps," available at http://www.simplesteps.org/#tk-featured-questions, accessed 12/3/10.

71 Society for Human Resource Management, "Green Workplace Survey," January 16, 2008, available at http://www.shrm.org/searchcenter/Pages/Results.aspx?k=green%20workplace%20survey, accessed 12/3/10.

72 Olivier Boiral, "Greening the Corporation Through Organizational Citizenship Behaviors," *Journal of Business Ethics*, 87, 2 (2009): 221–236.

73 Starbucks, "Environmental Mission Statement," available at www.starbucks.com/aboutus/environment.asp, accessed 12/3/10.

74 Tom Zeller, "Clothes Makers Join to Set 'Green Score,'" *New York Times*, March 1, 2011.

75 Darcy Hitchcock and Marsha Willard, *The Business Guide to Sustainability* (Sterling, VA: Earthscan, 2006).

76 *Walmart Supplier Sustainability Assessment*, available at http://walmartstores.com/Sustainability/9292.aspx, accessed 12/3/10.

77 International Organization for Standardization website, available at www.iso.org/iso/home.htm, accessed 12/3/10.

78 Daniel David Edwards and Nicole Darnall, "Averting Environmental Justice Claims? The Role of Environmental Management Systems," *Public Administration Review*, 70, 3 (2010): 422–433.

79 Richard Florida and Derek Davison, "Gaining from Green Management: Environmental Management Systems Inside and Outside the Factory," *California Management Review*, 43, 3 (2001): 64–84.

80 Pete Engardio, "Beyond the Green Corporation," *Business Week*, January 29, 2007.

81 Daniel C. Esty and Andrew S. Winston, *Green to Gold* (New Haven, CT: Yale University Press, 2006), p. 17.

82 Nattrass and Altomare, *The Natural Step for Business*; The Natural Step website, available at www.naturalstep.org, accessed 12/3/10.

83 Hilary Bradbury and Judith A. Clair, "Promoting Sustainable Organizations with Sweden's Natural Step," *Academy of Management Executive*, 13, 4 (1999): 63–74.

84 The Natural Step, "Case Studies on Strategic Sustainability Principles and Processes," available at http://www.naturalstep.org/en/usa/case-studies, accessed 12/3/10.

85 The Natural Step, "A Natural Step Case Study: Madison, WI," available at http://www.naturalstep.org/sites/all/files/Madison_TNScasestudy.pdf, accessed 12/3/10; Sherrie Gruder, Anna Haines, Jerry Hembd, Lisa MacKinnon, and Jane Silberstein, *Toward a Sustainable Community: A Toolkit for Local Government* (Madison, WI: UW Extension, 2007), available at http://www4.uwm.edu/shwec/publications/cabinet/reductionreuse/SustainabilityToolkit.pdf, accessed 12/3/10.

86 Emergo Europe website, available at www.greendotcompliance.eu/en/packaging-waste-directive-94-62-ec.php, accessed 12/3/10.

87 McDonough and Braungart, *Cradle to Cradle*.

88 MBDC, "Certification Overview," available at http://mbdc.com/detail.aspx?linkid=2&sublink=8, accessed 12/3/10.

89 Walmart Corporate, "Wal-Mart Unveils 'Packaging Scorecard' to Suppliers," available at http://walmartstores.com/pressroom/news/6039.aspx, accessed 12/3/10; Walmart Corporate, "Packaging," available at http://walmartstores.com/Sustainability/9125.aspx, accessed 12/3/10.

90 U.S. Green Building Council, "Building Design Leaders Collaborating on Carbon-Neutral Buildings by 2030," available at http://www.usgbc.org/News/PressReleaseDetails.aspx?ID=3124, accessed 12/3/10; Home Construction, Inc., "Building

Green," http://www.mainehomeconstruction.com/green.shtml, accessed 12/3/10.

[91] U.S. Green Building LEED website, available at http://www.usgbc.org/DisplayPage.aspx?CMSPageID=51, accessed 12/3/10; U.S. Green Building, "LEED Building Certification System: FAQ," available at http://www.usgbc.org/ShowFile.aspx?DocumentID=3330, accessed 12/3/10.

[92] Green Building Certification Institute (GBCI) Press Release, "One Billion Square Feet of LEED Certified Building Projects Worldwide," November 10, 2010, available at http://www.usgbc.org/Docs/News/One%20Billion%20Release%202010.pdf, accessed 12/3/10.

[93] Auden Schendler and Randy Udall, *LEED is Broken … Let's Fix It* (Aspen, CO: Community Office for Resource Efficiency, 2005), available at: http://www.aspensnowmass.com/environment/images/LEEDisBroken.pdf, accessed 12/3/10.

[94] U.S. Green Building Council, 2009, *LEED Green Building Rating System, Version 3*, available at http://www.usgbc.org/ShowFile.aspx?DocumentID=5546, accessed 12/3/10.

[95] Climate Care Green Calculator, available at https://www.jpmorganclimatecare.com/business/business-co2-calculator/, accessed 12/3/10.

[96] Samantha Putt del Pino and Pankaj Bhatia, *Working 9 to 5 on Climate Change: An Office Guide* (Washington, DC: World Resources Institute, 2002), available at: http://pdf.wri.org/wri_co2guide.pdf, accessed 12/3/10.

[97] Baxter, 2009 *Sustainability Report*, available at http://sustainability.baxter.com/EHS/2009_environmental_performance/index.html, accessed 12/3/10.

[98] Global Reporting Initiative, "G3 Guidelines" available at http://www.globalreporting.org/ReportingFramework/G3Guidelines/, accessed 12/3/10; Global Reporting Initiative, "FAQ," available at http://www.globalreporting.org/AboutGRI/FAQs/, accessed 12/3/10.

[99] Travelocity, "Offset Your Carbon Emissions Now," available at http://www.travelocity.com/TravelForGood/gz-main.html, accessed 12/3/10.

[100] 1% for the Planet website, available at http://www.onepercentfortheplanet.org/en/, accessed 12/3/10.

CHAPTER OUTLINE

12

COMMUNITY OUTREACH AND RESPECT

What would you do?

Employee Relations

Upon graduation, you obtain a staff position with a bank. Your bank is engaged in many community activities and maintaining a positive image in the community is a high strategic priority. Managers and employees volunteer to assist nonprofit organizations with technology issues, participate in fund-raisers, and are active contributors to the United Way.

On a sunny Tuesday afternoon, you have a lunch meeting with a potential client at an out-of-the-way bar and restaurant. While being escorted to your table, you notice a married colleague sitting in a rear booth with his arm around someone, not his spouse. The colleague does not see you. You also notice that the colleague is drinking a bottle of wine on a workday and playing footsies with the unknown lunch date,

both of whom are giggling. You know the colleague's spouse and children.

As you sit at your table, you find it difficult to give your full attention to the client because of what you saw on the way to being seated.

What would you do? Would you (you may indicate more than one)

1. Stop by the colleague's lunch booth and say hello?
2. Speak with the colleague about the incident later in the day?
3. Report the incident to the bank president?
4. Report the incident to the colleague's spouse?
5. Do nothing?
   Why?

Chapter Objectives

After reading this chapter, you will be able to

- Describe four types of social responsibilities businesses have
- Articulate the competitive advantages of community involvement
- Understand the six phases of issues-driven multi-stakeholder dialogues
- Develop a diverse portfolio of giving opportunities—money, products or services, skills, and job opportunities
- Choose community organizations for strategic partnerships
- Administer the community involvement process

The English poet John Donne noted that "no [hu]man is an island." People exist in relationship to others. Similarly, no organization is an island. Organizations are embedded in the communities where they operate. In addition to the geographic community, organizations are members of supplier and customer communities, professional and industry communities, and a host of virtual Internet communities that communicate through email, websites, and other technological mechanisms.

Ethical organizations aspire to be model community citizens. This chapter is primarily concerned with an organization's geographic community. The well-being of the host community profoundly impacts an organization, and vice versa. On the one hand, organizations are the beneficiaries of community development and disadvantaged by community decay. On the other hand, organizations can contribute to community well-being or decay. According to business strategists Michael Porter and Mark Kramer, "Ultimately, a healthy society creates expanding demand for business, as more human needs are met and aspirations grow. Any business that pursues its ends at the expense of the society in which it operates will find its success to be illusory and ultimately temporary."[1]

This chapter begins with a discussion on the extent to which businesses have social responsibilities and describes the business case for community involvement. An organization's reputation is critical to its success. Public criticisms against an organization generate a negative stigma that can be difficult to undue. Managers can engage multiple community stakeholders on a wide variety of issues. Philanthropy and employee volunteerism are the most common forms of community involvement. Managers must determine how much and what to give to whom. The chapter also explores how to manage the community involvement process, and what community impacts to assess and report.

Extent of Social Responsibilities

To what extent do businesses have social responsibilities? Is obeying the law and making a profit sufficient, or must an organization also engage in philanthropy and other community involvement activities?

The Nobel Prize–winning economist Milton Friedman famously articulated the viewpoint that the only social responsibility for business is to maximize profits within the guidelines of the law.[2] Managers have a fiduciary duty to always act in the best interests of shareholders. Stay focused on your organization's mission, Friedman instructs managers, and don't be distracted by activities not associated with core operations. Sneaker manufacturers, for example, fulfill their social responsibilities by efficiently and effectively meeting consumers' sneaker needs without violating any laws. By doing so, the sneaker company provides employment and pays taxes, which benefit the local community. The more profitable an organization becomes, the more consumer needs it meets, the more people it employs, and the more taxes it pays.

Friedman's narrow conceptualization of social responsibility has been criticized by many scholars.[3] Business ethicist Brian Schaefer argues that

> Corporations often stand to profit from polluting water, overcharging customers, treating suppliers coercively, [and] downsizing without warning. . . . [T]o argue this position on the duties (or lack thereof) of shareholders is

incompatible with the foundations and conclusions of some of the most widely respected and influential moral theories in the Western tradition, namely utilitarianism, Kantianism, virtue ethics, and Judeo-Christian ethics.[4] Critics of Friedman argue that managers may not have a legal obligation to be kind to customers or the local community, but they do have a moral obligation to be socially responsible in their interactions with customers and community members.

Corporate tax avoidance raises similar issues. *Tax evasion* refers to illegally not paying taxes, whereas tax avoidance refers to legally not paying taxes. According to the U.S. Government Accountability Office, 83 of the 100 largest public companies had subsidiaries in territories and nations, such as the Cayman Islands and Bermuda, which legally allow corporations to move their income into tax-free accounts.[5] Citigroup, which in 2009 claimed $45 billion in federal bailout money, had 427 subsidiaries in tax-haven locations. Ingersoll-Rand legally claimed a P.O. box in Bermuda as its corporate headquarters address to avoid paying more than $40 million annually in U.S. taxes.[6] Tyco applied the same strategy to avoid paying $450 million in taxes. Corporations may legally avoid paying taxes to maximize profits by employing accountants well versed in tax loopholes. But does this behavior violate a civic duty to pay taxes in the nation where the company really operates, particularly if it is a recipient of federal bailout money?

Another common example helps differentiate whether social responsibility extends beyond profit making and legal compliance. Assume that pollutants from a company operating within federal and state laws contaminate the adjacent river running downstream and the air that enters the gulf stream wind pattern. An inexpensive new technology is available that could significantly reduce the pollution. Should the company purchase the new technology?

According to Friedman, the answer is no. Laws are being obeyed and the additional costs detract from profit maximization. Yet, purchasing the new technology is not burdensome and would greatly benefit the well-being of employees, neighbors, and many other people. Although managers are not required to purchase the new technology, both utilitarian (what is the greatest good for the greatest number of people) and deontology (treat every stakeholder with respect and integrity) strongly suggest that managers should.

Professor Archie Carroll differentiates four components of social responsibility: economic responsibilities, legal responsibilities, ethical responsibilities (activities and practices that society expects even though they are not codified by law), and philanthropic responsibilities (voluntary and discretionary activities that give back to the community, such as corporate giving, product and service donations, and employee volunteerism).[7] According to Carroll's conceptualization, a socially responsible business is profitable, law abiding, ethical, and a good corporate citizen.

An important management challenge is determining the extent of an organization's philanthropic activities. Financial capability, as well as managerial philosophy, matter. When starting a new business, there is usually little excess income to donate. As the business becomes more profitable, managers must decide how much of the additional profits should be reinvested in the company, distributed to shareholders or employees, or donated. Different managers will reach different distribution conclusions.

The national average for corporate philanthropy is 1 percent of pretax income. In 1976, the Minneapolis Chamber of Commerce created the 5-Percent Club, in which corporations agreed to donate 5 percent of their pretax income. Renamed the Keystone Club, 134 members donate 5 percent and 80 members donate 2 percent of pretax income.[8] Target, one of its members, donated more than $155 million in 2009, which amounts to approximately $3 million a week.[9]

In terms of bottom-line impacts, researchers report an inverse U-shape relationship between philanthropy and financial performance.[10] Up to a point, philanthropy and financial performance increase together. As financial performance improves, there is more excess income available for philanthropy. The additional philanthropy enables an organization to secure critical resources controlled by various stakeholders. At a certain point, the relationship levels off and then declines. In the declining stage, additional philanthropic contributions simply increase organizational costs without generating any additional financial benefits.

Work-Life Balance

As a manager, conceptualize the organization's social responsibilities beginning with your own employees' pursuit of happiness. Employees need adequate time off from work to care for their families and participate in civic organizations. Work-life balance refers to achieving the appropriate balance between time spent working and one's personal life. No matter how enjoyable or essential work may be, employees need time away from work to develop their personalities, replenish their energy, and avoid burnout.

In Book I of *Nicomachean Ethics,* Aristotle surmises that "happiness is the meaning and the purpose of life, the whole aim and end of human existence."[11] Happiness is the only thing human beings desire for its own sake. All other items of desire—such as wealth, prestige, and love—are pursued in hopes of achieving happiness. In a well-balanced society, organizations and the political economy are structured so that happiness can be achieved. The failure to do so results in unhappiness and community turmoil. The path to individual and community happiness, Aristotle reasons, requires the development of four factors: physical well-being (health), financial well-being (wealth), intellectual virtue, and moral virtue, as well as responding appropriately to the misfortunes that are inevitable when pursuing these. The most important of these factors is moral virtue, which includes love for family, neighbors, community, and nation.

The developmental psychologist Erik Erikson complemented Aristotle's conception of happiness by noting that happiness is achieved through the appropriate balancing of work, love, and play.[12] As paraphrased by the historian Doris Kearns Goodwin:[13]

> The richest and fullest lives attempt to achieve an inner balance between three realms: work, love and play. To pursue one to the disregard of the others is to open oneself to ultimate sadness in older age, whereas to pursue all three with equal dedication is to make possible a life filled not only with achievement but with serenity.

On average, Americans work 350 hours a year (nine full weeks) more than their European counterparts.[14] As discussed in Chapter 2, during the late 1800s, unions provided the impetus to achieve an eight-hour workday, five days a week. But in 2003, 33 percent of American employees worked more than 40 hours a week, and 20 percent worked more than 50 hours a week. Many women bear an extra burden because they are also primarily responsible for family and child care duties.[15]

Long working hours contribute not only to poor health conditions and emotional exhaustion, but also less time for family activities and civic engagement. Take Back Your Time, a national coalition to reduce work hours, has been lobbying governments for a variety of work-life balance benefits, including guaranteed *paid* leave for parents after the birth or adoption of a child, one week of paid sick leave, and three weeks of paid annual vacation leave.[16]

Progress is being made. Since 1986, *Working Mother* magazine has annually published a list of the best companies for working mothers.[17] In 1986, only two companies on the list allowed telecommuting (employees working from home). In 2010, 100 percent of the companies on the list did. In 1990, only 4 percent of the best companies offered paid paternity leave. In 2010, 75 percent offered paid paternity leave to both mothers and fathers. IBM and Johnson & Johnson have been on the list all 25 years. Specific examples of family-friendly and community-friendly policies include the following:[18]

- Eighty-nine percent of Abbott employees have flexible work schedules and 64 percent telecommute.
- Arnold & Porter provides onsite child care and employees may visit their children during the workday.
- Credit Suisse allows primary caregivers of new children to take 12 fully paid weeks off and an additional eight weeks to phase back to work.
- Principal Financial Group employees can work part time for up to 12 weeks per year, while maintaining full benefits and guaranteed job security.
- Whole Foods Market employees accrue paid time off for every two weeks they work.
- Timberland employees receive up to 40 hours per year of paid leave for community service.

Business Case for Community Involvement

Organizations implementing the Optimal Ethics Systems Model (Exhibit 2.7) will enhance their reputation within a community. As discussed throughout this textbook, implementing the Optimal Ethics Systems Model means hiring highly qualified and ethical job applicants, training employees in ethical decision making, holding employees accountable to Codes of Ethics and Conduct, enhancing sensitivity and training in diversity, empowering employees, treating customers respectfully, and skillfully managing the organization's relationship with the natural environment.

Isn't that enough? Why not save resources by letting other businesses bear the extra burden of improving community well-being while your organization receives the benefits?

Managers who reason like that overlook the strong business case for being a model corporate citizen. Corporate citizenship is the extent to which a business meets its economic, legal, ethical, and philanthropic responsibilities in the community, or communities, in which it operates by creating a higher standard of living and quality of life. A company's reputation as a good citizen favorably impacts employee, customer, community, and investor relations in the following ways:[19]

Benefits to Employee Relations

- Attracts and retains employees
- A more engaged, productive, and healthier workforce
- Employees develop a deeper sense of purpose and mission

Benefits to Customer Relations

- Increases brand awareness and recognition
- Enhances customer loyalty
- New business opportunities from collaborating with other involved companies

Benefits to Community Relations

- Recognition as a responsible neighbor of choice
- Community goodwill and support

Benefits to Investor Relations

- Attracts socially responsible investment funds
- Preferences with local banks

In terms of employee relations, researchers report that employees of organizations known for their community citizenship contributions are more engaged in their work tasks, have higher levels of camaraderie, and are more prone to creative and innovative thinking.[20] The "millennial generation"—people born between 1980 and 2000—are a key constituent in many long-range business plans because they are replacing the mass outmigration of baby boomers in employment and consumer markets. According to research, a company's philanthropic reputation and community involvement are important selling points to millennial job seekers and consumers.[21]

Being socially responsible also benefits marketing and customer relations. Companies can use all the positive marketing help they can get to increase consumer awareness. A wide range of people and organizations seeking to create a better world advertise the products and services of socially responsible organizations. *The Good Shopping Guide* highlights companies that respect the environment, animals, and people.[22] For many years, Walmart seemed oblivious to the negative publicity it received regarding low wages and insufficient employee benefits. It became more socially responsible, in part, after a consulting company found that 8 percent of its customers had stopped shopping at Walmart because of its bad reputation.[23]

Investors are also paying greater attention to a company's social performance. In December 2004, Southeast Asia was devastated by a tsunami tidal wave. Researchers report that companies donating money to the relief efforts experienced a positive five-day cumulative abnormal stock price return following their press releases.[24] According to a survey conducted by McKinsey & Company and Boston College's Center for Corporate Citizenship, more than 74 percent of the socially responsible institutional investor respondents claimed that the presence of social, environmental, and stakeholder governance programs enhanced shareholder value in the long term.[25]

The Socially Responsible Investment (SRI) financial market is huge. SRI funds screen companies for (1) financial performance—meets financial goals, solid return on investment *and* (2) social performance—generates social benefits through good employer-employee relations, strong environmental practices, safe products, and respect for human rights.

In 2007, the SRI market in the United States accounted for approximately $2.7 trillion, 11 percent of all investment assets under professional management, up from $639 billion in 1995.[26] This 324 percent SRI market increase exceeded the 260 percent overall stock market growth during this 12-year time period.

In 1988, KLD's Domini 400 Social Index (renamed FTSE KLD 400 Social Index in 2009) became the first socially responsible investment fund, screening publicly held companies based on environmental, social, and governance performance criteria.[27] The FTSE KLD 400 Social Index firms are selected by a committee for having met financial screens (such as earnings, liquidity, stock price, and debt to equity ratio) and social screens (excellent records for community relations, diversity, employee relations, human rights, product quality and safety, and environment and corporate governance).[28] The firms are evaluated relative to other companies in their industries and the broader market. Companies with significant holdings in alcohol, tobacco, firearms, gambling, nuclear power, and military weapons are not eligible for inclusion.

International Corporate Citizenship

Every nation has different corporate citizenship standards and expectations based on its political, economic, regulatory, and social historical evolution. *The World Guide to CSR: A Country-by-Country Analysis of Corporate Sustainability and Responsibility* provides comparable national profiles for nearly 60 countries.[29]

The Corporate Responsibility Officers Association (CROA) annually evaluates and recognizes the "100 Best Corporate Citizens." Companies are assessed based on seven criteria—environment, climate change, human rights, employee relations, governance, philanthropy, and financial. The top five for 2010 were Hewlett-Packard, Intel, General Mills, IBM, and Kimberly-Clark.[30]

From an international perspective, should multinational corporations establish one standard of citizenship in the United States and a different standard in developing nations? Or, should one standard apply everywhere? This issue is addressed in the following two sections.

Double Standards Problem

Social activists have long accused American businesses of unethical behavior in underdeveloped and developing nations by exploiting laborers, engaging in government corruption, and taking advantage of lax environmental regulations. Managers of these companies have adopted a "double standard"—one set of behaviors that meets high expectations in the United States and a different set of behaviors that meets low expectations in underdeveloped and developing nations.

Nike, for instance, has received many business ethics and corporate social responsibility awards.[31] In 2010, Nike was rated among the "100 Best Corporate Citizens" by *CRO Magazine*, and among the "World's Most Ethical Companies" by

Ethisphere magazine. The company, however, has been targeted by labor activist groups such as Global Exchange for contracting with factories in Vietnam and Indonesia that operate under sweatshop working conditions that would be illegal in the United States.[32]

Sweatshops in developing nations epitomize the difficulty of imposing a universal standard on all organizations in all nations. A sweatshop is a business facility that employs workers at low wages, for long hours, and in unhealthy working conditions. Chinese and Indonesian sweatshops manufacture products purchased by U.S. companies for sale in the United States and elsewhere. In these factories, peasant girls, paid by the piece, work from six o'clock in the morning until nine o'clock at night, seven days a week, for three months before getting a day off.[33] These conditions are in clear violation of U.S. labor laws but not necessarily host country laws.

Managers and political, economic, and moral theorists defend the double standard based on cultural relativism and utilitarianism. According to cultural relativism, it is ethical to adopt standards based on the norms of the host community—when in Rome do as the Romans do.

Sweatshops are also defended based on utilitarianism, the greatest good for the greatest number—sweatshops in developing nations allow thousands of peasants to earn a local living wage.[34] Sweatshop jobs in China and Indonesia are lucrative compared to the alternative—prostitution or starvation. Sweatshops are an evolutionary phase in the industrialization of underdeveloped nations. If the sweatshop goes bankrupt, the unemployed women revert back to searching through garbage at hazardous dumps with their children to find items to sell that would earn the $1 necessary to live another day.

But from a deontological (human rights) and virtue ethics (practicing virtues) perspective, these working conditions are unacceptable. An unfair double standard is being invoked—if it is wrong to employ Americans under these unhealthy and abusive working conditions, then it is also wrong to employ those living in developing nations this way. The rights of all employees in the world must be respected, and virtuous behaviors should be applied to all employees in the world, not just those working in the United States.

Nike has made many changes in its supplier relations in response to sweatshop issues raised by activist groups and NGOs.[35] Nike now employs independent auditors to certify that its products are not manufactured under sweatshop conditions. But its public image remains tarnished because of other types of unethical supplier behaviors. As recently as 2010, United Students Against Sweatshops targeted Nike for two subcontractors in Honduras who refused to pay approximately $2 million in severance payments to 1,800 employees following plant closings.[36] Shortly after the University of Wisconsin–Madison terminated its licensing agreement with Nike, the company agreed to create a $1.54 million relief fund, provide vocational training, and finance health coverage for the laid-off workers.

United Nations Global Compact Principles

The United Nations (UN) has developed guiding principles for conducting business anywhere in the world. In 1999, then UN Secretary-General Kofi Annan presented the UN Global Compact Principles to business leaders attending the World Economic Forum in Davos, Switzerland. As of 2010, more than 7,700 businesses from more than 130 countries had officially committed to the principles.[37] The 10 principles are in the areas of human rights, labor, environment, and corruption (see Exhibit 12.1).[38] Signatories share best practices and report progress in these areas.[39] Businesses that fail to report progress are delisted from the compact.

Exhibit 12.1 United Nations Global Compact Principles

HUMAN RIGHTS

- Principle 1: Businesses should support and respect the protection of internationally proclaimed human rights; and
- Principle 2: make sure that they are not complicit in human rights abuses.

LABOR

- Principle 3: Businesses should uphold the freedom of association and the effective recognition of the right to collective bargaining;
- Principle 4: the elimination of all forms of forced and compulsory labor;
- Principle 5: the effective abolition of child labor; and
- Principle 6: the elimination of discrimination in respect of employment and occupation.

ENVIRONMENT

- Principle 7: Businesses should support a precautionary approach to environmental challenges;
- Principle 8: undertake initiatives to promote greater environmental responsibility; and
- Principle 9: encourage the development and diffusion of environmentally friendly technologies.

ANTICORRUPTION

- Principle 10: Businesses should work against corruption in all its forms, including extortion and bribery.

Hewlett-Packard requires its suppliers to submit a self-assessment questionnaire developed in partnership with the Global e-Sustainability Initiative Supply Chain Working and the Electronic Industry Code of Conduct Implementation Group, copyrighted by the United Nations Environment Programme.[40] Questions to ask suppliers about their labor and health and safety practices appear in Exhibit 12.2.

Exhibit 12.2 Supplier Labor and Occupational Health and Safety Practices

1. Does your company utilize, or is it developing, a **management systems** approach (including policies, goals, procedures, and review processes) to assure proper management of **labor and occupational health & safety?**
2. Do you have a company-wide management system registered to SA 8000, Ethical Trading Initiative, or other recognized codes of social conduct?

(Continued)

Exhibit 12.2 Supplier Labor and Occupational Health and Safety Practices (Continued)

3. To what extent are your labor and occupational health & safety management systems **documented**?

4. How often does the management of your company **periodically review** the status of the labor and occupational health & safety management systems and identify improvement opportunities?

5. Do your labor and occupational health & safety policies apply to **all** of your **facilities** regardless of country location?

6. Do your labor and occupational health & safety policies express a commitment to **continuous improvement**?

7. Has your company established a **tracking system** to identify and monitor labor and occupational health & safety laws and regulations that apply to your company?

8. Is a **management representative** of the company assigned responsibility for assuring and facilitating compliance with labor and occupational health & safety laws, regulations and codes across all of your facilities?

9. Does your company place a **contractual requirement on its suppliers** to be in compliance with occupational health and safety laws and regulations?

10. Does your company have written **performance objectives** for labor and occupational health & safety practices, including metrics and targets with implementation plans for achieving them?

11. Does your company have a **risk assessment** process to identify, prioritize, and mitigate the potential labor and occupational health & safety risks associated with your operations and activities?

12. Does your company conduct **periodic audits** of labor and occupational health & safety practices at its operating facilities in order to assess conformance with regulatory and other requirements?

13. Does your company have a process to implement timely **corrective actions** for labor and occupational health & safety deficiencies identified by internal or external assessments, audits, and reviews?

Managing Stakeholders

Interpenetrating Systems Model

Activists, the media, NGOs, and government agencies hold organizations accountable for the social consequences of their activities. Liberal and conservative activists draw attention to a particular social problem, solicit support from others, and then seek to change the behavior of offending organizations through the media and changes in public policy.

As shown in Exhibit 12.3, the Interpenetrating Systems Model segments human activities into four major subsystems: government, business, nonprofits, and personal-communal, each with its own purpose.[41] Governments exercise control

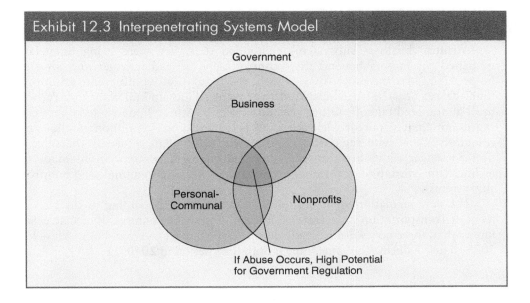

Exhibit 12.3 Interpenetrating Systems Model

Government

Business

Personal-
Communal

Nonprofits

If Abuse Occurs, High Potential
for Government Regulation

over populations by developing and enforcing rules and regulations, businesses provide goods and services by generating wealth for owners, and nonprofits provide goods and services not met by governments and businesses. The personal-communal subsystem refers to individuals behaving within the context of a family or neighborhood.

The four subsystems impact one another. What happens in the business subsystem often impacts the other three subsystems. During a business recession, individuals have less discretionary income, nonprofits lose funding, and incumbent politicians lose elections. Government is the most powerful subsystem because it finalizes the rules for behaviors within its own subsystem and imposes them on the other three subsystems.

No subsystem is monolithic. Multiple views and perspectives are evident within each. Health care legislation, for instance, impacts government, businesses, nonprofits, and individuals. Some businesses favor national health care and some do not. Some people, nonprofits, and political leaders favor national health care and some do not.

The Interpenetrating Systems Model area where all four subsystems overlap is typically one of regulatory interest if abuse occurs. The request for regulation can come from any person or group in any subsystem.

In 2006, for example, Kate Hanni, her husband, and two children (personal-communal subsystem) were stranded on a plane at the Austin, Texas, airport for nine hours. Outraged at her lack of rights in this situation, Hanni created flyersrights.org as a nonprofit consumer organization representing airline passengers (nonprofit subsystem) and lobbied political leaders and regulators to remedy the situation (government subsystem).[42] Three years later, the U.S. secretary of transportation announced a "Passenger Bill of Rights" for domestic flights. The new regulation requires an airline to provide passengers with food and water after waiting two hours on the tarmac and the opportunity to leave the plane after three hours.[43] The fine for not doing so: $27,500 per passenger.

Airlines (business subsystem) responded that they were being financially punished for factors beyond their control, such as bad weather and air traffic problems. Furthermore, they argued, the regulation would create additional flight delays because airplanes would not want to line up and wait on a runway until guaranteed takeoff. Otherwise, an airplane with 100 passengers experiencing unanticipated takeoff delays risked being fined $2.75 million. Airline representatives met with regulators (government subsystem) to clarify the rules so that passenger rights are respected with reasonable accommodations made for airlines (the overlap of government, business, personal-communal, and nonprofit subsystems).

The new regulation went into effect in May 2010. According to the Department of Transportation's Air Travel Consumer Report, the number of tarmac delays longer than three hours dramatically declined by 98 percent, from 463 in May–July 2009 to just 7 during the same three month time period in 2010.[44]

Multiple Stakeholder Demands

It is very challenging for managers to respond appropriately to multiple stakeholders making simultaneous demands. All stakeholders matter. But from a practical perspective, managers cannot address all, and sometimes conflicting, stakeholder demands.

Scholars have differentiated primary and secondary stakeholders to help deal with this problem.[45] Primary stakeholders are those who have an economic relationship with the organization, such as owners, employees, customers, and suppliers. Without them, the organization would fail to exist. Secondary stakeholders are those who indirectly affect or are affected by the company's activities, such as community members, nonprofits, the media, and the governmnt.

Out of the plethora of stakeholders and issues, to which ones should companies pay the most attention? Ronald Mitchel, Bradley Agle, and Donna Wood have developed a typology of stakeholder characteristics to help managers sort through demands from primary and secondary stakeholders.[46] They categorize stakeholders and issues based on three attributes: power, legitimacy, and urgency (see Exhibit 12.4).

Power refers to the ability of a stakeholder to impose its will on the business. The power can be transitory, more important in some periods, and less important in other periods. Labor unions, for example, exhibit tremendous power during contract negotiations when the economy is growing and labor supply is low. But during a recession, labor unions possess less power because many employees are desperate to maintain their jobs.

Legitimacy, which at times is similar to power, refers to the stakeholder's standing in society or to the claim being made. The Red Cross, for instance, has high legitimacy in the eyes of the public. Its recommendations for emergency aid typically matter more than those of recently created nonprofits with similar purposes.

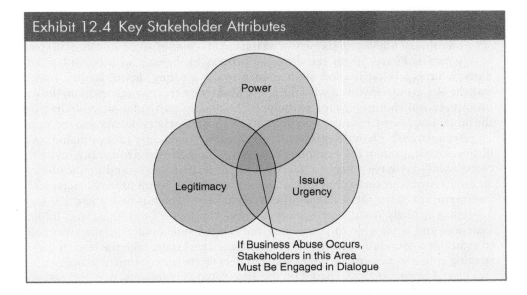

Exhibit 12.4 Key Stakeholder Attributes

Urgency refers to the immediateness of the issues being raised. For many years, some small business owners on the Gulf of Mexico complained about the negative impact of BP's oil drilling on their recreational activities. Shortly after the oil-well tragedy, their concerns received attention.

Managers need to scan their environment to determine when these three stakeholder characteristics—power, legitimacy, and urgency—exist. Joining industry and professional organizations, such as the Chamber of Commerce, provides managers access to relevant national social, political, and environmental trends. Appropriately managing these trends and changing stakeholder expectations can prevent damaging newspaper headlines, consumer boycotts, and burdensome new regulations. But do not neglect stakeholders who lack power. If their claims are legitimate and urgent, others are likely to join them, as happened in the case of Kate Hanni.

Stakeholder Dialogues

Companies can pursue three different strategies for managing stakeholders: reactive, proactive, or interactive.[47] Managers can wait for problems to arise (reactive), anticipate problems and implement plans before the problems arise (proactive), or engage with key stakeholders and jointly determine the appropriate course of action (interactive).

The most difficult, yet possibly the most meaningful, approach is interactive dialogue with stakeholder groups. To begin this process, managers must reach an understanding that unilateral decision making, which excludes stakeholder input and dialogue, can generate more intense conflict and create both short-term and long-term organizational problems. The UN Global Compact is an interactive approach whereby businesses, politicians, social justice activists, and NGOs meet under the auspices of the United Nations to discuss how best to deal with issues such as suppliers in developing nations employing child laborers.

Julia Roloff highlights six phases of issues-driven multi-stakeholder dialogues.[48]

Initiation Phase: Begin the dialogue process by having an independent third party with expert facilitation skills moderate the meeting. Invite leaders from all stakeholder groups involved with the issue. Make sure representatives from the most prominent stakeholder groups participate. Excluding particular stakeholders from the initial discussion will raise questions about the business's sincerity and intentions.

Acquaintance Phase: Representatives of each stakeholder group, including the business itself, present their unique perspectives. Stakeholder groups can invite "experts" who may have a better understanding of factual details and implications. In an uninterrupted round-robin format, each stakeholder group presents facts, and its interpretation of the facts, to the other stakeholders. The business and other stakeholders will likely learn new knowledge about capacity limitations and impacts. Listening and being able to paraphrase the various stakeholder perspectives begins to establish a foundation for trust. Business managers must take the lead in demonstrating empathy toward the other stakeholders to ensure continued dialogue.

First Agreement Phase: Based on the articulated perspectives, participants, guided by the facilitator, reach agreement on the problem definition. Do not progress to other issues until after consent is first achieved on the problem definition.

Second Agreement Phase: After understanding the competing viewpoints, stakeholder group representatives propose potential solutions to the defined problem. For this phase to succeed, representatives must be willing to entertain potential win-win scenarios. The credibility of the dialogue process is damaged if participants are not open to exploring alternative solutions. At this point, some stakeholders may disengage from further deliberations because their important demands are not being addressed.

Implementation Phase: Begin this phase by recognizing that every stakeholder, including the business, may have sacrificed something in reaching the agreement. The channels of communication must remain open to ensure commitments are upheld. Any broken promises by the business, whether intentional or unintentional, can ignite protests, negative publicity, or lawsuits if not rectified immediately. Be transparent about new and unexpected developments and disclose the information to the stakeholder group as soon as possible.

Consolidation Phase: Next, institutionalize successful dialogue formats and procedures until the issue is resolved. Establish weekly meetings or list-serve communications whereby contentious issues that arise can be addressed. Stakeholder leaders benefitting from this process may inform others about the sincerity of the process, which could attract other stakeholders to become dialogue participants.

Institutionalization or Extinction Phase: As the initial issue reaches the end of its life cycle, participants in the stakeholder dialogue can either end their participation or institutionalize the dialogue process to address other issues on their potentially conflicting agendas. The end goal is not "winning," it is understanding different expectations and perspectives and improving processes and policies for addressing social issues.[49]

In conclusion, business representatives must be transparent, engage in two-way communication, be fair, and be held accountable for ensuring that the dialogue succeeds.

Philanthropy and Volunteerism

In addition to engaging in multi-stakeholder dialogues, companies exhibit good citizenship through philanthropy and volunteerism. Philanthropy is the donation of money or property to assist a nonprofit organization or people in need. Volunteerism is the donation of time for similar purposes. When well managed, corporate philanthropy and volunteerism provide employees an opportunity to fulfill their altruistic needs, which deepens employee identification with both the company and the community.[50]

Frame philanthropic efforts as part of the organization's public relations strategy and link the reputational benefits to improving organizational performance. The field of public relations focuses on maintaining an organizational presence among consumers, investors, and community members. Philanthropy and volunteerism can be a prominent part of an organization's public relations portfolio and a driver of success rather than just an outcome of success.[51] In a survey of 721 corporate executives conducted by *The McKinsey Quarterly*, approximately 90 percent use their philanthropic efforts to achieve business benefits, primarily through enhancing corporate reputation and brand identity and by generating goodwill among employees, customers, and community members.[52]

Philanthropy provides a buffer when things go wrong. Researchers report that, whereas public notice of an EPA or Occupational Safety and Health Administration violation damages an organization's reputation, the damage is less among those organizations engaged in community philanthropy, reducing the negative effect.[53]

Philanthropy and volunteerism have been around since the arrival of European settlers.[54] A belief that the wealthy had a social obligation to care for the poor was prominent among the Puritans. In 1636, John Harvard donated his entire library and half his land to found Harvard University, the first institution of higher education in the American colonies. Paul Revere was a Minuteman and member of the Sons of Liberty, an association of people willing to volunteer in a minute to form a local militia against the British army. For three years, George Washington donated his time to serve as the commanding general of the Continental Army.

Noblesse oblige, the belief that the wealthy are obligated to exercise the virtue of generosity, was common among wealthy Americans by the mid-1800s. Industrialist Andrew Carnegie, in an 1889 essay titled "The Gospel of Wealth," argued that wealthy individuals, particularly the self-made rich, had a moral responsibility to invest their fortunes for the well-being of society.[55]

Carnegie proposed community-based philanthropy as an ethical way to assist laborers and their families. Business fortunes, Carnegie maintained, should be distributed during a person's lifetime to harmonize relationships between the rich and poor. Poverty was a scar on capitalist society that could be offset through strategic philanthropic contributions.

Carnegie denounced ostentatious living and indiscriminate giving. Wealthy businesspeople should apply their "superior wisdom, experience, and ability to administer" to spending excess wealth in a way that enriched the lives of the poor through public projects, particularly the building and funding of libraries, schools, and universities. God, he insisted, would reward those who pursued this path in the afterlife. In 1901, Carnegie sold his U.S. Steel stock for $300 million ($12 billion in 2009 dollars adjusted for inflation) and disbursed it over the last 20 years of his life, including $5 million for an employee pension and benefit fund and the building of 2,507 free public libraries.

Let's Build a Building

Customer Service

You are a partner-in-charge for a firm that provides accounting, tax, and consulting services. Lois, a subordinate, informs you about a problem involving two clients. Big Construction, a large construction company, is a new client. Medium Retail Store has been your company's accounting client for 15 years.

While reviewing Big Construction's accounting documents, Lois found a memo of agreement stating that Big Construction would not earn more than 15 percent profit on a new building for Medium Retail Store. Lois analyzed everything very thoroughly and has determined that Big Construction is overcharging Medium Retail Store for materials and labor hours, resulting in 25 percent profit on the project. You look over the documents and agree with Lois's analysis. You instruct Lois to address this problem with Big Construction's chief accounting officer (CAO).

Meanwhile, you are a neighbor of, and good friends with, Medium Retail Store's CAO. The two of you attend Rotary meetings, play golf, and have adjacent season tickets at football games. The CAO even gave you a heads-up about a recent store-wide sale.

During a football game, Medium Retail Store's CAO starts complaining to you about the higher than expected costs for Big Construction's retail store building project. You wonder if you should tell the CAO what Lois found out about Big Construction's significantly higher than agreed-upon building profits.

What would you do? Would you

1. Tell Medium Retail Store's CAO about the memo of agreement violation?

2. Not say anything and change the topic? Why?

What to Give

The who, what, when, where, and why of an organization's philanthropic efforts say a lot about its values.[56] For small organizations, the owner's personal preferences usually determine the nature of philanthropic efforts. As organizations grow in size, these choices often reflect those of the employees as well.

What do nonprofit organizations and the community need from businesses?

1. Money

2. Products or services

3. Skills

4. Job opportunities

A systematic giving program would cover all four areas. Giving money and products or services is a meaningful way to contribute that requires minimal time and effort. Giving skills and job opportunities require significantly more time and effort.

Salesforce.com, which provides on-demand customer relationship management services, applies a "1/1/1 Model" for giving money, products, and skills: 1 percent of new shares of stock is placed in the company foundation for philanthropic purposes, 1 percent of the company's products is donated to nonprofit organizations, and 1 percent of employee working hours (four hours a month, or six days annually) is allocated to community service.[57]

Giving Money

Many nonprofit organizations operate with minimal financial resources and depend on philanthropic donations to serve clients. Intermediary charity organizations arose in the late 1880s to help businesses more efficiently pool their resources for the benefit of nonprofit organizations.[58] Initial efforts began in 1887 when a priest, two ministers, and a rabbi joined forces to address social welfare problems in Denver, Colorado. Other cities formed Community Chests and these merged into the United Way, which raises money from local businesses and distributes the donations to nonprofit organizations. In 2010, *Forbes* rated the United Way #26 among the world's 50 most valuable brands.[59]

Wealthy individuals give generously to social causes through a variety of methods. In 1982, Paul Newman created Newman's Own to sell salad dressing, pasta sauces, and other products for which all after-tax profits are donated to charities.[60] At the time of Paul Newman's death in 2008, the company had donated more than $250 million.

The amount of giving can be quite staggering. In 2009, total philanthropy amounted to $303.7 billion. Individual giving accounted for 75 percent, $227.4 billion, of this total. Corporate giving totaled $14.1 billion.[61] In 2007, the United Way raised $4 billion.

In 2010, the Bill & Melinda Gates Foundation was the second largest foundation in the world, behind only the Stichting INGKA foundation in the Netherlands, created by the founder of IKEA. The Bill & Melinda Gates Foundation had $33 billion in assets and, in 2009, distributed funds totaling $3 billion.[62] The financier Warren Buffett pledged 10 million shares of Berkshire Hathaway Inc. stock worth $31 billion to the Bill & Melinda Gates Foundation, beginning with $1.6 billion in 2006.[63]

Managers can arrange for employees to donate money through payroll deductions. IBM employees, for instance, have donated more than $800 million since 1978 from payroll deductions.[64] IBM's nonprofit beneficiary list continually grows via employee nominations.

Some organizations put a special effort into lobbying employees to donate money when annual bonuses are disbursed. Researchers report that although employees are happy to receive bonuses, they are even happier after voluntarily donating a portion of the bonus to charity.[65]

Giving Products or Services

Many community organizations can benefit from receiving company products or supplies. Low-income community centers, for instance, welcome school supplies from retail stores, food from grocery stores, books from publishers, and so on.

Timberland, which makes boots, shoes, clothes, and gear for the outdoors, has an extensive product donation program.[66] The company proactively solicits product donation requests from organizations connected with the company's mission, such as environmental volunteer programs. Footwear samples and similar products are donated to underprivileged youth and homeless shelters. The company also encourages nonprofits to leverage Timberland's product donations as fund-raising auction items.

Tips and Techniques

A Highly Integrated Win-Win Donation

Mattel's American Girl division, formerly the Pleasant Company, created a win-win opportunity for the environment, a nonprofit organization, children, and itself. The unique partnership integrates product donations, volunteers, and philanthropy.*

Rather than disposing product returns into a landfill, the company donates returned American Girl dolls to the Madison Children's Museum, which then recruits volunteers to repair the dolls. The repaired dolls are resold, at discounted prices, during an annual benefit sale. The proceeds fund Madison Children's Museum programs and other children's organizations.

This arrangement expands the American Girl customer base. The discounted prices make the dolls more affordable to a wider range of consumers.

———

*Denis Collins and Lisa Goldthorpe, "Smart Seconds," *Madison Magazine*, February 2007: 32–33.

Giving Skills

In 2009, 63.4 million Americans age 16 and older volunteered a total of 8.1 billion hours of service with an estimated dollar value of nearly $169 billion.[67] Companies can tap into an employee's desire to help others by supporting volunteer activities and offering sabbaticals.

Some companies set aside one day a year for all employees to serve the community. All employees of a small company usually work on the same project, such as a Habitat for Humanity project or painting for nonprofits or the elderly. Larger companies typically provide a menu of community involvement opportunities. PNC Financial Services Group provides employees with contacts at 200 nonprofits nationwide.[68] Have employees or departments choose the activity they find most interesting.

The United Way sponsors a "Day of Caring" in many communities during which it coordinates a host of projects with nonprofit organizations that makes it easy for company employees to participate. In addition, the United Way provides individualized opportunities.[69] Its computerized system collects data about an employee's skill set and then matches the potential volunteer to the needs of nonprofits. Accountants can perform bookkeeping duties, marketing employees design communication materials, and information technology specialists update computer systems. The United Way also recruits business leaders and mid-level managers to sit on the boards of nonprofit organizations. The federal government's Corporation for National and Community Service maintains a similar volunteer database.[70]

Invoke the three "Cs"—compatibility, commitment, and communication—when forming long-term volunteer partnerships, such as delivering food weekly for Meals-on-Wheels or serving food monthly at a homeless shelter.[71] Employee volunteers must be *compatible* with the nonprofit's culture, *committed* to the project, and maintain ongoing *communication* with the organization to minimize misunderstandings.

Walmart's volunteerism in response to the Hurricane Katrina catastrophe in New Orleans is particularly noteworthy.[72] In addition to quickly pledging $15 million to the disaster relief fund and donating more than $3 million in products, the company applied its supply chain management skills and expertise in transportation logistics to coordinate the delivery of merchandise to emergency relief organizations. The resultant positive media coverage contributed to changing Walmart's previously negative reputation.

A growing number of companies offer employees short- or long-term sabbaticals, or leave programs, for community involvement activities.[73] Among *Fortune's* 2007 "100 Best Companies to Work For," 20 percent offered fully paid sabbaticals.[74] The sabbatical program at Intel is mandatory. Employees earn two fully paid months off every seven years.

Sabbaticals are a retention policy that appeals to people who are in high-stress jobs, on the verge of burnout, travel a great deal, are looking for new challenges to apply and develop their skills, or simply want to give back to the community. Have the sabbatical-bound employee train a replacement, which provides the company an excellent opportunity to develop another high-potential employee. Some companies also use sabbaticals during economic downturns, as an alternative to laying off a highly skilled employee whose job task is temporarily not needed.

Link sabbaticals to the employee's skills and career goals. Direct benefits to the employee include improving leadership and project management skills, obtaining a broad perspective of the local community, and gaining new community contacts. Pfizer offers volunteer opportunities in developing nations to give employees a first-hand experience with economic development and political dynamics.

Key issues to consider when creating a sabbatical program include the following:

Who qualifies: Will the employee be chosen based on years of employment, performance achievements, or some other criterion?

For how long: Will the sabbatical be for one week, three weeks, two months, or a year?

Where: Will the activity be performed locally, nationally, or internationally?

Type of activity: Will the activity be community service, small-business assistance, travel immersion, or nothing at all?

Compensation: Will the employee receive full pay, reduced pay, or no pay?

Post-sabbatical obligation: Does the employee have to remain with the company for a certain period of time after the sabbatical?

Giving Job Opportunities

In addition to giving money, products, and skills, businesses can give back to the community by providing jobs to people in need. One of the most important aspects of a person's life is having a job. Applying a skill for the benefit of an organization contributes to the development of a meaningful life. People tend to take this for granted until they are without a job.

Soon after Hurricane Katrina hit the Gulf Coast in 2005, Walmart promised a job for every one of its displaced workers. Walmart could have simply laid them off due to the natural disaster but didn't. Some companies also create special job positions for people with disabilities, the elderly, and returning war veterans. These efforts are supported by nonprofit organizations that train people with mental or physical disabilities to reenter the workforce. Job coaches assist them at the workplace and, when needed, fill in if the person with disabilities is unable to work a particular day.

Ex-convicts are a group of people most in need of job opportunities. Many prisons offer vocational training and prisoners can earn technical and advanced degrees while serving time. One reason for high recidivism rates is that ex-cons have difficulty obtaining employment. The government encourages the employment of former prisoners. Companies can receive a federal tax credit of up to $2,400 the first year employing a formerly incarcerated person. Companies can also apply for government-provided insurance to protect against theft by a recently hired ex-convict.

Social Entrepreneurship

Social entrepreneurship—entrepreneurs with a social mission—is another way that businesspeople can contribute their skills. Social entrepreneurship refers to using business principles to directly meet basic human needs.[75]

Many social entrepreneurs participate in nonprofit organizations, although some develop for-profit ventures. For instance, a micro-lending organization that benefits economic development in poverty-stricken areas could be a nonprofit or for-profit business. What these two types of organizations have in common is their social aim—poverty eradication.

Initially, social entrepreneurs came out of nonprofit organizations that realized they needed innovative long-term fund-raising activities to support their organizations. For instance, Save the Children, a nonprofit that helps disadvantaged children, developed a line of clothing as a source of revenue.[76]

The One Laptop Per Child Association, another social entrepreneurship venture, is a nonprofit created to develop and distribute inexpensive low-power laptops for poor children living in developing nations.[77] The organization's goal is to supply a laptop to 2 billion children. In 2010, after three years of existence, the organization had distributed 1.6 million laptops, half of them in Uruguay, Peru, and Rwanda.[78]

As is the nature of entrepreneurs, social entrepreneurs continually look for new opportunities to leverage their skills. Trek Bicycles "Earn-A-Bike" program provides job training for at-risk youth who recycle bikes and bike parts.[79] These activities led to the creation of DreamBikes, a nonprofit used-bicycle store located in a low-income neighborhood. The store employs local youths from a nearby Boys and Girls Club to fix and sell affordable bicycles.[80]

To Whom to Give

Small-business owners operating on Main Street and corporate foundation officers secluded in headquarters are both inundated with requests for assistance from nonprofit organizations. Which nonprofit should a business give to?

Managers can (1) reactively give on a first-come first-serve basis, (2) outsource giving to the United Way and other intermediary organizations that select recipients, or (3) proactively develop a few key strategic partnerships with nonprofit organizations. An integrative approach that involves all three situates a company as a community leader and enhances employee satisfaction.

Reactive Giving

Set aside some community giving resources to support local nonprofit organizations and causes that are meaningful to employees and community members. These organizations may have unforeseen emergencies that companies can help address. For example, due to an unanticipated sudden budget shortfall, the public high school's theater program might find itself on the verge of being eliminated. A company can have a tremendous impact, and gain favorable local publicity, by meeting this emergency need. Employee goodwill is generated if several employees have children who benefit from the program. Supporting community organizations that directly impact employees generates company pride.

Other times, a national emergency, such as Hurricane Katrina, may create a need for immediate assistance. Involving employees in developing a company response to these emergencies unites them in a high-profile cause. The goodwill can spill over into everyday work relationships.

Companies must ensure that their charitable donations do the most good and actually benefit the intended recipients. The American Institute of Philanthropy (AIP) *Charity Rating Guide & Watchdog Report* grades more than 500 national charities based on how nonprofits spend donations.[81] A list of the top-rated charities organized based on their cause—for example, cancer, human services, youth development—is available on AIP's website.[82]

Attributes of the top-rated charities include:

- Spends 75 percent or more of its budget on programs
- Spends no more than $25 to raise $100 in public support
- Does not hold excessive assets in reserve
- Discloses financial information and documents to AIP

Charity Navigator, an independent nonprofit organization, rates the financial health of more than 5,500 of the largest charities for daily operations and program sustainability.[83] The organization publishes a list of the "10 Top-Notch Charities"[84] and "10 Charities in Deep Financial Trouble" whose total liabilities exceed total assets, and the bills they owe exceed available assets that can be used to pay them.[85]

Charity Navigator recommends that company executives address the following six questions before donating money to a particular charity:[86]

1. Can the charity clearly communicate who it is and what it does?
2. Can the charity define its short-term and long-term goals?
3. Does the charity report progress made toward its goals?
4. Are the charity's programs rational and productive?
5. Can the charity be trusted?
6. Is the company willing to make a long-term commitment to the charity?

Outsource Giving

Set aside some community giving resources to support the local United Way or other highly credible intermediary organizations that select and monitor donation recipients. The United Way performs community needs assessments and ensures that nonprofit recipients appropriately manage donations. The United Way is strongly supported by many local government officials and is an important business networking opportunity. Be careful, though, not to force employees to give to the United Way. Doing so damages employee morale.

Companies can also donate money to *international* social projects (GlobalGiving), individual microloan recipients (Kiva), and scholarship recipients (Vittana).

GlobalGiving, created in 2002 by former World Bank executives, links donors to specific projects.[87] By 2010, 119,722 donors had given $31.7 million to 3,128 projects. A company's community outreach committee can browse the GlobalGiving website and research causes either by topic (e.g., children, environment) or location. The recipient organizations are legally accountable to GlobalGiving for meeting standardized compliance measures.

GlobalGiving ensures that 85percent to 90 percent of the tax-deductible donation is put to use by the recipient organization within 60 days. Donors are given quarterly updates from the recipient organization about the project's progress. GlobalGiving offers donors a satisfaction guarantee of up to $10,000 annually. If not pleased with the project's progress, the donor can request a voucher for the original donation amount and reallocate the money to a different project.

Kiva, founded in 2005, is a person-to-person microloan lending website that links donors/lenders to entrepreneurs in underdeveloped or developing nations who are unable to obtain loans from regular banking institutions.[88] Technically, this is not a donation because the money is being loaned to the recipient with the intent of repayment. The donor can browse entrepreneur profiles, select one, and then send the money to Kiva, which deposits the money with a nearby microfinance institution. The microfinance institution also offers the local entrepreneur training and other assistance. After the entrepreneur pays back the loan, the donor can reissue another loan to the entrepreneur, lend the money to a different entrepreneur, or withdraw the funds.

Vittana also works with local microfinance organizations, but the beneficiaries are college scholarship recipients.[89] Headquartered in Seattle, Washington, Vittana donors make person-to-person loans to students seeking a college education in a developing nation that lacks adequate student loan programs. Vittana reports a loan repayment success rate of 95 percent.

Another option is to allocate money to an investment fund that makes loans to businesses operating in disadvantaged communities. The Calvert Social Investment Foundation lends money to more than 250 community organizations.[90] Started in 1988, Calvert Investment Fund recipients had built or rehabilitated 17,000 homes and created 430,000 jobs by 2010. The foundation has also financed 25,000 cooperatives, social enterprises, and community facilities. Loan candidates must have three years of operating experience, a solid base of net assets or net worth, evidence of good operating performance, audited financial statements, and a track record of raising and repaying debt capital.[91]

Strategic Philanthropy

Also set aside some community giving resources for strategic partnerships with nonprofits aligned with the company's mission. Strategic philanthropy is the partnering of a company and nonprofit organization to achieve a communal good that also benefits the company. Michael Porter and Mark Kramer maintain that "each company must select issues that intersect with its particular business. . . . Typically, the more closely tied a social issue is to a company's business, the greater the opportunity to leverage the firm's resources—and benefit society."[92] Porter and Kramer differentiate three social issue categories that may impact business operations:

- *Generic social issues* that do not significantly affect a company's operations or long-term competiveness
- *Value chain social impacts* that significantly affect a company's activities in the ordinary course of business
- *Competitive context social dimensions* that significantly affect the underlying drivers of a company's competitiveness in the locations where it operates

Strategically determine which social issues have the greatest impact on business operations.[93] Value chain social impacts and competitive context social dimensions are usually ranked higher than generic social issues.

Porter and Kramer, for example, note that it generally makes more strategic sense for a credit card company, rather than a public utility, to financially support a dance company. For a public utility, a dance company addresses a generic social issue—supporting the arts improves quality of life in a community. For a credit card company, however, a dance company is a competitive context issue because attendees are likely to charge expenditures for the performance, transportation, and eating out, which increases credit card revenue.

But don't underestimate the strategic importance of generic social issues. Although 99 percent of the U.S. population can read and write,[94] the National Center for Family Literacy reports that 23 percent of American adults are functionally illiterate.[95] Functional illiteracy is defined as the lack of reading and writing skills needed to manage daily living and employment tasks, which is typically at the fourth-grade level. Researchers estimate that two-thirds of the students who cannot read proficiently by the fourth grade end up in jail or on welfare.[96] According to the U.S. Department of Education, 60 percent of adults in prison read at or below the fourth-grade level.[97] Such a high level of functional illiteracy damages the quality of life in the community and significantly limits labor force skill sets. This is, in part, why Facebook CEO Mark Zuckerberg, at the age of 26, donated $100 million to improve the Newark, New Jersey, public school system.[98]

Examine how the company can leverage its assets and expertise to

- select the most effective recipient
- signal to other funders that they should also assist the recipient
- improve the recipient's performance
- advance knowledge and practice related to the recipient's activities

Then rigorously monitor and evaluate results.[99]

The ideal strategic partnership is a "win-win" situation whereby the recipient nonprofit organization and the company can most benefit from associating with each other. To achieve optimal benefits for both the company and the recipient, there needs to be alignment between the missions of both organizations. Exhibit 12.5 provides questions to help managers determine which community organizations would benefit the most by being aligned with the company.

> ### Exhibit 12.5 Community Organizations That Benefit the Most from a Strategic Partnership
>
> Determine a nonprofit strategic partner by answering the following questions:
> 1. *Mission Match:*
>   a. What is your company's mission?
>   b. What community organizations have a mission that intersects this mission?
> 2. *Product or Service Match*
>   a. What is your company's product or service?
>   b. What community organizations would benefit from this product or service?
> 3. *Employee Skills Match*
>   a. What skills can your employees offer a community organization?
>   b. What community organizations would benefit from these skills?
>
> An optimal partner is a community organization with a similar mission that can benefit from the company's product, service and employee skills.

Also determine which community organizations can supply inputs to the company or purchase the company's products or services. Companies need high-quality laborers. Donating money, products, or skills to educational institutions that develop future employees enhances a company's competitive advantage.

Similarly, a company that wants to expand its customer base can donate to organizations whose managers or employees are associated with key target markets. By forming a strategic partnership with the American Red Cross, the Nationwide Insurance Foundation can more effectively serve natural disaster victims.[100] Scholastic Books, which markets products for new readers, funds literacy programs. Klinke Cleaners collects coats for kids during the winter holiday season. In the latter two circumstances, the donation beneficiaries are potential customers.

Dell and Verizon have well-integrated strategic partners that impact potential future employees and customers, and significantly benefit the donation recipients. By donating computers to educational institutions, Dell develops the labor skills of potential future employees and creates a future customer base among the student population. Verizon, which provides high-speed Internet access, developed partnerships with several educational associations to develop the "Thinkfinity" website.[101] The website provides educators, students, parents, and after-school programs with more than 50,000 free K–12 classroom lesson plans, interactive activities, and other online resources. The website serves community needs, reduces instructional costs, and connects millions of potential employees and customers to the company's services. The free service is also intended to increase the need for fiber-optic networks, supplied by Verizon.

Exhibit 12.6 provides questions that can help managers determine which community organizations would contribute the most to the company achieving its strategic goals.[102]

Exhibit 12.6 Community Organizations That Benefit the Company the Most	
Partnership Factor	Probing Questions: What Community Organizations . . .
Sources of Potential Employees or Other Resources	• Have similar labor and product supply chains? • Train and develop potential employees? • Attract high-quality potential employees to the community? • Serve as incubators for research and development of relevant ideas? • Develop and protect necessary natural resources? • Are associated with current and potential sources of capital? • Attract potential suppliers to the community? • Can contribute to cost reductions? • Have similar infrastructure needs?
Sources of Potential Customers	• Currently, or could, purchase products or services? • Serve current and potential customers? • Make the location a more attractive place for potential customers? • Stimulate business development and economic growth?

A community organization that rises to the top after applying the questions in Exhibit 12.5 (community organizations that benefit the most from partnering with the company) and Exhibit 12.6 (community organizations that benefit the company the most) is an optimal choice for a win-win strategic partnership.

The ideal partnership is also an equal partnership. Company managers must be empathetic to the problems of managing community organizations. Acknowledge and respect the community organization's limitations, and work within those limits to develop quality win-win projects. Strategic partnership objectives must be transparent, fair, and realistic, with two-way communication between the community organization and the business.

Cause-related marketing is a win-win strategic partnership whereby nonprofits benefit by revenue generated through the sales of the donor's product or service.[103] Cause-related marketing took off during the 1980s, when American Express donated a penny to the Statue of Liberty restoration project each time a consumer used the company's credit card. Ben & Jerry's upped the ante, donating 1 percent of the profits from its Peace Pop ice cream novelty bar to peace organizations. Nabisco innovatively produced a series of Animal Crackers in the shape of endangered species and donated product sales to the World Wildlife Fund.

In 2006, Bono, the U2 rock group singer, and Bobby Shriver launched (RED). A portion of profits for all licensed (RED) products are donated to the Global Fund, which finances AIDS programs focused on women and children in Africa.[104] None of the (RED) money can be used to pay overhead expenses. Early corporate partners include Converse, Gap, Motorola, Apple, Hallmark, and Dell. By 2010, (RED) products contributed more than $150 million to provide AIDS inoculation for over over 50 million people.

Community Involvement Management Process

Similar to the process with ethics, integrate corporate citizenship endeavors as part of the company's vision and mission rather than as an afterthought done to please local politicians and activist groups. Make responsible business practices toward employees, customers, and the community central to organizational operations. This is particularly important to small businesses, whose employees and customers live in the community.

Philip Mirvis and Bradley Googins describe a five-stage corporate citizenship developmental process: elementary, engaged, innovative, integrative, and transforming.[105] Most companies begin at the *elementary* level, occasionally helping out the community when requested by local governments and powerful community constituents. To gain greater credibility, companies become more *engaged* by monitoring community needs and developing policies clearly articulating their intentions to be good citizens. Engagement in the community raises the issue of organizational capacity to follow-through on its commitments. Companies become *innovative* by brainstorming solutions, planning programs, and developing metrics that measure impacts. Next, organizations create coherence among their initiatives by *integrating* them under a common theme that enables the company to brand its efforts.

By fully committing to being good citizens, some organizations undergo a *transformative* experience whereby core business products and services are modified, or new products and services created, to meet community needs. When this occurs, corporate citizenship becomes a central aspect of the organization's identity, as has happened at Ben & Jerry's, the Body Shop, and Patagonia.[106]

Deciding what to give which organization could be determined by the human resources office, a philanthropic foundation, or a team of employees. Even if a company is large enough to support its own foundation, involve employees in the outreach decision-making pocess.

The process for authentic engagement between the company and the community closely parallels the Managing Environmental Change process that appeared in Exhibit 11.7. The expanded model appears in Exhibit 12.7.

Exhibit 12.7 Community Involvement Management Process		
Step	Action	Explanation
1	Assign a community involvement champion	This is an opportunity to provide leadership training to a go-getter at the middle management or nonmanagement level.
2	Obtain management support	Have executives provide visible and vocal support for the program.

3	Form a "Community Involvement Team"	A cross-functional employee team can obtain participation throughout the company.
4	Conduct a company asset analysis	Determine the amount or type of money, time, product, and skills the company can contribute.
5	Gather information on community needs	Obtain information from the employees and the United Way.
6	Match *company* assets and *community* needs	Determine potential links between company assets and community needs, and prioritize these win-win possibilities.
7	Match *community* assets and *company* needs	Determine potential links between community assets and company needs, and prioritize these win-win possibilities.
8	Develop a strategic partnership with a community organization	Form a strategic alliance with a community partner, gather suggestions on the type of assistance it needs most, and reach agreement on an action plan.
9	Create a vision and goal statement	In partnership with the community organization, create an overall vision statement and several goals for the highest-priority items.
10	Determine a practical application	Focus on a low-hanging fruit whereby the company's involvement can make a difference or a high-profile issue employees strongly support.
11	Involve other employees in the community involvement process	Share the vision and goal with other employees and provide outlets for employee input.
12	Assess performance	Develop measures to assess performance, gather other relevant feedback for continuous improvement, and make changes as needed.
13	Support other opportunities	Provide flexibility for employees to take responsibility for other community involvement initiatives.

Community Involvement as Employee Training

Community involvement provides an opportunity for team building, leadership training, and teaching project management, all of which directly impact a company's daily operations. Go-getters, in particular, need diverse opportunities to use their creativity, develop talents, and hone managerial skills, and they can meet these needs through community involvement options.

Volunteering on a common cause benefitting the community enhances employee morale. Workplace relationships can get monotonous and frayed over time. Employee interactions while serving food at a homeless shelter or building a Habitat for Humanity home create common experiences that keep relationships fresh and meaningful.

Timberland uses community service projects to teach employees project management skills. The employee leading the project defines its scope, researches community needs and assets, selects the service partner, develops the project, prepares a budget and plan, motivates participants, manages the event, measures outcomes, and celebrates the accomplishments.[107] As highlighted in the "Best Practice in Use" exhibit, the company provides the team leader with tools and worksheets to enable successful completion of the project.

BEST PRACTICE IN USE

Timberland's Service Toolkit

At Timberland, we believe in making a difference in the communities where we live and work. By engaging dedicated volunteers in service events that develop civic leadership and build civic pride and by finding opportunities to invest in our resources, we share our core values of humanity, humility, integrity and excellence.

Timberlands Path of Service™ program provides our employees with the opportunity to use 40 hours of paid time to commit their skills and energy to a cause, issue or organization that is important to them. In addition, we initiate and execute a number of company-wide service events designed to build better communities around the globe.

This Service Tool Kit has been created from our firsthand experience to help you develop and execute meaningful service events from start to finish. We have included information to help you get organized, recruit and manage volunteers and deliver superior results for your service partner.

Table of Contents
1.0   Define Project Parameters
    1.1   Identify Vision, Goals and Scope of Project
    1.2   Establish a Budget and Prepare a Plan
    1.3   Recruit the Operations Team
2.0   Research Community Needs and Assets
    2.1   Internet Research
    2.2   Community Outreach
    2.3   Recognize Community Assets
    2.4   Use a Request for Proposal (RFP) Process
3.0   Select Service Partners
    3.1   Conduct First Site Visit
    3.2   Use Available Tools to Assess Partner
    3.3   Review Partnership Agreement and Clarify Expectations
4.0   Develop Project
    4.1   Define Clear Objectives
    4.2   Complete Service Partner and Roles and Responsibilities Checklists
    4.3   More Key Steps

Networking

Community involvement provides many opportunities for networking with other businesses and community leaders. Managers can join the Rotary, Chamber of Commerce, Better Business Bureau, and other business associations, including Businesses for Social Responsibility, Lions Club, Kiwanis Club, and Optimist Club.

Rotary International is a professional networking and service organization that was founded in 1932.[108] As mentioned in Chapter 5, more than 1.2 million business, professional, and community leaders are members of 32,000 Rotary International clubs around the world. The organization's mission is to "provide service to others, promote integrity, and advance world understanding, goodwill, and peace through our fellowship of business, professional, and community leaders." Local rotary affiliates usually meet weekly for breakfast, lunch, or dinner and engage in local service projects. Meals are typically followed by a speaker discussing topics of interest. Rotary International's two primary service projects are the eradication of polio worldwide by immunizing children and increasing literacy. Rotaries conduct outreach to college and university students through Rotaract, a Rotary-sponsored service club.[109]

Chambers of Commerce, which began in Europe in 1599, exist on the national, state, and local levels. Nationally, the U.S. Chamber of Commerce represents the interests of more than 3 million businesses, 96 percent of them small businesses with 100 or fewer employees.[110] It advocates on behalf of the business community, supplies relevant information, and engages in public policy lobbying. The Chamber of Commerce's top public policy issues on the national level include energy, legal reform, health care, international trade, taxes, and labor relations.[111] Local affiliates provide networking opportunities to meet new clients, suppliers, and mentors, and they generate awareness of member products and services.

The Better Business Bureau, founded in 1912, is an international organization with independently governed affiliates that establish, monitor, and uphold standards for conducting business. They improve community well-being through fraud prevention, ensuring truth-in-advertising, resolving customer disputes, and supplying consumers with relevant information. Better Business Bureau membership signals that a business operates according to eight standards of trust: Build Trust, Advertise Honestly, Tell the Truth, Be Transparent, Honor Promises, Be Responsive, Safeguard Privacy, and Embody Integrity.[112] Members are monitored for adherence to these standards and can lose their accreditation if these standards are violated.[113]

Businesses for Social Responsibility (BSR) is a global networking organization formed in 1992 and focuses on sharing best practices in social responsibility and sustainability.[114] The more than 250 member companies include Coca-Cola, Ford, General Electric, IBM, IKEA, McDonald's Microsoft, Nike, Starbucks, Walmart, and Walt Disney. Although a nonprofit organization, membership fees are not tax deductible because businesses receive services from BSR, such as assistance in developing a corporate responsibility strategy, creating sustainability reports, greening the supply chain, and energy improvement projects.

Some business networking organizations fund public policy lobbying efforts. Carefully choose which lobbying activities to support. Ethically, lobbying groups tend to be dominated by social group relativism analysis, which sometimes results in proposing rules and regulations that benefit businesses to the detriment of community well-being.

In the 1980s, for instance, many business groups lobbied against 60-day plant closing prenotification legislation, which had been proposed to limit the hardship suffered by dislocated employees and local communities following massive layoffs of more than 100 workers.[115] Business lobbyists predicted that publically giving a 60-day plant closing notice would force businesses to close prematurely and devastate the national economy. The legislation, formally called "The Worker Adjustment and Retraining Notification Act," passed Congress and took effect in 1989.[116] It benefitted many laid-off workers and communities and neither of the forecasted worst-case scenarios put forth by business lobbyists occurred.

Community Reputation Assessment

Assess key constituents to ensure that an important intended benefit of community involvement—a better reputation—is being accomplished. The Council on Foundations has created a Corporate Philanthropy Index (CPI) for companies to assess their reputation within the community. Send the three-item survey, measured on a 1–5 Likert scale, to multiple stakeholders or administer the survey at a focus group meeting.[117] The survey includes the following items:

- Compared to other companies, (*Company Name*) does its fair share to help the community and society.
- Overall, (*Company Name*) is the kind of company that helps the community and society by contributing things like time, volunteers, money, and sponsorships of nonprofit events and causes.
- (*Company Name*) really seems to care about giving and making contributions to help the community and society.

Social Performance Reporting

A company can also demonstrate respect for the community by being transparent about its operations and impacts. More than 3,500 corporate responsibility reports are published annually.[118] The Global Reporting Initiative (GRI), discussed in Chapter 11, offers a standardized framework for community impact reporting, in addition to environmental performance.[119] GRI examined 72 sustainability reports and found that most companies reported community impacts in the areas of education and training, philanthropy and charitable giving, community services and employee volunteering, total community expenditure, and community engagement and dialogue.

The top three indicators used to measure performance in each of the five areas appear in Exhibit 12.8.[120] Adopting this format enables companies to make comparisons with other firms in their region or industry.

Exhibit 12.8 Top Three Indicators for Five Community Impact Topics

EDUCATION AND TRAINING

1. Number of people benefited/reached by education initiatives
2. Amount of money invested/donated in the education initiatives
3. Number of education-related activities (seminar, classes, conferences, etc.) held

PHILANTHROPY AND CHARITABLE GIVING

1. Sum of money donated/raised/contributed to community initiatives
2. Percentage or number of people (organizations) granted/sponsored/covered by donated services
3. Number or quantity of scholarships/materials/services donated

COMMUNITY SERVICES AND EMPLOYEE VOLUNTEERING

1. Number of people/organizations/projects benefitted, served, or implemented
2. Number of volunteers
3. Number of volunteering hours

TOTAL COMMUNITY EXPENDITURE (THREE-WAY TIE FOR THIRD)

1. Amount of money spent in community investment
2. Percentage of profit/revenue/income spent
3. Percentage increase of money spent on social investment, compared to past year
3. Number of people benefitted in community investment activities
3. Number of projects developed and completed

COMMUNITY ENGAGEMENT AND DIALOGUE

1. Number of visitors, audience and participants reached
2. Percentage/number of sites where community engagement activities were performed
3. Frequency of meetings

Ben & Jerry's,[121] Timberland,[122] and Starbucks,[123] three leading companies in the area of social reporting, publicize their community involvement reports on the Internet and offer them as models for other companies to adapt. CorporateRegister.com, founded in 1998, profiles more than 23,000 social responsibility reports from 116 nations.[124] An annual award voted on by the website's registered users is given to the best social responsibility reports. The winner of the 2010 CRReporting Award was Vodafone Group and first runner up, ironically, was BP.[125]

SUMMARY

Companies possess tremendous power in their host communities and can influence community well-being or decay. Nonprofit organizations, which usually arise because of market failures, depend on the generosity of companies to serve their clients. Community outreach, a hallmark of ethical organizations, is a win-win opportunity for companies, nonprofit organizations, and the host community. The relationship among outreach partners must be based on respect, fairness, and transparency.

Managers must determine to what extent their organizations should engage in community activities. This chapter recommends a diverse approach to community outreach, beginning with employee work-life balance. Companies can give money, products and services, skills, and job opportunities to the community. Companies can also give to community organizations that are supported by employees, outsource giving to organizations that carefully monitor how recipients use donations, and develop strategic partnerships with community organizations that are aligned with the company's strategic goals and objectives.

Community outreach provides an opportunity for companies to conduct team-building exercises, train future managers in project management, and provide leadership opportunities to go-getters. Carefully measure and assess outcomes, and report the results to the community.

KEY WORDS

Tax avoidance; work-life balance; corporate citizenship; Socially Responsible Investment (SRI); sweatshops; UN Global Compact Principles; Interpenetrating Systems Model; primary stakeholders; secondary stakeholders; philanthropy; volunteerism; noblesse oblige; "The Gospel of Wealth;" United Way; sabbatical; social entrepreneurship; strategic philanthropy; cause-related marketing.

CHAPTER QUESTIONS

1. What are the four types of social responsibilities that businesses have?

2. Discuss the ethical pros and cons of doing business with a sweatshop in a developing nation.

3. What are the competitive advantages of community involvement?

4. Describe the six phases of issues-driven multi-stakeholder dialogue?

5. Discuss the four ways that businesses give to the community and the three strategic approaches they can take.

6. How can managers determine an optimal win-win community partner?

7. Describe the steps a manager should take to develop a highly effective community involvement program.

In the Real World: Enron

Arthur Andersen's Document Retention Policy—October 2001

On October 16, 2001, Ken Lay violated federal law by lying to shareholders. He announced that Enron had third-quarter operating losses of $618 million and $1.01 billion in nonrecurring write-offs. He failed to report an additional $5 billion in hidden losses. The nonrecurring write-offs attracted public attention. The SEC began an "informal" investigation, and the *Wall Street Journal*'s investigative journalists began publishing articles describing how CFO Andy Fastow profited from managing SPEs that did business with Enron.

Arthur Andersen found itself in a bind. Andersen was already under a cease-and-desist order from the SEC for its role in an accounting fraud at Waste Management, the giant trash-removal firm. The SEC threatened to disbar Andersen from practicing public accounting if it did not cease and desist from other fraudulent activities. Now it was becoming obvious that, a mere four months later, Andersen had been fraudulently certifying the books of another client—Enron.

Nancy Temple, Andersen's in-house lawyer, was among those creating a paper trail documenting Andersen's concerns about the Enron audit. Four days prior to Lay's October 16 financial statement announcement, Temple sent an email to Andersen's Houston office reminding it about Andersen's "documentation retention and destruction policy."

According to the policy, all nonessential audit materials could be destroyed prior to the initiation of a formal SEC investigation. Nothing could be destroyed after the SEC announced a formal investigation. The email was forwarded to David Duncan, the lead auditor on the Enron account, for his consideration.

Duncan's engagement team had been very lax. The team failed to remove redundant and nonessential documents after completing its two most recent quarterly audits. A formal SEC investigation seemed imminent, but it had not yet been declared. Duncan still had the legal right to destroy redundant and nonessential documents.

DECISION CHOICE. If you were the lead external auditor engagement partner, would you

1. Implement Andersen's document retention and destruction policy and destroy redundant and nonessential documents?

2. Preserve all Enron documents to assist any future SEC investigation?

   Why?

ANCILLARY MATERIALS

Websites to Explore

- Timberland, "Corporate Responsibility: Service Toolkit," available at http://www .timberland.com/graphics/media/tbl/Timber landServiceToolKit.pdf.
- Salesforce.com Foundation, "Share the Model," available at www.salesforcefoundation .org/sharethemodel.
- (RED), available at www.joinred.com.
- United Nations Global Compact, available at http://www.unglobalcompact.org/.
- Philanthropy
  - United Way, available at http://liveunited .org/.
- Council on Foundations, available at www .cof.org.
- Giving USA, available at http://www .givingusa.org/.
- Bill & Melinda Gates Foundation, available at http://www.gatesfoundation.org/.
- American Institute of Philanthropy, available at www.charitywatch.org.
- Charity Navigator, available at www .charitynavigator.org.
- Volunteering In America, available at http:// www.volunteeringinamerica.gov/.
- Socially Responsible Investing (KLD), available at http://www.kld.com/.

- International Opportunities
  - GlobalGiving, available at www.global giving .com.
  - Kiva, available at www.kiva.org.
  - Vittana, available at http://www.vittana .org/.

Best Place to Work Video

- Best Place to Work—Zappos, available at http://money.cnn.com/video/fortune/2009/ 01/21/fortune.bctwf.zappos.fortune/.

Business Ethics Issue Video

- "Ten Million and Counting," *Frontline*, about the politics behind the federal government's huge debt; March 24, 2009, 57 minutes, available at http://www.pbs.org/wgbh/ pages/frontline/tentrillion/view/?utm_ campaign=viewpage&utm_medium= grid&utm_source=grid.

TEDTalks Videos

- Work Sabbatical: Designer Stefan Sagmeister, who every seven years closes his New York studio for a yearlong sabbatical to rejuvenate and refresh their creative outlook, explains the often overlooked value of time off and shows the innovative projects inspired by his time in Bali; July 2009,18 minutes, available at http://www.ted.com/talks/stefan_sagmeister_ the_power_of_time_off.html.
- Kiva: Jessica Jackley, the co-founder of Kiva .org, talks about how her attitude about people in poverty changed and how her work with microloans has brought new power to people who live on a few dollars a day; July 2010, 19 minutes, available at http://www.ted.com/talks/jessica_jackley_ poverty_money_and_love.html.

Conversations with Charlie Rose

- A conversation with Bill Gates, Melinda Gates, and Warren Buffett about "The Giving Pledge" to donate half of a person's net worth to charity; June 16, 2010, 60 minutes, available at http://www.charlierose .com/view/interview/11063.
- A discussion about philanthropy and foundations in the United States; August 22, 2007, 24 minutes, available at http://www.charlierose .com/view/interview/8655.

NOTES

[1] Michael E. Porter and Mark R. Kramer, "Strategy & Society: The Link Between Competitive Advantage and Corporate Social Responsibility," *Harvard Business Review*, 84, 12 (2006), 83.

[2] Milton Friedman, "The Social Responsibility of Business Is to Increase Its Profits," *New York Times Magazine,* September 13, 1970.

[3] Keith Davis, "The Case For and Against Business Assumption of Social Responsibilities," *Academy of Management Journal*, 16, 2 (1973), 312–322; Colin Grant, "Friedman Fallacies," *Journal of Business Ethics*, 10, 12 (1991), 907–914; Thomas Mulligan, "A Critique of Milton Friedman's Essay 'The Social Responsibility of Business Is to Increase Its Profits,'" *Journal of Business Ethics*, 5, 4 (1986), 265–269; Brian Schaefer, "Shareholders and Social Responsibility," *Journal of Business Ethics*, 81, 2 (2008), 297–312.

[4] Schaefer, "Shareholders and Social Responsibility."

[5] U.S. Government Accountability Office, "Large U.S. Corporations and Federal Contractors with Subsidiaries in Jurisdictions Listed as Tax Havens or Financial Privacy Jurisdictions," December 2008, available at http://www.gao.gov/new.items/ d09157.pdf, accessed 12/10/10.

[6] David Cay Johnston, *Perfectly Legal* (New York: Portfolio Trade, 2003).

[7] Archie B. Carroll, "A Three-Dimensional Conceptual Model of Corporate Social Performance," *Academy of Management Review,* 4, 4 (1979), 497–505.

[8] Joe Nocera, "Emerald City of Giving Does Exist," *New York Times,* December 22, 2007.

[9] Target, "2009 Corporate Responsibility Report," available at http://sites.target.com/images/corporate/

about/responsibility_report/2009/full_report
.pdf, accessed 12/10/10.

10 Heli Wang, Jaepil Choi, and Jiatao Li, "Too Little or Too Much? Untangling the Relationship
Between Corporate Philanthropy and Firm Financial Performance," *Organization Science*, 19, 1
(2008), 143–159.

11 Aristotle, *Nicomachean Ethics*, translated by W. D.
Ross (New York: World Library Classics, 2009).

12 Erik Erikson, *The Life Cycle Completed* (New
York: W.W. Norton, 1982).

13 Quoted by Doris Kearns Goodwin in TEDTalks,
"Learning from Past Presidents," available at
http://www.ted.com/talks/lang/eng/doris_kearns_
goodwin_on_learning_from_past_presidents.html,
accessed 12/10/10.

14 John de Graaf (Ed.), *Take Back Your Time: Fighting Overwork and Time Poverty in America* (San
Francisco, CA: Berrett-Koehler, 2003).

15 Juliet Schor, *The Overworked American: The
Unexpected Decline of Leisure* (New York: Basic
Books, 1991).

16 "Time to Care Public Policy Agenda" available at
http://www.timeday.org/time_to_care.asp, accessed
12/10/10.

17 "2010 Working Mother 100 Best Companies,"
Working Mother, available at http://www.working
mother.com/BestCompanies/node/7818/list, accessed
12/12/10.

18 Kristina A. Bourne, Fiona Wilson, Scott W. Lester,
and Jill Kickul, "Embracing the Whole Individual: Advantages of a Dual-Centric Perspective of
Work and Life," *Business Horizons*, 52, 4 (2009),
387–398; "2010 Working Mother 100 Best Companies," *Working Mother.*

19 Council on Foundations website, available at
www.cof.org, accessed 12/10/10.

20 Ante Glavas and Sandy Kristin Piderit, "How
Does Doing Good Matter?: Effects of Corporate
Citizenship on Employees," *Journal of Corporate
Citizenship*, 36, 4 (2009), 51–70.

21 Sarah E. Needleman, "The Latest Office Perk,"
Wall Street Journal, April 29, 2008.

22 Charlotte Mulvey, *The Good Shopping Guide*
(London, Eng.: The Ethical Company Organization, 2009).

23 Marc Gunther, "The Green Machine," *Fortune*,
July 27, 2006.

24 Dennis M. Patten, "Does the Market Value Corporate Philanthropy? Evidence from the Response to

the 2004 Tsunami Relief Effort," *Journal of Business Ethics,* 81, 3 (2008), 599–607.

25 Sheila Bonini, Noemie Brun, and Michelle Rosenthal, "McKinsey Global Survey Results: Valuing
Corporate Social Responsibility," *McKinsey Quarterly,* July 2009, available at http://mkqpreview1
.qdweb.net/Corporate_Finance/Valuing_social_
responsibility_programs_2393, accessed 12/10/10.

26 Social Investment Forum, "Overview for Financial
Professionals," available at http://www.socialinvest
.org/resources/professionals.cfm, accessed 12/10/10.

27 KLD Indexes, available at http://www.kld.com/
indexes/ds400index/index.html, accessed 12/10/10.

28 KLD Indexes, "FTSE KLD 400 Social Index,"
available at http://www.kld.com/indexes/data/fact_
sheet/DS400_Fact_Sheet.pdf, accessed 12/20/10.

29 Wayne Visser and Nick Tolhurst (Eds.), *The World
Guide to CSR: A Country-by-Country Analysis of
Corporate Sustainability and Responsibility* (Shef-
field, UK: Greenleaf Publishing, 2010).

30 Dirk Olin and Jay Whitehead, "CR: How Fast It's
Growing, How Much It's Spending, and How Far
It's Going," *CR*, March/April 2010, 25–32, available at http://www.thecro.com/content/100-best-
corporate-citizens, accessed 12/10/10.

31 Nike website, "Awards and Recognition," available at http://www.nikebiz.com/company_over
view/awards_recognition.html, accessed 12/10/10.

32 Global Exchange website, "Nike Campaign," available at http://www.globalexchange.org/campaigns/
sweatshops/nike/, accessed 12/10/10.

33 Nicholas D. Kristoff and Sheryl WuDunn, *Thunder from the East: Portrait of a Rising Asia* (New
York: Alfred A. Knopf, 2000).

34 Allen R. Myerson, "In Principle, A Case for More
'Sweatshops,'" *New York Times,* June 22, 1997.

35 Nike Inc., "Social Responsibility Report: FY
07/08/09, available at http://www.nikebiz.com/
crreport/content/pdf/documents/full-report.pdf,
accessed 12/10/10.

36 Steven Greenhouse, "Pressured, Nike to Help Workers in Honduras," *New York Times*, July 26, 2010.

37 United Nations Global Compact, "Overview of
the UN Global Compact," available at http://www
.unglobalcompact.org/aboutthegc/index.html,
accessed 12/10/10.

38 United Nations Global Compact, "The Ten Principles," available at http://www.unglobalcompact
.org/AbouttheGC/TheTenPrinciples/index.html,
accessed 12/10/10.

39 United Nations Global Compact, *United Nations Global Compact Annual Review 2008*, available at http://www.unglobalcompact.org/docs/news_events/9.1_news_archives/2009_04_08/GC_2008AR_FINAL.pdf, accessed 12/10/10.

40 Global e-Sustainability Initiative Supply Chain Working and the Electronic Industry Code of Conduct Implementation Group, *The Information and Communications Technology (ICT) Supplier Self-Assessment Questionnaire,* June 19, 2007, available at http://www.hp.com/hpinfo/globalcitizenship/environment/pdf/ICT_Self-AssessmentQuestionnaire.pdf, accessed 12/10/10. The questions have been slightly modified for presentation purposes.

41 The Interpenetrating Systems Model in this book expands similar models developed in Lee E. Preston and James E. Post, *Private Management and Public Policy* (Englewood Cliffs, NJ: Prentice Hall, 1975), and Lyman Reed, Kathleen Getz, Denis Collins, William Oberman, and Robert Toy, "Theoretical Models and Empirical Results: A Review and Synthesis of JAI Volumes 1–10," in Lee Preston (Ed.), *Corporation and Society Research: Studies in Theory and Measurement* (Greenwich, CT: JAI Press, 1990), pp. 27–62.

42 FlyersRights.org website, available at www.flyersrights.org, accessed 12/10/10.

43 Matthew L. Wald, "Stiff Fines Are Set for Long Wait on Tarmac," *New York Times,* December 22, 2009.

44 FlyersRights.org, "Stuck on the Tarmac? Not Anymore!" September 14, 2010, available at http://strandedpassengers.blogspot.com/2010/09/stuck-on-tarmac-not-anymore.html, accessed 12/10/10.

45 R. Edward Freeman, *Strategic Management: A Stakeholder Approach* (New York: Basic Books, 1984).

46 Ronald K. Mitchell, Bradley R. Agle, and Donna J. Wood, "Toward a Theory of Stakeholder Identification and Salience: Defining the Principle of Who and What Really Counts," *Academy of Management Review*, 22, 4 (1997), 853–886.

47 Preston and Post, *Private Management and Public Policy.*

48 Julia Roloff, "Learning from Multi-Stakeholder Networks: Issue-Focused Stakeholder Management," *Journal of Business Ethics*, 82, 1 (2008), 233–250; see also Esben Rahbek Pedersen, "Making Corporate Social Responsibility (CSR) Operable: How Companies Translate Stakeholder Dialogue into Practice," *Business & Society Review*, 111, 2 (2006), 137–163.

49 Jeanne Logsdon and Harry Buren, "Beyond the Proxy Vote: Dialogues Between Shareholder Activists and Corporations," *Journal of Business Ethics*, 87, 4 (2009), 353–365.

50 M. Todd Henderson and Anup Malani, "Corporate Philanthropy and the Market for Altruism," *Columbia Law Review,* 109, 3 (2009), 571–627.

51 Michael E. Porter and Mark R. Kramer, "The Competitive Advantage of Corporate Philanthropy," *Harvard Business Review,* 80, 12 (2002), 56–69; Leonard L. Berry, "The Best Companies Are Generous Companies," *Business Horizons*, 50, 4 (2007), 263–269.

52 Sheila Bonini and Stephanie Chenevert, "The State of Corporate Philanthropy: A McKinsey Global Survey," 2008 McKinsey & Company, available at http://www.disabilityfunders.org/webfm_send/13, accessed 12/10/10.

53 Robert J. Williams and J. Douglas Barrett, "Corporate Philanthropy, Criminal Activity, and Firm Reputation: Is There a Link?" *Journal of Business Ethics*, 26, 4 (2000), 341–350.

54 National Philanthropic Trust, "History of Philanthropy," available at http://www.npt.org/philanthropy/history_philanthropy.asp, accessed 12/10/10.

55 Andrew Carnegie and Gordon Hunter, *The Autobiography of Andrew Carnegie and the Gospel of Wealth* (New York: Signet Classics, 2006).

56 Marc Benioff and Karen Southwick, *Compassionate Capitalism: How Corporations Can Make Doing Good an Integral Part of Doing Well* (Franklin Lakes, NJ: Career Press, 2004).

57 Salesforce.com Foundation, "Share the Model," available at www.salesforcefoundation.org/sharethemodel, accessed 12/10/10.

58 Live United, "History," available at http://liveunited.org/pages/history/, accessed 12/10/10.

59 Kurt Badenhausen, "The World's Most Valuable Brands," *Forbes,* July 28, 2010.

60 Newman's Own Foundation, "History," available at http://www.newmansownfoundation.org/basics/history.php, accessed 12/10/10.

61 The Center on Philanthropy at Indiana University, *Giving USA 2010: The Annual Report on Philanthropy for the Year 2009* (Glenview, IL: Giving USA Foundation, 2010), available at http://www.givingusa2010.org/products/GivingUSA_2010_ExecSummary_Print.pdf, accessed 12/12/10.

62 Bill & Melinda Gates Foundation, "Foundation Fact Sheet," available at http://www.gatesfoundation

.org/about/Pages/foundation-fact-sheet.aspx, accessed 12/10/10.

63 Bill & Melinda Gates Foundation, "Implementing Warren Buffet's Gift," available at http://www.gatesfoundation.org/about/Pages/implementing-warren-buffetts-gift.aspx , accessed 12/10/10.

64 Ron Lieber, "How Much to Donate? God Knows," *New York Times*, April 30, 2010.

65 Michael I. Norton and Elizabeth W. Dunn, "Help Employees Give Away Some of That Bonus," *Harvard Business Review*, 86, 7/8 (2008), 27.

66 Timberland, "Corporate Responsibility: Product Donation," available at http://www.timberland.com/category/index.jsp?categoryId=4039655, accessed 12/10/10.

67 Corporation for National and Community Service, *Volunteering in America 2010: National, State, and City Information*, available at http://www.volunteeringinamerica.gov/assets/resources/IssueBriefFINALJune15.pdf, accessed 12/10.10.

68 Sarah E. Needleman, "The Latest Office Perk," *Wall Street Journal*, April 29, 2008.

69 United Way of Dane County, "VolunteerYourTime.org," available at http://volunteeryourtime.org/, accessed 12/10/10.

70 Corporation for National & Community Service, "United We Serve," available at http://www.serve.gov/index.asp, accessed 12/10/10.

71 Dadit Hidayat, Samuel Pratsch, and Randy Stoecker, "Principles for Success in Service Learning—The Three Cs," in Randy Stoecker and Elizabeth A. Tryon (Eds.), *The Unheard Voices: Community Organizations and Service Learning* (Philadelphia: Temple University Press, 2009), pp. 147–161.

72 Michael Barbaro and Justin Gillis, "Wal-Mart at Forefront of Hurricane Relief," *Washington Post*, September 5, 2005.

73 Andrew E. Carr and Thomas Li-Ping Tang, "Sabbaticals and Employee Motivation: Benefits, Concerns, and Implications," *Journal of Education for Business*, 80, 3 (2005), 160–164.

74 Kristina A. Bourne, Fiona Wilson, Scott W. Lester, and Jill Kickul, "Embracing the Whole Individual: Advantages of a Dual-Centric Perspective of Work and Life," *Business Horizons*, 52, 4 (2009), 387–398.

75 Peter A. Dacin, M. Tina Dacin, and Margaret Matear, "Social Entrepreneurship: Why We Don't Need a New Theory and How We Move Forward From Here," *Academy of Management Perspectives*, 24, 3 (2010), 37–57.

76 J. Gregory Dees, "Enterprising Nonprofits," *Harvard Business Review*, 76, 1 (1998), 54–67.

77 One Laptop Per Child website, available at http://laptop.org/en/, accessed 12/10/10.

78 Randall Stross, "Two Billion Laptops? It May Not Be Enough," *New York Times*, April 17, 2010.

79 Trips for Kids website, available at http://www.tripsforkids.org/, accessed 12/10/10.

80 DreamBikes website, available at http://www.dream-bikes.org, accessed 12/10/10; Patricia Simms, "Nonprofit Aims to Do Good," *Wisconsin State Journal*, April 10, 2008.

81 American Institute of Philanthropy website, available at www.charitywatch.org, accessed 12/10/10.

82 American Institute of Philanthropy, "Top Rated Charities," available at www.charitywatch.org/toprated.html, accessed 12/10/10.

83 Charity Navigator website, available at www.charitynavigator.org, accessed 12/10/10.

84 Charity Navigator, "10 Top-Notch Charities," available at http://www.charitynavigator.org/index.cfm?bay=topten.detail&listid=113, accessed 12/10/10.

85 Charity Navigator, "10 Charities in Deep Financial Trouble," available at http://www.charitynavigator.org/index.cfm?bay=topten.detail&listid=12, accessed 12/10/10.

86 Charity Navigator, "6 Questions to Ask Charities Before Donating," available at http://www.charitynavigator.org/index.cfm?bay=content.view&cpid=28, accessed 12/10/10.

87 GlobalGiving website, available at www.globalgiving.com, accessed 12/10/10.

88 Kiva website, available at www.kiva.org, accessed 12/10/10.

89 Vittana website, available at http://www.vittana.org/, accessed 12/10/10; see also Stephanie Strom, "College Loans as Development Aid," *New York Times*, December 5, 2009.

90 Calvert Foundation website, available at http://www.calvertfoundation.org/, accessed 12/10/10.

91 Calvert Foundation, "Lending Criteria," available at http://www.calvertfoundation.org/who-we-help/criteria, accessed 12/10/10.

92 Porter and Kramer, "Strategy & Society."

93 Porter and Kramer, "The Competitive Advantage of Corporate Philanthropy."

94 Central Intelligence Agency, "The World Factbook," available at https://www.cia.gov/library/publications/the-world-factbook/geos/us.html, accessed 12/10/10.

[95] Jessica Reaves, "Fighting Illiteracy in Chicago, With Enthusiasm," *New York Times*, January 14, 2010.

[96] Begin to Read, "Literacy Statistics," available at http://www.begintoread.com/research/literacy statistics.html, accessed 12/10/10.

[97] United States Department of Education, *The Health Literacy of Adults,* available at http://nces.ed.gov/pubs2006/2006483.pdf, accessed 12/10/10.

[98] Richard Perez-Pena, "Facebook Founder to Donate $100 Million to Help Remake Newark's Schools," *New York Times,* September 22, 2010.

[99] Porter and Kramer, "The Competitive Advantage of Corporate Philanthropy."

[100] Anonymous, "A Unique Approach to Corporate Citizenship," *Impact*, 16, 1 (2010), 12–14.

[101] Verizon Foundation, "Thinkfinity," available at www.thinkfinity.org, accessed 12/10/10.

[102] Porter and Kramer, "The Competitive Advantage of Corporate Philanthropy."

[103] Matthew Berglind and Cheryl Nakata, "Cause-Related Marketing: More Buck Than Bang?" *Business Horizons*, 48, 5 (2005), 443–453.

[104] (RED) website, available at www.joinred.com, accessed 12/10/10.

[105] Philip Mirvis and Bradley Googins, "Stages of Corporate Citizenship," *California Management Review*, 48, 2 (2006), 104–126; Boston College Center for Corporate Citizenship, "Stages of Corporate Citizenship," available at http://www.bcccc.net/index.cfm?pageId=2009, accessed 12/10/10.

[106] David Bollier, *Aiming Higher: 25 Stories of How Companies Prosper by Combining Sound Management and Social Vision* (New York: AMACOM, 1996).

[107] Timberland, "Corporate Responsibility: Service Toolkit," available at http://www.timberland.com/graphics/media/tbl/TimberlandServiceToolKit.pdf, accessed 12/10/10.

[108] Rotary International, "About Us," available at http://www.rotary.org/EN/ABOUTUS/Pages/ride fault.aspx, accessed 12/10/10.

[109] Rotary International, "Rotaract," available at http://www.rotary.org/en/StudentsAndYouth/YouthPrograms/Rotaract/Pages/ridefault.aspx, accessed 12/10/10.

[110] U.S. Chamber of Commerce, "About the U.S. Chamber of Commerce," available at http://www.uschamber.com/about, accessed 12/10/10.

[111] U.S. Chamber of Commerce, "Issues Center," available at http://www.uschamber.com/issues, accessed 12/10/10.

[112] Better Business Bureau, "BBB Standards for Trust," available at http://www.bbb.org/us/bbb-standards-for-trust/, accessed 12/10/10.

[113] Better Business Bureau, "Frequently Asked Questions," available at http://www.bbb.org/us/bbb-faqs/, accessed 12/10/10.

[114] Businesses for Social Responsibility (BSR) website, available at http://www.bsr.org/, accessed 12/10/10.

[115] Denis Collins, "Plant Closings: Establishing Legal Obligations," *Labor Law Journal*, 40, 2 (1989), 67–80.

[116] U.S. Department of Labor, "The Worker Adjustment and Retraining Notification Act," available at http://www.doleta.gov/programs/factsht/warn.htm, accessed 12/10/10.

[117] Council on Foundations, "Making the Case for Corporate Philanthropy," available at http://classic.cof.org/members/content.cfm?itemnumber=761&navItemNumber=2409, accessed 12/10/10.

[118] CorporateRegister.com website, available at http://www.corporateregister.com/about.html, accessed 12/10/10.

[119] Global Reporting Initiative, "G3 Guidelines," available at www.globalreporting.org/Reporting-Framework/G3 Guidelines, accessed 12/10/10.

[120] 2008 Global Reporting Initiative, *Reporting on Community Impacts*, available at www.globalreporting.org/NR/rdonlyres/6D00BC14-2035-42AB-AB6A-5102F1FF8961/0/CIReportfinalnew.pdf, accessed 12/10/10.

[121] Ben & Jerry's, "Social Environmental Assessment Reports," available at http://www.benjerry.com/company/sear/, accessed 12/10/10.

[122] Timberland Company, *2007–2008 Corporate Social Responsibility Report*, available at http://www.timberland.com/graphics/media/tbl/2007-2008_Timberland_CSR_Report.pdf, accessed 12/10/10.

[123] Starbucks, *Global Responsibility Report 2009*, available at http://assets.starbucks.com/assets/ssp-g-p-full-report.pdf , accessed 12/10/10.

[124] CorporateRegister.com, "About CorporateRegister.com," available at http://www.corporateregister.com/about.html, accessed 12/10/10.

[125] CorporateRegister.com, *CR Reporting Awards 2010*, available at http://www.corporateregister.com/pdf/CRRA10.pdf, accessed 12/10/10.

Case Studies

Additional Cases available online
www.wiley.com/college/collins

Nortel: The Rise and Fall of a Telecommunications Company

Asbestos Compensation: The James Hardie Group

China: Economic Development and Employee Wages

Experimenting on Monkeys: Is it Ethical?

Product Trademarks: Apple vs. Cisco over iPhone Name

Case Study

BP and the Gulf of Mexico Oil Spill

By Mark Barnard   Mark Barnard is an associate professor of management in the School of Business at Edgewood College in Madison, Wisconsin. His research interests include employment relationships, organizational behavior, and strategic management. Contact: mbarnard@edgewood.edu

> We have to get the priorities right. And Job 1 is to get to these things that have happened, get them fixed and get them sorted out. We don't just sort them out on the surface, we get them fixed deeply.[1]
>
> John Browne, BP CEO, 2006

> [S]afe and reliable operations are BP's number one priority today. They will remain BP's number one priority while I am the CEO of BP.[2]
>
> Tony Hayward, May 2008

> There is a complete contradiction between BP's words and deeds. You [Tony Hayward] were brought in to make safety the top priority of BP. But under your leadership, BP has taken the most extreme risks. BP cut corner after corner to save a million dollars here and a few hours there. And now the whole Gulf Coast is paying the price.[3]
>
> Henry A. Waxman, Chair, Committee for Energy and Commerce, House of Representatives, June 2010

Overview

After discovering oil in British Petroleum's Mississippi Canyon Block, the crew on the Deepwater Horizon started working to temporarily seal the well. There had been delays and cost overruns during the drilling process, but the significant oil and gas reserves that were discovered made the effort worthwhile. Everything quickly changed, however, on the night of April 20, 2010, when an explosion and fire rocked the oil rig, killing 11, injuring 17, and starting what would become the largest oil spill in U.S. history.

For the next five months, British Petroleum (BP) faced constant criticism for the disaster and resultant environmental and economic fallout. Every decision before and after the well exploded was examined and questioned. Federal and state governments were challenged as they tried to mitigate the impact on individuals, businesses, and the environment. Residents of the Gulf States, having survived Hurricane Katrina, again had to cope with an environmental disaster whose impact would be felt for years to come.

BP's History[4]

BP has an internationally complex organizational history. After securing the rights to drill for oil in Persia (present-day Iran), William D'Arcy, a wealthy British entrepreneur, funded the search for oil. In May 1908, after seven years of searching, oil was finally discovered. This was the start of the Anglo-Persian Oil Company. In 1914, the British government became the major stakeholder in Anglo-Persian and saved the company from bankruptcy. In the early 1920s, Anglo-Persian began opening gas stations in Britain and by 1925 owned more than 6,000 pumps.

Anglo-Iranian (renamed after Persia changed its name to Iran) began investing in refineries after World War II and marketed its products in Europe. Iran nationalized all oil operations in 1951, including those of Anglo-Iranian. After extended negotiations, a consortium of oil companies was established in 1954 to oversee oil operations in Iran. Anglo-Iranian owned a 40 percent stake in the consortium. Soon afterwards, the company changed its name to British Petroleum Company.

In 1969, BP struck oil on the North Slope of Alaska, the largest oil reservoir ever found on the North American continent. Although BP now had significant access to oil, it did not have refineries or gas stations in North America. BP struck a deal with Standard Oil of Ohio (Sohio), which had refineries and stations but little oil, for a 25 percent stake in the company. In 1987, BP acquired the entire company, which it then used to expand nationwide as BP America. BP continued to expand its operations by merging with Amoco in 1998, making the company the largest producer of oil and natural gas in the United States.

In 2009, BP was the largest oil producer in the Gulf of Mexico, operating 89 production wells, sharing ownership in 60 others, and pumping 182 million barrels of oil from the Gulf. It is estimated that the Gulf generated $5 billion to $7 billion in profits annually for BP, about a quarter of the company's total.[5]

BP's Environmental, Social Responsibility, and Safety Record

Protection of the environment and safety are strongly emphasized in BP's Values and Code of Conduct.[6] The Responsibility value states, "We aim for no accidents, no harm to people and no damage to the environment." The Performance value affirms, "We deliver on our promises through continuous improvement and safe, reliable operations."[7] BP's extensive Code of Conduct provides numerous guidelines and examples of how to deal with a broad array of ethical concerns. The section on Health, Safety, Security, and the Environment lays out the "fundamental rules and guidance to help us protect the natural environment, the safety of the communities in which we operate, and the health, safety and security of our people."

BP was the first oil company to acknowledge the relationship between energy usage and global warming. In 1997, Lord John Browne, CEO of BP, called for "a balance between the needs of development and the need for environmental protection."[8] He also acknowledged that BP had to share the responsibility for addressing global warming. BP committed to reducing its greenhouse emissions 10 percent by 2010. A new unit, BP Alternative Energy, was devoted to researching and developing low-carbon energy—solar, wind, natural gas, and biofuels. BP became one of the world's largest producers of solar panels and solar power.

In 2000, BP unveiled a new global brand featuring a green, yellow, and white sunburst logo or Helios (Greek god of the sun) meant to "symbolize the living, organic form of a sunflower to the greatest source of energy . . . the sun itself."[9] Using the tagline *Beyond Petroleum*, BP ran ads focused on carbon footprints, alternative energy sources, and global climate change. A survey conducted by Landor Associates found that 21 percent of consumers thought BP was the greenest of oil companies compared to 15 percent for Shell and 13 percent for Chevron. From 2000 to 2007, BP's brand awareness grew from 4 percent to 67 percent.[10]

In 2009, BP cut corporate expenses by shutting down its alternative energy headquarters in London, and reducing its budget for alternative energy development from $1.4 billion to between $500 million and $1 billion. Several solar power manufacturing plants in the United States and Spain were also closed.[11]

BP has frequently been recognized for its environmental and social responsibility activities and has received numerous accolades for its efforts (see Exhibit 1).

Exhibit 1 Sample List of Awards and Recognition Received by BP
2010 – *Barron's* and *MSN Money* rank BP as the 47th most respected company among the world's top 100 largest companies.*
2010 – BP is ranked first among the 10 largest oil companies in the world in Tomorrow's Value ranking based on how well companies "manage their most pressing social and environmental issues."**
2009 – BP received second place honors for "Best Corporate Responsibility Report" based on addressing corporate social responsibility issues related to the company's performance, risks, and opportunities, and for identifying both strong and weak aspects of its corporate social responsibility activities.***
2006, 2007, 2008 – BP ranked in second, first, and ninth places respectively for the extent to which its strategy considered and then managed its social and environmental impact.+
2005 – *The Financial Times* ranked BP seventh on its list of Most Respected Companies.++

* "The World's Most Respected Companies," *MSN Money Central*, February 15, 2010, available at http://articles.moneycentral.msn.com/Investing/Extra/the-worlds-most-respected-companies.aspx?page=3, accessed 11/1/10.
** Two Tomorrow's, *2010 Tomorrow's Value Rating of the World's Largest Oil and Gas Companies: Summary Report*, available at http://www.tomorrowsvaluerating.com/Page/OilandGas, accessed 11/1/10.
*** CR Reporting Awards '10, available at http://www.corporateregister.com/pdf/CRRA10.pdf, accessed 11/1/10.
+ The Accountability Rating, available at http://www.accountabilityrating.com/past_results.asp, accessed 11/1/10.
++ *Financial Times*, "World's Most Respected Companies, 2005," available at http://www.ft.com/cms/indexPage/dc5c2cec-5c2a-11da-af92-0000779e2340.html, accessed 11/1/10.

Despite BP's stress on safety, the environment, and social responsibility, the company has been plagued by numerous accidents and safety failures since 2005. In 2005, an explosion at BP's refinery in Texas City, Texas, killed 15 workers, injured 180 others, and forced the evacuation of 43,000 people. For this accident, BP was fined $50 million for violating the Clean Air Act and an additional $21 million by the Occupational Safety and Health Administration (OSHA) for safety violations.[12] Although BP invested $1 billion to upgrade the Texas refinery, the company was fined an additional $87 million in 2009 by OSHA for continued deficiencies, the largest fine in OHSA's history.[13]

In 2005, cracks and breaks were found in pipes on BP's newly installed Thunder Horse oil platform. An engineering consultant who worked on the platform blamed BP for rushing construction in order to "demonstrate to their shareholders that the project was on time and on schedule."[14]

A year later, 267,000 gallons of oil leaked from BP's oil pipeline in Alaska. BP was fined $20 million in criminal penalties after prosecutors said the company had neglected corroding pipelines. An even larger leak occurred five months later due to extensive corrosion. An Environmental Protection Agency (EPA) agent who led the probe of the accident explained that "There was a corporate philosophy that it was cheaper to operate to failure and then deal with the problem later rather than do preventive maintenance."[15]

An OSHA inspection of a BP refinery in Toledo, Ohio, in 2006 revealed problems with pressure-relief values. In 2008, the same problems were found with valves in other areas of the refinery. BP was fined $3 million for not proactively addressing these issues. In March 2010, BP was again fined $3 million for "willful safety violations"[16] at the refinery. In a review of BP's safety performance since Tony Hayward became CEO, it was found that OSHA had cited BP for "760 egregious willful safety violations in its refineries."[17]

Offshore Drilling and Federal Laws

Early drillers noticed that wells located nearest the ocean produced more oil than those located inland. In 1887, one driller decided to build an oil derrick on a wharf extending 300 feet into the ocean. As expected, the well proved to be successful and others drillers began to build similar derricks.

Ocean drilling continued to push farther and farther offshore. Kerr-McGee Corporation is credited with drilling the first well from an offshore fixed platform out of sight of land in 1947. This marked the beginning of the modern offshore industry. By 1949, 11 oil fields were located in the Gulf of Mexico along with 44 exploratory wells.[18]

The U.S. Submerged Lands Act of 1953 established the federal government's ownership of submerged lands beginning three miles from a state's coast. The Outer Continental Shelf Lands Act (OCSLA), also passed in 1953, authorized the secretary of the interior to grant leases for oil exploration, drilling, and extraction.

After the Santa Barbara, California, oil spill in early 1969, during which 200,000 gallons of oiled spilled, the National Environmental Policy Act (1969) was passed to ensure that environmental impacts were considered in the decision-making process of federal agencies and all regulated activities, including oil exploration and drilling. The Clean Water Act (1977) regulated the discharge of toxic and nontoxic pollutants into surface waters.

Deepwater oil production, defined as drilling in waters greater than 1,000 feet in depth,[19] started in the Gulf of Mexico in 1979 and expanded much faster in the mid-1990s with new technology and federal incentives. Platform design continued to improve and drilling depths reached 7,500 feet. In 1982, Congress passed the Federal Oil & Gas Royalty Management Act, requiring oil companies to protect and conserve the environment when building oil and gas platforms in the ocean. The Mineral Management Service (MMS) was charged with supervising leasing and offshore oil operations.

In 1983, President Reagan signed Proclamation 5030, expanding the government's rights to 200 miles off the coastline and allowing drilling to move farther from shore and into deeper waters. In 2008, 108 deepwater wells were drilled in the Gulf of Mexico and there were 141 deepwater producing wells. In 2009, 80 percent of the oil pumped from the Gulf of Mexico was from deepwater wells.[20]

Drilling on the Deepwater Horizon

The Deepwater Horizon was drilling in waters approximately 5,000 feet deep. The drill pipe and bit extended from the derrick that sat on top of the oil platform, through the water and into the earth. The blowout preventer (BOP), which safeguarded against well blowouts, was placed on the sea floor with the drill pipe passing through its center and into the sea floor.

The bit used to drill the well was wider than the drill pipe, which allowed pieces of rock and waste to be removed. Mud pumped downward through the drill pipe pushed rocks and debris back up the well in the space between the drill pipe and rock wall, thus keeping the well hole clear. The drilling mud also helped maintain sufficient downward pressure within the well to keep gas and oil from rising through the well and causing a blowout. Maintaining such a balance required constant attention to the pressure level within the well.[21]

As drilling progressed into the earth, metal casings were used to line and stabilize the walls of the well. To keep the metal casings in place, cement was pumped into the space between the rock wall and the metal casing. O-rings or liner hangers were placed in the space where one sized diameter casing ended and the next smaller sized casing began. The O-rings and the cement safeguarded against gas and oil escaping from the well.

Once the well reached the oil reservoir, the drilling apparatus was removed and tests were performed to confirm that oil and gas were present in sufficient quantities. Since sufficient quantities were determined to be present, work started on a temporary seal.

Before sealing the well, a production casing was installed in the well hole that would allow oil and gas to be pumped out when BP was ready to extract it. Either of two types of production casing could be used, a long string (single pipe) or a liner tieback (a pipe within a pipe). The production casing would be cemented in place, and if a liner tieback casing was used, cement would also be pumped into the space between the two pipes, providing an additional seal against

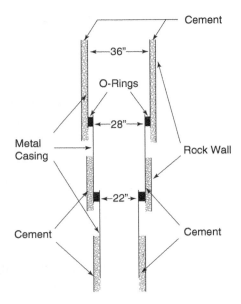

gas and oil leakage. The liner tieback also used mechanical seals to center the pipe and ensure that the cement set properly.[22] The disadvantage of using a liner tieback rather than a long string is that the tieback costs an additional $5 million to $7 million and takes several days longer to install. Approximately 75 percent of the deepwater wells use a liner tieback.[23] For this well, BP decided to use a long string casing.

Besides placement of the production casing, a cement plug would be placed at the bottom of the well (approximately 300 feet high), a second cement plug closer to the sea floor would be poured, and drilling mud would be placed between the two plugs. This would seal the well and keep oil and gas from leaking.

Companies Working on the Deepwater Horizon Well

Minerals Management Service (MMS)

MMS conducts the bidding process for leasing offshore areas to oil companies and provides regulatory oversight of the industry. Successful bidders pay fees to MMS along with royalties on all the minerals they extract. MMS also reviews and approves drilling and operational and maintenance plans for the well. MMS has often been criticized for its lax oversight of the drilling industry and its corrupt culture. Some employees in the agency have permitted oil companies to write their own environmental impact statements and accepted expensive gifts. There have also been drug and sex scandals involving employees of MMS and oil companies.[24]

BP

BP's responsibilities for the well included geologic assessment, engineering design, and getting regulatory approvals required for construction and operation of the well. Transocean owned the drilling rig, not BP. BP employees gave instructions on where and how Transocean employees should drill. BP employees also represented the company's interests in all operations related to the well. BP retained right of inspection and approval of work performed on its behalf. BP also retained contractors to provide various services. Contractors operated under their own management systems and provided their own personnel, equipment, and materials. Of the 126 people present on the day of the explosion, only 8 were BP employees.[25]

Transocean

Transocean, a Swiss-based company, is the world's largest offshore drilling contractor. Transocean leased the Deepwater Horizon drilling rig to BP and provided personnel to operate it. Transocean was responsible for the day-to-day drilling operations, operations safety, and maintaining well control. In 2009, BP was Transocean's largest single customer, accounting for 12 percent of its $11.5 billion in operating revenue.[26]

Halliburton

Halliburton's major area of responsibility dealt with cement work carried out at the well, including the work that was done when closing down the well. Halliburton provided engineering and design services, materials, testing, and mixing and pumping for cementing operations.

Other Companies

A number of other companies had a hand in various aspects of the operations on the Deepwater Horizon. Schlumberger Ltd. ran tests to make sure that the cement performed as expected. Cameron International constructed, installed, and maintained the blowout preventer. Speery-Sun, a Halliburton-owned company, was responsible for mud logging equipment, which records drilling activities, and personnel. M-I SWACO provided engineering services, mud supervisory personnel, mud products, and measured mud properties. Transocean crews conducted mud handling at the direction of M-I SWACO's mud engineers. Weatherford International supplied personnel, equipment, and components for the casing, including centralizers. Dril-Quip provided the well-head equipment and supervised the installation, servicing, modifications, and maintenance of the equipment. Oceaneering supplied the remote operated vehicles (ROVs) and the employees to operate them.

The Disaster: BP's MC252 Well

In 2008, BP paid the U.S. government $34 million for exploration and drilling rights for Mississippi Canyon Block 252 (MC252), a nine-square-mile area of ocean in the Gulf of Mexico, approximately 50 miles from Louisiana coast.[27] BP sold 25 percent of the lease to Anadarko Petroleum Corporation and 10 percent to Mitsui Oil Exploration Company of Japan. Neither company had day-to-day involvement with operations. BP budgeted approximately $96 million and 78 days for drilling. BP's actual target time for completing the well, however, was about 51 days.[28] Drilling began on October 6, 2009, using Transocean's Marianas drilling rig.

A month after drilling began, Hurricane Ida forced the evacuation of workers from the rig. Subsequently, the Marianas was damaged by the hurricane and had to be towed to port for repairs. BP leased the Deepwater Horizon drilling rig from Transocean and drilling resumed on February 6, 2010.

In early March, workers had difficulty controlling pressure in the well and gas started seeping into the well, a potentially dangerous situation. While attempting to bring the well under control, the drill pipe became stuck and could not be freed. The decision was made to fill approximately 2,000 feet of the well hole with cement and begin drilling in a different direction. This pushed back the completion of the well. Each day's delay cost BP approximately $1 million for additional rental fees for the rig and contractor costs.

On April 9, after reaching a depth of 18,360 feet below sea level, approximately 13,000 below the sea floor, tests were done to determine if sufficient oil was present to extract. On April 14, analysis confirmed that the well was at the proper depth to allow extraction and operations began to temporarily seal the well. The well hole was cleaned and determined to be in good condition with no gas leaking.

Since there had not been problems with gas seeping, BP decided to significantly shorten a mud circulation procedure. In this process, drilling mud would be circulated through the drill pipe and back up the well hole so that workers could make sure that no gas was entering the well. Although the American Petroleum Institute stated that it is "common cementing best practice" to circulate the mud at least once,[29] the mud was circulated for only 30 minutes, far too short a time to completely circulate it.

On April 18 and 19, the long string casing was placed and readied for the cementing. There were discussions about the cementing that would need to be done during the preliminary preparations for closing down the well. Halliburton indicated in a job log concerns that the long string casing would prevent a "successful cement job."[30] A later version of the BP document written after further testing was done, however, stated that "It is possible to obtain a successful cement job" and "possible to fulfill MMS regulations."

Halliburton had also advised BP to install 21 centralizers, a device used to center the casing in the well. If the pipe was not centered, the cement might not set properly, increasing the possibility that gas could seep into the well. As late as April 18, Halliburton warned that if BP did not authorize the use of more centralizers, the well would likely have "a SEVERE gas flow problem."[31] Rather than using 21 centralizers, BP installed only 6.

Beginning on the evening of April 19, cement was pumped into the well to cement the casing in place. A cement plug was poured to seal the bottom of the well and a seal assembly was installed. Pressure tests conducted to check that no gas was leaking indicated that everything appeared to be normal. Based on these results, BP sent workers from Schlumberger Ltd., who were on board to conduct a cement bond test that would ensure that the cement had set properly, back to shore without conducting the test.

At approximately the same time, a meeting was held between officials from BP and Transocean regarding the next steps in sealing the well. A heated disagreement ensued between Donald Vidrine, the most experienced and top-ranking BP manager assigned to the rig, and Jim Harrell, Transocean's rig manager. Harrell raised concerns about whether precautionary measures had been taken to ensure that no gas would escape from the well. Since BP was in charge of the well, the Transocean manager lost the argument.

At around noon, the mud displacement procedures were reviewed and drilling mud began to be replaced with seawater. At 5:00 p.m., Robert Kaluza, the second in charge on the rig for BP, and Jim Harrell oversaw a key test called a negative pressure test to ensure that the well had been properly cemented and that no gas was seeping into the well. Although the results of the test seemed to indicate that gas might be entering the well, Harrell considered the test successful. Kaluza, who was on the rig to "learn about deep water,"[32] apparently agreed.

When Vidrine came back on shift, he demanded that a second pressure test be conducted based on the unacceptable results of the first test. Although others disagreed, Vidrine insisted that it be done. During the test, pressure levels were again outside the acceptable range. Transocean employees, however, explained that the pressure results were normal and due a "bladder effect." Vidrine, seeking further input, discussed the situation with a superior at BP's Houston office. The supervisor, Mark Hafle, assured Vidrine that "If there had been a kick in the well, we would have seen it."[33] Vidrine gave the go ahead to continue replacing the drilling mud with seawater.

Starting at approximately 8:00 p.m., and continuing for the next 90 minutes, a number of mud control events occurred that indicated that gas was entering the well. No action was taken by BP or Transocean employees and drilling mud continued to be removed from the well.

At around 9:30 p.m., events quickly started to spiral out of control. At 9:31, increased levels of pressure were observed along with continued mud flows. Soon after, the chief mate and tool pusher were seen discussing "differential pressure." At approximately 9:40, mud started overflowing onto the rig and a minute later started to shoot up the derrick. Vidrine was notified that drilling mud was spewing from the well. Efforts were made to activate the BOP, which would seal the well. Although lights indicated that the BOP was activated, oil and gas continued to flow unabated from the well.

Minutes later, gas was heard escaping from the well and gas alarms sounded. Since the fire and gas prevention/suppression system was not configured to automatically trigger a shutdown of the HVAC system, outside air continued to be drawn into the engine room, a potential flash point for igniting the escaping gas. At 9:47, a roaring noise was heard and the rig vibrated. Power failed at 9:49, followed quickly by two explosions and a fire.

A Mayday call went out at 9:52 p.m. The oil rig started to become unstable and the order was given to abandon the rig to the ship *M/V Damon Bankston* that had been on site to assist with the mud displacement. Of the 126 workers on the drilling rig, 17 were injured, and 11 were reported missing. It was later determined that these 11 men had been killed in the explosion and fire.

Aftermath of the Spill

During the first few days after the disaster, efforts were focused on searching for the 11 men who were missing and extinguishing the fire on the drilling rig. On April 22, two days after the explosion, the Deepwater Horizon sank. On the same day, BP announced that it was sending more than 30 vessels to the area in order to skim oil from the ocean surface. BP also initiated a plan for drilling a relief well to seal the well if it was leaking.

Initially, it was uncertain whether oil was leaking from the well. Even though there was oil on the surface of the water, it was thought to have come from the initial blowout. On April 24, however, oil was discovered to be flowing from the drill pipe 5,000 feet below sea level.

BP, working with the Coast Guard and other agencies, attempted a number of different methods to seal the well and collect oil gushing from the well. Although initial efforts failed to reduce the flow of oil from the well, later efforts allowed increasing amounts of leaking oil to be pumped to surface ships. Finally, on July 15, a total of 86 days after oil and gas had started spewing into the Gulf, BP announced that the cap was completely closed and that oil was no longer flowing into the surrounding water.

With the flow of oil completely stopped, BP made plans to temporarily seal the well while continuing to drill the relief wells that were still needed to permanently seal it. On September 16, the first relief well intersected the oil reservoir. Cement was pumped through the relief well to permanently seal the leaking well. On the evening of September 19, the well was pronounced permanently sealed, five months after oil had started spilling into the Gulf. An estimated 4.1 million to 4.9 million barrels of oil spilled into the Gulf of Mexico from this tragedy.[34]

Cleanup Efforts and Economic Impacts

During the attempt to seal the well, BP was also involved in numerous cleanup efforts. In areas where oil accumulated in sufficient quantity and density, it was burned; skimmers collected thinner accumulations of oil. More than 500 miles of protective booms were used to protect shorelines and gather oil.[35] Chemical dispersants were sprayed on the surface of the water and directly into oil spewing from the well to break it into droplets that would disperse in the water and be eaten by microbes naturally present in the water.

The oil spill created severe economic hardships. Fishing, a livelihood of many in the Gulf States, was banned in areas affected by the oil slick. By the time that the oil stopped flowing into the Gulf on July 15, federal and state officials had closed more than 35 percent of the Gulf to fishing. Estimated losses for the fishing industry were $2.5 billion.[36]

Tourists' bookings in Alabama and Mississippi were down 40 percent to 75 percent during the summer. Researchers in Mississippi estimated the state's tourism losses would total $119 million for the summer. Florida was expected to lose $3 billion in tourism income in 2010. The U.S. Travel Association estimated that the economic impact of the oil spill on tourism across the Gulf Coast region would be $22.7 billion over a three-year period.[37]

On May 27, President Barack Obama announced a six-month moratorium on deepwater drilling that was set to last through November 30. The ban, lifted on October 12, 2010, six weeks early, idled 33 drilling rigs and led to the loss of approximately 23,000 jobs.[38]

After the disaster, consumers took action using Facebook and other means to organize protests and boycott BP stations. Tom Kloza, chief oil analyst for the Oil Price Information Service, estimated revenues for BP distributors and retailers dropped 10 percent to 30 percent during June 2010. Sales later recovered though there was still an average decline of approximately 5 percent.[39] Since BP owns fewer than 2 percent of the 10,000 BP branded gas stations, these actions mainly hurt independently owned BP stations.

BP stockholders suffered a rapid and sharp reduction in the value of their stocks. At their lowest point on June 25, BP's stock was selling for $27.02 a share, down from $60.48 a share on April 20. The equity partners for the well, Anadarko and Mitsui Oil, as well as Transocean, also saw their stock prices plunge 40 percent or more. BP stockholders were further hurt when BP discontinued dividend payments, estimated to be approximately $10 billion.

On June 16, after meeting with President Obama, BP agreed to create a $20 billion escrow fund to pay damage claims and government penalties stemming from the disaster and subsequent oil spill. After a one-time charge of $32.2 billion for costs related to the spill, including the escrow funds, BP reported a second-quarter loss of $17 billion, its first in 18 years.

BP has also agreed to contribute $100 million to a foundation to support rig workers who lost their jobs because of the drilling moratorium. It pledged $500 million for a 10-year research program to study the impact of the spill. To promote tourism in the Gulf area, BP donated $32 million to Florida's marketing efforts and $15 million each to Louisiana, Mississippi, and Alabama.[40]

In addition to the other costs, under the Clean Water Act, BP faces civil fines that could range from $1,000 per barrel of oil spilled up to $3,000 per barrel, if gross negligence is established. Thus, fines can range from $4.1 billion to $4.9 billion, or if gross negligence is found, from $12.3 billion to $14.7 billion.

The ultimate cost of the disaster remains uncertain. Some estimates have put the cost for BP at $17 billion to $60 billion, including penalties, damages, and cleanup costs for the Deepwater Horizon disaster.[41]

Environmental Impact

More than 1.4 million gallons of chemical dispersants were used to break the oil into small droplets, far more than has ever been used before.[42] Although the dispersant is toxic, BP and government agencies decided that applying the solution was a better and less toxic option than leaving the oil untreated. The chemical dispersants, however, did not cause the oil to disappear, only to be broken down into small droplets. Large plumes of droplets have been found in the Gulf. A study in the journal *Science* reported one oil plume more than 20 miles long, more than a mile wide, and 600 feet thick.[43] Reports appearing in other news sources reported the discovery of other large plumes, one of which was 22 miles long and 6 miles wide.[44] There was little evidence that microbes were quickly consuming the oil.

As microbes feed off the oil droplets, the danger is that oxygen will be depleted from the water, possibly killing sea life near the plumes. The droplets could also be eaten by animals or organisms in the water or get into the skin of fish.

A large layer of oil has been found on the sea floor, up to two inches deep in some places, indicating that a large amount of oil has not evaporated or dissipated as reported. Oil also made landfall along hundreds of miles of the Gulf Coast in Louisiana, Mississippi, Alabama, and Florida. Given the millions of gallons of oil that spilled into the Gulf, scientists believe that the ecosystem in the Gulf could require years or even decades to recover.[45]

Investigations

Investigations were undertaken by the Coast Guard, the U.S. House Committee on Energy and Commerce, the National Academy of Engineering, the National Commission on the BP Deepwater Horizon Oil Spill and Offshore Drilling, the Justice Department, BP, and other companies involved in drilling and operations on the rig to determine the cause of the Deepwater Horizon disaster.

U.S. House of Representatives

In a letter to Tony Hayward, lawmakers on the House's Committee on Energy and Commerce cited "five crucial decisions" BP made in designing and completing the well that may have led to vulnerabilities in the well's design:[46]

1. Using a long string pipe instead of a liner tieback, which provided only two barriers against the escape of gas or oil into the well
2. Relying on safety procedures with unclear emergency procedures
3. Using fewer centralizers than recommended
4. Not completely circulating mud through the well hole
5. Not conducting a cement bond test to determine if the cement was properly set

The House Committee strongly criticized BP for placing costs ahead of safety, noting that "the common feature of these five decisions is that they posed a trade-off between cost and well safety." The letter concluded, "Time after time, it appears that BP made decisions that increased the risk of a blowout to save the company time or expense."

National Commission on the BP Deepwater Horizon Oil Spill and Offshore Drilling

During the National Commission's investigation of the disaster, it was revealed that on December 23, 2009, four months before the Deepwater Horizon disaster, an oil rig in the North Sea owned by Transocean had a similar incident when drilling mud was being replaced by seawater. On that rig, dangerous pressure fluctuations went unnoticed, mud and oil flowed from the well onto the rig, and an order to evacuate the rig was given. Fortunately, the blowout preventer worked and the well was sealed before a blowout and spill.

Transocean identified a "'lack of clear' procedures for controlling well pressure, 'weakness in planning' the job's risk assessment and an absence of data about conditions in the well."[47] In response to these findings, Transocean revised its procedures for replacing drilling mud with seawater, the same process that was a factor in the disaster on the Deepwater Horizon. Unfortunately, it does not seem as if the crew on the Deepwater Horizon was aware of the safety changes. Daun Winslow, Transocean's performance manager on the Deepwater Horizon, claimed that he had never heard of the event with the other rig.[48]

BP's Investigation

On September 8, 2010, BP released the results of its own internal investigation. BP's report states that the accident was the result of "a complex and interlinked series of mechanical failures, human judgments, engineering design, operational implementation, and team interfaces [that] came together to allow the initiation and escalation of the accident."[49] Unlike the findings of the House Committee that focused on BP's failures and poor decision making, of the eight faults identified in BP's report, BP took partial blame for only one of the failures (misreading the pressure readings from the negative well tests). Blame for the other seven factors was attributed to Transocean and Halliburton. Further, the faults that were identified by BP seemed to reduce its own responsibility in the disaster. BP's report stated that the oil and gas exited through the center of the well rather than outside the casing.[50] Such a finding shifts blame away from BP's decisions to use a long string pipe and fewer centralizers, two areas of negligence identified by the U.S. House of Representative's investigation as being key factors that led to the disaster.

Future of the Well

BP can still tap into the well in the future to extract the oil and gas that have been discovered. BP, however, may hesitate to return to the well and may sell its 65 percent stake to another company. Based on BP's estimates that the well contains at least 50 million barrels of oil, it could be a worthwhile investment. At March 31, 2011, prices ($81.90), the oil would be worth more than $5 billion.

QUESTIONS

1. Identify the ethical and unethical actions and behaviors of BP, Transocean, and Halliburton. Based on your analysis, which company bears primary responsibility for the well blowout and ensuing events?

2. In a situation in which multiple companies are working together (contractor/subcontractors), what would be the best approach to ensure that ethical decision making takes place?

3. What steps can a company take to make sure that an employee will make the best decision possible in situations in which delays are costly or pressure from other employees, executives, or partners to continue working can be intense?

4. How can a company's executives balance their fiduciary responsibilities to earn as high a rate of return as legally possible against the need to use more costly materials or processes that, although not legally required, may potentially reduce risks?

5. Should BP reopen the well or sell it? Would it be ethical for BP to profit either by extracting and processing oil from the well or by selling the well to another company?

NOTES

1 Matthew L. Wald, "BP Says It Will Address Safety and Legal Problems," *New York Times,* July 27, 2006.

2 *Sustainability Review 2007: Our Key Priorities—Safety, People, Performance* (London, Eng.: BP, 2008), p. 5, available at http://www.socialfunds.com/shared/reports/1211305630_bp_sustainability_review_2007.pdf, accessed 11/1/10.

3 U.S. House of Representatives Committee on Energy and Commerce, Subcommittee on Oversight and Investigations, "The Role of BP in the Deepwater Horizon Explosion and Oil Spill: Opening Statement of Rep. Henry A. Waxman, Chairman, Committee on Energy and Commerce," June 27, 2010, available at http://energycommerce.house.gov/documents/20100617/Waxman.Statement.oi.06.17.2010.pdf, accessed 11/1/10.

4 BP, "Our History," available *at* http://www.bp.com/extendedsectiongenericarticle.do?categoryId=10&contentId=7036819, accessed 11/1/10.

5 Clifford Krauss and John M. Broder, "BP Says Limits on Drilling Imperil Spill Payouts," *New York Times*, September 2, 2010.

6 BP, *"Our Commitment to Integrity: BP Code of Conduct,"* 2005, available at http://www.bp.com/sectiongenericarticle.do?categoryId=9003494&contentId=7006600, accessed 11/1/10.

7 BP, "Our Values," available at http://www.bp.com/sectiongenericarticle.do?categoryId=9002630&contentId=7005204, accessed 11/1/10.

8 John Browne, "Addressing Global Climate Change," address given at Stanford University, Stanford, CA, available at http://www.bp.com/genericarticle.do?categoryId=98&contentId=2000427, accessed 11/1/10.

9 BP, "Our Logo," available at http://www.bp.com/section genericarticle.do?categoryId=9028307&contentId=7019193, accessed 11/1/10.

10 "'Beyond Petroleum' Pays Off for BP," *Environmental Leader*, January 15, 2008, available at http://www.environmentalleader.com/2008/01/15/beyond-petroleum-pays-off-for-bp/, accessed 11/1/10.

11 Terry Macalister, "BP Shuts Alternative Energy HQ," *The Guardian*, June 29, 2009.

12 Melanie Trottman and Guy Chazan, "BP to Pay $50.6 Million for Texas Safety Lapses," *Wall Street Journal*, August 13, 2010.

13 Guy Chazan, "BP Already in Safety Spotlight," *Wall Street Journal*, April 22, 2010.

14 Sarah Lyall, "In BP's Record, a History of Boldness and Costly Blunders," *New York Times*, July 12, 2010.

15 Michael Isikoff and Michael Hirsh, "Slick Operator—Political Connections," *Newsweek*, May 7, 2010.

16 Jad Mouawad, "For BP, a History of Spills and Safety Lapses," *New York Times*, May 8, 2010.

17 Joe Nocera, "BP Ignored the Omens of Disaster," *New York Times*, June 18, 2010.

18 Bureau of Ocean Energy Management, Regulation and Enforcement (BOEMRE), "OCS Lands Act History," available at http://www.boemre.gov/aboutmms/OCSLA/ocslahistory.htm, accessed 11/1/10.

19 Leslie D. Nixon, Nancy K. Shepard, Christy M. Bohannon, Tara M. Montgomery, Eric G. Kazanis, and Mike P. Gravois, *Deepwater Gulf of Mexico 2009: Interim Report of 2008 Highlights,* U.S. Department of the Interior, Minerals Management Service, Gulf of Mexico OCS

Region, p. xi, available at http://www.gomr.boemre.gov/PDFs/2009/2009-016.pdf, accessed 11/1/10.

20. Bureau of Ocean Energy Management, Regulation, and Enforcement, *Deepwater Production Summary by Year,* available at http://www.gomr.boemre.gov/homepg/offshore/deepwatr/summary.asp, accessed 11/1/10.

21. Aimee Whitcroft, "What Actually Went Wrong on Deepwater Horizon?" May 31, 2010, *Sciblogs* available at http://sciblogs.co.nz/terms/?s=what+actually+went+wrong+on+deepwater+horizon%3F, accessed 11/1/10.

22. Neil King Jr. and Russell Gold, "BP Crew Focused on Costs: Congress," *Wall Street Journal,* June 15, 2010.

23. Russell Gold, "BP Relied on Cheaper Wells-Analysis Shows Oil Giant used 'Risky' Design More Often than Most Peers," *Wall Street Journal,* June 19, 2010.

24. Sharon Begley, "Boycott BP! Because It's Much Better to Give your Money to Exxon," *Newsweek,* June 7, 2010.

25. Ian Urbina, "In Gulf, It Was Unclear Who Was in Charge of Rig," *New York Times,* June 5, 2010.

26. Barry Meier, "Owner of Exploded Rig Is Known for Testing Rules," *New York Times,* July 7, 2010.

27. Henry Fountain, "Reservoir in Gulf May Still Be Used," *New York Times,* September 18, 2010.

28. Ben Casselman and Russell Gold, "Unusual Decisions Set Stage for BP Disaster," *Wall Street Journal,* May 27, 2010.

29. Ibid.

30. Urbina, "In Gulf, It Was Unclear Who Was in Charge of Rig."

31. Casselman and Gold, "Unusual Decisions Set Stage for BP Disaster."

32. Ibid.

33. James C. McKinley Jr., "Documents Fill in Gaps in Narrative on Oil Rig Blast," *New York Times,* September 7, 2010.

34. U.S. Coast Guard, "Deepwater Horizon MC252 Gulf Incident Oil Budget: Government Estimates—Through August 01. (Day 104)," available at http://www.noaanews.noaa.gov/stories2010/PDFs/DeepwaterHorizonOilBudget20100801.pdf, accessed 11/1/10.

35. Carl Bialik, "The Numbers Guy: Oil Spill May Be Still Bigger," *Wall Street Journal,* May 29, 2010.

36. Bryan Walsh, "With Oil Spill (and Blame) Spreading, Obama Will Visit Gulf," *Time,* May 1, 2010.

37. Press Release, "Gulf Travel Likely to Last 3 Years and Cost $22.7 Billion," *U.S. Travel Association* July 10, 2010, available at http://www.ustravel.org/news/press-releases/bp-oil-spill-impact-gulf-travel-likely-last-3-years-and-cost-227-billion, accessed 11/1/10.

38. Stephan Power and Andann Zimmerman, "Gulf Drilling Ban Is Lifted. Oil Industry Still Concerned About Costs, Delays in New Federal Regulations," *Wall Street Journal,* October 13, 2010.

39. John Collins Rudolf, "BP Station Owners Face Long Road to Recovery," *New York Times,* August 10, 2010.

40. Clifford Krauss and John M. Broder, "BP Says Limits on Drilling Imperil Spill Payouts," *New York Times,* September 2, 2010.

41. Jad Mouawad and Clifford Krauss, "For BP, Toll Likely to Extend Past Cleanup," *New York Times,* June 14, 2010.

42. Jeffrey Ball, "The Gulf Oil Spill: Success on Surface, Questions Below," *Wall Street Journal,* August 4, 2010.

43. Amanda Mascarelli, "Extent of Lingering Gulf Oil Plume Revealed," *Nature News,* August 19, 2010, available at http://www.nature.com/news/2010/100819/full/news.2010.420.html?s=news_rss, accessed 11/1/10.

44. "Third Giant Underwater Oil Plume Discovered," *Washington's Blog,* May 28, 2010, available at http://georgewashington2.blogspot.com/2010/05/third-giant-underwater-oil-plume.html, accessed 11/1/10.

45. Jeffrey Collins and Jason Dearen, "BP: Mile-Long Tube Sucking Oil Away from Gulf Well," *Washington Times,* May 16, 2010.

46. Representative Henry A. Waxman and Representative Bart Stupak, "Letter to Tony Hayward, CEO of BP," June 14, 2010, available at http://energycommerce.house.gov/documents/20100614/Hayward.BP.2010.6.14.pdf, accessed 11/1/10.

47. Robbie Brown, "After Another Close Call, Transocean Changed Rules," *New York Times,* August 16, 2010.

48. Robbie Brown, "Adviser Says He Raised Concerns to BP on Well," *New York Times,* August 24, 2010.

49. "Deepwater Horizon Accident Investigation Report," September 8, 2010, p. 11, available at http://www.bp.com/liveassets/bp_internet/globalbp/globalbp_uk_english/incident_response/STAGING/local_assets/downloads_pdfs/Deepwater_Horizon_Accident_Investigation_Report.pdf, accessed 11/1/10.

50. Ian Urbina, "BP Spill Report Hints at Legal Defense," *New York Times,* September 8, 2010.

Case Study

Mining: Respecting Sacred Sites

By Maria Humphries and Dale E. Fitzgibbons Maria Humphries is an associate professor of management at Waikato Management School at Waikato University in New Zealand. She takes close interest in the changing rhetoric and practice of responsibility for people and planet, including the situation of indigenous people the world over and the call for a more responsible education in management. Contact: Mariah@waikato.ac.nz

Dale Fitzgibbons is an associate professor of management at Illinois State University, Normal, Illinois. His research interests include corporate social responsibility, sustainability, and what Western management education can learn from indigenous worldviews. Contact: defitz@ilstu.edu

Waihi: Pronounced **why-he** Meaning: **wai:** water; **hi:** raise or draw up[1]

Overview

Moving a fragile 2,000-ton concrete historical icon 26.5 meters (87 feet) south and 275 meters (902 feet) west over unstable terrain is not an easy or inexpensive exercise. In the little New Zealand town of Waihi, however, the Newmont Mining Company did just that. The building that housed the early pumps that drained the goldmine at Martha Hill was to be moved at a cost of more than NZ $3.2 million. It involved the sophisticated engineering work of securing the crumbling building, designing the technology to move it, strengthening the terrain over which it would travel, and preparing its new resting site.

This case study describes Newmont's corporate social responsibility activities in the little town of Waihi where a mountain once known as Pukewa has been mined away. Newmont is committed to enhancing recreational facilities, environmental restoration, and historical conservation of the region and is proud of its reputation as a socially and environmentally responsible global corporation.[2]

New Zealand/Aotearoa

New Zealand, or Aotearoa as it is sometimes known, is a country of great natural beauty. The country prides itself on being committed to robust democratic ideals; environmental sustainability; economic progress at home; and economic, scientific, and diplomatic leadership internationally.

Originally, the country was settled by people who organized themselves into self-determining tribes or "iwi"—each with its own name, claim to territory, and highly developed organizing principles, ethical codes, lore, and custom. Collectively, they are now known as Maori. After earliest contact with European explorers, traders, and settlers, these tribes united in 1835 to form a sovereign nation, and thus a legal capacity to sign the Treaty of Waitangi with the Crown of England in 1840. This treaty asserts that the queen of England confirms and guarantees to the tribes the absolute *tino rangatiratanga* (self-determination or sovereignty) at *hapu* (extended family) level and the authority for *hapu* to manage their own affairs.

Although there have been debates about the translation of the words of the treaty from Maori to English, the Maori did not sign away their authority over their people, resources, or treasures. Today, the descendants of these tribes and the later settlers who now share this land are attempting to generate processes to govern people and resources in ways that honor the ideals expressed in a wide spectrum of diverse values.

Mining, fishing, communication technology, water, and land care are just some of the areas in which the issues of cohabitation in this land require significant corporate attention.[3] Responsibility for the governance, management, and determination of who should benefit draws in a wide range of stakeholders. Among the stakeholders is the Ngati Tamatera tribe,[4] for whom Pukewa was a limb of Mother Earth, the resting place of their dead, and a place of healing for the living. Pukewa is the region from which Ngati Tamatera draw their identity and for which they assumed stewardship responsibilities and accountability.

Ko Pukewa Te Maunga. Pukewa the Mountain

Clothed in shades and hues of green, sparkling 'neath the brilliant rays of Tama-nui-te-ra her body lay outstretched, beautiful, serene. . . . She was Papatuanuku, the Earth Mother, lifelong love of Ranginui, the sky father. Within the folds of her generous gowns of green, birds and insects found food and shelter. . . . The curves of nga maunga provided the hills and valleys which helped determine the habitats of birds and insects. Such was the partnership between the creatures that lived upon her generous body that each of the many maunga which were part of Papatuanuku was named and carried its own mauri. Pukewa was one such maunga.

As time went by the shape of Papatuanuku changed as she adapted to the needs of the elements, all of which were products of her own sons. So too did her clothing change. For te maunga Pukewa this meant that an outcrop, a tamore, became visible from beneath the gown of Papatuanuku. For the Maori who co-habited with and inhabited the area, this outcrop had little significance, except as another landmark and as a further adornment upon the body of Papatuanuku. They continued to reside in the area and used Pukewa as an area to bury rangatira.[5]

But soon, incoming strangers discovered gold in this mountain. Not all were in agreement that this meant Pukewa should be mined.

Waihi—Home of Ngati Tamatera

I will not consent. If you give me what is not life, I shall know. Of what is the use of the land after it is broken? When the land is broken the owner perishes. This is my place, why do you seek after it? It is only a little piece. Let it remain to me.

These are the words of Te Hira Te Tuiri, a chief of the Ngati Tamatera, spoken in 1869 while attempting to stop the further private acquisition of land for gold mining and kauri logging. The speech came just 29 years after the signing of the treaty.[6] Over time, similar calls were made by many Maori but most failed to halt the land grabbing of their time. The process included outright confiscation, the individualizing of titles in preparation for sale of land by the Native Land Court, and the taxing of land at such a high price that its indigenous owners were left no option but to sell. Like so many other indigenous tribes, Ngati Tamatera lost their land. Many were dispersed. Those who remained struggled to hold onto life, particularly life *as* Maori. As a result, mining and kauri tree logging were able to progress unchecked.[7]

Gold at Pukewa

Despite Te Hira Te Tuiri's plea for the land to be left unmined, the Waihi Plains Goldfield was formally opened in 1875. In 1878, prospectors John McCombie and Robert Lee found gold on Pukewa. The samples McCombie and Lee sent for analysis suggested there was little value in the find. They left the area and in 1879 their claim was taken over by William Nicholl. Nicholl pegged out five acres and renamed the claim "Martha" after a family member. Later, a few small claims were amalgamated to form the Martha Company and underground mining commenced.

In 1890, the Martha Company and other claims in the area were bought by the Waihi Gold Mining Company of London. A great deal of capital was invested in the mine. The mine became the town's principal employer for more than 50 years. A workforce averaging 600 men was employed over the 70-year life span of the mine. When gold production peaked in 1909, a total of 1,500 people were employed in the mine and battery.[8]

The beautiful curve that bore the name Pukewa was slowly and methodically disembowelled. Heedless of the injuries being heaped upon Pukewa and therefore Papatuanuku, for years the mining was relentless.[9]

Mining operations negatively impacted the environment above and below ground. A honeycomb of underground tunnels and mine shafts developed as a network of 175 kilometres (110 miles) of tunnels spread over 15 levels. In 1913, electricity was introduced, facilitating the pumping of groundwater to the surface, thus allowing miners to work more efficiently. The landmark Cornish Pumphouse housed steam engines to power the dewatering pumps. Waihi was indeed aptly named. Once pumped up, the water flowed through deep gutters lining town streets and filled the public swimming pool.

Pukewa screamed out for help. She screamed out to her whanaunga, the creatures of Tane Mahuta, the children of Haumiatiketike, the children of

Rongomatane, but all to no avail. Finally the tears of rage and shame from Pukewa joined with those of Papatuanuku and the deep wounds within her were flooding too fast for the miners to make any material gain.[10]

The original Martha Mine closed in 1952 when a combination of factors suggested it was no longer profitable to mine low-grade ore. These factors included a fixed international gold price, depleting manpower, and a difficult economic climate. Once pumping ceased, the groundwater returned to pre-mining levels. In 1961, an area of land on Martha Hill subsided into earlier underground workings, leaving a crater approximately 40 meters (132 feet) in diameter.[11]

In the 1970s, gold prices began to rise, sparking renewed interest in gold prospecting at Waihi.

With renewed fervor and a methodology which defied the defences of Papatuanuku mining was once again imposed upon the body of Pukewa. This time, however, there was no chance of recovery. Her body was disembowelled and dismembered. Her very essence exposed and devastated.[12]

The modern Martha Mine is an open pit. Measured at the surface, the pit is 850 meters (2,800 feet) long, has a width of 600 meters (2,000 feet), and a depth of 250 meters (820 feet). The open pit is both massive and daunting.

The mine dominates Waihi and the surrounding area. The processing plant, waste disposal area, and water treatment plant are located 2 kilometres (1.2 miles) away in a rural area. Because of its location, the mining operation has received a high level of public scrutiny.

Mining today is an industry enabled and constrained by complex technical, economic, social, and legal conditions. The latter are now firmly grounded in the Western capitalist framework controlled by instruments of courts and administrative bodies. Working with these instruments is costly for corporations and communities.

The Newmont Mining Corporation

The Newmont Mining Corporation is a leading producer of gold, silver, copper, and zinc with operations on five continents. It also is engaged in the exploration and acquisition of more potential mine sites. Founded in 1921 in New York, Newmont has been trading on the New York Stock Exchange since 1925. It also now trades on the Australian and Toronto stock exchanges. The company employs approximately 35,000 employees and contractors. It has expressed an overt commitment to good social and environmental practices: "Newmont is committed to high standards and leadership in the area of environmental management and health and safety for its employees and neighboring communities."[13]

It was clear from the outset of Waihi operations that Newmont was committed to accruing stakeholder respect and responsiveness. The company is publicly sensitive to a variety of religious, environmental, community, contractor, and human rights issues. In addition, Newmont created a Five-Star Assessment system to continuously improve performance in the safety and health, community relations, and environmental aspects of an operation based on the principles of ISO 14001, the international standards for best practices in environmental management. At the very beginning of operations at a new site, Newmont plans carefully for the future closure of sites and the reclaiming of disturbed lands. This reclaiming begins and continues while the mine is being developed.

To operate in Waihi, Newmont has had to work its way through a number of legal requirements to deal with the legacy of the past and to set in place its aspirations for the future. The complexity and the cost of operations can be imagined by thinking about the implications of some of the many compliances Newmont must honor, including the Water & Soil Conservation Act of 1967, the Mining Act of 1971, the Clean Air Act of 1972, the Local Government Act of 1974, the Resource Management Act of 1991, and the Crown Minerals Act of 1991. These government regulations ensured that mining activities did not adversely affect the amenity of the area or natural environment, and the local communities were consulted.

Newmont's corporate social responsibility engagement with the community has been vigorous and ongoing. In 1990, the company built the Waihi Information Center for visitors. Newmont provides information on gold mining for secondary school curricula, sponsors sporting events, and donates money to a variety of local organizations. More than 20,000 people have toured the gold and silver mine.[14]

Newmont's website is full of technical, social, environmental, and economic information, giving it the image of being one of the more transparent mining operators in the world. Among the most publicly visible commitments to the community is its agreement to move the Cornish Pumphouse, a relic of the past and a landmark of note in the small town, to a new site.

The Pumphouse: Move It or Lose It[15]

The Cornish Pumphouse was constructed in 1904 to house the steam engines and pumps that kept the 400-meter (1,300 foot) deep No. 5 mine shaft dry. Designed to pump 6,375 liters (1,684 gallons) of water per minute, the pumps were fully in use from 1904 until 1913 when electric centrifugal pumps replaced them. However, due to the miners' deep mistrust of that "newfangled electricity," the pumps were operated only until 1929. The building was then stripped and gradually succumbed to the elements— becoming the stark monument seen today.

Some have likened the building, with its arched windows, to an ecclesiastical ruin, a quality that has helped the Pumphouse become Waihi's principal icon. Until recently, this Gothic-looking shell with tall imposing lines and cathedral scale sat perched right next to the unstable No. 5 shaft, tilting almost a foot. According to geotechnical experts, it was at risk of falling victim to any number of possible events—from the collapse of the shaft to pit slope failure, wall collapse, or movement at the Martha mine.

The Pumphouse, now registered as a Category I historic place, has been a Waihi landmark for nearly 100 years. It was endangered and a danger to others. Relocation was an option under consideration by Newmont. To separate the above ground parts of the structure from its foundations would considerably reduce the Pumphouse's heritage value. However, with 400 meters (1,300 feet) of uncertainty beneath, no amount of shoring up, reinforcement, and engineering ingenuity would save the building in the event of a mine collapse.

But moving the Pumphouse would be a feat in itself, and quite likely a very expensive one. What to do?

A number of stakeholders were drawn into the conversation. Local Historic Places Trust area co-coordinator Gail Henry and Hauraki District Council General Manager Langley Cavers, for example, expressed their preference for the structure to stay in its original location. To leave the relic safely where it was would be costly and perhaps impossible to do.

Regardless of the remedy, who would foot the bill? Cavers maintained that the close proximity of the Pumphouse to the open-cast Martha Mine meant that the activities of Newmont Waihi Operations contributed to the vulnerability of the Pumphouse. If true, the company would be liable for costs of removal under the terms and conditions of its land-use consent. Newmont funded an archaeological assessment of the Pumphouse and immediate environs.

Local interest in the issue was enormous. Whatever the decision, it would certainly be controversial. Some people wanted the Pumphouse saved regardless of cost. Others believed that moving it may not be worth the effort and that nature should take its course. Some locals strongly opposed any mining activity—historic or recent—because of what the town had already experienced. In the end, the decision was made to move the Pumphouse. Its movement would be a feat of engineering achievement.

And so it came to pass. The Pumphouse was moved. Citizens and tourists can observe this great and expensive feat of engineering from the closed circuit television set up for this purpose in the Newmont Education Center. Subsequent public relations and education material produced by Newmont include a DVD of breathtakingly beautiful scenes of the environment and the heroic feat of engineering as the structure moved to its new resting place. The music is grand as the sun is filmed rising gloriously over the majestic monument on the move. Indeed, it is a massive achievement.

In the Shadows

There are many unfinished chapters in this story. In August 2003, at a meeting of the Waihi Community Consultation Committee (WCCC), John McIver, the CEO/GM of the Runanga (Council) of Ngati Tamatera,[16] presented the context from which *tangata whenua* see their relationship with the land, their perspective of the history of the Waihi, and the issues that arise from the conflict among the philosophy of Maori as *tangata whenua*, the effects of the taking of land for mining, and the mining itself.[17]

The taking away of Pukewa represents a huge spiritual loss for Ngati Tamatera. They are no longer able say *ko Pukewa toku maunga* (Pukewa is the mountain) and point to what had become better known as Martha Hill.[18] The *maunga* is gone and the spiritual significance of the space that was this mountain is no longer. This is a core issue for Ngati Tamatera, who experience the hurt and loss themselves, and who, in McIver's words "have to account to others for the loss of the mountain/for the land that was lost."[19]

Based on the records of this meeting, Newmont demonstrated a high level of interest in this conversation. Questions were asked about what could be achieved out of this WCCC process to give something back to *tangata whenua* for what was taken away. McIver's response suggested that talking about what happened was a good thing. "It's a start" he said. *Rangatira* (leadership) is there and stands as a tribute to those who have struggled. Something like a Pa Site (fortified settlement) would be significant and provide the notion of a shelter for visitors and represent what has gone before. He suggested that if something positive was done, contemporary *tangata whenua* would be able to hold their heads up, to be proud.

When asked about the motivation of Maori, McIver said it was not about asking for anything. It was about wanting to see acknowledgement for past wrongs. He reminded Newmont that *tangata whenua* are "not so in favor of mining." Providing a sanctuary containing native plants and birds was a good thing, but that an acknowledgment of the historical concerns that explains why people cannot see the mountain was also needed. Such an acknowledgment would need to be more of a focal point and atone for that loss.

The conversations continue. Senior staff from Newmont Waihi met with Ngati Tamatera at Te Pai o Hauraki marae in Paeroa. The *hui* was held so that each group could achieve a better understanding of the other—their history, philosophy, and objectives. "It was very useful for Newmont staff to learn about Ngati Tamatera beliefs, concerns and aspirations at first hand," said External Affairs Manager Malcolm Lane. "In return we were able to explain how modern gold mining works and allay a number of concerns."[20]

Adriaan van Kersen, Waihi Gold general manager at that time, stated that the company is committed to working alongside *iwi* for the benefit of all involved. According to van Kersen,

> *We would like to think that we have an understanding of the unique relationship Maori people have with the land and water—with Pukewa and the Ohinemuri River—and ongoing communication can only enhance that understanding. It is important that we all understand the culture, heritage and spiritual values of* tangata whenua. *This* hui *has provided a solid foundation on which to continue to develop that understanding. We are currently investigating ways of raising cultural awareness amongst all employees and contractors. We are also committed to involving* iwi *in various opportunities that arise from our operation, and* iwi *are involved in closure planning at Martha.*[21]

QUESTIONS

1. Should Newmont have gone through the trouble and expense of NZ $3.2 million to move the Cornish Pumphouse, which to some people seemed to be simply a pile of rubble?

2. The Pumphouse is only one of a number of icons for which the people of Waihi wanted protection. Some claim that the transformer building that sat alongside the Pumphouse was of greater significance and should be equally protected. Should Newmont also have incurred costs to protect other icons?

3. The United Nations estimates that 300 million to 350 million indigenous peoples, derived from 5,000 distinct peoples living in at least 72 countries, inhabit the Earth.[22] To what extent are other indigenous peoples not having their voices heard in important decisions that affect them?

4. How would that many people, spread over that many countries, ever have a hope of being heard?

5. Are we witnessing the emergence of a new generation of managers who are more alert to, and responsible for, the impact of their activities on communities, more mindful of their responsibilities, and less driven by a sense of entitlement associated with the economic might and the power of their corporate presence? Or are communities at risk of being harnessed by the vanguard of newly sensitized executives and advocates who understand that to maintain their privileged existence they must appear to be responsive to those affected by their activities?

6. Is Newmont a socially and environmentally responsible corporation or simply an astute generator of good public relations in search of profit making? By what criteria would you make this assessment?

NOTES

1 Waihi's website is at http://www.waihi.org.nz, accessed 9/17/10; in order to enhance the reading of this case, we have included the original Maori or Pacific Island word or phrase while also providing a rough translation.

2 Newmont Mining website is at http://www.newmont .com/, accessed 9/17/10.

3 Condensed from *Standing Tall on Te Tiriti O Waitangi*, available at http://www.greens.org.nz/ features/standing-tall-te-tiriti-o-waitangi, accessed 9/17/10.

4 See "Ngāti Rongoū, Ngāti Tamaterā and Ngāti Whanaunga," available at http://www.teara.govt .nz/en/marutuahu-tribes/2, accessed 9/17/10.

5 See "Pukewa," available at http://www.marthamine .co.nz/WCCC/pukewa010903.html, accessed 9/17/10.

6 Condensed from *Standing Tall on Te Tiriti O Waitangi*.

7 Most Maori claims of injustice remain hidden from a Pakeha (New Zealanders not of Maori blood lines) dominated media. There are still *wahi tapu*—Maori sacred places—being desecrated. A Thames swimming pool is permanently out of bounds to some children of the Hauraki and Thames iwi Ngati Maru. It was built on a burial ground. Sewage is still discharged over traditional shellfish beds.

8 Website is at http://www.waihi.org.nz, accessed 9/17/10.

9 See "Pukewa," available at http://www.marthamine .co.nz/WCCC/pukewa010903.html, accessed 9/17/10.

10 See "Pukewa," available at http://www.marthamine .co.nz/WCCC/pukewa010903.html, accessed 9/17/10.

11 In later years local authorities filled the crater with various items, including old car bodies. Further subsidence occurred in the same area in 1999.

12 See "Pukewa," available at http://www.marthamine .co.nz/WCCC/pukewa010903.html, accessed 9/17/10.

13 See News Release, "CSC Signs $180 Million Services Agreement With Newmont Mining Corporation," November 14, 2006, accessed 10/6/10.

14 See Newmont, "Mining and the Community," available at http://www.marthamine.co.nz/martha_ com.html, accessed 9/17/10.

15 See Martha Mine website at http://www .marthamine.co.nz/, accessed 9/17/10; and Penelope Carroll, "Stations on the Move, *New Zealand Historic Places Trust*, Winter 2003, available at http://www.historic.org.nz/Publications/ HeritageNZMagazine/HeritageNz2003/HNZ03- StationsMove.aspx

16 See Ngati Tamatera available at http://www.tkm.govt .nz/iwi/ngati-tamatera/, accessed 10/6/10.

17 John McIver, Tangata Whenua Presentation, WCCC, August 18, 2003, available at http://www .marthamine.co.nz/WCCC/McIver180803.html, accessed 9/17/10.

18 For Maori, when introducing themselves, their identification of self with mountain, river, or sea comes prior to affiliation with ancestors and parents. Only once these are articulated, does the person take/state his or her name. By taking away the mountain, a deeply held sense of identity has been destroyed.

19 The significance of his speech requires a deep understanding of the ontological connections made by Maori to Earth and all energies.

20 Newmont Waihi Gold, "Ngati Tamatera Hui," available at http://www.marthamine.co.nz/29_03_05 .HTM, accessed 9/17/10.

21 Ibid.

22 International Work Group for Indigenous Affairs, "Indigenous Peoples—Who Are They?" available at http://www.iwgia.org/sw641.asp, accessed 10/6/10.

Case Study

Bernie Madoff's Ponzi Scheme: Reliable Returns from a Trustworthy Financial Adviser

By Denis Collins   Denis Collins is a professor of management in the School of Business at Edgewood College in Madison, Wisconsin. His research interests include business ethics, management, and organizational change. Contact: dcollins@ edgewood.edu

> *A [person] is incapable of comprehending any argument that interferes with his revenue.*
>
> Rene Descartes

Overview

This case study is a chronology of the largest Ponzi scheme in history. Bernie Madoff began his brokerage firm in 1960 and grew it into one of the largest on Wall Street. While doing so, he began investing money as a favor to family and friends, though he was not licensed to do so. Over a period of fifty years, these side investments became an investment fund that mushroomed into a $50 billion Ponzi scheme. Bernie[1] pled guilty without a trial on March 12, 2009, and was sentenced to 150 years in prison. Thousands of wealthy clients, philanthropic organizations, and middle-class people whose pension funds found their way into Bernie's investment fund lost their life savings.

What to Do?

Bernie Madoff, at age 69, owned three very successful financial companies—a brokerage firm, a proprietary trading firm, and an investment advisory firm. On December 10, 2008, the brokerage and proprietary trading firms, managed by his brother and two sons, were performing as well as could be expected in the middle of a deep recession. His investment advisory firm, however, was on the verge of collapse. Investors in Bernie's investment fund had requested $7 billion in withdrawals, and he did not have the cash to pay them. Known only to Bernie and a close circle of loyal employees, the investment fund was a $50 billion Ponzi scheme in operation for at least twenty years.

Bernie met with his sons—Mark, age 44, and Andrew, age 42—in his office to discuss his contentious plan to issue annual employee bonuses in December rather than in February, as was typical. Bernie insisted they be chauffeured with him 12 blocks to his $7.4 million penthouse apartment to discuss the matter in greater privacy. Shortly after arrival, Bernie broke down and confessed, "I'm finished. I have absolutely nothing. [The investment fund is] all just one big lie."[2] The Ponzi scheme consisted of tens of thousands of falsified balance sheets and client statements.

The brothers were shocked. They admired their father and looked forward to inheriting the company. They, along with other family members and close friends, were heavily invested in the fund. Now they were all broke, and their father would have to spend the rest of his life in jail. Andrew collapsed in tears. Their mother, Ruth, hovered nearby.

Bernie made one request of his sons. He asked them to remain quiet about the Ponzi scheme for one week, allowing him time to distribute what little money remained left into investment accounts held by family, friends, and a few special clients. Then he would turn himself in to the Securities and Exchange Commission (SEC) and FBI. After forty-five minutes of screaming and heartache, the sons left the apartment. Should Mark and Andrew grant their obviously distraught father the one week he requested, or should they immediately notify government officials about their father's criminal activities?

Becoming a Stockbroker

Bernie Madoff was born on April 29, 1938, the second child of Ralph and Sylvia Madoff.[3] Ralph and Sylvia, married at the nadir of the Great Depression in 1932, were children of eastern European immigrants who had fled the anti-Semitism—persecution and murder of people who are Jewish—in their homeland. The family lived in a small lower eastside Manhattan apartment. Following the birth of Peter, their third child, in 1946, Bernie's parents bought a small home in the Laurelton section of Queens. Laurelton was a predominantly working-class Jewish community near what is now Kennedy Airport.

Ralph worked, mostly off-the-books, as a plumber. The IRS found out, ordered him and two partners to pay $13,000 in back taxes (equivalent to $103,000 in 2010 dollars),[4] and placed a lien on his home. In the late 1950s, desperate for money, Ralph and Sylvia, a homemaker, opened Gibraltar Securities. The business was registered in Sylvia's name to protect its assets from the IRS. Sylvia obtained a stockbroker license, but not an investment adviser license. Ralph had neither license.

A stockbroker and an investment adviser differ according to the type of obligations they have to clients. An investment adviser has a fiduciary duty to *always act in the client's best interest*. A stockbroker, on the other hand, is a salesman who brokers a deal between buyers and sellers. A stockbroker must provide the client "*suitable advice*," which may not necessarily be the best advice.[5]

In 1959, while majoring in political science at nearby Hofstra College, Bernie made a series of decisions that shaped the rest of his life. First, he decided that he, too, wanted to become rich working as a stockbroker. Second, he married Ruth, his high school sweetheart, and they moved into an inexpensive one-bedroom apartment in Bayside, Queens. Third, two days after the wedding ceremony, he registered Bernard L. Madoff Investment Securities as a brokerage firm with $200 of assets and no liabilities. Bernie had $5,000 in working capital, money he saved from summer jobs as a lifeguard and installing lawn sprinkler systems. Ruth agreed to do the bookkeeping.[6]

Growing the Business through Some Illegal Trading on the Side

In 1960, who would trust a 22-year-old political science major trading stocks out of his apartment? Initially, hardly anyone. Ruth's father, Saul Alpern, helped Bernie establish some legitimacy by giving him office space in his mid-town Manhattan accounting firm.

A publicly traded company listed on the New York Stock Exchange (NYSE) and American Stock Exchange (AMEX), had to meet certain size requirements and pay substantial fees. Bernie focused on trading "over-the-counter" penny stocks, valued at less than $1.00, that were traded outside the NYSE or AMEX. An investor would telephone Bernie wanting to buy or sell penny stock. Bernie would then contact other investors or stockbrokers to make the trade at the best price for Bernie's client.

In a short time, Bernie got several big breaks. Alpern, impressed by his son-in-law's work ethic, loaned him $50,000 ($364,000 in 2010 dollars) to invest. Then, a mutual acquaintance introduced Bernie to Carl Shapiro, the very successful owner of a Boston women's apparel company. Shapiro, worth more than $22 million ($3.0 billion in 2010 dollars) at age 45, was intrigued by Bernie's ability to complete trades in three days; most stockbrokers took three weeks.[7] Shapiro gave him $100,000 to invest on his behalf. Bernie used the money he made trading for Alpern and Shapiro to subsidize his penny stock brokerage firm.[8]

Bernie earned substantial fees by investing Alpern and Shapiro's funds, and sought to increase business by offering to pay his father-in-law for each new client he recruited. Alpern told family members, business friends, accounting clients, and acquaintances he met during summer vacations in the Catskills, that Bernie could get them an 18 percent return on their investment. At the time, the SEC had a rule that exempted investment advisers with less than 15 clients from being licensed. Bernie exceeded this limit and was required to obtain a license; this meant passing an examination, paying fees, and filing statements with the SEC. Instead, Bernie joined the ranks of illegal unlicensed investment advisors—including his parents—who escaped the scrutiny of the SEC and state securities regulators.

By 1962, after only two years of operation, Bernie was overwhelmed by the paperwork required for managing his growing number of small investments. Bernie told his father-in-law to do him a favor by collecting money from various investors and then give the total amount to Bernie as one account to invest.[9] This also made it appear to the SEC as though he had fewer clients. Soon, Alpern's accounting business unofficially merged with Bernie's investment business. Alpern assigned Jerry Horowitz, one of his accountants, as Bernie's personal accountant. This allowed Ruth to reduce her company involvement to writing checks and managing her husband's work expenses. Frank Avellino, another Alpern accountant, not only invested with Bernie for a guaranteed 20 percent return rate, but also earned a commission for recruiting other clients. Both Alpern and Avellino were, like Bernie, unlicensed investment advisers.

In 1963, Bernie focused on growing his brokerage clients. That year, the SEC investigated 48 brokerage firms, including Bernie's mother's Gibraltar Securities business, for not filing financial reports. His mother, though not fined, lost her business license and was banned from the securities industry.[10] Nonetheless, Bernie's father continued to earn money as an investment adviser.

As for Bernie, he could have obtained an investment advisory license then to avoid what happened to his mother. But if he did, the SEC or other securities regulators might audit his financial books and discover that Bernie also had been violating SEC licensing laws. He feared that, just like his mother, this could result in being banned forever from the securities industry.

More Growth and Illegalities

Businesses borrow money from banks to pay for expansion. Bernie didn't have to do this because he had a bank account with money flowing in and out from his illegal investment advisory business. He used some of this money, without his client's permission, to avoid interest payments. Bernie moved money between his Bank of New York brokerage bank account and his Chase investment adviser bank account as needed. Whenever he fell short of the guaranteed 20 percent investment advisory returns, he made up the difference by taking money out of his brokerage bank account. If he needed income to grow the brokerage firm, he took money from the investment advisory bank account.[11]

Bernie got another big break when his father-in-law hired Michael Bienes as an accountant in 1968. Bienes' brother-in-law was Jeffrey Picower, a wealthy Wall Street investor.[12] Bienes earned hundreds of thousands of dollars in commissions from money Picower invested with Bernie over the next forty years.

How did Bernie explain his remarkable results to sophisticated investors like Picower? Bernie now sold blue-chip stocks and claimed he invested client money using a complicated three-part "split strike conversion" investment strategy. He told clients that first he purchased common stock from a pool of 35 to 50 Standard & Poor's 100 Index companies whose performance paralleled overall market performance. The S&P 100 Index represents the 100 largest publicly traded companies based on market capitalization, and represented a very sound investment. Second, he bought and sold option contracts as a hedge to limit losses during sudden market downturns. Third, he left the market and purchased U.S. Treasury Bills when the market was declining, and then sold the U.S. Treasury Bills and reentered when the market was rising.[13] Bernie never shared his mathematical calculations for determining when to buy or sell. He considered the information proprietary and did not want competitors to copy it. Later, financial experts would question whether Bernie ever used this method.

Key to Bernie's success was the efficiency and speed of his trading operations. Bernie was one of the first brokers to recognize the role computers could play in the financial industry. In 1970, he hired his younger brother, Peter, to help computerize operations.[14] The speed of their trading transactions attracted a growing number of clients, such as other brokerage firms and investment advisers, to do business through Bernie's operations.

Investment advisers were also intrigued by Bernie's unique one or two pennies commission for each share invested with his company. Although legal, competitors maintained that these commission payments created a conflict of interest for investment advisers, equivalent to paying financial kickbacks to a supplier. As noted earlier, an investment adviser is legally obligated to make the best deal for a client. The possibility of investment advisers earning a commission for directing their client's money to Bernie introduced another motive—doing what was in the investment adviser's financial interest rather than the client's financial interest.

While Bernie was pushing other investment advisers into ethically grey areas with his commission offers, the SEC was trying to break up the virtual trading monopoly the NYSE and AMEX had in the investment community. The SEC encouraged Bernie and others to create a "third market" for trading over-the-counter stocks of small public companies. In 1971, the National Association of Securities Dealers and Automated Quotations (NASDAQ) was founded for public companies not listed on NYSE or AMEX. As the name implies, the buy and sell prices for these stocks were automated by computers. Bernie became one of the first five brokers to join NASDAQ.[15]

Bernie also made trades on small regional stock exchanges. The Cincinnati Stock Exchange, founded in 1885 to raise funds for Cincinnati area businesses, was one of the many regional stock exchanges that floundered under the shadow of the NYSE. Bernie revived the exchange in the 1970s by investing $250,000 ($950,000 in 2010 dollars) to upgrade its computer system. By 1976, the Cincinnati Stock Exchange increased its volume of trades significantly by closing its trading floor and becoming an all-electronic stock market.

Bernie's Ponzi Scheme

Most analysts, particularly litigators, believe Bernie began operating a Ponzi scheme much earlier than 1991, the year he claimed during his sentencing trial. Some date it as early as the mid-1960s.[16] Ponzi schemes are named after a scheme developed by Charles Ponzi. In 1920, Ponzi promised to double the money of investors within forty-five or ninety days if they invested in a complicated security that only he knew how to manage. However, he never invested the money. Instead, he deposited their money into his bank account and paid investors the promised return using new investor income. His scam was uncovered within a year. Investors who withdrew their funds early earned a large profit, while those who had not withdrawn money lost their investment.

A successful Ponzi scheme requires a network of trusted co-conspirators. In 1975, Annette Bongiorno, hired 10 years earlier at age 19 as Bernie's secretary, recommended her Queens neighbor, Frank DiPascali, Jr., an 18-year-old recent high school graduate, for a job assisting Bernie's investment advisory business. DiPascali quickly advanced to managing Bernie's computer systems. DiPascali and Daniel Bonventre, originally hired seven years earlier as Bernie's auditor, created fraudulent records to verify trades that never occurred.

Unlike Ponzi, Bernie owned a successful and legitimate brokerage firm. He used the activities of his booming brokerage business to shield his fraudulent activities. The computer software program developed by Bernie's brother determined optimal trades within four seconds.[17] Clients visiting the brokerage company observed a great deal of trading hustle-and-bustle that generated tremendous profits.

Bernie's fraud was a rather simple scheme. Assume a client, promised a 20 percent annual return, gave Bernie $1 million to invest on January 1. Bernie deposited the client's money in his own bank account. As more clients invested over the course of the year, the amount in Bernie's bank account grew. If the client decided to redeem the entire investment on December 31, Bernie wrote the client a check for $1.2 million from the company's bank account. Then DiPascali and several loyal investment fund employees fed price data from the previous 12 months for stocks, options, and Treasury Bills into a computer to derive a long list of trades that indicated a $200,000 profit. DiPascali mailed these documents and fictitious trading tickets to the client as supporting evidence.[18]

Why would potential clients trust Bernie? Investors are drawn to successful fund managers trusted by others. Bernie had a long track record of successful investing, and was at the forefront of the computerization of stock trading. He served on SEC advisory committees, held a four-year elected term on the NASD Adviser Council, and was elected as non-executive chairman of NASDAQ.[19]

In addition, people were drawn in by Bernie's personality. He was quiet yet charismatic and did not boast about his financial success. Bernie exhibited a strong sense of family, loyalty, and honesty, and did not drink alcohol. Elderly clients treated Bernie as a son, peers treated him like a brother, and younger clients treated him like a friendly uncle.

Bernie also played hard to get. When approached by potential investors, Bernie typically told them his investment fund was closed, having reached its peak capacity. Then he'd re-contact them and offer a huge favor by reopening the fund just for them. For all these reasons, having Bernie manage their money became a status symbol.

Flush with cash, Bernie opened a London office in 1983 to attract European investors. But that was not his only reason: the London office would play a key role in his money laundering operation. Bernie and his co-conspirators deposited client investment money in Bernie's New York City Chase bank account and then transferred the money to his London bank account, creating the appearance of investing in London-based securities. He then transferred the money back to his personal Chase bank account.

The Apex of Hedge Funds

Bernie's investment fund performance caught the attention of large hedge fund managers seeking to maximize their client's financial returns. This put Bernie's fund at the apex of the investment pyramid.

The investment pyramid begins with individuals deciding whether to conservatively deposit money in a highly liquid bank account and earn low interest rates, or pay a broker's fee and invest in riskier mutual funds, consisting of a portfolio of investments. Mutual funds combine money from many investors, are professionally managed, charge management and withdrawal fees, and are highly regulated by the SEC. The most conservative mutual funds contain blue-chip stocks and Treasury Bills, the type Bernie allegedly bought and sold.

Hedge funds, unlike mutual funds, can invest in anything, such as midwestern farmland.[20] They are only available to "accredited investors" with individual income over $200,000, and a net worth of over $1 million. Hedge funds are less regulated than mutual funds and charge higher management, performance, and withdrawal fees. Some hedge funds are very risky and involve aggressive buying and selling and more speculative positions in derivative securities. Other hedge funds are very conservative, they hedge, or reduce, market exposure inherent when investing in stocks.

Bernie's business strategy consisted of marketing his investment fund to feeder hedge funds. A feeder hedge fund is a hedge fund that earns profits by feeding its clients' investments into another investment fund. Feeder hedge fund managers found investing their clients' money with Bernie very appealing because of his consistently high annual returns.

In addition, Bernie paid feeder hedge fund managers a commission instead of charging them fees. [21] Hedge fund managers, then, earned money on both ends of their transactions. They charged their clients a 2 percent fee on assets and 20 percent fee on profits and then passed the money along to Bernie, who paid them commissions instead of charging them fees. However, Bernie would only do business with feeder hedge fund managers if they agreed not to mention his name in their marketing materials. Bernie insisted on this condition because, unknown to the feeder hedge fund managers, he was still an unlicensed investment adviser.

Bernie's feeder hedge funds strategically operated out of New York City, Boston, Palm Beach, Hollywood, Austria, and Greenwich, Connecticut. Bernie's largest feeder hedge fund suppliers included Fairfield Greenwich Group, Ascot Partner, Bank Medici of Austria, and Cohmad Securities. Ascot Partner, owned by Ezra Merkin, had invested a total of $2.4 billion with Bernie before his arrest. [22] Merkin, a well-known money manager, philanthropist, and leader within the Jewish New York City community, was trusted to manage investments for many Jewish charities, Yeshiva University, the American Jewish Congress, and holocaust survivor Elie Wiesel, among others. The Cohmad Securities hedge fund, which rented office space from Bernie, combined the first letters of the last names of its two founders—Maurice "Sonny" Cohn and Bernie Madoff. Robert Jaffee, the son-in-law of Bernie's long time client Carl Shapiro, became the primary recruiter for Cohmad Securities. Professionally, all seemed to be going well for Bernie. In 1986, Bernie's earnings of $6 million put him among the 100 highest paid people on Wall Street. [23] His new computer system, one of the best in the world, could calculate the best price for stock orders of up to 3,000 shares in just 10 seconds. [24] Both of his sons, after graduating from college, worked for Bernie and learned about the legitimate business from the bottom up. The SEC also honored Bernie for staying open for business on "Black Monday," October 19, 1987, when the Dow Jones Industrial Average dropped 508 points (22.6 percent) in one day of chaotic trading. [25] Unknown to the SEC, Bernie was able to remain open because he had a large amount of cash from his illegal investment fund account.

Solidifying Operations

With all this success, Bernie relocated to three floors in the new prestigious Lipstick Building on Third Avenue in mid-Manhattan. The red-granite, 34-story, receding oval skyscraper is considered an architectural masterpiece and, as the nickname implies, looks like a tube of lipstick. The main entrance to Bernie's business was on the eighteenth floor, which housed a conference room, information technology and administrative offices, Ruth's office, and the Cohmad Securities office. A state-of-the-art, glass-enclosed trading floor was on the nineteenth floor, along with offices for Bernie, his brother Peter, and his sons Mark and Andrew. Bernie's traders made 15,000 trades a day, accounting for five percent of total daily business on the NYSE. The illegal investment advisory business was on the seventeenth floor, where DiPascali managed a dozen employees behind locked doors with signs noting "Do Not Enter" and "Do Not Clean."[26] Their operations were so secretive that Bernie's personal secretary of eight years did not know he managed an investment fund until reading about it in the *Wall Street Journal*.

Bernie's company owned two computer servers, "House 05" for the legitimate business and "House 17" for the illegal business. In the early 1990s, Jerome O'Hara and George Perez were hired to develop computer programs and maintain the "House 05" server. Upon earning the trust of Bernie and DiPascali, they were assigned to manage the "House 17" server on the mysterious seveneenth floor. They became responsible for creating fraudulent client statements.[27]

Around the same time, Horowitz retired as Bernie's auditor and personal accountant. Horowitz gave the business to David Friehling, his son-in-law. Friehling quickly became a key member of Bernie's scam. Friehling gave Bernie signed blank SEC forms to complete; when questioned about his auditing duties, Friehling lied to the American Institute of Certified Public Accountants (AICPA).

Almost Caught

Bernie's father-in-law, Saul Alpern, retired in the early1970s and handed his CPA business over to his two employees. They renamed the company after themselves, Avellino & Bienes. The two accountants inherited Alpern's investment advisory clients, recruited more investors, and gave Bernie their own money to invest. Thanks to Bernie, both accountants earned $10 million a year.[28]

In 1992, a client being recruited by Avellino & Bienes shared the company's marketing material with an investment adviser in Seattle. The competing investment adviser researched Avellino & Bienes and found out it was an unregistered investment advisory company. Suspecting a Ponzi scheme, the Seattle-based investment adviser filed a complaint with the SEC.[29] The ensuing SEC investigation revealed that, since 1962, Avellino and Bienes had created nine accounts for 3,200 clients totaling $441 million. Their apparently falsified paperwork claimed the funds had been invested with Bernie.

Bernie admitted conducting some business with Avellino & Bienes, but told the SEC that he had assumed they were a registered investment advisory business, which was an outright lie. Avellino and Bienes, who shielded Bernie from further investigation, were fined $350,000 and required to return $441 million to their victims.

Bernie, seemingly magnanimous, offered to recoup any money Avellino & Bienes could not return. He did this by using his own fraudulent investment advisory client money as collateral for a loan with which to pay them.[30] Bernie also offered victims the opportunity to invest directly in his fund rather than being reimbursed. Many of them accepted the offer. Unknown to the SEC, Bernie also continued to pay Avellino and Bienes a commission for any new clients they directed to another of his feeder funds.

Ironically, Bernie's involvement in this case enhanced his reputation on Wall Street. In a *Wall Street Journal* article about the Avellino & Bienes scandal, Bernie was referred to as an "ace money manager."[31] Bernie not only avoided getting caught, but received free advertising in the nation's largest and most respected financial newspaper, attracting additional clients.

Three years later, in 1995, Bernie purchased a $9.5 million mansion in Palm Beach, Florida, which complemented his Manhattan penthouse and summer home in France. He joined the Palm Beach Country Club and paid the $350,000 initiation fee with company money. One-third of the members would eventually invest with him.[32]

Soon after, Bernie added a second legitimate business to his growing financial empire, a proprietary trading firm that traded stocks, bonds, and other financial instruments using the company's, rather than client, money. Mark and Andrew managed both the new proprietary trading firm and the original brokerage firm.[33]

Almost Caught Again

In 1999, Frank Casey of Rampart Investment Management Company sought to do business with René-Thierry Magon de la Villehuchet, a wealthy French investment fund manager and owner of Access International Advisers. Villehuchet had been investing with Bernie since the mid-1980s and told Casey that Bernie's premier fund outperformed anything Casey had to offer.[34] Casey then gave Harry Markopolos, a highly skilled Rampart hedge fund manager, all of Bernie's marketing materials he could find and asked him to replicate Bernie's investment fund for Rampart. Markopolos studied the materials and within four hours mathematically proved that Bernie's fund was a fraud.[35]

A major red flag noted by Markopolos was that Bernie reported being down only three months out of an 87 month time period. The S&P 500, over the same time period, had been down 28 months. In later testimony before Congress, Markopolos concluded "That would be equivalent to a major league baseball player batting .966 [with] no one suspecting that this player was cheating."[36]

Markopolos hypothesized that Bernie was running one of two possible types of fraud: (1) front-running, which is buying and selling stocks from the broker's account based on having previous knowledge about how the broker's clients would buy and sell, thus profiting from trades the broker planned to make for them,[37] or (2) a Ponzi scheme. Markopolos stood to receive a whistleblower reward windfall of millions of dollars for having reported a multi-billion dollar fraud to federal authorities if either theory was correct.

In May 2000, Markopolos submitted an eight-page complaint explaining his findings to the SEC. The understaffed and underfunded SEC, which received a record 13,599 complaints in 2000,[38] decided not to initiate an investigation of his complaint.

Casey and Markopolos remained persistent in exposing Bernie's fraud. Fortuitously, Casey shared a taxi ride from the airport to a Barcelona conference with financial reporter Michael Ocrant and presented the case against Bernie. Ocrant wrote an article titled "Madoff Tops Charts; Skeptics Ask How" about Casey's concerns in the May 1, 2001 financial newsletter *MARHedge*. The story caught the attention of investigative reporter Erin Arvedlund. She further questioned Bernie's methods in an article titled "Don't Ask, Don't Tell" that appeared in the financial weekly *Barron's*.

Markopolos filed a second complaint to the SEC following the publication of these two articles in highly respected outlets. Once again, the SEC took no action.

Financial and SEC Problems

Bernie's two legitimate businesses lost money in the early 2000s when the economy entered a recession after the dot.com industry collapse. Bernie continued to regularly transfer money among his various bank accounts as needed. He started putting more pressure on feeder funds to recruit new investment advisory clients for his now $7 billion fund.[39]

Deposits in Bernie's bank accounts were treated like the family piggy bank. Over a period of four years, he deposited $21 million in Ruth's account to pay for her Paris shopping sprees and a $2.8 million yacht.[40] Bernie's brother, Peter, purchased an expensive weekend home in the Hamptons for his daughter, and Bernie's sons acquired a manufacturer of fly-fishing equipment, a sport they both enjoyed.[41]

In 2003 and 2004, the SEC received two more complaints alleging that Bernie operated a Ponzi scheme. The SEC finally decided to investigate. Bernie reminded the investigators he had served three years as NASDAQ chairman, had several times provided expert opinions to the SEC on complicated financial issues, and that he was on the short list of people under consideration to be the next SEC chairman, which was a lie.[42]

The SEC investigators were surprised by the tremendous size of Bernie's billion dollar fund, and caught Bernie in several obvious lies and contradictory statements. When questioned about not being a licensed investment adviser, Bernie stated that he had less than 15 clients, the threshold required for licensing, which was a lie. DiPascali falsified records to support Bernie's fraudulent statements.[43] The SEC closed the case without additional follow-up.

After the SEC investigation ended, Bernie rewarded his two computer programmers, O'Hara and Perez, with $116,950 and $108,530 disguised as an investment advisory account transfer.[44] A more chastened Bernie banned the use of company e-mail on the seventeenth floor, and required employees to use their personal accounts for e-mail communications.[45]

November 2, 2005 brought unexpected bad news. For the first time, Bernie had a major liquidity problem with his fund. He had $105 million in client redemption claims but only $13 million in his bank account.[46] Bernie used the balance as collateral for a $95 million loan to cover the difference.

During this crisis, Bernie tried desperately to borrow huge amounts of money from European banks. Frank Casey found out and informed Markopolos, who now worked for a different employer.[47] Markopolos valued Bernie's fund at $50 billion and filed his third SEC complaint. He titled the complaint "The World's Largest Hedge Fund is a Fraud" to catch everyone's attention. Markopolos detailed more than 25 red flags strongly suggesting that Bernie operated a Ponzi scheme. After a short inquiry, the SEC dismissed the complaint.

Why did the SEC dismiss complaints filed against Bernie? A list of factors played into their decision making:

- The SEC annually receives more than 10,000 complaints against brokers. The understaffed SEC assigned cases to investigators who had little experience with Ponzi schemes. As a result, they focused on the more familiar "front-running," which Bernie was not doing.

- The SEC had difficulty understanding the complexity of Bernie's operations. Bernie lied to them multiple times to keep them off track.

- They gave Bernie the benefit of the doubt because he had an impressive track record with NASDAQ and had assisted the SEC on complex issues.

- Bernie never requested the presence of a lawyer when speaking with SEC agents, signaling that he had absolutely nothing to hide.
- When questioned about his consistently high returns, Bernie explained he had a personal "feel" for market fluctuations, which is why he had been a successful investor for decades.
- Markopolos unsuccessfully competed against Bernie, thus leaving himself vulnerable to the "sour grapes" accusation.
- SEC managers and Markopolos had an adversarial relationship.
- The SEC believed Markopolos was primarily motivated by a desire for the whistleblowing reward windfall.

A frustrated Markopolos contacted Taxpayers Against Fraud about getting the *Wall Street Journal* to investigate his findings. The *Wall Street Journal* editors rated the topic a low priority due to other pressing economic issues.[48] Markopolos considered going to the FBI, but dismissed the idea because the issue fell under the purview of the SEC, which had already decided not to investigate further.

Scared Employees and Rule Changes

The SEC investigations made some of Bernie's key conspirators very nervous. In 2006, O'Hara and Perez tried covering up their involvement by deleting 218 of the 225 special programs they had designed for the House 17 server.[49] They refused to create any new programs for producing fraudulent records. Bernie authorized DiPascali to meet O'Hara and Perez' 20 percent salary increase demand to buy their silence.[50] O'Hara withdrew $976,000 and Perez withdrew $289,000 from their respective investment fund accounts.

Joann "Jodi" Crupi, who had worked more than twenty years for Bernie, stepped in and agreed to help DiPascali record fictitious trades and client statements. Crupi also received a 20 percent salary increase for her efforts.

A new SEC rule banned the practice of allowing an entire feeder fund to count as one client. Instead, feeder funds had to be counted according to the number of investors in the fund. Bernie ignored the law because he feared counting one feeder fund as hundreds of clients would lead to greater SEC scrutiny.[51] When the SEC directly asked Bernie for a client count, he lied, stating that he had only nine clients. After further questioning, Bernie admitted he exceeded the 15 client minimum. On August 25, 2006, Bernie finally registered with the SEC, ending 45 years of illegally operating as an unlicensed investment adviser.[52]

Beginning of the End

The onset of a major recession in 2007 marked the beginning of the end for Bernie. Warren Buffet often jokes that you only learn who is swimming naked when the tide goes out. Within two years, Bernie would be caught swimming naked.

At the beginning of 2007, Bernie reported $613 million in net capital and 146 employees, making his the fortieth largest Wall Street brokerage firm.[53] Ruth kept busy doing Bernie's expense accounts and helping to manage the $19 million Madoff Family Foundation.[54]

Then the home mortgage market collapsed and credit availability tightened. The stock market declined dramatically. By August, every major hedge fund reported losses, but not Bernie's investment fund.[55] The growing recession had two contradictory impacts on Bernie's fund. On the one hand, some wealthy clients and hedge funds shifted almost all their money to Bernie's investment fund because it was the only fund reporting positive results. On the other hand, some clients withdrew money to cover expenses because stock they used for collateral had declined in value.

Due to these financial fluctuations, Bernie needed new computer programs. O'Hara and Perez compromised on their earlier refusal to help and created a program for altering data on the House 17 server for DiPascali and Crupi to use.[56] Crupi received another 20 percent salary increase for her involvement, plus money to purchase a $2.2 million beach house in New Jersey.

As the recession deepened, more clients withdrew their money for immediate cash needs, such as margin calls. They intended to reinvest with Bernie when the value of their other investments increased again. Bernie reduced his investment fund's guaranteed payouts to 4.5 percent to discourage this trend.[57]

Two more complaints against Bernie were filed with the SEC during this tumultuous period, one from a "concerned citizen" reporting that Bernie kept two sets of books, and another from Markopolos with new details. The SEC, overwhelmed with trying to stabilize the economy, did not investigate either complaint.

In August 2008, JPMorgan Chase withdrew $250 million from their account, noting that Bernie's investment fund lacked transparency. JPMorgan did not inform the SEC that some of their employees suspected Bernie might be operating a Ponzi scheme. In mid-September, Lehman Brothers' bankruptcy further tightened credit, the stock market continued its slide, and more clients withdrew their investment.

Bernie's Ponzi scheme fell apart in November 2008. Client requests for redemptions reached $1.45 billion, but he only had $487 million in his investment fund bank account.[58] Every day his secretary called the bank at 5:30 p.m. and reported more bad news—the gap between redemption requests and cash on hand kept widening.[59] If the Ponzi scheme collapsed, thousands of clients would lose billions of dollars, family members and friends would lose everything, 200 employees would lose their jobs, Bernie would spend the rest of his life in jail, and his family would spend the rest of their lives in court cleaning up his mess. Bernie's blood pressure soared. He relieved the stress by lying down on the floor in his glass-enclosed office, exposed to all his employees, for extended periods of time.[60]

In a last ditch attempt to save all three businesses, Bernie created a new fund the week of the Thanksgiving holiday. He marketed the new investment fund exclusively to five special clients and required each to invest $100 million.[61] Two of the five, the co-founder of Home Depot and a feeder fund in Spain, declined immediately.[62] Doom seemed inevitable and, on November 25, Bernie instructed Ruth to withdraw $5.5 million from their Cohmad Securities account.

On November 30, Bernie reported $64.8 billion in his hedge fund. However, he had only $266 million in his bank account with $7 billion in redemptions waiting to be paid.[63] Bernie admitted the inevitable. He set up a December 12 meeting with his lawyer, Ira Sorkin, when he planned to turn himself in to federal authorities for operating a Ponzi scheme.[64]

Then an old friend provided some temporary relief. Carl Shapiro, who helped launch Bernie's investment adviser career nearly 50 years earlier, was now 95 years old. His son-in-law, Robert Jaffee of Cohmad Securities, unaware Bernie was operating a Ponzi scheme, convinced Shapiro to invest an additional $250 million with Bernie. This was followed by a $10 million investment from the president of a Bronx fuel company.[65] Bernie deposited the money into his personal account. Both investors would lose it all within a week—Bernie's fund was insolvent.

On December 3, Bernie informed DiPascali there were no assets available to pay the billions of dollars clients requested to withdraw.[66] A distraught DiPascali met Crupi outside the building and told her the investment fund was bankrupt. They coordinated plans to ensure consistency in their explanations to the SEC and FBI. Crupi insisted they should lie and tell federal authorities that they assumed all trading transactions occurred at Bernie's London office.

Bernie wanted to make sure that his family members and a few clients were taken care of before he turned himself in to authorities. On December 9, he informed Mark that he wanted to break with tradition and pay $173 million in employee bonuses immediately, rather than waiting until February when bonuses were typically paid. Mark, concerned about his father's stress level, told Andrew. They demanded an explanation and Bernie agreed to meet with them the following day. That night Bernie confessed everything to Peter, his loyal younger brother, now 62.

First thing on December 10, Bernie instructed Ruth to withdraw another $10 million from their Cohmad account. Then Bernie invited his sons to join him for a car ride to his apartment where he confessed everything.

Mark always thought Bernie and the small group of employees on the seventeenth floor were investing a few billion dollars on behalf of a handful of wealthy friends. He found out otherwise.

After the Fall

Bernie went back to the office after informing his sons. He became suspicious when neither Mark nor Andrew attended the annual holiday party that evening. Mark and Andrew had sought legal advice immediately after leaving Bernie's apartment that morning. Mark contacted his wife's stepfather, a retired lawyer who had also invested with Bernie, who connected them to a litigator. The litigator informed Mark and Andrew that they would be considered partners to Bernie's on-going crimes if they did not inform federal authorities immediately. Acting on this advice, the brothers notified the U.S. Attorney and the SEC that their father had been operating a $50 billion Ponzi scheme.[67]

At 8:30 a.m. on December 11, 2008, two FBI agents knocked on the door of Bernie's luxurious $7.4 million penthouse apartment. They asked Bernie if there was an innocent explanation for what his sons had reported to federal authorities the previous day. Bernie, still in his pajamas, declined the opportunity to contact his lawyer and confessed. He stated that he alone was responsible for the fraud, which was a lie. After nearly 50 years, Bernie no longer had to worry about getting caught.

News about Bernie's arrest spread quickly. Peter informed Bongiorno and DiPascali, and then told the entire trading floor that Bernie had been arrested by the FBI for securities fraud.[68] The shocked feeder fund owners notified their wealthy and influential clients that all of their money invested with Bernie had been lost.

At least 13,500 people had money being managed by Bernie at the time of his arrest.[69] Many were in disbelief.[70] They did not know that their investment adviser had invested client money with Bernie. All their money was gone. Pension funds, retirement accounts, and children's trust funds were worthless. Philanthropic organizations had to cancel millions of dollars in promised or ongoing donations. Outraged clients hounded Bernie and his family members after he posted a $10 million bail. The judge ordered him under house arrest and 24-hour electronic monitoring. His assets were frozen and all three businesses liquidated.

A significant amount of the reported $50 billion in losses, which soon rose to $65 billion in newspaper headlines, was paper profit. Bernie had received $36 billion from investors and paid out approximately $18 billion, which meant $18 billion was missing.[71] The difference between the invested $36 billion Bernie received and the $65 billion reported by the media consisted of unclaimed profits from 20 percent annual fund increases.[72]

Not everyone in Bernie's Ponzi scheme lost money. Jeffrey Picower, for instance, had invested $1.7 billion with Bernie and withdrew $6.7 billion, earning $5 billion in profits.[73]

Among the biggest financial winners, at least until Bernie's arrest, were feeder fund managers, Bernie's co-conspirators, and family members. Cohmad Securities earned $67 million in commissions,[74] and six employees earned more than a combined $12 million between 2003 and 2008.[75] Sonja Kohn and Bank Medici of Austria earned $62 million in commissions,[76] and Ezra Merkin earned annual fees of $25 million to $35 million.[77] Annette Bongiorno, who had deposited $920,000 in her account since 1975, withdrew $14.5 million.[78] Among family members, according to litigator David Sheehan, Peter deposited only $14.00 in his account between 1995 and 2008 and withdrew $16 million.[79] Mark and Andrew also made only a few small deposits into their accounts and withdrew more than $5 million.[80]

As shown in Exhibit 1, the feeder funds that earned substantial fees from their clients and commissions from Bernie during the Ponzi scheme were, after Bernie's confession, the largest financial losers. Exhibit 1 also lists the largest reported losses among nonprofit organizations and individuals.[81] Bernie's former married mistress had been the Chief Financial Officer of Hadassah, which lost the most money among the nonprofit organizations.[82]

Exhibit 1 Largest Financial Losers

Feeder Funds	Non-Profit Organizations	Individuals
Fairfield Greenwich Advisors: $7.5 billion	Hadassah: $90 million	Carl Shapiro: $500 million
Tremont Group Holdings: $3.3 billion	New York University: $24 million	Phyllis Molchatsky: $17 million
Banco Santander: $2.9 billion	Jewish Community Foundation of Los Angeles: $18 million	Richard Spring: $11 million
Bank Medici: $2.1 billion	Elie Wiesel Foundation: $15.2 million	Zsa Zsa Gabor: $10 million
Ascot Partners: $1.8 billion	Yeshiva University: $14.5 million	Ira Roth: $1 million

A more extreme loss is the loss of life. Thierry de la Villehuchet, the French aristocrat who refused to believe Casey or Markopolos' theory that Bernie operated a Ponzi scheme, lost $1.5 billion. This included his personal fortune along with substantial funds from European royalty and aristocrats. On December 22, 2008, unable to pay his 28 employees or office rent, Villehuchet committed suicide in his downtown Manhattan office.[83]

Family Ramifications

The day before Christmas, while still under house arrest, Bernie instructed Ruth to mail five uninsured packages containing watches, necklaces, bracelets, rings, and other jewelry valued at millions of dollars. The recipients included Mark, Andrew, and Peter. Mark, wanting nothing to do with his father, informed government officials.[84]

On March 10, 2009, the government formally indicted Bernie on 11 counts for securities fraud, money laundering, false statements, perjury, investment adviser fraud, mail fraud, wire fraud, and theft from an employee benefit plan. Two days later, Bernie pled guilty to all counts. In his statement to the court, Bernie told the packed courtroom:[85]

> As I engaged in my fraud, I knew what I was doing was wrong, indeed criminal. When I began the Ponzi scheme I believed it would end shortly and I would be able to extricate myself and my clients from the scheme. However, this proved difficult, and ultimately impossible, and as the years went by I realized that my arrest and this day would inevitably come. I am painfully aware that I have deeply hurt many, many people, including the members of my family, my closest friends, business associates and the thousands of clients who gave me their money. I cannot adequately express how sorry I am for what I have done.

Bernie claimed that the Ponzi scheme began in 1991, after which he made no legitimate investments with client money. Government prosecutors believe Bernie used 1991 as the beginning date to protect properties he bought for Ruth and his sons prior to that date. Bernie left the courtroom as prisoner No. 61727-054. He was locked down 23 hours a day while awaiting sentencing.

On July 29, 2009, Bernie received the maximum sentence allowable, 150 years in jail. His projected release date was November 14, 2139, which included reduction for good behavior. Bernie was ordered to forfeit $170 million in assets. Ruth was ordered to forfeit $85 million in assets, leaving her with $2.5 millon.

Bernie refused to cooperate with authorities or to name any conspirators. His indicted co-conspirators had other ideas, particularly considering the anticipated prison sentences they faced if they did not cooperate (see Exhibit 2).

The court granted Irving Picard power of attorney to recover lost money for victims. Picard initiated a $198 million lawsuit against Mark, Andrew, Peter, and Peter's daughter Shana for negligence and breach of fiduciary duty. He sued Ruth for $44.8 million on the grounds that she enriched herself with company funds.[86]

Picard also filed lawsuits against the beneficiaries of Bernie's investment fund, enough to collect $50 billion if he won them all.[87] The defendants included feeder

Exhibit 2 Indicted Co-Conspirators		
Name	Role	Maximum Prison Term
Frank DiPascali	CFO	125 years
David Friehling	Accountant/Auditor	108 years
Daniel Bonventre	Director of Operations	82 years
Annette Bongiorno	Manager	75 years
Judi Crupi	Assistant	65 years
Jerome O'Hara	Computer Programmer	30 years
George Perez	Computer Programmer	30 years

fund managers and clients for having failed to perform due diligence. Picard's general philosophy was that people who invested with Bernie should only get what they put in. If they withdrew more than they deposited, the difference should be given to victims who put in money and got nothing out.[88] The lawsuits claim that sophisticated investors, banks, and accounting firms "chose to simply look the other way" rather than investigate some obvious red flags.[89]

Victims gained renewed hope when Picard reached a $7.2 billion settlement with the estate of Jeffrey Picower, making it the largest forfeiture to date in legal history.[90] As noted earlier, Picower had invested $1.7 billion with Bernie and withdrew $6.7 billion.

Bernie's imprisonment took a toll on him. In October, he experienced his first jail fistfight. In December, he was hospitalized at Duke University Medical Center in North Carolina for high blood pressure, though others reported he had a broken nose and ribs from another prison fight.[91]

Bernie's crimes also continued to take a toll on his family. Mark refused to see Bernie or Ruth after his father's arrest. He could not obtain another job on Wall Street and was named in multiple lawsuits amounting to hundreds of millions of dollars. His wife, Stephanie, filed with the New York Supreme Court to change her last name and those of their two children to her maiden name, Morgan. Reporters and news cameras were staked outside his home and scorned family members wherever they went. Victims harassed Mark and his family as they walked along the streets of Manhattan or attempted to eat in restaurants.

December 11, 2010 was the second anniversary of Bernie's arrest. A few days earlier Stephanie left for a Disney World vacation with her and Mark's 4-year-old daughter. At 4 a.m., Mark e-mailed Stephanie asking that she send someone to care for their 2-year-old son, who had stayed home with him. Then Mark, at age 46, attached his dog's leash to a metal ceiling beam in their $6 million downtown Manhattan apartment and committed suicide by hanging himself.[92] His tragic death will negatively impact another generation of Madoffs. Upon hearing the news in prison, Bernie cried.

QUESTIONS

1. Should Mark Madoff have granted his father's request for a one week delay before notifying government authorities about his crime?

2. Describe the chronological evolution of Bernie Madoff's Ponzi scheme.

3. Why did sophisticated investors trust Bernie Madoff with their funds? Why didn't they perform appropriate due diligence?

4. Why didn't the SEC, which received several complaints about Bernie Madoff, uncover the fraud?

5. Do you believe Mark and Andrew Madoff didn't know about their father's Ponzi scheme prior to their December 10, 2008 discussion at Bernie Madoff's apartment? Why?

6. Should sophisticated investors who withdrew millions from their Madoff accounts forfeit the undeserved gains to people who lost the millions of dollars they invested?

NOTES

[1] Throughout this case, "Bernie" will be used to differentiate Bernie Madoff from Ruth Madoff (his wife), Peter Madoff (his brother), and Mark and Andrew Madoff (his sons). This is not meant in disrespect. He told others to call him Bernie, which endeared him to others.

[2] Andrew Kirtzman, *Betrayal: The Life and Lies of Bernie Madoff* (New York: HarperCollins, 2009), p. 232.

[3] Most of the information about Bernie Madoff's life and Ponzi scheme comes from: Erin Arvedlund, *Too Good To Be True: The Rise and Fall of Bernie Madoff* (New York: Penguin, 2009); James Bandler and Nicholas Varchaver, "How Bernie Did It," *Fortune*, April 30, 2009; Diana B. Henriques, *The Wizard of Lies: Bernie Madoff and the Death of Trust* (New York: Times Books/Henry Holt & Company, 2011); Andrew Kirtzman, *Betrayal: The Life and Lies of Bernie Madoff* (New York: HarperCollins, 2009); Brian Ross, *The Madoff Chronicles: Inside the Secret World of Bernie and Ruth* (New York: Hyperion, 2009); *United States of America v. Bernard F. Madoff* available at http://www.justice.gov/usao/nys/madoff/20090310criminalinfo.pdf; and *Wall Street Journal* articles about Bernie Madoff, available at http://online.wsj.com/public/page/bernard-madoff.html, accessed 4/11/11.

[4] Inflation conversion calculator is available at http://www.westegg.com/inflation/infl.cgi, accessed 4/12/11.

[5] W. Scott Simon, "The Critical Difference Between a Stockbroker and Registered Investment Advisor," 2005, available at http://www.arkadvisor.com/_docs/fiduciary_library/fiduciary.pdf, accessed 4/11/11.

[6] Mark Seal, "Madoff's World," *Vanity Fair*, April 2009.

[7] Seal, "Madoff's World."

[8] Andrew Kirtzman, *Betrayal: The Life and Lies of Bernie Madoff*.

[9] "The Madoff Affair," *Frontline*, Timeline, available at http://www.pbs.org/wgbh/pages/frontline/madoff/cron/, accessed 4/11/11.

[10] Seal, "Madoff's World."

[11] Erin Arvedlund, *Too Good To Be True: The Rise and Fall of Bernie Madoff* (New York: Penguin, 2009).

[12] Diana B. Henriques, "Deal Recovers $7.2 Billion for Madoff Fraud Victims," *New York Times*, December 17, 2010.

[13] *United States of America v. Bernard F. Madoff* available at http://www.justice.gov/usao/nys/madoff/20090310criminalinfo.pdf, accessed 4/11/11.

[14] Peter Chapman, "Before the Fall," *Traders Magazine*, March 2009.

[15] Arvedlund, *Too Good To Be True: The Rise and Fall of Bernie Madoff*.

[16] *Matthew Greenberg, Walter Greenberg, Doris Greenberg, and the Estate of Leon Greenberg v. Friehling & Horowitz, KPMG UK, KPMG International, JPMorgan Chase & Co., The Bank of New York Mellon, Paul Konigsberg, Annette Bongiorno, Frank DiPascali, Andrew Madoff, Mark Madoff, Peter Madoff, and John Does 1 through 30* available at http://www.oakbridgeins.com/clients/blog/madofflawsuits/greenberg.pdf, accessed 4/11/11.

[17] Arvedlund, *Too Good To Be True: The Rise and Fall of Bernie Madoff*.

18 *United States of America v. Frank DiPascali, Jr.* available at http://www.justice.gov/usao/nys/madoff/20090811dipascaliinformationsigned.pdf, accessed 4/11/11.

19 "The Madoff Affair," *Frontline*, Timeline.

20 Sebastian Mallaby, *More Money than God: Hedge Funds and the Making of a New Elite,* (New York: Penguin, 2010).

21 Arvedlund, *Too Good To Be True: The Rise and Fall of Bernie Madoff.*

22 Aaron Elstein, "Bernie Madoff's Bagman Had Everything to Lose," *Crains,* January 9, 2009.

23 Arvedlund, *Too Good To Be True: The Rise and Fall of Bernie Madoff.*

24 Chapman, "Before the Fall."

25 Arvedlund, *Too Good To Be True: The Rise and Fall of Bernie Madoff.*

26 Brian Ross, *The Madoff Chronicles: Inside the Secret World of Bernie and Ruth* (New York: Hyperion, 2009).

27 *United States of America v. Daniel Bonventre, Annette Bongiorno, Joann Crupi, a/k/a "Jodi," Jerome O'Hara, and George Perez* available at http://www.justice.gov/usao/nys/madoff/20101118s2supersedingindictment.pdf, accessed 4/11/11.

28 Arvedlund, *Too Good To Be True: The Rise and Fall of Bernie Madoff.*

29 "Investigation of Failure of the SEC to Uncover Bernard Madoff's Ponzi Scheme," Report of Investigation, United States Securities and Exchange Commission, Office of Inspector General available at http://www.sec.gov/news/studies/2009/oig-509-exec-summary.pdf, accessed 4/11/11.

30 *United States of America v. Daniel Bonventre, Annette Bongiorno, Joann Crupi, a/k/a "Jodi," Jerome O'Hara, and George Perez.*

31 Randall Smith, "Wall Street Mystery Features a Big Board Rival," *Wall Street Journal,* December 16, 1992.

32 Seal, "Madoff's World."

33 James Bandler and Nicholas Varchaver, "How Bernie Did It," *Fortune,* April 30, 2009.

34 Andrew Kirtzman, *Betrayal: The Life and Lies of Bernie Madoff.*

35 *Testimony of Harry Markopolos Before the U.S. House of Representatives Committee on Financial Services,* February 4, 2009, p. 7, available at http://www.house.gov/apps/list/hearing/financialsvcs_dem/markopolos020409.pdf, accessed

4/11/11; Harry Markopolos, *No One Would Listen* (Hoboken, NJ: John Wiley & Sons, 2010).

36 *Testimony of Harry Markopolos Before the U.S. House of Representatives Committee on Financial Services,* p. 10.

37 Markopolos, *No One Would Listen.*

38 Marcy Gordon, "Complaints to SEC Against Brokers Set High in 2000," *ABC News,* January 26, 2001.

39 *United States of America v. Frank DiPascali, Jr.* available at http://www.justice.gov/usao/nys/madoff/20090811dipascaliinformationsigned.pdf, accessed 4/11/11.

40 *Securities Investor Protection Corporation v. Bernard L. Madoff Investment Securities LLL* available at http://www.slideshare.net/breakingnews/lawsuit-against-ruth-madoff-irving-picard, accessed 4/11/11.

41 Seal, "Madoff's World."

42 *Investigation of Failure of the SEC to Uncover Bernard Madoff's Ponzi Scheme,* Report of Investigation, United States Securities and Exchange Commission, Office of Inspector General available at http://www.sec.gov/news/studies/2009/oig-509-exec-summary.pdf, accessed 4/11/11.

43 *United States of America v. Frank DiPascali, Jr.*

44 *United States of America v. Daniel Bonventre, Annette Bongiorno, Joann Crupi, a/k/a "Jodi," Jerome O'Hara, and George Perez.*

45 Bandler and Varchaver, "How Bernie Did It."

46 *United States of America v. Daniel Bonventre, Annette Bongiorno, Joann Crupi, a/k/a "Jodi," Jerome O'Hara, and George Perez.*

47 *Testimony of Harry Markopolos Before the U.S. House of Representatives Committee on Financial Services*; Markopolos, *No One Would Listen.*

48 *Testimony of Harry Markopolos Before the U.S. House of Representatives Committee on Financial Services,* p. 10.

49 *Securities and Exchange Commission v. Jerome O'Hara and George Perez* available at http://www.sec.gov/litigation/litreleases/2009/lr21292.htm, accessed 4/11/11.

50 *United States of America v. Daniel Bonventre, Annette Bongiorno, Joann Crupi, a/k/a "Jodi," Jerome O'Hara, and George Perez.*

51 Arvedlund, *Too Good To Be True: The Rise and Fall of Bernie Madoff.*

52 *United States of America v. Frank DiPascali, Jr.*

53 Chapman, "Before the Fall."

54 David Segal and Alison Leigh Cowan, "Madoffs Shared Much; Question Is How Much," *New York Times,* January 14, 2009.

55 *Testimony of Harry Markopolos Before the U.S. House of Representatives Committee on Financial Services*; Markopolos, *No One Would Listen.*

56 *United States of America v. Daniel Bonventre, Annette Bongiorno, Joann Crupi, a/k/a "Jodi," Jerome O'Hara, and George Perez.*

57 Andrew Kirtzman, *Betrayal: The Life and Lies of Bernie Madoff.*

58 *United States of America v. Daniel Bonventre, Annette Bongiorno, Joann Crupi, a/k/a "Jodi," Jerome O'Hara, and George Perez.*

59 Ross, *The Madoff Chronicles: Inside the Secret World of Bernie and Ruth.*

60 Kirtzman, *Betrayal: The Life and Lies of Bernie Madoff.*

61 Seal, "Madoff's World."

62 Kirtzman, *Betrayal: The Life and Lies of Bernie Madoff.*

63 *United States of America v. Frank DiPascali, Jr.*

64 Kirtzman, *Betrayal: The Life and Lies of Bernie Madoff.*

65 Ibid.

66 *United States of America v. Frank DiPascali, Jr.*

67 David Margolick, "Did the Sons Know?" *Vanity Fair,* July 2009.

68 Ross, *The Madoff Chronicles: Inside the Secret World of Bernie and Ruth.*

69 Robert Chew, "The Bernie Madoff Client List Is Made Public," *Time,* February 5, 2009.

70 Erin Arvedlund (editor), *The Club No One Wanted to Join: Madoff Victims in their Own Words* (Andover, MA: Doukathsan Press, 2010).

71 "Bernie Madoff," *Business Insider* available at http://www.businessinsider.com/blackboard/bernie-madoff, accessed 4/11/11.

72 Ross, *The Madoff Chronicles: Inside the Secret World of Bernie and Ruth.*

73 Ibid.

74 Commonwealth of Massachusetts Office of the Secretary of the Commonwealth Securities Division, *Cohmad Securities Corporation,* Administrative Complaint available at http://www.sec.state.ma.us/sct/sctcohmad/cohmad_complaint.pdf, accessed 4/11/11.

75 Arvedlund, *Too Good To Be True: The Rise and Fall of Bernie Madoff.*

76 Diana B. Henriques and Peter Lattman, "Madoff Trustee Seeks $19.6 Billion from Austrian Banker," *New York Times,* December 10, 2010.

77 Steve Fishman, "The Monster Mensch," *New York Magazine,* February 22, 2009.

78 *United States of America v. Daniel Bonventre, Annette Bongiorno, Joann Crupi, a/k/a "Jodi," Jerome O'Hara, and George Perez.*

79 "The Madoff Scam: Meet the Liquidator," *60 Minutes,* September 27, 2009 available at http://www.cbsnews.com/stories/2009/09/24/60minutes/main5339719.shtml?tag=currentVideoInfo;segmentUtilities, accessed 4/11/11.

80 Ibid.

81 "Madoff's Victims," *Wall Street Journal,* March 6, 2009.

82 Sheryl Weinstein, *Madoff's Other Secret* (New York: St. Martin's Press, 2009).

83 Kirtzman, *Betrayal: The Life and Lies of Bernie Madoff.*

84 David Margolick, "Did the Sons Know?" *Vanity Fair,* July 2009.

85 *United States of America v. Bernard L. Madoff,* "Statement of Guilt" available at http://www.justice.gov/usao/nys/madoff/madoffhearing031209.pdf, accessed 4/11/11.

86 *Securities Investor Protection Corporation v. Bernard L. Madoff Investment Securities LLL* available at http://www.slideshare.net/breakingnews/lawsuit-against-ruth-madoff-irving-picard, accessed 4/11/11.

87 Diana B. Henriques and Peter Lattman, "Madoff Trustee Seeks $19.6 Billion from Austrian Banker," *New York Times,* December 10, 2010.

88 "The Madoff Scam: Meet the Liquidator," *60 Minutes,* September 27, 2009 available at http://www.cbsnews.com/stories/2009/09/24/60minutes/main5339719.shtml?tag=currentVideoInfo;segmentUtilities, accessed 4/11/11.

89 Alison Leigh Cowan and Richard Sandomir, "Madoff Profits Fueled Mets' Empire, Lawsuit Says," *New York Times,* February 4, 2011.

90 Henriques, "Deal Recovers $7.2 Billion for Madoff Fraud Victims."

91 Steve Fishman, "Bernie Madoff, Free at Last," *New York,* June 6, 2010.

92 Diana B. Henriques and Peter Lattman, "Mark Madoff's Name Became Too Big a Burden to Bear," *New York Times,* December 16, 2010.

Case Study

Goldman Sachs and the Financial Crisis of 2007–2010

By Frank L. Winfrey Frank L. Winfrey is the Clark N. and Mary Perkins Barton
Professor of Management at Lyon College in Batesville, Arkansas. His research interests include corporate governance, executive compensation, and corporate social
responsibility. Contact: frank.winfrey@lyon.edu

> . . . just a banker doing God's work.
>
> Lloyd C. Blankfein, Chairman and CEO[1]

> The world's most powerful investment bank [Goldman Sachs] is a great vampire squid
> wrapped around the face of humanity, relentlessly jamming its blood funnel into anything
> that smells like money.
>
> Matt Taibbi, Rolling Stone[2]

> We recognize that there is a disconnect between how we view the firm and how the
> broader public perceives our roles and activities.
>
> Lloyd C. Blankfein, Chairman and CEO[3]

Overview

This case examines events leading up to the financial crisis of 2007–10, with special emphasis on the behavior of Goldman Sachs, one of the largest investment
companies on Wall Street. The case focuses on the ethical implications of economic
conflicts of interest. In 2010, Goldman Sachs received the largest civil fine in history by the Securities and Exchange Commission for its role in selling the ABACUS
collateralized debt obligation.

Background

Goldman Sachs is a bank holding company and a global financial services firm
providing investment banking, securities, and investment management services to a
client base of corporations, institutional clients, governments, and high net worth
individuals. The company describes its core mission as "growing our franchise as a
leading global investment banking, securities, and investment management firm."

Goldman Sachs segments its activities into three areas: investment banking, trading and principal investments, and asset management and securities services. Headquartered in New York City, Goldman Sachs is a Delaware-based corporation with offices in the major financial centers around the world, including London, Frankfort, Tokyo, and Hong Kong.[4]

The firm was founded in 1869 as a partnership between Marcus Goldman, a German immigrant, and his son-in-law, Samuel Sachs, for the purpose of being an originator and clearinghouse for commercial paper. In 1999, under the leadership of Henry M. Paulson Jr., Goldman Sachs transitioned from a partnership into a public corporation. The firm credits its partnership background for an elite corporate culture providing its people with a sense of personal ownership. This partnership ethos supports the firm's approach to risk management, encouraging accountability, communication, and independence among its control areas. The ethos is also reflected in its self-discipline of using rigorous mark-to-market accounting of its positions— which uses current market prices to determine the value of assets and liabilities—and in the firm's 14 business principles (see Exhibit 1).

Exhibit 1 Goldman Sachs' 14 Business Principles*

Principle 1: Clients' interests always come first.

Principle 2: Goldman's assets are its people, capital, and reputation.

Principle 3: The goal is to provide superior returns to shareholders.

Principle 4: Pride in the professional excellence of the firm's work.

Principle 5: Constantly strive for creativity and imagination to better serve clients.

Principle 6: Identify and recruit the very best person for every job.

Principle 7: Provide rapid advancement opportunities based on merit and responsibilities.

Principle 8: Stress teamwork to produce the best results.

Principle 9: Dedication and intense effort by Goldman people.

Principle 10: Consider the size of any asset in any project undertaken.

Principle 11: Strive to anticipate rapidly changing client needs.

Principle 12: Maintain client confidentiality.

Principle 13: Always be a fair but aggressive competitor seeking to expand.

Principle 14: Maintain high ethical standards because integrity and honesty are at the heart of the business.

---

*Business Standards Committee, available at http://www2.goldmansachs.com/our-firm/on-the-issues/bsc/index.html, accessed 9/17/10.

Goldman Sachs has a history of adapting to global financial crises and economic dislocations. During the Asian contagion crisis initiated by the collapse of Thailand's financial system in 1997, it made several significant investments in consumer and real estate assets. In the aftermath of the Long Term Capital Management implosion in the late 1990s, Goldman increased its fixed income market share. Following the dot-com and telecom bubbles in the early 2000s, Goldman built up its private equity investments. After the failure of Houston-based Enron in 2001, Goldman invested in power plants.

Goldman Sachs also has a history of encouraging its senior partners to leave the company at a relatively young age after making their fortune in order to take powerful leadership roles in government and public service.[5] A number of them served the government immediately prior to, and during, the 2007–10 financial crisis (see Exhibit 2).

Exhibit 2 Former Goldman Sachs Partners

Henry M Paulson: U.S. secretary of the treasury, 2006–09

Joshua B. Bolten: chief of staff for President George W. Bush, 2006–09

Neel T. Kashkari: special assistant to Treasury Secretary Paulson and interim assistant secretary of the treasury for financial stability in the U.S. Department of the Treasury, which supervised the $700 billion fund the government used to buy toxic bank accounts

Ruben Jeffrey: interim chief investment officer of the bailout program

Dan Jester: Supervised government takeover of Fannie Mae and Freddie Mac

Robert K. Steel: undersecretary for domestic finance of the U.S. Treasury Department; reviewed Fannie Mae and Freddie Mac problems and became CEO of troubled Wachovia Corporation

Steve Shafran: Focused on troubled student loan program and involved in initiative to guarantee money market funds

Kendrick R. Wilson III: Treasury Department liaison to bank CEOs

John A. Thain: Briefly took the leadership position at troubled Merrill Lynch before it was pressured to merge with Bank of America

Edward M. Libby: Selected by Secretary Treasury Paulson as CEO of financially troubled American International Group (A.I.G.)

Edward C. Frost: Briefly served as advisor to Treasury Secretary Paulson on setting up bailout fund

Mark Patterson: chief of staff for Treasury Secretary Timothy Geithner

Robert E. Rubin: U.S. secretary of the treasury, 1995–99

In September 2008, Goldman decided to restructure itself as a bank holding company with permanent access to borrowing from the Federal Reserve System. The transition meant that Goldman would face increased regulatory oversight with the attendant constraints of greater disclosure requirements, higher capital reserves, and less risk taking. After regulators approved the change, Goldman became one of the world's largest bank holding companies with $20 billion in deposits between its U.S. and European operations.[6]

Goldman reported that it ended the third quarter of 2008 with a "tier 1" capital ratio of 11.6, well above the 6 percent required to be a "well-capitalized" bank. In October 2008, Goldman received $10 billion from the U.S. Treasury Department under the Troubled Asset Relief Program. It also received $12.9 billion in payment for credit derivatives from its major trading partner, the troubled insurer A.I.G., which had received some $180 billion in emergency loans from the government.[7]

Government Regulation of Depository (Commercial) Banks

Economist John Kenneth Galbraith noted in his economic history of the Great Depression that

> *The most notable piece of speculative architecture of the late twenties . . . was the investment trust or company. . . . [The investment trust] brought about an almost complete divorce of the volume of corporate securities outstanding from the volume of corporate assets in existence . . . [and] the difference went into . . . the pockets of the promoters. . . . Sponsorship of a trust was not without its [direct] rewards. The sponsoring firm normally executed a management contract with its offspring. Under the usual terms, the sponsor ran the investment trust, invested its funds, and received a fee based on a percentage of the capital or earnings. Were the sponsor a stock exchange firm, it also received commissions on the purchase and sale of securities for its trust. . . . There was also leverage . . . [where] the compounding effect of a geometric series led to a rush to sponsor investment trusts which would sponsor investment trusts, which would sponsor investment trusts."[8]*

In the late 1920s, within a one-year period Goldman, Sachs & Company organized and sold nearly a billion dollars worth of securities in three interconnected investment trusts—Goldman Sachs Trading Corporation (December 1928), Shenandoah Corporation (July 1929), and Blue Ridge Corporation (August 1929). By October 1929, trust leverage was in full reverse and had become a "form of firm self-immolation." All eventually depreciated to virtually nothing when the stock market crashed. Ironically, "Goldman, Sachs and Company rescued its firm name from its delinquent [investment trust] offspring and returned to an earlier role of strict rectitude and stern conservatism. It became known for its business in the most austere of securities."[9]

The Glass-Steagall Act of 1933 was passed to bar the conflicts of interest created when commercial (deposit-taking) banks underwrite securities. The law prohibited depository banks from engaging in investment bank activities. The Bank Holding Company Act, passed in 1956, extended the restrictions on banks, forbidding bank holding companies owning two or more banks to engage in non-bank activities. It also stipulated that bank holding companies could not buy banks in other states.[10]

Thirty years later, the trend reversed itself and depository banks were slowly given permission to engage in investment bank activities. In 1986, the Federal Reserve Board reinterpreted Section 20 of the Glass-Steagall Act and decided that banks could have up to 5 percent of their gross revenues from investment banking business. Subsequently, in the spring of 1987, the Fed Board eased the regulations further by allowing banks to handle several underwriting businesses, including commercial paper, municipal revenue bonds, and mortgage-backed securities. In January 1989, the Fed Board allowed bank holding companies to deal in debt and equity securities and later in that year issued an order raising the limit to 10 percent of gross revenues.[11]

In December 1996, the Fed Board expanded the loophole even further by permitting bank holding companies to own investment bank affiliates with up to 25 percent of their business in securities underwriting. By August 1997, the Fed Board eliminated many of the remaining restrictions on Section 20 subsidiaries, effectively making Glass-Steagall obsolete.[12]

On November 4, 1999, the U.S. Congress approved a final version of the Financial Services Modernization Act of 1999, known as the Gramm-Leach-Bliley Act (GLBA). The act repealed the parts of the Glass-Steagall Act that separated commercial banking from the securities business and repealed the parts of the Bank Holding Company Act of 1956 that separated commercial banking from the insurance business. GLBA also explicitly exempted security swap agreements from regulation.[13]

William Kaufmann, writing in the political newsletter *CounterPunch,* stated that "the Glass-Steagall Act worked fine for fifty years until the banking industry intensified its lobbying efforts for its repeal during the 1980s, the go-go years of Reaganesque market fundamentalism."[14] He noted the complicity of "neoliberal Democrats" in its 1999 repeal, which included Senators Christopher Dodd (Connecticut), Ted Kennedy (Massachusetts), John Kerry (Massachusetts), Harry Reid (Nevada), Charles Schumer (New York), and Joseph Biden (Delaware) as well as President Bill Clinton. The repeal of Glass-Steagall was generally a bipartisan effort.

Subsequently, the culture of commercial banks was overwhelmed by the culture of investment banks, such as Goldman Sachs. A scenario similar to the one that preceded the Great Depression happened again with banks engaging in high-risk financial gambles. In addition to making large profits from advising companies on mergers and taking them public, real money—staggering money—is made trading and investing capital through a global array of mind-bending products and strategies unimaginable a decade ago.[15]

In October 2007, economist Robert Kuttner testified before the House Committee on Financial Services:

> *Since repeal of Glass-Steagall in 1999, after more than a decade of de facto inroads, super-banks have been able to re-enact the same kinds of structural conflicts of interest that were endemic in the 1920s—lending to speculators, packaging and securitizing credits and then selling them off, wholesale or retail, and extracting fees at every step along the way. And, much more of this paper is even more opaque to bank examiners than its counterparts were in the 1920s. Much of it isn't paper at all, and the whole process is supercharged by computers and automated formulas.*[16]

The Financial Crisis of 2007–10

The root causes of the financial markets crisis originating in late 2006 included mistakes from a number of institutional actors. Financial institutions such as Countrywide Financial and Washington Mutual offered home mortgage loans to borrowers who lacked the financial resources to repay them. Two government-sponsored enterprises (GSEs), Fannie Mae and Freddie Mac, encouraged these subprime housing loans with the support of members of the U.S. Congress and both Democratic and Republican presidential administrations.[17]

The subprime loans were repackaged (securitized) by investment banking firms (Bear Stearns, Lehman Brothers, Merrill Lynch, Goldman Sachs) and sold with high investment ratings from government-approved rating agencies (Moody's, Standard and Poor's, and Fitch's) to domestic and foreign investors who failed to perform due diligence on the underlying securities. Insurers, such as A.I.G., provided hedge funds and investment speculators, such as Goldman Sachs, with assurance of profits whether the housing market was performing well or poorly. While these activities occurred, the Federal Reserve and the U.S. Securities and Exchange Commission (SEC) pursued a *laissez faire* approach to their regulatory policies and responsibilities.[18]

According to financial market experts Niall Ferguson and Ted Forstmann, the subprime mortgage bust turned into a global financial crisis because there was excessive bank leverage (on and off bank balance sheets), and the financial derivative markets allowed massive, opaque side bets on the future value of U.S. homes (amounting to $604.6 trillion in June 2009). The synthetic collateralized debt obligations in the derivatives market were nothing more than "elaborate wager[s] on the future price of some mortgage-backed securities."[19] It was inappropriate to treat the credit default swaps between two private parties as though they were standardized and traded on transparent exchanges. In addition, the Federal Reserve failed to correctly recognize "the extent to which inflationary pressures had relocated themselves from consumer prices to asset [housing] prices."

Meanwhile, an enormous growth in the amount of foreign capital seeking safe and liquid assets, such as U.S. treasuries, pushed down relatively low long-term interest rates, which made subsidizing home ownership in the United States even more attractive. This happened at a time when many financial institutions and investors decided to outsource their risk management by relying on ratings agencies rather than on their own research and analysis. But rating agencies were no longer as rigorous as they had been previously. For example, although the much-coveted AAA-rating was held by only 12 companies in the entire world in January 2008, there were 64,000 structured finance instruments, such as CDO (credit default obligations or swaps) tranches (slices), rated AAA at that same time. These AAA ratings attracted investors.[20]

The creation and introduction of new financial products in the late 1990s, such as basket indices (a bundle of commodity price indices) and credit default swaps (created to offset certain risks), added new layers of risk. These financial products assumed that liquidity would be readily available. Financial risk was further compounded over the previous two decades because most financial institutions did not account for asset values through fair value accounting. Risk and control functions often were not independent from the business units in financial institutions.[21]

Marketing and Purchasing Credit Default Obligations/Swaps

In 2007, hedge fund manager John Paulson of Paulson & Company approached several investment banks, including Goldman Sachs and Bear Stearns, with the proposal that they could create securities composed of subprime mortgages.

Paulson explained to the banks that based on an analysis by one of his employees, Paolo Pellegrini, he had discovered a perfect trade by betting against housing market securities through credit default swaps and thus profiting from them.[22]

Paulson's idea was to handpick the worst possible assets for a housing market security by selecting "residential mortgage-backed securities [RMBS] that included a high percentage of adjustable rate mortgages, relative low borrower FICO scores, and a high concentration of mortgages in states like Arizona, California, Florida and Nevada that had recently experienced high rates of home price appreciation." Paulson predicted that these people had mortgages they could not afford and would soon default on them.[23]

The resulting security, known as ABACUS 2007-AC1, was based on "a static portfolio of 90 mortgage-backed securities (RMBSs) rated Baa2 by Moody's Investors Services." ACA Capital Management was named as the portfolio selection agent. In addition to itself, Goldman Sachs found two other "sophisticated" participants to purchase the ABACUS CDO: ACA Capital holdings (a bond insurer backstopped by the Dutch Bank ABN-Amro) and IKB Deutsche Industriebank (a German specialist in mortgage securities).[24]

Paulson and Goldman Sachs subsequently purchased credit default swaps as insurance policies on the portfolio that would pay out when the borrowers defaulted. Within a year, the assets in ABACUS 2007-AC1 CDOs were downgraded in quality by ratings agencies at a cost to its investors of $1 billion.[25]

Goldman Sachs trader and vice president Fabrice "Fab" P. Tourre apparently knew that there were problems with the ABACUS 2007 AC-1 CDOs at the same time he was selling them to investors. He wrote in a March 7, 2007, email (one month before the deal closed), "That [subprime] business is totally dead, and the poor little subprime borrowers will not last so long!!!"[26]

Political Inquiries and Public Explanations

As observed by William Cohan on his *New York Times* Web Log, "politicians seized on Goldman Sachs for easy political gain" as there were perceptions that Goldman Sachs, through a combination of conflicts of interests and political influence, had not only escaped the misery of the financial crisis and the recession but also actually profited from it.[27]

Both the U.S. House of Representatives and the U.S. Senate scheduled and held hearings and set up a Financial Crisis Inquiry Commission to file an independent report to the Congress by December 2010. Additionally, the SEC filed charges against Goldman Sachs in April 2010.[28]

In what were characterized as tortuous Senate hearings, Goldman Sachs executives stuck to the company talking points that the company acted as a "market maker" in many transactions so there was no obligation to reveal certain information about the firm's own investment views or those of its clients on the other side of the deal. Senator Susan Collins (R., Maine) asked the panel of Goldman Sachs executives whether they had a duty to act in the best interests of their clients when selling CDOs. Daniel L. Sparks, the former head of the company's mortgage department, replied, "I believe we have a duty to serve our clients." Fabrice Tourre added, "I do not believe we are acting as investment advisors for our clients."[29]

In testimony to a Senate subcommittee, John C. Coffee Jr., the Adolf A. Berle Professor of Law at Columbia University, stated, "Conflicts of interest played a key role in causing the 2008 financial meltdown."[30] However, Coffee stated, Goldman Sachs's broker-dealers "did not owe a fiduciary duty to their clients." He explained that "investment banks owe[d] a much lesser obligation . . . known as suitability rules.'" Coffee elaborated that "the suitability norm required that the recommended security only be 'within the ballpark' in terms of what the broker knows (if anything) about the investor's needs and financial position." Further, "under a suitability standard the broker is under no obligation to disclose (1) its own investment strategies (even when they are adverse to the client's), or (2) that it believes, or has reasons to know, that a particular security is likely to underperform the general market for such securities." Coffee concluded his testimony urging legislatively mandated market transparency to protect investment banking clients from "derivatives and esoteric financial engineering."

In late April 2010, in an interview with Goldman Sachs's CEO Lloyd C. Blankfein, Bloomberg's Charlie Rose inquired as to whether Goldman Sachs ever took the opposite side of a trade that it had advised its clients to take. Blankfein stated that "as a market maker, we are making buying and selling a thousand times a minute, probably. . . . Advising is where people are coming to us for advice—people are asking us for our opinion, where we have an obligation and duty. . . . When the bank is acting as a market maker, [clients] are not asking us for our opinion, we are not providing [it], we are simultaneously sell, buy, sell, buy."[31]

In a 30-minute conference call to the customers of Goldman Sachs's private-wealth management group, Blankfein said that as a market maker, "we are not telling [clients] what to do . . . that the way we put the client first is to get them the best price under all market circumstances." Blankfein also said that "it would never be acceptable to us to create an investment designed to fail to anyone in the market."[32]

On April 16, 2010, the SEC alleged that Goldman Sachs misstated and omitted key facts when marketing the ABACUS 2007-AC1 CDO. The SEC filing submitted to the U.S. District Court for the Southern District of New York stated that Goldman Sachs failed to disclose the role that the hedge fund Paulson & Company played in the creation of the portfolio, and the fact that John Paulson had taken a short position against the CDO.[33]

At a hearing of the Financial Crisis Inquiry Commission, which Congress created to investigate the causes of the financial crisis of 2007–10, Goldman executives repeated that their firm had minimal obligations to look after its customers' interests in its role as a market maker.[34]

On July 15, 2010, the SEC announced that Goldman Sachs would be fined $550 million, the largest civil fine in SEC history. Goldman Sachs consented to the entry of a final judgment of the charges without admitting or denying the allegations. The fine amounted to 1.1 percent of Goldman Sachs's $51.7 billion revenue and 4.1 percent of the firm's profits in 2009, and the equivalent of 5 percent of the bonuses it paid to employees that year.[35] The settlement also required Goldman to review its offerings of certain mortgage securities and institute remedial actions.[36]

By conceding that its marketing materials were deficient, Goldman Sachs essentially admitted to negligence, but not to fraud. According to Pravin Rao, a former SEC branch chief and current partner at Perkins Coie in Chicago, the admission is "a bit nuanced . . . but from a legal perspective it makes sense. There's a significant difference between negligence and fraud."[37] Former SEC enforcement lawyer and current Wayne State University law professor Peter Henning stated that individual investors would likely not be able to use the acknowledgment to further their own suits. Under the terms of the settlement, Goldman avoided having to report to a court-appointed corporate monitor.

Concluding Comments

In an interesting article from the UK journal *Credit*, John Reynolds, the chairman of the London-based investment bank Reynolds Partners and chairman of the Church of England's Ethical Investment Advisory Group, stated the following:[38]

> *I do not think ethics is something that lawyers and auditors—who are generally the people who deal with compliance issues—are best placed to inculcate into banks. It is a different type of issue. Compliance is about whether you have acted in accordance with the law, and if not, can you find a way around it? Ethics is not about finding that way around.*

Reynolds noted that one of the major conundrums facing large banks "is identifying and meeting the needs of multiple clients, whose interests may conflict." He pragmatically cautioned that "[u]nless thought about in advance, it is very difficult to have an ethical framework in place when you are in the heat of a deal."

Stefianai Perrucci, the founder and CEO of the Pennsylvania-based hedge fund New Sky Capital, commenting on the ABACUS CDO, stated, "There is a qualitative difference between compliance to regulations and ethical behavior. Compliance is about obeying the letter of the law; ethics is about living according to the spirit of it, and may I dare to say, the common good."[39]

Goldman Sachs CEO Blankfein acknowledged this when he took the stage at the firm's annual meeting in April 2010 and stated that it was "clear that our firm must renew the core principles that have sustained us for 141 years. . . . Questions have been raised that have gone to the heart of our most fundamental value: How we treat our clients."[40]

QUESTIONS

1. Did Goldman Sachs deviate from any of its 14 business principles during the 2007–10 financial crisis?

2. Was it unethical for Goldman Sachs to sell the ABACUS CDO to clients?

3. Why did the U.S. government refuse to intervene to save Bear Stearns and Lehman Brothers, and then step in at the last minute when Goldman Sachs was in jeopardy? Did Goldman have undue influence due to its alumni in government positions?

4. Should the Glass-Steagall Act be reinstated?

5. What is the role of mark-to-market accounting in creating inflations (or devaluations) in derivative instruments?

6. What legitimate purpose does a synthetic CDO serve for the capital markets or society?

NOTES

1 Sian Harrington, "Big Bonuses for Doing God's Work," *Human Resources* (London), December 1, 2009.

2 Matt Taibbi, "The Great American Bubble Machine," *Rolling Stone*, July 6–23, 2009.

3 Investment Brokerage—National "Goldman Sachs Announces Details of Business Standards Committee," *Business & Finance Week*, June 5, 2010.

4 Charles D. Ellis, *The Partnership: The Making of Goldman Sachs* (New York: Penguin Press, 2008).

5 Michael J. De la Merced, "Goldman's Shadow Extends Far Past Wall St.," *New York Times*, November 15, 2007; and Julie Creswell and Ben White, "The Guys From 'Government Sachs,'" *New York Times*, October 19, 2008; and Elizabeth Williamson and Brody Mullins, "Goldman Shows It Can Still Lobby Hard," *Wall Street Journal*, April 29, 2010.

6 Andrew Ross Sorkin and Vikas Bajaj "Radical Shift for Goldman and Morgan," *New York Times*, September 22, 2008; and Ben White and Louise Story, "Last Two Big Investments Shift Course," *New York Times*, September 23, 2008.

7 White and Story, "Last Two Big Investment Shift Course."

8 John K. Galbraith, *The Great Crash 1929* (Cambridge, MA: Riverside Press, 1954), pp. 48–70.

9 Ibid., pp. 71–172.

10 James R. Barth, Dan Brumbaugh Jr., and James A. Wilcox, "The Repeal of Glass-Steagall and the Advent of Broad Banking," Economic and Policy Analysis Working Paper 2000-5, April 2000, available at http://www.comptrollerofthecurrency.gov/ftp/workpaper/wp2000-5.pdf, accessed 9/17/10.

11 "The Long Demise of Glass-Steagall," *Frontline*, PBS, accessed at www.pbs.org/wgbh/pages/frontline/shows/wallstreet/weill/demise.html, 9/17/10.

12 Ibid.

13 Ibid.

14 William Kaufmann, "Shattering the Glass-Steagall Act," *CounterPunch*, September 19, 2008.

15 Marcus Baram, "Who's Whining Now? Gramm Slammed by Economists," *ABC News*, September 19, 2008, available at http://abcnews.go.com/Politics/story?id=5835269&page=1, accessed 9/17/10.

16 Robert Kuttner, "Testimony of Robert Kuttner Before the Committee on Financial Services," U.S. House of Representatives, October 2, 2007, available at http://financialservices.house.gov/hearing110/testimony_-_kuttner.pdf, accessed 9/17/10.

17 David O. Beim, "The Spirit of Glass-Steagall," Columbia Business School, February 26, 2010, available at http://www4.gsb.columbia.edu/ideasatwork/feature/7210409/The+Spirit+of+Glass-Steagall, accessed 9/17/10; David Brooks, "The Goldman Drama," *New York Times*, April 27, 2010; and William D. Cohan, "Let Goldman Be Goldman," *New York Times*, July 7, 2010.

18 Ibid.

19 Niall Ferguson and Ted Forstmann, "Back to Basics on Financial Reform," Wall Street Journal, April 23, 2010.

20 Remarks by Lloyd C. Blankfein, Chairman and CEO, The Goldman Sachs Group to the Council of Institutional Investors, Spring Meeting, April 7, 2009, available at http://www2.goldmansachs.com/our-firm/on-the-issues/cii-remarks.pdf, accessed 9/17/10.

21 Ibid.

22 Gregory Zuckerman, "Profiting From the Crash," Wall Street Journal, October 31, 2009.

23 Arthur Delaney, "Goldman Sachs 'Fraud' Explained: How They Pulled Off the Alleged Scheme," *The Huffington Post*, April 16, 2010.

24 Peter Madigan, "Spotlight on Goldman," *Risk* (London), June 2010, pp. 64–67.

25 Delaney, "Goldman Sachs 'Fraud' Explained."

26 Ibid.

27 William D. Cohan, "Big Profits, Big Questions," *New York Times*, April 15, 2009.

28 John D. McKinnon and Susanne Craig, "Finance Panel Accuses Goldman of Stalling," *Wall Street Journal*, June 7, 2010.

29 Peter J. Henning, "What's Next for Goldman Sachs," *New York Times*, April 29, 2010.

30 John C. Coffee Jr., "Testimony of Professor John C. Coffee Jr. Before the Subcommittee on Crime and Drugs of the United States Senate Committee on the Judiciary," Hearing on S.3217, "Wall Street Fraud and Fiduciary Duties: Can Jail Time Serve as an Adequate Deterrent for Willful Violations," May 4, 2010, available at http://judiciary.senate.gov/hearings/hearing.cfm?id=4560, accessed 9/17/10.

[31] Cyrus Sanati, "Debate Flares on Goldman's Role as Market Maker," *New York Times*, April 29, 2010.

[32] Joe Bel Bruno and Brett Philbin, "Blankfein Defends Goldman's Ethics," *Wall Street Journal*, May 5, 2010; and Joe Bel Bruno and Brett Philbin, "Blankfein Tells Clients That They Come First," *Wall Street Journal*, May 6, 2010.

[33] Stephan Grocer, "The SEC Statement on Goldman: A Stark Lesson to Wall Street," *Wall Street Journal*, July 15, 2010.

[34] McKinnon and Craig, "Finance Panel Accuses Goldman of Stalling."

[35] Editorial, "Fistful of Dollars: Goldman Sachs Got Off With a Slap From the SEC," *Pittsburgh Post Gazette*, July 20, 2010.

[36] Grocer, "The SEC Statement on Goldman."

[37] Ashby Jones, "But Who Won? Sizing Up Goldman's Deal With the SEC," *Wall Street Journal*, July 15, 2010.

[38] Katy Barnato, "A Morality Play," *Credit* (London), June 2010, pp. 30–33.

[39] Peter Madigan, "Spotlight on Goldman," *Risk* (London), June 2010, pp. 64-67.

[40] Joe Bel Bruno and Brett Philbin, "Blankfein Says Goldman Must Renew Core Principles," *Wall Street Journal*, May 7, 2010.

Case Study

Cigarette Regulation: Who Is Responsible for What?

By Ruth T. Norman   Ruth T. Norman is an assistant professor and director of the Doctor of Business Administration program at Wilmington University in Delaware. Her research interests include business policy, business ethics, and media coverage of science and business issues. Contact: ruth.t.norman@wilmu.edu

Overview

Corporations have responsibilities to customers, employees, communities, and other stakeholders. Stakeholders also have obligations as well as rights. What is the appropriate balance between the rights and duties of the various parties? As a society, how do we decide where to draw the line? Do our ideas change over time, and, if so, what are the processes by which they change?

This case study examines a complicated arena of corporate social responsibility—cigarettes. It looks at a number of ethical or normative issues, including uncertainty of risk, manipulation of science, free speech, free markets, adult free choice, marketing practices, protection of children and vulnerable populations, and responsibility for physical and financial harm. In doing so, the case examines actions taken by the cigarette companies, smokers, antismoking activists, regulatory bodies, and the courts in the United States over the past 60 years.

Marketing Unhealthy Products

Although smoking has declined in the United States, millions of current and former smokers still continue to be at risk for smoking-related disease, and a number of parties still reap significant financial benefits from the industry, including state and federal governments (settlement payments and excise taxes), members of Congress (campaign contributions), retailers, and employees. Taking a global perspective, despite an antismoking treaty brokered by the World Health Organization, cigarette smoking is increasing in developing countries.[1] The World Health Organization reports that 5 million people die annually from tobacco consumption and that 80 percent of the world's 1 billion smokers live in low- and middle-income countries.[2]

Activists are using the cigarette case as a template for other corporate social responsibility campaigns. Similar rhetoric, norms, and tactics are used in other areas, such as the antiobesity campaign. To what extent is Coca Cola or McDonald's responsible for making people fat? Or, are parents responsible for ensuring that their children have good eating habits? Legal precedents established in cigarette litigation set the stage for future litigation relating to other products, just as asbestos precedents (and tort revenues) set the stage for cigarette suits.

This is the dynamic ethical and legal arena in which all organizations operate today. Marketing and other activities that may have been tolerated in the past are increasingly under scrutiny, and legal damages can run into many billions of dollars.

History of Tobacco and Cigarettes in the United States

The history of tobacco in the United States goes back to colonial days when it was a key export commodity. In that era, health concerns relating to smoking were minor compared to disease, accidents, and other causes of deaths. However, some people did voice ethical concerns about the slave labor that was integral to the cultivation of tobacco and other plantation crops.

Whereas tobacco has been consumed for centuries in pipes, cigars, and snuff, smoking cigarettes is a relatively recent phenomenon, emerging commercially around 1870. The U.S. government helped establish the habit by supplying cigarettes to World War I and World War II soldiers. By the early 1960s, 42 percent of adults smoked cigarettes—52 percent of men and 34 percent of women.[3]

People had long suspected some negative health impacts from smoking (hence the slang term "coffin nails" for cigarettes), but it was also believed that there were physiological benefits such as relaxation, alertness, virility, and protection against colds. Such positive health claims were often incorporated in cigarette advertising.

It was difficult to establish a statistically significant relationship between smoking and disease, in part because the effect is delayed, with cancer and other diseases often occurring more than 20 years after smoking begins. Some members of the medical community thought that industrial pollution was responsible for the rising prevalence of lung cancer, and no proven physiological mechanism could explain how smoking might cause cancer.

However, by the mid-twentieth century, several factors combined to increase the suspected, though not yet proven, significance of smoking as a public health problem. First, since antibiotics and improved hygiene reduced premature mortality caused by infectious diseases, other causes of premature death were becoming relatively more important. Second, due to the rise in cigarette smoking following World War I, large numbers of people had been smoking long enough to experience the consequences.

During the early 1950s, more sophisticated medical research techniques started to be used, and evidence that smoking caused disease was building. Cancer scare articles were carried by popular publications. In response, cigarette companies, which had previously operated in a highly competitive fashion, banded together to conduct a public relations counterattack. The industry maintained that scientific findings on the health hazards of smoking were inconclusive and pledged to do research to ensure that its products were safe.[4]

The industry responded to customer health concerns by offering new products with filters, menthol additives, and reduced tar and nicotine. These new products became very popular, and cigarette consumption resumed its growth pattern.

Both the Federal Trade Commission (FTC) and the public believed that lower tar and nicotine cigarettes were safer than traditional products. However, independent studies subsequently showed that smokers compensate for reduced nicotine content and filters by inhaling more deeply, blocking ventilation holes, or smoking more cigarettes, hence largely neutralizing any risk reduction. Based on this new information, cigarette companies ceased promoting reduced nicotine and tar products as being safer, but they continued to use the terms "light" and "mild" in reference to flavor.

Smoking May Be Harmful to Your Health

As epidemiological evidence was becoming more convincing, the U.S. surgeon general commissioned a review by 10 medical experts. Their report, issued in January 1964, identified a strong association between cigarette smoking and substantially higher death rates in men. They concluded that the data supported a judgment of causality and called for remedial action.

The tobacco industry countered that the scientific evidence was indeterminate. In support of this position, the industry's research arm sponsored its own carefully designed studies. The industry's sponsorship was not always revealed when these studies were published.

As negative medical evidence started to mount, the percentage of the public viewing tobacco as a relatively harmless pleasure declined. However, there was not a groundswell of support for regulation because adult smoking was perceived to be a matter of personal choice.

As a result of the power of Southern representatives in Congress, who were highly influenced by tobacco lobbyists and their campaign contributions, policy development proceeded with difficulty. The FTC proposed warning statements on packages and advertisements. Congress responded by ruling that the FTC did not have jurisdiction. Although the industry lobbied for self-regulation, Congress remained under pressure to formally take remedial measures. The resultant legislation was a highly compromised measure. The bill did mandate warning labels on the side of cigarette packs and cartons but did not require warning statements in advertisements. Furthermore, the mandated package warning, "Caution: Cigarette Smoking May Be Hazardous to Your Health," implied that there was some doubt. Congress declared that its bill preempted the FTC (for five years) and the states (for an indeterminate period) from requiring additional or more stringent tobacco warnings.

Although the FTC was temporarily preempted from action, other federal agencies were not prevented from stepping into the fray. In 1967, the Federal Communications Commission applied the fairness doctrine of public broadcasting, previously employed to ensure that both sides of controversial political issues were presented, to provide free airtime for antismoking announcements. Smoking declined during this counteradvertising period, so the industry may have actually benefited when Congress banned television and radio advertising in 1971, thus ending free antismoking announcements.

Congress strengthened the wording and prominence of the package warning statement in 1969 and again in 1984. In 1971, after the congressional preemption expired, the FTC mandated warning statements in cigarette print advertisements.

Marketing Regulation

Regulatory interference in marketing practices and product design tends to meet public resistance in the United States. Government, however, is perceived as having an obligation to protect children and other vulnerable populations. This obligation outweighs the free market and free speech rights of businesses. Many smokers start when they are teens; hence, government may have a legitimate role in regulating access and marketing practices.

Similar to other manufacturers of consumer products, cigarette companies have spent large amounts of money on marketing. Sophisticated advertising campaigns created glamorous images for smoking and smokers. Establishing numerous retail outlets, including ubiquitous vending machines, and promoting multipack cartons helped ensure that smokers would always have convenient access to cigarettes. King-size cigarettes were promoted to increase the amount of tobacco consumed per cigarette.

Antismoking proponents maintained that children were exposed to and strongly influenced by cigarette advertising even if it was targeted at adults. They claimed that children were vulnerable to the glamorous images portrayed and were too young to make informed choices about health risk.

Products such as Virginia Slims were developed to appeal to females. Target marketing programs are common in many consumer products. In the case of cigarettes, however, marketing to specific segments, such as women or blacks, started to be viewed as manipulative and unacceptable.

Regulation of youth access to cigarettes occurred at the state and local levels, where grassroots political activity was more effective and the industry's lobbying power was reduced. As a result of advocacy by various groups, all states have passed laws restricting minors' access to cigarettes.

In 1971, Congress banned cigarette advertising on television and radio. Despite this ban, the industry was able to market effectively through other avenues. It continued to walk a thin line, however, on whether its promotional activities were targeted solely to adults.

In 1987, R.J. Reynolds stepped over the line when it started a $75 million marketing campaign featuring Joe Camel, a hip cartoon character. The campaign included branded items such as T-shirts and beach sandals. The campaign garnered considerable criticism because of its apparent orientation toward children. California filed a lawsuit against the Joe Camel campaign citing unfair competition, and the company was forced to discontinue the Joe Camel promotions there.

Product Regulation

Although consumer protection laws from the 1960s and 1970s specifically excluded tobacco from Food and Drug Administration (FDA) regulation, a number of antismoking advocates continued to believe that cigarettes should be regulated by the agency. In February 1994, FDA Commissioner David Kessler resurfaced the issue by announcing his intention to regulate the nicotine in cigarettes. The agency moved forward with an exhaustive investigation of industry conduct. Its efforts were assisted by whistle-blowers and legal discovery. Four thousand pages of incriminating, internal Brown & Williamson (B & W) documents were stolen by a contract paralegal and made public. The investigations documented that B & W was purposely using Y-1, a nicotine-rich, hybrid tobacco, in some of its brands. It was also revealed that ammonia was commonly added to cigarettes to enhance the release of nicotine.

Integrating addiction with the ever-popular theme of protecting children, FDA Commissioner Kessler labeled smoking as a "pediatric disease." In response, the industry filed a lawsuit against the FDA. The action eventually worked its way up to the U.S. Supreme Court, where, in March 2000, it ruled by a 5–4 margin that the FDA did not have jurisdiction over tobacco unless congressional legislation was enacted to grant the power.

Such legislation did pass in the House in 2004 but failed in the Senate. In 2009, however, a bill authorizing FDA to regulate (but not to ban) cigarettes was finally passed. The reasons the bill passed this time include the declining power and image of the tobacco industry and support by Philip Morris USA, the largest U.S. cigarette company. The bill specifies a number of marketing restrictions but does not provide any protection against litigation even if a company is in compliance with all FDA content and labeling requirements.

The new advertising and promotion restrictions will make it more difficult for the smaller cigarette companies to increase market share. Hence, it is not surprising that plaintiffs including Reynolds American and Lorillard filed a suit in federal court to block some of the marketing restrictions because they abridge their First Amendment rights to free speech. In addition to helping Philip Morris lock in its dominant market share, the restrictions make it difficult to provide information about smokeless products, which might be safer alternatives for current adult smokers of cigarettes.

A federal district court judge ruled that the FDA cannot block the use of color and graphics in cigarette advertisements but upheld the constitutionality of other parts of the bill including requirement of warnings graphically showing health risks covering the top half of packages and bans on sponsorships and branded merchandise.

Nonsmoker Rights

A key element to the success of the antismoking campaign has been the advancement of a new concept, "nonsmoker rights." In this view, smokers are at fault because they put innocent people at risk.

This campaign benefitted from previous public consciousness-raising by environmentalists, who had successfully framed pollution as a public policy issue in the 1960s and established the concept of a right to clean air and water.[5] Although environmental tobacco smoke health risks are lower than those encountered by smokers themselves, the concept of protecting innocent and vulnerable people from unpleasant and unhealthy tobacco smoke has had strong resonance with nonsmokers.[6]

The industry has attempted to undercut the scientific basis of this campaign by claiming that the evidence of health risks from secondhand smoke is inconclusive. It has argued against policy initiatives by maintaining that this is a social rather than a regulatory issue, and that the desires of both parties can be amicably addressed through courtesy and tolerance.

Although the cigarette industry's financial and lobbying power continued to be significant at the congressional level, nonsmoker rights policies advanced slowly but surely at the state and local levels and through federal agency action. For example, Arizona, Connecticut, and Minnesota passed laws in the 1970s restricting smoking in public places. Early federal agency regulation involved no smoking zones in public transportation. In 1988, Congress banned smoking on domestic flights that were less than two hours in duration. In 1990, this ban was extended to most domestic flights.

Government facilities and private employers, often voluntarily, started to restrict smoking to certain areas. State and local governments started to pass laws for no-smoking areas in public and commercial facilities, such as restaurants. Gradually, public opinions changed. There is now less tolerance for smokers, and policy is switching from no-smoking zones to complete smoking bans in commercial buildings, including restaurants and bars.

A factor contributing to privileging nonsmoker rights is the decline in smokers' political influence. This decline has occurred for three reasons. First, the voting power of smokers has been cut in half, as the percentage of adults who smoke cigarettes has shrunk from 42 percent to 21 percent. Second, people who continue to smoke are disproportionately in lower socioeconomic groups and are thus less politically influential. Third, smokers have been increasingly viewed in a negative light. They are perceived as lacking the will power to quit and as being inconsiderate to nonsmokers.

As a result of viewing smokers more negatively, some employers, such as the states of Alabama and North Carolina and General Electric, charge smokers a higher health insurance co-pay. Some states or local jurisdictions allow employers to refuse to hire smokers. For example, in Ohio, where such employment policies are allowed, the Cleveland Clinic, Summa Health, Scotts Miracle-Gro, and USI Financial Services do not hire smokers.[7]

Corporate Liability

The basic premise supporting corporate liability is that cigarette companies have failed to behave responsibly, so the legal system should force them to pay for the social costs (externalities) of smoking. Early attempts to establish corporate liability occurred through a series of personal injury lawsuits. For nearly 40 years, the U.S. tobacco industry was able to outspend and outlast litigants, despite steadily increasing knowledge about the health effects of smoking. From 1954 until 1992, 813 cases were filed against cigarette companies, but only 23 went to trial. During this period, the companies never settled out of court and never paid a penny to plaintiffs, although their legal expenses were large.

The early suits claimed that tobacco companies were negligent in not warning customers or that there was an implied warranty of safety. The industry's initial defense was that the scientific studies were inconclusive. Although this defense may have been legitimate early on, it became increasingly unviable as both public and concealed in-house information mounted.

Starting in 1983, plaintiffs changed their arguments to focus on strict liability. At this time, the industry switched its defense to a position that the health risks were common knowledge, and the defendant should have been aware of these risks and therefore had assumed responsibility for his or her health outcomes. The package warning labels that had been mandated since 1966 buttressed the industry's defense. Comparative fault principles were beginning to be applied to product liability cases in this period, with many states disallowing damages unless more than 50 percent of the responsibility could be assigned to the defendant. Although many juries did believe that the companies were partly at fault, they overwhelmingly believed that individual smokers bore more than 50 percent of the responsibility for their own health outcomes.

Starting in the 1990s, antismoking advocates focused on a new tool for corporate liability framing: intentional nicotine addiction. It had long been recognized that quitting smoking was difficult. In fact, some members of the 1964 surgeon general's committee wanted to label cigarettes and nicotine as addictive, but the decision was that the evidence was insufficient. Instead, the report indicated that tobacco was habituating. This was the official position until the 1988 Surgeon General's Report, which declared that nicotine exhibited addictive properties similar to hard drugs.

Flush with money from asbestos litigation, tort lawyers viewed nicotine addiction as an opportunity for profitable class-action personal injury lawsuits. Such suits accused cigarette companies of manipulating nicotine to enhance addiction, intentional misrepresentation, concealment, and failure to disclose information.

Other class-action suits accused cigarette companies of defrauding current and former smokers of "light" brands by suggesting that these were less hazardous than higher tar cigarettes. It was not necessary that the plaintiffs had experienced negative health outcomes, but merely that they were deceived and hence suffered economic damages.

Light cigarette and other litigation continue to take place in both state and federal courts. Notably, a large number of personal injury suits in Florida have been spun off from a disallowed class action suit. Decisions in the initial trials have largely been going against the tobacco industry, but these and many other decisions are being appealed.[8]

State Government Litigation

Following the lead of the attorneys general from Florida, Minnesota, Mississippi, and Texas, in June 1997, attorneys general from 39 states (supported by a battery of contingency fee-based tort lawyers) sued for penalties, punitive damages, and recovery of Medicaid costs associated with smoker illnesses. They cited a conspiracy to mislead smokers and the public. In particular, they claimed that the companies had violated antitrust and consumer fraud laws by withholding information, had manipulated nicotine levels to maximize addiction, and had conspired to prevent introduction of lower risk products.

Interestingly, some expert analyses show that state expenditures for smokers are actually lower than for nonsmokers because reduced life expectancy decreases nursing home and pension expenses, and this more than offsets other costs. This is clearly an ethically unsustainable argument, and the industry's ethical and legal positions were already rapidly deteriorating. Many incriminating internal documents were now available to the public, and millions more pages became available during the states' litigation. The stonewalling strategy that had enabled the industry to weather more than 30 years of attacks was now crumbling.

Considerable uncertainty remained relative to the ultimate outcome of the states' suits. Juries still tended to support the industry, laws in most of the states were not favorable to this type of suit, and many of the attorneys general were lukewarm to the approach. Nonetheless, the industry was likely to lose in at least some of the states. Given the considerable resources of the states and the impressive war chests of tort lawyers, it was questionable whether the industry could afford to go the distance.

Accordingly, the industry decided to pursue a negotiated settlement with the states for the purpose of managing its liabilities. Four states settled individual lawsuits for a total of $40 billion. The remaining states, most of which had weak cases, banded together to negotiate the Master Settlement Agreement of 1998 (MSA).[9]

The MSA required payments of $206 billion over 25 years to the participating states in exchange for protection from suits by the state governments. This still left them vulnerable to federal suits and private class actions, as well as individual suits. The settlement also contained marketing restrictions and required the industry to disband its lobbying and research organizations.[10]

Federal Litigation

Soon after the dust settled on the MSA, the federal government filed its own lawsuit, charging fraud and concealment and seeking reimbursement of its health care costs. The health care cost actions were dismissed, but the Justice Department was permitted to proceed with its "unlawful conduct" case under the Racketeer Influenced and Corrupt Organizations Act (RICO).

The federal government sought equitable relief via disgorgement of $280 billion in allegedly ill-gotten gains. The government's economic consultants claimed that this was the invested value of $76 billion they calculated that the industry earned between 1971 and 2001 from smokers who were lured into nicotine addiction before age 21 because they were manipulated by tobacco advertising. Prosecution arguments attempted to establish an ingrained pattern of fraudulent behavior by demonstrating that the industry concealed information about cancer and addiction, manipulated nicotine delivery, marketed to children, and misled people into thinking that "light" cigarettes were safer.

In 2006, a federal judge ruled that the cigarette companies had violated racketeering laws by deceiving the public about the harm caused by cigarettes but stated that she did not have the authority to order major financial remedies. The companies were ordered to stop using terms such as "light" and "low tar" and to put additional warning labels on cigarette packs. The Justice Department petitioned for Supreme Court review of the decision but was turned down.[11]

Current Activities

In addition to ongoing litigation and appeals at federal and state levels, a number of current activities relate to cigarettes. For example, recently considerable focus has been placed on raising both state and federal excise taxes on cigarettes. The most frequent justification offered by antismoking advocates for higher taxes is that higher retail prices discourage youth smoking. There is also some rhetoric that the higher retail prices provide more incentive for adult smokers to quit. The inference here is that excise taxes are needed to send pricing signals to "protect" people who are apparently not sufficiently rational to respond to medical evidence. Occasionally, it is inferred that smokers should help pay for the medical cost burdens they impose on government and society. The bottom line is, however, that both state and the federal government are becoming increasingly dependent on cigarette-related revenues.

Cigarette companies are shifting their focus to smokeless tobacco products, asserting that they are safer because they have lower levels of carcinogens and are not absorbed in the lungs. In addition to traditional snuff, these products include snus (spit-free tobacco in pouches) and flavored, dissolvable pellets and strips.[12]

A number of public debates concern smokeless products. The first is whether they are, in fact, safer. Even if they are safer, a second debate is whether any tobacco product is sufficiently safe. A third concern is whether the mint- or cinnamon-flavored pellets, which look rather like Tic Tacs, are designed to lure young people into smoking. Even though the containers have child-proof designs, another concern is whether the pellets should be illegal because the products could be poisonous to small children due to the high level of absorbable nicotine. The FDA is working on a policy regarding dissolvable nicotine products and has asked Reynolds to provide its market research findings.

One of the most sensitive issues facing the FDA is establishing a policy on menthol flavoring. Menthol products make up around 70 percent of the U.S. market. Menthol masks the harsh taste of tobacco, and critics claim that menthol increases teen smoking. Because menthol products are particularly popular with African Americans, charges of predatory marketing have been raised. Congress was not able to resolve the menthol issue in its legislation and passed this political hot potato on to the FDA, requiring it to develop a policy by 2012.

Because smoking has been on the decline in the United States, cigarette companies increasingly are looking toward other countries where growth opportunities still exist, particularly developing countries. In order to focus on these growth opportunities, Philip Morris International (PMI) has been completely split off from Philip Morris USA. This allows PMI to pursue growth strategies free of U.S. political and litigation problems.

Antismoking activists, however, are gaining strength in the international arena, supported by an antismoking treaty brokered by the World Health Organization. The treaty requires the 168 signatory countries to implement excise taxes, warning labels, and marketing restrictions. Consequently, PMI is moving quickly to gain share before marketing restrictions are fully phased in. The company claims that it is not wooing new smokers, but rather encouraging existing smokers to switch to higher-quality cigarettes. Other international cigarette companies are also seeking to grow their businesses before more marketing restrictions are implemented.

QUESTIONS

1. Who is primarily responsible for a teenager's decision to smoke—the individual teen, peers, parents, school, church, government, cigarette companies, or retailers? Why?

2. Should cigarettes be illegal? Which stakeholders would be impacted by such a law? Which rights must be weighed?

3. How ethical or unethical are the actions and behaviors of the following parties in this case study: cigarette companies, antismoking activists, smokers, politicians, retailers? Provide examples to support your position.

4. Identify a consumer product that can cause physical, economic, or social harm. What marketing constraints should be in place? Should these be voluntary or regulated? Should some consumer segments receive more protection?

5. Should governments levy excise taxes on other products that can have negative health impacts, such as soft drinks? Why? If so, what products should be taxed and how high should the tax be?

6. What should be done about menthol-flavored cigarettes? Why?

7. What policies should be enacted concerning flavored tobacco pellets?

NOTES

[1] *WHO Report on the Global Tobacco Epidemic, 2009* (Geneva, Switzerland: World Health Organization, 2009), available at http://whqlibdoc.who.int/publications/2009/9789241563918_eng_full.pdf, accessed 8/31/10.

[2] http://www.who.int/mediacentre/factsheets/fs339/en/index.html, accessed 8/31/10.

[3] Centers for Disease Control and Prevention, "Surveillance for Selected Tobacco-Use Behavior—United States, 1900–1994," *CDC Surveillance Summaries*, MMWR 1994; 43, No. SS-3 (Washington, DC: U.S. Government Printing Office, 1994).

[4] Excellent sources for historical information on the cigarette industry include Martha A. Derthick, *Up in Smoke: From Legislation to Litigation in Tobacco Politics,* 2nd ed. (Washington, DC: CQ Press, 2005); A. Lee Fritschler, *Smoking and Politics: Policy Making and the Federal Bureaucracy,* 4th ed. (Englewood Cliffs, NJ: Prentice Hall, 1989); Richard Kluger, *Ashes to Ashes: America's Hundred-Year Cigarette War, the Public Health, and the Unabashed Triumph of Philip Morris* (New York: Vintage Books, 1997); Fred C. Pampel, *Tobacco Industry and Smoking* (New York: Facts on File, Inc., 2004); and Robert L. Rabin and Stephen D. Sugarman (Eds.), *Regulating Tobacco* (New York: Oxford University Press, 2001).

[5] Ronald Bayer and James Colgrove, "Children and Bystanders First: The Ethics and Politics of Tobacco Control in the United States," in Eric A. Feldman and Ronal Bayer (Eds.), *Unfiltered* (Cambridge, MA: Harvard University Press, 2004), pp. 8–37.

[6] Maia Szalavitz, *Secondhand Smoke: Nuisance or Menace?* Statistical Assessment Service, June 2, 2003, available at http://stats.org/stories/2003/secondhand_smoke_jun3_03.htm, accessed 8/31/10.

[7] Jim DeBrosse, "Ohio Employers Saying No to Smokers to Reduce Costs," *Dayton Daily News,* February 22, 2010.

[8] Bob Van Voris, "Big Tobacco Gets Its Many Days in Court," *Bloomberg Businessweek*, May 24, 2010.

[9] The Master Settlement Agreement is available at http://www.ag.ca.gov/tobacco/pdf/1msa.pdf, accessed 8/31/10.

[10] W. Kip Viscusi, *Smoke-Filled Rooms: A Post-Mortem on the Tobacco Deal* (Chicago, IL: University of Chicago Press, 2002).

[11] Duff Wilson, "Supreme Court Rejects Appeals of Tobacco Ruling," *New York Times*, July 29, 2010.

[12] Duff Wilson, "Tobacco," *New York Times*, May 4, 2010; and David Kesmodel, "In Tobacco Giant's Makeover, No Smoke, But Plenty of Fire," *Wall Street Journal*, March 26, 2010.

Case Study

Fast Food, Childhood Obesity, and Local Government Regulations: No More Fun and Games

By Michael Germano and Ivan Montiel   Michael Germano is an assistant professor in the University Library at California State University, Los Angeles. His research interests include social marketing and sales. Contact: mgerman@ calstatela.edu

Ivan Montiel is an assistant professor at the College of Business Administration at Loyola Marymount University. His research interests include corporate socially responsible and sustainable strategies. Contact: ivanmontiel@gmail.com

Overview

This case examines what is widely considered the first law of its kind: the vote by the Santa Clara County, California, Board of Supervisors to require fast-food chains to remove toys from high-calorie children's meals or make the meals meet nutritional standards by May 2010. Concerns about the increasing rate of childhood obesity prompted the local government to act. Restaurants operating in Santa Clara County must either eliminate toys from their meal packages or reduce the amount of calories to a certain threshold established by the county. Not surprisingly, the response from businesses has been less than supportive. Harlan Levy of McDonald's disagreed with the local government's approach saying: "It substitutes the county's judgment for the judgment of parents. It does nothing to address a holistic response to the problem."[1]

Lookout Ronald, the Toy Police are After You!

Fed up with the high economic and social costs related to childhood obesity, Santa Clara County's Board of Supervisors took action in a novel way during the spring of 2010 by enacting a local ordinance that prohibits restaurants from using toys to promote unhealthy foods. Specifically, the law requires compliance with the following nutritional values in order to bundle a toy with a meal:[2]

- 485-calorie limit for entire meal
- 120-calorie limit for drinks accompanying the meal
- 200-calorie limit from a single food item
- 600 milligrams of sodium limit for entire meal
- 480 milligrams of sodium limit for a single food item
- No more than 35 percent of all calories from fat
- No more than 10 percent of all calories from added sugar
- Violators face a fine of $1,000 for each meal served that does not meet the requirements

Not surprisingly, although the law had some support from parents and dieticians, the Santa Clara County local government faced significant backlash from some businesses and individuals. The negative reactions ranged from head-shaking dismissal to outrage over the excessive burden government placed on businesses affected by the new law and the implied intrusion into people's lives. These businesses and customers resented what they considered heavy-handed government efforts to require or force people to eat healthier foods and questioned the law's benefits.

Santa Clara County's Board of Supervisors countered that the regulation was aimed at arming parents with a concrete tool that would mitigate the overwhelming desire of children to eat unhealthy and potentially dangerous fast food. The local government's reasoning echoed the frustration of many parents who feel powerless in their attempts to steer their children toward healthier food choices. Parents claim there are few resources at their disposal to counter the massive amounts of money and resources that restaurants, particularly fast-food chains, use to create brand preference for their products among children. Ken Yeager, a county supervisor, clarified that:[3]

> Under this ordinance, restaurants are still permitted to give out toys. This ordinance merely imposes very specific, common-sense nutrition standards that are linked to these incentives . . . [the ordinance] prevents restaurants from preying upon children's love of toys to peddle high-calorie, high-fat, high-sodium kid's meals.

The California Restaurant Association fired back with large full-page ads in local newspapers, including the San Jose–based *Mercury News*, asking: "Who made politicians the toy police?" In addition, the trade group surveyed local residents in Silicon Valley and San Jose, of which Santa Clara is in the geographic center, and reported in subsequent advertisements that an overwhelming 80 percent considered the issue of bundling toys and fast food an unimportant one.[4]

Is the burgeoning specter and explosive epidemic of childhood obesity itself an unimportant issue? What role do restaurants, particularly fast-food ones, play in the role of the epidemic? What are the obligations of restaurants, parents, and government? Are regulations that seek to limit children's exposure to unhealthful, calorie-laden fast foods actually useful or simply inadequate to the task? Lastly, what strategies beyond industry self-regulation should governments impose on businesses that have a negative impact on public health and result in increased health care costs for everyone? To answer these questions, it is helpful to examine the fast-food industry in general, and its role in childhood obesity specifically.

Fatty Fast Food and Fun: A Failing Recipe for Kids?

It seems hard to imagine, but for many people over the age of 40, fast food played a minimal, if any presence at all, in their childhood. This group, like all generations of children, did indulge in their preferred junk foods, such as candy, chips, soda, and snack cakes. But those born before the 1970s received relatively limited attention from food manufacturers and marketers.

Food-related marketing directed at children prior to the 1970s was mostly in the form of television advertising for breakfast cereals and processed meats such as hotdogs and cold cuts. Fast food was only beginning to emerge as a high-growth industry with outlets throughout the United States. Its presence in terms of brands and outlets represented a fraction of what it is currently. Children were more likely to eat foods made at home from fresh ingredients than highly processed foods, including fast foods.

All of this changed dramatically, along with childhood eating habits, in the early 1970s with the innovation of Ronald McDonald and, eventually, the Happy Meal. In the years before the yellow and red spokesperson of the largest fast-food franchise in the United States emerged, restaurants and their marketing rarely targeted children directly. McDonald's changed all of that by creating a likeable, easily identifiable character that spoke directly to children.

Ronald McDonald took to the airwaves for the first time in 1966. But it wasn't until he was joined with a cast of characters including Hamburglar, Grimace, Captain Crook, and Mayor McCheese—denizens of the child-friendly McDonaldland in 1971—that McDonald's hit marketing gold. These characters created an imaginative sparking universe that allowed for overwhelming brand preference by children that would carry well into their teens and adulthood.

The groundbreaking innovation in appealing directly to children recognized the way parents spent money and fueled McDonald's explosive growth during the 1970s. According to McDonald's website, the business hit upon several other key innovations that lead to explosive growth that culminated in the opening of 5,000 stores by 1980.[5] These game changers included the drive-through window, which accounted for more than half of McDonald's revenues within three years, along with its iconic breakfast menu. At the same time, other fast-food brands, including Burger King, Wendy's, Taco Bell, and Kentucky Fried Chicken, experienced laudable, but hardly comparable, growth.

Fast food came of age in the United States during the 1970s. The combination of convenience, taste, and price made these fast-growing chains the leading source of revenue in the restaurant industry.[6] As the industry became more competitive with more and more choices and an increasing number of outlets competing for consumer dollars, McDonald's again found itself in the forefront of marketing innovation when it combined its marketing message to children with product development. The result was the Happy Meal, which debuted in 1979. The Happy Meal became a paradigm of fast-food marketing that left parents virtually powerless to the oft-repeated plea, as well as the implied convenience, of dinner out at a fast-food restaurant.

The simple combination of a toy or trinket in a colorful box decked out in stories, games, and puzzles became the paradigm for the fast-food industry to market meals to children. The promotions became increasingly sophisticated with movie and television tie-ins that created a marketing juggernaut for fast food, entertainment, and even, ironically, the toys themselves. Media outlets, such as movie studios and television programs, recognized the value of being associated with a Happy Meal as a means of program promotion. Toy manufacturers also saw the benefit of introducing their product lines by partnering with McDonald's to give away a free version of their toy.

The end result was that fast-food companies, led by McDonald's, became tastemakers when it came to marketing toys and entertainment to children. In the process, they exercised substantial control over parental purse strings and, maybe not intentionally, children's waistlines.

As McDonald's and other fast-food restaurants developed their businesses and product offerings, a funny thing happened: meal size and portion size increased as children became an increasingly vital portion of their business. The average fast-food adult meal includes on average more than 1,200 gut-busting, nutritionally suspect calories.[7] Kids' meals, although substantially smaller, have evolved into what might have been an adult-sized portion in the past. A total calorie count of 700 when other amenities are added is not uncommon.[8] The amount of fat, sodium, and added sugar increased as well. One fast-food meal accounts for half the daily calories recommended for children under the age of 8 (see Exhibit 1).

Exhibit 1 Nutritional Needs of Healthy Children

Boys and Girls Ages 2 to 3

Calories	1,000 to 1,400, depending on growth and activity level
Protein	5 to 20% of daily calories (13 to 50 grams for 1,000 daily calories)
Carbohydrates	45 to 65% of daily calories (113 to 163 grams for 1,000 daily calories)
Total fat	30 to 40% of daily calories (33 to 44 grams for 1,000 daily calories)
Sodium	1,000 milligrams a day
Fiber	19 grams a day
Calcium	500 milligrams a day

Boys Ages 4 to 8	
Calories	1,400 to 2,000, depending on growth and activity level
Protein	10 to 30% of daily calories (35 to 105 grams for 1,400 daily calories)
Carbohydrates	45 to 65% of daily calories (158 to 228 grams for 1,400 daily calories)
Total fat	25 to 35% of daily calories (39 to 54 grams for 1,400 daily calories)
Sodium	1,200 milligrams a day
Fiber	25 grams a day
Calcium	800 milligrams a day
Girls Ages 4 to 8	
Calories	1,200 to 1,800, depending on growth and activity level
Protein	10 to 30% of daily calories (30 to 90 grams for 1,200 daily calories)
Carbohydrates	45 to 65% of daily calories (135 to 195 grams for 1,200 daily calories)
Total fat	25 to 35% of daily calories (33 to 47 grams for 1,200 daily calories)
Sodium	1,200 milligrams a day
Fiber	25 grams a day
Calcium	800 milligrams a day

Source: Mayoclinic.com

Based on the information in Exhibit 2, most kids' meals are not in compliance with Santa Clara County requirements. For instance, the Happy Meal contains a total of 660 calories, 175 more than the 485 Santa Clara limit. Also, the burger served to kids at Burger King contains 330 calories; the regulation establishes a 200-calorie limit for a single food item. Therefore, most food items served in different fast-food chains nowadays would have to be modified to be in compliance with the new ordinance.

There seems to be a growing awareness of the potentially harmful effects of fast food on adults and children, but the realization may be too late for millions of children raised on fast-food kids' meals. As fast-food organizations raked in the profits, children and adults alike packed on the pounds. The fast-food industry is not the only cause of the obesity epidemic in the United States. Nonetheless, it may be a major contributing factor in the current public health nightmare that results from unhealthful eating, especially among children.

Exhibit 2 Selected Fast-Food Restaurants' Nutrition Facts for Meals or Menu Items Marketed to Children

McDonald's Happy Meal (burger, kid's size soda, kid's size fries)

Nutrition Facts
Serving Size: 1 meal

Amount per Serving

Calories 660   Calories from Fat 225

	% Daily Value*
Total Fat 25g	38%
Saturated Fat 8g	40%
Trans Fat 4g	
Cholesterol 40 mg	13%
Sodium 900mg	38%
Total Carbohydrate 92g	31%
Dietary Fiber 5g	20%
Protein 17g	34%

Est. Percent of Calories from:
Fat 34.1% **Carbs** 55.8%
Protein 10.3%

Taco Bell Kid's Tacos (tacos only)

Nutrition Facts
Serving Size: 1 burger (121 g)

Amount per Serving

Calories 330   Calories from Fat 0

	% Daily Value*
Total Fat 16g	25%
Saturated Fat 7g	35%
Trans Fat 1g	
Cholesterol 55mg	18%
Sodium 780mg	32%
Total Carbohydrate 31g	10%
Dietary Fiber 1g	4%
Sugars 6g	
Protein 17g	34%

Vitamin A	6%
Vitamin C	2%
Calcium	15%
Iron	15%

Est. Percent of Calories from:
Fat 43.6% **Carbs** 37.6%
Protein 20.6%

Burger King Kid's Burger (hamburger only)

Nutrition Facts
Serving Size: 3

Amount per Serving

Calories 420   Calories from Fat 100

	% Daily Value*
Total Fat 100g	154%
Saturated Fat 10g	50%
Monounsaturated Fat 60g	
Polyunsaturated Fat 10g	
Trans Fat 20g	
Sodium 0mg	0%
Total Carbohydrate 25g	8%
Dietary Fiber 4g	16%
Sugars 10g	
Protein 0g	0%

Est. Percent of Calories from:
Fat 214.3% **Carbs** 23.8%
Protein 0.0%

Subway's Kids Pack Meal Combo (turkey sandwich without cheese, yogurt, and bottled water)

Nutrition Facts
Serving Size: 1 meal

Amount per Serving

Calories 370   Calories from Fat 40

	% Daily Value*
Total Fat 4.5g	7%
Saturated Fat 1.5g	8%
Cholesterol 15mg	5%
Sodium 800mg	33%
Total Carbohydrate 72g	24%
Dietary Fiber 3g	12%
Sugars 31g	
Protein 13g	26%

Vitamin A	4%
Vitamin C	145%
Calcium	16%
Iron	20%

Est. Percent of Calories from:
Fat 10.9% **Carbs** 77.8%
Protein 14.1%

Source: Livestrong.com

What do Cigarettes and Burgers Have in Common?

According to a 2006 Federal Trade Commission (FTC) estimate based on federal subpoenas, $1.6 billion was spent in a single year on food and beverage marketing to children and adolescents.[9] Sixty-five percent of this money was spent promoting carbonated beverages, breakfast cereals, and fast food.

The FTC, which has regulatory authority over marketing and advertising practices of food and beverage companies, has made several attempts to create specific rules for marketing aimed at children. The American Psychological Association's Taskforce on Advertising to Children determined that children as old as eight accept commercial claims as truthful because they are unaware, or lack comprehension, of the intent of advertising generally.[10] Despite such scientific evidence that suggests children have no understanding of the persuasive and sometimes manipulative intent of advertising, the FTC has had minimal success limiting commercial messages to children because affected individuals and businesses claim protection from regulation based on the First Amendment of the U.S. Constitution and commercial freedom of speech rights.[11]

If marketing and advertising practices are poorly understood and accepted as truthful by most children, does this translate into culpability for an epidemic of childhood obesity brought on by unhealthful eating? Or perhaps a lesser level of responsibility that requires some form of accountability? Are purveyors of fat-laden, calorie-rich fast foods, such as McDonald's or other fast-food restaurants, particularly responsible for the nation's obesity problems?

According to survey after survey, Americans don't believe so. An overwhelming majority of respondents, when asked whether they agree with class-action lawsuits aimed at fast-food restaurants that seek damages under the same theory of liability used to successfully sue tobacco firms for deceptive practices, think these lawsuits are frivolous.[12] The class-action lawsuits claim that McDonald's and other fast-food restaurants target children illegally and mislead the public about the ill effects of their foods.

These same surveys reveal that Americans agree that fast food is unhealthy and does not contribute to a healthful diet. However, Americans prefer to place the burden of responsibility for addressing this problem squarely on the shoulders of the individual rather than relying on lawsuits or government regulation. Although cigarettes and fast food may both represent public health threats, albeit in varying degrees of seriousness and quantity, the similarities end there because fast-food companies did not actively deceive consumers about the commonsense dangers of eating salty, high-fat, highly processed foods along with sugary soft drinks.

Help! I've Fallen and Can't Get Up—and I'm Only 12!!!

Anyone who has spent time with a child intuitively knows that kids, like most people, prefer a chicken finger to a carrot stick. They also know that the current setup, when it comes to fast food and parental control, seems like a lost cause. With limited time, picky eaters, low costs, and the difficulty of preparing meals from fresh ingredients, fast food is often the hands-down winner for busy, cash-strapped families on the go. Throw an irresistible toy into the mix and the battle is lost. But at what cost? Childhood obesity and the deleterious health effects of a fatty, salty, sugary diet are enormous.

Obesity has become one of the most troubling health issues of the country in the past few years. Americans are continuing to get fatter, with obesity rates reaching 30 percent or more in nine states in 2009, as opposed to only three states in 2007. This increase means that 2.4 million more people became obese in a two-year period, bringing the total to 72.5 million (26.7 percent of U.S. population).[13]

Public health experts are concerned because obese children are increasingly developing weight-related health problems that normally show up only in adults, such as type 2 diabetes, high cholesterol, and heart disease. Whereas the short-term effects of unprecedented numbers of severely overweight children are weighing heavily on the health care system, the long-term effects could be catastrophic, according to some experts. Some suggest that average lifespan in the United States could decline for the first time in history due primarily to the shortened lifespan associated with excessively heavy children who become even heavier adults with a slew of chronic health problems that result from the excess weight brought on by a lifetime of poor nutrition and bad eating habits.[14]

In Santa Clara County, where more than one in four children under age 12 are considered obese, Public Health Director Dan Peddycord put it bluntly when supporting the ban on free toys with unhealthy meals:[15]

This ordinance breaks the link between unhealthy food and prizes. Obesity is literally an epidemic. If food meals sold in restaurants contain too many calories, high fats, high sugars and high sodium and are attached to an incentive item like a toy, that is part of the environment we make our decision in.

Santa Clara County supervisor Liz Kniss compared the ordinance to curbing dangerous behaviors such as smoking or speeding. Ken Yeager, the original drafter of the law, summarized the frustration of parents:[16]

It's unfair to parents and children to use toys to get them hooked on high-calorie, high-fat foods so early in life . . . this ordinance prevents restaurants from preying on children's love of toys . . . it turns the tables and asks fast food restaurants to tie incentive like toys to good behavior or eating healthier meals.

Although these arguments seem to be viable, the fast-food industry is skeptical and believes it is being targeted and blamed for a problem that is much more widespread than the law implies. Additionally, businesses are skeptical because it takes away the responsibility of parents to ensure their children eat healthful foods. Harlan Levy, a spokesperson from McDonald's, summarizes the industry's frustration: [17] "It substitutes the county's judgment for the judgment of parents. It does nothing to address a holistic response to the problem of childhood obesity."

Childhood obesity and unhealthful eating are tied together. But the solutions to ending both of these problems are unclear. Although some argue that the Santa Clara ordinance is a step in the right direction, others think it is wasted effort or simply window dressing on a larger problem that needs to be addressed in a much broader way. The nearby city of San Francisco passed a similar fast food meal toy law, effective December 2011.[18]

DISCUSSION QUESTIONS

1. Whose responsibility is it to solve the societal problem of obesity, especially with regard to children: individuals, parents, government, or businesses? Exactly what roles should each stakeholder play in correcting the problem?

2. Should businesses, especially ones that seek children and their parents as customers, take a leadership role in doing "what's right" as a strategy that's good for business?

3. Do businesses owe their customers a responsibility to provide only safe, healthy products at all times?

4. How effective do you think local regulations are in promoting changes in industries, especially those that are consumer driven?

NOTES

1 Anonymous, "California's Santa Clara County Bans Happy Meal Toys to Stem Child Obesity," *Vancouver Sun,* April 28, 2010.

2 Karen Kaplan, "Santa Clara County Votes to Remove Toys from Salty, High-Calorie Fast Food Kids' Meals," *Los Angeles Times,* April 27, 2010.

3 Carmen Rita Nevarez, "Opinion: Santa Clara County Toy Law Allows Incentives for Healthy Food," *Mercury News,* May 6, 2010.

4 Sara Bonisteel, "Toys Banned in Some California Fast Food Restaurants," *CNN,* April 28, 2010.

5 McDonald's website: www.mcdonalds.com.

6 Peter Romeo, "The Road Taken," *Restaurant Business,* 100, 14 (July 15, 2001).

7 Janet Raloff, "Americans Eat Faster, and More," *Science News,* 165, 24 (2004), 381–382.

8 Jayne Hurley, Bonnie Liebman, Tamar Genger, Heather Jones, Sarah Wade, and Nicole Ferring, "Kids' Cuisine," *Nutrition Action Health Letter,* 31, 2 (2004), 12–15.

9 Parke Wilde, "Self-Regulation and the Response to Concerns about Food and Beverage Marketing to Children in the United States," *Nutrition Reviews,* 67, 3 (2009), 155–166.

10 Jennifer Pomeranz, "Television Food Marketing to Children Revisited: The Federal Trade Commission Has the Constitutional and Statutory Authority to

Regulate," *Journal of Law, Medicine & Ethics,* 38, 1 (2010), 98–116.

11 Jan Wicks, Ron Warren, Ignatius Fosu, and Robert Wicks, "Dual-Modality Disclaimers: Emotional Appeals and Production Techniques in Advertising Airing During Programming Rated for Children," *Journal of Advertising,* 38, 4 (2009), 93–105.

12 Anonymous, "Ronald McDonald, A Monster in a Clown Suit?" *Consumers' Research Magazine,* 86, 8 (2003), 41.

13 Denise Grady, "Obesity Rates Keep Raising, Troubling Health Officials," *New York Times,* August 3, 2010.

14 National Institutes of Health, "Obesity Threatens to Cut US Life Expectancy, New Analysis Suggests," available at http://www.nih.gov/news/pr/mar2005/nia-16.htm, accessed 9/9/10

15 Anonymous, "California's Santa Clara County Bans Happy Meal Toys to Stem Child Obesity."

16 Kaplan, "Santa Clara County Votes to Remove Toys from Salty, High-Calorie Fast Food Kids' Meals."

17 Anonymous, "California's Santa Clara County Bans Happy Meal Toys to Stem Child Obesity."

18 Anonymous, "SF Supervisors Pass 'Happy Meal' Regulations," *Associated Press,* November 2, 2010.

Case Study

Chiquita in Colombia: Funding Paramilitary Groups to Protect Business and Employees[1]

By Virginia G. Maurer Virginia G. Maurer is the Huber Hurst Professor of Business Law and Legal Studies in the Warrington College of Business Administration, at the University of Florida. Her research interests include corporate governance, mentoring, and business ethics. Contact: virginia.maurer@warrington.ufl.edu

Overview

This case examines Chiquita Brands behavior in Colombia. From 1989 to 2004, Chiquita provided financial support and weapon delivery to various guerilla and paramilitary organizations in Colombia that had killed and threatened to continue killing Chiquita employees. These organizations used the support to slaughter one another as well as hundreds of civilians, including Chiquita workers and American missionaries, all with the intention of establishing control over areas of Colombia that the national government could not control. These payments stopped for good in 2004 as a result of possible criminal prosecution in the United States under the antiterrorism laws.

Chiquita Brands International

Chiquita Brands International, headquartered in Cincinnati, Ohio, is a successor corporation to the United Fruit Company, which was formed in 1899 through a merger of small banana growers and shippers to export and haul bananas from Central America to North America and Europe. Within just two years—by 1901—United Fruit had 75 percent of the combined United States and European markets for bananas. In 1955, United Fruit still retained 40 percent of these huge markets, handling 2.7 million pounds of fruit, and employing 60,000 people. The company "operated the world's largest private shipping fleet, and owned more than 1.7 million acres of land and 1,100 miles of railroad in Guatemala, Honduras, Costa Rica, Panama, Colombia, and Ecuador."[2]

The history of United Fruit is disturbing and fraught with contradiction. On the one hand, it was on the forefront of food marketing, use of pesticides and herbicides, and use of refrigerated vessels in the twentieth century. It built infrastructure—housing, schools, railroads, and ports—throughout the Central American region. On the other hand, it has a sordid history of political intrigue, corruption, and poor practices in labor, safety, and human rights. The term "banana republic," attributed to the American humorist O. Henry and commonly used in the mid-twentieth century to describe certain Central American countries, had its origin in United Fruit's political and economic dominance of the region.

In 1984, through a series of mergers and control changes, United Fruit became Chiquita Brands and relocated its headquarters from Boston, Massachusetts to Cincinnati, Ohio. For several years, the company expanded its holdings in land and shipping. The company anticipated increased access to European markets as the expected economic policy of the European Union (EU) would adjust or eliminate the trade preferences former colonial powers granted for bananas from former colonies. By 1993, it had become clear that such access would not soon materialize, and Chiquita was left with a mountain of debt to finance the expansion. The expected growth of the European market did not occur until the twenty-first century, leaving Chiquita in a difficult financial position in the 1990s. Chiquita responded by fighting trade restrictions through the World Trade Organization and international trade diplomacy. This process, popularly known as "The Banana Wars," culminated in May 2001, when the EU agreed to phase out the quota and tariff regime that disadvantaged non-colonialist-based sources of bananas in Europe.

In 1998, the *Cincinnati Enquirer* ran a series of articles about Chiquita that constituted a scathing indictment of Chiquita's labor practices, environmental record, bribery and corruption, and human rights record in fruit-growing areas of Central America. The articles were retracted when the newspaper learned that although much of the material was derived from firsthand observations of the two *Enquirer* reporters, some of the information was leaked from Chiquita employees, in breach of both confidentiality agreements and journalism ethics. The retraction, however, did not remove the stain on the company's reputation.

Whether or not in response to these accusations, Chiquita top management led the firm through a comprehensive review of corporate values. The CEO and the Senior Management Group involved more than 1,000 employees in a consensus-seeking process to develop a statement of "Corporate Core Values: Integrity, Respect, Opportunity, and Responsibility." Under the core value of "Responsibility," the company included, "We act responsibly in the communities and environments in which we live and work."

In addition, Chiquita appointed a senior officer for corporate responsibility and developed a Code of Conduct consistent with Social Accountability standard 8000 (SA8000). SA8000 is an international standard for decent working conditions developed by Social Accountability International, based on the United Nations Universal Declaration of Human Rights. Chiquita's Code of Conduct specifically emphasized "the areas of food safety, labor standards, employee health and safety, community involvement, environmental protection, ethical behavior, and legal compliance."[3] Corporate responsibility became one of Chiquita's long-term strategic goals.

By 2002, the result of this process had become evident. Chiquita reduced accidents, improved workplace safety, reduced the use of pesticides, engaged in extensive recycling programs, planted trees, and attended to sustainable production and distribution practices consistent with environmental standards of the Rainforest Alliance and the labor standards of SA8000. These initiatives remain important to Chiquita's corporate identity, and the commitment to corporate responsibility continues to guide Chiquita's management practices.

In 2001, Chiquita underwent a Chapter 11 bankruptcy reorganization to manage its debt and stagnant sales and emerged from bankruptcy the following year. By 2003, however, the progress made in the banana wars, in corporate ethical identity, and in restabilized financial health was undermined by problems arising out of a Colombian banana plantation.

Chiquita in Colombia

From 1989 to the present, successive Chiquita managers and directors made a series of decisions that threatened the reputation, if not the possible existence, of the company. The problem involved payments made to non-governmental security forces to protect banana plantations and their workers in the South American country of Colombia.

Colombia has been in conflict amounting to a civil war for decades. Organizations of the extreme right and extreme left have fought one another and the national government over control and power, financing their hostilities with money extorted from the illegal drug industry and from legal businesses such as Chiquita and other multinationals. At any point in recent years, the democratically elected Colombian government has been unable to control large areas of the country, and throughout the case study's relevant time period, the Colombian government did not control the region in which Chiquita grew bananas.

Paramilitary groups have been formed to conduct many of these battles. A paramilitary group is composed of people who function and organize in a way similar to a professional military force but is not considered part of a nation's formal military. In Colombia, paramilitary groups were formed by landowners to protect their property from left-wing guerillas trying to seize their land and political power, by drug cartels to protect their illegal drug trade, and by the government to avoid scrutiny from the democratic political process.[4]

United Fruit left the Urabá region of Colombia in 1982 because of the civil war. Chiquita returned to the Urabá region, which consists of 24 municipalities in northwestern Colombia, in 1989 through a wholly owned subsidiary, Banadex. Chiquita's Banadex plantation in Urabá was a model facility in many respects. It subscribed to international standards promulgated by international non-governmental organizations (NGOs) on worker compensation, safety, concern for public health, education, and the environment.

To operate the plantation, Banadex paid paramilitary groups, first FARC (Revolutionary Armed Forces of Colombia) and later ELN (National Liberation Army) to protect its workers and operations from local terrorists. Eventually, Banadex transported weapons and provided financial support to other guerilla and paramilitary organizations, namely AUC (United Self-Defense Forces of Colombia).

The paramilitary organizations used the Banadex/Chiquita support to conduct paramilitary warfare on one another and terrorist attacks on civilian noncombatants. In 1993, for example, FARC brutally murdered five American missionaries. In 1995, FARC stopped a busload of Chiquita employees and murdered 28 of them, forcing others to watch the massacre. On another occasion, AUC entered a small farming village, "round[ing] up all of the male civilians, and smash[ing] their skulls with stones and sledgehammers."[5] On yet another occasion, in 1998, two AUC members entered the Chiquita plantation on motorcycles. When work began, they pulled a banana picker out of a tree, cut off his head with a machete, and then rode away. In short, these organizations were serious in their intention either to collect money outright or else to reek horror and extract payments.

AUC is an exemplar of the Colombian government's lack of sovereign control. In the mid-1990s, the government formed and supported AUC as a private paramilitary group to fight FARC. Soon, however, AUC went rogue and engaged in brutal massacres of its own to control the area where Chiquita and FARC operated. At most times between 1989 and 2003, Chiquita was paying one paramilitary group or another to secure the safety of its plantation and its workers and managers. At its peak, Chiquita had more than 4,000 employees in Colombia. The company paid almost $1.7 million to AUC over a seven–year period.

Eventually, Chiquita's engagement with FARC, ELN, and AUC created serious legal and ethical problems. A timeline of relevant events includes the following:

October 1997: The U.S. Department of State placed FARC and ELN on the Foreign Terrorist Organization (FTO) list. Providing payments of any kind to identified foreign terrorist organizations is a serious federal crime for which both business organizations and their responsible individuals may be prosecuted. Chiquita ceased payments to these groups immediately and soon after began paying AUC for protection.

September 10, 2001: The U.S. Department of State placed AUC on the FTO list. This went unnoticed at Chiquita, probably because legal counsel and others were distracted by the attack on the World Trade Center and the Pentagon on September 11, 2001, and by the company's declaration of Chapter 11 bankruptcy for being unable to pay interest on its $862 million debt. During this period, in November 2001, after AUC had gone on the FTO list but before legal counsel's notice, a Chiquita subsidiary smuggled several thousand AK-47s and perhaps a million rounds of ammunition into Colombia from Panama for AUC and other paramilitary groups as part of a "cocaine for weapons" exchange.[6] The munitions were carried back to Colombia on banana transports returning from deliveries to North America.

February to April 2003: A junior lawyer at Chiquita ran across the FTO list and checked entries against Chiquita's and Banadex's security practices. At all times after September 10, 2001, top management, the Audit Committee, and the board of directors knew of the relationship with AUC, but presumably did not know that the payments were illegal under U.S. law. One can safely assume that financial support for insurgent paramilitary or terrorist organizations was illegal under Colombian law, although an arguable case could be made that early on the payments were the product purely of extortion, a defense under Colombian law. The security payments were reported in all relevant public company disclosures as "security payments," and apparently no attempt was made to conceal the relationship from the government or from shareholders. General Counsel Robert Olson immediately took the new information from his office to Chiquita's Audit Committee, chaired by Roderick Hills, a highly respected Washington lawyer, who, in turn, took it to the Audit Committee and to the board of directors.

After conducting a basic internal investigation to ascertain the most important facts, the board directed Hills to take what he knew to the U.S. government and seek direction. The board was reluctant to cease payments and place its workers, and its profits, at sure and certain risk, and yet it recognized the company's precarious legal position. Hills met with Michael Chertoff, head of the U.S. Department of Justice's (DOJ) Criminal Division and laid out the results of an internal investigation.

Recollections of the attendees at the meeting do not agree on all points, but they do agree that DOJ regarded the payments as constituting a violation of federal criminal law that it could not endorse. By some attendees' recollections, the DOJ directed that the payments be stopped. Other recollections are more ambiguous. Nonetheless, in May 2003, fearful of the consequences, Chiquita decided to continue making the payments. Chiquita's outside legal counsel, headed by Eric Holder (who became U.S. attorney general in the Obama administration), advised Chiquita in September 2003 that the DOJ would not tolerate continued payment and that it would prosecute violations of U.S. federal law on terrorist organizations.

January 2004: Chiquita ceased payments to AUC. Soon after, it sold its Colombian holdings to CI Banacol, SA, of Colombia, for $51.1 million in cash, deferred payments, and assumption of pension obligations.

March 14, 2007: The DOJ filed criminal charges against Chiquita under the U.S. antiterrorist law. Chiquita pled guilty and agreed to a $25 million fine the next day, providing a thorough and detailed internal investigation report that became part of the legal record.

The Other Shoe Drops: The Aftermath

For about two years, the threat of individual prosecution hung over the heads of several top executive officers of Chiquita in Cincinnati. Ultimately, the U.S. government declined to press charges against these individuals.

In March 2007, a Colombian prosecutor formally sought access to the record of the Chiquita criminal case and threatened to request extradition from the United States of top Chiquita managers in Cincinnati to face criminal charges and possible life imprisonment in Colombia. Eventually, this threat was dropped.

Chiquita has been sued in U.S. federal courts under the Alien Tort Claims Act and other U.S. laws for civil claims totaling nearly $8 billion by U.S. citizens and the estates, survivors, and heirs of deceased U.S. citizens who were victims of AUC violence, including torture, the death of fetuses cut from pregnant women's wombs, human heads stuck on fence posts, and similar atrocities. These claims have been joined by other similar claims, including those of the families of the missionaries killed by FARC. Plaintiffs allege that the company sponsored and provided support to terrorists who committed atrocities, and that it did so knowingly and for its own financial gain. These cases have been consolidated to be tried in the U.S. Court for the Southern District of Florida.[7]

Chiquita shareholders have filed multiple derivative suits in state and federal courts against officers and directors of the company. A shareholder derivative suit seeks damages on behalf of Chiquita against officers and directors who caused the company to suffer losses as a result of their alleged wrongful actions. In April 2008, the Chiquita board of directors appointed a Special Litigation Committee composed of outside members of the board. In February 2009, this committee filed a report in Florida federal court in conjunction with pending lawsuits.[8] The report is remarkably forthcoming about the facts and the company's sequential decision points between 1987 and 2004.

On February 4, 2010, the federal court refused many of Chiquita's claims to dismiss the lawsuit submitted by the victims of FARC atrocities. Additional plaintiffs joined the crowd of lawsuit claimants, seeking additional money in total damages. As of August 2010, the civil suits remain pending.

QUESTIONS

1. Describe Chiquita's actions in Colombia.

2. Chiquita's Banadex plantation in Urabá was a model facility in many respects and addressed international standards promulgated by international NGOs on worker compensation, safety, concern for public health, education, and the environment. Why would the company not have attended to the human rights atrocities its security payments supported?

3. Quite apart from the legal issues, explain exactly how Chiquita does or does not bear moral responsibility for these atrocities. Consider the analytical frameworks of virtue ethics, deontology, utilitarianism, and others that you have studied.

4. If you were a Chiquita executive, would you have paid Colombian paramilitary groups to protect the lives of your employees, particularly after other paramilitary groups had already massacred some of them? Why?

5. The case highlights the practical ethical and legal challenges of doing business in a politically unstable foreign environment. What lessons might you derive from your analysis of this case? What advice would you give to a firm entering a similarly volatile environment?

NOTES

1 Much of the substance of this case derives from an article written by the author, Virginia G. Maurer, "Corporate Social Responsibility and the 'Divided Corporate Self': The Case of Chiquita in Colombia," *Journal of Business Ethics*, 88, Supplement 4 (2009), 595–603.

2 Nicholas Stein, "Yes We Have No Profits," *Fortune*, November 26, 2001.

3 Marco Werre, "Implementing Corporate Responsibility—The Chiquita Case," *Journal of Business Ethics*, 44, 2/3 (2003), 247–260, at 254.

4 Mauricio Romero, "Reform and Reaction: Paramilitary Groups in Contemporary Colombia," in Diane E. Davis and Anthony W. Pereira (Eds.), *Irregular Armed Forces and Their Role in Politics and State Formation* (New York: Cambridge University Press, 2003), pp. 178–208.

5 Theresa A. Diperna, "Small Arms and Light Weapons: Complicity 'With a View' Toward Extended State Responsibility," *Florida Journal of International Law*, 20, 1 (2008), 25–77.

6 Ibid.

7 *Tania Julin, et. al., v. Chiquita Brands International*, available at http://www.osen.us/upload/104902-04-10%20Chiquita%20Decision.pdf, accessed 8/30/10.

8 Howard W. Barker, William H. Camp, and Clare M. Hasler, "Report of the Special Litigation Committee of Chiquita Brands International, Inc.," February 25, 2009, in Re: Chiquita Brands International, Inc. Alien Tort Statute and Shareholder Derivative Action, Doc 2/02 Case No.: 08-01916-MD, United States District Court for the Southern District of Florida. The report is available at http://chiquitabrandsinternational.com/pdfs/SLC_Report.pdf, accessed 8/30/10.

Case Study

Plan Togo: Human Trafficking Dilemmas

By Asbjorn Osland Asbjorn Osland is a professor of business at San Jose State University in California. His research interests include business and society cases, international human resources management, and sustainability. Contact: asbjorn. osland@sjsu.edu

> *I gave my daughter to her father's cousin so that she could have a better future. I was divorced and felt overwhelmed. . . . She has come back to me as empty-handed as the day she left. I acknowledge that I have wronged my daughter. I never imagined that her aunt would maltreat her.[1]*
>
> Mother of Carole, who was 14 when she was trafficked from Togo to Bangui, Central African Republic

Overview

This case study highlights a strategic ethical dilemma facing the director of Plan Togo, a non-governmental organization (NGO), which serves the community in varied ways, including anti-trafficking advocacy in Togo, Africa. It presents the extent and causes of slavery and illegal human trafficking in the world. Efforts to eliminate trafficking by the United Nations, the United States, and Plan International are summarized. The case concludes with a focus on human trafficking in one nation, Togo, and some strategic problems faced by Plan Togo.

Slavery and Human Trafficking

Free the Slaves, a nonprofit organization devoted to ending slavery, estimates that 27 million people live in slavery worldwide, more than at any time in history.[2] In its 2010 annual *Trafficking in Persons Report*, the U.S. State Department estimated that 12.3 million adults and children were victims of forced labor, bonded labor, and forced prostitution around the world.[3]

Human trafficking refers to the illegal trade of human beings for the purposes of commercial sexual exploitation or forced labor. The process typically entails tricking, kidnapping, or coercing someone into slavery. The U.S. Department of Justice estimates that 14,500 to 17,500 people are trafficked annually into the United States.[4] Free the Slaves has documented cases in at least 90 U.S. cities, with most of the cases involving enslaved prostitutes and domestic servants.

Worldwide, the majority of slaves are in South Asia—in India, Pakistan, Bangladesh, and Nepal—and large numbers are also in some areas of South America and Africa. In 2009, there were 4,166 successful trafficking prosecutions, of which 335 were related to forced labor involving 49,105 victims.

The U.S. State Department categorizes five types of human trafficking—sex trafficking, bonded labor, involuntary domestic servitude, forced child labor, and child soldiers:

- *Sex trafficking* entails the coercion of women into prostitution.

- *Bonded labor*, sometimes referred to as peonage, refers to exploiting workers to pay off a debt they incur when they begin working, such as money loaned for transportation, housing, and food, or debt incurred by an ancestor. Workers are obligated to work off the debt and aren't free until the debt is repaid.

- *Involuntary domestic servitude* occurs when domestic workers are forced against their will to work or are abused sexually. Domestic workers usually make little and live in poor quarters if provided by the employer.

- *Forced child labor* occurs when children are sold and trafficked and the child is not paid. Some African countries such as Niger still have large numbers of slaves, some of whom are children.

- *Child soldiers* are exploited in specific countries suffering conflict, such as Burma, Chad, Democratic Republic of the Congo, Somalia, Sudan, and Yemen. The youngest of these unpaid soldiers, at age seven, start as porters, messengers, and spies and then advance to combatants.[5]

Causes of Trafficking

A wide variety of factors contribute to the illegal trafficking business. Demand-side factors contributing to trafficking include the customers benefitting from the forced labor, businesspeople profiting from human trafficking, and corrupt government officials receiving bribes to allow the trafficking to occur despite laws prohibiting it. On the supply side of the equation, the major contributor is poverty. According to the World Bank, in 2005 about 1.4 billion people lived in extreme poverty, defined as living on less than $1.25 a day.[6]

Trafficked children usually come from subsistence farming families. The parents are too poor to keep the children in school and there are few opportunities for growth or employment in their villages. Sometimes HIV/AIDS is a factor in that the children are orphaned or feel pressured to support their families economically if a parent is disabled by disease. Children may also be envious of returned laborers who come to the village with a bicycle, radio, more contemporary clothing, and the sophistication that comes with travel and experience.

Migration is a normal state of affairs for some families in which adult men and women have customarily sought work elsewhere when they couldn't work locally. So, too, children are prone to migrate when they can't attend school and their families need support. Families have historically sent children to live with relatives in cities hoping that their children would be able to attend school and progress.

Plan International conducted a study in 2002 of 400 child victims of trafficking, three-quarters of them girls.[7] Promises of education for younger children and employment for older ones were the most powerful recruitment tools used by traffickers. Forty-seven percent of their parents were illiterate, which often made them less supportive of their children's education. When girls drop out of school, they become easier targets for traffickers. Some parents unwittingly facilitated trafficking out of desperation or misplaced trust in relatives who serve as traffickers. Sometimes girls left home because they need the extra money to buy utensils so they are desirable to suitors.

Returning children who had been trafficked were often in deplorable conditions, sometimes infected with HIV/AIDS. Some of the returning children, however, reportedly were happy, which could contribute to other children hoping that they too could prosper elsewhere.

Following is Christelle's brief testimony. She is the eldest of five Togolese children and was in fifth grade when she left with traffickers going to Gabon:[8]

> *One day a woman named Yawa came to visit a woman in my village. . . . Yawa told me I could make a lot of money working in Gabon, and that I would continue my education at the same time. . . . Three of us were later confided to another lady who took us to Benin by bus . . . crossed the border on Togo-Benin border on foot . . . and were put with about 30 other girls for three days . . . we took a boat . . . spent seven days at sea . . . we reached Gabon . . . and arrived with nothing. . . . I was placed with a Togolese-Gabonese couple. . . . The woman owned a shop. . . . I was required to run the shop for her. . . . She beat me and called me names; she said I was a thief. . . . When she was absent, her husband would come to the shop. He would squeeze my breast and my behind. . . . Finally, one night, he succeeded in raping me. I stopped having periods and knew I was pregnant. He wouldn't accept his responsibility and I was sent away.*

Christelle eventually escaped, went to the Togolese embassy, and was returned to her family in Togo. Plan-Togo, in collaboration with government offices, provided Christelle with an apprenticeship to become a seamstress.

Response by the United Nations and United States

In 2000, the United Nations negotiated international standards against transnational organized crimes, including trafficking in persons. The "Protocol to Prevent, Suppress, and Punish Trafficking in Persons, Especially Women and Children" became known as the Palermo Protocol, named after the Italian city where it was opened for signature by member states at a conference in 2002. The Palermo Protocol is an effort to foster convergence among the approaches taken by different countries and to create international cooperation to investigate and prosecute offenders by incorporating a "3P" paradigm: *prevention*, criminal *prosecution*, and victim *protection*.[9]

In conjunction with the international standards, the U.S. Congress enacted the Trafficking Victims Protection Act (TVPA) of 2000 to eliminate human trafficking in the United States and to protect undocumented people who may be victims of human trafficking.[10] Modeled after the Palermo Protocol, TVPA focuses on violence against the then estimated 50,000 poor women and children trafficked in the United States each year, most as part of the international sex trade.

TVPA has three goals: (1) prevent human trafficking overseas, (2) protect victims and help them rebuild their lives in the United States with federal and state support, and (3) prosecute traffickers with stiff federal penalties. The protection and assistance clauses include providing housing, educational, health care, job training, and other social service programs available to non–U.S. citizen victims to the same extent as refugees, and allowing up to 5,000 victims each year to obtain permanent residence status.

The law also requires the State Department to issue an annual *Trafficking in Persons Report* on worldwide progress[11] and the Department of Justice to submit a biennial report summarizing data collected from state and local law enforcement agencies regarding human trafficking in the United States.[12]

TVPA applies a three-tier system to rank nations in their efforts to meet compliance standards for eliminating human trafficking. The standards include prohibiting trafficking; vigorously investigating, prosecuting, and sentencing traffickers; and cooperating with other governments engaged in eliminating trafficking. A Tier 1 classification refers to countries in full compliance, such as Nigeria. A Tier 2 classification refers to countries in which progress is being made but serious problems remain, such as Togo, Benin, and Burkina Faso. A Tier 3 classification refers to countries not in compliance and not making progress. Tier 3 nations include the Dominican Republic, Cuba, North Korea, Burma, Iran, Saudi Arabia, Democratic Republic of the Congo, and Zimbabwe.

Togo and Human Trafficking

The Togolese Republic, referred to as Togo, is a small sub-Saharan West African nation of 6 million people that borders Ghana, Benin, and Burkina Faso.[13] Togo's southern border is the Gulf of Guinea. Togo and its neighboring coastal countries were referred to as the "Slave Coast" when slaves were taken abroad during the fifteenth and sixteenth centuries. Togo gained independence from France and Great Britain in 1960, and has since experienced decades of military dictatorship.

Subsistence agriculture employs roughly 65 percent of Togo's labor force. An estimated 32 percent of the population lives below the poverty line. Cocoa, coffee, and cotton are the primary export crops. Approximately 70 percent of males and 44 percent of females are literate, and 75 percent of the children ages 6 through 11 are enrolled in school. Life expectancy is 51 for males and 55 for females. In terms of religion, 47 percent are Christian, 33 percent Animists, and 14 percent Muslim.

As mentioned earlier, Togo has a TVPA Tier 2 compliance ranking, which means it is making progress with the standards but serious problems remain. The 2010 U.S. State Department report noted that Togolese children are trafficked to Burkina Faso, Democratic Republic of the Congo, Côte d'Ivoire, Gabon, and Niger. Their forced labor activities include prostitution, bar attendants, restaurants workers, domestic servants, street venders, mechanics, and construction workers. Human Rights Watch, a nonprofit human rights advocacy organization, described Togo children as also being trafficked to Benin and Nigeria, with girls enslaved as domestic and market laborers and boys as agricultural workers.[14]

Victims tend to have rural roots. Most are recruited to work in Lomé, Togo's capital, as servants, vendors, or prostitutes. Traffickers approach villagers with attractive offers of paid labor and education. Boys are often approached directly and girls tend to be recruited through family members.

Traffickers of Togolese are often from Togo but some are from Benin and Nigeria as well. Some Togolese women have reportedly been forced into domestic servitude and prostitution in Lebanon, Saudi Arabia, European countries, and the United States. In 2009, two Togolese men and one woman living in New Jersey were prosecuted for trafficking offenses. They trafficked 20 girls from Togo and Ghana ranging in age from 10 to 19 to work unpaid 14-hour days seven days a week in two hair-braiding salons.[15]

In 2007, Togo enacted a Child Code that prohibits child trafficking and started training authorities on how to recognize trafficking. There is not as yet a prohibition of adult sex trafficking. The government recently convicted 13 trafficking offenders, but some were released after paying bribes.

In 2009, the government's hot line received 85 calls from trafficking victims. The Ministry of Social Affairs' Tokoin Community Shelter serves the victims by offering them a place to stay while in transition prior to transferring victims to facilities managed by NGOs. NGOs cared for 156 victims during the year. The government encourages victims to press charges against traffickers, but few do because they fear retaliation against them and their family members. Other recent government efforts include requiring child travelers to carry identification and parental authorization information, and collaborating with a UNICEF workshop on trafficking.

Plan Togo's Approach

Plan International is a non-governmental organization active since 1937 in child welfare.[16] Its American affiliate is classified as a 501c3, an IRS classification for charitable organizations. In the 1970s, Plan International evolved from a charitable approach to development assistance with a focus on child welfare to operating programs. The NGO launched its first programs in Africa in Ethiopia in 1974.

The organization works with more than 3.5 million families in 48 countries. Plan International's work reflects the UN Convention on the Rights of the Child, which includes the rights to survive; develop to the fullest; protection from abuse and exploitation; and participate fully in family, cultural, and social life. Plan International receives most of its income from child sponsorships but also receives many government grants. In 2009, the organization spent approximately $550 million on its activities.

Plan International has been working in Togo since 1988. In 2009, the NGO's activities benefitted 26,320 Togolese children in 242 communities.[17] Plan Togo, the national branch, participates in the collective fight against trafficking in terms of prevention and victim protection, with criminal prosecution left to the state.

Plan Togo's strategic framework for Africa includes investing in human capital, encouraging learning, and collaborating with government and other agencies in projects such as birth registration. Birth registration is important in the fight against child trafficking because children can have identity documents. Fifty-five percent of sub-Saharan African children are not registered at birth. Identity documents enable authorities to repatriate victims of trafficking. In 2004, Plan Togo assisted in the registration of more than 30,000 children. It has also been training members of children's clubs how to use a new text-messaging service to report any violence against them.

In 2010, Plan Togo partnered with Plan Benin to launch a cross-border project aimed at addressing cross-national aspects of trafficking, including border controls, support of repatriation of trafficked children, and larger-scale awareness raising in the two countries.

What Should Stefanie Do?

Stefanie Conrad, country director of Plan International in Togo, considered the dilemmas associated with human trafficking in West Africa and the role Plan Togo could play.[18] The organization has to work closely with community leaders, children, and others to prevent trafficking. She and her staff have to build trusting relationships with the communities while continually denouncing trafficking.

She had two questions—one policy oriented and the other specific to the lives of individuals:

1. Plan Togo had long supported a law against child trafficking. When it became a reality, the Togolese authorities were so aggressive in their communication regarding enforcement of the law that trafficking became more clandestine. The communities Plan Togo worked with became less willing and open to admit that trafficking was still ongoing. Sensitization work at the community level became more difficult, including access to key people such as community leaders. Young people likely to follow traffickers in hope for easy money or youth recruiting children into trafficking became more clandestine. Should Plan Togo tone down its denunciation of trafficking activity in the hope of being better able to work closely with community leaders, children, and others to prevent trafficking?

2. Plan Togo agreed to support the Ministry of Social Affairs' effort to reunite children intercepted in trafficking with their families but encountered awkward situations from time to time. Some children did not want to be reunited with their families. Plan Togo could not create independent living situations for returned victims, and Togo lacks the foster child system that exists in the United States. What should Stefanie and her staff do in the following situations?

   • A girl nearly 18 years old had been intercepted but she vehemently refused to return to her family because she voluntarily left home and followed traffickers to escape a forced marriage.

   • A 13-year-old intercepted girl refused to return to her family because she was forced into trafficking by her stepmother, with the father's consent.

QUESTIONS

1. Should Plan Togo tone down its denunciation of trafficking activity in the hope of being better able to work closely with community leaders, children, and others to prevent trafficking?

2. What should Stephanie and her staff do in the two situations at the end of this case involving the 13 and 18 year old girls?

3. Collaborating with African governments is not easy. The authorities often see foreign assistance providers as sources of vast resources. Stealing from foreigners is not the same as taking from a relative, in the eyes of many government officials, just like some Americans will steal from employers or cheat the IRS but not steal from their family. Governmental authorities can also be very slow and unresponsive. Suppose that you are the NGO representative—how can you gain the trust and cooperation of a corrupt government official in order to be effective?

4. What examples have you observed that did not as yet constitute trafficking but could conceivably become problematic? What

would exacerbate the situation so that it passed from legal exploitation to trafficking? For example, exotic dancing is something students will sometimes do to earn money, yet criminal elements in such clubs can also facilitate the transition of exotic dancers to prostitution through drug dependency.

5. On vacations abroad, one can readily observe young prostitutes working in red light district bars. One sometimes doesn't know their ages or if they are enslaved by a pimp. What would you do if in the company of drunken friends one of them decided to enlist the services of such a girl?

6. Harsh labor conditions exist in the United States as well. Farm workers die from heat stroke and agricultural accidents. Factory workers are exposed to toxic substances, repetitive motion injuries in meat-packing and other plants, and perilous conditions. How can society ensure that labor abuses don't occur with vulnerable people, such as undocumented workers fearful of informing on the abusers to the authorities?

NOTES

[1] Wendy Davies (Ed.), *For the Price of a Bike* (Plan International, 2005), available at http://plan-international.org/files/global/publications/protection/togotraffick.pdf, accessed 7/8/10.

[2] Kevin Bales, *Disposable People: New Slavery in the Global Economy* (Berkeley, CA: University of California Press, 2004).

[3] U.S. State Department, *Trafficking in Persons Report*, 10th ed., 2010, available at http://www.state.gov/documents/organization/142979.pdf, accessed 7/8/10.

[4] *Attorney General's Annual Report to Congress on U.S. Government Activities to Combat Trafficking in Persons Fiscal Year 2005*; the 2009 report is available at http://www.justice.gov/ag/annualreports/tr2008/agreporthumantrafficing2008.pdf, accessed 7/8/10.

[5] Coalition to Stop the Use of Child Soldiers, *The Use of Children as Soldiers in Africa,* 2002, available at http://www.reliefweb.int/library/documents/chilsold.htm, accessed 7/8/10.

[6] World Bank, *Understanding, Measuring, and Overcoming Poverty*, 2002, available at http://web.worldbank.org/WBSITE/EXTERNAL/TOPICS/EXTPOVERTY/EXTPA/0,contentMDK:20153855~menuPK:435040~pagePK:148956~piPK:216618~theSitePK:430367,00.html, accessed 7/8/10.

[7] Davies, *For the Price of a Bike.*

[8] Ibid.

[9] UN Office on Drugs and Crime, *United Nations Convention against Transnational Organized Crime and its Protocols*, 2010, available at http://www.unodc.org/unodc/en/treaties/CTOC/index.html, accessed 7/8/10.

[10] Trafficking Victims Protection Act (TVPA) of 2000 is available at http://www.state.gov/g/tip/laws/61124.htm, accessed 7/8/10.

[11] U.S. State Department, *Trafficking in Persons Report.*

[12] Allen J. Beck, Thomas H. Cohen, and Tracey Kyckelhahn, *Characteristics of Suspected Human Trafficking Incidents, 2007–08*, Department of Justice Report, January 15, 2009, available at http://bjs.ojp.usdoj.gov/index.cfm?ty=pbdetail&iid=550., accessed 7/8/10.

[13] Information on Togo available from the U.S. State Department at http://www.state.gov/r/pa/ei/bgn/5430.htm and the CIA at https://www.cia.gov/library/publications/the-world-factbook/geos/to.html, accessed on 7/8/10.

[14] Human Rights Watch, *Borderline Slavery: Child Trafficking in Togo*, 2002, available at http://www.hrw.org/en/reports/2003/04/01/borderline-slavery, accessed 7/8/10.

[15] Joe Ryan, "East Orange Man Admits Helping Run Human Trafficking Ring for Hair Salon," *The Star-Ledger*, August 26, 2009.

[16] http://plan-international.org/, accessed 7/8/10.

[17] http://plan-international.org/where-we-work/africa/togo, accessed 7/8/10.

[18] Stefanie Conrad currently serves Plan International in Dakar, Senegal, as regional communication manager, Plan West Africa. She was country director in Togo at the time of this case study.

Case Study

Movimiento Congruencia: Serving Mexican Workers with Physical Disabilities

By Otavio Carrera Santa Cruz, Alejandra Guzmán Barraza, and Asbjorn Osland Octavio Carrera Santa Cruz serves as the organization development manager at CEMEX, Mexico. His interests include employment for people with disabilities. Contact: octavio.carrera@cemex.com

Alejandra Guzmán Barraza is responsible for the design and execution of social initiatives at CEMEX. Her interests include corporate social responsibility and sustainability. Contact: alejandra.guzmanb@cemex.com

Asbjorn Osland is a professor of business at San Jose State University in California. His research interests include business and society cases, international human resources management, and sustainability. Contact: asbjorn.osland@sjsu.edu

Having a job can result in a significant change in one's life; one becomes more self-sufficient. It's important for the disabled because living expenses go beyond all the customary expenses and contributions to the family; the disabled pay additional health care costs, special accommodations, and transportation costs. When I began, I remember an interview where the HR representative told me that even though there were elevators, I couldn't be hired because the accountants worked on the second floor and it would be too risky in the event of a fire since I couldn't walk down the stairs. I didn't get that job but in the other companies where I've worked they've created special fire or emergency brigades to assist the disabled in the event of a problem. For me it's been more than just getting a job in that I've been promoted and now I'm an executive. I've learned to travel for work and today the limitations are minimal. . . . The disabled are generally loyal and committed employees that enrich their teams and offices with their support and optimism. . . . I thank God for the lessons that my disability has given me and for teaching me that people's ability is greater than their disability. I'm grateful to my family for their unconditional support, and to the Movimiento Congruencia and to CEMEX, for giving me the chance to grow as a professional as well as contribute to Movimiento Congruencia.[1]

Reflections of Rodolfo Efraín Ramírez Cuéllar

Overview

Mexico-based Movimiento Congruencia (MC) is an alliance among companies, hiring agencies, and other institutions in Mexico focused on the integration of people with physical disabilities into the workforce and society.[2] The leadership of MC wrestled with two dilemmas:

1. MC members do not all coach their employees with physical disabilities adequately. It's essential that a coaching process be offered to employees with physical disabilities so their possibility of workplace success increases. How can this be accomplished?

2. Initially, MC decided not to push other companies for specific objectives regarding the employment and retention of people with physical disabilities or the creation of accessible buildings. Committing to targets may have caused some companies to avoid MC because they may have suffered embarrassment at not having been able to achieve the desired results. Should MC limit itself to member companies that adopt objective targets and assist them, or should MC remain welcoming to all companies that want to join regardless of objective commitment to meeting targets?

MC

According to the 2000 Mexican census, nearly 2 percent of Mexico's population has a physical disability, which amounts to almost 1.8 million people.[3] In 1999, CEMEX, through its Programa Congruencia, began attempting to reduce the barriers that limited the integration of people with physical disabilities into the workplace.[4]

The need to hire people with disabilities was acute because in 2000, of the estimated 31,035 people with physical disabilities who had a professional education, only 7,618 were employed.[5] This gap represented a loss of highly qualified candidates to the overall Mexican labor pool, and it also was a great personal tragedy for people with disabilities who earned an educational degree and then were unable to find employment.

CEMEX is a global building materials (mainly concrete) company serving markets throughout the Americas, Europe, Africa, the Middle East, and Asia. CEMEX was founded in Mexico in 1906 and has grown from a local player to one of the top global companies in the construction industry, with close to 47,000 employees worldwide.

CEMEX employs people with physical and mental disabilities. It launched a car wash project where people with mental disabilities offered car wash services to CEMEX employees. CEMEX networked with other Mexican organizations to expand its Programa Congruencia into Movimento Congrucia (MC), an association that includes various companies helping to reduce the barriers for employing people with disabilities.[6]

MC began in 2000 with 11 participating companies. MC collaborates with the government, academic institutions, and non-governmental organizations (NGOs) to achieve its goal of obtaining employment for people with disabilities so they can add value to society. People with physical disabilities have many useful capabilities and seek employment with companies and organizations that need their talents. For them to succeed in the workplace, employers need to gradually provide accommodations by creating a physical infrastructure that is handicapped accessible. The goal is that eventually employing people with disabilities will become routine and no longer a special issue.

MC companies communicate the responsibility the private sector has toward people with disabilities. In 2010, 10 years after its founding, MC listed 62 member companies, organizations, and universities. Member companies include other large Mexican employers and a number of foreign-based companies, such as British American Tobacco, Dow, Quaker, Whirlpool, Carl's Junior, and Manpower.

MC has benefitted more than 500 people with disabilities. It has expanded operations from Mexico to Panama and Colombia. Every year, MC has an annual meeting at which more companies are integrated into the movement.

Physical disabilities, like other socioeconomic problems, require multisector, multidisciplinary and multicomponent efforts. Each member of MC works from its own perspective to integrate people with physical disabilities into the workplace:

- Universities promote programs to improve the living and educational conditions of students with disabilities. By making modifications to their facilities and programs, universities collaborate in educating professionals to enter the workforce.

- Companies make their facilities and policies accessible in order to promote job opportunities.

- Federal and state governments are responsible for legislative actions needed to implement the aforementioned changes and create incentives to make them attractive from an economical point of view.

- NGOs and other organizations play a key role by raising awareness and promoting various initiatives.

MC members voluntarily take on many obligations. They plan their new facilities to be handicapped accessible, as well as remodeling existing installations to make them accessible as well. Within their social networks, members promote the theme of employment of people with disabilities. Within their supply chain management, MC members try to include businesses that employ people with physical and mental disabilities and make appropriate accommodations.

MC's services to people with physical disabilities seeking employment are free of charge. MC also provides a complimentary comprehensive manual that can be downloaded from its website to instruct people with disabilities on how to make use of MC's services. Once a person with physical disabilities is in the MC database, only members have access to search the database for a new employee. MC helps educate members about building accommodations and provides an accessibility manual for the job candidate and employers.

Rodolfo's Story

As a social movement, MC has noble intentions. But to fully understand MC's impact, it is essential to understand the organization from the perspective of a person with a physical disability, such as Rodolfo Efraín Ramírez Cuéllar.

Rodolfo, the elder of two children, was born into a middle-class family from Monterrey, located in Nuevo Leon, the industrial heart of northern Mexico. Rodolfo was born premature at six and a half months. The lack of adequate oxygen led to a brain injury. Months later, his family noticed that he could not stand like other children his age. His family sought medical solutions that could enable him to be ambulatory. For years, he endured futile medical treatment but in 1985 he was admitted into a Shriners' program in Houston, Texas. For 11 years, he received treatment and 12 surgeries that allowed him to slowly become more independent.

While undergoing treatment, Rodolfo continued studying and going to school with his peers. Upon completing his "bachillerato" (roughly equivalent to a community college associates degree), he entered the Valley Baptist Academy, in Harlingen, Texas, for nine months of English as a Second Language training. The experience of being independent and living away from his parents exposed Rodolfo to important challenges of caring for himself (e.g., laundry, cleaning his room). This phase made him more independent and helped him grow. After Valley Baptist Academy, he returned to Mexico where he started his university studies to become a public accountant.

Upon completing his internship and earning a degree, Rodolfo set out to obtain employment as an accountant. But finding a job in a small city proved too complicated because local organizations didn't assist people with physical disabilities in finding employment. Rodolfo decided to become an independent public accountant working with an associate. He learned a great deal over the next two years while earning an income. But the local growth opportunities were limited. In 2002, with the support of his family, Rodolfo moved to Monterrey, Nuevo Leon, enthusiastically looking for work. Months passed without an interview.

Rodolfo sent his resume through the Internet to the executives of various companies and became acquainted with many corporate employees at Femsa, CEMEX, Alfa, Vitro, Banamex, Fundación Teletón, and British American Tobacco, among others. At the end of one year of searching, CEMEX called him in for an interview. Upon arrival, Rodolfo was surprised to see that one of the executives had a physical disability.

"Seeing a disabled executive at CEMEX kept me from giving up on my search for work," Rodolfo said. CEMEX didn't have a vacant position, but the company informed him about an internal program called Programa Congruencia that promoted the integration of people with physical disabilities within CEMEX.

In September 2003, the British American Tobacco Group, after receiving information from CEMEX, created a program called "People without Barriers" to hire people with physical disabilities. The umbrella for this effort was the company's Social Responsibility and Diversity Initiatives. Actions taken included (1) eliminating architectural barriers in the building, (2) HR policies that support the integration of people with physical disabilities, and, most important, (3) creating awareness among employees about people with physical disabilities to successfully integrate them as new team members.

In March 2004, Rodolfo began employment at British American Tobacco as an analyst in the comptroller's office. He worked there until the end of 2007. In 2008, Rodolfo moved to SEAO, a company of Arancia Group, to serve as its northeast administrative chief, with a team that achieved important administrative goals in the regional operation. Rodolfo continued with his own personal efforts to contribute to the integration of people with physical disabilities. Then in October 2009, he moved to CEMEX Shared Services Americas as an external employee contributing to innovation projects. In March 2010, Johnson Controls hired Rodolfo to work in its finance area. He progressed up the corporate ladder with every move.

Being a part of British American Tobacco allowed Rodolfo to develop professionally in addition to permitting him to continue contributing to the "People without Barriers" program. Rodolfo served on a team of representatives from MC for nearly five years and shared many lessons learned.

Rodolfo observed:

From my arrival in Monterrey, going from interview to interview in various organizations, I found it enriching to see that companies are becoming more concerned about corporate social responsibility. Clients, suppliers, investors, employees, and society in general prefer that companies move beyond financial goals and show concern for society's welfare, including hiring the disabled.

Rodolfo mentioned that when speaking with an HR manager about his satisfaction with the additional elevator the company had installed, the HR manager stated, "Rodolfo, the building elevator is operational, but when will we activate the heart's elevator?" This comment made Rodolfo reflect on how sensitized people had become to the theme of integrating people with physical disabilities, and how important they feel to be able to compete for a job vacancy, a promotion, or other opportunities. Yet there was still much more to do to "activate the heart's elevator" of critics and people who do not believe people with physical disabilities can contribute.

Rodolfo concludes:

Employees and companies need to work together on diversity and integration strategies where the organization can be a model for other companies. Each person has different capabilities according to his disability, but there are a lot of ways to make a contribution to the goals of the company. Understanding each disability individually can help us assign the correct positions to employees with disabilities and get the best of each person being integrated.

CEMEX and MC Member Commitments

CEMEX and other leaders within MC want to integrate people with physical disabilities into the workforce. CEMEX's program was developed to add value to participating organizations, rather than as a charitable organization. Three major fronts of action were determined to be vital for the success of the Programa Congruencia:

Sensitivity: information and training to enhance awareness related to the topic of disability for the audiences involved

Productive opportunities: employment or training for employment opportunities, direct and indirect

Accessibility: consideration of architectural and easy access to facilities issues, regardless of the physical or sensorial condition of a person

In terms of sensitivity, CEMEX made a commitment to raise awareness internally and externally. The world of people with physical disabilities is unfamiliar to most Mexicans. Culture and the attitude toward people with physical disabilities often pose a barrier that limited opportunities for them.

In terms of accessibility, CEMEX offered advice to architects, engineers, and the construction industry in its total accessibility guide and the special award, "Congruencia en Accesibilidad," to recognize builders and designers.

The goal of *accesibilidad total* (i.e., total accessibility) is to eliminate physical, architectural, and educational barriers in public and private buildings. According to the Organización de Libre Acceso, roughly 70 percent of the Mexican population lives in places where there are no services or accessibility for people with physical disabilities.[7] This inaccessibility contributes to the unemployment of people with physical disabilities in private and public organizations. Lack of access goes beyond the simple entrance to a building; it involves restrooms, doors, parking, signaling, and the height of objects.

CEMEX decided to document its experience with Congruencia to share with other enterprises, including the following key factors:

1. Knowledge of the appropriate regulatory offices was crucial. In Mexico, the appropriate entities are the Secretariat of Labor and Social Security, Mexican Social Security Institute, and the Secretariat of the Treasury and Public Credit. The later agency deals with financial and tax-related issues.

2. Awareness inside the company was crucial because physical disabilities in the workplace require attention from those directly and indirectly involved. In addition to the job candidate, future coworkers play key roles in this process. Some company policies and procedures need to be modified.

3. CEMEX had to make reasonable modifications to accommodate certain needs.

4. CEMEX created a multidisciplinary committee consisting of employees from Human Resources, Institutional Relations, Marketing, Supply Chain, Legal Affairs, and the Financial Office to lead Congruencia. Committee members had to learn about people with physical disabilities and how to accommodate their needs within the office. They also had to have the time and commitment to implement the project.

People with Disabilities Legislation in the United States

In Mexico, employing people with disabilities is a voluntary action. In the United States, federal and state governments have passed laws to protect the rights of people with disabilities to obtain employment.

The Americans with Disabilities Act of 1990 prohibits employment discrimination against disabled and qualified individuals by employers, both private and governmental, with 15 or more employees.[8] A disability can be a physical or mental impairment that limits one or more major life activities. Qualified individuals are those who can perform the job duties required. Some disabled but qualified individuals need reasonable accommodations to do so. This could mean physical accessibility, job restructuring, the use of equipment or devices (but not personal items such as glasses or hearing aids), changing examinations (including the provision of suitable training materials), and making qualified readers (e.g., for the blind) or interpreters (e.g., for the deaf) available.

Reasonable accommodations vary. A deaf applicant may need an interpreter during the job interview and a blind person could need a reader when sight is essential (e.g., reading a bulletin board). Employees with illnesses (e.g., diabetes) that require regular monitoring and maintenance may need appropriately scheduled breaks to attend to their needs. An ill employee (e.g., cancer patient) may need to attend treatment sessions. Employers do not need to make reasonable accommodations that impose an undue hardship, given the size, finances, and nature of its operation. Employees who need reasonable accommodations have to request them. Various tax incentives are available to employers to make reasonable accommodations.

Employers can ask if applicants can perform specific essential job functions, but they cannot ask direct questions about disabilities. Employee requests for reasonable accommodations are considered confidential information.

Immediate Concerns

The population of employed people with physical disabilities has grown slowly and not enough upgrades have been made in member buildings to make them accessible. MC's leadership had not lobbied for legislation to reform national or state disability laws to require employment of people with physical disabilities and architectural changes to make buildings more accessible. MC seemed to be stuck at the level of several members hiring people with physical disabilities and making buildings more accessible for them. Too many MC members seemed to merely speak about hiring but were not following through on their commitment.

QUESTIONS

1. MC members do not all coach their disabled employees adequately. Rodolfo Efraín Ramírez Cuéllar, discussed earlier, is an excellent example of success in terms of emotional balance and professional excellence, but not all people with physical disabilities are as capable. As result of their disabilities, they have a greater probability of being fired from their companies or not being considered for a promotion. It's essential that a coaching process be offered to employees with physical disabilities so their possibility of workplace success increases. How can this be accomplished?

2. Initially, MC decided not to push other companies for specific objectives regarding the employment and retention of people with physical disabilities or the creation of accessible buildings. Committing to targets may have caused some companies to avoid MC because they may have suffered embarrassment at not having been able to achieve the desired results. Should MC limit itself to member companies that adopt objective targets and assist them, or should MC remain welcoming to all companies that want to join regardless of objective commitment to meeting targets?

3. Should MC leadership lobby for political legislation to reform national or state disability laws to require employment of people with physical disabilities and architectural changes to make buildings handicapped accessible? This could result in a national dialogue to raise awareness, but the risk is that the governmental authorities could pass onerous requirements that some organizations and companies are not yet prepared economically or socially to meet.

4. What can individuals do to help integrate people with physical disabilities into the workforce?

NOTES

[1] Rodolfo Efraín Ramírez Cuéllar welcomes opportunities to speak about his experiences. He may be contacted at rodolfoe75@hotmail.com.

[2] MC website, available at http://www.congruencia.org.mx/index.asp, accessed 8/15/10.

[3] INEGI (Instituto Nacional de Estadística Geográfica e Informática), available at http://www.inegi.gob.mx, accessed 8/15/10.

[4] Social services prefer the term "people with disabilities" to "disabled people" because the former term highlights the people dimension first, and disabilities as just one aspect of their unique persona.

[5] INEGI.

[6] Programa Congruencia, available at http://www.congruencia.org.mx/index.asp, accessed 8/15/10.

[7] Organización de Libre Acceso, available at http://www.libreacceso.org, accessed 8/15/10.

[8] This section is paraphrased from the U.S. Equal Employment Opportunity Commission, September 9, 2008. *Facts About the Americans with Disabilities Act*, available at http://www.eeoc.gov/facts/fs-ada.html, accessed 8/15/10.

Case Study

Degussa AG: When a Corporation's Holocaust History Intrudes on the Present[1]

By Al Rosenbloom and Ruth Ann Althaus Al Rosenbloom is an associate professor of marketing and international business at Dominican University in River Forest, Illinois. His research interests include corporate social responsibility, social entrepreneurship, and marketing in the least-developed countries in the world. Contact: arosenbloom@dom.edu

Ruth Ann Althaus is a professor of health administration at Ohio University in Athens, Ohio. Her research interests include comparative health systems, corporate social responsibility, business ethics, and the business of health care. Contact: althaus@ohio.edu

Overview

This case is about whether the German company Degussa AG should submit a bid to supply Protectosil®, its anti-graffiti coating, for a new memorial being planned in Berlin to honor the memory of Jews murdered by Nazis. Degussa AG is a multispecialty chemical company headquartered in Dusseldorf, Germany. Degussa's ethical dilemma is that a former Degussa subsidiary, Degesch, manufactured and supplied Zyklon B, the nerve gas used by the Nazis to kill Jews in the concentration camps during World War II. Although Degussa has made attempts both to acknowledge and atone for its wartime Nazi collaboration, public disclosure of its bid has the potential to engulf Degussa in controversy when activists and Jewish leaders learn of it. How relevant should the company's historical legacy be to contemporary decision making?

The CEO's Dilemma

In 2001, Utz-Hellmuth Felcht became CEO of Degussa AG, the world's largest specialty chemical company, headquartered in Dusseldorf, Germany. Felcht was well suited to lead Degussa AG. Not only did he have a Ph.D. in chemistry, he also was a skilled corporate executive. But in 2002, Felcht faced a difficult decision: Should Degussa AG bid to have its graffiti-resistant coating, Protectosil®, applied to the 2,700 pillars of the new Memorial to the Murdered Jews in Europe in Berlin?

505

Felcht believed that Degussa should bid on all possible jobs. Yet, Felcht also knew that, from its beginning, the memorial had been controversial. German newspapers and TV routinely reported the conflicts over it. These included its location, design, funding, and even whether it was appropriate to have a Holocaust memorial dedicated only to Jews and not to other groups, such as gypsies, political dissidents, and homosexuals, who were also persecuted and killed by the Nazis during World War II. The requirement for an anti-graffiti coating on the memorial, in fact, resulted from fear by the Memorial Foundation Board that neo-Nazi demonstrators would deface the monument.

One other consideration immediately intruded into Felcht's thoughts. He knew that during World War II, Degussa had collaborated with the Nazis. This, by itself, was not unusual. Most German companies, including Volkswagen, Siemens, Daimler-Benz, Deutsches Bank, and Bosch, were involved with the Nazis. Although he was born after World War II, Felcht, like other Germans his age, knew of Nazi atrocities. More central to his current concern was Degussa's controlling interest in Degesch, a now-defunct company. Degesch was the only producer of Zyklon B, the gas used by Hitler and the Nazis to murder millions at the Auschwitz, Madjanek, and other Nazi concentration camps.

Felcht worried about how the Jewish community, his own board, and the media would react to Degussa bidding to be a supplier for a memorial to honor the very European Jews who were killed by one of its products. He, himself, was frankly concerned about the ethics and propriety of even bidding on the job. Bids on construction projects were routine at Degussa and would, under normal circumstance, never involve the CEO. Yet Felcht knew that as CEO, he had a fiduciary and ethical responsibility to discuss this particular bid option with his board. His challenge was to prepare a balanced board presentation that considered the contradictory responsibilities for Degussa to be both profitable and contrite.

The Nazis and the Jews

Adolph Hitler, the person most closely associated with the National Socialist or Nazi Party, believed that humanity could be divided into racial groups and that the Nordic Aryan group, from which "true Germans" were descended, was superior.[2] In particular, he believed that the Jews were "evil incarnate"[3] and in his 1925 book, *Mein Kampf (My Struggle)*, he outlined ways to eliminate them. Hitler's unwavering anti-Semitism, his overt racism, and his commitment to Aryan superiority became cornerstones of Nazi ideology. The Holocaust, the systematic extermination of more than 6 million Jews and other "undesirable" groups throughout Europe during World War II, resulted from Nazi action.

As the Nazis gained power in Germany in the 1930s, anti-Jewish actions and laws proliferated. Nazi ideology held that the Jews simply had too much political, cultural, and economic power and, therefore, needed to be removed completely from Europe. At first, the Nazis used restrictive anti-Jewish laws and decrees to encourage Jews to leave Germany voluntarily. Shortly after Hitler became chancellor of Germany in January 1933, the Nazis organized a one-day nationwide boycott against Jewish businesses and then placed quotas on the number of Jewish students allowed in higher education.

Two years later, the Nuremberg Laws were passed, which defined who was legally a German citizen and banned all contact, including marriage, between Germans and Jews. In 1938, all Jewish property in Austria was confiscated, Jewish physicians in Germany were restricted to treating only Jewish patients, Jewish lawyers were banned from practicing law in Germany, and Jewish children were expelled from German schools. On January 1, 1939, the German government passed the Measure of Elimination of Jews from the German Economy, which banned Jews from working with Germans.

The Nazis also isolated Jews in ghettos (small, restricted, highly controlled neighborhoods). Overcrowding, lack of food, lack of sanitation, and brutality by Nazi guards were common in the Jewish ghettos. The Jews, however, proved more adaptable to this increased isolation than the Nazis' expected.[4] Nazi efforts to further ostracize the Jews occurred through the Aryanization of Jewish businesses, the transfer of business ownership (often forced) from Jews to German Aryans. Frustrated by the Jews' resilience, the Nazis needed a more thorough solution to "the Jewish question." The Nazis eventually came up with a wide-ranging plan— known as the "Final Solution"—to kill every Jew systematically.[5]

Degussa AG

Degussa AG began in 1843 when Friedrich Roessler, then an employee of the German mint in Frankfurt-am-Main, set up a smelting and refining business that would sell refined gold and silver back to the German mint to be made into coins.[6] Degussa grew over the years through diversification, mergers, acquisitions, and joint ventures. By the early twenty-first century, Degussa AG had become the world's largest maker of specialty chemicals, and Germany's third largest chemical company.[7] In 2001, Degussa operated more than 200 facilities in 50 countries, employed more than 53,000 individuals and had total revenue from operations of €12.9 billion or about US $10.8 billion.[8]

In the early 1930s, Degussa attempted to balance a business strategy of acquisition and expansion with the Nazis' domestic demands to comply with national policies. For example, Degussa announced, in 1933, that it had no Jews employed, when, in fact, several board members and scientists were converts to Judaism. Degussa retained these individuals until the Nazis forced their ouster. Until the mid-1930s, Degussa did not have any Nazi board members; eventually there would be three. When explaining this change in corporate policy, Degussa's then Chairman of the Board Ernst Busemann said, "There's no point in swimming against the current."[9]

Degussa ended up collaborating with the Nazis in four ways. It (1) acquired firms and parcels of real estate that Jews were forced to sell because of Nazi Aryanization efforts, (2) acquired rights to process gold and silver plundered from Europe's Jews, (3) used compulsory laborers, and (4) owned the company called Degesch.

First, as Aryanization was imposed, Degussa tried to pay former business partners near-market prices for their firms, keep the former Jewish owners on as managers, and help them resettle after Nazi demands for their removal became more persistent. By 1938, though, Degussa's approach had changed markedly. It was more vigorous in actively working to attain Jewish companies, paid only a fraction of the company's real value to Jewish owners, and owned more and more plundered stock and real estate.[10] Near the end of his life in 1937, Walter Roessler, one of the last family members associated with Degussa, expressed regret about company concessions made to the Nazis. He acknowledged "the correctness of all those who were against all concessions from the beginning."[11]

Second, Degussa's smelting operation also actively acquired rights to process gold and silver stolen from Europe's Jews.[12] A postwar study revealed that the firm's leaders "probably" knew the metals' origins. There is no evidence to indicate whether they would have resisted the work had they known definitely.[13]

Third, Degussa used compulsory laborers from concentration camps to build new facilities in central and eastern Germany late in the war.[14] In Gleiwitz, these laborers comprised 76 percent of Degussa's workforce.[15] Most laborers died on site or, when they were no longer able to work, were sent back to the concentration camps.[16]

Fourth, Degussa acquired the German company Degesch (short for Deutsche Gesellschaft fur Schadlingsbekampfung) in 1922. Degussa divested part of its ownership in 1930 but retained a controlling, managerial interest throughout Degesch's existence. Degesch manufactured Zyklon, a cyanide-based pesticide made from prussic acid, routinely used as a fumigant against lice, horticultural pests, and other vermin because it brought quick death to any animal that inhaled it. Prussic acid works by interfering with the transfer of oxygen into living cells. Although completely effective as an insecticide, the acid was unstable, thus making it dangerous to produce, transport, and use. Degesch made significant manufacturing improvements to Zyklon by saturating the gas in pellets and by including an odorant to warn people of the gas's presence. This new version was named Zyklon B to differentiate it from its predecessor.

Initially, the Nazis used Zyklon B to remove lice from military barracks, uniforms, ship holds, and concentration camp barracks. But, as the Nazis implemented the Final Solution to exterminate all Jews, they needed a more efficient method of killing people than shooting, using car exhaust, and other methods they had tried.[17] The Nazis ordered Degesch to produce Zyklon B with a blue dye but without the warning odorant (which was required by German law) for them to use in the gas chambers in the concentration camps.[18] At Auschwitz, Madjanek, and other camps, mass exterminations were carried out using Zyklon B, dispensed in what looked like shower rooms to the victim.

Degussa After World War II

World War II devastated the German economy. At war's end, Degussa had only a third of its production capacity left intact.[19] In terms of personnel, Degussa demoted some Nazi managers and fired, then rehired, others. As the Cold War quickly gained prominence, Western democracies desired to see a strong West Germany to combat communist imperialism rather than identifying, finding, and punishing former Nazis in positions of power.

Research conducted by Peter Hayes, a Northwestern University historian, found that Degussa profited by $4 million (in 2002 adjusted dollars) from its wartime acquisition of Jewish businesses but lost much of it to restitution and confiscation after the war. Hayes also estimated that Degussa's profits from processing precious metals confiscated from Jews to be about $8 million (in 2002 adjusted dollars).

By international law, responsibility for allowing slave labor was ascribed to the German people and the paying of claims was assigned to the German state.[20] In 2000, without government coercion, Degussa, along with 16 other companies and the German state, created the Foundation for Remembrance, Responsibility and the Future. This foundation allocated millions of dollars to distribute to survivors of slave labor and their heirs. Had Germany won the war, it was estimated that Degussa's gain from slave labor usage would have been $16 million (in 2002 adjusted dollars).

In terms of Zyklon B, the war crimes trials at Nuremburg sentenced the director of Degesch to five years imprisonment and sentenced officials of companies that distributed Zyklon B to death.[21] Neither the Nuremberg trials nor postwar investigations could disprove Degussa leaders' claims that they did not know that Zyklon B was being used for purposes other than pest extermination.[22] Even if they had noticed the larger quantities ordered, they would not necessarily have been alerted to its unauthorized use.[23] Hayes found that Degussa made minimal profit from the Zyklon B used in the concentration camps, with sales totaling perhaps $168,000 (in 2002 adjusted dollars) or less than 1 percent of the Degesch contribution to Degussa.[24]

Remembering the Holocaust

The term "Holocaust" increasingly has became associated with the widespread murder of European Jews by the Nazis. Historians have estimated that in addition to approximately 6 million Jews murdered during the war, another 5 million "undesirables," as the Nazis termed them, were exterminated.[25] By 2002, memorials to Holocaust victims had been dedicated in many countries, including the United States, Canada, the United Kingdom, Australia, France, and Israel. These memorials honored the individuals killed and reminded society to never let an event like this happen again. Holocaust museums were also built. These museums helped preserve the historical record connected with these events and provided opportunities for understanding, remembrance, and education.

In 1988, Lea Rosh, a German TV journalist, launched a campaign to build a memorial to the murdered Jews of Europe.[26] Rosh's idea for the memorial was inspired by a visit she and historian Eberhard Jakel had made the previous year to Yad Vashem, the Israeli memorial to Jewish Holocaust victims. Upon their return to Germany, they both agreed that a similar memorial was needed in the country of the perpetrators.[27]

Almost immediately, the memorial was embroiled in controversy. Representatives of groups that were also killed in concentrations camps, such as the gypsies and homosexuals, wanted the memorial to be more inclusive. Directors of other existing Holocaust memorial sites, such as the concentration camps themselves, claimed that funding for a memorial dedicated to Jewish victims would diminish their annual funding from the state.[28] Other controversies plagued the memorial's progress—not the least of which was its design.

In April 1994, a design competition was held. Although 500 entries were submitted, no single design was declared the winner. In April 1997, there was a second design competition. This time a design by American architect Peter Eisenman and American artist Richard Serra was selected the winner. Their design was to install more than 4,000 concrete pillars throughout the memorial site, which was larger than two football fields. Each pillar would be 9'9" in length and 37" wide; the height would range from 18" to 15'. The pillars would be spaced so close together that only a single person could pass between them, thereby heightening feelings of oppression and disorientation. In the end, the final memorial design, as simplified by Eisenman, would be a series of 2,700 concrete pillars of varying heights, with each pillar standing on an undulating, uneven concrete foundation.

Decisions

Felcht thought carefully about the issues. He knew the following:

- Protectosil® was the best anti-graffiti spray in the world; it would last for 8 to 10 years, whereas competing products would last for only 3 to 5 years before they needed to be reapplied.

- PSS Interservice AG, a Swiss company, was also bidding on the memorial project. PSS Interservice made a competing anti-graffiti spray, PSS-20. PSS's proposed bid price would be approximately €450,000, and Degussa's current bid was €812,000.[29]

- The Coatings and Advanced Fillers Division of the company, the division that manufactured Protectosil®, had suffered a 5 percent decline in sales from 2000 to 2001.

- Degussa already had taken many actions that honestly acknowledged its past, such as helping to create the Foundation for Remembrance, Responsibility and the Future. Additionally, Degussa had hired Peter Hayes to objectively research and report on Degussa's involvement with the Nazis. Hayes had been given free access to all Degussa archives and his report was due soon.

As Felcht thought about his upcoming board presentation, he still had questions: How should Degussa behave given its activities and actions during the war? Should economic gain and shareholder interests override other concerns? Should Degussa modify its bid price based on the information it had about PSS Interservice? Should Degussa even bid on this project? Would bidding help "clear the air," or would it be an insult to the world's Jews? Would the bid justify the potential public relations nightmare? Could Degussa and Germany ever get past their association with the Nazis, or would these historical associations continue to haunt both forever?

As he wrestled with his own thoughts, Felcht knew he had a fiduciary responsibility to present this bid to the board. He needed to present the facts and the ethical dilemmas inherent in the project. Was there a way to reach both an ethically and a fiscally sound solution?

Lastly, Felcht thought about how much his company had already done and how much more it should do to participate as a "good citizen" in atoning for its World War II misdeeds. He certainly recognized Degussa's rather unique dilemma—that its association with Zyklon B, one of the most powerful symbols associated with the murder of Europe's Jews, could, perhaps, never be forgiven.

QUESTIONS

1. Who are the stakeholders that Felcht and the Degussa board must consider in deciding whether or not to bid on the memorial project? Describe the claims that each stakeholder may have in this situation.

2. Assess the relevance to the current situation, if any, of Degussa's efforts to date to acknowledge and atone for its participation in World War II.

3. What are the various options Felcht might propose to his board? How might each of these options be supported using a utilitarian and/or a deontological ethical framework?

4. If you were a Degussa AG board member and presented with the variety of options, which option would you choose?

5. How have other companies in other countries, particularly the United States (e.g. slavery) and South Africa (e.g. apartheid), behaved under pressure, either governmental or societal, to conduct unethical business? What can be learned from their behaviors and their later attempts at atonement?

NOTES

[1] Some of the substance of this case derives from Al Rosenbloom and Ruth Ann Althaus, "Degussa AG and Its Holocaust Legacy," *Journal of Business Ethics*, 92, 2 (2010), 183–194.

[2] Dan Cohn-Sherbok, *Understanding the Holocaust: An Introduction* (London, Eng.: Cassell, 1999).

[3] Jack R. Fischel, *The Holocaust* (Westport: Greenwood Press, 1998).

[4] Ibid.

[5] Steven Lehrer, *Wannsee House and the Holocaust* (Jefferson, NC: McFarland & Co., Inc., 2000).

[6] http://history.evonik.com/sites/geschichte/en/chemicals/timeline/1840-1869/Pages/default.aspx, accessed 8/21/10.

[7] Richard Bernstein, "Holocaust Legacy: Germans and Jews Debate Redemption," *New York Times*, October 29, 2003.

[8] *Degussa Annual Report 2001.*

[9] http://history.evonik.com/sites/geschichte/en/chemicals/history/degussa/degussa-ns/pages/default.aspx, accessed 8/21/10.

[10] Peter Hayes, "The Degussa Ag and the Holocaust," in Ronald Smelser (Ed.), *Lessons and Legacies V, the Holocaust and Justice* (Evanston, IL: Northwestern University Press, 2002).

[11] Ibid.

[12] Peter Hayes, *From Cooperation to Complicity: Degussa and the Third Reich* (Cambridge, Eng.: Cambridge University Press, 2004).

[13] Ibid.

[14] Hayes, "The Degussa Ag and the Holocaust."

[15] Ibid.

[16] Kara Ryf, "Burger-Fischel v. Degussa AG: US Courts Allow Siemens and Degussa to Profit From Holocaust Slave Labor," *Case Western Reserve Journal of International Law*, 33 (2001), 155–178.

[17] "Zyklon B," in Israel Gutman (Ed.), *Encyclopedia of the Holocaust*, Vol. 4: 1749–1750 (New York: Macmillan, 1990).

[18] Ibid.

[19] http://history.evonik.com/sites/geschichte/en/chemicals/timeline/1940-1949/Pages/default.aspx, accessed 8/21/10.

[20] Hayes, *From Cooperation to Complicity.*

[21] Konnilyn G. Feig, *Hitler's Death Camps: The Sanity of Madness* (New York: Holmes & Meier, Publishers, 1981).

[22] Hayes, "The Degussa Ag and the Holocaust."

[23] Ibid.

[24] Ibid.

[25] Martin Gilbert, *The Second World War: A Complete History* (New York: Henry Holt, 1989); Raul Hilberg, *The Destruction of the European Jews* (New York: Holmes & Meier, 1985).

[26] Joachim Schlör and Jurgen Hohmuth, *Memorial to the Murdered Jews in Europe* (Munich, Germany: Prestel, 2005).

[27] Caroline Gay, "The Politics of Cultural Remembrance: The Holocaust Monument in Berlin,"

International Journal of Cultural Policy, 9, 2 (2003), 153–166.

28 Gerd Knischewski and Ulla Spittler, "Remembering in the Berlin Republic: The Debate About the Central Holocaust Memorial in Berlin," *Debatte*, 13,1 (2005), 25–43.

29 Ulrich Paul, Degussa-Konkurrent will gegen den Senat klagen. *Berliner Zeitung*, November 18, 2003, available at http://www.berlinonline.de/berliner-zeitung/archiv/.bin/dump.fcgi/2003/1118/berlin/0014/index.html accessed 8/21/10.

Case Study

Kiva and Its Field Partners

By Asbjorn Osland   Asbjorn Osland is a professor of business at San Jose State University in California. His research interests include business and society cases, international human resources management, and sustainability. Contact: asbjorn .osland@sjsu.edu

Overview

Kiva, a nonprofit organization founded in 2005, facilitates loans as small as $25 from individuals to entrepreneurs primarily in third-world countries through its website. Kiva has experienced rapid growth in loan funds received and loans made through field partners. Matthew Flannery, Kiva's co-founder, is questioning the way Kiva works with its field partners abroad. How can Kiva improve its management systems so that field partners continue to serve as a channel for lending money and also focus on the social aspects of microfinance (i.e., the double bottom line—not just financial but social too)?

Starting Kiva

Kiva, headquartered in San Francisco, California, allows anyone to lend money through the Internet to microfinance institutions that, in turn, lend the money to small businesses in developing countries. The word "kiva" means "unity" in Swahili.

Matthew and Jessica Flannery co-founded Kiva when they were 28 and 27 years old respectively. Before starting Kiva, Matt Flannery was a computer programmer at TiVo, having earned a bachelor's degree in symbolic systems and a master's degree in analytic philosophy from Stanford.[1] In 2003, Jessica, then Matt's fiancée, worked on the staff of the Stanford Business School and invited him to accompany her to a speech given by Dr. Muhammad Yunus.[2] Yunus founded the Grameen Bank in the early 1980s to help empower rural impoverished people in Bangladesh by providing small loans to groups of women for operating a business without requiring collateral.

Yunus's talk resonated with their idealism. Matt thought it was a great story told by an inspiring person, but for Jessica it was a call to action that focused her life goals. Both Matt and Jessica had previously sponsored children in Africa through their church and families. The following year, after Matt and Jessica married, Jessica quit her Stanford job and travelled to East Africa as an employee with the Village Enterprise Fund (VEF) where she and Matt saw firsthand that the unavailability of credit was a major impediment to economic development. Jessica returned a few months later and enrolled for her MBA at Stanford.

Matt and Jessica concluded that three factors would make an organization such as Kiva possible:

1. Technology could connect Kiva to the developing world quite readily.

2. The poor were very entrepreneurial.

3. Potential lenders would find the stories of developing world entrepreneurs compelling.

Matt's religious background contributed to his motivation to help those less fortunate, but he didn't want to pursue a charitable approach. Instead, he wanted to capitalize on the entrepreneurial desire and ability he observed visiting Jessica in East Africa and meeting small business owners in other third-world countries. Matt and Jessica launched Kiva and sent an email out to their wedding list appealing for small loans to fund seven entrepreneurial businesses in Uganda. Within a week, they received enough money to fund all seven entrepreneurs. Word spread over the Internet and $10,000 was raised in one day after Kiva was mentioned on a political blog. Matt quit his job and with Jessica became fully dedicated to making Kiva a success.

The founders knew how to approach potential partners now listed on Kiva's website for support. They also knew how to create a board of action-oriented people with the skills and connections to make Kiva prosper through their social networks in Silicon Valley. Matt said,

> I'm glad we didn't just add members to our board without thinking about [whom] we wanted. . . . We've decided to seek out board members [who] are very influential. We want several young angel investors or venture capitalists, one microfinance luminary, a high-tech executive, and a chair [who's] a good steward with relevant experience who can represent us publicly.

Kiva's value proposition of using the Internet to link lenders with third-world entrepreneurs resonated with the media and Kiva received extensive free public relations coverage. Matt's father had been a CEO of a large company, so he had been around business leaders growing up. Strategizing seemed to come easy to him. Matt speaks in an engaging self-effacing manner, so his audience tends to believe his commitment and trust him. One can follow Matt on both Twitter and Facebook. Matt and other social entrepreneurs are part of various networks in the San Francisco Bay Area. Matt said, "I meet people at conferences and as part of fellowship programs. Ashoka, Skoll and Draper Richards come to mind."

The best way to understand Kiva is to visit its website (www.kiva.org). Kiva has shown itself to be masterful in three important areas: financial support, loans for entrepreneurs, and microfinance field partners.

First, Kiva has created partnerships with influential and useful corporations that provide extensive free support. The free public relations it has received would have cost millions of dollars.

Second, in late 2009, Kiva reached the $100 million mark in loans, dramatic testimony to what social entrepreneurs can accomplish in just a few years. Users readily understand Kiva's value proposition—link lenders to low-income entrepreneurs through the Internet.

Third, Kiva's reliance on microfinance field partners has enabled it to grow rapidly. This strength is also a weakness in that some of these partners have proven dishonest.

Kiva's success has been remarkable. Exhibit 1 summarizes Kiva's activity as of June 22, 2010. In just five years, Kiva has generated $143.4 million in loans to 368,928 entrepreneurs with an average loan of $389 and a 98 percent repayment rate.

Exhibit 1 Kiva's Outcomes as of June 22, 2010	
Total value of all loans made through Kiva	$143,417,135
Number of Kiva Users	726,149
Number of Kiva users who have funded a loan	462,171
Number of countries represented by Kiva lenders	199
Number of entrepreneurs who have received a loan through Kiva	368,928
Number of loans that have been funded through Kiva	198,022
Percentage of Kiva loans that have been made to women entrepreneurs	82.15%
Number of Kiva field partners (microfinance institutions Kiva partners with)	119
Number of countries in which Kiva field partners are located	53
Current repayment rate (all partners)	98.26%
Average loan size	$389.73
Average total amount loaned per Kiva lender (includes re-loaned funds)	$197.95
Average number of loans per Kiva lender	5.79

Kiva as Social Entrepreneurship

Social entrepreneur refers to someone who applies entrepreneurial principles to address social problems, such as Muhammad Yunus and the Grameen Bank.[3] Social entrepreneurs measure performance based on furthering social and environmental goals by creating social capital. Most social entrepreneurships are nonprofit or voluntary organizations, but they can also be for-profit businesses with social goals.

Assorted scholars and organizations active in social entrepreneurship have identified characteristics that typify social entrepreneurs. Kiva's leaders are social entrepreneurs because they present innovative and systemic solutions to the world's most pressing social problems, such as the unavailability of credit in areas in desperate need of economic development. They attack problems with commitment by fulfilling a visionary role and mobilizing people to embrace their vision.

Kiva performs its virtuous act for virtuous reasons, with no ulterior motive, such as profit. Kiva's leaders also followed through until the program was established—it's not merely an idea or concept. They apply balanced judgments, displaying a clear and coherent vision coupled with a unity of purpose and action in the face of the socioeconomic challenges of operating in what can be a chaotic world.

Kiva's leaders demonstrate tolerance for risk and are proactive and innovative in their decision making. They have relentlessly pursued new opportunities related to the basic value proposition and have engaged in a process of continuous innovation, adaptation, and learning. Kiva's leaders have acted boldly without being constrained by limited resources. They have also shown accountability to the constituencies served and for the outcomes created. Working with its field partners entailed risk and bold action on the part of Kiva. It couldn't afford to establish its own presence abroad, thereby forcing the organization to seek out partners.

Lending Process

The process for a Kiva lender appears in Exhibit 2. The prospective lender goes to www.kiva.org and chooses a particular entrepreneur/small businessperson whose story he or she finds compelling. The lender then transfers funds using his or her credit card and is gradually repaid according to a schedule. Lenders receive periodic

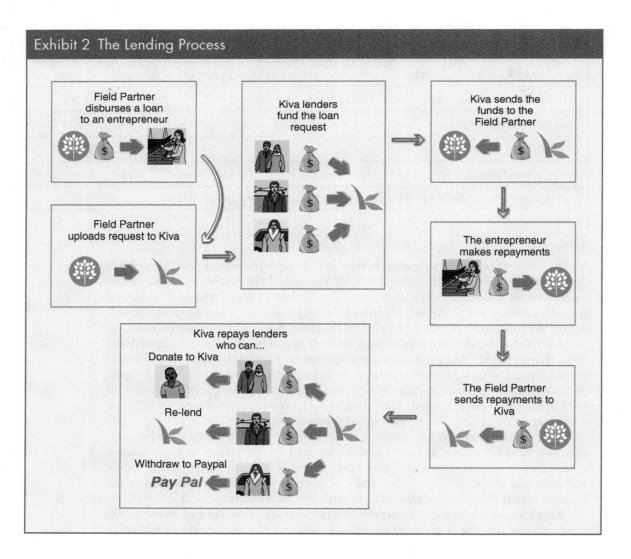

Exhibit 2 The Lending Process

Field Partner disburses a loan to an entrepreneur

Field Partner uploads request to Kiva

Kiva lenders fund the loan request

Kiva sends the funds to the Field Partner

The entrepreneur makes repayments

The Field Partner sends repayments to Kiva

Kiva repays lenders who can...
Donate to Kiva
Re-lend
Withdraw to Paypal
Pay Pal

email updates about the entrepreneur or small businessperson. Once the entire loan has been repaid, the lender can reclaim the money, re-lend the money to someone else in need, or donate the repaid loan to Kiva to cover some of the organization's expenses. All of these transactions occur over the Internet.

Field Partners

Kiva is a conduit for funneling money from lenders to individuals using local field partners (i.e., nonprofits); it does not lend directly. A key to Kiva's growth is its partnership with field partners, the existing microfinance institutions that choose the entrepreneurs or small businesspeople and service the loans. The field partners screen potential borrowers and provide services to minimize losses.

Borrowers pay interest rates to the field partners that manage the loans overseas. The interest rates cover the cost of the money the microfinance institution lends; the cost of loan defaults; and transaction costs incurred by the field partner, such as for the loan appraisal, processing the loan disbursement and repayments, and follow-up monitoring.

Kiva does not receive any of the interest payments. Nor does Kiva pay interest to lenders, to do so would require approval from the Securities and Exchange Commission (SEC) to attract investors and pay returns, something charitable organizations typically do not do. Once active, lenders have access to detailed information on the borrowers, including descriptions of their businesses and balances. Lenders can also review all the historical activity of their portfolio.

Several years ago, Matt talked about creating a for-profit micro-lending platform or having Kiva pay interest to lenders, which MicroPlace of eBay does. He wanted to avoid the paternalistic or charitable perspective of third-world development assistance and thought a for-profit model would be more dignified. When asked if Kiva was still considering a for-profit platform, Matt responded, "We are not thinking about that anymore. It seems like the SEC has decided to regulate our peers Prosper and Lending Club. With financial regulation, things may get even stricter." The SEC issued a cease and desist order on November 24, 2008,[4] for Prosper.com because it found the organization in violation of securities laws. Lending Club also had to conform to SEC regulations.[5]

Kiva recruits microfinance institutions to serve as field partners through its website. As of 2010, Kiva had more than 119 field partners in 53 nations. In order to become a field partner with Kiva, a microfinance institution must, at a minimum[6]

- Serve at least 1,000 active borrowers with microfinance services
- Have a history (at least 2 to 3 years) of lending to poor, excluded, and/or vulnerable people for the purpose of alleviating poverty or reducing vulnerability
- Be registered as a legal entity in its country of operation
- Have at least one year of financial audits

Lender Risks

Kiva has achieved a remarkable 98.26 percent repayment rate on $93.4 million of loans with completed terms. Despite this impressive outcome, lending through Kiva entails three types of risks: entrepreneur risk, field partner risk, and national risk.

First, entrepreneur risks are limited because the local field partner screens every entrepreneur before posting on the Kiva website. In addition, Kiva reduces some of the entrepreneurial risk and enhances the social benefit by lending primarily to women entrepreneurs. Women tend to be more responsible and are also more likely to use the proceeds for the benefit of their families. Nonetheless, individual entrepreneur risks still remain, with the most common being business issues (e.g., crop failure), health issues, theft, and pressing household needs such as school fees that preclude timely loan repayment.

Second, field partners present risks as a result of potential bankruptcy, fraud, and mismanagement (e.g., poor systems and procedures in loan management). Kiva reduces this risk to lenders by assigning every field partner a risk rating, from 1-Star (higher risk) to 5-Star (lower risk).[7] The financial statements of field partners are audited by respected auditing firms. Nonetheless, some field partners have suffered internal control problems including fraud, while others were buffeted by violence or chaos:

- "Kiva has discovered that MIFEX (i) improperly inflated the loan amounts it posted for entrepreneurs on the Kiva website and (ii) kept the excess amount of the posted loan to fund its own operational expenses. . . . Based on a sample of visited entrepreneurs, Kiva estimates that MIFEX inflated posted loans by approximately 35% on average."[8]

- Due to turmoil in Gaza "and trouble collecting repayments, Shurush paused their lending operations in 2006. The partnership is now closed."[9]

- "Kenya suffered the devastating effects of post-election violence and Ebony Foundation's target area, Nakuru, was severely affected. Ebony Foundation reported that approximately 58% of their Kiva portfolio was unrecoverable."[10]

- "HELP Africa . . . In 2008, a number of key staff members left the institution to pursue further education or better paying positions, thereby weakening HELP Africa's internal capacity. New staff were hired to replace departing employees, but some were fired shortly thereafter as it was discovered that they were embezzling the institution of funds, further contributing to HELP Africa's challenges."[11]

Third, national issues create risks. Kiva determines the country risk and reports the risks on its website. As noted, Gaza experienced political turmoil and Kenya had postelection violence. Kiva tries to reduce this risk by not exceeding more than 10 percent of total loans outstanding in any one nation. Guarantee mechanisms are garnered if this limit is exceeded.

Kiva is transparent about problems that arise. In 2008, Premal Shah, Kiva's president, told a group of University of Chicago business students that,

> As our auditors uncover this [fraud] information all over the world, we want to put it right back on the website and email you. Last year, we had $250,000 embezzled in Uganda. We emailed 5,000 people who had loaned the money to tell them what had happened. The most shocking thing to me was that people loved that we told the truth and that we were checking on their money.

Kiva seems to have a Teflon-like quality when it comes to funds lost due to fraud. The organization communicated what went wrong and the steps it took to remedy the problem, and the media did not focus on the issue. Why? According to Matt,

> We had many partner problems, a lot in East Africa. We made it through that period and now have risk under control pretty much. We made it through by being transparent and getting lots of great press that helped us grow beyond it. . . . We've done many audits and borrower verifications in the last couple years. It's been going well and has helped us get ahead of the fraud problems we used to have.

Kiva Fellows

The Kiva Fellows program is another innovative aspect of Kiva's operations.[12] These unpaid volunteers travel abroad to experience the impact and realities of microfinance firsthand. They work directly with the local field partner and loan recipient, interviewing at least 15 businesses per week to assess loan impact and gather and verify information. The Kiva Fellows serve a public relations purpose by writing blogs and filming YouTube videos about their experiences. They also post borrower profiles, advise the field partner, and provide services to the field partner as needed.

More than 337 people have served as Kiva Fellows, many of them graduates of private colleges and universities. Their short biographies and field activities appear on the Kiva website.[13] The ideal Kiva Fellow is someone who has had some overseas experience, fluency in the host nation's language, background knowledge in economics and finance, business consulting experience, and excellent writing and web application skills.

Social Performance Monitoring

Kiva is starting to monitor field partners based on a new social performance monitoring system. Kiva already provides extensive narrative information about its borrowers through the profiles and journal updates. Kiva now wants to assess the social performance of its field partners (referred to as MFI) by asking the following:[14]

- Who is the MFI reaching with its services?
- What products does the MFI offer (variety of loans and beyond loans)?
- What are the benefits to the clients?
- How socially responsible is the MFI?

Social performance monitoring includes the ethical treatment of clients. In addition, potential field partners have to demonstrate that they use ethical business practices.

Kiva is in the process of reviewing the CERISE SPI (Social Performance Indicators Audit tool) for monitoring the social performance of its field partners and wants its long-term field partners to report CERISE SPI results.[15] CERISE, a microfinance knowledge exchange network focused on disseminating best practices, created a microfinance social performance auditing tool in 2001 based on the United Nations "Principles for Responsible Investing" to hold microfinance institutions accountable to their broader social goals. A wide variety of organizations already use the CERISE SPI tool, including more than 250 MFIs.

MFIs are determined to be socially responsible by

1. Being transparent and accountable
2. Establishing a clear social mission and strong governance structure
3. Providing a range of well-adapted financial and nonfinancial services
4. Treating employees, clients, community, and environment in an ethical manner

Kiva Fellows will play a key role in information gathering for the CERISE SPI, and Kiva plans to provide the Fellows with training on its social performance monitoring system. The intent is to focus on a double bottom line: financial progress through the business-oriented loan as well as ensuring that social benefits occur.

In summary, Kiva has implemented five policies and procedures to reduce risks associated with field partners and clients that lender's incur:

1. Financial audits by reputable accounting firms of field partners
2. Risk assessment and rating of the field partner
3. On-site visits to clients by Fellows
4. Performance by the field partners in terms of paying Kiva back and complying with the additional Kiva reporting requirements
5. Social performance monitoring to ensure that the field partner understands the importance of the double bottom line.

Personal Experience

I have participated in more than 400 Kiva loans. The $25 loans offered by Kiva are distributed so that lenders cannot really lend a large amount to one person. Nonetheless, I initially selected and lent $1,050 to one person and then $1,200 to another person. I later modified my approach to Kiva's recommended $25/loan. This spreads the risk for lenders into a portfolio of loans so that it's improbable that one lender would suffer a catastrophic loss. Now I simply click on the list of $25 loans for the people Kiva presents. Some people carefully choose the entrepreneur, which engages them in the process of deciding what kind of person, business, and location to support. But that is somewhat misleading because the funds lent go to a pool that Kiva distributes to its field partners.

The detail Kiva provides each lender is extensive—one spreadsheet for my account has close to 4,300 transactions. Basic information provided by Kiva on my lender page about my loan activities appears in Exhibit 3.

Exhibit 3 Lender Page Loan Information	
Loan summary information	My loans
Total amount lent	$16,750
Total amount repaid	$13,931
Total amount lost	$156.34

I can download information about all my loans or individual loans. Of my 404 loans to date, 12 ended with a loss totaling $156.34. I have "deposited" $7,625 in three deposits that have been recycling for several years. I have no intention of reclaiming the money and recycle it every time a few hundred dollars accumulate.

After each set of loans, Kiva asks how much the lender wants to donate. I've donated $577.23 in small amounts after the various loan transactions. These are charitable contributions, whereas the money deposited for loans is not. My lender page describes what I want to share. I receive emails on my lender page from various groups that invite me to join them.

QUESTIONS

1. Is it more ethical to donate money to the United Way, which then distributes the money raised locally, or to lend money internationally through Kiva to entrepreneurs in underdeveloped and developing nations?

2. MicroPlace pays interest to lenders. Kiva, on the other hand, decided not to pursue interest payments to lenders because of SEC regulations. Do you think Kiva should pay loan interest to lenders? Would doing so increase, or decrease, its lender base?

3. Kiva's website is highly functional but Matt wants it to be more viral. What should Kiva do to make its website more viral?

4. Kiva and the Grameen Bank exhibit a strong preference to lend money to women entrepreneurs. Is this discrimination against men unethical?

5. How can Kiva improve its systems so field partners continue to serve as a channel for lending and also focus on the social aspects of microfinance (i.e., the double bottom line—not just financial but social too)?

NOTES

[1] Matthew Flannery, "Kiva and the Birth of Person-to-Person Microfinance," *Innovations: Technology, Governance, Globalization*, 2, 1–2 (2007), 31–56. For interviews with Jessica Flannery, see http://www.gsb.stanford.edu/news/perspectives/2007/flannery_kiva.html and Cynthia Haven, "Small Change, Big Payoff," *Stanford Magazine,* November/December 2007, available at http://www.stanfordalumni.org/news/magazine/2007/novdec/features/kiva.html. Matt's blog is available at http://www.socialedge.org/blogs/kiva-chronicles, accessed 6/24/10.

[2] Yunus later shared the 2006 Nobel Peace Prize with the Grameen Bank, which he founded. The prize was awarded "for their efforts to create economic and social development from below."

[3] J. Gregory Dees, "The Meaning of 'Social Entrepreneurship,'" unpublished paper revised May 30, 2001, Kauffman Center for Entrepreneurial Leadership, available at http://www.caseatduke.org/

documents/dees_sedef.pdf, accessed 6/24/10; Ana Maria Peredo and Murdith McLean, "Social Entrepreneurship: A Critical Review of the Concept." *Journal of World Business*, 41, 1 (2006), 56–65; and Jay Weerawardena and Gillian Sullivan Mort, "Investigating Social Entrepreneurship: A Multidimensional Model," *Journal of World Business*, 41, 1 (2006), 21–35.

[4] See http://www.sec.gov/litigation/admin/2008/33-8984.pdf, accessed 6/24/10.

[5] See https://www.lendingclub.com/extdata/secFilings/10-K/10-K-MAR-31-2009.pdf, accessed 6/24/10.

[6] See http://www.kiva.org/partners/info, accessed 6/24/10.

[7] See http://www.kiva.org/about/risk, accessed 6/24/10.

[8] See http://www.kiva.org/partners/7, accessed 6/24/10.

[9] See http://www.kiva.org/partners/2, accessed 6/24/10.

[10] See http://www.kiva.org/partners/25, accessed 6/24/10.

11 See http://www.kiva.org/partners/45, accessed 6/24/10.

12 See http://www.kiva.org/fellows, accessed 6/24/10.

13 See http://www.kiva.org/fellows/bios, accessed 6/24/10.

14 See http://www.kiva.org/blog/2010/03/03/2010-social-performance-baseline-for.html, accessed 6/24/10.

15 See http://www.cerise-microfinance.org/-tools-, accessed 6/24/10.

Case Study

Cafédirect: The Marketing Evolution and Market Penetration for Fair Trade Products

By Bob Doherty, Iain A. Davies, and Simon Knox Bob Doherty is an associate professor at Liverpool Hope University, United Kingdom. His research interests include ethical marketing and fair trade business models. Contact: dohertb@hope .ac.uk

Iain A. Davies is a lecturer in marketing at Bath University, United Kingdom. His research interests include ethical marketing and business networks. Contact: i.davies@bath.ac.uk

Simon Knox is a professor of brand marketing at Cranfield University, United Kingdom. His research interests include strategic marketing, branding, and sustainable marketing. Contact: s.knox@cranfield.ac.uk

Overview

This case study investigates the performance of the fair trade pioneer Cafédirect and how it achieved its prominent position in the United Kingdom's mainstream coffee market based on ethical positioning. The case explores how Cafédirect's marketing and communications channels resulted in rapid growth from niche player to a mainstream product. The company, however, is now experiencing a market growth slowdown. Some question whether it is possible for Cafédirect to regain its former momentum with its current marketing strategy.[1]

Background to Cafédirect

Following World War II, coffee prices fluctuated significantly. When prices peaked, nations exporting coffee earned windfall profits, but when prices collapsed, their economies collapsed. In 1962, coffee exporters and importers sought to achieve a reasonable balance between the supply and demand of coffee by signing the International Coffee Agreement, brokered at the United Nations.[2] The agreement stabilized the price of coffee over a five-year period by establishing a quota system prohibiting coffee exports from exceeding consumer demand.

This international agreement temporarily collapsed in 1989, when coffee prices fell to record lows of just one-third of their pre-1989 level. The price decline had a devastating effect on the incomes of small-scale coffee farmers globally.[3] Small family-owned farms were producing three-quarters of the global supply of coffee, and many of them could no longer earn a subsistence income from their coffee beans. The cost to provide coffee beans far exceeded the revenue being generated.

In response to this crisis, Oxfam, a British-based non-government organization (NGO), and three alternative trading organizations (ATOs)—Traidcraft, Equal Exchange, and Twin Trading—got together in 1991 and formed Cafédirect as a branded "fair trade" coffee company to ensure adequate wages for those providing coffee beans.[4] Each of the four partners owned 25 percent of Cafédirect.

Cafédirect's specific aim has been to pioneer fair trade products into the mainstream United Kingdom (UK) hot beverage market. By 2007, Cafédirect had become the UK's largest fair trade hot drinks company and the fourth largest hot beverage company in the UK with annual sales of £21.8 million.[5] Its fair trade brands include Cafédirect Coffee, Teadirect, and Cocodirect (drinking chocolate), which are sold through major supermarket chains and alternative channels of distribution, including Oxfam shops. Cafédirect is the fifth largest coffee brand in the UK with an 8 percent market share of the roasted and ground coffee market and sources coffee beans from 39 producer organizations across 13 different countries, which benefits more than 250,000 coffee producers.

There are several fair trade product certification organizations. Cafédirect chose the standards developed by the Fairtrade Labelling Organisation (FLO) for establishing its brand. FLO determines standards for Fairtrade[6] commodity products, including minimum prices for specific types of coffee beans, and FLO-CERT conducts supplier audits to ensure compliance with these standards.[7]

To further assist coffee growers, Cafédirect exceeds FLO minimum price standards by paying an additional 10 percent above the Fairtrade Certification price. Cafédirect refers to this as its "Gold Standard." When in 2004 and 2005, tea prices fell from US $1.60 to US $1.35 per kilogram (equivalent to 2.2 pounds) in Tanzania and as low as US $1.18 in Uganda, Cafédirect bought these products for US $1.95 per kilogram.[8]

In 2007, Cafédirect paid nearly £1.0 million above the market price for its coffee, tea, and cocoa raw materials. The company then paid an additional £600,000 to producers through its Producer Partnership Programs, which build the organizational capacity of producer organizations. The programs include providing investment for marketing capability, quality control, and improved agricultural practices.

What is Fair Trade?

Under the standard market mechanism, many of the growers of commodities such as coffee live in poverty. Competitive forces drive down product costs, and under the standard market mechanism, large variations in the price for coffee exist. This can result in unsustainable income levels; poor working conditions; exploitation; and limited health, safety, and environmental protection for coffee growers.[9] A major contributor to these problems are international commodity markets, which often set prices that fail to provide growers with a sustainable livelihood.[10]

The most recent coffee crisis (2000–05) was so extreme that coffee prices and farmers' incomes were depressed to such an extent that many coffee farmers faced starvation and the loss of their land.[11] The cost of production was twice the price received via the standard market mechanism. For example in Nicaragua, 245,000 workers in the coffee industry lost their jobs, and the families of 30,000 small coffee producers suffered chronic hunger. The lack of income on farms prompted massive rural-to-urban migration, increasing the poverty belts around Nicaragua's major cities.

In contrast, *fair trade* aims to be a transformative tool for modifying the economic model toward more social ends.[12] Fair trade has been described as

> *a trading partnership, based on dialogue, transparency and respect that seeks greater equity in international trade. It contributes to sustainable development by offering better trading conditions to, and securing the rights of, marginalized producers and workers—especially in the South. Fair Trade organizations (backed by consumers) are engaged actively in supporting producers, awareness raising and in campaigning for changes in the rules and practice of conventional international trade.[13]*

Fair trade differentiates itself from the standard market mechanism according to several key principles and practices, including[14]

- direct purchasing from producers
- the payment of both a fair trade minimum price and a social premium
- long-term relationships and supply contracts
- co-operative, not competitive, dealings with producers
- access to capital, such as the provision of credit, for producers when requested, usually in the form of pre-financing
- provision of market information to producers
- democratic organization of producers and
- practicing sustainable production

In 1991, the Fairtrade Foundation was created in the UK by a number of charities, including Oxfam, Christian Aid, and the World Development Movement. The foundation's primary responsibility was to oversee the Fairtrade Certification Mark, a product label informing consumers that a product's supply chain complies with the Fairtrade standards established by FLO.[15] The Fairtrade standards aim to ensure both better working conditions and more sustainable farming practice in grower communities. The standards establish minimum prices for a range of products and prohibit the use of certain materials, such as toxic insecticides.

Coffee and tea prices are volatile. The FLO sets minimum market prices (a floor price) paid for Fairtrade certified products that cover the cost of production. For example, in November 2006, the Fairtrade minimum price for Arabica coffee beans was US $1.31. When world market prices go above these minimum prices, growers of Fairtrade certified products are guaranteed a higher–than–market price through an additional "social premium" of between 5 cents and 15 cents per kilogram, depending on the product. For coffee, this equates to paying the market price plus 10 cents per pound. Through minimum market prices and social premiums, Fairtrade certification aims to guarantee a long-term sustainable commitment to growers, giving them more opportunity to plan for the future and to invest in their farms and communities.

Cafédirect and Three Phases of Fair Trade Marketing

Scholars have identified three evolutionary phases in the marketing of fair trade products: the *Solidarity Era* (1970–90), the *Market Development Era* (1990–2002), and the *Mass-Market Era* (2002–09).[16] During the Solidarity Era, fair trade businesses highlighted their solidarity with third-world producers. Buying fair trade products was akin to charity. During the Market Development Era, fair trade businesses tried to shake their charity image and competed openly on the market with quality products, using Fairtrade certification as a product differentiation selling point. In the current Mass-Market Era, fair trade businesses compete in the mainstream with a wide range of fair trade brands positioned at different pricing points and qualities (from budget to premium). They also compete with long-established multinational coffee brands that now include a fair trade brand in their portfolio.

The following sections describe Cafédirect's evolution through the three phases of industry marketing development.

Fair Trade Solidarity: Marketing Ethics, 1993–99

Although Cafédirect's high product quality has remained constant over the years, the sales, distribution, advertising, branding, and packaging have gone through some major changes. Early packaging tended toward simplicity, but with large amounts of text educating customers about the product and the producers. This fits well with a solidarity view of the products by bringing the consumers and producers closer together. It also supports Cafédirect's aim to market the core ethics of its products. Customers demonstrated compassion for the lives of coffee growers by paying extra for the certified products.

Poster campaigns during this six-year period highlighted the living and working conditions of coffee growers. Cafédirect suppliers demonstrated pride in their accomplishments, whereas exploited mainstream suppliers suffered through poverty living conditions. The advertisements tended to contain a testimony and portray how purchasing Cafédirect helps coffee farmers and their communities. This links closely with attempts to draw consumers into feeling solidarity with producers and to commence the process of showing how Cafédirect provides a more ethical and sustainable alternative choice.

As brand recognition increased, Cafédirect became more controversial by suggesting that not only was its coffee ethical but, by its very nature, the mainstream competition was not. Big-brand competitors were attacked for having a "fat-cat" mentality. In a stroke of creativity, on September 8, 1997, Cafédirect ran an anti–fat cat mentality advertisement in the *Guardian* newspaper. The advertisement appeared on an almost full-page obituary for Mobuto Sese Seke, one of Africa's most corrupt dictators.

A problem with this type of branding is that consumers are being asked to be charitable, rather than purchasing a product based on its quality. Prior to the Fairtrade Certification Mark, consumers assumed that fair trade products were of "poor quality," and the charity approach reinforced this image. Cafédirect shook off the stigma associated with poor-quality charity products by benchmarking product quality to mainstream competitors, such Kenco's medium roast. This could be achieved because Cafédirect's Producer Partnership Programs helped suppliers through quality control initiatives. As a result, Cafédirect achieved recognition as a premium quality brand with retail prices 20 percent to 30 percent higher than its competition.

In 1994, the company entered the less prestigious freeze-dried coffee market because market research revealed that the majority of UK consumers were drinking freeze-dried coffee. Cafédirect's instant coffee product enabled the company to make its first profits in 1995 and heralded the start of Cafédirect's strong growth continuously fuelled by new product launches.

During this era, Cafédirect's sales relied heavily on product distribution through its ATO founding partners Traidcraft and Equal Exchange. Employees were often recruited from these ATO organizations. Cafédirect depended heavily on ATO marketing campaigns to increase consumer awareness about its products. The company's primary marketing efforts had been through public relations, journalism, and print advertising. Marketing success was achieved through the skilled use of partners, volunteers, and network associates.

Market Development: Marketing Quality, 1999–2002

There is a perceived limit within the fair trade community as to how much market share a "core ethics" marketing strategy can gain a company. Market experts estimate that socially conscious consumers account for a small percentage of the buying public, just 3 percent of the cocoa and coffee market in Europe. Other fair trade initiatives such as Max Havelaar, Transfair, Rättvisemärkt, and Reilun Kaupan have all struggled to grow beyond 3 percent market share.

In 1999, in an effort to increase its sales above the 3 percent level, Cafédirect dramatically changed its advertising messages. Rather than focusing on portraits of small-scale coffee farmers, the new Cafédirect advertisements focused on its high-quality product offerings. Its premium coffees were shown related to the pristine environmental scenes in which they were produced. The company even changed the name of Cafédirect Instant to 5065—the average height at which its coffee beans were grown—to make a clear transition to the premium end of the market.

Over the following two years, progress continued in new advertising methods and media. In the first highly evocative cinema advertisement produced for any fair trade company, Cafédirect showed the peak of Machu Picchu waking up in the morning to the smell of its coffee. In another first, Cafédirect was granted advertising rights on the London Underground for its new brand 5065. The success of Cafédirect's innovative marketing culminated when the company, with its limited marketing budget, won the Marketer of the Year Award in 2004 from the Marketing Society.

The main aim of Cafédirect's new advertising and packaging was to move the focus away from the experience of the producer (or the "core ethics" message previously noted) to the experience of the consumer. Consequently, there was a major decrease in the amount of fair trade text on the advertisements and packaging. The space allocated to the Fairtrade Certification Mark was significantly reduced. This new customer experience message sparked a rapid growth in sales and much greater brand awareness. Cafédirect's market share rose above the 3 percent barrier. During this growth stage, Cafédirect began to rely less on the founding partners for sales and distribution and secured significant supermarket distribution.

As each product was rebranded to reflect this new positioning, the company began to have a new problem. Fair trade competitors began to follow Cafédirect's lead by rebranding and adopting product-quality messages, so more marketing expense was needed to differentiate Cafédirect from other fair trade companies. Each brand now needed its own marketing and sales support, which led to rapidly increasing costs.

New competition arose from mainstream coffee companies wanting to capitalize on increased consumer demand for fair trade products. The fair trade market experienced a vast increase in the number of fair trade brands on the supermarket shelf, including premium coffees from major roasters, own-label brands from supermarkets, fair trade lines from Nestlé, and similarly branded "sustainable" coffee from Kenco. Cafédirect's competitive advantages from the "core ethics" of its product were being eroded. With trusted brands bringing out quality products, the product quality message was no longer as effective. Cafédirect's revenue growth began to slow down.

Internal market research attributed some of the stagnant growth to consumers not being aware that Cafédirect's coffees, teas, and cocoas came from the same company. As a result, Cafédirect had been unable to leverage the success of its coffee to sell newer products. With product quality now established, the next step was for Cafédirect to leverage its organizational values and corporate brand communications to fuel sales growth and help reduce marketing expenditures.

Mass-Markets: Marketing Uniqueness, 2004–09

Commencing in 2004, Cafédirect undertook a three-year corporate product and rebranding program with its brand portfolio being presented as a family of products sharing a common value system. In making this move, the company departed from product brand marketing toward corporate brand marketing.

Cafédirect's uniqueness embraced both innovation and ethical products. Cafédirect was the first fair trade company to advertise, the first supplier of fair trade instant coffee, and the first fair trade company to have an initial public share offering. The company could also identify a number of ethical market initiatives, such as setting up the Gold Standard by exceeding Fairtrade certification minimum price standards.

This shift in focus was symbolized by Cafédirect's effort to raise £5 million by offering shares of stock through an initial public offering (IPO) on Triodos Bank's "ethical exchange" Ethex.[17] The IPO provided Cafédirect an opportunity to extend a financial ownership stake in the company's ethical business model to its consumers. IPO press releases emphasized that Cafédirect invested 70 percent of its pretax profits in growers' organizations. Within just two months, Cafédirect raised the £5 million. Sixty percent of Cafédirect was now publicly owned. Cafédirect's four founding partners each reduced its ownership from 25 percent to 10 percent. Combined, the founding partners now shared one seat on the board of directors.

Over the next three years, Cafédirect invested £1.9 million, or 60 percent of operating profit, into its Producer Partner Programs. The company also handed over a portion of its share issue to producer partners—accounting for 4.9 percent of the company's equity—in order to give producers a role in the governance of Cafédirect.

During the Mass-Market Era, the vast majority of Cafédirect's advertising has been based on "events" and big extravaganzas, such as the Glastonbury Rock Festival and the Edinburgh Fringe, a large arts festival in the Scottish capital city.

Cafédirect also used the London Eye for an event in 2005 and provided entertainment in each pod of this Ferris wheel.

Three other noteworthy changes have occurred during this phase.

First, Cafédirect expanded its social concerns from fair trade to include climate change.

Second, Cafédirect expanded its employee base. The company initially recruited employees from its ATO partners, such as Equal Exchange. Cafédirect now recruits former sales and marketing managers from major blue-chip companies.

Third, Cafédirect has made significant changes in the types of companies with which it networks. Cafédirect now forms partnerships with more traditional businesses to sell and represent its brand in the mainstream market. As the range of partners that Cafédirect works with increases dramatically, the company is beginning to look more like any other small coffee business. Cafédirect is concentrating less on advocating for the fair trade movement as it makes more traditional business connections to advance the commercial aspects of the firm.

Current Issues

Cafédirect has been a huge marketing success story. The company expanded into the tea market in 1998 and the chocolate-drinking market in 2002. Cafédirect introduced many gourmet single-source-of-origin coffees (some of them organic), and a range of premium instant coffees and speciality teas. By 2007, Cafédirect had become the UK's largest fair trade hot drinks company, fourth largest hot beverage company, and fifth largest coffee brand. In 2008, the Cafédirect's former CEO was made an Officer of the Order of the British Empire, a prestigious award for service to the British Empire bestowed by the queen of England

As shown in Exhibit 1, Cafédirect has consistently grown faster than the total market, although not necessarily as fast as some competitors.

Exhibit 1 Market Share (by Value) of Coffee by Manufacturer: 2003–07					
Company	£m 2003	£m 2005	£m 2007	% change 2003–07	% change 2005–07
Nestlé	294	308	304	3.4	−1.3
Kraft	126	128	139	10.3	8.6
Douwe Egberts	27	40	47	74.1	17.5
Cafédirect	**7**	**8**	**10**	**28.6**	**12.5**
Taylors	8	8	10	37.5	37.5
Lavazza	8	8	11	37.5	37.5
Gala (Lyons)	6	5	4	−33.3	−20

(Continued)

Exhibit 1 Market Share (by Value) of Coffee by Manufacturer: 2003–07 (*Continued*)				
Food Brands Group (Percol)	5	5	5	0	0
Own-label	88	104	122	38.6	17.3
Others	44	56	68	54.5	21.4
Total	613	670	720	17.5	7.5

Source: Adapted from Mintel, 2008.

However, in 2006, the company experienced its first after-tax loss since 1995 (see financial results in Exhibit 2). During 2007, retail sales actually fell 4 percent for the first time in the company's history to £17.0 million, and down again to £16.8 million in 2008, which must be viewed with some concern because 70 percent of total annual sales is via the retail channel. Fairtrade Certification coffee sales

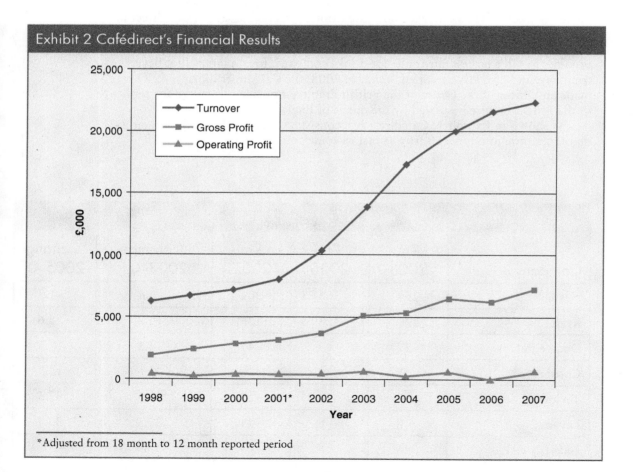

Exhibit 2 Cafédirect's Financial Results

*Adjusted from 18 month to 12 month reported period

continued to grow at 33 percent total volume and 24 percent through retail outlets.[18] However, Cafédirect does not seem to be capitalizing on this and is experiencing the effects of the increased competition.

For instance, 64 percent of the fair trade coffee sales are now accounted for by supermarket own-label fair trade brands.[19] Forecast data for Fairtrade Certification coffee do not look encouraging with a steady slowing of growth, which could reduce even faster if the 2006–07 trend continues (see Exhibit 3, long-dash line). Since 2005, Cafédirect has actually underperformed in terms of growth compared to fair trade in general (6 percent to 7 percent versus 8 percent) and has grown conservatively compared to the rest of the coffee market.

A problem also exists in the target age group for coffee consumption among the demographic group called the Thirdage (hashed line of Exhibit 3), people age 45 and older. There is a predicted fall in this age bracket. This may have a double impact on Cafédirect because fair trade products are more attractive to Thirdage consumers than to other demographic groups.[20]

Rival certification systems are now also entering the market. For instance, Rainforest Alliance labels coffee products produced without rainforest destruction, a certification system used by Kenco. The coffee industry's 4C code, created by the world's four largest coffee roasters and grinders, promises many of the same advantages as

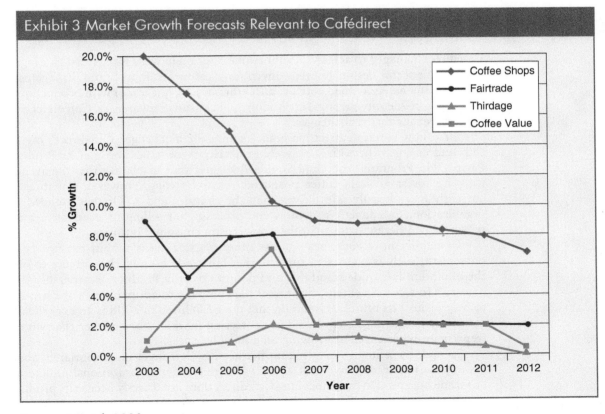

Exhibit 3 Market Growth Forecasts Relevant to Cafédirect

Source: Mintel, 2008.

Fairtrade Certification but without any auditing or requirements on which to judge compliance.

As a response to the falling retail sales and the new competition from other fair trade brands, own-label supermarket brands, and competing ethical labels, Cafédirect embarked on a further rebranding (a fourth fair trade marketing phase) in May 2009. The new branding identified as promoting Cafédirect's "Provenance,"[21] or advertising its heritage as a longstanding fair trader, to help protect its existing market share from these competitive products. It remains to be seen whether this return to proximity-to-farmers type branding will pay off for Cafédirect. Ethical consumption theory would suggest it should fail because of market size limits.[22] Indications are that sales of Cafédirect have been consistently shrinking since June 2009.[23] However, it is impossible at the present time to define whether this fall in sales is due to product brand or unfavorable economic conditions.

The company also has to deal with some negative publicity about fair trade products that appears in the media from time to time that questions the standards and processes used to determine that a product is really fair trade. Cafédirect itself has been accused in the media of protecting coffee growers and damaging free trade across the whole coffee market.[24] This argument is weak, however, because it assumes that the standard market mechanism had been working in the first place. It wasn't. Small-scale coffee farmers had been receiving less for their product than it cost them to produce sustainably.[25]

Cafédirect: Where To Next?

Cafédirect managed to achieve a competitive position in what is regarded as a highly competitive sector despite limited conventional resources. In its brand management, the company has combined core product ethics (being fair trade) with product quality, corporate identity, strong distribution, and consumer awareness. Cafédirect now faces three new major challenges.

First, how can Cafédirect maintain its unique ethical edge? Cafédirect's ownership and engagement with supply chain development issues through its Producer Partnership Programs and Gold Standard suggest that its claim to be the authentic voice for small-scale coffee producers remains strong. However, Cafédirect is currently more heavily sales driven than the charities and ATOs that founded the organization. Cafédirect's structures and processes for selling its products are not particularly different from any other mainstream consumer business.

Cafédirect now competes against other organizations within the fair trade movement, such as own-label supermarket fair trade brands, that adhere to only the minimum fair trade standards and do not invest in Producer Partnership Programs.[26] To a certain extent, this forces the company to adopt a defensive strategy to help protect its brand. It is telling that the CEO hired in 2008 is an experienced consumer goods marketer skilled in protecting market share, rather than an entrepreneur experienced at growing an ethical business.

Second, by selling in mainstream markets, is Cafédirect inappropriately abandoning the fair trade movement and its former partner organizations? Unlike the fair trade business Divine Chocolate, Cafédirect does not directly license its products to other organizations for their own-label production. Cafédirect also provides the opportunity for mainstream organizations in its network partnership to gain ethical credentials while contributing very little. An extreme example would be an airline demonstrating a commitment to sustainability by having fair trade coffee onboard, which could deflect attention from the environmental problems airlines cause.

Third, can consumers differentiate between not only competing ethical claims (i.e., the new ethical labels) but also between the fair trade pioneer brands, such as Cafédirect, and fair trade products from multinational corporations? Some experts believe that consumers are not sufficiently savvy to comprehend multiple messages on ethical or sustainability issues. For instance, consumers often assume that pesticide-free organic products are fair trade products. Fair trade activists are calling for fair trade businesses to demonstrate greater unity in fair trade messaging to ensure its survival as a distinct product offering.

QUESTIONS

1. Identify the tangible and intangible resources utilized by Cafédirect to support its competitive position in the UK hot beverage market.

2. Cafédirect is a successful archetype for an "ethical business," but it is now facing some extreme competitive pressures from traditional businesses providing similar products. Do you think companies in an ethical niche have to compromise their ethics to compete successfully in mainstream markets?

3. Should Cafédirect become more involved in the fair trade movement again?

4. Should the company be getting involved in climate change discussions or is this diluting its core purpose?

5. Assume you were appointed the new marketing director of Cafédirect and given specific instructions to get both profits and sales back on track. What marketing strategies would you pursue?

NOTES

[1] Most of the data used in this case study come from two longitudinal, exploratory studies into the management and implementation of strategy in Cafédirect over the periods of 1999–2004 and 1999–2008, respectively.

[2] http://www.ico.org/history.asp, accessed 8/3/10.

[3] Michael Barratt Brown, "Fair Trade with Africa," *Review of African Political Economy*, 34, 112 (2007), 267–277.

[4] Cafédirect company website, available at http://www.cafedirect.co.uk/index.cfm, accessed 8/3/10.

[5] Mintel International, *Coffee—UK* (London: Mintel International Group Limited, 2008).

[6] "Fairtrade" as one word refers to Fairtrade Labelling Organization's product certification system.

[7] For ease of communication, these two related bodies will be referred to as FLO; FLO website available at http://www.fairtrade.net/, accessed 8/3/10.

[8] Cafédirect, *Cafédirect plc Report and Financial Statements 2003–2004* (London, Eng.: Baker Tilly International, 2005).

[9] Michael Barratt Brown, *Fair Trade: Reform and Realities in the International Trading System* (London, Eng.: Zed Books Ltd, 1993); Sheila Page and Rachel Slater, "Small Producer Participation in Global Food Systems: Policy Opportunities and Constraints," *Development Policy Review*, 21, 5–6 (2003), 641–654.

[10] Anil Hira and Jared Ferrie, "Fair Trade: Three Key Challenges for Reaching the Mainstream," *Journal of Business Ethics*, 63, 2 (2006), 107–118; Pauline Tiffen, "A Chocolate-Coated Case for Alternative International Business Models," *Development in Practice*, 12, 3 & 4 (2002), 383–397.

[11] Robert Rice, "Coffee Production in a Time of Crisis: Social and Environmental Connections," *SAIS Review*, 23, 1 (2003), 221–245.

[12] Marie-Christine Renard, "Fair Trade Quality, Market and Conventions," *Journal of Rural Studies*, 19, 1 (2003), 87–96.

[13] Geoff Moore, Jane Gibbon, and Richard Slack, "The Mainstreaming of Fair Trade: A Macromarketing Perspective," *Journal of Strategic Marketing*, 12, 4 (2006), 329–352.

[14] Geoff Moore, "The Fair Trade Movement: Parameters, Issues and Future Research," *Journal of Business Ethics*, 53, 1–2 (2004), 73–87.

[15] The combined term "Fairtrade" is used for FLO's certification and labeling systems to differentiate it from the phrase "fair trade," which refers to an economic social movement.

[16] Iain A. Davies, "The Eras and Participants of Fair Trade: An Industry Structure/Stakeholder Perspective on the Growth of the Fair Trade Industry," *Corporate Governance*, 7, 4 (2004), 455–470.

[17] Donna Werbner, "Campaign: Cafédirect Attracts Investors for Its IPO," *PR Week UK*, June 11, 2004.

[18] Fairtrade Foundation website, available at http://www.fairtrade.org.uk/what_is_fairtrade/facts_and_figures.aspx, accessed 8/3/10.

[19] Datamonitor, *UK Coffee Market Report* (Manchester, Eng.: Datamonitor, 2010).

[20] Alex Nicholls and Charlotte Opal, *Fair Trade: Market-Driven Ethical Consumption* (London, Eng.: Sage Publications, 2005).

[21] We wish to thank Dr. Caroline Wright of University of Warwick for this term, which she used at a presentation in October 2009.

[22] Marylyn Carrigan and Ahmad Attalla, "The Myth of the Ethical Consumer—Do Ethics Matter in Purchase Behavior?" *Journal of Consumer Marketing*, 18, 7 (2001), 560–577; Patrick De Pelsmacker, Lisebeth Driesen, and Glenn Rayp, "Do Consumers Care about Ethics? Willingness to Pay for Fair Trade Coffee," *Journal of Consumer Affairs*, 39, 2 (2005), 363–385.

[23] According to initial sales figures at the 2010 Annual General Meeting.

[24] Kappler, D. Quoted in "Fair Trade Chocolate—The Argument Continues," *Corporate Finance*, 204 (2004), 18.

[25] Brown, *Fair Trade*.

[26] Darryl Reed, "What Do Corporations Have to Do with Fair Trade? Positive and Normative Analysis from a Value Chain Perspective," *Journal of Business Ethics*, 86, 1 (2009), 3–26.

INDEX*

*All page references above p. 533 refer to Case Studies posted to the Instructor Companion Site.

Public trust surveys, 7
Puritans, 43
Purity, ethical intuition
    and, 141
Putnam Investments, 250

Questions, interview, 93–94, 98
Quiet time, 284
Qui tam, 256

Racial discrimination, 211–212.
    see also Discrimination
Racketeer Influenced and Corrupt
    Organizations Act
    (RICO), 472
RADR, 194
Raleigh, Walter, 42
Rampart Investment Management
    Company, 443
Rand, Ayn, 149
Rao, Pravin, 461
Rational ethical decision making,
    145–161
Raven, Bertram, 272
Raytheon, 146
Reactive giving, 393
Reagan, Ronald, 58, 256,
    342, 417
Realistic job preview, 94
Reasoning, ethical, 147–148
Reciprocity, 141
Recreational Equipment
    Incorporated (REI), 56
Recruitment
    costs, 14
    diversity and, 218
    word-of-mouth, 78
(RED), 397
Red Cross, 396
Reference checks, 82–83, 97
Referent power, 272
Refrigerators, 351
Regional Greenhouse Gas
    Initiative (RGGI), 344
Regulation, government, 57,
    341–342, 457–458,
    465–473
Regulators, role of, 4
REI. see Recreational Equipment
    Incorporated (REI)
Reid, Harry, 458

Reid Psychological Systems, 81
Reid Report, 85
Reina, Christopher, 276
Relativism
    assessment of, 188
    cultural, 149, 152–153
    social group, 149, 151–152
Religion
    discrimination based
        on, 212
    ethical decision making
        and, 140
    values and, 157
Reporting
    assist lines in, 253–255
    chaplain in, 251
    in Code of Conduct, 120
    employee silence vs., 240–245
    Ethics & Compliance Officer
        and, 247–249
    failure in, 30
    manager approachability and,
        245–246
    ombudsperson in, 250–251
    system management, 249
    whistleblowing in, 255–260
Reputation, 402
Reputation costs, of unethical
    behavior, 13
Respect
    common decencies and, 276
    diversity and, 208
    ethical intuition and, 141
    for others, 208
    as workplace quality, 280
Responsibilities, social, extent of,
    374–376
Rest, James, 137, 187
ResumeDoctor.com, 81
Resumes, 81–82, 97
Retail industry, employee theft
    in, 12
Retaliation
    for discrimination, 217
    for reporting of
        misconduct, 244
    for whistleblowing, 260
Retention, diversity and, 218
Revere, Paul, 387
Reverse discrimination, 79, 211
Revolutionary War, 43–44
Reward power, 272

Rewards, ethical decision making
    and, 144
Reynolds, John, 462
RGGI. see Regional Greenhouse
    Gas Initiative (RGGI)
RICO. see Racketeer Influenced
    and Corrupt
    Organizations Act
    (RICO)
Riggio, Ronald, 276
Risk assessment, environmental,
    358–359
R.J. Reynolds, 468
Roanoke Settlement, 42
Role models, managers as,
    269–271
Roloff, Julia, 384
Roman Catholicism, 20, 43
Roosevelt, Franklin, 51, 54
Rosh, Lea, 509
Rotary International, 146, 401
Roth, John, 536, 538–539, 541,
    542, 544
Rousseau, Jean-Jacques, 19
Rubin, Robert E., 456

Sabbatical, 391
Sabin, Albert, 573
Sachs, Samuel, 455
Saint Augustine, 20
SAIP. see Self-Assessment and
    Improvement Process
    (SAIP)
Sales, unethical behavior in, 8
Salesforce.com, 388
Saliva analysis, for drug
    testing, 95
Sanctions, ethical decision making
    and, 144
Sanctity, ethical intuition
    and, 141
Sand County Almanac, A
    (Leopold), 340
Santa Clara County, 475–482
Sarbanes-Oxley Act (SOX),
    110, 259
SAS, 307
Satisfaction, employee,
    306–307
Save the Children, 392
Scanlon-type gainsharing plans,
    322–324